MOON HANDBOOKS®

ILLINOIS

FIRST EDITION

CHRISTINE DES GARENNES

♫ AVALON TRAVEL

TRUTH — JUSTICE — THE AMERICAN WAY

CONTENTS

Discover Illinois

Explore Illinois

Chicago 24

Know Illinois

MAPS

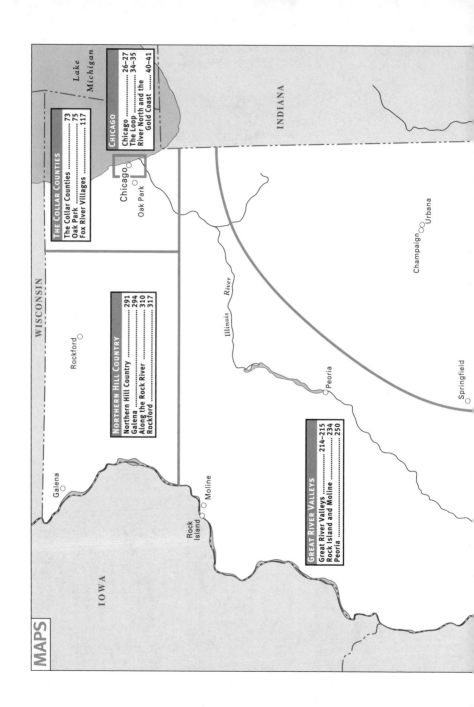

Lake
Michigan

WISCONSIN

IOWA

INDIANA

Galena

Rockford

Rock
Island

Moline

Chicago

Oak Park

Peoria

Illinois River

Champaign
Urbana

Springfield

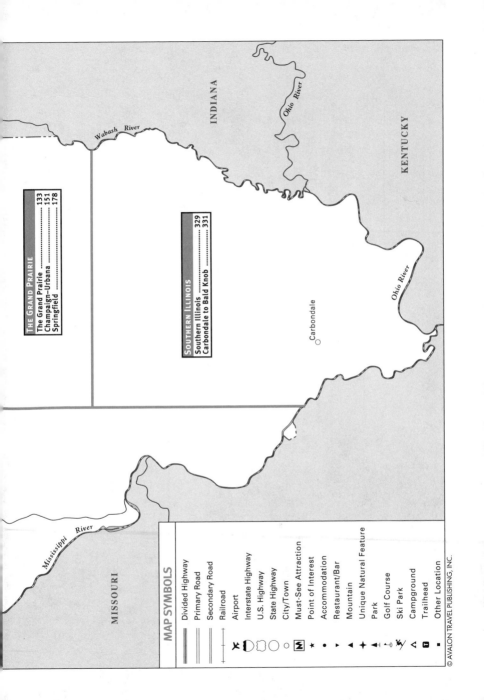

INDIANA

KENTUCKY

MISSOURI

Wabash River

Mississippi River

Ohio River

Ohio River

Carbondale

MAP SYMBOLS

	Divided Highway
	Primary Road
	Secondary Road
	Railroad
✈	Airport
🄸	Interstate Highway
◯	U.S. Highway
◯	State Highway
○	City/Town
Ⓜ	Must-See Attraction
★	Point of Interest
●	Accommodation
▼	Restaurant/Bar
▲	Mountain
◀	Unique Natural Feature
+○	Park
⚑	Golf Course
⋀	Ski Park
⌂	Campground
🚩	Trailhead
■	Other Location

© AVALON TRAVEL PUBLISHING, INC.

Discover
Illinois

You'd be hard-pressed to find a more classic American place than Illinois. Vintage car rallies in downtown squares. Sweet corn festivals. Crowded blues clubs that get grooving around 2 A.M. The genius of Muddy Waters and Frank Lloyd Wright was developed here. It's where Abraham Lincoln grew to believe slavery was immoral, where Carl Sandburg wrote about the simple beauty of natural events such as the fog coming on, where Mother Jones fought for workers' rights, and where Ronald Reagan dreamt of Hollywood while working as a lifeguard.

The state stretches for almost 400 miles north to south, from the Galena area, with its limestone cliffs, windy rivers, dairy farms, and artisan communities, to the impressive Shawnee Hills, with its fruit orchards, family wineries, all-terrain hiking trails, and quiet canoe paths. In between and along the way, you'll come upon the wide Mississippi and Illinois River Valleys, home to eagles and other wildlife, and the remains of an ancient, mound-building culture. There are impressive flatlands in the midsection where much of the country's corn and soybeans are grown.

And then there is Chicago—a world-class city and melting

pot for all types of people, business, art, and culture. Chicago is a vibrant, youthful city of neighborhoods where visitors can attend countless musical festivals and dine and drink al fresco. A city of high and low culture, Chicago has a little of everything. Admire Impressionist paintings at the Art Institute. Take in an outdoor film in Grant Park. Order a brew and learn to polka in a South Side club.

As far as recreation opportunities go, what'll you have? Bicycle along the Hennepin or Illinois and Michigan canals. Discover an unspoiled bog. Have a go at spelunking. At night pack into a remote campsite, rent an air-conditioned cottage, or spend the night in a state park lodge built by the Civilian Conservation Corps. Shopping more your thing? From Chicago's Michigan Avenue to the historic village of Bishop Hill, Illinois towns will satisfy, whether you're shopping for folk art or ultra-mod furniture.

Aside from the occasional traffic jam on a Chicago-area expressway and perhaps a spirited argument with another driver over a downtown parking space, visiting and living in Illinois is easy and, for the most part, hassle-free. There's space out here, space you might not be able to see or feel on the East or West coasts. You just can't beat the sight of the sun setting over the prairie when a thunderstorm is rolling in, or a train carrying grain or coal rumbling through a small town, or a red-winged blackbird following a pair of bicyclists as they pedal on county roads past fields of corn and soybeans.

All the while you may meet people who gladly offer you directions to their favorite coffee shop or bar or engage you in conversation and complain about the weather or the Chicago Bears. Throughout your adventures in Illinois, you'll meet some pretty humble, practical people. During the fall it's not uncommon for farmers to get together and harvest the fields of a neighbor who fell ill. Instead of waxing poetic about their volunteer efforts, they're more likely to shrug it off, saying, "Well, the beans have to be cut sometime," or "He'd do it for me if I were sick." Although technically a Midwestern state, Illinois also has an easygoing, Southern feel in its downstate towns, where many residents have roots in Tennessee and Kentucky. Don't be surprised when a gas station clerk calls you "Honey."

Sure, there's a lot to do, but sometimes all you'll want to do is roll down the car window, slow down, and rumble down an old two-lane highway. Or better yet, unfold a lawn chair at the edge of a lake and sit. And that's all right with us.

Illinois is definitely a road trip–friendly state, popular among motorcyclists, RVers, minivans packed with kids, and the occasional re-outfitted Volkswagen. Whatever your mode of transportation, be sure to leave extra time for traveling. Somehow it always seems to take longer than expected to travel through Illinois, whether it's because of traffic delays around Chicago or the sheer size of the state. Several interstates crisscross Illinois, making them an efficient way to travel the state. But remember, the state is long. Even a drive along interstates from Chicago to Carbondale in the south can take about six hours. Two-lane highways dominate southern Illinois and the state's eastern and western borders. These routes, such as the Great River Road near the Mississippi, are often more scenic and offer better glimpses into the state's towns and residents, but they take considerably longer to drive from one place to another, especially when you keep stumbling upon detours such as roadside cafés or antiques shops.

Depending on how ambitious you are, it is possible to cover the state's best sights in a two- or three-week period. But you may not be able to stand or operate a motor vehicle after doing so. You can breeze through the big sights in Chicago or the Lincoln sights in Springfield, but the best things about Illinois are some of the out-of-the-way places that deserve more than a quick stop to appreciate, such as the Little Grand Canyon Hiking Trail in southern Illinois or the Under the Prairie museum and adjacent café in Elkhart.

WHEN TO GO

Ideally you'll want to visit Illinois sometime between late spring through early fall. Otherwise, the scenery is, quite frankly, uninteresting. Things don't shut down November–March, but they sure are quiet. Instead, from April or May–November, museums, historic sites, and restaurants are guaranteed to be open. The grass is green, flowers are blooming, and we Illinoisans are feeling swell. Spring is an exciting time for residents. When the mercury rises above 50 degrees, suddenly everyone digs out his or her shorts and T-shirts and starts jogging and biking. The mood lightens.

As we head into June, the festival season kicks in. All around the state, weekends are packed with blues and bluegrass concerts, pie-eating and watermelon seed–spitting contests. Chicago in the summertime is pulsing and packed with things to do—air and water shows, bike races, ethnic festivals, you name it. The population swells in the summertime, largely because every weekend there's a major concert or sporting event, museum or theater opening. It's always cooler by the lake, so if the heat of the city gets to you, grab a towel and stake out a place in the sand.

</

If

're

Illinois

The

Sh

National

Forest

Schedule

Because the state is so long from north to south, winters in Illinois can run the gamut from heavy snowfalls in the north to slick, icy rains in the south. There are a few ski hills in the northern part of the state, plus plenty of cross-country ski trails throughout. Snowy weather is more likely to happen along the lakeshore, and travel delays are a given whenever any precipitation starts to fall, particularly in the Chicago area. Hoteliers tend to discount their rooms at this time of year. If you visit in the winter, you'll find that many sites that aren't seasonal in nature (such as theme parks) are still open, but at reduced hours. Always call ahead.

WHAT TO TAKE

Unless you plan to dine in places such as Wolfgang Puck's place in Chicago, dress is casual in Illinois. Obviously if clubbing in Chicago is on the agenda, you'll probably dress differently than if backpacking in southern Illinois. On the whole, though, the state and the people are not particularly fancy or snobbish. Want to make friends with the natives? Wear a little orange and blue, the color of the University of Illinois Fighting Illini. Jeans and shorts are acceptable in most places, unless perhaps some nightclubs in Chicago. Wherever you go, whenever you go, layering is a good idea, especially if you're driving from one region to another and have plans to hop in and out of museums and restaurants, stroll along the lakeshore, or hike through the prairie.

Most stores and restaurants will take major credit cards, and most gas stations have automated teller machines if you need cash fast. But bring along extra change. Several toll highways run through the northern part of the state. And if you're a student, pack your student identification card to receive discounts at museums or historical sites.

You can request a free state map from the Illinois Department of Transportation, but DeLorme's Illinois Atlas and Gazetteer is a must-have if you plan to veer off the main highways or travel through Shawnee National Forest.

If hiking, biking, or canoeing is on the agenda, bring a cooler and keep it in your car. Pack it with ice, drinks, and snacks. Most of the trails, especially in southern Illinois, are a good distance from towns. And not all of the nearby towns have restaurants or gas stations.

Bring along a hat, sunglasses, and sunblock if you're out and about in the summer, and especially if you plan to lounge along the Lake Michigan shoreline or any of the other lakes in the state.

Whatever you do, do not forget insect repellent for mosquitoes and ticks. Many cities spray for mosquitoes, especially since the West Nile virus has arrived here. But mosquitoes will sneak up on you everywhere you go, from an evening walking along the Lakefront Trail in Chicago to an outdoor café in Champaign.

Unless you plan to rent a cottage for a week or so in the rural part of the state, such as in the Shawnee National Forest, most bed-and-breakfasts and hotels will have a supply of soap and towels for you.

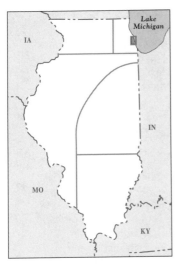

CHICAGO

It's OK to drop your jaw and lean back in awe at this city. A city of more than three million people, stretching over 28 square miles, it's one big city—the biggest in the Midwest. Chicago is a vibrant city with 30 miles or so of Lake Michigan frontage, perfect for sunning, biking, and walking. There's historic Grant Park with the gorgeous Buckingham fountain, and there's an array of funky, chic, and ethnically diverse neighborhoods. While in town, admire the stunning collections of paintings and sculpture in the Art Institute of Chicago and fossils and historical artifacts at The Field Museum. Root, root for the home team at Wrigley Field. Prepare yourself for some of the best hotdogs and pizza ever made, not to mention Mexican, Brazilian, Moroccan, and Ukrainian food. A visitor-friendly place, Chicago offers personalized tours with natives, trolley tours, and information booths around downtown where you can pick up a map and explore on your own. We hope you'll leave shouting, "Man, I love this town."

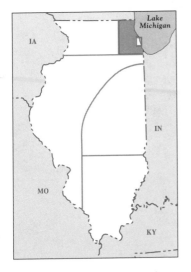

THE COLLAR COUNTIES

Although often overshadowed by their big-city neighbor, many towns that surround Chicago can stand on their own merit. Some are wealthy bedroom communities such as Lake Bluff, others are self-sustaining cities such as Elgin. As far as highlights go, let's start with the awesome architecture of inner-ring suburb Oak Park, where not only can you see dozens of Frank Lloyd Wright–designed homes, but his very own former home and studio. On the north shore of Chicago is Evanston and Northwestern University and just north of there, the impressive Baha'i Temple in Wilmette. Megamalls such as

Woodfield in Schaumburg to the northwest draw hundreds of thousands of shoppers to the 'burbs. But recreation opportunities are not limited to mall walking. The Chicago Botanic Garden in Glencoe are especially dazzling in the spring, and Morton Arboretum in Lisle amazes in the fall. Out in the western suburbs, you can bicycle along the Prairie Path near Warrenville, past restored wetlands and prairies. Or there's the multirecreational Fox River Trail near Geneva and St. Charles. Conservation-minded Lake County has numerous forest preserves open to the public. Dining options are not limited to chain restaurants or buffet or family-style places but include some independent storefront cafés and award-winning fine dining establishments such as Carlos' in Highland Park.

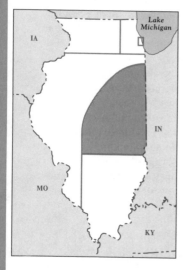

THE GRAND PRAIRIE

Perhaps the most Illinois of all regions, the Grand Prairie encompasses the center of the state. Hundreds of years ago it was a wet and muddy place where tall prairie grasses grew and wildflowers bloomed. Drainage has changed all that and it's among the most fertile farmland in the nation now, with more corn and soybean fields than you can imagine. The region makes up for its lack of hills with lots of awe-inspiring open spaces. Sunsets above farmsteads and across the huge sky are almost always unbeatable. The region is home to several small town gems, such as Elkhart, which has an artful archae-ological museum and pioneer cemetery, as well as Arthur and Arcola, where most of the state's Amish live. In between the rural towns are larger cities like the capital of Springfield, home to the new Abraham Lincoln Presidential Library and Museum, plus Lincoln's former home. Diverse arts and music scenes are thriving within the university towns of Champaign-Urbana and Blooming-ton-Normal. And finally, don't miss a trip to the magnificent Allerton Park in Monticello, a European-style manor in the middle of the prairie.

GREAT RIVER VALLEYS

The Illinois River Valley is somewhat of a dichotomous corridor. You've got working cities such as Peoria, where equipment manufacturers and utility plants generate power and products. Then, not far from them are wildlife refuges where the only fellow visitors spotted for miles may be a pair of migrating swans. The star of the LaSalle and Peru area is Starved Rock State Park, with its hiking trails, scenic overlooks of the river, campsites, cottages, and historic lodge. Coming in a close second is nearby Matthiessen State Park, an ideal spot for horseback riding. The city of Peoria, once known for its hog markets, is developing a growing reputation for its revitalized riverfront with boat rides, antiques shops, coffee shops, and restaurants. Moving south along the river, visitors can go way back in time with a visit to Dickson Mounds near Havana, once the site of an ancient mound-building American Indian culture.

From the Cahokia Mounds World Heritage Site near Collinsville to the well-preserved town of Nauvoo, the Middle-Mississippi River valley oozes history. Historic river towns such as Alton and Quincy, with their brick-lined streets and stately old homes, overlook the river, a river that for many years brought prosperity to the region with fishing, shipping, pearl button manufacturing, and other industries. The French were the first white people to settle in this area, particularly east and south of present-day East St. Louis. For a good history lesson on the area, stop by the old French Fort de Chartres in Prairie du Rocher.

NORTHERN HILL COUNTRY

As this region's name implies, the distinguishing features of the Northern Hill Country are gently undulating hills, with small towns tucked into the valleys and the occasional farmstead folded into the mix. Drive U.S. 20 between Rockford and Galena or Highway 2 along the Rock River near Castle Rock State Park for quintessential glimpses of this region. The far northwest corner of the state near Galena was untouched by glaciers (it's called the driftless region) and the landscape contrasts sharply with the smooth farmland in the central part of the state. Here are numerous state parks and trails for hiking along the river and atop cliffs, especially at Mississippi Palisades State Park. Towns such as Dixon, Elizabeth, and especially Galena are especially picturesque with their historic downtowns, towering old trees, vintage homes with flower boxes, and city parks with band shells. Arguably one of the most scenic parts of the state, the hill country is all somewhat bucolic, and because of its pastoral beauty, threatened by sprawl as others realize the quiet beauty of northwestern Illinois.

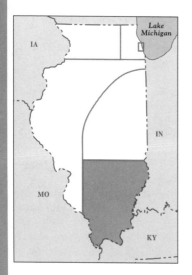

SOUTHERN ILLINOIS

Leave your dress shoes at home. Southern Illinois is an informal kind of place. Four-star restaurants and hotels are rare here, but fruit stands brimming with juicy peaches and hillside cabins with views of the Shawnee National Forest abound. After many of the coal mines shuttered, the local economies of many towns and the livelihoods of residents took a hit, forcing many to reinvent themselves and focus on other things, such as growing grapes and making wine. Some have bounced back and others still struggle. Southern Illinois is definitely Southern. Residents speak with an easy drawl; tend to be a bit more conservative than their northern neighbors; love, just love, their environment; and fish, hunt, and hike. Southern Illinois is a magical kind of place where just around the bend is another hilly vista, hiking trail, family winery, or barn full of antiques for sale. Crowds? What are those? You can go rock climbing or canoeing without running into mobs of other people. If you go Cache River canoeing among cypress and tupelo swamps, you'd swear you were in Louisiana.

The 14-Day Best of Illinois

So it's not as vast as Montana, but Illinois is a big state, from the rocky and hilly Shawnee National Forest in the south, the expansive prairie in the middle, and the buzzing Chicago metropolitan area in the northeast. It's chock-full of big-city museums, small-town antiques shops, fancy and homespun restaurants. It might be asking a lot to see all this in two weeks, but load up the car, fill up the gas tank, and give it a shot. This is an ambitious tour and hits the state's must-sees. Be sure to set aside extra time for driving and for the occasional veering off for the flea market, fruit stand, or roadside restaurant that piques your interest.

DAY 1

Begin your trip in Chicago, where you'll admire paintings and sculpture at the Art Institute of Chicago and get lost in other great museums downtown, such as the Field Museum or Shedd Aquarium. Take in an architectural boat tour or wander along Navy Pier and the lakefront.

DAY 2

Still in Chicago, explore some of the city's eclectic neighborhoods such as Wicker Park, Chinatown, or Hyde Park. Spend the afternoon or evening in one of the historic, inner-ring suburbs of Oak Park or Evanston.

DAY 3

Drive northwest from Chicago toward the former mining town of Galena. On your way to Galena, stop at Castle Rock State Park near Oregon and hike up the limestone cliffs to view the Rock River valley. Continue northwest, with another stop at the small but scenic Apple River Canyon State Park for a another short hike through the woods. Drive along Highway 20 and through the little towns of Stockton and Elizabeth. Check into an inn, bed-and-breakfast, or resort in Galena.

DAY 4

Spend the day in Galena. Tour Ulysses S. Grant's former home, have lunch in the historic DeSoto House Hotel, sample regional wines, shop in the galleries downtown. See a play or musical. Stroll along the river.

DAY 5

Depart Galena and drive south along Great River Road. South of the Quad Cities, go east to the former Swedish colony Bishop Hill. Spend the day browsing artisan shops and admiring Swedish-American folk art. In the afternoon drive east through the river towns of Hennepin, La Salle, and Peru toward Ottawa and the popular Starved Rock State Park. Check into the state park lodge or private cabin.

DAY 6

Hike the trails at Starved Rock State Park. Rent horses and explore the nearby Matthiessen State Park. Cruise the Illinois River on a paddle-wheel boat.

DAY 7

Drive to scenic Nauvoo for a visit to the Joseph Smith Historic Site, the rebuilt Mormon Temple—the Nauvoo Illinois Temple, and a nearby winery. Stay overnight in a hotel or lodge overlooking the Mississippi River.

DAY 8

Head south along the Great River Road to the small but bustling river town of Grafton. Hop on your bike (or rent one) and ride along the Mississippi River and through Pere Marquette State Park. Stay in the grand state park lodge.

DAY 9

Continue south and west of St. Louis to the town of Collinsville for a must-see visit to Cahokia Mounds. Wander the museum, hike Monks Mound, and walk the nearby trails. Spend the afternoon driving the scenic back roads to Carbondale.

Castle Rock State Park, Oregon

DAY 10

Grab a hard hat and some tough boots. This morning you'll explore the wild Illinois Caverns State Natural Area near Red Bud.

DAY 11

Hike or horseback ride along the bluffs of Giant City State Park. Try your hand at rock climbing. Dine and stay in the historic lodge or one of the state park's cabins. Browse boardwalk shops in Makanda.

DAY 12

Canoe the Cache River, stroll along a floating boardwalk through wetlands, and amble along on a drive through the region, pausing at the occasional scenic overlook.

DAY 13

Hike the stupendous trails on the eastern end of the Shawnee National Forest in the Garden of the Gods and Cave-in-Rock State Park, where bluffs tower above the Ohio River.

DAY 14

Drive north to Springfield for a walk through the Lincoln Home and surrounding historic district, followed by a visit to the new Lincoln Presidential Library and Museum.

Chicago: Your Kind of Town

You could live in Chicago an entire year and still not see all there is to see in this constantly changing, morphing town. The standouts are the Art Institute and an architectural boat tour of the city's great buildings, but Chicago is often called a city of neighborhoods, so don't forget to spend a few hours strolling through one or two of them. It's here where you'll get a sense of the city, its residents, its vivacity, its realness, its dreams.

DAY 1

Morning

Start your weekend downtown in the "Loop" district with an architectural boat tour along the Chicago River. Follow that up with a visit through the gorgeous Art Institute of Chicago and a walk through nearby Grant Park, pausing for a stop in front of Buckingham Fountain. Grab a sandwich and beer at the historic Berghoff, a German-American pub and restaurant open since 1898.

Afternoon

Rent bicycles at Navy Pier and ride along the lakefront trail. Take off your shoes and test the Lake Michigan water. Head back to the pier and then over to the fabulous Michigan Avenue to ogle at the shops.

Evening

Watch the sun set from atop the Hancock Observatory or Sears Tower. Dine in award-winning Mexican-American restaurant Topolobampo. Take in a show at the Goodman Theatre or Steppenwolf Theatre.

DAY 2

Morning

Spend the morning touring the Field Museum, Adler Planetarium, or Shedd Aquarium, all within walking distance of each other downtown.

Afternoon

Take off for the north-side neighborhood of Lincoln Park for a visit to the free Lincoln Park Zoo. From there head north to Wrigleyville and the friendly confines of Wrigley Field. Browse the bookstores and boutiques and duck into a coffee shop in Andersonville.

Evening

At night dine in the Wicker Park or Southport neighborhoods. Then slip into a jazz, blues, or alt-rock club.

DAY 3

Morning

Go south to the burgeoning Prairie District to visit the Clarke House, the oldest house in the city. Continue farther south to bustling Chinatown for lunch.

Afternoon

And onward to the Hyde Park neighborhood and the University of Chicago campus. Get lost in bookstores, and wander through the gothic quad. Finish with a tour of Frank Lloyd Wright's Robie House or a visit to the DuSable Museum of African American History.

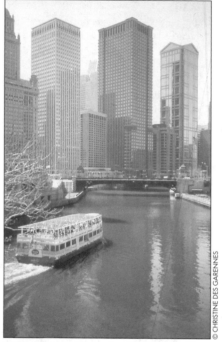

© CHRISTINE DES GARENNES

architectural boat tour along the Chicago River

Evening

Stick around the Hyde Park neighborhood for a theater production or music concert at one of the University of Chicago's performance spaces.

OAK PARK

Boasting more than a dozen Frank Lloyd Wright homes, Oak Park is a mecca for fans of Prairie-style architecture. Free shuttle buses between the major sights and shopping districts make this town easy to navigate. You can get there from downtown Chicago on the Chicago Transit District's elevated trains or the Metra suburban train line.

Morning

Begin your visit with a tour of Wright's Home and Studio, followed by a walking, biking, or driving tour of the surrounding neighborhoods. From there you can walk to downtown Oak Park, grab lunch from a deli, and picnic in one of the many parks in the village.

Afternoon

Spend an hour or so browsing the shops along Lake Street, Harrison Street, or Chicago Avenue. Each district offers a mix of clothing and gift boutiques, second-hand music and book stores, and coffee shops. Next it's on to the birthplace of Ernest Hemingway, also within a short walking distance of downtown. When you've finished the home tour, walk down the street to visit a small museum dedicated to the writer.

Ernest Hemingway's birth home, Oak Park

COURTESY OF THE ERNEST HEMINGWAY FOUNDATION OF OAK PARK/NANCY HLAVACEK

Evening

Top off your visit to Oak Park with dinner at one of the award-winning storefront restaurants such as La Bella Pasteria or Khyber Pass. Then follow that with a play at Circle Theatre in Forest Park or, if you're visiting in the summer, an outdoor Shakespearean play at Festival Theater in Austin Gardens.

EVANSTON

Bordering Chicago on the north side, Evanston manages to be part college town (Northwestern University is here), well-to-do north-shore suburb (lots of grand homes on the lakeshore), and a vibrant, diverse community of progressive artists and other folks. Visitors are drawn to the lakeshore, which stretches for four miles in Evanston. There are plenty of sandy beaches, lakefront trails for walking, biking, jogging, or in-line skating. You can take the Chicago Transit Districts elevated train to Evanston or the Metra suburban train line.

Morning

Begin your trip visiting the scenic lakeshore and Grosse Point Lighthouse, a National Historic Landmark on the north side of Evanston. Tour the adjacent Evanston Arts Center and lounge awhile on the sandy beach. If you're feeling ambitious, walk along the lakeshore path.

Afternoon

Head back into town for lunch at one of dozens of restaurants within walking distance of the lakeside parks. Shop for used books, travel accessories, and music along Chicago and Orrington avenues. Rest your feet in one of the many coffee shops. Check out exhibits at Kendall College's Mitchell Museum of the American Indian or wander through the chateaulike Charles Gates Dawes House.

Evening

Indulge in a big meal at Davis Street Fish Market or Dave's Italian Kitchen. Catch a theater production or music concert at Northwestern University or at one of the community venues.

FOX CITIES

Forty miles west of Chicago along the rolling Fox River, the villages of St. Charles, Geneva, and Batavia are postcard towns: tree-lined streets with tidy bungalows and ornate, renovated Victorians, and historic downtowns with shops, restaurants, and watering holes. All three are connected by the multirecreational Fox River Trail, which meanders along the river. From downtown Chicago you can take the Metra train line to Geneva. Otherwise, follow I-88 west to Batavia or North Avenue west.

Morning

Start on the south end with a stroll along Batavia's riverfront park, which allows you to get up close to the river and admire a collection of windmills.

Afternoon

Drive north to Geneva for lunch at a riverside restaurant, followed by an hour or so of browsing art galleries and gift shops.

Evening

Continue your shopping in St. Charles, which has numerous antiques shops and the popular Kane County Flea Market. Stroll along the riverfront and dine at one of the downtown restaurants or within the historic Hotel Baker.

CHAIN O' LAKES

About 45 miles northwest of Chicago, the Chain O' Lakes region is, as the name implies, a land dotted with countless lakes. Formed by the last retreating glacier, the lakes and the parks along their shores provide lots of opportunities for boating, fishing, and hiking.

Morning

Rent a rowboat or canoe at Chain O' Lakes State Park and explore the backwaters. Or, lace up your hiking boots for a walk through the park.

Afternoon

After a picnic at Chain O' Lakes, drive to the rare Volo Bog, a National Natural Landmark, for a leisurely stroll. Look for orchids and listen for frogs. Drop by the Glunz Family Winery and Berry Farm in Grayslake.

Evening

Take advantage of late-day discounts and take a spin on one of the many roller coasters at the Six Flags Great America theme park in Gurnee.

STARVED ROCK

Craving fresh air and eager to exercise? About 1.5 hours west of Chicago along I-80 are several state parks packed with horseback riding and hiking trails.

Morning

The largest and most popular state park in the region is Utica's Starved Rock State Park. Begin your visit with a tour of the visitors center, which has excellent exhibits on the region's Native American history. Hike up Starved Rock. Then, take a trolley ride for an overview of the park or a paddle-wheel boat ride along the Illinois River.

Afternoon

Scout for eagles or admire the fall foliage of the region while on the back of a horse. Starved Rock Riding Stables offers several horseback-riding trips in the area.

Evening
Visit nearby downtown Ottawa for dinner followed by a walk through Washington Square, where Abraham Lincoln and Stephen Douglas debated slavery. Before leaving, drop by Buffalo Rock State Park between Utica and Ottawa. The small park has an outstanding scenic overlook of the Illinois River Valley.

Outdoor Adventure in Southern Illinois

Scale rocks. Canoe cypress swamps. Hike through ravines. Drive along a two-lane scenic highway. This is what the southern third of the state is all about. Almost everywhere you turn you'll find top-notch hiking and biking trails, quiet campsites, and amazing rock formations. And along the way, a winery or orchard here and there.

DAY 1
Spend the morning exploring the only cave open to the public in the state, Illinois Caverns State Natural Area, near Redbud. The wild cave has several miles of trails to follow. They're lit only by the light of your flashlight .

After your time underground, drive southeast toward Carbondale and Giant City State Park. Pitch a tent or rent a room in the historic lodge in the heart of the Shawnee National Forest. Hike the Red Cedar Hiking Trail or take a brief jaunt along the Stone Fort Nature Trail. Otherwise, rent a horse at the park stables and follow one of the horse trails.

DAY 2
After a full breakfast at the lodge, drive south through the Shawnee Hills to Natural Bridge Park for a short hike through woody ravines. Wind through the back roads and stop at Little Grand Canyon, also southwest of Carbondale. The steep, four-mile loop has several scenic overlooks of the forest. Unwind with a glass of wine at the nearby Pomona Winery or Von Jakob on Jakob Vineyards.

DAY 3
Drive east a short distance to Drapers Bluff and Vertical Heartland Climbing School, where instructors will teach you the ropes about rock

Tunnel Hill State Trail near Karnak

© CHRISTINE DES GARENNES

climbing on their private outdoor course or take you to the best boulders and cliffs in the area, including those at Ferne Clyffe State Park.

DAY 4

Today you'll turn south toward Metropolis. The shallow seas that once covered Illinois millions of years ago are long gone, but you've still got a chance to explore underwater life. Mermet Springs, between Vienna and Metropolis, is a spring-fed quarry that has been transformed into a scuba destination for beginner or experienced divers.

DAY 5

Wake up early and rent a canoe in Ullin, and then paddle into the otherworldly Cache River State Natural Area near Belknap in the far southern part of the state. Reminiscent of the swamps in Louisiana and other Gulf states, the natural area has quiet canoe trails through tupelo and cypress swamps. Keep an eye out for orchids and egrets.

DAY 6

Jog over to Karnak or north to Harrisburg, where you'll unload your bike for a trip down Tunnel Hill State Trail. The trail challenges riders for 45 miles from Harrisburg to Karnak. Pedal through tunnels, over trestles, and along the bottomlands of the Cache River basin.

DAY 7

Discover remains of a Native American village and an ancient rock shelter while hiking along 80- to 100-foot-high bluffs at Lusk Creek Canyon Nature Preserve and Indian Kitchen, east of Eddyville in Southern Illinois. If you've got some strength left, go east toward the Ohio River for one final hike through the Garden of the Gods.

From the ancient Mississippian mound culture to Abraham Lincoln, the state of Illinois has plenty of sights for history buffs. If you love Lincoln, you're so in luck. Springfield is loaded with Lincoln's old haunts, as are several other towns where Lincoln once debated Stephen Douglas or practiced law. Many of the history-rich towns are a joy to visit. The former lead-mining town of Galena, once home to Ulysses S. Grant, has been transformed into a burgeoning artisan community. Historic Nauvoo, once a settlement to Mormons and later French Icarians, has an amazing number of well-preserved brick homes and storefronts.

DAY 1

Begin with a visit to the Chicago Historical Society on the near north side of Chicago. It's stocked with permanent and rotating exhibits about the city and state's history and legendary figures from the past. Head south to Hyde Park and Pullman Historic District, two primarily residential neighborhoods.

DAY 2

Visit the former lead mining town of Galena, now a bustling arts community. Wander through the home of Civil War hero and former U.S. President Ulysses S. Grant. Stay or dine in the historic DeSoto House Hotel, where Abraham Lincoln, Grant, Mark Twain, Teddy Roosevelt, and other famous Americans have stayed.

DAY 3

Drive south to Galesburg and the Knox College campus. It is in front of the Old Main building, where Lincoln and Stephen Douglas held the fifth in a series of political debates on topics such as slavery. Drop by Carl Sandburg's former home in Galesburg. Stay overnight in a Toulon bed-and-breakfast, where Lincoln once reportedly stayed.

DAY 4

Learn about the Mormons and Icarians with a visit to Nauvoo, a historic Mississippi River town north of Quincy. Then drive east to get a feel for pioneer life in the 1800s by walking through New Salem, a recreated village north of Springfield. With horses, vegetable gardens, weavers, and millers, the town is modeled after the days when Lincoln lived here, working as postman and general store manager.

One of the best Lincoln sites in Illinois is New Salem, his old stomping grounds near Petersburg.

DAY 5

Dive into all the Lincoln sights Springfield has to offer, among them Lincoln's former home, the Old State Capitol, and Lincoln Presidential Library and Museum.

DAY 6

Drive west and south to Jacksonville for a personalized tour of former Underground Railroad sites. Continue to the amazing Cahokia Mounds, where you'll discover ancient Native American burial mounds and a comprehensive museum on Native Americans from the Mississippi River valley.

DAY 7

Before they set out on their journey west, Meriwether Lewis and William Clark rounded up volunteers and supplies in Illinois. To find out more about their time here, tour the Lewis and Clark Interpretive Center near Hartford. Continue south along the Mississippi River to the ghostly Fort de Chartres near Prairie du Rocher. The recreated stone fort stands as a reminder that Illinois once belonged to France. The site includes archaeological remains and a recreation of the wooden and stone fort built and occupied in the mid-1700s.

Explore Illinois

Chicago

Let's be frank. Chicago winters can get wet, bitterly cold and windy. Chicago "rush hour" traffic delays often develop as early as 3 P.M. And really, who likes to pay $20 a day to park their car?

But oh, I love this town. And I bet you will too. Step off the plane, train, or car, and Chicago rises before you. The lake stretches out to the east, and in the Loop, the birthplace of the skyscraper, steel and glass pierce the clouds. Down below you'll discover an array of dining, cultural, recreation, and shopping possibilities. Most visitors to Chicago tend to stick to the downtown Loop area and North Shore neighborhoods of Lincoln Park and Lakeview. But the city encompasses approximately 28 square miles and stretches for about 30 miles along Lake Michigan. In one corner of the city a hot dog vendor sells juicy dogs, and in another a chef designs art nouveau cuisine. At the historic Lyric Opera, an internationally renowned singer takes stage; in a tiny, storefront theater uptown, an actor reads from a new, groundbreaking script. From the popular Shedd Aquarium to the offbeat holography museum, this rich city has it all.

Above all, Chicago is a fun city. Just take a look at the list of annual music and food festivals, where all walks of life from the Midwest gather every summer. Even if you aren't a sports fan, spending an afternoon in the bleacher seats at the friendly confines of Wrigley Field is a great way to experience the character of the city. For more refined tastes, Chicago has great opportunities for shopping in glitzy boutiques, dining in five-star restaurants, or just strolling along tree-lined residential streets. Walk down to the lower level of the Art Institute of Chicago and view a moving photography exhibit. Check out the ornate

Must-Sees

Look for M to find the sights and activities you can't miss and Ⅺ for the best dining and lodging.

M Museum Campus: A majority of Chicago's major museums lie within what is called Museum Campus, a cluster of huge buildings east of Lake Shore Drive and near the Lake Michigan shoreline. In particular, don't miss the Field Museum, the gigantic Oceanarium at John G. Shedd Aquarium, and the historic Adler Planetarium and Astronomy Museum (page 33).

M The Art Institute of Chicago: Perhaps best known for its extensive collection of 19th-century French impressionist art, the Art Institute, which contains more than 300,000 works of art, is also home to fine modern paintings (such as a few Picassos), contemporary photography, textiles, and a collection of medieval armor (page 36).

M Grant Park: Grant Park is where the city plays. You can salsa as part of SummerDance, watch vintage movies during the Chicago Outdoor Film Festival, listen to the symphony orchestra, chomp on hot dogs, or smell the lilacs. During the summer, the iconic Clarence Buckingham Memorial Fountain, a huge, bronze wrought-iron sculpture, displays a spectacular light and water show (page 37).

M Wrigley Field: The "Friendly Confines," as the baseball stadium is known around town, was built in 1914 and is one of the few remaining ballparks in the country that can boast ivy-covered brick walls. An evening or afternoon game here is a treat even for people who aren't fans of the sport (page 44).

M Garfield Park Conservatory: On the National Register of Historic Places, this sometimes-overlooked conservatory is a jewel box of a complex. Built in 1906, the conservatory was renovated in 2003 and features art glass by Dale Chihuly (page 44).

M Hyde Park: A great way to spend the day is walking through the diverse Hyde Park neighborhood on the city's south side. Take a peek inside the university's Gothic Rockefeller Memorial Chapel and Quadrangle. Go ice-skating or picnicking at Midway Plaisance, the extra wide and extra long parkway at the southern tip of the campus. Take a tour of Frank Lloyd Wright's Robie House (page 45).

M Lake Michigan Beaches: This isn't Santa Monica, but Chicago has plenty of parks and beaches along the Lake Michigan shoreline for dozing in the sun, jogging, bicycling, or engaging a stranger in a game of chess (page 53).

Chicago

CHICAGO

Lake Michigan

SEE "RIVER NORTH" MAP

SEE "THE LOOP" MAP

Lincoln Park

LASALLE ST

THE LOOP

WISHBONE

GREEKTOWN

ANDERSONVILLE

WRIGLEYVILLE

BROADWAY

LINCOLN AVE

RIDGE AVE

CALIFORNIA AVE

EMERSON ST

DODGE AVE

CENTRAL ST

MCCORMICK BLVD

CRAWFORD AVE

SKOKIE

FOSTER AVE

LAWRENCE AVE

TOUHY AVE

LINCOLN AVE

DEVON AVE

PETERSON AVE

ELSTON AVE

MILWAUKEE AVE

FULLERTON AVE

Humboldt Park

PULASKI RD

GRAND AVE

CHICAGO AVE

★ GARFIELD PARK CONSERVATORY

GLENVIEW

GOLF RD

Forest Preserve

DEMPSTER ST

OAKTON ST

CROSS POINT RD

CALDWELL AVE

CICERO AVE

IRVING PARK RD

ADDISON ST

BELMONT AVE

CENTRAL AVE

NORTH AVE

RIDGELAND AVE

NARRAGANSETT AVE

HARLEM AVE

EUCLID AVE

MILWAUKEE AVE

NORTHWEST HWY

GREENWOOD AVE

TALCOTT RD

LAWRENCE AVE

CUMBERLAND AVE

FOREST PRESERVE AVE

THATCHER AVE

WASHINGTON BLVD

DEE RD

E RIVER RD

Forest Preserve

BUSSE HWY

(TOLL)

Forest Preserve

DES PLAINES RIVER RD

MANNHEIM RD

25TH AVE

MANNHEIM RD

CHICAGO O'HARE INTERNATIONAL AIRPORT

WOLF RD

(TOLL)

Chicago

© AVALON TRAVEL PUBLISHING, INC.

architecture of the Pullman National Historic District on the far south side, the historic Garfield Park Conservatory to the west, or the bookshops and cafés in Andersonville on the far north end of the city. Board a boat for a fascinating tour of the Chicago River and a look at some of the city's most notable buildings. Bring your bike (or rent one), pedal along the lakeshore path, and unwind for about an hour or so on a rock ledge or sandy beach. Take in a show at one of the dozens of award-winning Broadway or storefront theaters. And if you want to eat like the locals, be sure to drop by a hot dog stand for a beefy dog or into a pizza joint and bite into the cheesiest, thickest pizza you could ever imagine.

PLANNING YOUR TIME

Like other major urban areas in the United States, Chicago has become much more of a welcoming place for visitors in recent years. Recreation trails have been expanded, parks have been remodeled, farmers markets have been added, and trolleys shuttle tourists from one attraction to the other. Public transportation in the city is swift and reliable. You should be able to take an elevated train or bus to all the sights highlighted in this chapter. Driving will most likely take longer and just cause headaches.

You can do Chicago in a weekend, but chances are you might not be able to walk afterward. However, if you do it all in two or three days, stick to the downtown and near north area. Museums and attractions such as the Art Institute of Chicago and Shedd Aquarium are huge and you could spend hours upon hours admiring their collections. Pick up interior maps of these places and hit the exhibits you're interested in first.

Chicago is a city of neighborhoods and it's a good idea to see the city neighborhood by neighborhood. Start downtown and then move north one day, then south on another day. Plan for traffic delays and long lines in front of popular museums such as the Shedd and Field.

Access

Chicago is fairly easy to navigate. It's laid out like a grid. If you ride to the top of the Sears Tower or John Hancock Center, or arrive via airplane and fly above during a clear day or a clear night, you'll be able to see this extensive grid system. Madison Street downtown is the dividing line between north and south; State Street divides east and west. East-west streets south of Congress Parkway, which is at the south end of the Loop, are numbered in descending order as you drive or walk south. A handful of avenues, such as Lincoln, Grand, and Milwaukee, run diagonally to and from the Loop. These streets, it seems, are always flooded with cars.

As in any major metropolitan city, driving in Chicago is a hassle, despite the ongoing expansions of the area's highways and tollways. Chicago is serviced by a number of interstates and tollways. I-294, otherwise known as the Tri-State Tollway, skirts the western edge of the city and the western suburbs. I-290, the Eisenhower or Ike, runs from Congress Parkway in downtown Chicago west to the western suburbs and places such as the Brookfield Zoo and Oak Park. Traffic backs up in both directions of the Ike starting at 6 A.M., tapers off around 9 A.M., and starts up again at 3 P.M. The main highway through town is I-94, called the Dan Ryan Expressway from the south side to downtown, and the Edens Expressway on the north side. I-90 runs from the Loop out to O'Hare and beyond. Avoid it if at all possible. It is notorious for long travel times.

Don't bother driving through the city unless you have to. Drivers aren't necessarily as speedy or territorial as they are in Los Angeles, but they aren't exactly considerate either. It's common for drivers to roll through stop signs and honk at those in front of them who have come to complete stops. And unfortunately, it's not uncommon for cars to drive in a bicycle lane to pass other cars.

Parking in the Loop can cost you about $20 per day. The cheapest lots tend to be those run by the city near Grant Park. There are some metered spaces on the streets, but these are strictly monitored. On-street parking is restricted in some areas, such as the neighborhoods around Wrigley Field and Lincoln Park. Parking there will require residential zone stickers and city stickers. Read the signs before you park anywhere. Parking enforcers will hunt you down, and tickets are expensive. If you park during street cleaning, expect a $50 ticket. Your best bet is to avoid traffic and parking problems by riding on Metra, the suburban train line, or trains and buses run by the Chicago Transit Authority. Trains and buses are fairly regular and reliable. One-way tickets will cost $1.75.

Resources

Pick up sightseeing and attraction brochures (including free Chicago Transit Authority system maps) at the Tourist Information Centers throughout the city: **Chicago Water Works** (163 E. Pearson Ave.); **Chicago Cultural Center** (78 E. Washington St.); and the **James R. Thompson Center** (100 W. Randolph St.).

The **Chicago Convention and Tourism Bureau** and the **City of Chicago Office of Tourism** manage the tourism hotline 877/

CHICAGO (877/244-2246) and the website www.877chicago.com. The tourism bureau has offices in the huge convention hall **McCormick Place** (2301 S. Lake Shore Dr.). The Office of Tourism is at 78 East Washington Street.

ORIENTATION
Neighborhoods

Many visitors to Chicago start their vacations here in the **Loop,** or downtown. All highways, subway, and elevated train lines lead to the Loop. The **Greyhound Bus Station** is here. So is **Union Station,** where suburban and Amtrak train lines depart and embark. The Loop is the area south and east of the Chicago River, north of Congress Parkway, and west of Lake Michigan. If you take a look at a Chicago Transit Authority Map, you'll see the train lines make a circle around this area. If you transfer bus or L (what we call the elevated trains) lines, chances are you'll transfer lines downtown.

The Loop is where the city does its business and where most convention and business

© CHRISTINE DES GARENNES

Wicker Park on a Sunday afternoon

travelers stay. It's easy to get around (plenty of taxis, trains, and buses) and boasts amazing architecture. But it clears out in the evening and lacks some of the charm that other areas of the city have.

North of the Loop are **River North** and the **Gold Coast** neighborhoods, home to the Museum of Contemporary Art, galleries, slick bars and restaurants, ritzy condominium buildings and hotels, department stores on Michigan Avenue and chic boutiques and salons on Oak Street. West of there is **Bucktown** and **Wicker Park,** once an affordable neighborhood popular among artists, musicians, and antiques dealers and now an increasingly expensive distric—still with great music venues and a mix of clothing and art shops. North of the Gold Coast are **Old Town** and **Lincoln Park,** gentrified areas home to Lincoln Park Zoo and several neighborhood parks, remodeled brownstones and Victorians, and a mix of storefront theaters, sports bars, and white-tablecloth restaurants popular among the 20- and 30-something crowd. Other neighborhoods to explore are youthful **Wrigleyville,** home to the world-famous Wrigley Field, and **Andersonville** and **Rogers Park** on the far north side, where a mix of people with Southeast Asian, Indian, Jewish, and Swedish roots live. To the south of downtown, and easily accessible via public transportation, is **Chinatown,** followed by **Hyde Park,** home to the University of Chicago campus, Frank Lloyd Wright's Robie House, and the Museum of Science and Industry. Finally, at the southern tip of the city is the historic **Pullman** neighborhood, a must-see for all preservationist buffs.

When to Go

Anytime! Chicago is always pulsing, no matter what time of day or season. In May, the city streets, cafés, and lakeside beaches become packed with residents who have been itching to soak up the sun's rays. In early summer the city is bursting with activity and into July and August it seems there's a festival every weekend. The average high in July is 83°F and 82°F in August. But sometimes it can get quite humid

and hot in August. (In fact, a heat wave was blamed for hundreds of deaths in 1995.) When the humidity and temperatures rise, stick by the lakeside, where it's cooler in the summer (and warmer in the winter). Chicago is splendid in the fall, but the weather tends to be fickle in October and November. One day it could be 70°F, the next day it could be in the 40s.

Chicago tends to attract frugal and hardy travelers during the winter. The average high in January is 29°F and the low is 14°F. Average snowfall in January is about two inches; however, in 1967 it snowed 23 inches in 29 hours. The museums are still open, and there are still a few excellent festivals, such as the outdoor Christkindlmarket downtown. Visit during this time and you'll get a lot more for your money. Hotels offer great deals during the chilly and snowy months of January and February. During this time of year check out the city's historic pubs and load up on comfort food. Snow storms don't shut down the city, but folks who like to travel on foot might be slowed down by the residents and businesses slow to shovel the sidewalks. On snowy days, it's best to avoid the expressways and keep to the elevated trains and the Metro suburban trains.

HISTORY

Chicago gets its name from the Potawatomi Indian word *checagou,* which has been translated to mean wild onion and swamp grass. Before the settlers, the flat, marshland area was home mainly to members of the Potawatomi tribe, who migrated from Michigan and the northeast region of the continent. Indians, fur traders, and explorers passed through the area, including Father Jacques Marquette and Louis Jolliet, who journeyed through the area on their way back from traveling down the Mississippi River. Most of the early pioneers to the state settled hundreds of miles south of Chicago, near Shawneetown.

It wasn't until the opening of the Erie Canal in 1825 that Chicago (and other parts of the former Northwest Territory) began to see their

THE DALEYS AND MACHINE POLITICS

The Machine. In Chicago this phrase doesn't refer to any sort of iron and steel structure. It's politics, baby. Machine politics is essentially rewarding people with jobs and other favors for supporting (and getting out the vote) for chosen political candidates. While this most certainly goes on in other cities and states, Chicago is famous for it. The guy who is most often linked to machine politics is Richard J. Daley, Chicago's mayor from the 1950s until 1976, when he died in office from a heart attack. His son, Richard M. Daley, has been mayor since 1989.

The Daley Dynasty, you might say, has had a hold on Chicago politics for decades. The Daleys and staff within the Daley administrations tend to think big, do big things, and they're not shy about taking stances on certain issues. During Richard J. Daley's tenure, a slew of buildings were erected, including the Sears Tower, McCormick Place, several interstates, and the notorious high-rise housing projects. He was much admired as a politician, but it wasn't hard to find critics. In 1968, he drew fire for taking a tough stance on dealing with protests during the Democratic National Convention, which involved violent clashes between protesters and police.

Richard M. Daley has also been behind several multimillion-dollar projects, such as the Soldier Field renovation, the brand-new Millennium Park, and the proposal to expand O'Hare International Airport. To the horror of many small-plane pilots, Daley ordered a team to bulldoze Miegs Field, the small airfield southeast of the Loop, in the middle of the night. It's now a park called Northerly Island. Among Daley's supporters: whites, blacks, Hispanics, Poles, gays. He talks frankly, like a real person, not always a politician. He's also a self-professed bicycling fan and a big proponent of making Chicago a bike-friendly city. The second Daley's administration has also not been without controversy. One of the more recent scandals, dubbed the hired truck program, involved the city's hiring private trucking companies to do work for the city. Investigations uncovered incidences in which trucks would carry nothing at all and truck companies with possible connections to the Mob.

populations grow. From 1830 to 1840 the city's population increased from 100 residents to 4,470. They came via steamboats and the railroad. Another boon to development was the opening of the Illinois and Michigan Canal in 1848, which connected the Great Lakes to the Mississippi River. At the same time the first railroad—the Galena and Chicago Union—linked Chicago with the Galena lead mines in the northwestern part of the state.

As the city grew, officials realized that they would need to make major changes to the infrastructure to keep pace with its growth. In 1855 the city undertook the huge task of raising the street level by several feet. Until that point most of the city's buildings were constructed hastily on swampy ground, leaving no room for sanitary sewers (which did not bode

well for the health of the residents). That year crews moved through the city, lifting buildings, adding foundations, building sewer lines, and planking the streets. The result was a more modern and clean city.

By that point the city was really taking off and emerging as an industrial city with McCormick's reaper factory, the Pullman Palace Car factory, textile factories, lumber companies, grain-storage facilities, and food companies. In 1865 the Union Stock Yards opened on the southwest side. The businesses employed thousands of workers, mostly German and Irish immigrants, and eventually included Eastern Europeans, Mexicans, and African Americans. As chronicled by Upton Sinclair in *The Jungle,* these workers toiled at their tasks in unsanitary conditions for long days. The yards were surrounded by miles and miles of railroad lines, which is how most of the animals were transferred into the city. Nearby was also a branch of the Chicago River, dubbed Bubbly Creek because of what was dumped into the river from the plants. Beyond the yards were meat-packing and meat-byproduct plants such as Armour, and finally, the neighborhoods where the workers lived: Back of the Yards, Whiskey Point, and Packingtown.

Then one night in early October 1871, after a long, hot, and dry summer, a fire was ignited in a barn on the city's West Side. (Legend says Mrs. O'Leary's cow kicked over a lantern.) Within hours the flames migrated to the city's south side and eventually leapt the Chicago River and struck the north side. By the time it was extinguished the following day, the fire claimed the lives of 300 people and left about 90,000 without homes. The fire, however devastating it was to the city, would provide Chicago the opportunity to rebuild itself in grand style. Architects such asDaniel Burnham, Louis Sullivan, Jens Jensen, Frank Lloyd Wright, and others devised lofty plans for the city. They built lavish hotels, music halls, and skyscrapers.

But the quality of life for the city's working class people and the poor was pretty grim. The Gold Coast and Prairie Avenue District flourished with mansions, parks, and department stores, but much of the city was mired with muddy, dirty streets and houses for drinking, gambling, and prostitution. Throughout the 19th and early 20th centuries residents battled smallpox, cholera, typhoid fever, tuberculosis, scarlet fever, and more. Hours at the factories or rail yards were long and wages were often cut.

It was during these years that social activists came onto the scene. Among them were Mary Harris "Mother" Jones, a union and labor organizer who founded the Industrial Workers of the World, and Jane Addams, who founded Hull House in 1889. Addams and her staff taught English to recent immigrants, organized social and recreation opportunities, and lobbied for the city to improve services to the poor areas of town, such as demanding regular garbage collection.

In the decades that followed the Depression and World War II, Chicago became a modern city. Richard J. Daley ruled as mayor 1955–1976. While he was mayor, O'Hare Airport was built and a number of expressways developed, further ensuring the city's place as a transportation hub. The 912-foot-tall Prudential Building was erected in 1955, the John Hancock Center in 1969, followed by the Sears Tower in 1974. During these years the city built massive housing projects on the south and west sides, many of which have been razed in recent years.

After Daley's death in 1976, the city's residents went on to elect their first female mayor, Jane Byrne, in 1979, followed by the first African-American mayor, Harold Washington, in 1983. Daley's son, Richard M., took control in 1989 and started his fifth four-year term in 2003.

The Loop

The Loop is where much of the city does its business. Many city, county, and state offices are here. The area is mobbed during the weekdays, generally 8 A.M. to 6 P.M., but is a bit more quiet during the weekends. Many of the big, must-see sights are here: Museum Campus, Grant Park, The Art Institute of Chicago, plus it's home to a Broadway theater district.

MUSEUMS

M Museum Campus

Home to the Field Museum, Adler Planetarium, and Shedd Aquarium, Museum Campus is a cluster of three amazing museums on the lakefront. You can get there by walking along the sidewalks from Michigan Avenue, by bus, taxi, or car. (There are some street parking spaces by Adler Planetarium, plus a lot by the Field Museum. If you want a space, go as early as possible in the morning.)

The vast **Field Museum** (1400 S. Lake Shore Dr., 312/922-9410, www.fmnh.org, 9 A.M.–5 P.M. daily, $14–25) was built to house many of the anthropological and biological items that were on display during Chicago's Columbia Exposition in 1893. More than 15 million artifacts are stored here, including meteorites, seed vials, Aztec pottery, Papua New Guinea dance masks, Egyptian mummies, and dinosaur fossils, the most impressive of which is Sue, reportedly the largest, most complete, and best-preserved *Tyrannosaurus rex* in the world.

When it opened in 1930, the **Adler Planetarium and Astronomy Museum** (1300 S. Lake Shore Dr., 312/922-STARR— 312/922-7827, www.adlerplanetarium.org, 9:30 A.M.–6 P.M. daily Memorial Day–Labor Day; 9:30 A.M.–4 P.M. daily Labor Day–Memorial Day; 9:30 A.M.–10 P.M. first Fri. of the month; $16), was the first planetarium of its kind in the Western Hemisphere. Since then it

The Shedd Aquarium and Sears Tower, Chicago

Chicago

THE LOOP

Lake
Michigan

NAVY PIER

FAMILY GOLF CENTER

Chicago River

Lincoln
Park

41

LAKE SHORE DR

E LOWER IL ST

▼ FOX & OBEL

N McCLURG CT

N DeWITT PL
N DELAWARE PL

E SUPERIOR ST
E HURON ST
E ERIE ST
E ONTARIO ST
E OHIO ST
E ILLINOIS ST
E WATER ST

★ MUSEUM OF
CONTEMPORARY ART

E CHICAGO AVE

N MIES VAN DER ROHE

N FAIRBANKS CT

E GRAND AVE

E WALTON ST
E CHESTNUT ST

N ST CLAIR ST

N STETSON AVE

JOHN HANCOCK
CENTER ■

★ WATER TOWER PLACE

MAGNIFICENT MILE

E WACKER DR

N RUSH ST

E PEARSON ST

N MICHIGAN AVE

CHICAGO
WATER TOWER ■

N RUSH ST

N WABASH A

E DIVISION ST
E ELM ST
E CEDAR ST
E BELLEVUE PL

N RUSH ST

N WABASH AVE

BILLY GOAT
TAVERN ▼

N WABASH A

N OAK ST

N STATE ST

CHICAGO THEATRE ★

W ELM ST
W MAPLE ST

N DEARBORN ST

PIZZARIA UNO ▼

MARSHALL FIELD'S ■

N CLARK ST

FRONTERA GRILL &
TOPOLOBAMPO ▼

★ MUSEUM OF BROADCAST
COMMUNICATIONS

W HILL ST

N LASALLE ST

CAFÉ
IBERICO ▼

N WELLS ST

HOWARD
● JOHNSON INN

W GRAND AVE

W WACKER DR

W LAKE ST

W COUCH PL

OHIO HOUSE
MOTEL ■

W ILLINOIS ST
W HUBBARD ST

N ORLEANS ST
N FRANKLIN ST
N INSTITUTE

N CHICAGO AVE

W SUPERIOR ST
W HURON ST
W ERIE ST
W ONTARIO ST
W OHIO ST

N WACK

W WALTON ST
W LOCUST ST

BRETT'S KITCHEN ▼

W DIVISION ST

N SEDGWICK ST

N HUDSON
AVE

N CLEVELAND AVE
N MOHAWK CT
N CAMBRIDGE AVE

N CLEVELAND AVE

N KINGSBURY ST

W KINZIE ST

W OAK ST

N LARRABEE ST

W KINZIE ST

Chicago

© AVALON TRAVEL PUBLISHING, INC.

has expanded quite a bit. The historical astronomical exhibit with its sundials and astrolabes is still stunning, but there are also the interactive digital StarRider Theater and an interactive computer graphic theater.

Designers didn't hold back when planning exhibits at the **John G. Shedd Aquarium** (1200 S. Lake Shore Dr., 312/939-2438, www.sheddaquarium.org, $8–25), particularly the $45 million Pacific Northwest exhibit, which opened in 1991. The three-million-gallon Oceanarium is home to seals, dolphins, and Beluga whales. Then there's the 2003 Wild Reef exhibit, which features sharks, from blacktip reef to zebra sharks, in a 400,000-gallon shark habitat. The place is pretty amazing. Listen as divers swim through the tanks and chat with visitors about the biology and social habits of passing fish and mammals via underwater microphones. The museum is open 9 A.M.–6 P.M. Memorial Day–Labor Day, and until 10 P.M. on Thursdays June–August. It is open 9 A.M.–5 P.M. weekdays and 9 A.M.–6 P.M. weekends Labor Day–Memorial Day.

The Art Institute of Chicago

The Art Institute (111 S. Michigan Ave., 312/443-3600, www.artic.edu, 10:30 A.M.–4:30 P.M. Mon.–Wed., Fri., 10:30 A.M.–8 P.M. Thurs., 10 A.M.–5 P.M. Sat.–Sun, $12 except on Tues., when it's free) is probably best known for its collection of 19th-century French impressionist art, including a number of Claude Monet paintings. You'll see Vincent van Gogh's self-portrait, Georges Seurat's *A Sunday on La Grande Jatte,* Pablo Picasso's *The Old Guitarist,* and Grant Wood's *American Gothic.* But the Institute contains more than just paintings. The collection of armor, including swords and iron helmets, from the 15–19th centuries is awe-inspiring. The museum plans to open a huge north-wing addition in 2009; it will feature about 65,000 more square feet of exhibit space specifically focusing on modern and contemporary art.

Other Museums

Originally in the Chicago Cultural Center,

the **Museum of Broadcast Communications** (State and Kinzie, 312/629-6000, www.museum.tv) was set to reopen in 2006 in a fancy new River North building. The museum was to contain 30,000 square feet of exhibit space for its collection of antique radios, televisions, and broadcast equipment. The Radio Hall of Fame pays homage to oldies such as Gene Autrey and the folks from National Public Radio's *All Things Considered.*

The **Spertus Museum** (618 S. Michigan Ave., 312/322-1747, www.spertus.edu, 10 A.M.–5 P.M. Sun.–Wed., 10 A.M.–7 P.M. Thurs., 10 A.M.–3 P.M. Fri., $5), has Jewish artifacts, such as silver Torah cases, 19th-century paintings depicting Jewish life, and items suchs as funerary objects and drinking vessels from as far back as the Bronze Age.

ARCHITECTURE AND HISTORIC BUILDINGS

Sears Tower

The art deco Board of Trade is an eye-catcher, the Art Museum is famous for its lions perched outside, but the most dominant building downtown is the Sears Tower (233 S. Wacker Dr., 312/875-9696, www.the-skydeck.com, 10 A.M.–10 P.M. May–Sept., 10 A.M.–8 P.M. Oct.–April, $12), which houses a variety of financial companies. When it was built in 1973, the 110-story Sears Tower was the tallest in the world at 1,450 feet high. Owners can no longer make that claim, but it's still a trip to ride on the speedy elevator to the observatory. The best time to visit is before sunset, when the lines are shorter. Don't waste your time on overcast, foggy days.

Chicago Cultural Center

Another grand building is the Chicago Cultural Center (78 E. Washington St., 312/FINE-ART or 312/346-3278, 10 A.M.–7 P.M. Mon.–Thurs., 10 A.M.–6 P.M. Fri.–Sat., 11 A.M.–5 P.M. Sun.; free). The center acts as one of the city's official visitors centers and is stocked with free maps and brochures for tours and hotels. But it is also a stunning

Street, which leads to Jackson Boulevard and the **Chicago Board of Trade** (141 W. Jackson Blvd., 312/435-3500, www.cbot.com), where millions of commodities and bonds are traded every day. Founded in 1848, it is the world's oldest and largest futures and options exchange. Look for the statue of Ceres, the goddess of grain, at the top of the art deco building. Along Wacker there's the **Chicago Mercantile Exchange,** where more futures are traded. The smaller **Chicago Stock Exchange** and **Chicago Board of Options Exchange** are on La Salle Street.

Other Notable Buildings

Many workers and visitors arrive downtown in **Union Station,** the train station on Canal Street, between Jackson Boulevard and Adams Street. Built in 1925, the station's best feature is The Great Hall, with its marble floors, wooden benches, and high ceilings. The room has appeared in films such as *The Untouchables* and *The Fugitive.* Even if you don't travel through Union Station, take a peek at this room. It's a great spot for watching people.

Built in 1991, the **Harold Washington Library Center** (400 S. State St., 312/747-4876 or 312/747-4300, www.chipublib.org, 9 A.M.–7 P.M. Mon.–Thurs., 9 A.M.–5 P.M. Sat. and Sun., 1–5 P.M. Sun., free) caused quite a stir among residents. The red-brick, neoclassical building has more than 750,000 square feet and humongous ornamental owls at the corners of the building. You'll find plenty of warm, cozy spots to read or write in your travel journal, such as the sunny Winter Garden on the ninth floor.

PARKS AND PLAZAS
Grant Park

East of the Loop, beyond Michigan Avenue, is Grant Park, a huge park where concerts, festivals, impromptu soccer games, and picnics take place. The park district calls Grant Park the city's front yard. You can spend hours strolling through here. The most distinctive feature of the park is the

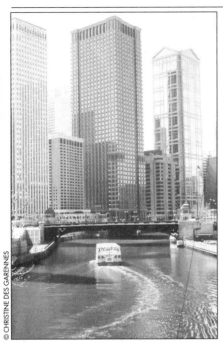

architectural boat tour along the Chicago River

Beaux-Arts building where hundreds of free concerts, art exhibits, lectures, and readings are held every year. Built in 1897 as a library for the city, the building contains sparkling mosaics on the floors and ceilings, marble stairways, and a Tiffany stained-glass dome estimated to be worth $35 million.

Chicago Architecture Foundation

To check out scale models of Chicago's beautiful landmark buildings and hot new ones, head over to the Chicago Architecture Foundation's **ArchiCenter** (224 S. Michigan Ave., 312/922-3432, www.architecture.org, 9:30 A.M.–5 P.M., Mon.–Sat. free). Here you can view rotating exhibits on architecture, buy tickets for the foundation's boat, bus, and walking tours, plus shop for Prairie-style design items such as coasters and clocks.

Financial Landmarks

The financial center is mainly along La Salle

iconic **Clarence Buckingham Memorial Fountain and Garden,** at Lake Shore Drive, Balbo Drive, Columbus Drive, and Jackson Boulevard. The 1927 Beaux-Arts–style fountain is made of wrought bronze and depicts sea horses. Sculptor Francois Marcel Loyau modeled it after the fountains at the palace of Versailles in France. The fountain's water runs 10 A.M.–11 P.M. daily. A water and light show starts around 7 P.M., lasts about 20 minutes, and continues every hour on the hour until 11 P.M. City Hall turns off the water during the winter but decorates the fountain with holiday lights.

The most recent addition to Chicago's park scene is **Millennium Park,** on the northwest corner of Grant Park at Michigan Avenue, between Randolph and Monroe streets. There are an outdoor music concert hall designed by Frank Gehry, more fountains, sculpture, a restaurant, and ice-skating rink.

Across the street from Marshall Field's on State Street is a large open space referred to as **Block 37** (Washington, Dearborn, and State Sts.). Buildings were razed to make way for a major mixed-use development that never got off the ground. But the city has made use of the space. During the winter it's home to an ice rink and outdoor German market. In the summer Chicago Public School students work on art projects there.

Plazas and Outside Art

Perhaps the most well-known and most-photographed sculpture in Chicago is Picasso's 50-foot-high, 167-ton structure outside Richard J. Daley Plaza (Washington and Dearborn Sts., 312/744-6630), known simply as *The Chicago Picasso.* Installed in 1967, the steel structure resembles a woman's face (or, some say, a horse's head). Throughout the year, Daley Plaza hosts free noontime concerts on some weekdays. It is also the spot of a farmers market.

Built in 1985 and designed by Helmut Jahn, the glass and steel **James R. Thompson Center** (100 W. Randolph St., 312/814-6660) contains mostly State of Illinois offices, but it also holds the **Illinois State Museum gallery,** which spotlights art by Illinois artists. Outside the shiny, modern building is Jean Dubuffet's *Monument with Standing Beast,* a black and white fiberglass project completed in 1985.

Marc Chagall depicts scenes from the Russian countryside in his *Les Quatre Saisons,* a glittering mosaic at First National Plaza on Dearborn Street, between Madison and Monroe streets. With plenty of benches and stairs on hand, this plaza makes for a good spot for a picnic lunch.

The sloping, red steel structure *Flamingo* at **Federal Center Plaza** (Dearborn and Adams streets) was designed by Alexander Calder and erected in 1974.

River North and the Gold Coast

The area immediately north of the Chicago River consists of skyscraper hotels, headquarters for businesses such as the *Chicago Tribune,* and a dizzying array of shops and restaurants. Michigan Avenue is lined with shops and hotels. River North is chock-full of galleries and loft apartments. This is an area of the city where you can find plenty of million-dollar townhouses and mansions (including the former Playboy Mansion at State Street and Lake Shore Drive) and plenty of beautiful people. The tanned and toned shop at Barney's on Oak Street and sun themselves on the Oak Street beach, at Oak Street, east of Lake Shore Drive. Just south and east of Oak Street is Navy Pier, an indoor and outdoor entertainment complex that tends to attract families and conventioneers.

SIGHTS

Navy Pier

Opened in 1916, Navy Pier (600 E. Grand Ave., 312/595-PIER or 312/595-7437, www.navy pier.com), formerly known as Municipal Pier, is where Navy ships docked during World Wars I and II. Before it fell into disrepair in the 1970s, it contained a hospital, streetcar line, and the University of Illinois campus. Mayor Richard M. Daley authorized a massive redevelopment of it in the 1990s and now much of the pier feels like a shopping mall. You'll find souvenir shops, an IMAX theater, and Bubba Gump Shrimp Company. Sightseeing boats also dock here. Oddly enough, not all of it feels commercial. The pier is home to the **Chicago Shakespeare Theatre** and **SOFA Chicago** (Sculpture Objects and Functional Art), an event in the fall at which modern and contemporary artists sell their stuff.

The pier is mobbed in the summertime, day and night. But the Ferris wheel offers some of the best views of the city and sunsets. On summer evenings, bands play for free at the far eastern end of the pier. You can buy beer and stroll along the pier. A fireworks show is held offshore Wednesday and Saturday evenings in the summer. You can walk to the pier from Michigan Avenue or take a bus or cab there. Summer hours are 10 A.M.–10 P.M. Sunday–Thursday, 10 A.M.–midnight Friday and Saturday. Fall hours are 10 A.M.–9 P.M. Monday–Thursday, 10 A.M.–11 P.M. Friday and Saturday, 10 A.M.– 7 P.M. Sunday. Winter hours are 10 A.M.–8 P.M. Monday–Thursday, 10 A.M.–10 P.M. Friday and Saturday, 10 A.M.–7 P.M. Sunday.

Chicago Water Tower and Michigan Avenue

One of the most recognizable landmarks on the city's north side is the old water tower on the 800 block of North Michigan Avenue. The cream-colored, castlelike tower was the only structure in the area that survived the 1871 fire. The minipark surrounding it attracts buskers, school groups, and couples waiting for one of the horse-drawn carriages that tend to park nearby. Inside the tower is a city-sponsored gallery that features photographs of Chicago. A few years ago the **Lookingglass Theatre** (821 N. Michigan Ave., 312/337-0665, www.lookinglasstheatre.org) moved into the adjacent and renovated Chicago Water Tower Water Works. Up and down Michigan Avenue from the tower are vertical malls and upscale shops such as Burberry's, Sak's Fifth Avenue, or Tiffany's. (See *Shopping* for more information.)

John Hancock Center

The **Hancock Observatory at John Hancock Center** (875 N. Michigan Ave., 888/875-VIEW or 888/875-8439, www.hancockobservatory.com, 9 A.M.–11 P.M. daily, $10) offers views of the city and lake. The lines here are usually shorter than those at the Sears Tower. The view from the top—1,000 feet high—can span 80 miles. The annual Hustle up the Hancock, held in February, challenges runners to see how fast they can climb 1,632 stairs, or 94 floors, in February. If you want to

Chicago

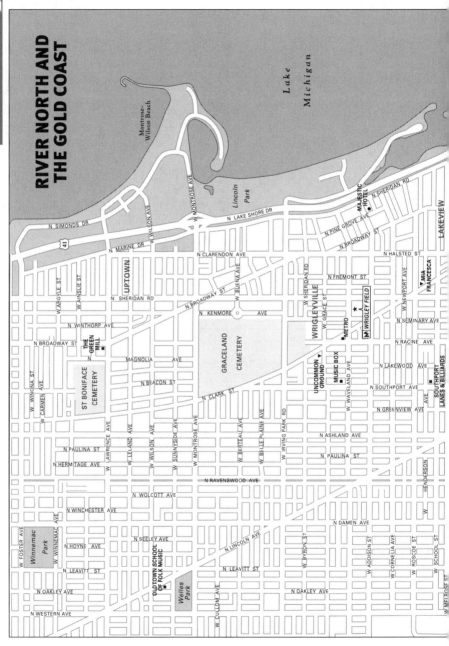

RIVER NORTH AND
THE GOLD COAST

take in the sights, but you don't want to wait in line and pay the admission fee, order drinks at the **Signature Room,** a bar on the building's 95th floor. Instead of paying $9.75 to visit the observatory room, you'll pay about $8 for a cocktail and a seat in a cushy lounge.

Museum of Contemporary Art

Somehow the exhibits at the MCA (220 E. Chicago Ave., 312/280-2660, www.mcachicago.org, 10 A.M.–5 P.M. Wed.–Sun., 10 A.M.–8 P.M. Tues., $10, free 5–8 P.M. Tues.) just keep getting more impressive and evocative every year. Open since 1945, the museum, one block east of the water tower, contains paintings, sculpture, photography, and video installations by artists such as Chuck Close, Sol Lewitt, Ann Hamilton, and Andreas Gursky. The museum's store is one of the best places to buy original, functional art such as dinner plates, jewelry, and vases.

Chicago Historical Society

Writer and radio legend Studs Terkel maintains an office at the Chicago Historical Society (Clark St. at North Ave., 312/642-4600, www.chicagohistory.org, 9:30 A.M.–4:30 P.M. Thurs.–Sat., noon–5 P.M. Sun., $5, free Mon.). Writers and historians spend hours researching here, but it's also a great spot for visitors. The society organizes impressive rotating and permanent exhibits throughout the year. American-history buffs will not want to miss exhibits such as *America in the Age of Lincoln,* which contains the bed on which Abraham Lincoln died and letters Lincoln penned to his rival Stephen A. Douglas and first-hand military man Ulysses S. Grant. Another informative exhibit is *Out of the Loop,* which features artifacts, photographs, and stories about the city's many diverse neighborhoods. Spend some time here before exploring areas such as Little Italy or Devon Avenue. The historical society also arranges excellent rotating exhibits that show off items that are usually in storage the rest of the year, such as a Chicago sports exhibit featuring jerseys worn by baseball player Ernie Banks and basketball star Michael Jordan. The historical

society sponsors numerous bus tours and seminars throughout the year. You can visit some of the city's architecturally stunning churches or listen in on a talk on John Dillinger in Chicago. The store has vintage photographs and posters for sale, eclectic accessories, and a good book selection for those interested in reading more about the city.

Newberry Library

Bibliophiles will fall in love with the historic Newberry Library (60 W. Walton St., 312/943-9090, www.newberry.org, free). Founded in 1887, it houses 1.5 million books and an impressive map collection. It attracts scholars of Chicago history, Native American history, genealogy, Renaissance studies, and other subjects. The Newberry is a noncirculating library, but you can request a book and take it with you into the reading room, where you can lounge for hours. Don't leave without taking a stroll through the exhibit galleries for a look at the historic maps. Throughout the year you can catch the Newberry Consort chamber ensemble. To visit the library, you'll need to show identification and fill out a registration form. The lobby and exhibit galleries are open 8:15 A.M.–5:30 P.M. Monday, Friday, and Saturday and 8:15 A.M.–7:30 P.M. Tuesday–Thursday. Public tours are at 3 P.M. Thursday and at 10:30 A.M. Saturday.

If you're looking for a place to rest your feet or munch on some snacks, head to **Burghouse Square,** a small park across from the library. Before the days of televised debates, politicians and aspiring politicians stumped here.

Merchandise Mart

Another building of note is the hulking Merchandise Mart (Kinzie and Wells Sts., 312/527-7732, www.merchandisemart.com). Unless you are shopping for pricey, designer furniture (or are an interior designer), there's really no reason for you to spend much time here. But with almost 100 acres of space, it's so huge it's worth a look if you're in the neighborhood or if you need to mail some postcards. (There's a U.S. Postal Service branch there.)

The North Shore

It's safe to say most of the city's young professionals live within the neighborhoods immediately north of the Gold Coast. Old Town, as its name implies, has an old-school feel to it. It's from Division Street north to the start of Lincoln Avenue. There are a handful of coffee shops, neighborhood pubs, florists, and bookstores, such as Barbara's Booksellers and the famous Second City comedy club. Lincoln Park and Lakeview have countless restaurants, bars, theaters, parks, boutiques, plus the Old Town School of Folk Music and Wrigley Field.

LINCOLN PARK

Arguably the best park on the north shore, Lincoln Park is a sprawling public green space that winds along the Lake Michigan coastline from North Avenue to Hollywood Avenue. It holds the Lincoln Park Zoo, Conservatory, Theater on the Lake, softball diamonds, soccer fields, beaches, areas for playing chess, and more.

Lincoln Park Zoo

Lincoln Park Zoo (2200 N. Cannon Dr., 312/294-4660, www.lpzoo.com, free) is one of the few free zoos in the country. You'll find polar bears, monkeys, gorillas, and elephants here. But to be frank, it doesn't compare to other, more modern zoos such as the San Diego Zoo. (Some of the small cages don't exactly look too comfortable for the animals.) But it's good for a walk-through, and if you're traveling with kids, they should enjoy the Farm-in-a-Zoo. Grounds are open 9 A.M.–6 P.M. daily. The buildings and the farm are open 10 A.M.–5 P.M. until 7 P.M. on weekends Memorial Day–Labor Day. Buildings close at 4:30 P.M., grounds at 5 P.M. November 1–March 31.

Notebaert Nature Museum

Open since 1999, the Peggy Notebaert Nature Museum (2430 N. Cannon Dr., 773/755-5100, www.naturemuseum.org, 9 A.M.–4:30 P.M. Mon.–Fri., 10 A.M.–5 P.M. Sat.–Sun., $7, free

the "Friendly Confines" of Wrigley Field

on Thurs.) in Lincoln Park promotes green living. The building, some of it made with solar panels, contains exhibits on composting, high-speed rail, and water conservation. It also houses excellent visiting exhibits, one of which focused on Jane Goodall's research.

Lincoln Park Conservatory

Lincoln Park Conservatory (2400 N. Stockton Dr., 312/742-7436, www.chicagoparkdistrict.com), built in 1891, is right out of the Victorian age. The annual flower shows, such as the winter azalea and model train show, are worth checking out. The conservatory is a good place to take a break from touring; it's always peaceful here.

NORTH OF LINCOLN PARK
M Wrigley Field

To get a feel for what Chicagoans are like, spend an afternoon within the "Friendly Confines," Wrigley Field (1060 W. Addison St., 800/THE-CUBS or 800/843-2827,

www.cubs.com). Take in the lake air, view the city's rooftops, and listen to a guest sing "Take Me out to the Ball Game."

Andersonville

The **Swedish American Museum Center** (5211 N. Clark St., 773/728-8111, www.samac.org, 10 A.M.–4 P.M. Tues.–Fri., 11 A.M.–4 P.M. Sat.–Sun., $4) is a little museum in the heart of Andersonville filled with photos of the area that show how the area has changed throughout the decades, plus arts and crafts by Scandinavian artists.

Uptown

Another diverse neighborhood in the far north is Uptown, sometimes called "Chicago's United Nations." Walk or drive along Devon Avenue and you'll come across Jewish butcher shops and fabric stores selling material for saris. Free weekly events and changing exhibits on Native American culture and history are always on tap at the **American Indian Center** (1630 W. Wilson Ave., 773//275-5871, www.aicchicago.org).

The South and West Sides

WEST SIDE
Sights and Activities

Clustered around Halsted Street and Jackson Boulevard, the small West Loop neighborhood of **Greek Town** thrives with cafés, gyros stands, and restaurants. You can spend a day sampling Mediterranean fare with all the restaurants packed into this area. Two of the best places to sample affordable Mediterranean fare and hear Greek being spoken is at the **Pan Hellenic Pastry Shop** or **Artopolis,** where you can nibble on sesame cookies and indulge in strong coffee. Both are on the 300 block of South Halsted Street.

You can hear a number of foreign languages being spoken in the Old World–style **Division Street Russian and Turkish Bathhouse** (1916 W. Division St., 773/384-9671). Lounge around here and you might run into

Mike Ditka or Jesse Jackson. Take your pick from hot and cold baths, showers, and massage areas. Men and women are welcome but are separated into their own areas.

M Garfield Park Conservatory

West of downtown, just off I-290 toward Oak Park, is the Garfield Park Conservatory (300 N. Central Park Ave., 312/746-5100, www.garfield-conservatory.org, 9 A.M.–5 P.M. daily, until 8 P.M. Thurs., free). Built in 1906, the 3.5-acre conservatory (within 184-acre Garfield Park) features four major flower shows every year, plus special exhibits. (An exhibit showcasing art glass by Dale Chihuly was hugely popular.) Inside the historic buildings are rare items such as a 44-pound seed from the double coconut palm and a fern that is reported to be one of the oldest plant species on earth.

PRAIRIE AVENUE HISTORIC DISTRICT

The Prairie Avenue District, about two miles south of downtown, is where you'll find the oldest house in Chicago, the **Clarke House** (1827 S. Indiana Ave.) and the **Glessner House Museum** (1800 S. Prairie Ave., www.glessnerhouse.org, $10 for either house, $15 combo ticket, free Wed.). The stately, Greek-revival Clarke House was built by Henry and Caroline Clarke in 1836. Since then it has survived two moves and two fires. Nearby is the Glessner House, a National Historic Landmark built in 1886 for John and Frances Glessner by Boston architect Henry Hobson Richardson. The style is unadorned English arts and crafts, and the house's presence in a district crowded with elaborate Queen Anne mansions annoyed many neighbors when it was built. The house has quite a collection of decorative arts, specifically ceramics. Tours of the Glessner are at 1, 2, and 3 P.M. Wednesday–Sunday. Tours of the Clarke House are at noon and 1 and 2 P.M.

While you're in the neighborhood, consider taking a **guided walking tour** of the Prairie Avenue Historic District. The tour center is in the coach house, west end of the building at 18th Street; tours at 1 and 2 P.M. first and third Saturdays and Sundays May–October.

Jane Addams and Helen Gates Starr founded Hull House in 1889 on the near West Side of the city. It was at Hull House that Addams fought for immigrant and worker rights. During her lifetime the pacifist won a Nobel Peace Prize and helped found the National Association for the Advancement of Colored People and establish the American Civil Liberties Union. Owned and operated by the University of Illinois at Chicago, the **Jane Addams' Hull House Museum** (800 S. Halsted St., 312/413-5353, 10 A.M.–4 P.M. Thurs.–Fri., noon–4 P.M. Sun., free) consists of two original Hull House buildings (out of 13). They are the Charles J. Hull mansion, the first building Addams used as a health and education center for the neighborhood, and the residents' dining hall. The museum is closed during university breaks.

HYDE PARK

On the city's south side, the historic neighborhood of Hyde Park is home to college students, professors, young professionals, and some working class families. It runs from 60th Street and the Midway Plaisance on the south to Hyde Park Boulevard on the north, between the lakeshore and Washington Park.

The University of Chicago

The University of Chicago is in the center of it all, and it's surrounded by bookstores jam-packed with new and used books. Two bookstores to get lost in are **57th Street Books** (1301 E. 57th St., 773/684-1300, 8:30 A.M.–9 P.M. Mon.–Fri., 10 A.M.–6 P.M. Sat., noon–6 P.M. Sun.) and **Seminary Co-Op** (5757 S. University Ave., 773/752-4381, 10 A.M.–10 P.M. Mon.–Sat., 10 A.M.–8 P.M. Sun.)

Frank Lloyd Wright's Robie House

Another highlight of Hyde Park is Frank Lloyd Wright's Robie House (5757 S. Woodlawn St., 773/834-1847, www.wrightplus.org, $12). Frank Lloyd Wright referred to the house, built in 1909, as the "cornerstone of modern architecture." (He never was a modest fellow. And neither was the original owner, Frederick C. Robie, a millionaire bicycle manufacturer.) The Prairie-style home features Wright's trademark low-pitched roofs, balconies, and art glass. (There are 174 art-glass windows and doors.) After the Robie family sold it to the Chicago Theological Seminary in 1926, the mansion was transformed into a dorm. Thanks to the University of Chicago, the National Trust for Historic Preservation, and the Frank Lloyd Wright Foundation, the mansion is undergoing an extensive, 10-year renovation project begun in 1997. Tours start every 30 minutes 11 A.M.–3 P.M. Saturday and Sunday, and at 11 A.M., 1 P.M., and 3 P.M. weekdays.

Museums

Affordable and informative, the **DuSable Museum of African American History** (740 E.

56th Pl., 773/947-0600, www.dusablemu-seum.org, 10 A.M.–5 P.M. Mon.–Sat., closed Mon., June–Jan.; $3) has friendly staff and well-done exhibits. Here you can learn about subjects such as the late Harold Washington, the city's first (and only one, so far) black mayor, and blacks in aviation, such as the Tuskegee Airmen. DuSable is one of the few remaining museums in Chicago that doesn't cost double-digit entrance fees.

The **Museum of Science and Industry** (57th St. and Lake Shore Dr., 773/684-1414, 800/GO TO MSI or 800/468-6674, www.msichicago.org, 9:30 A.M.–4 P.M. Mon.–Sat., 11 A.M.–4 P.M. Sun., $9, Omnimax tickets extra, occasional free days throughout the year) boasts some fairly significant and large mechanical equipment from history. There are the sleek 1934 Pioneer Zephyr, a high-speed streamliner; a Boeing 727, where you can check out the fuselage and engine; a working coal mine shaft elevator; the Aurora 7 Mercury spacecraft, one of the first manned spacecraft to orbit the Earth; and a German U-505 submarine captured in 1944. In the spring of 2005 the museum reopened the exhibit after spending millions on restoring the U-boat and putting together an elaborate multimedia display. In addition to the science exhibits and artifacts, the museum has an Omnimax theater.

PULLMAN

Historic preservation buffs will fall in love with the buildings within the **Pullman National Historic Landmark District** on the city's far south side. Start your visit to the district by touring the **Historic Pullman Foundation Visitor Center** (112th St. and Cottage Grove Ave., 773/785-8181, www.pullmanil.org, 11 A.M.–3 P.M. Tues.–Sun.) Tours are at 12:30 P.M. and 1:30 P.M. on the first Sunday of each month May–October.

Pullman was established as a town in 1880 by railroad car executive George M. Pullman and annexed to Chicago in 1889. It was the first planned community in the United States, owned by stockholders and managed by the Pullman Land Association. It was here that most of Pullman's workers lived and worked. Pullman envisioned it to be a model, idyllic community. There were flower gardens and open-air markets. But things didn't turn out as well as he planned. After Pullman laid off part of his workforce, cut back hours, and refused to lower rents on his workers' homes, employees went on strike. After troops marched in to quell the strikers, eventually the town was annexed into the city and the homes sold to their owners.

In all, there are about 1,000 properties in the Pullman National Historic Landmark District. Some have been renovated and others are in need of a visit from the guys from the PBS show *This Old House*. There's the grand and ornate Hotel Florence, which is being renovated; Market Hall, where the produce markets were originally held; stables; and executive homes. A standout is the Romanesque Greenstone Church, a church unlike any other found in Chicago. (It's made of green serpentine stone.) Annual tours include The Pullman House Tour in October and Christmas Candlelight House Walk.

Entertainment and Events

PERFORMING ARTS

The Loop theater district has had its ups and downs throughout the years. It was the place for entertainment in the 1920s, languished a bit in the 1980s, and has become a vibrant spot in the late 1990s and into the 21st century after several theaters were renovated. The 1921 **Chicago Theatre** (175 N. State St., 312/462-6363, www.chicagotheatre.com), most noticeable for its dazzling marquee and vertical "Chicago" sign, brings in everyone from members of the Buena Vista Social Club to Deep Purple. The modern yet classical **Goodman Theatre** (170 N. Dearborn St., 312/443-3800, www.goodman-theatre.org) presents plays by August Wilson and Mary Zimmerman. The **Ford Center for the Performing Arts** (24 W. Randolph St., 312/855-9400, www.broadway-inchicago.com), formerly known as the Oriental, and **Shubert Theatre** (22 W. Monroe St., 312/977-1700, www.broadwayinchicago.com) present Broadway shows, such as *Rent* and *Thoroughly Modern Millie* in gilded venues where Orpheum stars such as Harry Houdini and Jack Benny performed.

Another rich and stunning venue is the Louis Sullivan–designed **Auditorium Theatre** (50 E. Congress Pkwy., 312/922-2110, www.auditoriumtheatre.org), in the south Loop. It has had dancers with the Joffrey Ballet cross its stage as well as singers such as Erykah Badu.

Rising on the west end of the Loop near the Chicago Mercantile Exchange and other financial centers is the massive **Lyric Opera of Chicago** (20 N. Wacker Dr., 312/332-2244, wwww.lyricopera.org) building, where great operatic performers have taken stage and symphonies and musicals have been presented to its adoring (and almost always well-dressed) audience.

Lookingglass Theatre (821 N. Michigan Ave., 312/337-0665, www.lookinglasstheatre.org) moved into the renovated Chicago Water Tower Water Works space, into an $8 million theater. The theater, cofounded by *Friends* star David Schwimmer, has developed a loyal local following for its cutting-edge, thinking plays.

In addition to the theaters mentioned in the Loop, there are a number of award-winning theaters around town. Featuring ensemble members such as John Malkovich and Gary Sinise, the **Steppenwolf Theatre** (1650 N. Halsted St., 312/355-1650, www.steppenwolf.org) stages productions such as *Hedda Gabler* and *A Streetcar Named Desire*.

Expect swift, biting comedy at the **Neo-Futurarium** (5139 N. Ashland Ave., 773/275-5255, www.neofuturists.org) on the north side of the city.

Originally started by a group of University of Chicago students in 1955, the improv comedy theater **Second City** (1608 and 1616 N. Wells St., 312/337-3992, www.secondcity.com) has become a Chicago institution. It has helped launch the careers of comedians such as Jerry Stiller and the late Chris Farley. Skits involve some audience participation, are usually related to current events, and the troupe members almost always poke fun at the country's current president.

Established in 1956, the touring dance company **Joffrey Ballet** (312/902-1500, www.joffrey.com) presents, year after year, cutting-edge, classical dance productions at venues throughout the city. The choreography, costume designs, and music scores have the ability to inspire and infuse joy into audiences.

Not just folk music is on tap at the **Old Town School of Folk Music** (4544 N. Lincoln Ave. and 909 W. Armitage Ave., 773/728-6000, www.oldtownschool.org). Local, national, and international jazz, Latin, and South American musicians stop by for concerts. Dance and music lessons are also offered here. Stop by for a lesson in flamenco dancing or on how to play the banjo.

Movie Theater

A few blocks from Wrigley Field is a lovely old

movie theater, the **Music Box** (3733 N. Southport Ave., 773/871-6604, www.musicbox-
theatre.com). The 1929 movie palace shows
midnight movies, new art-house films, and classic Hollywood movies. Check out the cool ceiling—blue sky with stars and moving clouds.

Resources

Want to attend a show, but don't want to pay
full price? Visiting town at the last minute? The
League of Chicago Theatres (312/554-9800,
www.chicagoplays.com) offers a limited number
of reduced-price tickets on the day of the show.
These tickets are sold in person at select locations, such as the Chicago Water Works Visitors
Information Center (163 E. Pearson St.). For
more information, visit www.hottix.org.

To find out about upcoming concert performances, contact the **Chicago Fine Arts Hot
Line** (312/346-3278, www.chicagomusic.org.)

EVENTS

The majority of Chicago's free festivals take
place in Grant Park and are sponsored by

the city. If you're looking for more information about an event, check with **The May-
or's Office of Special Events** (312/744-3370,
www.cityofchicago.com). Otherwise, the
Chicago Reader (11 E. Illinois Ave., 312/828-
0350, www.chireader.com), a weekly alternative newspaper, keeps track of happenings. You
can pick up a copy at any convenient store or
casual restaurant or café.

Chicago's largest event is probably **Taste of
Chicago** (312/744-3370), a snacking extravaganza held around the Fourth of July every
year. Dozens and dozens of restaurants and
food vendors pitch tents in Grant Park hock-
ing everything from cheesecake slices and ribs
to egg rolls. As people chow down, blues, rock,
and country bands perform.

Grant Park also plays host to a wide variety
of free musical festivals in the summer. One
popular event is **Blues Festival** (312/744-
3370), or, as some people refer to it, Booze Fest,
because the crowds tend to get a little sloppy in
the evening. Musicians such as Charlie Musselwhite, Otis Rush, and Bonnie Raitt have taken
the stage here. Blues Fest is held in June. A

the Taste of Chicago food festival in Grant Park

© CHRISTINE DES GARENNES

more subdued atmosphere can be found at the **Grant Park Music Festival** (312/742-4763), where the celebrated Grant Park Orchestra plays for free on various evenings late June–late August in Millennium Park. Other free music events at Grant Park include **Viva Chicago,** a Latin music festival at the end of August, and **Jazz Festival** in early September.

Also at Grant Park during the summer is the popular **Chicago Outdoor Film Festival** (877/CHICAGO or 877/244-2246), which features films such as *It Happened One Night* and *In the Heat of the Night* on a huge screen. Arrive early to stake out a spot on the lawn by Butler Field. Films start at sunset and are shown on Tuesday evenings in July and August.

Pilots and parachuters with the U.S. Air Force and other flying groups such as the Blue Angels breeze into town in mid-August for the **Chicago Air and Water Show.** While helicopters and fighter jets zoom through the air there are waverunner and wakeboard demos at the lake. Another spectacular water-related event is **Venetian Night** in July, when boats parade through Monroe Harbor with twinkling, white lights.

Inland, the Printers Row District, in the south Loop area, hosts the largest free outdoor book show in the Midwest, the **Printer's Row Book Fair** (on Dearborn St. from Congress Pkwy. to Polk St., 312/222-3986, www.printersrowbookfair.org) in June. There are author readings, book signings, and antiquarian and out-of-print books for sale.

On the north side, Lincoln Square hosts a jolly **Oktoberfest,** with draft beer, fish sandwiches, and oompah bands. Tons of parades are held throughout the city every year. Some of the best ones are the **Chinese New Year Parade** in January, the **South Side Irish Parade** in March, Little Village's **Mexican Independence Parade** in September, and Andersonville's **St. Lucia Festival of the Lights** in December.

During December, residents and tourists flock to **Christkindlmarket Chicago** (Dearborn, Washington, and State Sts., open daily from Thanksgiving to a few days before Christmas). Modeled after the outdoor Christmas market in Nürnberg Germany, Christkindlmarket Chicago is a four-week event at which you can shop for nutcrackers, munch on pretzels, sip dark beer, watch glass-blowing demonstrations, and listen to choirs singing carols.

NIGHTSPOTS

Dance clubs come and go in the Windy City, but a select few jazz, blues, and yes, polka clubs have persevered throughout the decades. The places listed below are almost always hopping, especially after midnight, and attract colorful audiences, from Northwestern University students to white-haired couples.

Live Music

One of the best late-night spots for music is the intimate **The Green Mill** in Uptown (4802 N. Broadway, 312/878-5552), which hosts, in addition to smooth jazz quartets, regular poetry jams.

The author's personal favorite is the easy-to-miss **Underground Wonder Bar** (10 E. Walton St., 312/266-7761), literally below the street level in the Gold Coast. Cover charges are reasonable (usually less than $10) and the drinks strong. The staff is professional and not there to look good. The Wonder Bar features local and visiting talents and it's not uncommon for musicians to walk in for impromptu sessions.

Regional bands such as Wilco play for enthusiastic crowds at the **Abbey Pub** (3420 W. Grace St., 773/478-4408, www.abbeypub.com) on the northwest side of the city. The Lambay Island Dining Room next door serves decent Irish fare for lunch and dinner in a surprisingly quiet atmosphere, considering it's next to a bar and small concert venue. The Abbey hosts St. Patrick's Day doings to write home about.

Green Dolphin Street (2200 N. Ashland Ave., 773/395-0066) is part restaurant, part jazz club, with a Latin bent. It's suitable for couples on dates or small groups who want to have conversations while listening to music.

CHICAGO BLUES

On the stage of a south Loop club, Buddy Guy wails on Lucille, his electric guitar. In a north side club, Big Time Sarah, in a brilliant red sweat suit, belts out the notes. On the Red Line train, a busker entertains riders with the always popular tune "Sweet Home Chicago." Welcome to the Chicago blues scene, with its blend of performers and clubs, where you can hear a little bit of everything, from classic Delta blues to the electrified Chicago version. Name the major blues musicians—Junior Wells, Muddy Waters, Buddy Guy—and just about all of them have lived, recorded, or played in Chicago.

Chicago blues originated during the Great Migration, when Southern blacks moved north beginning in the 1920s in search of better jobs and opportunities. It came of age in the 1940s and 1950s when musicians from the Mississippi Delta region and Southern cities such as Memphis, Tennessee, moved to Chicago. They hooked up with other musicians, plugged in their guitars, and added drums, piano, and other instruments to the mix. Early musicians performed in clubs along Madison Street and at outdoor markets such as the old Maxwell Street Market. Recording studios, such as Chess and Alligator records, set up shops here. (Alligator still produces blues music with the likes of Koko Taylor and Luther Allison.) In 1980, John Belushi and Dan Ackroyd introduced a younger generation to the city of the blues with their movie *The Blues Brothers*. Today, Buddy Guy still performs occasionally at his club. Regulars such as Big Time Sarah draw a loyal crowd. And the Blues Festival is still going strong after more than 20 years. During the huge weekendlong music and food event held in mid-June, local and national blues artists such as Charlie Musselwhite and Bonnie Raitt take the stage. Most of the festival concerts, which are held in Grant Park, are free.

While in Chicago, you can catch a blues show at clubs such as Buddy Guy's Legends, Blue Chicago, Rosa's Lounge, Kingston Mines, Eddy Clearwater's Reservation Blues, or House of Blues. To find out who's playing where and for a more comprehensive listing of clubs, check concert listings in the free weeklies, the *Chicago Reader* or *Newcity Chicago* or the daily newspapers, the *Chicago Tribune* and *Chicago Sun-Times*.

Serious blues aficionados might want to set aside some time to peruse the **Chicago Blues Archives in Harold Washington Library.** The archives contain live recordings of shows from the Chicago scene that date back decades. The library also hosts blues concerts. Although Chicago does not have a station that plays all blues, all the time, some stations will play blues music occasionally. They include WCKG 105.9, WXRT 93.1, and WBEZ 91.5, which showcases blues music on late Saturday nights.

Drinks at **B.L.U.E.S.** (2519 N. Halsted St., 773/528-1012, www.chicagobluebar.com) tend to be overpriced, but you can't beat the up-close-and-personal atmosphere of these small-stage venues.

If you're in the mood to dance and don't mind the sweaty crowds, **Kingston Mines** (2548 N. Halsted St., 773/477-4646) is the place to go in Lincoln Park to listen to energetic blues.

If you're lucky, Buddy Guy himself will take the stage at his club and soul food restaurant **Buddy Guy's Legends** (754 S. Wabash Ave., 312/427-0333).

The kitschy **Baby Doll Polka Club** (6102 S. Central Ave., 773/582-9706) is always festive. Even if you're not a fan of the accordion, somehow you'll find yourself stomping your way across the packed dance floor.

The Wrigleyville club **Metro** (3730 N. Clark St., 312/549-3604, www.metrochicago.com) showcases up-and-coming alternative and retro bands. The Smashing Pumpkins, Flaming Lips, Dandy Warhols, and The Assassins all played here.

The bar and stage at **Double Door** (1572 N. Milwaukee Ave., 773/489-3160, www.double-door.com) are nothing to write home about. But the place tends to book some great bands that you might not otherwise get to see in a small venue. The Rolling Stones stopped by on their 1997 tour.

Both **Schuba's Tavern** (3159 N. Southport Ave., 773/525-2508, www.schubas.com) and the nearby **Southport Lanes and Billiards** (3325 N. Southport Ave., 472-6600) were Schlitz Brewery buildings. (Look for the vertical Schlitz signs.) Schuba's attracts a 20- and 30—something crowd for its live rock, alt-rock, alt-country, and sometimes bluesy concerts. Inside Schuba's is the surprisingly good Harmony Grill, which serves solid American and Southern food for lunch and dinner. Southport Lanes is an old-school, four-lane bowling alley, with real, live pin-setters working in the back.

Bars

The subdued **Webster's Wine Bar** (1480 W. Webster, 773/868-0608, www.websterwinebar.com) is a subdued wine bar with more than 400 wines by the bottle and 30 available by the glass. If you're not sure what you like, drop by for one of the tastings throughout the week or order a wine flight. Different wines are featured every month, focusing on a wine region or grape variety. A growing selection of food is available, such as plates of triple-cream brie or stilton. A small entrée will cost about $9. Live music every Monday night completes the mood.

If you're thinking of proposing or celebrating an anniversary, the place to do it is **Pops for Champagne** (2934 N. Sheffield Ave., 773/472-1000, www.popsforchampagne.com), which has more than 100 champagnes to choose from and desserts such as chocolate fondue.

Shopping

MAGNIFICENT MILE

The city's largest (and probably best-known) shopping district is the Mag Mile, the stretch of glamorous department stores on Michigan Avenue, north of the Chicago River. Most of the stores in this area are national chain stores, such as Nieman Marcus and boutiques such as Tiffany and Company and Burberry. The wide sidewalks and extravagant plant and flower beds make shopping here easy and pleasant. During the holidays the street is gleaming with twinkling white lights. If it's February and blustery out, take cover in one of the street's vertical malls, such as the 900 North Michigan Avenue Shops, which is anchored by Bloomingdale's.

Just a few blocks north and west of Michigan Avenue is **Oak Street,** where the *uber*-rich shop for clothing and home decor in shops such as Barneys New York and unwind in day spas. See how many limousines or chauffeured town cars you can count.

STATE STREET AND THE LOOP

State Street, "that great street" (as the 1922 song "Chicago" goes) is still pretty great. The landmark **Marshall Field's** (111 N. State St., 312/781-1000, www.marshallfields.com, hours vary per season but are generally 9 A.M.–8 P.M. Mon.–Fri., 9A.M.–9 P.M. Sat., and 11 A.M.–6 P.M. Sun.) has been around since 1868. During the Christmas shopping season it's nearly impossible to walk down the sidewalk because everyone is checking out the store's extravagant window displays. Inside, the atrium is also lavishly decorated and many shoppers take a break in the fabled Walnut Room, a touristy but decent lunch spot.

You'll find affordable items sold in stores such as Sears along State Street from Lake Street to Jackson Boulevard. The discount chains TJ Maxx and Filene's Basement also have locations along State Street. One block east of State Street is Wabash Avenue, also known as **Jeweler's Row,** where you can often find bargain prices for engagement rings, cuff links, or rare coins.

Michigan Avenue is the place to shop in Chicago.

ARTS, ANTIQUES, AND BOUTIQUES

Treasure-hunters can get lost in the maze of antiques stores lining **Belmont Avenue,** west of Clark Street to I-90/94, and along Lincoln Avenue, north of Fullerton Avenue to Irving Park Road.

A number of gift shops, home-decor shops, and the independent bookstore Women and Children First are in the northern neighborhood of **Andersonville,** along the 5000 block of North Clark Street.

Retro clothing shops (along with gay-friendly cafés, bars, and salons) dominate the **North Halsted Street** business district from Barry Street to Sheridan Road. More vintage and one-of-a-kind clothing shops are also packed into the West Side neighborhoods of **Bucktown** and **Wicker Park,** around the 1500 block of North Milwaukee Avenue and 2000 block of North Damen Avenue. These areas also have a number of galleries and framing shops. **River North,** from Chicago Avenue south to Illinois Street, has countless photography, home-decor, and fine art galleries.

Sports and Recreation

PARKS

In addition to the popular parks of Grant Park, just east of downtown, and Lincoln Park, which runs along the north shore, the **Chicago Park District** (312/742-PLAY or 312/742-7529, www.chicagoparkdistrict.com) oversees dozens of parks and beaches throughout the city.

Lake Michigan Beaches

On the city's far north side, the family-friendly **Montrose Avenue Beach,** at Montrose Avenue and the lake shore, has sandy beaches, picnic areas, soccer fields, a bathhouse, nature trail, and fishing pier. That blue and white ocean liner on **North Avenue Beach** is actually a beach house where you can change into your swimsuit, buy ice-cream cones, rent volleyballs, or talk to the lifeguards. This beach, east of the zoo, tends to attract the college-age set. Less than a mile south is the chichi **Oak Street Beach,** which really is just another beach. You can travel between all these beaches via bicycle, in-line skates, skateboards, or your feet, on the multiuse recreational **Lakefront Trail.**

Columbus and Jackson Parks

Columbus Park (500 S. Central Ave., 312/746-5046) and **Jackson Park** (6401 S. Stony Island Ave., 312/747-6187) may not have beaches, but they are historic parks worth a visit. Famed architect Jens Jensen designed the West Side Columbus Park in 1912 in full Prairie-style with walking paths, waterfalls, and an outdoor stage. Today there are also a golf course, tennis courts, and baseball diamonds. Frederick Olmsted and Calvert Vaux designed the grand South Park in the 1870s, part of which would become Jackson Park. During the 1893 Columbia Exposition some exhibits were held in Jackson Park. When you visit today you'll find a lagoon, bicycle path, baseball diamonds, tennis courts, and a golf course.

BICYCLING

Major Richard M. Daley is a big fan of bicycling, and as a result the city has become much more bike-friendly during his tenure, renovating trails, widening bridges, and installing bike racks. For a free map of bicycling trails and lanes, contact the City of Chicago Department of Transportation (312/742-2453, www.cityofchicago.org). The Chicagoland Bicycle Federation (312/42-PEDAL or 312/427-3325, www.chibikefed.org) also publishes bicycling maps and sponsors rides.

The **Lakefront Trail,** maintained by the park district, runs along the shore of Lake Michigan, past sunbathers, volleyball players, chess players, and anglers. The asphalt-paved path is not used only by bicyclists, but also by walkers, joggers, and in-line skaters. The trail is accessible from any major east-west street.

The **North Branch Trail Connection** (708/771-1050, www.fpdcc.com), a part paved, part gravel bike path, runs through Cook County Forest Preserve land on the far northwest side of the city and north to the suburbs. This trail is accessible at the corner of Milwaukee and Devon avenues.

Several city streets have bicycle lanes. A word of caution when riding in the bicycle lane: It is designated for bicycles only, but as you will find, particularly during peak traffic times, cars will speed past others using the bicycle lane. Biking in this lane does not necessarily mean worry-free biking. Here are some streets with bike lanes: Elston Avenue, which runs diagonally from the far northwest side to the near north end of the city; parts of Southport Avenue south of Belmont Avenue; Lincoln Avenue south of Diversey Parkway; Milwaukee Avenue south of Chicago Avenue; Damen Avenue from Irving Park Road to Summerdale; Wells, Clinton, and Canal streets; South Wabash Avenue from south of the Loop to Chinatown; and along parts of Lawrence Avenue.

You'll also find a smattering of bicycle paths

Chicago

through parks along the Chicago River, such as Horner Park and Legion Park on the city's north side.

Bike Chicago (at North Avenue Beach, Navy Pier and South Dock, 800/915-2453, www.bikerental.com) rents bicycles and offers tours.

The Chicago Transit Authority has installed some bike racks on buses serving 63rd Street and North Avenue. Bikes are allowed on the L trains at any time during the weekends and on weekdays during nonpeak times. For more information call 888/YOUR-CTA (888/968-7282) or visit www.transitchicago.com.

GOLF

The Chicago Park District has one 18-hole course, five nine-hole courses, three driving ranges, and a miniature golf course. The 18-hole golf course is on the south side in **Jackson Park** (6401 S. Stony Island Ave., 63rd and Lake Shore Dr., 312/747-2763 or 312/747-6187). Fees range from $12 twilight to $23 for a weekend round. In addition there are five nine-hole courses: **Columbus Park** (500 S. Central Ave., 312/746-5573 or 312/746-5046), **Marquette Park** (6734 S. Kedzie Ave., 312/747-2761 or 312/747-6469), **South Shore Cultural Center** (7059 S. South Shore Dr., 312/747-2536), **Robert A. Black** in Warren Park (2045 W. Pratt Ave., 312/742-7931 or 312/742-7888), and **Sydney Marovitz** along Lake Michigan (3600 N. Recreation Dr., 312/742-7930). Prices for nine-hole courses range from $7.50 twilight to $14 for one round with a golf cart.

Driving ranges are at Jackson Park, Marquette Park, and in Lincoln Park at the **Diversey Driving Range and Miniature Golf Course** (141 W. Diversey Pkwy., 312/742-7929).

CANOEING AND KAYAKING

Yes. People do paddle down the Chicago River. In fact, canoeing the river has grown in popularity in recent years, and it is a different way to see the city. You can rent canoes or kayaks and get tips on canoeing the area from the folks at **Chicagoland Canoe Base** (4019 N. Narragansett, 773/777-1489, www.chicagolandcanoebase.com, 9 A.M.–5 P.M. Mon.–Sat., 9 A.M.–9 P.M. Thurs.). It'll cost about $40 per day to rent a canoe, more if you need to rent a trailer, clothing, or other accessories. If canoeing along the Chicago River intimidates you, head just north of the city to Skokie and the quiet Skokie lagoons.

ICE-SKATING

During the winter the Chicago Park District maintains a number of outdoor ice-skating rinks. Two popular spots are at **Daley Bicentennial Plaza** (337 E. Randolph St., 312/742-7650) and **Millennium Park** (55 N. Michigan Ave., 312/742-5222). Depending on the weather conditions, the rinks are open from the end of November to the end of February. Admission is $4 for residents, $5 for nonresidents, except at Millennium Park, where admission is free. Skate rental is available at all parks. Rental costs $5 at Millennium Park and $4 elsewhere.

SPORTS TEAMS
Baseball
The two baseball teams are the **Chicago Cubs** and the **Chicago White Sox.** Most north side residents are fans of the Cubs, and most south siders adore the Sox. The hottest tickets during the baseball season, which runs April–September, are for the games when these teams play against each other. The Cubs play at **Wrigley Field** (1060 W. Addison St., 800/THE-CUBS or 800/843-2827, www.cubs.com), which was built in 1914 and is one of the oldest ballparks in the country. Diehard fans tend to sit in the sometimes raucous (but always a good time) bleacher seats. If you can't find tickets at the box office, take a walk on the streets leading up to the stadium on game day and you'll find plenty of scalpers hoping to unload.

A CITY BY ANY OTHER NAME

"The Windy City." "The Second City." "The City of Big Shoulders." "City on the Make." "My Kind of Town." "Chitown." Chicago has been called many things in the 200 or so years that pioneers started making their way to the southwest corner of Lake Michigan. The pictures they paint are not exactly flattering. One of the more common ones is the Windy City moniker. Although it's not unusual for the city to experience gusty days, Chicago does not rank at the top (or even close to the top) of the National Weather Service's list of windy metropolitan areas in the United States. What's behind the nickname? The tireless politicians and promoters who bragged endlessly about how fabulous the city was around the time of the Columbia Exposition in 1893. (Which prompted another nickname: "The White City.")

The second most-common nickname is "The Second City," the name now used by the legendary north side comedy club. Before Los Angeles came into the picture, Chicago was the second-largest city in terms of population (second to New York City). It was New York writer A. J. Liebling who popularized the term. Liebling lived in Chicago in 1952 and penned a series of essays for *The New Yorker* magazine about life in the city. Essentially he thumbed his nose at Chicago's residents and their habits, their politics, restaurants, theater scene, you name it.

Other nicknames include "City of Big Shoulders" and "Hog Butcher to the World," coined by Galesburg native Carl Sandburg in his *Chicago Poems* in 1916. And perhaps one of the more upbeat portrayals of the city is in Frank Sinatra's song, "My Kind of Town," which describes Chicago as a town that "won't let you down" and full of smiling people.

The **Chicago White Sox** play in U.S. Cellular Field, formerly Comiskey Park (333 W. 35th St., 312/831-1SOX or 312/831-1769), on the south side. Game-day tickets are usually available, although they tend to be in the nosebleed seats. Stick around after a weekend game; the stadium's management often puts on a fireworks show.

Football

The city's professional football team, the **Chicago Bears,** a team that dates back to the 1920s, still has a loyal following. You can catch a game in the renovated Soldier Field (3425 E. McFetridge Dr., 312/559-1212, www.chicagobears.com).

Basketball

Chicago Bulls games are still fun, even though stars such as Michael Jordan have been gone for years. The Bulls play at the United Center

on the city's West Side (1901 W. Madison St., 312/455-4000).

Hockey

The United Center is also home to the city's professional hockey team, the **Blackhawks**(312/445-4500, www.chicagoblackhawks.com).

If you love hockey but can't find tickets to a Blackhawks game (or can't afford a ticket), try the **Chicago Wolves,** a semiprofessional team that plays in the Allstate Arena (6920 N. Mannheim Rd., 800/THE-WOLVES or 800/843-9658, www.chicagowolves.com).

Soccer

The **Chicago Fire** (425 E. McFetridge Dr., 888/657-3473, www.chicago-fire.com), the city's major league soccer team, is developing a strong fan base. A multimillion dollar soccer stadium was planned to open in 2006 in the southwest suburb of Bridgeview.

Accommodations

LOOP

Under $50

One of the best lodging deals in Chicago, the **M J. Ira and Nikki Harris Family Hostel** (24 E. Congress Pkwy., 312/360-0300, www.hichicago.org) has single-sex, dorm-style, 14-bed rooms and four-bed rooms. This clean, hip hostel opened in 2000, although the building dates to the 1800s. The seven-story complex has a kitchen, coffee shop, luggage storage, and a library, and is near a number of L stops and the Amtrak and Greyhound stations. You don't need to be a member of Hostelling International to stay here, but members do receive cheaper rates. Rates are also cheaper if you book a room 30 days in advance.

$100–150

If you're planning to spend most of your time at Museum Campus, Grant Park, or the Art Institute and don't want to shell out a lot of money, a good bet is the **The Essex Inn** (800 S. Michigan Ave., 312/939-2800 or 800/621-6909). It doesn't compare to those amenity-laden (and pricey) hotels on Michigan Avenue, but it's a not a bad option for people who don't plan to hang out in a hotel room.

$150–250

Along with The Drake, dignitaries often find their way to **The Palmer House Hilton** (17 E. Monroe St., 312/726-7500) here while in town. The lobby is dazzling at this 1920s hotel, named for developer Palmer Potter. Some complain the rooms are small and outdated, but the location can't be beat. You're steps from L stops, the Art Institute, and State Street. Although some weekend room rates here can be pricey, bargains can be found depending on occupancy rates. On one weekend a room with two double beds can cost $129, the next it could fetch $279.

$250 and Up

Before it was renovated (transformed, really) into the **M Hotel Burnham** (1 W. Washington St., 312/782-1111 or 877/294-9712, www.burnhamhotel.com), the building at the corner of Washington and State streets was known around town as the Reliance Building, a National Historic Landmark designed by Daniel Burnham's firm. In 1999 and $28 million dollars later, it opened as a high-end boutique hotel. The 103 rooms and 19 suites are gorgeous, decorated in muted gold and royal blue colors. Architecture and history buffs will love the place, with its dark mahogany woodwork, mosaics, and marble touches throughout the building. It's a pretty pampering experience to stay here: There's free wine in the evening, and, if you've got your dog or cat in tow, the hotel provides pet beds and kitty litter service.

NEAR NORTH AND GOLD COAST

$50–100

Chain restaurants such as Planet Hollywood have come and gone, but **The Ohio House Motel** (600 N. LaSalle St., 312/943-6000) has become a bit of a landmark in the River North area, with its kitschy, white, 1950s-style design. No Egyptian cotton sheets, here, but if you're looking for a cheap hotel room in a central location, this one delivers.

Another neighborhood icon is the **Howard Johnson Inn,** (720 N. LaSalle St., 312/664-8100 or 800/446-4656, www.hojo.com), a genuine motor lodge right smack in the middle of tony River North. With room prices ranging $85–145, this place is a bargain. It's safe, clean, and best of all, there's free parking (a rarity in this town).

$100–150

Gold Coast Guest House B&B, (113 W. Elm St., 312/337-0361, www.bbchicago.com) is an 1873 town home in the chichi Gold Coast neighborhood. Big, comfy beds await you and allow you to catch up on sleep after a day of touring. Breakfasts are served in a quiet, little ivy-laden backyard.

$150–250

The Flemish House of Chicago, (68 E. Cedar St., 312/664-9981, www.chicago-bandb.com) is in the heart of Gold Coast, steps away from Oak Street beach and the Oak Street shops. The renovated 1890s building contains four smartly designed studio and three one-bedroom apartments. Owners Mike and Tom decorated the rooms in English arts and crafts style. They feature private baths, kitchens, hardwood floors, and fireplaces. You'll feel part of the neighborhood if you stay here.

Fitzpatrick Chicago Hotel (166 E. Superior St., 312/787-6000 or 800/367-7701, www.fitzpatrickhotels.com) is not too big and not too small, not too fancy and not too chintzy. The 100 suites (plus a few executive rooms and penthouses) feature canopy-style beds, pillowtop mattresses, and bathrobes. It's just south of the historic Water Tower and the Museum of Contemporary Art and a block off Michigan Avenue.

$250 and Up

The historic **Drake Hotel** (140 E. Walton Pl., 312/787-2200 or 800/55DRAKE, www.thedrakehotel.com) is where most celebrities, dignitaries, and royalty stay when in town (from Bono to Prince Charles). It's opulent, and according to some, snooty. If you've got money to throw around, spend it on a lakeview room at The Drake. As with many Chicago hotels, rates can vary widely at this hotel depending on when you are in town and what type of room you stay in.

One of the best features of the **Four Seasons Hotel** (120 E. Delaware Pl., 312/280-8800 or 800/332-3442) is the stunning 50-foot indoor pool. People wearing togas strutting around. Domed glass ceiling, palm trees. The Four Seasons is a superclean, classy joint above the fancy schmancy 900 North Michigan Avenue shops. It's one of the best bets along the Magnificent Mile. Rates for deluxe rooms can top $250.

LINCOLN PARK TO UPTOWN

Under $50

The Arlington House International Hostel (616 W. Arlington Pl., 773/929-5380 or 800/467-8335, www.arlingtonhouse.com) is within walking distance of Lincoln Park and all the shops and eateries along Lincoln Avenue and Clark Street. The hostel has basic, single-sex dorm rooms and some private rooms available for extra. A kitchen is on-site.

On the far north side of the city you'll find **Chicago International Hostel** (6318 N. Winthrop Ave., 773/262-1011, www.hostelinchicago.com) near the colorful Devon Avenue neighborhood and the inner-ring suburb of Evanston. Loyola University of Chicago is also nearby, and the place tends to attract the college set. Private single rooms and dorm-style and four-bed rooms are available. The hostel has lockers, a laundry room, and kitchen.

$100–150

Owned by local TV news reporter Andy Shaw and his wife, **Windy City Urban Inn** (607 W. Deming Pl., 773/248-7091, www.chicago-inn.com) has five guest rooms in the main house, plus three suites in the coach house (named after Illinois authors). Some suites have whirlpool baths and fireplaces. The 1886 brick home has an enclosed garden and common room with books, television, and refrigerator.

Neighborhood Inns of Chicago runs a handful of boutique hotels within residential areas on the city's north shore. Two good options are the 55-room **Willows Hotel** (555 W. Surf St., 773/528-8400 or 800/787-3108, www.cityinns.com) and the 52-room **Majestic Hotel** (528 W. Brompton St., 773/404-3499, www.cityinns.com). The Willows is a bright, French-style hotel blocks from the lake. The Majestic is an English-style hotel in northern Lakeview, within walking distance of home-decor boutiques, cafés, and intimate neighborhood restaurants. A highlight is tea and cookies served throughout the day.

GREEKTOWN TO AUSTIN

$100–150

The House of Two Urns (1239 N. Green-view Ave., 773/235-1408 or 877/896-8767, www.twourns.com) is in the heart of artsy Wicker Park and Bucktown neighborhoods, surrounded by galleries, restaurants, night-clubs, and boutiques. There are three options here: a one-bedroom room with fireplace and whirlpool bath, a two-bedroom suite, and a three-bedroom apartment that can sleep up to five adults. A little backyard patio and garden offer respite after a day of traveling. Winter rates here can drop below $100.

The Wicker Park Inn (1329 N. Wicker Park Ave., 773/486-2743, www.wickerparkinn.com) is the other option for staying in hip Wicker Park. The three rooms here are modern, clean, and feature private baths, hardwood floors, and homey touches such as quilts on the beds. It's by the Blue L line. Winter rates here can also dip below $100.

CHINATOWN TO PULLMAN

$150–250

Wooded Isle Suites consists of 14 apartment units in a courtyard building between the University of Chicago and Museum of Sci-ence and Industry in Hyde Park. Some of the units are studio apartments with Murphy beds and kitchens. Rates can vary from near $100 to near $200 depending on the size of the unit and time of year.

The Benedictine Bed and Breakfast (3111 S. Aberdeen St., 773/927-7424 or 888/539-4261, www.chicagomonk.org) is run by the Roman Catholic Monastery of the Holy Cross in Chicago's Bridgeport neighborhood (less than two miles from the Chicago White Sox's Comiskey Park). In Gothic and Renaissance-style buildings, the complex includes a two-bedroom loft with a kitchenette and living room, and a one-bedroom garden apartment.

$250 and Up

Built in 1870, the **Ⓜ Wheeler Mansion** (2020 S. Calumet Ave., 312/945-2020, www.wheel-ermansion.com) is a Second Empire–style Chicago landmark. It's south of Chinatown, by McCormick Place in the up-and-coming Prairie Avenue Historic District. For a real treat, check in here, where each one of the 11 rooms is different, some with claw-foot bath-tubs, sleigh beds, and floor-to-ceiling windows. In the morning you'll be treated to a heavenly gourmet breakfast with nice touches, such as fresh-squeezed oranges. Other pluses: a rose garden, bikes for rent, and free parking.

Food

Given Chicago's large number of residents with German and Polish ancestry, it's no surprise that the city's restaurants serve an ample supply of comfort food. There are steak and potatoes establishments such as Gene and Georgetti's Italian steakhouse and the Busy Bee Polish restaurant. But because of its diverse popu-lation, you can find numerous Asian restau-rants, particularly Thai spots, and Latin and South American restaurants. Some places do serve heart-healthy and dieter-friendly dishes, but for the most part, portions are large and butter-laden.

Two quintessential Chicago foods that are certainly not for the dieting type are pizza and hot dogs. A **Chicago-style hot dog** is robust, juicy, and spicy. It's an all-beef wiener placed in a poppy-seed bun and topped with green relish, chopped onions, sliced tomatoes, and serrano peppers. A good place to sample this Chicago favorite is at Superdawg (see listing). **Chicago-style pizza** has thick, dense crust and is incred-ibly cheesy. You need a fork and a knife to dive into a slice. Even if you've worked up an appe-tite, don't be surprised if you can eat only 1–2 slices. Here is how Chicago-style pizzas tend to be made, from bottom to top: a sprinkling of cornmeal, followed by pressed dough (lots of it), layers of mozzarella (lots of it), ingredients such as sausage or spinach (lots of it), then tomato sauce. Although always crowded with tourists, Pizzaria Uno serves a pie that never misses the mark.

If you want to sample some of the city's best cuisine, head over to one of Rick Bayless's restaurants, Frontera Grill or Topolobampo, which serve Mexican-American fare; Italian bistro Mia Francesca; Swedish spot Ann Sather for the massive, gooey cinnamon rolls; Manny's Coffee Shop and Deli for a turkey club sandwich; and the expensive, but outstanding, Charlie Trotter's for innovative cuisine.

LOOP AND RIVER NORTH
Casual
Manny's Coffee Shop and Deli (1141 S. Jefferson St., 312/939-2855, 5 A.M.–4 P.M. Mon.–Sat.) is a clattering, boisterous institution in the South Loop. It's been around for decades serving traditional deli food for breakfast and lunch. Try the corned beef on rye. You'll spend about $8 for lunch here.

John Belushi is credited with making the **Billy Goat Tavern** (430 N. Michigan Ave., 312/222-1525, 7–2 A.M. Mon.–Fri., 10–3 A.M. Sat., 11–2 A.M. Sun.) famous when he parodied the owner on a *Saturday Night Live* skit, shouting "cheezborger, cheezborger, no fries, chips!" Decades later, the grill has spawned a handful of other locations around the city and attracts tourists and newspaper employees. The food isn't spectacular, just greasy grill food, but the owners and the crowd (newspaper people, tourists, construction workers) is true blue. The Billy Goat is also the subject of local legend. The story goes that Billy Sianis, the tavern's original owner, and his goat were turned away from Wrigley Field during the 1945 World Series. A rebuffed Sianis cursed the team, saying it wouldn't ever play in the series again. Open for breakfast, lunch, and dinner. Average meal is $5.

Before they embark on a drive down Route 66, road-trippers often fuel up on pancakes at **Lou Mitchell's Restaurant and Bakery** (625

W. Jackson Blvd., 312/939-3111, 5:30 A.M.–3 P.M. Mon.–Sat., 7 A.M.–3 P.M. Sun.). Some say the place is overrated, but like Manny's, it's a good place to people-watch. Free doughnut holes. You can't beat the omelettes and French toast. You'll spend a little less than $10 for breakfast or lunch here.

Steaks
Chicagoans tend to love or hate **Gene and Georgetti** (500 N. Franklin St., 312/527-3718, 11:30 A.M.–midnight daily), an Italian steakhouse that has been in the River North neighborhood (and within sight of the Brown Line L train) since the 1940s. The clientele tends to be mostly salt-and-pepper–haired men in suits, and the servers usually reflect the clientele. The lunch and dinner menus feature items such as lamb chops and a 32-ounce T-bone. Average dinner entrée is $30. You can usually spot celebs and dignitaries here.

Mexican American
Celebrated chef Rick Bayless and his wife, Deann, run **N Frontera Grill** and its upper-end sibling, **Topolobampo** (445 N. Clark St., 312/661-1434, www.fronterakitchens.com). Both feature fresh, artistic dishes for lunch and dinner, such as chipotle-glazed scallops, stews, and chilis featuring homemade tortillas and organic ingredients. A dinner entrée at Frontera, the more casual of the two, will cost about $20. A five-course tasting menu at Topolobampo costs around $75. Topolobampo is open for lunch 11:45 A.M.–2 P.M. Tuesday, 11:30 A.M.–2 P.M. Wednesday–Friday. It is open for dinner 5:30–9:30 P.M. Tuesday–Thursday, 5:30–10:30 P.M. Friday and Saturday. Frontera Grill is open for lunch 11:30–2:30 P.M. Tuesday–Friday, for brunch 10:30 A.M.–2:30 P.M. Saturday and it is open for dinner 5:30–10 P.M. Tuesday, 5–10 P.M. Wednesday–Thursday, 5–11 P.M. Friday and Saturday.

German
A Loop landmark, the **Berghoff** (17 W. Adams St., 312/427-3170, www.berghoff.com) opened in 1898. A popular lunch and after-work spot,

Berghoff has traditional German fare such as sauerbraten and strudel, plus American dishes such as broiled halibut. The menu here is heavy on the meat and fish. Stop by the bar's lunch counter for a quick sandwich or hardboiled eggs. Meals are around $10.

GOLD COAST AND OLD TOWN

Casual

Breakfast and lunch sandwiches at **M Brett's Kitchen** (223 W. Superior St., 312/664-6354, 6 A.M.–4 P.M. Mon.–Fri., 8 A.M.–4 P.M. Sat.) are so satisfying. Everything is great: the toasted bagels, fried egg sandwiches, veggie pitas, and brownies, which are available only on Fridays. The staff are always smiling. Sandwiches are about $5.

Steaks

Many Illinois politicians rub elbows at **Gibson's** (1028 N. Rush St., 312/266-8999, www.gibsonssteakhouse.com) during lunch or dinner. (Mayor Daley and Bill Clinton have dined here.) Gibson's is a place to see and be seen, but unlike some other trendy places in Chicago, the restaurant serves mouth-watering food. Come for the scene or the food. The menu focuses, not surprisingly, on red meat, such as porterhouse steaks and London broils. For something "lighter" there are pork chops and wild salmon. Average entrée is $25. Gibson's is open for lunch at 11:30 A.M. Friday, Saturday, and Sunday. Dinner is served 3–11 P.M. Sunday–Saturday.

Asian

Traditional Thai dishes, such as *pad thai*, plus plenty of seafood entrées such as red snapper and snow crabs are on the menu at **Erawan** (729 N. Clark, 312/642-6888), an upscale Asian restaurant in River North. A lunch entrée can cost $20 and dinner twice that much.

Spanish

The sangria is always flowing at **M Café Iberico** (739 N. La Salle St., 312/573-1510),

a busy tapas restaurant in River North serving lunch and dinner. Little plates of red potatoes, marinated pork loin, or goat cheese range in price $3.75–5.95. If you're in a hurry, try the deli inside the restaurant and pack a picnic lunch to take with you to a park. Open 11 A.M.–11 P.M. Monday–Thursday, 11–1:30 A.M. Friday, noon–1:30 A.M. Saturday, noon–11:30 P.M. Saturday.

Italian

Scoozi (410 W. Huron St., 312/943-5900, www.leye.com, 5:30–9 P.M. Mon.–Thurs., 5:30–10 P.M. Fri., 5–10 P.M. Sat., 5–9 P.M. Sun.) is a large, fun, sometimes loud Italian restaurant that serves big, heaping dishes of pasta for lunch and dinner. Dine in the outdoor seating area if you're in River North sightseeing during lunch time. The average entrée is about $12.

Chances are you'll have to wait for a table at either **Pizzeria Uno** (29 E. Ohio St., 312/321-1000, 11:30–1 A.M. Mon.–Fri., 11:30–2 A.M. Sat., 11:30 A.M.–11:30 P.M. Sun.) or **Pizzeria Due** (619 N. Wabash Ave., 312/943-2400, 11–1 A.M. Sun.–Thurs., 11–2 A.M. Fri.–Sat.), and you'll have to wait for more than 30 minutes for your Chicago-style pizza to cook. Once you've had your fill (the cooks at these places whip up some heavy-duty pie), you probably won't be able to get up from the table.

Ranalli's (1925 N. Lincoln Ave., 312/642-4700; 24 W. Elm St., 312/440-7000; 337 S. Dearborn St., 312/922-8888, 11–2 A.M. Sun.–Fri., 11–3 A.M. Sat.) is a popular dining spot, particularly the Lincoln Avenue location because of its huge outdoor patio. Ranalli's serves crunchy thin-crust pizza and has a good beer selection.

Continental

Booth One is where celebs such as Judy Garland and Humphrey Bogart hung out when they dined at **The Pump Room** (in the Omni Ambassador East Hotel, 1301 N. State Pkwy., 312/266-0360, www.pumproom.com). The restaurant, lounge, and cigar saloon scream old school. (It's been around since the 1930s.)

Black-and-white celebrity photographs are plastered throughout the restaurant, and chandeliers dangle from the ceiling. The chefs serve European and Midwestern fare (king salmon, veal porterhouse) and arrange them so artfully on your plate that you're not sure how to begin eating. Dinner entrées are around $30; lunch is half that. The Sunday champagne brunch is about $30. Open for breakfast 6:30–11 A.M. Monday–Friday, 7–11 A.M. Saturday–Sunday, for lunch 11 A.M.–2 P.M. Monday–Saturday, for dinner 6–10 P.M. Monday–Sunday, and for brunch 11:30 A.M.–2 P.M. Sunday.

The **Bin 36** (339 N. Dearborn St., 312/755-9463, www.bin36.com) complex includes a restaurant, café, wine bar, and wine shop. It's a light and airy modern place where you can choose from more than 50 wines by the glass and dine on items such as tuna tartare. Arrive early and have a seat at the cool red and zinc bar. Breakfast, lunch, and dinner are served here daily. A five-course tasting menu is about $40; wine flights are approximately $15.

NORTH SIDE
Casual
Cubs fans pack late at night into **The Wiener's Circle** (2622 N. Clark St., 773/477-7444), where the sassy cooks serve Chicago-style dogs and extra-thick milk shakes. Don't hem and haw when you order, or expect a few expletives shouted your way.

Costello Sandwiches and Sides (2015 W. Roscoe Ave., 773/929-2323, 11 A.M.–9 P.M. Mon.–Sat., 11 A.M.–6 P.M. Sun.) is crowded for a reason. The sandwiches are big and veggie-friendly pasta dishes. Lunch or dinner will set you back about $8.

Stanley's Kitchen and Tap (1970 N. Lincoln Ave., 312/642-0007) serves food just like your mom and grandma used to make in a dining room out of the early 1970s. Stanley's serves fun dishes such as meatloaf and Tater Tots. Open 11:30 A.M.–11 P.M. Monday–Thursday, 11:30 A.M.–midnight Friday–Saturday, 11 A.M.–11 P.M. Sunday, and for brunch 11 A.M.–4 P.M. Saturday–Sunday.

The best fish and chips in the city are at **Duke of Perth** (2913 N. Clark St., 773/477-1741). Wash down your meal with some top-shelf scotch whiskey.

The Red Lion Pub (2446 N. Lincoln Ave., 773/348-2695) also serves decent fish and chips, and, if you're brave enough to try it, steak and kidney pie. The Red Lion hosts occasional poetry and fiction readings.

The marscapone-stuffed French toast at **Toast** (746 W. Webster Ave., 773/935-5600; and 2046 N. Damen Ave., 773/772-5600, 7 A.M.–3 P.M. Mon.–Fri., 8 A.M.–4 P.M. Sat.-Sun.) is just incredible and the breakfast burritos will tide you over until dinner. You can expect to spend less than $10 on breakfast or lunch at this popular and often-crowded Lincoln Park restaurant.

Spanish
Hot and cold Spanish tapas are on the menu at **Café Ba-Ba-Reeba!** (2024 N. Halsted St., 312/935-5000, www.leye.com, noon–10 P.M. Sun.–Thurs., noon–midnight Fri.–Sat.), a festive restaurant with an outdoor patio. Try one of the heaping, steaming dishes of paella (rice dishes originally from Valencia, Spain. Tapas range in price $2.95–7.95.

Italian
The focus is on Northern Italian cuisine at **Mia Francesca** (3311 N. Clark St., 773/281-3310, 5–10:30 P.M. Sun.–Thurs., 5–11 P.M. Fri.–Sat.) The bruschetta always tastes fresh and the pasta rich. The little courtyard is a great spot on summer evenings. Dinner entrées average $20.

Unlike Mia Francesca, **Sabatino's** (4441 W. Irving Park Rd., 773/283-8331, 11 A.M.–midnight Mon.–Thurs., 11–12:30 A.M. Fri.–Sat., noon–10:30 P.M. Sun.) isn't necessarily a scene with up-and-coming young professionals. It's an old-school Italian restaurant in Old Irving Park area with the look and feel of a supper club. The dining rooms are a bit cramped, but you can't beat the piano player welcoming you, crunchy, warm bread, and gracious hosts. Dinners are around $10.

Asian

Ⲙ Penny's Noodle Shop (3400 N. Sheffield Ave., 773/281-8222; 950 W. Diversey Pkwy., 773/281-8448; and 1542 N. Damen Ave., 773/394-0100, 11 A.M.–10 P.M. Tues.–Thurs. and Sun., 11 A.M.–10:30 P.M. Fri.–Sat.) is always bustling, no matter what time of day or day of the week. The dishes—*pad thai,* spicy basil noodles—are not only yummy and large, but affordable. A bowl or plate will cost about $7 for lunch or dinner.

The neighborhood and the building in which you'll find **Arun's** (4156 N. Kedzie Ave., 773/539-1909, 5–10 P.M. Tues.–Sat., 5–9 P.M. Sun.) are pretty unspectacular, but the cuisine, primarily Thai, gets rave reviews by restaurant critics from all around every year. Don't be surprised if you spend about $75 on dinner here.

Ethiopian

At **Ethio Café** (3462 N. Clark St., 773/929-8300, 3–11 P.M. Tues.–Thurs., 3–midnight Fri., 1 P.M.–midnight Sat., noon–11 P.M. Sun.), as a live band jams, diners sit together around one large platter and scoop lentil and split pea stewlike concoctions onto *injera* bread (instead of a utensil). Lunch and dinner (about $10) is served on the weekends, dinner on the weekdays.

Romanian

The folks at **Euro Café** (3001 N. Ashland Ave., 773/929-8640, 4 P.M.–midnight daily) will pick you up at your hotel in their limo (albeit a dated one) if you dine at their fun restaurant. Fill up on Romanian food such as homemade dumplings and stew as an accordion player sings. Average entrée is $12.

Fine Dining

Housed in a renovated townhouse on well-to-do Armitage Avenue, **Charlie Trotter's** (816 W. Armitage Ave., 773/248-6228, www.charlietrotters.com, 6–10 P.M. Tues.–Thurs., 5:30–10 P.M. Fri.–Sat.) is often called the best restaurant in the city. Trotter and his staff create French and Asian dishes using organic, free-range meat and heirloom vegetables. The menu

changes all the time, but here's a sampling of what you might dine on: cold smoked sturgeon with citrus crème fraîche or warm souffle of acorn squash. It's easy to drop more than $100 on dinner here.

For a romantic night out, Chicago couples love to nuzzle in **Geja's Café** (340 W. Armitage Ave., 773/281-9101, 5–10:30 P.M. Mon.–Thurs., 5–midnight Fri.–Sat., 4:30–10 P.M. Sun.), an intimate fondue spot near Lincoln Park.

Coffee Shops

Tucked into a residential area within Wrigleyville, **Ⲙ Uncommon Ground** (1214 W. Grace St., 773/929-3680, 9 A.M.–11 P.M. Sun.–Thurs., 9 A.M.–midnight Fri.–Sat.) is a great spot to visit any time of day. You can drop by in the afternoon for a cup of tea or mug of latte, sip on hot toddies while listening to a jazz band or folk singer in the evening, or dive into an omelet during Sunday brunches.

The only **Julius Meinl** (3601 N. Southport Ave., 773/868-1858, www.meinl.com, 6 A.M.–10 P.M. Sun.–Thurs., 6 A.M.–11 P.M. Fri.–Sat.) café in the United States is on north Southport Avenue, just by the Brown Line stop. The Austrian café sells its world-renowned coffee here in addition to pastries such as apricot strudel, some sandwiches, and soups. Classical or jazz groups perform for customers on some days.

UPTOWN

Casual

Breakfast is just delightful at **Ⲙ Ann Sather** (5207 N. Clark St., 312/217-6677; 929 W. Belmont Ave., 773/348-2378; and 3416 N. Southport Ave., 773/404-4475). The cinnamon rolls are enormous, the brownies fresh, eggs fluffy, and potatoes done just right.

Blue-haired ladies tend to frequent **Lutz Continental Café** (2458 W. Montrose Ave., 773/478-7785, www.lutzcafe.com, 11 A.M.–8 P.M. Sun.–Thurs., 11 A.M.–10 P.M. Fri.–Sat.), which has been open since 1948, for the coffee cakes. But the menu also features crepes, homemade ice cream, goulash soup,

Superdawg dancing hot dogs

and warm sandwiches such as the broiled ham sandwich on rye bread. Lunch or dinner will cost about $12.

As its name implies, the **Fireside** (5739 N. Ravenswood Ave., 773/561-SIDE—773/561-7433, 10 A.M.–4 A.M. Sun., 11 A.M.–4 A.M. Mon.–Fri., 11 A.M.–5 P.M. Sat.) restaurant boasts a warm hearth for you to sit beside during your meal. Or have a seat on the deck, a great spot during the winter or summer; the roof retracts. The kitchen serves barbecued ribs, burgers, pizza, and pasta for about $10 for lunch and dinner.

You can recognize **Superdawg** (6363 N. Milwaukee Ave., 773/763-0660; 3344 N. Kimball Ave., 773/478-7800 or 773/478-7214, 11–1 A.M. Sun.–Thurs., 11–2 A.M. Fri.–Sat.) by the two giant fiberglass hot dogs dancing on the roof. Superdawg weiners are solid Chicago dogs (all-beef dogs topped with green relish, onions, serrano peppers, and celery salt. The crinkly fries are salty and crunchy.

The first **Fluky's** hot dog stand (6821 N. Western Ave., 773/274-3652; and on the fourth floor of The Shops of Northbridge, 520 N. Michigan Ave., www.flukys.com) opened

on the city's West Side in 1929. The dogs are beefy, salty, and smoky.

Middle Eastern
Reza's (5255 N. Clark St., 773/561-1898; plus another location at 432 W. Ontario St., 312/664-4500) serves primarily Persian cuisine, such as kebabs, hummus, and thick, creamy yogurt. Whatever dinner you choose, top it off with a cup of Persian tea. Entrées are about $10.

Coffee Shop
Bring a book and slide into a window seat at **Kopi** (5317 N. Clark St., 773/989-5674), where you can watch people, sip great coffee, and nibble on chocolate cake or order a sandwich. Kopi is a place where you can lounge away the afternoon unnoticed.

WEST SIDE
Southwestern
One of the best Sunday brunches in Chicago is at **Flo** (1434 W. Chicago Ave., 312/243-0477, breakfast served 8:30 A.M.–2:30 P.M.

Tues.–Fri., brunch 9 A.M.–2:30 P.M. Sat.–Sun., dinner 5:30–10 P.M. Tues.–Thurs., 5:30–11 P.M. Fri.–Sat.), which features Southwestern-style breakfasts burritos. The chicken and green chili enchiladas are really tasty.

European

If you're in the mood for innovative French cuisine, head to the West Loop brasserie **Marché** (833 W. Randolph St., 312/226-8399, www.marche-chicago.com). The dining room is colorful (umbrellas hang from the ceiling), and so is the food. Dinner entrées, which average $18, can include monkfish medallions and duck confit strudel. Open for lunch 11:30 A.M.–2 P.M. Monday–Friday, and for dinner 5:30–10 P.M. Sunday–Wednesday, 5:30–11 P.M. Thursday, 5:30–midnight Friday and Saturday.

On a cool fall day, **Paprikash** (5210 W. Diversey Pkwy., 773/739-4949, www.paprikashrestaurant.com, 4 P.M.–midnight Tues.–Thurs., 11 A.M.–midnight Fri.–Sun.) will deliver Hungarian comfort food such as chicken *paprikash* with homemade noodles, cream of mushroom soup, and cheese spread, sprinkled with lots of paprika. Dinner entrées are about $10.

Southern

Wishbone (1001 W. Washington St., 312/829-3597; and 3300 N. Lincoln Ave., 773/549-2663) is the kind of place some people can visit every day and not grow tired of the food. The corn cakes and crab cakes are superb, the eggs and breakfast burrito fresh and satisfying. There's a reason they call it soul food. Open for breakfast and lunch 7 A.M.–3 P.M. Monday–Saturday, 8:30 A.M.–2:30 P.M. Saturday–Sunday, and for dinner 5–10 P.M. Tuesday–Friday and Sunday, 5–11 P.M. Saturday.

Greek

Traditional Greek pastries such as *diples* (fried pastry) are baked daily at **Pan Hellenic Pastry Shop** (322 S. Halsted St., 312/454-1886). The casual café **Artopolis** (306 S. Halsted St., 312/559-9000) is a gathering place for many residents of the area. Sip on a latte in this bustling joint or dine on a Greek sandwich such as *kotosalata,* walnut bread topped with mescluns, chicken salad, pine nuts, and pesto. Wood-fired pizza is also available. Sandwiches, made from fresh, wholesome breads baked on site, cost approximately $7.

If you're traveling with a large party or family, spend the evening in the festive **Greek Islands** (200 S. Halsted St., 312/782-9855). Feast on fresh seafood, lamb, and favorites such as *spanakopita,* which is spinach and feta cheese wrapped in pastry.

Polish

Hearty, stick-to-your ribs kind of food is dished up at the **NorthPoint Café and Grill** (2234 W. North Ave., 773/395-1111, 7:30 A.M.–8:30 P.M. Mon.–Sat., 9:30 A.M.–3 P.M. Sun.), an unpretentious restaurant that serves Polish and (yes) Mexican food, such as pierogies, borscht, and *tortas* that never disappoint.

Culinary School

See what the next Wolfgang Puck is conjuring by dining at one of the dinners presented by the **M Kendall College School of Culinary Arts** (900 N. Branch St., 312/752-2328, www.kendall.edu). This notable culinary school trains students and they present themed meals (vegetarian, Mexican). These are prix fixe menus with several courses and tend to be meat- and seafood-heavy, with such offerings as lobster risotto and braised lamb shank. Prices are about $20 per person.

SOUTH SIDE

Asian

Bubble teas have made Chinatown's **M Joy Yee's Noodle Shop** (2159 S. China Pl., 312/328-0001, www.joyyee.com, 11 A.M.–9:30 P.M. daily) famous. The affordable, youthful Pan-Asian restaurant also has spring rolls, noodle dishes such as black mushroom chow mein, and Korean barbecue ribs. Lunch or dinner will cost about $7 per dish.

For great dim sum, try **The Phoenix** (2131 S. Archer Ave., 312/328-0848) in the heart of Chinatown. The restaurant is upstairs, the more casual café downstairs.

The ambience at **Opera** (1301 S. Wabash Ave., 312/461-0161, www.opera-chicago.com, 5–10 P.M. Sun.–Wed., 5–11 P.M. Thurs., 5–midnight Fri.–Sat.) is definitely romantic and much like an opera house (imagine lots of silky red drapes throughout the dining rooms). Meals are cooked in Cantonese, Szechwan, Shanghai, and Hunan styles. A dinner entrée will cost about $20.

Southern

Cajun and Creole fare is on the menu at **Dixie Kitchen and Bait Shop** (5225 S. Harper Ave., 773/363-4943). Try the fried green tomatoes.

Gladys Holcomb, of **Gladys Luncheonette** (4527 S. Indiana Ave., 773/548-4566) died in 2003 at the age of 96, but her daughter has stepped in to run the restaurant, a south side tradition since 1946. You'll find items such as fried catfish, black-eyed peas, and peach cobbler on this restaurant's menu.

FOOD MARKETS

Farmers markets, with flowers, fruits, veggies, and arts and crafts, are held Tuesday, Wednesday, Thursday, Saturday, and Sunday in about 30 different locations throughout the city. For more information, contact the Mayor's Office of Special Events (312/744-3315, www.cityof-chicago.org).

The site of the original **Maxwell Street Market** has been cleared for town houses and boutiques, but the tradition of an open-air market continues at Canal Street and Roosevelt Road, southwest of the Loop. Vendors sell everything from *churros* to zucchini, as well as clothing and garage sale items such as used toasters. The market is held 7 A.M.–3 P.M. Sunday, year-round. For more information, contact the Mayor's Office of Special Events.

Warm, fresh breads and imported meats and cheeses are on display at **Fox and Obel** (401 E. Illinois St., 312/410-7301), a gourmet food market in River East (from Michigan Ave. to Navy Pier). The shop's café also sells mugs of coffee and glasses of beer and wine.

If you have plans to picnic, you'll find plenty of supplies in **Treasure Island** (3460 N. Broadway, 773/327-3880; and 680 N. Lake Shore Dr., 312/664-0400), which stocks food, wine, and beer from around the world.

Information

TOURISM AGENCIES

The **Chicago Convention and Tourism Bureau** and the **City of Chicago Office of Tourism** manage the tourism hotline 877/CHICAGO (877/244-2246) and the website www.877chicago.com. The tourism bureau has offices in the huge convention hall McCormick Place, 2301 South Lake Shore Drive. The Office of Tourism is at 78 East Washington Street.

You can pick up sightseeing and attraction brochures and free Chicago Transit Authority system maps at the Tourist Information Centers throughout the city: Chicago Water Works (163 E. Pearson Ave.); Chicago Cultural Center (78 E. Washington St.); and the James R. Thompson Center (100 W. Randolph St.).

MEDIA

Two newspapers dominate the Chicago market: the *Chicago Tribune* (www.chicago-tribune.com) and the *Chicago Sun-Times* (www.sun-times.com). The *Trib* is a broadsheet that costs $.50 and the *Sun-Times* is a tabloid-size paper that costs $.35. Both are fairly conservative in their political views, publish Thursday entertainment sections, and are available at newsstands throughout the city, in L stations, grocery stores, and coffee shops.

The Tribune Company also owns *Chicago* magazine (www.chicagomag.com), a slick monthly magazine that often highlights the best and the worst restaurants, most attractive bachelors and bachelorettes, most successful businesspeople, and other list-driven articles. It is available at grocery stores, drug stores, and convenience marts.

The most comprehensive entertainment and dining listings are in the weekly alternative, *The Chicago Reader* (www.chireader.com). The other alternative weekly is the *Newcity Chicago* (www.newcity.com). Both are available at most convenience stores, casual restaurants, and bookstores.

The weekly newspaper *Windy City Times* (www.wctimes.com) focuses its coverage on the city's gay, lesbian, and bisexual population. The newspaper and website have plenty of listings on the city's gay and gay-friendly restaurants, bars, and nightclubs.

You'll find NBC on Channel 5, ABC on Channel 7, CBS on Channel 2, Fox on Channel 32, WGN on Channel 9, and WTTW, the Chicago PBS affiliate, on Channel 12.

WBEZ 91.5 FM is Chicago Public Radio, WXRT FM 93.5 plays classic and alternative rock, and WFMT 98.7 FM is the classical music station. On the AM dial, the *Tribune*'s news and talk radio station is WGN 720 AM. Or, you can get the scoop on local news by listening to WBBM 780 AM.

HOSPITALS

On the West Side is **John H. Stroger, Jr. Hospital** (1835 W. Harrison St., 312/633-3000), formerly Cook County Hospital, which opened in 2002 at a price tag of $551 million. The hospital (named after the head of the Cook County board) is the oldest public hospital in the country. It served as the model for the television show *E.R.* The original 1914 building is still next door. You can reach Stroger Hospital on the Blue Line L's Forest Park branch. The stop is Medical Center.

In the Gold Coast is **Northwestern Memorial Hospital** (251 E. Huron St., 312/926-2000, www.nmh.org). In Lakeview and Lincoln Park, there's **Advocate Illinois Masonic Medical Center** (836 W. Wellington Ave., 773/975-1600, www.advocatehealth.com). And on the south side is the **University of Chicago Hospitals** (5841 S. Maryland Ave., 773/702-1000, 888/UCH-0200 or 888/824-0200, www.uchospitals.edu). You can reach the university hospital on the Green Line. The stop is Cottage Grove.

Services

TOURS

If you're not comfortable exploring the city on your own, a great option is the free **Chicago Greeter** (877/CHICAGO or 877/244-2246) tour-guide service run by the City of Chicago. The program links you with a Chicago native or resident and together you explore a neighborhood such as Lincoln Park or Chinatown. It is available for solo travelers and groups of up to six people.

For a formal tour of a neighborhood, hop aboard one of the **Chicago Neighborhood Tours** (312/742-1190, www.chgoci-tytours.com). Run by the Chicago Office of Tourism and Chicago Department of Cultural Affairs, these half-day bus tours highlight local landmarks, restaurants, and shopping enclaves, and focus on specific neighborhoods, from Devon Avenue to Pullman. Tours are $25 for adults, $20 for seniors and students. A few select, more comprehensive tours are $50. Tours are by reservation only.

A good way to check out the downtown area on rainy or snowy days is on the free **Loop Tour Train.** Docents from the Chicago Architecture Foundation narrate stories about the history of the city and the elevated trains. It runs Saturday afternoons May–September. Even though it's free, you'll need a ticket, available at the Chicago Cultural Center (77 East Randolph St., 877/CHICAGO or 877/244-2246.)

Guides with **Tour Black Chicago** (312/684-9034, www.tourblackchicago.com) will pick you up from one of the major hotels in the Loop and give you the African-American perspective on some of the city's sights.

If you're going to take a guided tour of Chicago, take an architecturally focused boat tour with the **Chicago Architecture Foundation** (224 S. Michigan Ave., 312/922-TOUR—312/922-8687 or 312/922-3432—bus tours, www.architecture.org). Its boat tours win rave reviews every year. Boat cruises run April–mid-November. The 1.5-hour narrated river cruises spotlight historical buildings in the Loop, including the Sears Tower and Wrigley building, plus docents give you the scoop on the city's most famous architects, such as Frank Lloyd Wright, Mies van der Rohe and Louis Sullivan and others. Cruises cost $23–25.

There aren't that many Al Capone- or mobster-related sites left in Chicago (many buildings have been torn down or extensively remodeled), but the guys with **Untouchable Tours** (312/881-1195, www.gangstertour.com, $24) make a mafia-focused tour of the city a blast. As Italian singers croon on the radio, you'll drive past places such as the site of the St. Valentine's Day Massacre aboard a black-painted school bus. Tours depart from the 600 block of North Clark Street.

A number of speedboats and cruise lines docked at Navy Pier and along the Chicago River offer shoreline cruises of Chicago. The best bet is to admire the skyline aboard the **Tall Ship Windy** (Navy Pier, 312/595-5555, www.tallshipwindy.com, $25 for a 1.5-hour cruise, $125 for a full-day tour), a 150-foot-tall majestic sailboat.

POST OFFICES

Most of the major office buildings have U.S. Postal Service offices: the Sears Tower (233 S. Wacker Dr.), John Hancock Building (835 N. Michigan Ave.), and Merchandise Mart (Kinzie and Wells Sts.). In the Gold Coast you'll find an office at 540 North Dearborn Street; in Lincoln Park at 2405 North Sheffield Avenue and 2643 North Clark Street.

Getting There

AIR

O'Hare International Airport

Chicago is serviced by two major airports: O'Hare International and Midway. O'Hare International Airport (773/686-2200, www.ohare.com) is one of the world's busiest airports. In 2002 66 million passengers traveled through its terminals and 922,000 planes landed or took off from O'Hare. In 2002 the city started acquiring land for a massive redevelopment of O'Hare, including reconfiguring the runways, adding high-speed rail service, more highway access, and extending the Blue Line L train.

To get to the city from O'Hare, catch the Blue Line L train, which operates 24 hours a day, seven days a week. Trains leave about every 10 minutes from the lower level of the main parking garage. To get to the station, you'll have to schlep through the pedestrian tunnels from Terminals 1, 2, and 3 or hop on the ATS from Terminal 5 to Terminal 3. A one-way ticket costs $1.75.

Parking at O'Hare is ridiculously expensive—$13–50 per day depending on how close you want to park to the airport and whether or not you choose valet service. The free Airport Transit System shuttles people between the four terminals, long-term parking, and Metra (the suburban train line) station. It operates 24 hours a day. Traveling from Terminal One to Lot E (the economy parking lot) takes less than 10 minutes.

Metra's North Central Line (312/222-6777 or 312/836-7000, www.metrarail.com) services northern Cook and Lake counties between the northern suburb of Antioch and Union Station in downtown Chicago. You can catch a shuttle from its O'Hare stop to the Remote Parking Lot F. A one-way fare between the shuttle stop and downtown costs a little more than $3. The Chicago Bicycle Federation is working to expand the program. Call Metra for additional information.

All the major rental-car companies have desks at O'Hare. They are on the lower level of the airport, near the baggage claim in Terminals 1, 2, and 3. If you are in Terminal 5, head to the lower level and you can call a rental-car agency on one of the free courtesy telephones stationed throughout.

You can catch a cab (fares run around $35 to the Loop depending on traffic) from the lower levels of all four terminals. Cabs don't offer flat rates to the Loop. If it's rush hour and traffic is backed up on the Kennedy (highly likely), expect a higher fare.

Midway International Airport

On the southwest side of the city, Midway (5700 S. Cicero Ave., 773/838-0600) is a hub for economy carriers Southwest Airlines and ATA. It's smaller than O'Hare, but by no means is it a small airport (17 million passengers fly through here every year). Two new concourses opened in 2002, as well as a new parking garage.

To get to the city from Midway, take the CTA's Orange Line L train (312/836-7000, www.transitchicago.com), which runs between the airport and the Loop. It's about a 30-minute ride to downtown, and a one-way ticket will cost you $1.75. The first train to downtown departs at 3:55 A.M. and last train to the city is at 12:55 A.M. Trains run about every 10 minutes during the day, and more frequently during rush hours and a little less often late evening or very early in the morning.

You can catch a taxicab into the city on the lower level of the arrivals area by door LL3. Taxi fare to downtown will run about $25 depending on traffic conditions. Most of the major rental-car companies have desks in the lower-level arrivals area. Parking at Midway costs $10–50 per day. A free shuttle will take you from the economy parking lots to the airport. **Continental Airport Express** (312/454-7800 or 800/654-7871) offers rides to and from Midway and downtown Chicago and some suburbs for $16 per person 6 A.M.–11:30 P.M. Shuttles leave about every 15 minutes from outside the LL3 door.

If you need to travel to and from O'Hare and Midway airports, **Omega** (773/483-6634) and **Coach USA Wisconsin** (877/324-7767) offer bus shuttles. Omega operates 7 A.M.–11:45 P.M. for $17. Coach USA Wisconsin runs 8 A.M.–10 P.M. for $12. Allow about one hour travel time. If you are staying at one of the hotels in the area, inquire about a shuttle. Some offer this service.

TRAIN

The vast **Union Station,** at Canal and Madison streets, is where suburban trains and Amtrak trains come and go. As of January 2004, **Amtrak** (225 S. Canal St., 800/USA RAIL or 800/872-7245, www.amtrak.com) had 13 train lines arriving and departing from Chicago, including the California Zephyr, City of New Orleans, Michigan, Missouri, Southwest Chief, and Empire Builder.

At Union Station, you can store your luggage, grab a bite to eat in one of the many fast-food joints, shop for trinkets, and rent a car. Three car-rental companies have offices in Union Station: Hertz (800/654-3131), Budget (800/527-0700), and Enterprise (800/736-8222). Short-term and long-term parking is available. You can catch a cab from anywhere outside Union Station. The closest Blue Line stop is at Clinton (and Congress Parkway) two blocks south of the station. The Orange, Blue, and Purple Lines are three blocks east at Quincy and Wells streets.

BUS

The main **Greyhound Bus Terminal** (630 W. Harrison St., 312/408-5800 or 800/229-9424, www.greyhound.com) is in the South

Loop and open 24 hours a day, seven days a week. Greyhound buses also stop at 95th Street and the Dan Ryan Expressway (14 W. 95th St., 312/408-5999) and on the north side at Cumberland Avenue (5800 N. Cumberland Ave., 773/693-2474).

Getting Around

About two million people ride on buses and trains of the **Chicago Transit Authority** (888/YOUR-CTA or 888/968-7282, www.transitchicago.com) every day. The quickest way around the city is aboard the L, Chicago's elevated train system, which consists of seven train lines (some run above ground, some below). All are designated by color: blue, red, purple, green, orange, brown, and yellow. A train sign at the front of each train shows its final designation. Stations can be found at all the major attractions and neighborhoods: Wrigley Field, State Street, Old Town, the University of Chicago, as well as into the inner-ring suburbs of Oak Park and Evanston.

Schedules vary per line, but trains generally run every 5–10 minutes. Most trains operate 4 A.M.–1 A.M., seven days a week. There are some exceptions. The Blue Line's Forest Park branch, which travels to and from O'Hare Airport and the western suburb of Forest Park, and the Red Line, which travels from the northern part of Chicago all the way south to 95th Street, operate 24 hours a day, seven days a week. The Yellow Line, a short route from the northern edge of the city to the suburb of Skokie, does not operate on weekends. One ride costs $1.75 for adults, a transfer is $.25. If you spend $10 on a Chicago or Transit card, you'll receive a 10 percent discount. A one-day pass is $5 and a seven-day pass is $20. You can buy passes at places such as the city's visitors centers, airports, and museums. In recent years the CTA has hinted that it will raise rates again.

The City of Chicago's Department of Transportation (877/CHICAGO or 877/244-2246, www.cityofchicago.org) offers **free trolley rides** in the summer and during the winter holidays. The trolleys run between major tourist destinations downtown such as Museum Campus, Navy Pier, and Union Station. Don't confuse these trolleys with paid operators that run sightseeing tours. Schedules vary every year.

There are more than 20 **taxicab companies** in Chicago. You can hail a taxi on the street or call one of the cab companies. Some companies include Yellow Cab (773/907-0020), Jitney Cab (773/548-6391), Checker Taxi Association (312/733-4790), and Chicago Carriage Cab (312/326-2221). Meters start at $1.90, and then increase by $1.60 for each additional mile. Each additional passenger is $.50. A ride to O'Hare from downtown is about $35, to Midway it's $25. Tipping is optional.

To travel to the near and far suburbs, you'll ride on the commuter rail line called **Metra** (312/836-7000, www.metrarail.com), which has 11 lines to six neighboring counties that depart from Ogilvie Transportation Center (Madison and Canal streets) and Union Station in downtown Chicago, and from Randolph Street Station between Michigan Avenue and Grant Park. Metra allows passengers to bring bicycles aboard some of its train lines at various times by reservations for an additional $5. Ogilvie Center has a currency exchange, automated teller machines, luggage storage, and phones.

The suburban bus line is **Pace** (847/364-PACE or 847/364-7223, www.pacebus.com).

The Collar Counties

Like many communities surrounding big cities, Chicago's suburbs sometimes face an image problem. When most people think of suburbs they think of monotonous subdivisions, strip malls, and golf courses. Sure, the region has some of those things, but Chicago's towns are surprisingly diverse places with rare, beautiful landscapes—from Volo Bog in the northwest, where you can stroll along a boardwalk, look for orchids, and listen for herons, to Illinois Beach State Park in the northeast, where you can hike past sand dunes. The inner-ring suburb of Oak Park boasts the nation's larg-

est collection of Frank Lloyd Wright–designed homes, plus an Ernest Hemingway home and museum (he was born here). The far west villages of Geneva, St. Charles, and Batavia are a string of arts and shopping villages on the Fox River connected by a riverfront trail.

The range of sights and activities in the collar counties is impressive. In the shopping nexus of Schaumburg, there's sprawling Woodfield Mall, but there's also Lynfred Winery, a winery and bed-and-breakfast. After a day of testing that iron stomach of yours at Six Flags Great America you can stop by a local farm and pick up a quart of raspberries. There's a lot to see and do other than shop—although that is a big thing to do out here. You can catch a Kane County Cougars game for less than $10 or an off-Broadway play at the Metropolis Center in Arlington Heights for about $20, cast a fishing line in a Lake County park, or view a multimedia art installation in Schaumburg.

PLANNING YOUR TIME

There's quite a lot to see and do in the collar counties. You'll need a week to hit all the best spots. If your time is limited to 2–3 days, focus your visit on one geographic area: the north shore, the near west, or the far west. If you're staying in Chicago and have a day or two free to explore outside the city limits, head to nearby Oak Park or Evanston. You can pack the north shore into a weekend, including a day in **Evanston** at the **Grosse Point Lighthouse,** lakeshore parks and beaches, downtown shops and restaurants, and a walk through Northwestern University, followed by a day driving north along windy **Sheridan Road** to the grand **Baha'i House of Worship** in Wilmette, and a walk through the **Chicago Botanic Gardens** in Glencoe. To the near west, don't miss the impressive **Brookfield Zoo** in Brookfield or **Morton Arboretum** in Lisle. To the far west the Fox River towns of **Geneva, St. Charles,** and **Batavia** boast riverside paths and parks, dozens of artisan and antiques shops, galleries, and storefront restaurants.

If you've got shopping on the brain, then make tracks to Schaumburg's **Woodfield Mall** and the enormous **Gurnee Mills** in the northwest. While planning your trip, check to see if the towns you plan to visit are on commuter train lines. You can waste a lot of time in traffic if you take the highways, especially in the summer.

Chicagoland covers a large area, roughly 30–40 miles from Chicago in all directions except east . It stretches north along Lake Michigan into northern Cook County and Lake County; and to the west and south, along the Des Plaines, Du Page, and Fox riv-

ers, into Du Page County, and beyond that, Kane County. South of the city, the suburbs extend into Will County.

If you plan to spend more than a day in the suburbs, particularly in towns that are within an hour's drive of the city, consider basing your vacation in lively **Oak Park,** which has plenty of attractions for literary and architecture buffs, boutique hotels, affordable, top-rated restaurants, and independently owned shops. Also, keep in mind restaurants in the suburbs tend to close earlier than those in Chicago (around 9–10 P.M.) and most shops keep banker hours (9 A.M.–5 P.M. daily). Sunday evenings are pretty quiet out here.

Access

If you plan to explore the inner-ring suburbs, you don't need to drive your car or hire a rental car. Suburbs such as Oak Park, Forest Park, and Evanston are on **Chicago Transit Authority** (888/YOUR-CTA or 888/968-7282, www.yourcta.com), so you could even stay in Chicago and take the L (elevated train) out to these cities for the day. The commuter train line **Metra** (312/836-7000, www.metrarail.com) runs a regular train schedule to the inner-ring cities as well as to towns in the collar counties of Du Page, Lake, Kane, and Will from downtown Chicago. Many of these towns have revitalized downtowns that you can explore right off the train.

If you want to visit sites beyond the downtowns situated along train lines, you will have to take one of the buses run by the suburban bus line **Pace** (847/364-7223, www.pacebus.com). Schedules for Pace buses vary per suburb, day, and time of year. With that said, you might be better off driving your car or renting one. But be warned. Driving through the suburbs will take time. On the map, Elmhurst and Naperville are about 15 miles apart and connected via interstate highway, but make this drive in the morning or early evenings and it could easily take you 30 minutes. Sometimes, traffic out here is just as snarly as it is in Chicago. I-290 is notorious for backups, as is I-55 from Chicago to Joliet. The "Hillside Strangler," where

Must-Sees

M Ernest Hemingway Birthplace and Museum: In 1899 Hemingway was born in a Victorian home on a tree-lined street in Oak Park. In recent years his birth home was restored and filled with furniture, books, letters, and displays about the writer's early years in the village (page 74).

M Frank Lloyd Wright Home and Studio: Built in 1889, Wright's renovated home and studio is where the architect launched his Prairie-style of design (page 76).

M Brookfield Zoo: The family-friendly zoo in Chicago's western suburb of Brookfield has constructed several different habitat areas, from Illinois marshes and prairies to the African savannah, for hundreds of animals (page 82).

M Grosse Point Lighthouse: This National Historic Landmark has been standing tall on the north side of Evanston since 1873. Climb the 113-foot-tall tower to take in views of Lake Michigan, stroll through the surrounding gardens, and visit the adjacent art center (page 86).

M Chicago Botanic Garden: English walled gardens, Japanese gardens, colorful spring bulb displays, vegetable gardens, waterfalls—you name it, the botanic garden (based in Glencoe, not Chicago) has got it. Add to the mix tram rides, walking trails, and indoor and outdoor cafés, and you've got a great way to spend a morning or afternoon (page 91).

M Baha'i House of Worship: Built in 1953, this stunningly beautiful building in Wilmette, near the Lake Michigan shoreline, is the first of its kind in the Western Hemisphere. Learn about the Baha'i faith or sit back and admire the architecture of the 135-foot-high dome and the surrounding rose gardens (page 92).

M Morton Arboretum: Once the estate of a Morton Salt executive, Morton Arboretum in Lisle is one of the best places in Chicago's western suburbs for taking a stroll. Choose among numerous trails through formal rose gardens, woodland trails past vibrant maple and birch trees, into tallgrass prairies or along a marsh boardwalk (page 107).

M Historic Village of Long Grove: In an area where most of the land has been developed into sprawling modern mansions or town-house developments, Long Grove is a picture-postcard town complete with a covered bridge, mill pond, and turn-of-the-20th century buildings home to boutiques and casual restaurants (page 129).

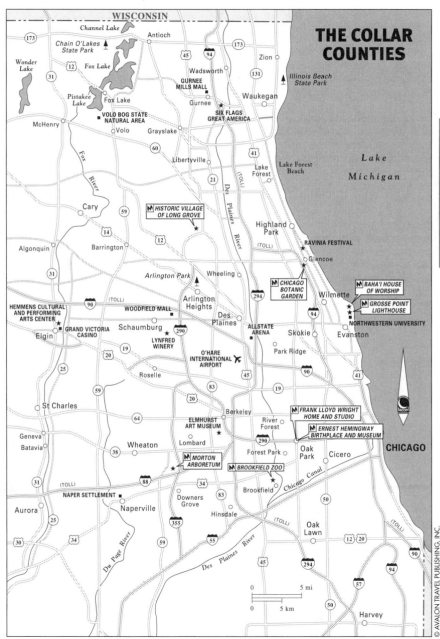

WISCONSIN

Channel Lake
Chain O'Lakes State Park
Antioch

(173)

(45) (94)
(173)
Zion

Wadsworth

(131)

Wonder Lake

(12)
Fox Lake

(31)

GURNEE MILLS MALL
Waukegan

Pistakee Lake
Fox Lake
Gurnee

VOLO BOG STATE NATURAL AREA
McHenry
Volo
Grayslake
SIX FLAGS GREAT AMERICA

(60)

THE COLLAR COUNTIES

Illinois Beach State Park

Cary
(59)

(14)

(12)

Algonquin
Barrington

(31)

Libertyville

(41)

(21)

Lake Forest
Lake Forest Beach

Lake Michigan

Fox River

HISTORIC VILLAGE OF LONG GROVE

Highland Park

Des Plaines River

(TOLL)

RAVINIA FESTIVAL

Arlington Park
Wheeling
Glencoe

Arlington Heights
(294)
CHICAGO BOTANIC GARDEN
Wilmette
BAHA'I HOUSE OF WORSHIP

HEMMENS CULTURAL AND PERFORMING ARTS CENTER

(TOLL)
(90)
WOODFIELD MALL
Des Plaines
(94)
GROSSE POINT LIGHTHOUSE
NORTHWESTERN UNIVERSITY

Elgin
GRAND VICTORIA CASINO
Schaumburg
(290)
ALLSTATE ARENA
Skokie
Evanston

(25)
(20)
(19)
LYNFRED WINERY
O'HARE INTERNATIONAL AIRPORT
Park Ridge

Roselle
(45)
(19)
(90)
(41)

(59)
(83)

St Charles
(64)
(20)
Berkeley
FRANK LLOYD WRIGHT HOME AND STUDIO

Geneva
ELMHURST ART MUSEUM
River Forest
ERNEST HEMINGWAY BIRTHPLACE AND MUSEUM

Batavia
(38)
Wheaton
Lombard
Forest Park
Oak Park
Cicero
CHICAGO

(31)
MORTON ARBORETUM
BROOKFIELD ZOO

(TOLL)
(88)
(34)
Chicago Canal

NAPER SETTLEMENT
Downers Grove
(83)
Brookfield

Aurora
Naperville
Hinsdale
(50)

(25)
(355)
(55)
(TOLL)
Oak Lawn

(30)
(34)
(59)
(45)
(12) (20)
(TOLL)
(90)

Du Page River
Des Plaines River
(294)
(94)

0   5 mi
0   5 km

(57)

(50)
Harvey

© AVALON TRAVEL PUBLISHING, INC.

The Collar Counties

I-290, I-294, and I-88 intersect near the west suburban town of Hillside, was reconfigured in recent years to relieve congestion, but drivers still encounter delays there.

Resources

The **Chicago Plus Regional Tourism Development Office** (60 W. Randolph St., Ste. 204, Chicago, 312/795-1700, www.chicagolandtravel.com) has information on attractions and accommodations within a 60-minute drive from Chicago, including to Lake County on the north, west to Elgin, St. Charles, and southwest to Joliet and other southern suburbs. It can send you tons of brochures, maps, and itinerary suggestions.

Oak Park, Forest Park, and River Forest

Known for their grand and decorative Victorian homes and Prairie-style mansions, Oak Park and River Forest are picturesque old towns, with streets lined with tall oak and elm trees, busy downtowns along commuter train lines, thriving arts scenes, and great little restaurants. Divided by Harlem Street, which runs north and south, Oak Park and River Forest share a high school and are often referred to together or as one town. Oak Park native Ernest Hemingway supposedly (the quote may be apocryphal) referred to his hometown as the city of "broad lawns and narrow minds." That image was probably true when Ernest was living there at the turn of the 20th century, when Oak Park was home to many conservatives, but today that statement is pretty far from the truth. Since the 1970s the city has been proactive about maintaining diversity and building a community where all races and sexes can coexist. Forest Park, which borders both to the south, is home to more working-class people and smaller homes. It is a bit livelier and less polished than its neighbors to the north. In recent years Forest Park has emerged as a diverse village with colorful and friendly young professionals, families, and older residents who were born and raised there.

SIGHTS

Although they comprise a relatively small area (Oak Park is about 4.5 square miles), the near west suburbs of Oak Park, Forest Park, and River Forest boast quite a few attractions, restaurants, and shops. Together, they have become quite the tourist destination. What draws most folks to Oak Park is the village's connection to two famous former residents: novelist and short story writer Ernest Hemingway, who was born here in 1899, and Frank Lloyd Wright, who built a home and studio in Oak Park in 1889.

Ernest Hemingway Birthplace and Museum

Let's start with Papa Hemingway, whom many residents (lots of whom are writers) adore. To commemorate his 100th birthday, local devotees scrounged up lots of money to renovate the Ernest Hemingway Birthplace (339 N. Oak Park Ave., Oak Park, 708/848-2222, www.hemingway.org, www.ehfop.org, 1–5 P.M. Sun.–Fri., 10 A.M.–5 P.M. Sat., $7, includes admission to Hemingway Museum).

The birth home and nearby Hemingway Museum (200 N. Oak Park Ave., same hours and admission for birthplace) are in a historic area of Oak Park, along tree-lined streets and near other Victorian or Prairie-style homes.

Ernest was born in the home on Oak Park Avenue and lived there with his family until 1905, when they moved to a house on Grove Street, followed by one on North Kenilworth Avenue. He graduated from the nearby Oak Park and River Forest High School in 1916 (it's still standing and producing writers such as Jane Hamilton). Hemingway left the village in 1919. The birth home is decorated with period furniture from the period when Hemingway lived there. (You'll see the nursery that Ernest shared

OAK PARK

NORTH AVE

▼ONION ROLL

LE MOYNE PKWY

GREENFIELD ST

DOMINICAN

UNIVERSITY

BERKSHIRE ST

Taylor
Park

DIVISION ST

THOMAS ST

AUGUSTA ST

IOWA ST

CLINTON PL

FOREST AVE

KENILWORTH AVE

OAK PARK AVE

LINDEN AVE

EAST AVE

ELMWOOD AVE

RIDGELAND AVE

CULVER AVE

LOMBARD AVE

CHICAGO AVE

AUSTIN BLVD

PETERSEN'S RESTAURANT
AND ICE CREAM PARLOR
▼

M FRANK LLOYD WRIGHT
HOME AND STUDIO
★

M ERNEST
HEMINGWAY
BIRTHPLACE
★

SUPERIOR ST

● GINKGO
TREE B&B

LONGWELL
HALL

ERIE ST

THE WRITE INN ●
ONTARIO

★ M ERNEST
HEMINGWAY
MUSEUM

ST

Austin
Gardens

Scoville
Park

BARBARA'S
BOOKSTORE ■

▼KHYBER PASS

LAKE ST

PUMPKIN MOON ■

▼UNITY TEMPLE

NORTH BLVD

SOUTH BLVD

LA BELLA PASTERIA▼

HISTORIC
PLEASANT
HOME

▼ VAL'S HALLA
RECORDS

THE CARLETON HOTEL ●
AND POOR PHIL'S

GRAPE LEAVES▼

PLEASANT ST

★

MARION ST

HARLEM AVE

Mills
Park

RANDOLPH ST

MARENGO AVE

CIRCLE AVE

WISCONSIN AVE

HOME AVE

KENILWORTH AVE

0   0.25 mi

0   0.25 km

MADISON ST

MONROE AVE

ADAMS ST

ADAMS ST

JACKSON

MAPLE AVE

JACKSON BLVD

S HIGHLAND AVE

S LYMAN AVE

Columbus
Park

BLVD

VAN BUREN ST

HARRISON EAST ARTS DISTRICT

HARRISON ST

HARRISON ST

▼BUZZ CAFÉ

GARFIELD ST

290 EISENHOWER EXPY

LEXINGTON ST

OAK PARK
CONSERVATORY ■

Rehm
Park

The Collar Counties

© AVALON TRAVEL PUBLISHING, INC.

with his sister Marcelline.) Among the items you will see displayed in the house and museum are toys donated by Hemingway's sister, a few family pieces such as a vase and rocking chair, Army fatigues, lots of photos and letters, and various editions of his many books.

Frank Lloyd Wright Home and Studio

About five blocks from Hemingway's birthplace is the Frank Lloyd Wright Home and Studio (951 Chicago Ave., Oak Park, 708/848-1976, www.wrightplus.org, guided tours only at 11 A.M., 1 P.M., and 3 P.M. weekdays, and every 20 minutes 11 A.M.–3 P.M. weekends, $12). Like Hemingway's birthplace, Wright's home has been restored. Built in 1889, the home and studio is where Wright crafted Prairie-style architecture, which would become his trademark style. The buildings and the accents in them, such as the art-glass windows, have been painstakingly and lovingly renovated by Wright devotees.

To see the house, you have to join a guided tour given by docents who know their stuff.

Tickets are sold first-come, first-served, and there are often folks lined up before the first tour of the day on weekends. You need to buy your tickets at the Under the Ginkgo Tree Bookshop adjacent to the home and studio. The bookshop has every Wright and Prairie-style–related product you could possibly imagine. You can even buy a CD-ROM of a Wright-designed computer font. The bookshop is open 10 A.M.–5 P.M. daily.

Wright's home and the Hemingway birthplace are in the heart of Oak Park, so take some time to wander through the neighborhood, dubbed the Frank Lloyd Wright Prairie School of Architecture Historic District. Thirteen more Wright-designed homes can be found in the surrounding area. But this area is marked by other impressive homes (one after the other, in fact) of Victorian, Tudor, and Greek-revival styles. Several guided and self-guided walking and bicycling tours are offered throughout the year via the Oak Park Visitors Center and Wright Home and Studio. You can pick up maps or cassette players at both spots.

© CHRISTINE DES GARENNES

Frank Lloyd Wright's home and studio, Oak Park

Unity Temple

The roof does not look stable and there are cracks in the walls, but Unity Temple (875 Lake St., Oak Park, 708/383-8873, www.unitytemple-utrf.org, 10:30 A.M.–4:30 P.M. Mon.–Fri., 1–4 P.M. Sat.–Sun., Mar.–Nov.; 1–4 P.M. daily Dec.–Feb., $7) is still a must-see for Frank Lloyd Wright aficionados. The architect reportedly said it was with this building that modern architecture was launched. (He was never a modest man.) Back when it was built in 1908, the cubicle-style building, made with reinforced concrete, was definitely different as far as church designs went. (For a contrast, check out the Gothic St. Edmund Church at 188 South Oak Park Avenue, about a 10-minute walk away). Unity Temple was undergoing a multimillion dollar renovation in 2004, but you can still visit. If you can't make it for a visit during the hours the temple is open, a good way to see the inside (the highlight is its auditorium) is by attending one of the temple's concerts held Saturday evenings fall through spring.

Historic Pleasant Home

Another example of early Prairie-style architecture can be found in the historic Pleasant Home (217 S. Home Ave., Oak Park 708/383-2654, www.pleasanthome.org, tours at 12:30 P.M., 1:30 P.M., 2:30 P.M. Thurs.–Sun., $5, free Thurs.), a 30-room mansion designed by George Maher in 1897. The National Historic Landmark features many of the telltale Prairie-style accents, such as decorative art glass and low-pitched roofs.

The second floor of the mansion is home to the **Historical Society of Oak Park and River Forest** (708/848-6755, call for hours). Rooms pay tribute to all the celebrated people who grew up in Oak Park or lived there at some point in their lives. There's a decent exhibit on Edgar Rice Burroughs, who created Tarzan while living in Oak Park 1914–1919. The historical society runs an excellent cemetery walk in Forest Park every year near Halloween. South of the Pleasant Home and historical society is **Mills Park,** which stretches for several acres. There are numerous tall elm trees to recline under or open spaces for sunning.

Oak Park Conservatory

Another good little rest stop can be found in the Oak Park Conservatory (615 Garfield St., Oak Park, 708/386-4700, www.oakparkparks.com, 10 A.M.–4 P.M. Tues.–Sun., 2–4 P.M. Mon., $1 donation). Stop by this beautiful, Edwardian-style conservatory in the middle of the afternoon and you may be the only person there. Just off I-90 in Oak Park, the conservatory is small compared to the Garfield Park Conservatory and Lincoln Park Conservatory in Chicago, but this one costs only $1 for admission and has stunning exhibits. Built in 1929, the conservatory has three different rooms: the tropical, fern, and desert. About 3,000 plants and flowers are on display here, from the exotic Birds of Paradise to more common begonias.

Scoville Park

Situated in the heart of Oak Park, the four-acre Scoville Park always seems to have some event going on in it, whether it is a food festival or a group of high school students playing with a Frisbee. The park, designed by landscape architect Jens Jensen, is on a little hill overlooking the town. One of the best ways to enjoy Scoville is by dropping by on a Sunday afternoon in the summer with a blanket or a few lawn chairs and listening to one of the **free music concerts,** where local jazz, bluegrass, or rock bands perform.

Trailside Museum

If you find an injured bird or squirrel while on your bike ride or walk through the woods, you can call forest preserve staff at the Trailside Museum (738 Thatcher Ave., River Forest, 708/366-6530, 10 A.M.–5 P.M. daily, donation); the staff rehab wildlife at the River Forest office. Trailside also houses a child-friendly nature center housed in a historic building. Built in 1874, the museum was once a finishing school for girls and private residence before the forest preserve district bought the building to use for offices.

The Collar Counties

ENTERTAINMENT AND EVENTS

Theater

Most nightlife in the near west suburbs is centered in Oak Park and Forest Park. Both host a number of well-attended community events throughout the year (both villages have spectacular Fourth of July fireworks shows), plus thriving community theater troupes and arts groups.

A troupe of professional actors performs Shakespeare's plays under the stars in Oak Park's Austin Gardens as part of the annual **Festival Theatre** (Austin Gardens, Forest Ave., one block north of Lake St., Oak Park, 708/524-2050 or 708/660-0633) on evenings July–mid-August.

For top-notch theater indoors, try **Circle Theatre** (7300 W. Madison St., Forest Park, 708/771-0700, www.circle-theatre.org). Circle was founded in the mid-1980s with the goal of presenting innovative theater to the western suburbs. Twenty years later and many Jefferson awards later (the Chicago version of the Tony award), the intimate theater is still producing smart and professional productions, such as *When You Comin' Back Red Rider?* to David Mamet's *American Buffalo*.

Events

The Oak Park and River Forest Historical Society hosts the popular **Tale of the Tombstones in Forest Home Cemetery** (863 Des Plaines Ave., Forest Park, 708/366-1900) every year in October. Local actors dress up as the deceased and share stories about life back in the Chicago area in the 1700s–1900s and highlight tragic events such as the Haymarket Riot and Iroquois Theatre Fire. Forest Home is the final resting place for a number of names that will ring a bell, such as members of Ernest Hemingway's family.

The big to-do for Wright aficionados is the **Wright Plus** house walk, held every year in Oak Park. For about $70, you get to tour the inside of about 10 homes designed by Wright. Many of them are private residences.

SHOPPING

Downtown Oak Park

The largest shopping district is downtown Oak Park, also known as the Lake Street shopping district. It lies along Lake Street, from Harlem Avenue to Oak Park Avenue, and is anchored by national chain stores Gap and Old Navy on the west end and independent and regional shops throughout. Here's a sampling of some of the shops you'll find in that district.

Earthy scents abound in **Penzeys Spices** (1138 Lake St., Oak Park, 708/848-7772, www.penzeys.com), a Midwest distributor of fine spices, herbs, and all kinds of goodies you need to make soups and sauces. Items such as tarragon, mint leaves, ginger, chili peppers, and saffron are stored in glass jars with recipe cards nearby to give you ideas on what to make with the stuff.

A few doors down from the Borders store is **Barbara's Bookstore** (1100 Lake St., Oak Park, 708/848-9140, www.barbarasbookstore.com), a regional independent bookshop where staff write passionate and witty reviews about books on little cards on the shelves for you. Barbara's has a good selection of locally published periodicals and regional books.

Marion Street Mall

South of downtown Oak Park is a little sub-shopping district called the Marion Street Mall, an outdoor pedestrian mall. You can get to Marion Street (which is closed off from vehicle traffic) from Lake Street to the north or North Boulevard to the south. Marion Street is a few blocks east of Harlem Avenue. Here you will find a few casual restaurants, an antiques mall, and two great little shops: **Fitzgerald's Fine Stationery** (131 N. Marion St., 708/445-8077) and **Pumpkin Moon** (1028 North Blvd., Oak Park, 708/524-8144, www.pumpkinmoon.com). Fitzgerald's has beautiful handmade journals, letter-writing paper, and greeting cards. And the designs are not all pastels and flowery. Pumpkin Moon carries whimsical tin toys and retro lunch boxes and action figures.

The Avenue

The Avenue shopping district is the area centered around Oak Park Avenue and Lake Street. Here there are more upscale antiques shops, women's clothing boutiques, and more restaurants. Val Camiletti has stashed away in her crowded music store **Val's Halla Records** (723 1/2 South Blvd., Oak Park, 708/524-1004, www.valshalla.com) thousands of 45s, LPs, cassettes, and compact discs. All music genres are represented here—we're talking from Neil Diamond to The Pixies.

Harrison Street

Once a string of empty, dilapidated storefronts, Harrison Street is now a lively arts district, home to art galleries and home-decor shops, featuring many original designs. (The Harrison East Arts District runs roughly from East Avenue to Austin Boulevard in Oak Park; Harrison Street is parallel to the Eisenhower Expressway, or I-290, on the north side.) One of the original, locally owned stores that has been around since the district started flourishing in the early 1990s is **Bead at Hand** (145 Harrison St., Oak Park, 708/848-1761, www.beadinhand.com). The shop sells semiprecious stones, African beads, glass beads, and bead kits for people who are new to the art of jewelry-making.

River Forest

Across Harlem Avenue in River Forest, the upscale tea shop **Todd and Holland Tea Merchants** (7577 Lake St., River Forest, 800/747-8327, www.todd-holland.com) has attracted quite a following in recent years for its wide selection of teas from all over the world, such as white tea from Sri Lanka or green tea from China. Prices range $20–220 for a quarter pound of tea. Bulk teas, teapots, cozies, and other accessories are for sale here.

ACCOMMODATIONS

$50–100

Built in 1890, the **Ginkgo Tree Bed and Breakfast** (300 N. Kenilworth Ave., Oak Park, 708/524-3237, $60) is an affordable bed-and-breakfast tucked into one of a mature and leafy residential neighborhoods. The house has a huge wraparound porch for spending time in the morning and evening. There are three rooms available here, each with a private bath.

$100–150

Another good bet for Hemingway fans is **Longwell Hall** (301 N. Scoville Ave., Oak Park, 708/386-5043, $60–100), which is in a beautiful residential area within a few blocks of Hemingway's birth home. Like the Gingko Tree, Longwell Hall is an affordable bed-and-breakfast in a beautiful residential area, decorated in English style and with a touch of femininity (white down comforters). Each has a private bathroom. One of the rooms has a screened-in porch. **M The Carleton** (1110 Pleasant St., Oak Park, 708/848-5000, www.carletonhotel.com, motel $90–100, hotel $128–198), a boutique hotel steps from the Green Line L stop and downtown Oak Park, has several lodging options for guests. Depending on how much money you are willing to spend and what kind of space you need, you can rent a room in the main boutique-style hotel, which was built in 1928, rooms in the adjacent Plaza Hotel, which was built in 1892 for visitors to the Columbia Exposition, or the economical option of staying at the motor lodge, in the rear of the hotel. Two restaurants (one casual, one upscale) are downstairs. Rooms are clean and comfortable, with nice accents such as cherry-finished desks and armchairs for reading.

The other boutique hotel in town is the **M Write Inn** (211 N. Oak Park Ave., 708/383-4800, www.writeinn.com, standard doubles $83–103), also near downtown Oak Park and a short walk to Hemingway's birth home, the Green line L stop, restaurants, and shops. There are 66 rooms here; some are suites that come with refrigerators, sinks, and microwaves. (Suites can cost up to $126.) Rooms are decorated sparsely, but with antiques and furniture from the 19th century and early 20th century. A French bistro is on the first floor.

The **Holiday Inn** (4400 Frontage Rd., Hillside, 708/544-9300, www.holidayinns.com, $97) doesn't have the charm of the boutique hotels in Oak Park, but with a spot just off I-290 and rates at around $100, it's not a bad deal if you're breezing through the area.

FOOD AND DRINK

Casual

Plump, juicy Chicago-style hot dogs and crispy fries are the specialty at **Ⓜ Parky's** (329 Harlem Ave., Forest Park, 708/366-3090, 10 A.M.–9 P.M. Mon.–Thurs., 10 A.M.–10 P.M. Fri. and Sat., 11 A.M.–9 P.M. Sun., $4).

Mmmm… the meatball sandwiches at **Starship Subs** (7618 Madison Ave., Forest Park, 708/771-3016, 8 A.M.–8 P.M. Mon.–Sat., 10 A.M.–6 P.M. Sun., $5) will fill you up. Starship, on Forest Park's main drag, whips up Italian and American-style hot and cold subs and is well known for its homemade soups, such as cream of asparagus, split pea, and tamale.

Café

Owned and operated by Laura and Andrew Maychruk, **Ⓜ The Buzz Café** (905 S. Lombard Ave., Oak Park, 708/660-0894, www.thebuzzcafe.com, 6 A.M.–9 P.M. Mon.–Fri., 7 A.M.–9 P.M. Sat., 8 A.M.–2 P.M. Sun.) is the place to go to hear the latest news in the village, controversy swirling about a new development, or ravings about a music or theater performance. The Maychruks have made this place welcoming for everyone. It manages to be bustling and relaxing at the same time. The main fare is coffee, but they also serve traditional coffeehouse fare (bagels, turkey sandwiches) with a focus on organic ingredients.

American

A popular local hangout, **Poor Phil's** (139 S. Marion St., Oak Park, 708/848-0871, 7 A.M.–1 A.M. Mon.–Thurs., 7 A.M.–2 A.M. Fri., 8 A.M.–2 A.M. Sat., 8 A.M.–midnight Sun.) is known mostly for its seafood. The fried calamari, mussels, and crab cakes are all good bets. The place is casual, loud (lots

of gabbing going on at all the tables), and a bit messy (much of the restaurant's free popcorn often ends up on the floor on busy Friday nights). During the summer, a table in its outdoor patio is a great spot to watch people. The Carleton Hotel is upstairs and the Green Line L is just down the block.

Try a slice of warm apple pie and cinnamon ice cream at **Petersen's Restaurant and Ice Cream Parlor** (1100 Chicago Ave., Oak Park, 708/386-6131, www.petersenicecream.com, 11 A.M.–10 P.M. Mon.–Thurs., 11 A.M.–11 P.M. Fri., 8 A.M.–11 P.M. Sat., 8 A.M.–10 P.M. Sun., $7), a friendly spot where the ice cream (which has been made here since 1919) is rich in butter fat, calories, and everything else you're not supposed to eat while on a diet. In addition to ice-cream sundaes, milk shakes, and other cool treats, Petersen's serves American food such as tuna melts and chicken salads in a dinerlike environment.

Walk into the **Onion Roll** (6935 North Ave., Oak Park, 708/383-2548, 6 A.M.–4:30 P.M. Tues.–Sat., and until 2:30 P.M. on Sun. and Mon.), a Jewish deli and bakery, and you'll be comforted by the smell of fresh-baked bread and a cup of the shop's chicken noodle soup.

Italian

For lunch, try **Cucina Paradiso** (814 North Blvd., 708/848-3434, lunch 11:30 A.M.–2 P.M. weekdays, dinner 5–10 P.M. Mon.–Thurs., 5–10:30 P.M. Fri.–Sat., 4–9 P.M. Sun., $10), for the fresh pastas and personal pizzas. The shop puts a spin on plain old pepperoni. Try the pear or artichoke.

A local favorite is **Ⓜ La Bella Pasteria** (109 N. Main St., Oak Park, 708/524-0044, www.labellapasteria.com, 4–10 P.M. Mon.–Wed., 11 A.M.–10 P.M. Thurs., 11 A.M.–11 P.M. Fri., 4–11 Sat., 4–9 P.M. Sun., $6–19 for lunch, $9–25 for dinner). This light and airy restaurant serves fine food in a atmosphere that is not too casual and not too pretentious. The menu is extensive and the dishes impressive. You can't go wrong with any dish. You've got plenty of pastas to choose from and sauces that are a little bit out of the ordinary (how about marinara with jalapeño peppers and prosciutto?) Then there are filet medallions, chops and chicken dishes, and seafood specials. For an appetizer try the bruschetta.

Indian and Middle Eastern

The affordable lunch buffet at **M Khyber Pass** (1031 Lake St., Oak Park, 708/445-9032, lunch 11:30 A.M.–3:30 P.M. daily, dinner 5–10 P.M. daily, $7–17), which runs about $7, features a variety of fresh, authentic Indian food, such as kebabs, fish curry, and fresh nan (bread). The restaurant, a favorite of area food critics, is know for its *dumbac* and tandoor *khana* cooking, which are techniques of cooking in a pot or over charcoal, respectively.

The cooks at **M Grape Leaves** (129 S. Oak Park Ave., Oak Park, 708/848-5555, 11:30 A.M.–10 P.M. daily, $7) know how to pack a falafel sandwich. The food is fresh and yummy at this small, cheap, and casual restaurant near the Oak Park Avenue Green Line L stop. Try the signature dish, stuffed grape leaves.

Food and Farmers Markets

Although it started as a grocery store catering to the West Siders with Italian roots, **Caputo's Fresh Markets** (2560 N. Harlem Ave., Elmwood Park, 708/453-0155, 7 A.M.–10 P.M. Mon.–Fri., 6 A.M.–9 P.M. Sat., 6 A.M.–8 P.M. Sun.) also sells Hispanic and Asian groceries. Here you will find a variety of pastries, produce, deli meat, and wine. The Elmwood Park store is just north of Oak Park and River Forest. Stores are also in the suburbs of Addison and Hanover Park.

Stop by the **Oak Park Farmers Market** (Pilgrim Church parking lot, 460 Lake St., Oak Park, 7 A.M.–1 P.M. June–Oct.) for home-made doughnuts, juicy peaches, and fresh-cut flowers.

Going picnicking? **River Forest Market** (7761 Lake St., River Forest, 708/366-7400, www.riverforestmarket.com, 8:30 A.M.–6:30 P.M. Mon.–Fri., 8:30 A.M.–5 P.M. Sat., 10 A.M.–2 P.M. Sun.) has deli meats and is a neat place to visit. It's an old-fashioned kind of meat market, with butchers who know their regular customers by name and who create extravagant crown roasts.

The national health-food chain **Whole Foods** (7245 W. Lake St., River Forest, 708/366-1045, 8 A.M.–10 P.M. Mon.–Sat., 8 A.M.–9 P.M. Sun.) has a River Forest store at the town center at the southwest corner of Lake Street and Harlem Avenue. There are a salad bar, coffee bar, bakery and deli sections, and a decent wine and beer selection.

Bars

As far as watering holes goes, Forest Park contains the most bars because of an Oak Park ordinance that limits certain types of drinking establishments in the village. The majority of Forest Park's bars (most are Irish and sports bars) are just west of Harlem Avenue on Madison Street. **Healey's West Side** (7321 Madison St., Forest Park, 708/366-4277, 11:30 A.M.–2 A.M. Sun.–Thurs., 11:30 A.M.–3 A.M. Fri.–Sat.) is a neighborhood bar where you can watch a ball game and play a game of darts.

INFORMATION

The **Oak Park Area Convention and Visitors Bureau** (158 N. Forest Ave., Oak Park, 708/848-1500 or 888/625-7275, www.visitoakpark.com, 10 A.M.–5 P.M. daily) maintains a visitors center just off Lake Street in downtown Oak Park. Here you can rent self-guided audio tours, pick up maps, and shop for Wright and Hemingway paraphernalia.

The Forest Park Main Street organization, which organized a renovation and revitalization of the street in the late 1990s, launched a website (www.forestparkmainstreet.org) that lists restaurants, bars, shops, and other sites.

SERVICES

The main branch of the **Oak Park Post Office** (901 Lake St., 708/848-7901, www.usps.com, 8 A.M.–5 P.M. weekdays, 8 A.M.–1 P.M. Sat.) is right next to Unity Temple in downtown Oak Park. Like many buildings in the city, it's quite beautiful to look at. Inside the 1930s-era, art

The Collar Counties

deco building are murals designed by Work Progress Administration employees depicting scenes from Illinois history.

GETTING AROUND
Train
Base your vacation in lively Oak Park, which has the most sights, with day trips or side trips to neighboring Forest Park for a visit to the innovative Circle Theatre or Brookfield Zoo, which is about five miles southwest of Oak Park.

Oak Park and Forest Park are connected to Chicago through the Green and Blue lines of the L train (888/YOUR-CTA or 888/968-7282, www.yourcta.com). The **Green Line** runs parallel to Lake Street, with stops at Austin Boulevard, Ridgeland, Oak Park, and Harlem avenues. The **Blue Line** runs between the east- and westbound lanes of the Congress Expressway (I-290), with stops at Austin Boulevard, Oak Park Avenue, and Harlem Avenue in Oak Park. The Blue Line ends in Forest Park at 711 South Des Plaines Avenue. Trains run about every five minutes during rush hour and 10–15 minutes during the rest of the day. One-way rides cost $1.75 per person. There is a CTA parking lot adjacent to the Forest Park station. It will cost $1.50 to park there for 12 hours.

Metra's Union Pacific Western line (312/836-7000, www.metrarail.com) runs between downtown Chicago (Madison and Canal streets) and the far west suburb of Geneva, on the Fox River. Generally, these trains run once an hour during the weekdays and every two hours on the weekends. A one-way ticket to or from Chicago costs $2.05. If someone is staffing the ticket booth, you will need to buy your ticket there. Otherwise, you will have to pay the conductor a $2 fee. If no one is on duty, you can buy your ticket on the train. The Oak Park Metra stop is at 1115 West North Boulevard. An agent is on duty 5:15 A.M.–1:15 P.M. Monday–Friday.

Bus
The suburban bus line **Pace** (847/364-7223, www.pacebus.com) operates buses in the suburbs, including Oak Park, River Forest, and the surrounding towns. Regular fare is $1.50; transfers and other specials are less. The **free Oak Park Shuttle** (Pace Route 906) runs passenger vans in spring and summer. It leaves every half hour with stops at places such as the Hemingway Museum, Carleton Hotel, and CTA train stations.

Riverside, Brookfield, and Vicinity

SIGHTS
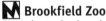 Brookfield Zoo
From the aardvark to the white-cheeked gibbon in "Tropic World," the 216-acre Brookfield Zoo (3300 Golf Rd., Brookfield, 708/485-0263 or 800/201-0784, www.brookfieldzoo.com, open daily; hours vary per year, $8, free Tues. and Thurs. Jan.–Feb., Mar., Oct.–Dec., parking extra) has a huge variety of animals and amphibians from all over the world. Every year it seems the zoo updates or alters its exhibits and brings in new animals either from other countries or from breeding. The family-friendly zoo has plenty of feeding demonstrations throughout the day and year. The dolphin shows are usually a good bet. Most major animal habitats are represented here, such as the African savannah and Asian rainforest. Less exotic, but just as educational, is the Salt Creek Wilderness area, which focuses on the state of Illinois's environment during the last two centuries. This area comprises the cool Dragonfly Marsh and some walking trails through wetland areas.

Riverside Historic District
Unlike Chicago and the majority of its surrounding suburbs, the village of Riverside was not designed in a grid system. Situated along the shore of the Des Plaines River (about a 10-minute drive south of Oak Park and River Forest), the village has streets that weave through

old neighborhoods. The town has 350 gaslit street lanterns, more than 40 little parks, and historic arts and crafts, Georgian-revival, and Victorian homes. The brains behind the plan was Frederick Law Olmsted, who would go on to design New York City's Central Park.

The **Riverside Landscape Architectural District** (which is clustered around downtown Riverside, east of the Brookfield Zoo) has 56 local landmarks. The entire village was designated a National Historic Landmark in 1970 because of its community and landscape plans. Downtown Riverside features numerous historic and renovated buildings. To learn more about Olmsted and the Riverside plan, stop by the **Riverside Historical Museum** (10 Pine Ave., Riverside, 708/447-2574, 10 A.M.–2 P.M. Sat.), in the historic Victorian Gothic pump house next to the water tower. In a storefront near the water tower is the **Riverside Arts Center** (32 E. Quincy Rd., Riverside, 708/442-6400, www.riversideartscenter.com, 11 A.M.–5 P.M. Wed. and Sat., 11 A.M.–7 P.M. Thurs. and Fri.), where a mix of contemporary art is always on display.

Cernan Earth and Space Center

Laser light shows are the specialty at Cernan Earth and Space Center (Triton College campus, 2000 5th Ave., River Grove, 708/583-3100, www.triton.edu, shows Fri., Sat., and Sun., $5–7), where staff have produced cool shows for all types of visitors. Take your pick from shows set to Pink Floyd and Jimi Hendrix music, pop, R&B, country, New Age, or even winter holiday music. The monthly earth and sky shows (schedules change monthly) highlight things such as planet movement, moon phases, or weather changes. Before the show, stop by the lobby to check out various artifacts from Apollo missions, a spacesuit donated by astronaut Gene Cernan, spacecraft models, and telescopes.

Chicago Portage National Historic Site

History buffs might want to make a quick detour to the Chicago Portage National Historic Site (4800 S. Harlem Ave., Lyons, 773/267-0948, www.civiccenterauthority.org, free). A statue of the explorers Louis Jolliet and Pere Jacques Marquette marks the spot where the two came to the conclusion in 1673 that there should be a canal built to connect Lake Michigan to the Illinois River to facilitate water travel.

Cermak Plaza

Fast-forward a few hundred years and a few miles north to Cermak Plaza (Cermak and Harlem Aves., Berwyn), where a visionary artist stacked eight cars on top of each other (a Volkswagen Beetle is on the top) with a pole through the center. A car kebab, you might say. The giant sculpture, titled *Spindle,* was commissioned in 1989 and is the largest and most famous of several sculptures you will find at this shopping plaza. Other modern, eye-catching sculptures, such as a large zoetrope, are placed throughout the center (which contains several discount stores, such as Marshalls).

SPORTS AND RECREATION
Biking

The best bicycle trail in the near west suburbs is the **Salt Creek Bicycle Trail,** a 6.6-mile paved trail between Brookfield Woods, just north of the zoo by 31st Street, and Bemis Woods, which is north of the town of Western Springs, on Wolf Road, between 31st Street and Ogden Avenue. The wide trail wanders along Salt Creek, through woods and meadows and under a railroad underpass.

If you didn't bring your bicycle with you on your trip, you can rent one at **Oak Park Cyclery** (1113 Chicago Ave., Oak Park, 708/524-2453).

Canoeing

So it may not be as scenic or thrilling as, say, the Colorado River, but the Des Plaines River does offer fun, easygoing opportunities for canoeing. You don't have to be an expert to canoe here, just a solid canoer. The **Forest Preserve District of Cook County** (headquarters 536 N. Harlem Ave., River Forest, 708/366-9420, www.fpdcc.com) comprises thousands of acres along both the east and west sides of the Des Plaines River. In Riverside you can launch your canoe at the preserve's Stony Ford ramp, by 1st Street, and float down to the Columbia Woods stop, which is 7.5 miles to the southwest, by Willow Springs Road in Willow Springs.

Kiddieland

A fixture on the north side since 1929, Kiddieland (8400 W. North Ave., Melrose Park, 708/343-8000, www.kiddieland.com, mid-Apr.–Oct., weekends only Apr., May, Sept. and Oct., hours vary per day, per year, $20.50 for ages six and up, $17.25 after 5 P.M.) is what amusement parks used to be: midway games, skeeball, train rides, and a roller coaster. The oldest amusement park in Chicago, Kiddieland has a carousel from the 1920s. It is just west of River Forest in nearby Melrose Park, about 10 minutes from downtown Oak Park.

Horse Racing

Maywood Park (8600 W. North Ave., Melrose Park, 708/344-4800, www.maywoodpark.com) has live horse racing on Monday, Wednesday, and Friday evenings July–March. The park is west of the Des Plaines River, a few minutes from River Forest.

It is not as glamorous as Arlington Park, but **Hawthorne Race Course** (3501 S. Laramie Ave., Cicero, 708/780-3700) can offer visitors an entertaining glimpse of the Illinois horse-racing industry as well as the colorful and sometimes unpolished West Side culture. Harness and thoroughbred races are held on the one-mile track.

FOOD AND DRINK

The publike **Irish Times** (8869 Burlington Ave., Brookfield, 708/785-8787, lunch and dinner daily), where the all-you-can-eat fish dinners draw loyal regulars, is hopping on Friday nights during Lent. During the win-ter this place can't be beat, with its cozy fireplace and live Irish music. Most dishes are under $10.

FitzGerald's (6615 Roosevelt Rd., Berwyn, 708/788-2118, www.fitzgeraldsnightclub.com, doors open at 7 P.M. Tues.–Sat. and at 5 P.M. Sun.) is a former hunting club and jazz club that has been transformed into a great spot to hear local, regional, and national acts. The performance schedule changes monthly, but on any given night you could hear soul, alt country, rock, or blues. Next door the grill serves sandwiches. You can eat outdoors in the patio during the warm months.

For more than three decades **Hala Kahiki** (2834 N. River Rd., River Grove, 708/456-3222, www.hala-kahiki.com, 7 P.M.–2 A.M. Mon.–Tues., 4 P.M.–2 A.M. Wed.–Thurs. and Sun., 4 P.M.–3 A.M. Fri.–Sat.) has been serving a dizzying array of stiff, rum-laden tropical concoctions. Drinks are reasonably priced (about $5) and served in a relaxing, somewhat amusing atmosphere (lots of bamboo and palm trees). There are hot and cool drinks, elaborate and simple drinks, and some made especially for couples that require you to drink out of the same bowl. Hala Kahiki is about five miles northwest of Oak Park.

INFORMATION AND SERVICES

The Frederick Law Olmsted Society (tours depart from the Riverside Train Station, 90 Bloomingbank Rd., Riverside, 708/447-2311, www.olmsteadsociety.org, $7 donation includes Riverside map and brochure) hosts walking tours of Riverside on the last Sunday of the month May–October. During the biennial house walk in May, people can tour inside several of the village's grand homes.

For more information about the village of Riverside, its history, and architectural landmarks, visit the community website, www.riverside-illinois.com.

Evanston

Evanston, like Oak Park, is a diverse village with a mix of wealthy residents, professors, day laborers, and up-and-coming artists. However, because Northwestern University is here, you can always find college students running down the Lakeshore Path and talking in coffee shops, lending energy to the town. The downtown is busy with a variety of restaurants, from hot dog stands to upscale cuisine. The lakeshore is lined with parks and stately, historic homes. Over on the campus in the northeastern part of town, students or visiting artists stage poetry readings, opera performances, and other performing arts events.

SIGHTS

Northwestern University Campus

The only private university in the Big Ten, Northwestern University (633 Clark St., Evanston, 847/491-3741, www.northwestern.edu) is one of the most prestigious universities in the Midwest. Although it has a Chicago campus in addition to the Evanston one, the 240-acre campus on Evanston's north shore is the more scenic of the two and designed like a college campus should be: situated along the lakeshore with Gothic buildings and spacious modern ones, and plenty of walking paths and trees.

The university was chartered in 1851 and was the university for the Northwest Territory, which included land west of the Appalachian Mountains. It opened in 1855 with 10 men students. It was later one of the first universities to admit women in 1869. Today there are about 17,000 students, including undergraduates and graduates, and part-time students in its business school, journalism school, liberal arts college, and other colleges. Alums include producer Garry Marshall, playwright Mary Zimmerman, politician Dick Gephardt, plus numerous business leaders and intellectuals. A great time to visit Northwestern is early fall, when you'll walk among eager stu-

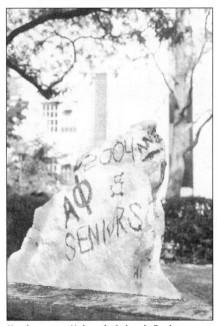

© CHRISTINE DES GARENNES

The Collar Counties

Northwestern University's iconic Rock

dents and under the canopy of large, colorful trees. However, during the summer, crowds are fewer.

The best way to tour Northwestern is on foot and a good start is at the iron **Arch,** a gate erected in 1993 at the southern edge of the campus, on the north side of Sheridan Road at Chicago Avenue (where Sheridan curves to the north). From there you can walk north along the sidewalk to **University Hall,** the oldest building on campus. This Gothic, limestone building was completed in 1869 and held dormitory rooms, classrooms, offices, and you name it. Renovated in the early 1990s, University Hall now contains seminar rooms and English Department offices and other offices for students and professors.

Just outside University Hall is the iconic **Rock,** a former fountain that students now coat with paint to promote various campus events and to honor graduating classes. This is a good spot to sit and watch people.

Another little architectural treasure nearby is **Annie May Swift Hall,** the building northeast of University Hall. Built in 1895 to house the school of oratory, the building is a little bit Romanesque, a little bit Gothic. (It has a striking red-tile roof.) Annie May Swift Hall now contains the campus radio station, WNUR, 89.3 FM.

Continuing north, past the theological seminary and Dearborn Observatory, you'll reach **Shakespeare Garden,** near Annenberg Hall (where the School of Education and Social Policy is housed). Listed on the National Register of Historic Places, this garden was designed by noted landscape artist Jens Jensen in 1915, the 300th anniversary of William Shakespeare's death. In it are flowers, herbs, and other plants mentioned in the playwright and poet's writings, such as roses, daisies, and poppies. The traditional English garden features a fountain and a sundial.

From there you can walk farther north to the quads and east toward the lakeshore. Heading back south you can follow along the lakeshore multipurpose trail for views of the campus (the library and arts buildings) and Chicago in the distance. You'll travel past athletic fields, a boathouse, and plenty of spots for sunbathing.

This tour sounds time-consuming, but the Evanston campus is fairly compact. Stopping by the aforementioned buildings should take no longer than two hours.

⃝ Grosse Point Lighthouse

Just off scenic Sheridan Road, which curves along the Lake Michigan coast, is Grosse Point Lighthouse (2601 Sheridan Rd., Evanston, 847/328-6961, www.grossepointlighthouse.net, grounds open daily, tours of the keeper's quarters museum 2, 3, 4 P.M. Sat. and Sun. June–Sept., $5), a National Historic Landmark. Built in 1873, the white and black lighthouse is surrounded by a beautiful park, with wildflower and butterfly gardens, right near the shoreline and a great sandy beach. You can climb the 113-foot tower (it's 141 steps to

the top) and tour the lighthouse keeper's house, which has been made into a little museum with photos and blueprints of the lighthouse.

Next door to the lighthouse is the **Evanston Art Center** (2603 Sheridan Rd., Evanston, 847/475-5300, www.evanstonartcenter.org, 10 A.M.–10 P.M. Mon.–Thurs., 10 A.M.–4 P.M. Fri.–Sat., 1–8 P.M. Sun., $3 donation from nonmembers of the center), a well-respected place where contemporary regional artists display their paintings, drawings, and photographs, and budding artists take classes.

Charles Gates Dawes House

Another stunning building near the lakeshore in Evanston is the Charles Gates Dawes House (225 Greenwood St., Evanston, 847/475-3410, www.evanstonhistorical.org, 1–5 P.M. Thurs.–Sun., $5), a chateaulike home that just exudes wealth. The place was home to Charles Dawes, Calvin Coolidge's vice president in 1925. The house, built in 1894, is quite impressive. Don't miss the gorgeous mahogany library with its historic books, Tiffany lamps, and paintings. But what's fascinating is learning about all this man accomplished during his life. Dawes was a banker and a businessman (he owned numerous power companies), he raised money to support the World's Fair in 1933, earned a Nobel Peace Prize, and in his spare time, played the flute and piano and composed music.

The Mitchell Museum of the American Indian

Kendall College's Mitchell Museum of the American Indian (2600 Central Park Ave., Evanston, 847/475-1030, www.mitchellmuseum.org, 10 A.M.–5 P.M. Tues.–Sat., Thurs. until 8 P.M., noon–4 P.M. Sun., closed last two weeks of Aug., $5 donation) highlights the history and culture of Indians from the Great Lakes, Plains, Southwest, and other regions in North America. Thousands of items are on display here (and the collection is always growing), including beadwork, blankets, dolls, and silver and turquoise jewelry. There's also a kid-friendly area where visitors can reach out and touch things such as birch bark.

Ladd Arboretum and Nature Center

Ladd Arboretum and Nature Center (2024 McCormick Blvd., Evanston, 847/864-5181, www.laddarboretum.org, ecology and nature center open 9 A.M.–4:30 P.M. Mon.–Sat., mid-Sept.–May, closed Sat. June–early Sept.) is a gem of park (park complex, really). The park stretches for about a mile along the North Shore Channel of the Chicago River. There are plenty of walking trails through woods of birch, maple, and oak trees, past the community gardens, and a little bird sanctuary. You'd hardly know you are about two miles from the Edens Expressway (I-94). In the middle of the arboretum (at Bridge Street) is the Evanston Ecology Center, a new building where community events are held. Many of the activities are geared toward children, but some adults will enjoy, such as birding by canoe. You don't need to be an Evanston resident to take advantage of its classes (many of them one-day classes), so check with the center in advance. There may be a yoga workshop or similar type of activity there while you're in town.

ENTERTAINMENT AND EVENTS
Theater

Next Theatre Company (Noyes Cultural Arts Center, 927 Noyes Ave., Evanston, 847/475-1875, www.nexttheatre.org, 2–6 P.M. Mon.–Fri., and two hours before curtain on days of performances, generally Thurs.–Sun., some Mon., $18–29) is a professional off-Loop troupe that produces dramas that prompt audience members to ponder social and political issues. Next has won a slew of Jefferson awards, a local version of the Tonys.

Gilbert and Sullivan musicals are often presented by the community theater group **Light Opera Works** (Noyes Cultural Arts Center, 927 Noyes St., Evanston, 847/869-6300, www.light-opera-works.org). The group, around since the early 1980s, performs shows such as *The Mikado* and *The Fantasticks*. Shows are presented at either the Cahn Auditorium (600 Emerson St.) or McGaw YMCA (1420 Maple Ave.).

Concerts and performances in Northwestern University's 1,000-seat **Pick-Staiger Concert Hall** (50 Arts Circle Dr., 847/467-4000 or 847/491-5441, www.northwestern.edu, 10 A.M.–6 P.M. Mon.–Fri., noon–3 P.M. Sat., hours change during academic breaks) feature students, faculty, and visiting artists. On any given evening you could see the opera *La Bohème*, a jazz concert, brass band performance, or choral concert.

Events

Originally designed clothing, pottery, and fine art are for sale at **Custer's Last Stand Art Fair** (Custer St., parallel to the Metra and CTA train lines, Evanston, 847/328-2204, www.custerfair.com, mid-June, free), a giant arts festival that has been held in Evanston for more than 30 years. The fair showcases the work of about 350 artists, dozens of food tents, and almost nonstop live music, including jazz, blues, and folk music.

The music of Johann Sebastian Bach and other baroque composers are highlighted every May during **Bach Week Festival** (concert locations vary per year throughout Evanston, 847/236-0452, www.bachweek.org, tickets $5–30 per concert). Chamber orchestras and choruses play in venues such as historic churches.

SHOPPING

Get lost amid the stacks at **Bookman's Alley** (in the rear of 1712 Sherman Ave., Evanston, 847/869-6999, noon–8 P.M. Sun. and Tues.–Thurs., noon–6 P.M. Fri., 10:30 A.M.–6 P.M. Sat.) where about 40,000 used and rare books are for sale. Tucked between the stacks are antiques such as rare records, prints, and uniforms from the armed services, as well as armchairs and tables and chairs where customers are welcome to lounge for as long as they'd like.

Got a rip in your backpack or did the airlines crumple your luggage? **Kaehler TravelWorks** (1724 Sherman Ave., Evanston, 847/328-0744, www.worldtraveler.com) is loaded with lots of brand-name backpacks, computer cases, and suitcases such as Hartman, Tumi, and Swiss Army. It also carries money belts, luggage locks, and other travel accessories. There are additional locations throughout the suburbs and downtown Chicago.

At **Uncle Dan's** (700 W. Church St., Evanston, 847/475-7100, www.udans.net, 10 A.M.–8 P.M. Mon.–Thurs., 10 A.M.–7 P.M. Fri.–Sat., 11 A.M.–5 P.M. Sun.) you can browse for camping and hiking gear, clothing and shoes, bags and bottles for bicycling, gloves and hats for winter, and more. It has two more locations: one in Highland Park, another in Chicago.

RECREATION
Parks and Beaches
Evanston stretches for about four miles along Lake Michigan, with several city parks and sandy beaches along the way (Evanston Parks Department, 847/866-2900, www.cityofevanston.com). Listed from north to south, there are five public beaches in Evanston: **Lighthouse Beach** (at Central St. and Sheridan Rd.), **Clark Street Beach** (at Clark and Sheridan Rd.), **Greenwood/Dempster Street Beach** (Greenwood St. at the lakeshore), **South Boulevard Beach** (at South Blvd. and the lakeshore) and **Lee Street** (Lee and Lakeshore Blvd.). You need a token to get onto the beach mid-June–Labor Day. Daily passes cost $7 and are sold at each beach. You can't go wrong with any of these beaches. Lighthouse Beach is probably the most scenic, but it can get crowded.

Burnham Shores (between Dempster and Hamilton Sts.) park is on the lakefront and has a sailboat launch (but no beach). Burnham is a nice quiet spot to picnic, take in the Chicago skyline, and look out onto the lake.

Merrick Park (at Lake St. and Oak Ave.), in downtown Evanston, is another good spot to take a break and read the newspaper for a while or take in the downtown scene. There's a fountain and rose garden.

Biking, Hiking, Jogging
The **Evanston Lake Shore Trail,** which extends the city limits, is the closest you'll get to Lake Michigan while riding your bicycle.

Most of the trail is on blacktop. Parallel to the trail is a gravel trail for joggers and walkers. At the southern end the trail links with Chicago's Lakefront Trail. So if you're not satisfied with the 3–4 miles in Evanston, you can head south. There are plenty of signs pointing you to the trail near Sheridan Road. Otherwise, you can head northwest to the **Green Bay Trail,** which runs along the Metra line starting near Shorewood Park in Wilmette, the suburb to the north.

Ice-Skating
Take a spin on the ice at **Robert Crown Community Center and Ice Rink** (1701 Main St., Evanston, 847/328-9400, www.cityofevanston.org, 8 A.M.–6 P.M. Mon., 8–8 P.M. Tues.–Thurs., 8 A.M.–9 P.M. Fri., 8 A.M.–10 P.M. Sat., noon–4 P.M. Sun.). You can rent ice skates at this indoor ice-skating rink.

Big Ten Sports
You can watch everything from fencing to football on Northwestern University's campus. The main attraction during fall and winter are Wildcats football games in the 40,000-seat Ryan Field, which can get a little rowdy with flying marshmallows. Contact the **Athletic Ticket Office** (1501 Central St., Evanston, 847/491-CATS or 847/491-2287, www.nusports.com, 9 A.M.–5 P.M. Mon.–Fri. Aug.–Apr., 9 A.M.–4 P.M. Mon.–Fri. May–July).

ACCOMMODATIONS
$100–150
If you're tired of chain hotels where all the rooms look the same, but you're not exactly a fan of bed-and-breakfasts, a good compromise is the **M Margarita Inn** (1566 Oak Ave., Evanston, 847/869-2273, www.margaritainn.com, $120), which bills itself as a European-style hotel. It's a boutique hotel with 42 rooms and five floors. The cheap rooms (about $80) require you to share a bathroom with other hotel guests on your floor. The more expensive suites (including mini and two-room suites) come with private bath. They cost up

to $160. Standards come with a single queen or two twins. You don't have to spend much time in your room, though. The hotel has a roof-top deck, parlor, and a gorgeous English-style library with built-in bookcases and armchairs. Extras are continental breakfast and high-speed Internet access is available in the lobby, library, and parlor.

The **Best Western University Plaza** (1501 Sherman Ave., Evanston, 847/491-6400 or 800/382-6786, www.bestwestern.com, $140) is a good bet because of its location, plus it has an indoor swimming pool and fitness room.

$150–250

If you plan to stay around for several days, try **N The Homestead** (1625 Hinman Ave., Evanston, 847/475-3300, www.thehome-stead.net), which offers studios with kitchens and one- and two-bedroom apartments. This is a fancy (there's a doorman), superclean hotel a few blocks from downtown, shoreline parks, and Northwestern's campus. Downstairs the well-reviewed **Trio** (847/733-8746, www.trio-restaurant.com, lunch noon–1 P.M. Fri., dinner 6–9 P.M. Wed.–Thurs., 6–10 P.M. Fri., 5–10 P.M. Sat., 5–9 P.M. Sun.) restaurant serves high-end, multicourse prix fixe menus of about $100 (that's per person).

The **Orrington Omni** (1710 Orrington Ave., Evanston, 847/866-8700 or 800/529-9100, www.omnihotels.com, $150) is perhaps one of the more exclusive spots to stay in the area, if you have money to throw around. The 269-room renovated hotel has a restaurant and fitness room inside.

FOOD
Italian

There are many pizza joints in and around the Evanston area, but **Carmen's** (1012 Church St., Evanston, 847/328-0031, 11 A.M.–10 P.M. Mon.–Thurs., 11 A.M.–11 P.M. Fri.–Sat., noon–10 P.M. Sun.) is one of the best because you can sample all different styles and flavors (stuffed, deep-dish, and thin) during the affordable lunch buffet.

N Dave's Italian Kitchen (1635 Chicago Ave., Evanston, www.davesik.com, 4–9:30 P.M. Sun.–Thurs., 4–10:30 P.M. Fri.–Sat., $6.75–12.75) is another popular place for college students, locals, and visitors. And no wonder. You get a lot of good food for a reasonable amount. A heaping plate of pasta averages $8. Options include the traditional spaghetti bolognese with carrots and onions in a beefy, red sauce, but also the tantalizing and unique dishes such as spaghetti carbonara (bacon and onion bits in a cream and egg sauce) or spaghetti calamari (with squid and garlic and olive oil). The pizza and homemade calzones are also yummy.

American

The veggie-friendly **Blind Faith** (525 Dempster St., Evanston, 847/328-6875, www.blind-faithcafe.com, breakfast, lunch, and dinner daily, under $10) cooks tempeh, tofu, textured vegetable protein, and soy smoothies for vegans and those dabbling in vegetarianism. There's also a self-serve section in the restaurant.

When you visit the **Dixie Kitchen and Bait Shop** (825 Church St., 847/733-9030, 11 A.M.–10 P.M. Mon.–Thurs., 11 A.M.–11 P.M. Fri.–Sat., 9 A.M.–10 A.M. Sun., $8), don't hold back, especially if you're there for its famous Sunday brunch. You could be there for hours stuffing yourself with sizzling Cajun food: catfish strips, gumbo, crawfish étouffé, shrimp, and grits. (Dixie Kitchen also has a location in the Hyde Park neighborhood of Chicago.)

There's something about a pulled-pork sandwich that is just so satisfying. At **N Merle's** (727 Benson Ave., Evanston, 847/475-7766, www.merlesbbq.com, 4:30–9:30 P.M. Mon., 11:30 A.M.–9:30 P.M. Tues.–Thurs., 11:30 A.M.–11 P.M. Fri.–Sat., noon–9 P.M. Sun., lunch and dinner), the kitchen staff barbecue pork, beef, and chicken, for days it seems. The meat is so tender and there's a wide variety of barbecue sauce flavors. If you're hungry (and not concerned about getting barbecue sauce stains around your mouth), try the baby back ribs or share the jumbo-size "barnyard platter," which is made for two. Otherwise, you won't be disappointed by a bowl of Brunswick stew (made with tomatoes, corn, potatoes, and pulled meats) and a side of potato salad.

The menu changes daily at ⓜ **Davis Street Fish market** (501 Davis St., Evanston, 847/869-3474, $13–22), one of the best places in the Chicago area to buy fresh fish. Seafood dishes may include Lake Superior whitefish or grouper, or oysters from the beautiful raw bar. There's a reason the Cajun brunch on Sundays is always packed.

The motto for **Prairie Moon** (1502 Sherman Ave., Evanston, 847/864-8328, lunch 11:30 A.M.–2 P.M. Wed.–Sat., dinner 4:30–10 P.M. Sun.–Thurs., 4:30–11 P.M. Fri.–Sat., Sun. brunch 9:30 A.M.–1:30 P.M., $8 average for lunch, a bit more for dinner) is "All-American Dining." That means cheeseburgers, sides of macaroni and cheese, but also surprising entrées such as tilapia fish tacos with avocado salad and Chesapeake blue crab cakes. Prairie Moon is big, with several dining rooms, two bars, and a patio, but friendly. Each month the restaurant celebrates a festival occurring somewhere in the United States.

Asian

After opening in a small storefront and expanded into a new space in 2003, ⓜ **LuLu's dim sum and then sum** (804 Davis St., Evanston, 847/869-4343, www.lulusdimsum.com, lunch and dinner daily, $7.95–14.95) serves contemporary pan-Asian food, including stir fry and noodle bowls. Don't leave without trying one of the funky drinks such as a Singapore Sling (gin, vermouth, ginger ale) or a frozen spiked lemonade.

Cafés

One of the coolest places in town to load up on java (or muffins and scones) is ⓜ **Kaffein** (1621 Chicago Ave., Evanston, 847/491-1621). Service is not exactly stellar here, but Kaffein is one of those places where you can feel free to pull out *Moby Dick* and read for hours. Occasional spoken-word performances are held here.

If you see a tiny table open at the often-crowded **The Unicorn Café** (1723 Sherman Ave., Evanston, 847/332-2312, 7:30 A.M.–11 P.M. Sun., 7 A.M.–11 P.M. Mon.–Thurs., 7 A.M.–midnight Fri., 7:30 A.M.–midnight Sat.), grab it. This busy café offers original art on the walls (and for sale), hot and cold coffee and tea drinks, plus a few panini options.

Ice Cream

Stop by this ice-cream shop for a cone or shake, and then head to the lakeshore or downtown for a stroll. **Hartigan's Ice Cream Shoppe** (2909 Central St., Evanston, 847/491-1232, 11 A.M.–11 P.M. daily June–mid-Sept. and 11 A.M.–10 P.M. mid-Sept.–May) has not only good cones, but a variety of drinks such as rich, thick milk shakes and sherbet coolers.

Farmers Market

Dozens of produce and flower vendors set up tents every Saturday at the Evanston Farmers Market (University and Oak Aves., 847/866-2936, 7:30 A.M.–1 P.M. Sat., mid-May–early Nov.).

INFORMATION

You can pick up hotel and event info from the **Chicago's North Shore Convention and Visitors Bureau** (Old Orchard Center, Arcade Level, Skokie, 847/763-0011, www.visitchicagonorthshore.com). The CVB maintains listings for Evanston and surrounding towns.

SERVICES

Newspapers

The weekly *Evanston Review* (1601 Sherman Ave., Evanston, 847/866-6501, www.pioneerlocal.com) has decent entertainment and event listings for the region, in addition to movie and stage reviews. It's published on Wednesdays by Pioneer Press, which runs a chain of weeklies in the Chicago region. (Pioneer is owned by Hollinger International.)

The Daily Northwestern (1999 Campus Dr., Evanston, 847/491-3222, www.dailynorthwestern.com) is published daily during the school year and weekly on Thursdays during the summer. It has a good city section for local news in addition to campus happenings. You can pick up a copy at most convenient stores and cafés.

The Reader's Guide to Arts and Entertainment (11 E. Illinois St., Chicago, 312/828-0350, www.chireader.com) is published by the Chicago weekly *The Reader* on Thursdays. It's free and available in cafés, restaurants, and convenient stores.

Hospital

Evanston Northwestern Healthcare (2650 Ridge Ave., Evanston, 847/570-5030, ww.enhc.org) operates a full-service hospital in Evanston (Evanston Hospital) as well as several in the region, including Highland Park Hospital to the north (718 Glenview Ave., Highland Park, 847/432-8000).

Computer Access

Screens (1730 Sherman Ave., Evanston, 847/332-1900, www.screenz.com, 9 A.M.–11 P.M. Sun.–Thurs., 9 A.M.–midnight Fri.–Sat.) is part Internet café, part Kinko's copy center. Here you rent a workstation by the hour, play video games, download music, and burn compact discs and print digital photos. And there's coffee, too. Locations are also in the Lincoln Park and Andersonville neighborhoods of Chicago.

GETTING AROUND

The Chicago Transit Authority's Purple Line elevated train (312/836-7000, www.yourcta.com) runs from Evanston to downtown Chicago and has several stops in Evanston (from north to south): Linden, Central, Noyes, Foster, Davis, Dempster, Main, and South Boulevard. Trains run about every 15 minutes 6 A.M.–1 A.M. on Sundays, 5 A.M.–1 A.M. weekdays, and 5 A.M.–2 A.M. Saturdays. A one-way ticket will cost $1.75.

CTA operates the "Evanston Circulator" bus route Monday–Friday. The bus operates roughly 6 A.M.–7 P.M. along Ridge and Dodge streets, with stops at the Metra Station. A one-way fare is $1.75.

Metra's Union Pacific Line stops at several locations in Evanston (Central Ave., 847/869-3622; 901 Davis St., 847/492-5066; and 600 Main St., 847/492-5066, www.metrarail.com). Trains run about every hour. During weekday rush hours, they run about every 15 minutes. A one-way ticket to Chicago's Ogilvie Transportation Center costs $2.90, and you must buy it in the station if it is staffed.

The North Shore

As the name implies, the North Shore region consists of towns along Lake Michigan. Most of them are quite elite, with mansions, well-manicured lawns, clean downtowns with boutiques and little cafés, and impressive schools. As you drive north on Sheridan Road, the scene might look familiar. Director John Hughes set many of his films here, including *Ferris Bueller's Day Off, Sixteen Candles,* and *Home Alone.* The towns have been home to big wigs such as advertising mogul Leo Burnett, the Walgreens drugstore family, basketball player Michael Jordan, and 1980s television star Mr. T, and many others. If you don't have time to visit the sights here, at least drive north along Sheridan Road (which follows Lake Michigan) to gawk at some mansions or have fun taking the curves.

SIGHTS

◪ Chicago Botanic Garden

A trip to the Chicago Botanic Garden (1000 Lake Cook Rd., Glencoe, 847/835-5440, www.chicagobotanic.org, 8 A.M.–sunset daily, free admission, parking $12 per car, tram tours extra) can last all day. The constantly evolving gardens are larger than they seem. Footpaths wind through Japanese and English gardens, onto little islands (accessible by little bridges), above miniature waterfalls, by vegetable gardens, formal flower gardens (in spring the tulips are dazzling), through prairie and woodlands. Flowers and plants aren't just on display here. The garden has a research and breeding center, where staff recently developed an orange *Echinacea* plant. Throughout the gardens you will find tons of spots for writing, reading, or chatting. Plus, there's an indoor and outdoor café and a well-stocked gift shop. You can avoid paying the car admission fee by taking the Metra train to the Braeside stop or by parking at the Braeside train station (10 N. St. John's Ave.). From there you can bike to the botanic garden. Head west from the train station on County Line Road; the botanic gardens are just west of Green Bay Road on the east side of County Line.

M Baha'i House of Worship

As you drive north on Sheridan Road, the view of the Baha'i House of Worship (100 Linden Ave., Wilmette 847/853-2300, www.us.bahai.org, gardens and auditorium 7 A.M.–6:30 P.M., visitors center 10 A.M.–5 P.M. daily, free) is just amazing. Built in 1953, not far from the Lake Michigan shoreline, it has a 135-foot-high white, lacey dome and is surrounded by colorful rose gardens. This building is the first Baha'i House of Worship built in the Western Hemisphere. The religion was founded by a Persian man by the name of Vaha'u'llah in the 1800s, and it teaches tolerance, acceptance, and peace. Some of his writings appear on the walls of the dome. There is no cross to which people kneel, nor are there statues lining all the walls. People tend to pick a seat (no pews, either) and sit quietly amongst themselves, looking upward. Curious? You can learn more about the religion and its followers in the building's visitors center on the lower level.

Skokie Sights

Another quiet place for reflection can be found west of Wilmette and the Baha'i temple in the town of Skokie. When residents of Skokie, home to a large Jewish population, heard that a neo-Nazi group planned to hold a rally in Skokie, they banded together and prevented

© CHRISTINE DES GARENNES

The magnificent Baha'i Temple in Wilmette

the rally. Afterward the group formed the **Holocaust Memorial Foundation** (4255 Main St., Skokie, 847/677-4640, www.hmfi.org, 9 A.M.–4:30 P.M.–Mon.–Thurs., 9 A.M.–3 P.M. Fri., noon–4 P.M. Sun.), which aims to educate the public about the Holocaust through educational programs, classroom visits, and exhibits at the Skokie center. At the center, visitors can hear firsthand accounts from survivors of the Holocaust and view artifacts from that era, including photographs, letters, and Jewish identification cards. A new 50,000-square-foot museum and center were planned.

Skokie also contains a great little **Sculpture Park** (just east of McCormick Blvd., from Dempster St. to Touhy Ave., 847/649-4265, www.sculpturepark.org, free). More than 70 sculptures line a two-mile walking and bicycling path along the north branch of the Chicago River. The sculptures are abstract figures, animals, people, and made of material such as steel, bronze, and wood.

ENTERTAINMENT AND EVENTS

Ravinia Festival

The quintessential evening for North Shore residents includes a gourmet, candlelight picnic of wine and cheese on the lawn of Ravinia Park, followed by a concert by the Chicago Symphony Orchestra, Tony Bennett, or Peter, Paul, and Mary. The Ravinia Festival (Green Bay and Lake-Cook Rds., Highland Park, 847/604-2414 or 847/266-5100, www.ravinia.org, lawn tickets $10, extra for seats in the pavilion, discounts for college students for certain concerts) is a summerlong series of outdoor concerts in Ravinia Park. You can buy seats in the 3,200-seat pavilion or the less-expensive lawn seats. Each season tends to focus on a specific composer, such as Sergei Rachmaninoff, a recent highlight. Visiting artists run the gamut and include legendary figures such as Itzhak Perlman and up-and-coming young artists. People can bring a picnic basket or buy food and drink at one of the many restaurants in the park (fare varies from basic hamburgers to fillets).

Lawn spaces fill up quickly. For a concert that starts at 8 P.M., you will want to stake out a spot at 6 P.M. Tickets go on sale starting at the end of May. Box office is open at 9 A.M. daily and 1 P.M. Sunday until the time of the show. Parking is available at the park, but those spots fill up rapidly. A good bet is to park around downtown Highland Park and take the free "park 'n' ride" shuttle. It runs every evening there is a concert, before and after the concerts. You can pick it up at the Metra Station. If you're staying in Chicago, you can take the Metra Union Pacific line on concert days; the train stops right at the park entrance.

Theater

If you want to avoid large crowds and are on a budget, one summer concert series you won't want to miss is the Park District of Wilmette's **Starlight Theatre** (Gillson Park, Michigan and Washington Aves., Wilmette, www.wilmette-park.org, 847/256-9656, weekend evenings July–Aug., free concert, parking is $5). Held in the Wallace Bowl, an outdoor stage and seating area in Wilmette's lakeside Gillson Park, Starlight concerts may feature '50s music, Polynesian music, or a patriotic big band show.

The **North Shore Center for the Performing Arts** (9501 Skokie Blvd., Skokie, 847/679-9501, www.northshorecenter.org) is not far from I-94 and a slew of ordinary shopping malls, but you can always find original, entertaining events here. The arts complex is home to the Northlight Theatre Company, Skokie Valley Symphony Orchestra, and Centre East, an arts programming company at the center. Centre East brings in a variety of performers, from Al Franken to Victor Borge. Northlight stages new musicals and plays, such as *Studs Terkel's The Good War* and some revivals, such as Oscar Wilde's *Lady Windermere's Fan*. Prices vary per show.

Since it began in 1993, **Writers' Theatre** (in the Glencoe Woman's Club, 325 Tudor Ct., Glencoe, and the rear of Books on Vernon, 664 Vernon Ave., Glencoe, 847/242-6000, www.writerstheatre.org) has been staging moving works of art in its intimate theaters. From its inaugural production, an adaptation of Anton Chekhov stories, the theater has been warmly received from critics and local theatergoers. The Writers' Theatre has produced work from writers such as William Blake and William Shakespeare.

You can catch an art film or second-run movie at the **Highland Park movie theater** (445 Central Ave., Highland Park, 847/432-3300, $3.50–5). Free parking is available in the lot next door.

SHOPPING

Downtown Highland Park and Lake Forest have a number of upscale boutiques, including locally owned and international chain stores. Lake Forest's town square near Western Avenue and Westminster Road has a Laura Ashley boutique and small version of a Marshall Field's department store. Highland Park's downtown shopping district is clustered around Central Avenue, between Green Bay Road and Saint Johns Avenue. You'll find a number of women's

© CHRISTINE DES GARENNES

Downtown Highland Park

clothing shops, such as Gap, as well as a handful of upscale children's boutiques.

Lake Forest and Highland Park

The **Lake Forest Book Shop** (624 N. Western Ave., 847/234-4420) is a crowded little bookshop near the Metra train station. The friendly, frank staff of this independent store are always eager to make recommendations.

Kids aren't the only ones gawking at the toys and trains in **The Toy Station** (270 Market Sq., Lake Forest, 847/234-0180, www.trains-toys-horses.com). Model-train enthusiasts can check out a variety of trains here—streamliners, locomotives, you name it. In addition to trains, the store carries a seemingly inordinate number of stuffed animals and dolls, including Madame Alexander dolls.

Reminiscent of the hat shops of Paris and London, **Ooh-La-La** (464 Central Ave., Highland Park, 847/433-5646, 10 A.M.–5 P.M. Mon.–Sat.) is a millinery shop that stocks fine, handcrafted hats, including basic pillboxes to decorative ones bearing silk flowers.

Skokie and Wilmette

If you can't live like the wealthy North Shore residents, at least you can dress like them. **De-** **signer Resale** (124 Skokie Blvd., Wilmette, 847/920-1565, 10 A.M.–6 P.M. Mon.–Fri., 10 A.M.–5 P.M. Sat., noon–5 P.M. Sun.) sells lightly used name-brand clothing.

Westfield Shoppingtown Old Orchard (Skokie Blvd. and Old Orchard Rd., Skokie, 847/673-6800, www.westfield.com, 10 A.M.–9 P.M. Mon.–Sat., 11 A.M. 6 P.M. Sun.), or Old Orchard, as it's known locally, is an open-air, ritzy shopping center. There are the usual suspects, such as Nordstrom and Marshall Field's, but also Brooks Brothers, known mostly for its men's suits, Christian Bernard jewelry, and Kate Spade purses.

RECREATION
The Skokie Lagoons

The Skokie Lagoons are a series of seven interconnected lagoons along the Skokie River totaling about 200 acres. They were constructed in the 1930s and 1940s by the Civilian Conservation Corps to control spring flooding in the area and to build a water recreational area for residents. The river runs parallel to the Lake Michigan coastline and the lagoons are situated from roughly Willow to Lake-Cook roads. (Eventually the Skokie River runs into the Chisunbathing, a concession stand, a playground, a shelter for picnics, and a place to wash your sandy feet. It's nearly perfect, except beachcombers who are not Lake Forest residents cannot park at the nearby parking lot or along nearby residential streets. Your best bet is paying a few bucks to park in the Metra Lot in town (at Deerpath Rd. and Western Ave.) and walk a little less than one mile to the beach along Deerpath. It's an easy stroll, through a residential neighborhood and past Lake Forest College.

The 60-acre **Gillson Park** (Michigan and Washington Aves., Wilmette, 847/256-9656, www.wilmettepark.org) has a sandy beach and spots on the lawn for lounging in the sun, plus a pavilion called the Lakeview Center. Admission for nonresidents of Wilmette is $6.50 per person, $3 after 6 P.M. Sailboats and kayaks are available for rent ($24–40 per hour) 9 A.M.–5:45 P.M. On weekend evenings July–August, the park district holds free concerts in the Wallace Bowl, a little stage by the lake.

Skokie River Nature Preserve

The quiet Skokie River Nature Preserve (from Green Bay Rd., turn west on Laurel Ave. until it ends, Lake Forest, 847/234-3880, www.lfola.org, 6:30 A.M.–sunset) has four miles of woodchip trails through woodlands and meadows, with plenty of benches and spots along the way to picnic or watch for wildlife. (There's a swinging bridge over the river). The preserve is managed by the Lake Forest Open Lands, a land trust organization.

ACCOMMODATIONS
$50–100

One of few hotels near Sheridan Road and Lake Michigan, the **Hotel Moraine** (700 N. Sheridan Rd., Highwood, 847/433-5566, www.hotelmoraine.com, $89) is tucked between the working-class town of Highwood and elite Lake Forest. It's a bit outdated, but there's an indoor pool here. A variety of rooms are available, including doubles, suites, and kings, and come with coffeemakers. Business conferences and banquets are often held here.

one of the many forest preserves in Lake County

© CHRISTINE DES GARENNES

cago River.) The lagoons are a popular spot for fishing (bass, walleye, northern pike) and for canoeing. There's a public boat launch just south of Tower Road, east of the Edens Expressway, between the towns of Wilmette to the east and Northbrook to the west. Or you can rent a canoe, kayak, or trailer from the **Chicagoland Canoe Base** (4019 N. Narragansett Ave., Chicago, 773/777-1489, www.chicagolandcanoebase.com, 9 A.M.–5 P.M. Mon.–Sat., 9 A.M.–9 P.M. Thurs., $40 per day, trailers extra).

Beaches

One of the best beaches on the Lake Michigan coastline is **Forest Park Beach** (Deerpath Rd. and Lake Rd., Lake Forest, 847/615-4284 or 847/615-4320, www.cityoflakeforest.com, open Memorial Day–Labor Day). There are long stretches of sandy beaches (a peach color, not white), a large stone fishing pier that is not only good for fishing but also for picnicking, boulders that jut into the water that are great for

The Collar Counties

The **Doubletree Hotel North Shore** (9599 Skokie Blvd., Skokie, 847/679-7000 or 800/222-8733, www.doubletreenorthshore.com, $89–109) is not too pricey, but it has an indoor and outdoor pool, fitness center, and restaurant. Because the hotel has a meeting center, it tends to attract the business traveler crowd. Suites can run up to about $200.

$150–250

Located the site of a former hunting lodge in Lake Forest, the **M Deer Path Inn** (255 E. Illinois Rd., Lake Forest, 800/788-9480, www.deerpathinn.com, $170) was built in 1929. Designed by Chicago architect William Jones, who also designed a number of buildings for the Chicago World's Fair, the Deer Path is an English manor type of inn. There are 54 rooms in a variety of layouts, including regular rooms plus suites and executive-level. Suites can cost up to about $300 per night. Depending on which room you stay in, you'll receive slippers and robes, turn-down service, and whirlpool baths. Each guest is treated to a breakfast buffet, but the Sunday champagne brunch is quite an extravagant feast and worth the $35.

How often do you get to stay in an Italian villa? The **Harrison Conference Center,** also called Harrison Manor House at Lake Bluff (136 Green Bay Rd., Lake Bluff, 847/295-1100, www.harrisonmanorhouse.com, $149), is the former estate of an Irish farmer transformed into a high-end boutique hotel. It's a great place to stay if you're looking for a retreat. Once called Stonebridge (for a stone bridge linking two lakes on the property), it was home not only to the Irish farmer who made it rich in the United States, but to a railroad company executive, Northwestern University, the Catholic Church, and now the Aramark Corporation. Situated on almost 50 acres, the Harrison House has 83 rooms (some of them suites), a fitness room, tennis courts, driving range, and a basketball court. There are also three well-run restaurants on-site. If you're looking to splurge, this is the place to do it.

FOOD

Casual

Try the crispy, thin-crust pizza at **Buffo's** (431 Sheridan Rd., Highwood, 847/432-0301), a casual spot to grab a bite to eat. Buffo's is a kid-friendly place, popular among local softball and soccer teams.

You can't beat the cheese steaks (or cheese fries or chocolate shakes) at **Hoagie Hut** (17 Bank Ln., Highwood, 847/432-3262), a casual and friendly little place near the Metra line.

M The Lantern (768 N. Western Ave., 847/234-9844, www.lakeforestlantern.com, kitchen open 11 A.M.–11 P.M., bar until midnight, $6) is where the locals go when they are not in the mood for foie gras. At this casual, intimate bar and restaurant you'll meet a mix of millionaire business professionals, college students, and folks who work in nearby towns. On the menu are burgers, sandwiches such as Reubens, and broasted chicken. Right by the Metra station, it's a good place to hang out before you catch the train.

Most dishes at **The Silo** (625 Rockland Rd., Lake Bluff, 847/234-6660, 11 A.M.–10 P.M. Mon.–Thurs., 11 A.M.–midnight Fri.–Sat., 4–10 P.M. Sun., pizzas $5–24, sandwiches $7), right off the Edens Expressway, seem to ooze cheese (the chili, the pizza, the patty melts). Portions are large and the atmosphere is welcoming to everyone—families, college students, and couples. Deep-dish pizzas are the specialty, but you'll also find some more unusual menu items, such as ostrich burgers.

Cafés

The apple pancakes are out of this world at **Walker Brothers Pancake House** (620 Central Ave., Highland Park, 847/432-0660). They're several inches thick, supersweet, dense, and chunky. They're worth the wait on a weekend morning. Other breakfast foods here, such as the waffles, are also able to fill you up and make you want to unfasten your belt a notch.

On a sunny morning, the outdoor patio at **M Southgate Café** (655 Forest Ave., Lake Forest, 847/234-8800) is a great spot to read the paper and feast on French toast or scrambled eggs.

Egg Harbor (512 N. Western Ave., 847/295-3449, Lake Forest, www.eggharborcafe.com, breakfast and lunch daily, $7), which features breakfast and lunch, is probably better known for its big, rich breakfasts, such as open-faced omelettes, eggs Benedict, and oatmeal-raisin French toast.

Mexican

For this writer, a perfect day would include time spent in the outdoor sidewalk café of **ⓜ Hot Tamales** (493 Central Ave., Highland Park, 847/433-4070, lunch Mon.–Fri., dinner daily, $10), munching on chips and *salsa verde* and sipping a cold beer. This brightly colored, lively restaurant serves amazingly fresh dishes (the tomatoes and peppers taste as if they were picked from a garden that morning), including corn chowders, quesadillas, and of course tamales.

Fine Dining

Former astronaut and Lake Forest resident Jim Lovell and his son, Jay, a chef, are behind the fancy **Lovell's of Lake Forest** (915 S. Waukegan Rd., Lake Forest, 847/234-8013, www.lovellsoflakeforest.com, 11 A.M.–2 P.M. Mon.–Fri., 5–9 P.M. Sun.–Thurs., 5–11 P.M. Fri.–Sat., $12–22 lunch entrée, $32 average dinner entrée). There's a manly man bent to this restaurant, with a martini and cigar bar, cognac list, and a menu that includes game, such as antelope loin. It's not that clubby, though. After all, there is a children's menu, which features chicken fingers. Lovell's last trip to space, by the way, was aboard Apollo 13. (Tom Hanks played him in the movie named after the mission.)

Carlos and Debbie Nieto's French restaurant **ⓜ Carlos'** (429 Temple, Highland Park, 847/432-0770, www.carlos-restaurant.com, dinner Tues.–Sun., $80) has been receiving rave reviews since it opened. It's a lovely restaurant, and eating here is a multicourse, carefully and beautifully designed event. Here's a sample from a recent degustation menu: "Rabbit Loin Wrapped in Prosciutto di Parma with Purple Potato Rosettes, Black Truffle and Leek Spaghettini and a Natural Jus." If only you could eat like this every night. The food is French and in addition to an extensive degustation menu, you can choose from a regular menu.

Nearby is **Café Central** (455 Central, Highland Park, 847/266-7878, 10:30 A.M.–9 P.M. Tues.–Thurs., 11:30 A.M.–10 P.M. Fri.–Sat., 8 A.M.–10 P.M. Sun., $10), also run by the Nietos. Like Carlos' Café Central serves French food, but this restaurant is the more casual (you can sit at a sidewalk table) and less expensive of the two. Dishes are less artsy but still great-tasting items such as a *croque monsieur* (a French version of grilled cheese).

Candy Shop

Colorful **ⓜ Sweets** (284 E. Deerpath Rd., Lake Forest, 847/295-1111) in downtown Lake Forest has jars stocked with all goodies you can imagine, from Gummi Bears to flavored licorice.

Markets

Don's Finest Foods (850 N. Western Ave., Lake Forest, 847/234-2700) in downtown Lake Forest sells fresh fruits and vegetables, deli meats and salads, chocolates, wines, and a variety of organic and healthy food products.

INFORMATION

The **Chicago's North Shore Convention and Visitors Bureau** (Westfield Shoppingtown Old Orchard Center, Skokie, 847/763-0011, www.visitchicagonorthshore.com) keeps track of what's doing in towns from Evanston to Lake Bluff.

The **Highland Park Chamber of Commerce** (508 Central Ave., Ste. 206, Highland Park, 847/432-0284, www.highland-park.com) publishes a decent shopping and dining guide.

The **Lake Forest/Lake Bluff Chamber of Commerce** (695 N. Western Ave., near Metra train line, Lake Forest, 847/234-4282, www.lakeforestonlinc.com) also maintains a shopping and dining guide, plus information about things to do in the two communities.

Media

North Shore Magazine (www.north-shoremag.com) is a colorful, glossy monthly magazine with restaurant reviews, performing arts information, and profiles of famous current and past residents. You can pick up copies at drugstores such as Osco, convenient stores such as White Hen, and bookstores such as Borders.

Pioneer Press (www.pioneerlocal.com) publishes weekly newspapers on Wednesdays in several North Shore towns.

SERVICES

If you are not a resident of Lake Forest, you won't be able to check out books from **The Lake Forest Library** (360 E. Deerpath Rd., Lake Forest, 847/234-0636, 9 A.M.–9 P.M. Mon.–Fri., 9 A.M.–5 P.M. Fri.–Sat., 1–5 P.M. Sun. Sept.–May), but that's no reason not to stop by this building. The library has an impressive art collection of American artwork, including John James Audubon engravings.

On a cold winter day you won't want to leave the reading room, with its crackling fireplace and armchairs.

While you're waiting to catch your train drop by a neat little barbershop in the Lake Forest train station: **Michael's Barber Shop** (950 Northwestern, Lake Forest, 847/234-9752).

Not feeling well? Pay a visit to the **Highland Park Hospital** (718 Glenview Ave., Highland Park, 847/432-8000).

GETTING AROUND

Metra's Union Pacific Line (312/496-4777, www.metrarail.com), which runs from Chicago to Kenosha, stops at all North Shore towns. Trains run about every hour 5 A.M.–1 A.M. Monday–Friday, except during rush hours, when they run about every 15 minutes. Trains run about every two hours 5 A.M.–1 A.M. Saturday and Sunday. Depending on where you catch the train, a one-way ticket to or from Chicago's Ogilvie Transportation Center can cost $2.90–4.50.

Northwest Suburbs

Connected to Chicago via commuter train lines and I-90, the northwest suburbs are a string of solid suburban communities, not quite the sprawling suburbs such as Schaumburg or Hoffman Estates farther out west, but not quite as eclectic as inner-ring suburbs such as Oak Park and Evanston. Homes here are well kept, streets are mostly quiet, and the schools are good. This is where many young families live. Highlights include Arlington Heights, with its quaint, bustling downtowns and the racehorse track Arlington Park; and the performance venues in Rosemont, which seems to cater to the conventioneer set.

DES PLAINES AND NILES

"First" McDonald's

So technically it is not the first McDonald's restaurant and no one serves hamburgers or

milk shakes here, but the **McDonald's #1 Store Museum** (400 N. Lee St., Des Plaines, 847/297-5022, www.mcdonalds.com, free) is a neat stop to drop by for a quick visit (like the Museum of Anesthesiology). The original store was actually torn down long ago, but this is a nifty recreation spot, complete with shiny cars from the 1950s outside the store. Mannequins model how McDonald's employees used to prepare food decades ago. (By gosh, they used to cut up potatoes before frying them.) A video on the lower level tells the story of Ray Kroc, the creator, and how the empire got its start. If you're itching for a cheeseburger after your visit, there's a working McDonald's just across the street.

Golf

Even in April, the Chicago area can be chilly, and temperatures of 45°F are not unheard of (even snow). With that said, golfers will appreciate the chance to get their golf games in gear at the **Golf Center of Des Plaines** (353 N. River Rd., Des Plaines, 847/803-4653, www.desplainesparks.org, 8 A.M.–10 P.M. daily, $9–11). The center has 80 heated stations at its three-level driving range.

Niles

Fool your friends back home by having your photo taken in front of the **Leaning Tower of Niles** (6300 W. Touhy Ave., Niles, 847/647-8222). This tower, a much smaller version of the original, was built in 1932 as part of a recreational complex. As it happens, Niles and Pisa, Italy, are "sister cities." The building now belongs to the YMCA and the village hosts evening concerts outside here in the summer.

Food

A favorite among the kids and the older train buffs, the ⚏ **Choo Choo Restaurant** (600 Lee St., Des Plaines, 847/391-9815, www.thechoochoo.com, 10:30 A.M.–8 P.M. Mon.–Fri., 7 A.M.–3 P.M. Sat.) has food delivered to some lucky customers on a toy train. Open since 1951, this breakfast and lunch spot serves milk shakes, pecan Belgian waffles, egg salad sandwiches, chili dogs (beef dog with turkey chili). Try the freight car of onion rings.

Another northwest side institution is **Affy Tapple** (7425 Croname Rd., Niles, 847/588-2900, www.affytapple.com, 9 A.M.–5 P.M. Mon.–Fri., 9 A.M.–2 P.M. Sat.) which also dates back more than 50 years. Visit the factory store and load up on caramel apples covered with peanuts.

ROSEMONT
Donald E. Stephens Museum of Hummels

In a town where the name Donald E. Stephens appears on almost every major building (Stephens has been mayor here since the town was incorporated in the 1950s), perhaps it shouldn't be too surprising there is a Hummel museum named after him. The Donald E. Ste-

phens Museum of Hummels (555 N. River Rd., Rosemont, 847/692-4000, www.stephenshummelmuseum.com) has thousands of those little ceramic figurines, cherub-faced boys and girls carrying umbrellas, books, flowers, with ceramic birds always perched nearby, on the fence post or on top of the child's hat. Surprise, some Hummels and other figurines are for sale.

Performance Venues

The **Allstate Arena** (6920 N. Mannheim Rd., Rosemont, 847/635-6601, www.allstatearena.com) is a 19,000-seat arena that holds major rock, pop, and country concerts, as well as events such as the Harlem Globetrotters and national circus shows.

The more intimate **Rosemont Theatre** (5400 River Rd., Rosemont, 847/671-5100, 11 A.M.–7 P.M. Mon.–Fri., noon–5 P.M. Sat.) has 4,300 seats. You can catch a wide variety of stars here, from Tom Jones to Tori Amos.

Sports

The semiprofessional hockey team, the **Chicago Wolves** (6920 N. Mannheim Rd., Rosemont, 800/THE-WOLVES or 800/843-9658, www.chicagowolves.com) play in the Allstate Arena in Rosemont, just off I-90. The season runs mid-October–mid-April.

Information

Rosemont is packed with national chain hotels and restaurants. Just about every hotel chain has a location here. For lodging or dining information, contact the **Rosemont Convention Bureau** (9301 W. Bryn Mawr Ave., Rosemont, 847/823-2100, www.rosemont.com).

ARLINGTON HEIGHTS
Arlington Park

Open since 1929, Arlington Park (2200 W. Euclid Ave., Arlington Heights, 847/385-7500, www.arlingtonpark.com, $6 admission, reserved seating extra $3–6, program guide extra) is a premier park to watch and bet on thoroughbred horse racing in the Midwest. After ownership changes, a fire in 1985 (which forced races to shift to Hawthorn racetrack for a while), and then a few years of closure in the late 1990s, Arlington Park seems to now attract a good mix of regular bettors, young couples, and even families out for a day. The park itself is well maintained, with plenty of flowers planted around the track area and staff cleaning up after bettors. Races are held every day except Tuesday mid-May–mid-September. If you're a novice, Arlington has special betting windows for beginners, plus a tutorial on its website.

Metropolis Performing Arts Center

Audiences can be treated to anything from a cabaret performance to a *Peter Pan* musical at the **Metropolis Performing Arts Center** (111 W. Campbell St., Arlington Heights, box office 847/577-2121, www.metropolisarts.com, 10 A.M.–5 P.M., or until show time on the day of an event, Tues.–Sun.). This 350-seat theater is one block from the Arlington Heights Metra stop.

The Metropolis Performing Arts Center is part of a village development called The Metropolis. In addition to the theater, you'll also find a club on the building's lower level called "The Boiler Room," as well as a supper club, shops, and apartments.

Janus Theatre (847/931-7247), affiliated with the Arlington Heights Park District, stages outdoor summer outdoor productions throughout the northwest suburbs.

Food

Irish pubs are a dime a dozen in Chicago and Chicagoland. **Peggy Kinnane's Irish Restaurant and Pub** (8 N. Vail Ave., Arlington Heights, 847/577-7733, www.peggykinnanes.com) is one of the newer ones in the area and has developed quite a following among northwestern residents. With its prime location and outdoor seating in downtown Arlington Heights, Peggy Kinnane's is a good

place to hang out on an afternoon in the sun and have a brew. There are plenty of beers available on tap, plus sandwiches and meals served in large portions, such as fried cod fillets, fish and chips, traditional Irish dishes such as shepherd's pie, and a decent selection of non-Irish food such as pasta and sandwiches. Live music Friday and Saturday evenings.

If you want to splurge on some glorious food, spend a few hours at **Le Titi de Paris** (1015 W. Dundee Rd., Arlington Heights, 847/506-0222, www.letitideparis.com, lunch Wed.–Fri., dinner Tues.–Sun.). Here are just two examples of its beautiful creations: grilled striped bass with wilted spinach, shaved fennel and red onions, carrot mousseline, shallot essence, and garlic aioli. Or how about duo of pheasant sausage and quail served with a wild mushroom and sweetbread mousse? Lunch entrées are around $20 and dinner entrées $35, but this really is a place to order the whole shebang, appetizers, wine, and dessert, which is appropriately called the grand finale.

Just north of Arlington Heights is **Le Français** (269 S. Milwaukee Ave., Wheeling, 815/541-7470, www.lefrancaisrestaurant.com, lunch Tues.–Fri., dinner Mon.–Sat.), another restaurant famous for its French cuisine. Open since 1973, Le Français's diners typically choose from among several degustation menus. A window to the kitchen allows guests to watch the chef prepare dishes such as foie gras with braised beef short rib and celery root puree, and black truffle and white asparagus salad. Entrées are around $35; multicourse meals are around $90 per person. This is a fancy place; guys will need to wear a coat on Saturday evenings.

Information

For tips on traveling to the region, contact the **Prospect Heights Convention and Visitors Bureau** (33 E. Palatine Rd., Prospect Heights, 847/325-4200 or 800/955-7259, www.chicagonorthsuburbs.com).

Busse Woods and Woodfield Corridor

At first glance tourism activities along I-90 and I-290 seem to center on shopping, shopping, and shopping, especially at the gigantic Woodfield Mall, where you can buy everything imaginable. However, there are some other sights worthy of a visit, namely Lynfred Winery, the Busse Woods park, and the Chicago Athenaeum at Schaumburg art gallery.

SIGHTS

Lynfred Winery

A few miles from huge shopping complexes such as Woodfield Mall, Lynfred Winery (15 S. Roselle Rd., Roselle, 630/529-WINE or 630/529-9463, www.lynfredwinery.com, 10 A.M.–P.M. daily, free) offers a nice little respite for folks looking for a break from the mall scene. Founded in the 1970s by the Koehler family, Lynfred Winery produces 25,000 cases of sweet red and white wines and some fruit wines. Some are made from Illinois grapes such as the chambourcin and chardonnel. The winery is housed on an approximately 100-year-old renovated, one-acre estate (it's a winery; there's no vineyard here). It holds tastings daily, tours on the weekends, and new-release parties and culinary events that pair food and wine throughout the year. A gift shop has boutique dipping sauces and jams. Five bucks gets you a taste of seven different wines. Dozens are featured in the tasting room. A bed-and-breakfast is on-site.

Chicago Athenaeum

In a world dominated by shopping malls and subdivisions, the Chicago Athenaeum at Schaumburg (190 S. Roselle Rd., Schaumburg, 847/895-3950, www.chi-athenaeum.org, $3) offers a refreshing respite from the buy, buy, buy atmosphere of Schaumburg. Inside the renovated barn (in the Schaumburg Town Center, which suspiciously resembles a shopping center), the Athenaeum presents innovative, thoughtful artwork. You'll find a host of

artwork to admire: architectural models, furniture, glass, paintings, and textiles.

The organization's 20-acre **sculpture park** is just south of the Village of Schaumburg's Robert O. Atcher Municipal Center, which includes the Prairie Arts Center. A walking path winds past about a dozen aluminum, fiberglass, bronze, regional, and international works, many more than six feet tall. The park is open sunrise–sunset daily.

Historical Museum

It may seem silly to have a historical museum about a town that has been around for about 50 years, but the **Rolling Meadows Historical Museum** (3100 Central Rd., Rolling Meadows, 847/577-7086, 10 A.M.–2 P.M. Wed., 1–4 P.M. Sun., donation) is what it is, a surprisingly interesting museum (house, really) that tells the story of how Rolling Meadows, a planned community, came to be. The house, a rebuilt-1950s ranch-style home, with furniture and decorations from that era, is a trip to visit.

ENTERTAINMENT AND EVENTS

Live Theater and Music

At **Medieval Times** (Roselle Rd. and I-90, Schaumburg, 888/WE-JOUST or 888/935-6878, www.medievaltimes.com, $50, includes dinner) men with long hair and long swords wield spiked balls and other such weapons and attempt to outmaneuver each other while riding well-trained Andalusian stallions. All the while, guests dine on chicken, potatoes, and assorted vegetables with their hands (this is medieval times, after all) and cheer for their favorite knight. It's all a bit unreal, but the kids will get a kick out of it.

The **Prairie Center for the Arts** (201 Schaumburg Ct., Schaumburg, 847/895-3600, www.prairiecenter.org, galleries open 8 A.M.–6 P.M. Mon.–Fri. and during events and performances, box office open 9 A.M.–4 P.M. Mon.–Fri. and 1.5 hours before shows) is the major performing arts venue in and around the Schaumburg area. Regional dance, music, and theater groups stage shows in its 442-seat theater, and local art students and professional artists exhibit their work in the gallery. The center also brings in a number of national touring musicians and the occasional speaker.

Even if you are not a fan of opera, you might be surprised by a visit to **Opera in Focus** (Rolling Meadows Park District Headquarters Theater, 3000 Central Rd., Rolling Meadows, 847/818-3220, www.operainfocus.com, shows at 1:30 P.M. Wed., Thurs., Sat., $12). Dedicated and talented volunteers bring rod puppets to life during a series of musical numbers choreographed on a small-scale but ornate and intricately designed stage. Each month they choose the best music and scenes from different operas and musicals; you won't sit through a three-hour production. Previous selections have included music from *Carmen, Faust, Porgy and Bess,* and *Fiddler on the Roof.*

Events

In the beginning, organizers of **Dodgeball Days** (Olympic Park, 1675 Old Schaumburg Rd., Schaumburg, 847/985-2115, www.dodgeballusa.com, mid-–late-July) were really just looking for something different to do other than getting together and playing softball or volleyball. The relatively new National Amateur Dodgeball Association's Championship annual tournament has really taken off. Teams of 6–10 players play with foam balls to enthusiastic crowds that grow every year. The annual event is run by the Schaumburg Park.

Christkindlesmarkt (Towne Sq., Roselle and Schaumburg Rds., 847/895-3600, free) is an open-air market with traveling minstrels, craft booths, carolers, and visits from Santa Claus.

Prairie Arts Festival (Prairie Center for the Arts, Memorial Day weekend) includes a juried artist show with watercolor paintings, ceramics, glassware, sculptures, and photography, plus live music (jazz, flamenco, you name it) and typical festival food such as ice cream and funnel cakes.

SHOPPING

Schaumburg

Woodfield Shopping Center (Golf Rd. and Hwy. 53, Schaumburg, 847/330-1537, www.shopwoodfield.com) has big-name department stores such as Lord and Taylor, Nordstrom, Sears, and chain after chain of clothing and knick-knack stores and entertainment outlets.

Woodfield Mall is surrounded by several shopping centers and megastores. They include **The Streets of Woodfield** (600 block of N. Martingale Rd., Schaumburg) shopping center and **Galyan's Trading Company** (847/995-0200, www.galyans.com), a giant sports equipment and sportswear store, complete with an indoor climbing wall.

The Schaumburg **Ikea** (1800 E. McConnor Pkwy., Schaumburg, 847/969-9700, www.ikea-usa.com) is the only Ikea retail store in the Midwest and it is always packed. The vast complex includes several levels of furniture and accents on display (for home or office). Decide what you want and staff will find it on the warehouse shelves on the bottom level. It's chaotic, with bargains on random items such as coat hangers and terra-cotta pots. The folks at Ikea made it easy for you to spend hours here. For example, there's the café upstairs that serves yummy Swedish meatballs. And there's the nursing room for mothers and babies.

Had it with new stuff? Make tracks to the **Antiques Mart of Elk Grove Village** (800 S. Rohlwing Rd., Elk Grove Village, 847/895-8900, 11 A.M.–6 P.M. Mon.–Fri., 11 A.M.–5 P.M. Sat.–Sun.) where 150–200 dealers sell their wares, including Depression glass, china, furniture, and collectibles.

SPORTS AND RECREATION

Nature Centers and Forest Preserves

Spring Valley Nature Sanctuary (1111 E. Schaumburg Rd., 847/985-2100, www.parkfun.com, museum and visitors center open 9 A.M.–5 P.M. daily in the summer, 8 A.M.–8 P.M. April–Oct., 8 A.M.–5 P.M. Nov.–March) has 135 acres through woodlands, a lake, wetlands, and prairie, plus a log cabin and 1880 farmstead the children will enjoy. A highlight of this park is its wheelchair-accessible trails; there are about three miles of them.

Ned Brown Forest Preserve, also known as Busse Woods (Golf and Arlington Heights Rds., Elk Grove Village, 708/366-9420, www.fpdcc.com) is a sprawling 6,000-acre park just east of I-290 and south of I-90. Park your car at the lot at Higgins and Arlington Heights Road, near the elk pasture (yes, an elk pasture). Then hop on your bike and hit the 11-mile trail around the park. The route is easy and fairly quiet (although you can hear the rumbling of cars on the nearby expressways). In the center of the park is Busse Lake Boating Center, where you can rent rowboats and fish. You can also reach the boat area off Higgins Road.

Baseball

The **Schaumburg Flyers** (1999 Springinsguth Rd., Schaumburg, 847/891-2255 or 847/891-4545, or 877/691-2255, www.flyersbaseball.com, $5–9) is a member of the independent Northern League and a relative newcomer to the minor leagues. Since the team started playing in Schaumburg (the stadium, Alexian Field, was built in 1999), the Flyers have attracted quite the loyal following, much like the Kane County Cougars to the west. Unlike at major league games, tickets are affordable here (less than $10), parking is free, and you can relax in the bleachers, lawn seats, or bucket seats. Or for a more private experience, fans can watch the game from within the Schaumburg Club, a glass-enclosed restaurant in view of first base. Alexian Field is just across the street from Metra's Milwaukee District West line.

Airplane Rides

Slip into a bomber jacket and strap on a pair of goggles—you are going flying in a bona fide biplane with **Red Baron Rides** (Schaumburg Regional Airport, 905 W. Irving Park Rd., Schaumburg, 866/FLY-BARON or 866/359-2276, www.redbaronrides.com, April–Nov.) Rides last 20, 40, or 60 minutes.

Golf

Indian Lakes Resort (250 W. Schick Rd., Bloomingdale, 630/529-0200, www.indian-lakesresort.com) has a little bit of something for everyone: two golf courses, indoor and outdoor pools, a miniature golf course, spa, plus more than 300 hotel rooms if you plan to make it a weekend visit. At the resort's hilarious Bad Pants Open, locals strut their finest and most obnoxious golf pants.

Two public courses worthy of a stop are **Schaumburg Golf Club** (401 N. Roselle Rd., Schaumburg, 847/885-9000, www.park-fun.com) and **Walnut Greens** (1150 N. Walnut Ln., Schaumburg, 847/490-7878, www.park-fun.com). The Schaumburg Golf Glub has one 18-hole course and a nine-hole course, putting green, and driving range. Walnut Greens has a nine-hole course and a putting green. Both are run by the Schaumburg Park District.

Water Parks

Schaumburg is a good three hours from Wisconsin Dells and all of its water parks, but a good substitute on hot days is **Rainbow Falls Water Park** (Elk Grove Blvd. and Lions Dr., Elk Grove Village, 847/437-949, www.parks.elkgrove.org, 10 A.M.–8 P.M. Mon.–Thurs., 10 A.M.–6:30 P.M. Fri., 11 A.M.–5 P.M. Sat.–Sun., times vary on Memorial Day Weekend, Fourth of July, and Labor Day weekends, $10, miniature golf an extra $3), a public water park with tons of activities: flume slides, paddleboat rides, and a place called The Fun House. Here water squirts out at you when you least expect it (although gauging by the squealing kids ahead of you, you can get an idea of when to expect the water spray). Rainbow Falls also has miniature golf.

Skiing

Here in the Midwest we make do with what we have. There are no mountains to speak of, at least any of significance in Illinois, but come winter, when the snowy stuff starts to fall and skiers feel the urge to move they head to **Villa Olivia Golf Course Ski Area and Country Club** (1410 W. Lake St., Bartlett, 630/289-

1000, www.villaolivia.com). Not everyone can afford to fly often to Colorado or drive six hours to northern Wisconsin and Michigan. Villa Olivia is relatively cheap for an afternoon of downhill skiing, snowboarding or snow tubing. As for skiing, the "mountain" has a 180-degree vertical drop, 12 lighted downhill runs, a chair lift, and several tow lifts. In addition to downhill skiing and snowboarding, there are groomed cross-country ski trails and a tubing hill.

The hill is open daily during the winter even when snow has not fallen, thanks to snowmaking machines. Slopes are closed for grooming 4:45–5:45 P.M. daily. Downhill skiing is 1–10 P.M. Monday–Thursday, Sunday and holiday evenings costs $26.50 for adults, plus $22.50 for equipment rental. Skiing during the day Friday, Saturday, and Sunday costs $32.50 for skiing, plus $24.50 for equipment rental.

Snowboarding board rental is $15.50 for one hour, $30 for 2–6 hours. Boot rental for snowboarders is $12.50 for one hour or $17 for 2–6 hours. Snow tubing for two hours costs $13.75 per person Monday–Thursday and $16.75 Friday, weekends, and holidays. Price includes the tube. During the warmer months, Villa Olivia maintains an 18-hole golf course.

ACCOMMODATIONS

Because Schaumburg has countless office parks and numerous business conferences a year, there are dozens of chain hotels here, and almost all of them cater to the business traveler. Continental breakfasts and fitness rooms are standard.

$50–100

Super 8 Chicago-O'Hare (2951 Touhy Ave., Elk Grove Village, 847/827-3133, $59–83) has standard accommodations for the budget-minded traveler. A block from Woodfield Mall, **Drury Inn** (600 N. Martingale Rd., Schaumburg, 847/517-7737 or 800/DRURY-IN, 800/378-7946, www.druryhotels.com, $69) is always a good buy. It's more expensive than the Super 8, but it has an indoor pool, fitness center, and a decent-size breakfast

buffet. The **Wingate Inn** (50 E. Remington Rd., Schaumburg, 847/882-5000, $69) is also a good bet and offers shuttle service to Woodfield Mall. It also has some suites in addition to standard rooms.

$100–150.

Eaglewood Resort and Spa (1401 Nordic Rd., Itasca, 630/773-1400, www.eaglewoodresort.com, $149) is a cool retreat in the middle of the suburbs. There are almost 300 rooms here, some with balconies and views of the resorts' golf course and nearby woods. Extras are terry cloth robes, high-speed Internet access, a spa and fitness center, plus restaurants on the grounds. You really don't have to leave the resort. There are also an 18-hole golf course and six-lane bowling alley.

$250 and Up

Lynfred Winery (15 S. Roselle Rd., Roselle, 630/529-WINE or 630/529-9463, www.lynfredwinery.com, $400–475) has four extravagant suites at its winery south of Schaumburg. Expect luxurious, Italian-themed, and decorative accommodations such as marble fireplaces and bathtubs.

FOOD

The **Bamboo Room** (616 E. Golf Rd., Schaumburg, 847/592-5959, $10–30) is a complex of sorts with three different scenes. The Bamboo Room's menu is the more extensive and elegant of the three, with Asian-fried oysters (coated with rice and with sweet soy syrup), Chilean sea bass, and jumbo-size prawns. The Koko Café is more casual, serving burgers and sandwiches. At the Tiki Lounge DJs spin dance music and beautiful people serve tropical drinks. All three parts of the club are sleek, decorated with tropical foliage, and frequented by a tanned, suburban set and conventioneers. The Bamboo Room and Tiki Bar are open for dinner Wednesday–Sunday. The café is open for lunch and dinner Tuesday–Friday and for dinner Saturday.

Sal and Carvao's (801 E. Algonquin Rd.,

Schaumburg, 847/925-0061, www.sale-carvao.com, 11:30 A.M.–2 P.M. Mon.–Fri., 4:30–10 P.M. Sun.–Thurs., 4:30–10:30 P.M. Fri.–Sat., $20) is a *churrascalia,* a large Brazilian restaurant where waiters carry meat on large skewers to tables. The meat (rump roast, leg of lamb, beef ribs, chicken, and pork) has been slow-roasted over charcoal, with dashes of salt and pepper. There are two other restaurants in Chicagoland, one in the city and another in Downers Grove.

At the colorful **🔟 Sabor** (160 S. Roselle Rd., Schaumburg, 847/301-1470, lunch Tues.–Fri., dinner Tues.–Sun.), in the Schaumburg Town Center, local chef Christina Hernandez whips up Latin cuisine, from Brazilian stews to Cuban, Peruvian, and Spanish dishes. On a given weekend you might see paella, empanadas, or mahimahi on the menu.

Just down the street from there is **Prairie Rock Brewing Company** (1385 N. Meacham Rd., Schaumburg, 847/605-9900, www.prairierockbrewingcompany.com, noon–9 P.M. Sun., 11 A.M.–10 P.M. Mon.–Thurs., 11 A.M.–11 P.M. Fri.–Sat., $8–27) a brew pub with more than just pizza and sandwiches for fare. Consider these options: salmon pasta, Malibu chicken (with a honey mustard and pineapple sauce), and tenderloin pasta. Bread is made daily in the restaurant. Brews include porter, bock, red ales, lagers, and more.

INFORMATION

More information about the area is available by contacting the **Greater Woodfield Convention and Visitors Bureau** (1430 N. Meacham Rd., Ste. 1400, Schaumburg, 847/490-1010 or 800/847-4849, www.visitgw.com).

SERVICES
Tours
Village Trolley and Tours (847/228-7662, www.villagetrolley.com) organizes tours throughout Elk Grove Village, through historic districts, to shops, and past homes lit up for the holiday season.

Hospital
St. Alexius Hospital (1555 N. Barrington Rd., Hoffman Estates, 847/843-2000, www.stalexius.org) is near I-90 and the suburbs of Hoffman Estates, Schaumburg, and Barrington.

Media
The ***Daily Herald*** (847/427-4300, www.dailyherald.com) covers northwest and west suburban news. You can find it at most gas stations, convenience stores, grocery stores, and news stands.

Library
The **Schaumburg Public Library** (130 S. Roselle Rd., Schaumburg, 847/985-4000, www.stdl.org) seems more like a Borders books and music store than a library. It is huge, often crowded with students and families, but it is staffed by friendly librarians and has a great periodicals and reference section, not to mention a coffee and sandwich café in the building.

GETTING AROUND
Train
Metra's Milwaukee District West Line (312/322-6777, www.metrarail.com) operates between Chicago's Ogilvie Transportation Center and Elgin, with stops in Itasca, Roselle, Schaumburg, and other northwest suburbs. Catch it at the Schaumburg station (2000 S. Springinsguth Rd., 847/895-9260, ticket office open 5 A.M.–12:45 P.M. Mon.–Fri.). A ticket to or from Chicago to Schaumburg costs $4.10. Trains run more frequently during rush hour weekdays and less frequently on holidays. You need to buy your ticket at the depot office when it is open; otherwise you will have to pay the conductor an additional $2. When the ticket office is closed, buy your ticket on the train from the conductor. There's plenty of parking at the depot.

Bus
From the Metra station, you can board a **Pace** bus (847/364-PACE or 847/364-7223, www.pacebus.com, $1.50), which can take you into Schaumburg and its neighboring

town, Roselle. Pace Northwest Transportation Center near Woodfield Mall is a hub of sorts for most of the bus system's suburban lines. There you can transfer to other lines, which run to most of the area's major shopping and hotel areas.

Trolley

The free Schaumburg Trolley connects Woodfield Mall and all the outlying shopping centers, in addition to the Pace Northwest Transportation Center. Known as Route 905, it operates daily.

I-88 Corridor: Elmhurst to Naperville

Out here, there's much more space compared with some of the inner-ring suburbs or even those in Lake County. There are plenty of forest preserves, golf courses, and well-manicured subdivisions and shopping centers with fine landscaping. Du Page County, in which most of the towns in this section are situated, is conservative and for the most part quite clean and more quiet compared with other suburbs. There are lots of families and stereotypical suburban activities of soccer games, nights at the movie complex, and mornings spent shopping. The wholesomeness of this area has attracted more and more families, and the area is booming.

NAPERVILLE

Riverwalk

The Riverwalk (500 W. Jackson Ave., 630/848-5000, www.napervilleparks.org) is an easy, popular way to spend time strolling on weekday evenings and weekend mornings. The 3.5-mile brick path follows the Du Page River and local landmarks such as the **Moser Tower Millennium Carillon,** which, with its musical bronze bells, soars to almost 160 feet tall. The Riverwalk is close to downtown. It's accessible at **Centennial Beach** (500 W. Jackson Ave., Naperville, 630/848-5000, www.napervilleparks.org, open end of May–early Sept., nonresident daily fee $10, $3 after 3 P.M.), where there is a quarry filled with water. The city has built a little beach here for residents, and it rents paddleboats.

Naper Settlement

The big attraction in downtown Naperville

is a historical village called Naper Settlement (523 S. Webster St., Naperville, 630/420-6010, www.napersettlement.org, 10 A.M.–4 P.M. Tues.–Sat., 1–4 P.M. Sun. Apr.–Oct., 10 A.M.–4 P.M. Tues.–Fri. Nov.–March, $7 spring and summer, $4.25 fall and winter). It is one of those "living museum" types of places where people are dressed up in costumes resembling clothes worn in the village Naperville once was. (Although the stone carvers and blacksmiths look a little too clean for living in the 1800s in a frontier town.) The 13-acre site is pretty impressive as far as historical villages go. There are about 30 structures, including a schoolhouse, chapel, meetinghouse, and the town's first post office, built in 1833. Throughout the year the settlement hosts numerous events popular with area families, such as Maple Sugar Days. Don't forget to check out an art gallery on the lower level of the Pre-Emption House Visitor Center (formerly a hotel and tavern in the town); fans of folk-art paintings will like the collection. During the winter, the settlement grounds are open, but the buildings are not.

Events

Naperville hosts several free outdoor concerts in the summer. The **Rolling on the River** (630/848-5000, www.napervilleparks.org) concerts are held at Civic Plaza, at the Riverwalk and Webster Street, downtown Naperville. They are held usually between 7–9 P.M. on Wednesday and Friday nights. At around 7:30 P.M. on Tuesdays in the summer, you can hear the bronze bells of the carillon play. The concerts are free and last about one hour (630/428-4239, www.visitnaperville.com). The **Naperville Municipal Band** (55 Concert

Ln., Central Park between Benton and Jefferson Aves., west on Van Buren Ave., Naperville, 630/778-9994, www.napervilleband.org) plays around 7:45 P.M. on Thursday evenings at the Community Concert Center, an outdoor band shell. The municipal band (the organization has been around since the mid-1800s) plays big-band tunes from the 1940s, music composed by John Philip Sousa, Broadway music, and other festive selections.

Accommodations

In the shadow of huge, fancy hotels you'll find the **Stardust Motel** (890 E. Ogden Ave., Naperville, 630/355-3467), a 70-room motor lodge with basic, clean rooms, coin-operated laundry, and a glittering sign in the shape of a star, reminiscent of the days when the Stardust opened back in the 1950s. Rates are around $50 per night and less during the week.

Bed-and-breakfasts are rare in the west suburbs, but a fine one can be found in Naperville at the **Harrison House B&B** (26 N. Eagle St., Naperville, 630/420-1117, www.harrisonhousebb.com). Most hotels lie along the interstates out here, but Harrison House is less than a mile to Naperville's Riverwalk and Centennial Beach. Renovated in 2002, the bed-and-breakfast has four light and airy, romantic rooms with modern touches such as high-speed Internet access. As expected, guests are treated to a full breakfast in the morning. Rates are above $200.

At 24,000 square feet, the **Holiday Inn Select** (1801 N. Naper Blvd., Naperville, 630/505-4900, www.holidayinnselect.com) is one of the largest if not the largest hotel in Du Page County. If you've got money to throw around in the suburbs, stay overnight in one of the rooms on the "Concierge Floor," where you have a choice between two-room suites or king studios. Free cocktails and appetizers are offered in the evenings. Rates are above $200.

Markets

Naperville hosts a **farmers market** at the 5th Avenue Station (5th Avenue, just east of Washington St., Naperville, 630/369-5638, 7 A.M.–noon Sat. June–late Oct.).

WHEATON AND LISLE

Morton Arboretum

During the fall, a walk or drive through the Morton Arboretum (4100 Hwy. 53, Lisle, 630/719-2400, www.mortonarb.org, 7 A.M.– 7 P.M. daily during daylight saving time and 7 A.M.–5 P.M. during central standard time, $5, reduced fee on Wed., tram tours extra) is a sight to behold: red maple trees, silver and yellow birch trees, and rusty oaks. (Then again, it's gorgeous in spring with all the blooming crab apples, in the summer with the rosebushes.) About a dozen trails wind through this 1,700-acre park, once the estate of a Morton Salt company executive. Trails cut through woodland areas and restored prairies that feature trees, shrubs, and flowers native to Illinois. During a trip down the boardwalk and Bur Reed marsh, you can hear what sounds like hundreds of frogs singing. There's also a herb garden on-site and a restaurant called the Ginkgo.

Cantigny Park

The former estate of *Chicago Tribune* publisher Colonel Robert McCormick has also been transformed into a place for the public to enjoy. **Cantigny Park** (1S151 Winfield Rd., Wheaton, 630/668-5161, www.cantignypark.com, $7 per car for parking, reduced in the evening hours) contains formal gardens, a war museum, and golf course, and hosts outdoor concerts. You could spend hours upon hours here. First, you can learn a little about the history of the estate by stopping by the former horse stables, which have been converted into a visitors center. There you can watch a 10-minute film and pick up a map. Next are the park's two museums. The McCormick museum is basically a tour of some rooms of the main house. The second is a museum extolling the bravery of the soldiers in the First Division. (McCormick commandeered the first battalion during World War I, part of the division.)

Finally, the gardens. Staff and volunteers

wandering through the maze at Morton Arboretum

© CHRISTINE DES GARENNES

maintain about 40 acres of gardens. In the spring literally thousands of tulips are blooming and in the summer the scents of about 800 roses fill the air. In addition to the flowers, staff has added wispy ornamental grasses, vegetable and herb gardens, ponds, a fountain, and a gazebo. Because of its beautiful gardens, Cantigny is a great place to spend half a day. It's rarely mobbed with people, and chances are you can find a quiet spot in the gardens to read or write. When you get hungry, head to the Tack Room Café, an equestrian-themed café that serves sandwiches in indoor and outdoor seating areas. Throughout the summer, at various times and days, the park hosts concerts in the estate's band shell or First Division museum. Concerts are free, but you still have to pay for parking.

In February, the park and grounds are open 9 A.M.–sunset Friday–Sunday, and the museums are open 10 A.M.–4 P.M. Friday–Sunday. March–Memorial Day, the park and grounds are open 9 A.M.–sunset Tuesday–Sunday, and the museums are open 10 A.M.–4 P.M. Tuesday–Sunday. June–August, the park is open 9 A.M.–sunset and the museums 10 A.M.–5 P.M.

Tuesday–Sunday; September–December the museums close at 4 P.M. Cantigny Park is closed in January.

Adjacent to Cantigny Park is its golf course, containing three nine-hole courses (27W270 Mack Rd., Wheaton, 630/668-3323, www.cantignygolf.com, $30 for nine holes, $85 for 18 holes).

Forest Preserves

At **Herrick Lake Forest Preserve** (Butterfield and Herrick Rds., just west of Arrowhead Golf Course and about one mile west of Naperville Rd., Wheaton, 630/933-7200, www.dupage-forest.com, open one hour after sunrise to one hour after sunset), more than six miles of limestone trails wind through Herrick Lake, with additional trails connecting it to nearby Danada and Blackwell forest preserves. On these trails you can hike or bike past woodlands, meadows, and marshy areas. In the winter several miles are groomed for cross-country skiing. At the center of the preserve is 21-acre Herrick Lake, surrounded by a handful of smaller lakes, where you can fish for bass and crappie. Herrick Lake rents canoes and rowboats by the hour and a concession stand sells drinks and snacks during the summer.

Next to Herrick Lake is another large Du Page County forest preserve, **Danada Forest Preserve and Equestrian Center** (35501 Naperville Rd., Wheaton, 630/668-6012, www.dupageforest.com). Before it became a forest preserve Danada was the estate of a wealthy Du Page family that raised racehorses. The farm estate consisted of an apple orchard, mansion, greenhouse, and riding stables. Today much of the estate remains, and there is still a focus on horses. Hayrides and sleigh rides are offered throughout the year at the Equestrian Center (open 9 A.M.–5 P.M. daily). And at the annual Fall Festival in October, visitors show various breeds and demonstrate riding styles. The preserve has three miles of trails for riding horses, hiking, jogging, or cross-country skiing, plus a display farm contains agricultural machinery and exhibits about the agricultural history of the county. Like Herrick Lake, Danada has property that runs through prairie, woodlands, and wetland areas.

A hidden gem in Wheaton is the **Lincoln Marsh Natural Area** (accessible from Harrison, Jewel, and Gary Aves., Wheaton, 630/871-2857). With just over 130 acres, the marsh is not nearly as vast as some of the forest preserves in the area, but it's a good detour while in the area. There are a quiet, short boardwalk trail through the marsh and a side trail through the restored prairie and wooded areas. The Illinois Prairie Path connects to trails within the marsh.

Other Parks
Railroad aficionados will want to drop by the town of Lisle's **Lisle Station Park** (915-925 School St., Lisle, 630/968-0499 or 630/968-2747, www.wwww.lisleparkdistrict.com). The park contains an 1881 wooden caboose, a railroad depot that dates to 1874, model trains, and gardens.

Billy Graham and Wheaton College
Billy Graham, who attended Wheaton College, is revered at the **Billy Graham Center**

Museum on Campus of Wheaton College (500 E. College Ave., Wheaton, 630/752-5905, www.wheaton.edu, 9:30 A.M.–5:30 P.M. Mon.–Sat., 1–5 P.M. Sun., donation). There's biographical information about Graham here, but also plenty about evangelism in general and how it developed in this country. In another exhibit, *Walk through the Gospel,* visitors, as the name implies, walk through a series of displays that illustrate major events written about in the gospel.

Entertainment
From June to August, several theater and music students from the College of Du Page and members of area community theater groups perform in the **McAninch Arts Center** (College of Du Page campus, Fawell and Park Blvds., Wheaton, 630/942-4000, www.atthemac.org, prices vary but generally range $10–30). Shows run the gamut, from Shakespeare's *As You Like It* to the musical *Into the Woods.*

Events
Held in early July, the **Eyes to the Skies Balloon Festival** (Community Park, Hwy. 53 and Short St., Lisle, 630/963-428, www.eyestotheskiesfestival.com, $8) entails about 20 hot air balloons taking off from the festival grounds captained by mostly Midwestern pilots. Balloons are in the shapes of footballs, the Energizer bunny, Felix the Cat, and yes, even a bottle of Jack Daniel. They launch early in the morning (around 5:30 A.M.) and early evening (around 6:30 P.M.), when it tends to be less windy and the skies are clear. Around 8:30 P.M. organizers light balloons for the balloon glow. Also on the festival grounds are dozens of arts and crafts booths, carnival rides, food vendors, and musicians. Past performers have included Davy Jones of The Monkees and The Spin Doctors (remember them?).

Golf
Run by the Wheaton Park District, **Arrowhead Golf Club** (26W151 Butterfield Rd., Wheaton, 630/653-5800, www.wheatonparkdistrict.com, 9 A.M.–dusk Mon., Tues.,

and Thurs., 9 A.M.–9 P.M. Wed. and Fri., 8 A.M.–dusk Sat. and Sun.) has 27 holes, plus a driving range. The courses are sandwiched between parks and wooded areas. Tee times are required on weekends and holidays. During the winter, staff groom cross-country ski trails and rent skis.

Accommodations

The Ⓜ **Wheaton Inn Bed and Breakfast** (301 W. Roosevelt Rd., Wheaton, 630/690-2600 or 800/447-4667, www.wheatoninn.com) may have the words "bed and breakfast" attached to its name, but the inn does not have the feel of a bed-and-breakfast. With 16 rooms, it does not feel as if you are living in someone's house, as is the case with some bed-and-breakfasts. Some rooms come with fireplaces, some with whirlpool tubs. In addition to the breakfast, the staff serve wine and cheese in the afternoons and cookies in the evenings.

Holiday Inn Glen Ellyn (1250 Roosevelt Rd., Glen Ellyn, 630/629-6000) is a 120-room hotel with outdoor heated pool. It's near I-88 and I-355, shopping centers, and grocery stores.

OAK BROOK
Graue Mill and Museum

Oak Brook is home to McDonald's, the sizeable Oak Brook Mall, and plenty of other shopping centers and office towers, so it does seem a bit odd that there is an actual, operating gristmill there, just off I-294. The Graue Mill and Museum (York and Spring Rds., Oak Brook, 630/655-2090, www.grauemill.org, 10 A.M.–4:30 P.M. Tues.–Sun. mid-April–mid-Nov.), listed on the National Register of Historic Places, is at Salt Creek in a brick building constructed in 1852. The working waterwheel gristmill is reportedly the only one operating in Illinois. The mill itself is interesting (as are the demonstrations on stone- and grain-grinding techniques), but what happened under the mill is worthy of note. The miller, Frederick Graue, housed slaves here as they made their way across the United States on the Under-

ground Railroad. An exhibit discusses this connection, as well as the claim that Abraham Lincoln stopped by the mill at one point. On the weekends, you might catch one of the regional history lectures or talks on the Underground Railroad occasionally held at the mill. In addition, staff or guests conduct craft workshops, such as on weaving. Next to the mill is the house where the Graue family lived, an Italianate house renovated for its 150th anniversary in 2002. Fresh-ground cornmeal is for sale in the museum shop.

Czech Museum

A variety of crystal, dolls, and folk costumes are on view at the little **Czechoslovak Heritage Museum** (122 W. 22nd St., Oak Brook, 630/472-9909, www.csafraternallife.org, 1 –4 P.M. Mon.–Fri., free). The museum has a research area for people searching for information on their Czech, Slovak, or Moravian ancestors, such as immigration documents and other historical documents.

Performing Arts

The flashy **Drury Lane Theatre** (100 Drury Ln., near Oakbrook Mall, Oak Brook, 630/530-8300, www.drurylaneoakbrook.com, $25–44) tends to host Broadway revivals such as *Fiddler on the Roof* and well-known children's theater or Neil Simon comedies. The theater, which seats almost 1,000, is lavish, with plush, red seats and several large chandeliers.

Oakbrook Center

Not as crowded or as large as Woodfield Mall, but with many of the same department stores, **Oakbrook Center** (Hwy. 83 and 22nd St., Oak Brook, 630/573-0700, www.oakbrookcenter.com, hours vary, but generally 10 A.M.–9 P.M. Mon.–Sat., 11 A.M.–6 P.M. Sun.) is an upscale outdoor mall, much like Old Orchard on the North Shore. There are 160 shops and 18 restaurants. Department stores include Neiman Marcus, Lord and Taylor, Marshall Field's, and specialty shops include Banana Republic, J. Crew, Crate and Barrel, and an Apple computer store. The shopping center is just off I-294 and I-88.

Polo

Sunday polo at the **Oak Brook Polo Grounds** (700 Oak Brook Rd., Oak Brook, 630/990-2394, www.chicagopolo.com, 1 P.M. Sun. mid-June–mid-Sept., $10) has been a tradition in Oak Brook since 1922. Local and international players compete on the grounds of the exclusive Oak Brook Sports Core, part of the Oak Brook Bath and Tennis Club. Some might consider the atmosphere to be clubby and preppy, but you don't need to be royalty or a member of the club to attend a match. So if you're in the area and have never seen a game of polo, here's your chance.

Accommodations

Shoppers will want to stay at the **Hilton Garden Inn Oakbrook Terrace** (1000 Drury Ln., Oakbrook Terrace, 630/941-1177, www.hiltongardeninn.com). Oakbrook Center is just steps away from this hotel, as is Drury Lane, a dinner theater complex.

ELMHURST
Wilder Park

In the 1990s the little (compared with the Chicago Art Institute or Milwaukee Art Museum) **Elmhurst Art Museum** (150 Cottage Hill Ave., Elmhurst, 630/834-0202, www.elmhurstartmuseum.org, 10 A.M.–4 P.M. Tues., Thurs., Sat., 1–8 P.M. Wed., 1–4 P.M. Fri. and Sun., $4, free Tues.) scored quite the collector's piece: the **McCormick House,** a house designed by famed modern architect Ludwig Mies van der Rohe. The house, with its telltale van der Rohe qualities of low ceilings, straight lines, and plenty of floor-to-ceiling windows, once belonged to Robert H. McCormick and was eventually transported to Wilder Park, where the art museum is. In addition to the McCormick House, the Elmhurst Art Museum has a decent collection of contemporary American art, from large-scale mixed media to watercolor paintings. The museum has a number of exhibitions each year, plus talks by visiting artists. At the annual Art in the Park in early May more than 100 artists sell work in Wilder Park.

Also in Wilder Park is the unusual **Lizzadro Museum of Lapidary Art** (220 Cottage Hill, in Wilder Park, Elmhurst, 630/833-1616, www.lizzadromuseum.org, 10 A.M.–5 P.M. Tues.–Sat., 1–5 P.M. Sun., $4, free admission Fri.). Lapidary art involves cutting, polishing, and arranging stones. It was a popular hobby in the 1950s–1970s, and Joseph Lizzadro was one of the most prominent lapidary hobbyists and collectors. His collection encompasses more than 200 carvings made from jade and other stones. There's a cool exhibit on fluorescent rocks, plus other small exhibits showing pieces of ivory or fossils.

Downtown Elmhurst

A highlight of downtown Elmhurst is the **York Theatre** (150 N. York Rd., Elmhurst, 630/834-0675, www.classiccinemas.com, $5–7.50), a Spanish-influenced theater that also features pipe organ music before weekend movies are played. The theater opened in 1924 and since then it has been extensively renovated and keeps Elmhurst's city center alive into the evening, long after the boutiques have closed. It's a beautiful theater, and worth a visit, especially for old-movie-theater buffs. The York shows first-run films and the Tivoli shows second-run movies (about a month or so after they first hit theaters). On the second floor of the theater is the **American Movie Palace Museum** (152 N. York St., Elmhurst, 630/782-1800, www.historictheatres.org, 9 A.M.–4 P.M. Mon.–Fri., free) run by the Theatre Historical Society of America. Volunteers have collected oodles of vintage movie posters, photographs of movie palaces from across the country, and pictures of shows performed in these historic theaters. A centerpiece of the museum is a scale model of the Avalon, a Chicago movie palace that was built in 1927.

Elmhurst City Centre

More information on the shopping district is available by contacting the district office (2 City Centre Plaza, Elmhurst, 630/993-2600, www.elmhurstcitycentre.com).

Textile shops such as **Blue Frog Beads** (136 W. Valette St., No. 2, Elmhurst, 630/530-8558, www.bluefrogbeads.com, 11 A.M.–6 P.M. Mon., Wed., Fri., 11 A.M.–7 P.M. Tues., Thurs., 10 A.M.–4 P.M. Sat., 1–4 P.M. Sun.) and **Have Ewe Any Wool** (120 N. York Rd., Ste. 220, Elmhurst, 630/941-9276, www.haveeweany-wool.com) offer knitting supplies, yarn, classes, and how-to kits.

Gourmet wines, chocolates, and teas are featured at **Tannins** (112 N. York Rd., Elmhurst, 630/834-4800, 11 A.M.–6 P.M. Tues.–Wed., 11 A.M.–7 P.M. Thurs.–Fri., 11 A.M.–5 P.M. Sat.), a storefront shop near the York Theatre. If you are lucky, you will stop by during one of the tastings held here occasionally. Have a seat in an armchair, flip through catalogs, and test your senses.

As the name implies, **Pastries Plus** (129 W. 1st St., Elmhurst, 630/530-2243, 11 A.M.–3 P.M. Mon., 10 A.M.–6 P.M. Tues.–Wed., 10 A.M.–7 P.M. Thurs., 10 A.M.–5:30 P.M. Fri.–Sat.) combines two things few women can resist: gourmet pastries and flowers. The pastry case changes daily and the flowers come in the form of fresh, silk, dried, and arranged on picture frames, in vases, and other objects.

The **Red Dragon** (117 W. 1st St., Elmhurst, 630/832-8326, www.reddragonchinese.com, 11:30 A.M.–9:30 P.M. Mon.–Thurs., 11:30 A.M.–10:30 P.M. Fri.–Sat., 4–9:30 P.M. Sun.) serves affordable Cantonese, Mandarin, and Szechuan dishes for lunch (about $7) and a bit higher for dinner. The restaurant, not exactly a casual restaurant and not yet fine dining, has comfortable red booths where you can enjoy your meal of beef with broccoli, lemon chicken, or a bowl of noodles. Couples will appreciate the "dinner for two" options in which you can share several dishes.

DOWNERS GROVE AND LOMBARD

During the first part of the 20th century, mail-order giant Sears, Roebuck and Co. not only sent out countless articles of clothing and appliances, but kits for homes. These self-assembled, mail-order kit homes came with tens of thousands of parts and were shipped by the railroads to neighborhoods across the country. The idea really caught on in the town of Downers Grove, a town about 18 miles west of Chicago. More than two dozen are here, many of which are in good shape. Most of these homes are within 1–2 miles of the downtown, which is centered around Main and Curtis streets. You can pick up a walking or driving tour map that showcases the homes from Downers Grove Tourism and Events (801 Burlington Ave., Downers Grove, 800/934-0615) or view photographs of some of the homes on the village's website, http://visitor.vil.downers-grove.il.us.

Entertainment

Classic Cinemas operates several restored movie theaters in downtowns throughout the suburbs. Two beautiful theaters in the western suburbs are the **Tivoli Theatre** (5021 Highland Ave., Downers Grove, 630/968-0219, www.classic-cinemas.com, $3), a French-style 1920s-style movie palace where you can listen to the music of a Wurlitzer pipe organ on weekends before the movies roll. You can catch 2-D and 3-D movies on the gigantic movie screen at **Cinemark IMAX Theatre** (6500 Hwy. 53, Woodridge, 630/434-2629, www.cinemark.com, $7–9). On the five-story-tall screen, watch first-run flicks and stunning nature films of gray whales swimming or butterflies migrating. Buy your tickets early; weekend lines can be long here.

Dancers with the well-respected **Salt Creek Ballet School and Company** (98 E. Naperville Rd., Westmont, 630/769-1199, www.saltcreek-ballet.org) perform classical ballet as well as what the company calls "artistically diverse" productions. Previous productions have included *The Nutcracker* (what dance company has not performed this one?) and *Sleeping Beauty.* Performance venues vary, from the College of Du Page in Glen Ellyn to Governors State University in University Park, a south suburb.

Shopping

Downtown Downers Grove, like most downtowns in the Chicago suburbs, is clustered around the Metra station. In Downers Grove, it can be found at the intersection of Main and Curtiss streets. Most of the shops are along Main Street. Downtown Downers Grove is nice in that it is not especially trendy and it has quite a mix of shops, a few slightly upscale boutiques, and a few craft stores in which Grandma should feel comfortable shopping. Along the way you'll find casual Italian restaurants, a hot dog and pizza joint, and a brewery.

Brain Snacks (6208 Main St., Downers Grove, 630/241-1040) is a small shop that stocks primarily mystery and history books, many of them in paperback.

Graham Cracker Comics (5223 Main St., Downers Grove, 630/852-1810) is loaded with, you guessed it, comic books.

The general bookstore in town is **Anderson's Book Shop** (5112 Main St., Downers Grove, 630/963-2665, www.andersonbookshop.com), which also has a shop in Naperville (123 W. Jefferson St., Naperville, 630/355-2665). Anderson's has a decent collection of new fiction and nonfiction, much of it reviewed by staff, a decent travel section, literary journals and magazines, plus children's toys and puzzles. Both stores host frequent author visits and readings.

Yorktown Shopping Center

With department stores such as JCPenney and Target, **Yorktown Shopping Center** (Highland Ave. and Butterfield Rd., Lombard, 630/629-7330, www.yorktowncenter.com, 10 A.M.–9 P.M. Mon.–Fri., 10 A.M.–7 P.M. Sat., 11 A.M.–6 P.M. Sun.) is slightly less ritzy than the Oakbrook mall. Here you can expect international chain shops such as Gap and The Disney Store, plus a movie theater, and several restaurants, such as Bucca di Beppo, a regional chain of family-style Italian restaurants.

Events

Sometimes referred to as Lilac Village, Lombard hosts a popular festival, **Lilac Time,** in early May in the lovely **Lilacia Park** (Parkside and Park Aves., near the Metra train line, Lombard, www.lombardparks.com). This 8.5-acre horticultural park was part of the estate of a family that planted lilac bush after lilac bush after seeing them in Europe in the 1800s. In addition to the lilac bushes, the park, designed by landscape architect Jens Jensen, also contains a butterfly garden. During the annual festival, you can buy lilac flowers and bushes and other plants, watch a parade, and listen to a variety of concerts in the park. You can monitor the flowers' progress on the "Bloom O' Meter" on the park district's website.

Whirlyball

What do you get when you cross bumper cars with a sport resembling lacrosse? Why, Whirlyball! (800 E. Roosevelt Rd., Lombard, 630/932-4800, 800/8WHIRLY or 800/894-4759, www.whirlyball.com, noon–10 P.M. Sun.–Thurs., noon–1 A.M. Fri. and Sat., walk-in price of $10 per person per 30 minutes or $160 per hour for court rental Mon.–Thurs., $180 per hour for Fri., Sat., and holidays.) Imagine two teams with players driving bumper cars, carrying scoops, and shooting a wiffle ball at a backboard. That's Whirlyball. Although many corporations reserve courts for "team building," Whirlyball is also frequented by people in their 20s stopping by after work for a pick-up game (followed by a little time spent at the bar there). Courts are rented out in advance; however, walk-ins are allowed. If you know you want to give Whirlyball a shot, you might want to call in advance to reserve a court or find out when a good time would be to walk in. Children younger than 12 years old are not allowed to play.

Accommodations

The 121-room **Comfort Inn of Downers Grove** (3010 Finley Rd., Downers Grove, 630/515-1500, www.comfortinn.com) is a couple of miles from Morton Arboretum and all of its trails, as well as several major highways (I-355 and I-88). Rooms come with coffeemakers, irons, data ports, and continental breakfast.

St. Therese Shrine

South of Downers Grove is the **National**

Shrine of St. Therese and Carmelite Visitors Center (8501 Bailey Rd., Darien, 630/969-3311, www.saint-therese.org, 10 A.M.–4 P.M. daily), a shrine to Therese Martin, a French Carmelite nun who wrote *Story of a Soul.* Martin, who died at 24 years old of tuberculosis, is known best for her writing about "doing the ordinary with extraordinary love." Admirers of her travel here from around the world to see photographs of her as a child, and to lay eyes on her prayer book and a chair she sat on while in the convent.

THE ILLINOIS PRAIRIE PATH

One of the best bicycling trails in the Chicago region is the Illinois Prairie Path (630/752-0120, www.ipp.org, free), an approximately 60-mile trail along a former railroad bed. The trail (much of it is crushed limestone) attracts serious bicyclists who race by you or parents toddling along with young children. Scattered along the way are picnic tables, benches, restrooms, water fountains, and garbage cans. The trail starts about 20 miles west of Chicago, just west of Maywood, and continues to Wheaton, where a northern section follows through to Elgin and another branch jogs south to Aurora through Naperville. There are dozens of access points along the path. Most Du Page County Forest Preserves have trails that connect to the trail, including Herrick Lake (see *Forest Preserves* in the *Wheaton and Lisle section)* and Blackwell (Butterfield Rd., just west of Winfield Rd.). These are good spots to park because there's always plenty of parking available and there are restrooms nearby. To reach the path from Herrick Lake, you can park at the lot at the southeast corner of Butterfield and Herrick roads. Otherwise, a good spot to start is in Wheaton at Liberty Drive and Carlton Street, near the Metra train line, or at Kline Creek Farm (County Farm and Geneva Rd., Wheaton), where you can bike along the Illinois Prairie Path or backtrack eastward to the Great Western Trail, which runs parallel to St. Charles Road, from Carol Stream to Villa Park.

INFORMATION

DuPage County Convention and Visitors Bureau (915 Harger Rd., Ste. 240, Oak Brook, 800/232-0502, www.dupagecvb.com) is the umbrella tourism organization for most western suburban towns. It publishes an annual travel guide, which contains numerous lodging lists, plus a calendar of events brochure. It does not maintain a visitors center.

In addition, several cities promote their attractions through tourism departments or local chambers of commerce: **Downers Grove Tourism and Events** (801 Burlington Ave., Downers Grove, 800/934-0615); **Elmhurst Visitor and Tourism Department** (630/530-3312, www.elmhurst.org/visitor); **Lisle Convention and Visitors Bureau** (800/733-9811, www.lislecvb.com or www.stayinlisle.com); **Naperville Convention and Visitors Bureau** (212 S. Webster, Naperville, 630/305-7701, 877/23-NAPER or 877/236-2737, www.visitnaperville.com).

Newspaper

Sun Publications publishes weekly and daily newspapers in several suburbs, such as Elgin, Antioch, and Naperville. *The Naperville Sun* (1500 W. Odgen Ave., Naperville, 630/355-8015, www.suburbanchicagonews.com) covers news in Naperville, Downers Grove, and other western suburbs.

SERVICES

Tours

The **Naperville Trolley and Tours** (630/420-2223, www.naperville.net) offers one-hour tours of downtown Naperville and the nearby Naper Settlement.

Hospital

If you're in need of immediate care, you can go to **Advocate Good Samaritan Hospital** (3815 Highland Ave., Downers Grove, 630/275-5900, www.advocatehealth.com).

Libraries

At both of the following libraries you can use

the Internet, flip through magazines, and more: **Downers Grove Library** (1050 Curtiss St., Downers Grove, 630/960-1200, www.downersgrovelibrary.org, 9 A.M.–9 P.M. Mon.–Fri., 9 A.M.–5 P.M. Sat., 1–5 P.M. Sun.) and **Naperville Library** (2035 S. Naper Blvd., Naperville, 630/962-4100, www.naperville-il.org, 9 A.M.–9 P.M. Mon.–Thurs., 9 A.M.–5 P.M. Fri.–Sat., 1–5 P.M. Sun.).

GETTING AROUND
Train
Metra's Burlington Northern Santa Fe Line (312/322-6777, www.metrarail.com) runs from downtown Chicago's Union Station to Aurora, with stops in Brookfield, Hinsdale, Downers Grove (5001 Main St., 630/969-0013), Lisle (1000 Front St., 630/968-3916), Naperville (105 E. 4th Ave., 630/355-4409), and other towns. A one-way ticket from the Downers Grove Main Street station to Chicago's Union Station is $3.70. **Metra's Union Pacific Western Line** runs from downtown Chicago to Geneva with stops in Elmhurst (128 W. 1st St., 630/834-2923), Lombard (9 S. Main St., 630/627-0099), Glen Ellyn (551 Crescent Blvd., 630/469-0353), Wheaton (402 Front St., 630/668-0176), and others. A one-way ticket from Wheaton or Elmhurst to Chicago's Ogilvie Transportation Center is $3.70. On both lines, trains leave about every hour, with more during weekday rush hours, and about every 1–2 hours on weekends and holidays.

Bus
Pace (847/364-7223, www.pacebus.com) runs several bus lines through the western suburbs. Schedules and routes vary per town. Fares generally run $1.50 per ride.

Taxis
For a lift to the airport or hotel, call one of several taxi or limo companies in the area: the **Airtran-O'Hare Shared Ride Limo** (630/961-5500); **Courtesy Cab** (Burlington and Main Sts., Downers Grove, 630/968-1323); or **AM Regional Taxi** (630/971-8888).

Fox River Villages

Situated about 40 miles west of Chicago, the communities along the Fox River until recently were not considered suburbs. These charming villages, especially Geneva and St. Charles, attracted people first for their shops (Geneva has a lot of galleries; St. Charles has plenty of antiques shops). People discovered old homes, tree-lined streets, and opportunities for recreation along the river. (Out here the topography changes and is a bit more hilly than, say, the Wheaton or Elmhurst areas.) Each town has a slightly different character. Geneva could be called the most yuppified of the three with its trendy boutiques and white-tablecloth restaurants. St. Charles, while also quite trendy and wealthy (the historic Hotel Baker is here) is a tad more youthful because it has more bars and restaurants with outdoor seating. Batavia on the southern end is probably the most diverse of the three. It's got a beautiful riverside park, but also a few fast-food restaurants.

SIGHTS
Fermi National Accelerator Laboratory
The fastest particle accelerator in the world is housed in Fermi National Accelerator Laboratory (Kirk Rd. and Pine St., Batavia, 630/840-3000, www.fnal.gov, 8 A.M.–6 P.M. daily, free). It's called the Tevatron, and using this along with other high-tech equipment at Fermi, scientists are essentially examining matter in its smallest form. You can't actually go into any working laboratories, but Fermi does have a science center that explains some of the work being done there. If you don't have any interest in particle acceleration, Fermi is a great place to go for a quiet hike. The laboratory is on a site measuring about 10 square

The Collar Counties

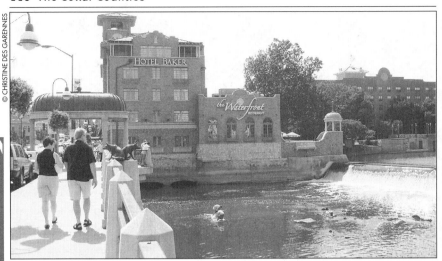

Hotel Baker, along the Fox River in St. Charles

acres. You can hike, bike, or ride horses through the property's many trails, go fishing in one of several ponds, or even check out the herd of buffalo in the restored prairie. In the winter, locals go cross-country skiing through the site.

Downtown Batavia

Just off Wilson and Houston streets in downtown Batavia, the **Batavia Riverwalk** (Houston St. and Island Ave., Batavia, 630/8795235, www.batpkdist.org) consists of a few nature trails winding through a 3.2-acre park on an island in the middle of the Fox River. The area has a few secluded spots for visitors to fish, admire wildflowers, or dip their toes in the water. During the winter, the park district maintains an outdoor ice rink here.

Perhaps the most noticeable attractions along the Riverwalk are several windmills dating from the 1880s to the 1940s. Batavia was once home to several windmill manufacturers and the ones in the park represent steel and wooden models manufactured here. On a sunny, windy day, the red, white, and blue mills are quite a sight.

Dutch Windmill

Speaking of windmills, there's a 68-foot-tall Dutch-style windmill in Geneva off Highway 35 (630/232-2631, open weekends Memorial Day–Labor Day, call for hours). It was built in the western suburbs, and Colonel George Fabyan brought it to Geneva in 1914. It's listed on the National Register of Historic Places.

Homes, Gardens, and Parks

Founded by Colonel Fabyan and his wife Nelle, **Fabyan Villa Museum and Japanese Gardens** (630/232-4811, Illinois 31, 1–4 P.M. Wed., 1–4:30 P.M. Sat.–Sun.) was built at the turn of the 19th century. The star of this 600-acre estate (formerly known as Riverbank) is the villa, redesigned by Frank Lloyd Wright in 1907, and the surrounding gardens. The house contains some local photographs of the area from decades ago.

The picturesque **LeRoy Oaks Forest Preserve** (37W330 Dean St., St. Charles, 630/584-5988) is tucked among 29 acres of woodlands and wetlands and along the babbling Ferson Creek (a perfect spot for cooling off in midsummer.) There are six miles of trails here, with one of those miles paved. Inside the preserve is an 1843 farmhouse, known as the Illinois 31, **Durant House Museum** (630/377-6424, 1–4 P.M. Sun. June

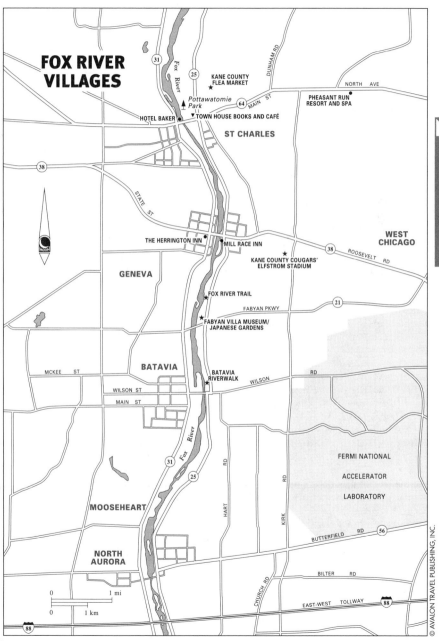

FOX RIVER VILLAGES

KANE COUNTY FLEA MARKET

Pottawatomie Park

PHEASANT RUN RESORT AND SPA

HOTEL BAKER

TOWN HOUSE BOOKS AND CAFÉ

ST CHARLES

WEST CHICAGO

THE HERRINGTON INN

MILL RACE INN

ROOSEVELT RD

KANE COUNTY COUGARS' ELFSTROM STADIUM

GENEVA

FOX RIVER TRAIL

FABYAN PKWY

FABYAN VILLA MUSEUM/ JAPANESE GARDENS

BATAVIA

BATAVIA RIVERWALK

WILSON RD

MCKEE ST

WILSON ST

MAIN ST

FERMI NATIONAL

ACCELERATOR

LABORATORY

MOOSEHEART

BUTTERFIELD RD

NORTH AURORA

BILTER RD

CHURCH RD

EAST-WEST TOLLWAY

0   1 mi

0   1 km

NORTH   AVE

MAIN ST

DUNHAM RD

STATE ST

Fox River

HART RD

KIRK RD

© AVALON TRAVEL PUBLISHING, INC.

15–Nov. 1, 1–4 P.M. Thurs. June 1–Aug. 31, and some Sun. in Feb. Admission is $3). This small house contains a smattering of remnants from the mid-1800s, such as a stove and kitchen table. Also in the preserve is the **Pioneer Sholes School** (1–4 P.M. Sun., June 15–Oct. 15), a one-room schoolhouse containing old school textbooks and other antique educational items.

ENTERTAINMENT AND EVENTS
Film and Performing Arts

A vaudeville playhouse built in 1926, the **Arcada Theatre** (105 E. Main St., St. Charles, 630/845-8900, www.o-shows.com) has been transformed into a multipurpose venue in downtown St. Charles. The theater shows second-run movies for kids and adults. During the evening "brewvies" series, the theater sells beer and wine you can take with you into the theater. Also, local and touring musicians play here and organ concerts have been held in the Arcada.

Headliners at the **Norris Cultural Arts Center** (1040 Dunham Rd., St. Charles, 630/584-7200, www.norriculturalarts.com, gallery open 10 A.M.–4 P.M. Mon.–Fri., 11 A.M.–4 P.M. Sat., free admission to gallery, show prices vary) have included jazzman Ramsey Lewis, the U.S. Air Force band, and the touring company of the comedy troupe Second City. This modern theater seats 1,000 people, and there's an art gallery that tends to highlight the work of regional artists.

The **Steel Beam Theatre** (111 W. Main St., St. Charles, 630/587-8521, www.steelbeamtheatre.com) is a 79-seat theater presenting community theater productions such as Steven Sondheim musicals and Noel Coward comedies.

Pheasant Run Resort and Spa (4051 E. Main St., St. Charles, 800/4-PHEASANT or 800/474-3272, www.pheasantrun.com), hosts dinner theater performances, musicals, comedian visits, and productions from Chicago's Noble Fool Theater Company.

Events

The highlight of the St. Charles **Scarecrow**

DRIVE-IN THEATERS OF ILLINOIS

Collar Counties

Cascade Drive-In (North Ave., 1.5 miles east of Hwy. 59, West Chicago, 630/231-3150 or 630/231-3151, www.cascadedrivein.com)
Hi-Lite 30 Drive-In (Montgomery and Hill Rd., Aurora, 630/898-5888, www.novacinemas.com)

Grand Prairie

Harvest Moon (Hwy. 47, Gibson City, 217/784-8770 or 877/54-MOVIE or 877/546-6843)
Route 66 Drive-In (Knight's Action Park, 1700 Recreation Dr., Springfield, 217/698-0066)
Skyview Drive-In (Route 66, Litchfield, 217/324-4451, www.litchfieldskyview.com)

Illinois and Mississippi Rivers Valley

Clark 54 Twin Pike Drive-In (U.S. 54 W, Summer Hill, 217/285-2805)
Skyview Drive-In (5700 N. Belt W, Belleville, 618/233-4400, www.skyview-drive-in.com)

Northern Hill Country

Midway Drive-In (91 Prairieville Rd., Dixon, 815/625-4099)
34 Drive-In (Old Hwy. 34, Earlville, 815/246-9700, www.rt34drive-in.com)

Southern Illinois

Fairview Drive-In (16045 Hwy. 33, Newton, 618/455-3100)

Festival (Lincoln Park, Main and 4th Sts., and throughout downtown St. Charles, www.scarecrowfest.com, early Oct., free) is row after row of scarecrows (more than 100 every year) crafted by area residents. In addition to the scarecrows, expect fall goodies such as apple muffins, and arts and craft booths.

For more than two decades **Pride of the Fox RiverFest** (held throughout St. Charles, 630/584-8415, www.prideofthefox.com, free) has featured live music, dance groups, carnival rides, and food tents. But perhaps the most interesting part of the fair is the dragon-boat racing. A Chinese tradition, dragon-boat racing involves teams of 18 paddlers racing along the river in hand-painted boats with dragon heads. They race for about 3,330 yards, with the participants paddling the water and beating drums.

SHOPPING

Geneva

Geneva's main shopping district is around 3rd Street, although you will find little storefront boutiques or galleries inside the first floors of restored homes from the 19th century throughout the town.

Like many shops in Geneva, **The Little Traveler** (404 S. 3rd St., 630/232-4200) is set up in a Victorian home. Each room is stocked with clothing and home-decor items from countries around the globe.

You can rent a bike, have your tire fixed, or buy tools and travel kits at **Mill Race Cyclery** (11 E. State St., Geneva, 630/232-2833, 10 A.M.–6 P.M. Mon.–Fri., 10 A.M.–5 P.M. Sat., noon–5 P.M. Sun.). Another shop is in Oswego.

St. Charles

Whereas the town of Geneva has countless boutiques and galleries, St. Charles has antiques shops and streetside shopping malls.

About two dozen shops are housed under one roof on the first block of 3rd Street. Known as the **3rd Street Shops,** they contain for the most part antiques dealers. You can find used books, furniture, china collections, and other collectibles here.

St. Charles Century Corners (Main St. and 2nd Ave., www.centurycorners.com) is a string of beautiful shops along the east side of the Fox River, from Highway 64 to State Avenue.

Town House Books and Café (105 N. 2nd Ave., St. Charles, 630/584-8600 and 630/584-8603—café, www.townhousebooks.com, 9 A.M.–5 P.M. Mon.–Sat., Thurs. until 8 P.M., 10:30 A.M.–4 P.M. Sun.) is an independent bookseller with a homey and collegiate atmosphere (within walking distance of other shops and restaurants). The shop features staff picks and the usual author signings. But Town House will take the author visits one step further, such as an inclusive dinner with an author. Inside it has a café that cooks up more than just good shots of espresso; it also offers sandwiches and brunch fare. Try the roasted chicken with apricots. In the evenings the café becomes a wine bar. Have a seat in the outdoor courtyard to begin reading the new book or magazine.

Stone House on Cedar (201 Cedar Ave., St. Charles, 630/762-0762, 10 A.M.–5 P.M. Mon., Tues., Wed., Fri., 10 A.M.–8 P.M. Thurs., noon–5 P.M. Sun.) specializes in functional art. This includes modular colored glass vases, primitive antiques, and writing journals made with handmade paper.

West of the Fox River is the old town commercial district known as **Old St. Charles** (Main and 3rd Sts., St. Charles) where more antiques markets have set up shop.

Flea Market

You could spend hours browsing over the oodles and oodles of antiques and collectibles for sale at the **The Kane County Flea Market** (Hwy. 64 and Randall Rd., St. Charles, 630/377-2252, www.kanecountyfleamarket.com, noon–5 P.M. Sat., 7 A.M.–4 P.M. Sun., schedule varies per year, but is generally the first weekend of the month, $5). Hundreds and hundreds of vendors set up tables under tents and in the buildings of the Kane County Fairgrounds for this hugely popular flea market. The flea market is one great treasure hunt for thousands of people each month. You can find everything from high-end furniture, linens, and glassware to boxes of cassette tapes from the 1980s. Parking is free, but you have to pay to get in.

SPORTS AND RECREATION

Multiuse Recreation Trails

The Fox River Trail runs along the river for roughly 30 miles between Algonquin and Aurora and is used by bicyclists, runners, in-line skaters, and walkers. The northern half is on the eastern shore of the Fox. At Fabyan Parkway, halfway between Geneva and Batavia, it crosses the river and follows the west shoreline until Aurora. In Geneva it connects with the Illinois Prairie Path, an approximately 60-mile trail through the western suburbs. As it snakes along the river, The Fox River Trail passes through several Kane County forest preserves and municipal parks.

Parks

Tekakwitha Woods (35W06 Villa Marie Rd., St. Charles, 847/741-8350, www.co.kane.il.us, 8 A.M.–sunset daily, free) is a 65-acre park at a bend in the Fox River. Before it became a county forest preserve, Tekakwitha, which is on the east side of the river, belonged to the Catholic Church and for decades retreats were held in its secluded setting. Because of its secluded nature, this park is a good, quiet spot for birders (staff also have set up several bird feeders). There's also a nature center here and about six miles of trails through the woods and ravines.

The first public park in Illinois, **Pottawatomie Park** (half mile north of Main St. on 2nd Ave., St. Charles, 630/584-1028, www.st-charlesparks.org) is on the east side of the Fox River near downtown St. Charles. At Pottawatomie you can catch a ride on a paddlewheel boat, rent canoes, play nine holes of golf, or sun alongside the swimming pool.

Baseball

You can't beat a baseball game in the summertime, and the **Kane County Cougars** (Elfstrom Stadium, 34W002 Cherry Ln., Geneva, 630/232-8811, www.kccougars.com, $7–9) never disappoint, even if they don't win a game. For one thing, an afternoon or evening here won't empty your bank account. Parking is free, and the pork chops and beer for sale in the concessions are not outrageously priced. There are several amusing side shows that are a hit with college kids and those of elementary-school age. Human bowling, for example, entails a person's being strapped inside a giant foam ball and rolled into six-foot plush pins. Roaming through the stands are

cartoon characters such as "Clammy Sosa" (a talking clam) and "Harry Canary" (a talking bird). The Cougars are affiliates of the Oakland A's, and some of the players have gone on to major league teams in the region, such as Joe Borowski of the Chicago Cubs. Take your pick of lawn seats, which are sold as general admission on a first-come, first-served basis, bleacher seats, or box seats. More than two dozen games throughout the summer are concluded by free fireworks shows.

Amusement Parks

Just off I-88, **Funway Entertainment Center** (1335 S. River St., Batavia, 630/879-8717, www.funwaybatavia.com, April–Sept.) has all the makings of paradise for preteens: go-carts, bumper boats, miniature golf, and batting cages.

ACCOMMODATIONS

Accommodations aren't cheap in the Fox River valley. But look here and you'll see you get a lot of what you pay for: luxury.

$100–150

The former country estate of a Chicago banker was transformed into a bed-and-breakfast called the **Oscar Swan Inn** (1800 W. State St., Geneva, 630/232-0173, www.oscarswan.com), a large brick home with an expansive lawn and eight rooms, some with private baths. Decorated modestly, it's along the Lincoln Highway (Highway 38) on the west end of town.

$150–250

Overlooking the Fox River and within walking distance of parks, antiques shops, and a variety of restaurants, is **M Hotel Baker** (100 W. Main St., St. Charles, 630/584-2100, www.hotelbaker.com, $152–172). Listed on the National Register of Historic Places, it opened in 1928 and has had notables including Louis Armstrong and John F. Kennedy stop by. It's a brick building with a patio and rose garden. Rooms come with data ports and whirlpool tubs. Luxury suites are also available. The Trophy Room restaurant serves steaks and seafood in a dining room overlooking the Fox River. It's awe-inspiring.

The Herrington Inn (15 S. River Ln., Geneva, 630/208-7433, www.herringtoninn.com, $165–230) is a 61-room riverside spa inn, if you can imagine such a wonderful place. With fireplaces, nightly turn-down service, and whirlpool tubs, this is a place for relaxation. The cheapest room ($164 during the week) is certainly not skimpy. It comes with a whirlpool and private balcony that overlooks the courtyard. Premiere suites can cost up to almost $400 per night. The hotel's restaurant, Atwater, also overlooks the Fox River.

Designed in Prairie-style, **Pheasant Run Resort and Spa** (4051 E. Main St., St. Charles, 800/4-PHEASANT or 800/474-3272, www.pheasantrun.com, $189) is a golf and spa resort with 473 rooms (some with whirlpools), performance spaces, and several restaurants onsite. Brush up on the sticks by hitting the 18-hole golf course, order massages and pedicures, and lift some weights at the fitness center. The latest dining addition to the resort is **Harvest,** a restaurant and bar serving American food in a renovated barn.

FOOD
American
𝗡 Mill Race Inn (4 E. State St., Geneva, 630/232-2030, www.themillraceinn.com) dates as a restaurant (it started as a tea room, actually) to 1933. With views of the river, this not-too-fancy country restaurant has great views of the Fox River. Lots of good comfort food here: slow roasted pot roast that's great during the cold months, simple open-faced sandwiches, and more complex pecan-encrusted fish fillets. Lunches are $7–17, and dinners $18–25.

A good quick place to grab a turkey or ham sandwich is **Smitty's on the Corner,** a deli in downtown St. Charles (15 E. Main St., St. Charles, 630/762-1080, 8–7 Sun.–Thurs., 8–10 Fri.–Sat., $6).

During the warm months, **𝗡 The Filling Station Pub and Grill** (300 W. Main St., St. Charles, 630/584-4414, www.filling-station.com, $6–9, 11–1 A.M. Mon.–Thurs., 11–2 A.M. Fri.–Sat., 11 A.M.–10 P.M. Sun.) is a decent spot to chow down on big hamburgers, lots of crispy fries, and share a pitcher of beer with friends. Near downtown St. Charles, within walking distance of the river and shops, the Filling Station is a casual, festive place with good food and good prices. It's reminiscent of roadside eateries that were common along the Lincoln Highway. As a tribute to that era, try the "58 Edsel Dog," a beef hot dog loaded with cheese, onions, and chili.

In addition, Hotel Baker, The Herrington Inn, and Pheasant Run Resort and Spa all have well-appointed restaurants on their grounds.

Mexican
El Taco Grande (6 N. River St., Batavia, 630/406-8415, lunch and dinner) is a casual spot near the Fox River where you can buy large plates of cheesy enchiladas or *tortas* (sandwiches).

Markets
You can buy picnic supplies at the **Blue Goose** (164 S. 1st St., St. Charles, 630/584-0900, www.bluegoosemarket.com, $6–18), on the west side of the Fox River, near downtown and the Fox River Trail. Blue Goose stocks juicy, ripe produce and has a good selection of deli meats and cheeses.

INFORMATION
The following chambers of commerce maintain shopping, dining, and lodging guides to their towns, as well as links to local festival information: **Geneva Chamber of Commerce** (8 S. 3rd St., Geneva, 630/232-6060 or 866/4-GENEVA—866/443-6382, www.genevachamber.com); **St. Charles Convention and Visitors Bureau** (311 N. 2nd St., Ste. 100, St. Charles, 630/377-6161 or 800/777-4373, www.visitstcharles.com); and **Batavia Chamber of Commerce** (100

N. Island Ave., Batavia, 6320/879-7134, www.bataviachamber.org).

SERVICES

Tours

Admire the Fox River aboard a paddlewheel boat. The *St. Charles Belle* and *Fox River Queen* (Pottawatomie Park, 2nd St., just north of State Ave., St. Charles, 630/584-2334, www.st-charlesparks.org) offer tours May–October and depart from the east side of the river.

GETTING AROUND

Train

Metra's Union Pacific Western Line runs from downtown Chicago to Geneva (station at 328 Crescent Pl., 630/232-0852, www.metrarail.com) with stops along the way in Lombard, Elmhurst, and other western suburbs. A one-way ticket from Geneva to Chicago's Ogilvie Transportation Center is $4.90. Trains leave about every hour, with more during weekday rush hours, and about every 1–2 hours on weekends and holidays.

Elgin

A diverse city on the Fox River, Elgin suffered from an image problem for many years. North of the Fox River Villages of St. Charles, Geneva, and Batavia, Elgin is not only a bigger city, but it has an industrial and manufacturing past (Elgin watches were made here) that doesn't make this blue-collar city as quaint as its neighbors to the south. In recent years, however, economic development has picked up a bit and people are rediscovering the city, especially taking to the affordable, Victorian-style homes and refinishing them. Downtown the main highlight is the riverboat casino, a blessing or a curse (depending on whom you talk to) to the city and region.

SIGHTS

Parks and Museums

You name it, **Lord's Park** (100 Oakwood, Elgin, 847/931-6120) has got it: a museum, petting zoo, pavilion, swimming pool, tennis courts, and more. This park, more than 100 years old, is named after a manager of the Elgin National Watch Factory and a former mayor. During the summer the park district sponsors free concerts on occasional Sunday afternoons at the Lord's Park pavilion. Also inside the park is the **Elgin Public Museum of Natural History and Anthropology** (Lord's Park, 225 Grand Blvd., Elgin, 847/741-6655, www.elginpublicmuseum.org, noon–4 P.M. Tues.–Sun., $2).

Listed on the National Register of Historic Places, the **Elgin Area Historical Society and Museum** (360 Park St., Elgin, 847/742-4248, noon–4 P.M. Wed.–Sat. March–Dec., $2) is in the former Elgin Academy (once connected to Northwestern University). Here you'll find a number of local-history exhibits, including lots of information on the watch company as well as amusing and intriguing photographs of the city from the past, such as a bridge collapsing from the weight of a herd of cattle in 1896. Got an Elgin watch and curious how much it's worth? The society will appraise it for a fee.

Fire Barn No. 5 (533 St. Charles St., Elgin, 847/931-1960, open weekends, call for hours) is an unexpected gem of a museum south of Elgin's downtown. Built in 1904, the classical-revival–style firehouse was decommissioned in 1991 and has been remade into a little museum with restored fire engines, vintage firefighter uniforms, and photographs.

The **South Elgin Trolley Museum** (361 S. LaFox St., South Elgin, 847/697-4676, www.foxtrolley.org, $2–7) has an impressive collection of vintage street cars, Pullman cars, engines, and cabooses. Highlights of the collection include a street railcar used to deliver mail in Chicago, Chicago Transit Authority cars from the 1950s, and a Soo Line caboose from 1887. Visitors board a train and take a four-mile ride along the Fox River Line, a line that used to run for 40 miles from Carpenter to Yorkville along the Fox River. The museum holds special events throughout the year, such as on Father's Day. The museum is open 11 A.M.–5 P.M. Sunday May–Nov., 11 A.M.–5 P.M. Saturday from the end of June–August. It's also open Memorial Day, Fourth of July, and Labor Day.

Grand Victoria Casino
You won't see it actually cruising down the Fox River, but Grand Victoria Casino (250 S. Grove Ave., Elgin, 847/468-7000, www.grandvictoria-elgin.com, 8:30 A.M.–6:30 A.M.) is technically a riverboat casino. Inside are rows upon rows of slot machines (more than 1,000 machines), video poker machines, plus tables of blackjack, craps, and roulette. If you need a break from gambling there are several restaurants (a steak and seafood restaurant, buffet, sandwich café) and some shops. Everyone must be 21 years old to enter the casino.

EVENTS AND ENTERTAINMENT
Performing Arts
The **Hemmens Cultural and Performing Arts Center** (150 Dexter Ct., 45 Symphony Way, Elgin, 847/931-5900, box office open 10 A.M.–4 P.M. Mon.–Fri., noon–4 P.M. Sat.) has had jazz, country, blues, rock, and bluegrass musicians, such as David Sanborn and the Cowboy Junkies, play here, as well as comedians, such as Paul Rodriguez. The 1,200-seat theater is on the Fox River and within walking distance of downtown shops and restaurants.

There are several other community theater and music groups that perform around the area. They include **Elgin Community Theatre** (355 E. Chicago St., Elgin, 847/741-0532) and the **Symphony Orchestra** (20 Du Page Ct., Elgin, 847/888-4000). Throughout the year students and visiting musicians take the stage in **Elgin Community College's Visual and Performing Arts Center** (1700 Spartan Dr., Elgin 847/622-0300).

Talisman Theatre (Wing Park band shell, 1000 Wing St., Elgin, 847/622-0300, www.tal-ismantheatre.org) produces Shakespeare in the Park during the summer.

Events
Held in mid-August, Elgin's **Fine Arts Fest** (Civic Center Plaza, 150 Dexter Ct., Elgin, 847/692-4000) brings out hundreds of juried artists, local food vendors, and music performers.

SHOPPING
State Street Market Shops (701 N. State St., Elgin, 847/695-3066, www.statestreetmarket.com, 10 A.M.–5 P.M. Tues., Wed., Fri., Sat., 10 A.M.–8 P.M. Thurs., 11 A.M.–5 P.M. Sun.) has a little more than 30 specialty shops, including gourmet food, costume jewelry, kitchen supplies, and a few collections such as cookie jars and glassware.

Schock's Greenhouse (508 N. McLean Blvd., Elgin, 847/742-7635) lies alongside a creek. You can buy flower bouquets and plants here. Also on the property: Our House Antiques, in the former home of one of the original owners of the greenhouse, which sells antiques, but also serves coffee, cookies, and slices of cake. Schock's also hosts occasional events on the property, such as musical concerts, theater productions, or weddings.

RECREATION
The Fox River Trail follows the river for about 30 miles from Algonquin to Aurora. For more information, see *Recreation* under Fox River Villages. Canoeists can launch their boats at **Blackhawk Forest Preserve** (35W003 Hwy. 31, South Elgin, 847/741-7883, www.kane.co.il.us), another park along the Fox River. From Blackhawk you can float southward to St. Charles's Ferson Creek Park, about four miles downriver, where there is also a boat launch. Or you can go all the way to Les Arends on the west shore or Glenwood Park on the east shore in North Aurora. Otherwise, there's plenty to do at Blackhawk, a 289-acre park with three miles of trails, including a

mowed grass trail for horseback riding. Plus, the Fox River Trail comes through here.

ACCOMMODATIONS

The bulk of Elgin's lodging options are clustered around the city's exits at I-90. Rates run $60–125 per night. Here are a few: **Country Inn and Suites by Carlson** (2270 Point Blvd., Elgin, 847/426-6400); and **Hampton Inn** (Airport Rd., Elgin, 847/931-1940.)

Camping

Burnidge and Paul Wolff Forest Preserve (campground is one mile west of Randall Rd. on Big Timber Rd., Elgin, 847/888-1361, www.co.kane.il.us) has 67 campsites (19 tent, 48 trailer) and the tent sites are in an area separate from the trailers. The forest preserve has 12 miles of mowed trails for horseback riding and a pond stocked with fish.

FOOD

With some of the best malts, milk shakes, and phosphates in the area, **Al's Cafe and Creamery** (43 Du Page Ct., Elgin, 847/742-1180, 11 A.M.–8 P.M. Mon.–Thurs., 11 A.M.–9 P.M. Fri.–Sat., $5) has been whipping up thick, rich dairy treats for decades. But there's more than just

ice cream here. Al's sells sandwiches (some veggie options) and sides such as sweet potato fries. The café is within walking distance of the river.

Also near the Fox River is **Mary's Market Café** (701 N. State St., Elgin, 847/741-6003, 10 A.M.–5 P.M. Tues., Wed., Fri., Sat., 10 A.M.–8 P.M. Thurs., 11 A.M.–5 P.M. Sun.). Mary's is another great casual sandwich-beverage café. Try the dilled egg salad sandwich or ham and apple grilled cheese, with an iced tea or coffee drink.

At **Randy's Vegetables** (15N440 Randall Rd., one quarter mile north of I-90, Elgin, 847/428-5244), you can roam the fields looking for the perfect pumpkin and buy flowers, gardening tools, and jars of jellies and jams.

GETTING AROUND

Train

Metra's Union Pacific Western Line runs from downtown Chicago to Geneva (station at 328 Crescent Pl., 630/232-0852, www.metrarail.com) with stops along the way in Lombard, Elmhurst, and other western suburbs. A one-way ticket from Geneva to Chicago's Ogilvie Transportation Center is $4.90. Trains leave about every hour, with more during weekday rush hours, and about every 1–2 hours on weekends and holidays.

Lake County

With sand dunes on the Lake Michigan coastline, a rare bog to the west, a historic village to the south, and a chain of lakes to the north, Lake County contains some of the most picturesque landscapes in all of Chicagoland. You can walk the nature trails in popular Illinois Beach State Park or Volo Bog. Rent a rowboat and paddle out on one of the Chain O' Lakes. Or, for a change of pace, drain your checking account at the huge Gurnee Mills mall and test your will at Six Flags Great America.

CHAIN O' LAKES AND GRAYSLAKE

Chain O' Lakes State Park

Formed by retreating glaciers thousands of years ago, the lakes that make up this region all came about naturally, unlike many of the big lakes in the rest of the state. **Chain O' Lakes State Park** (8906 Wilmot Rd., Spring Grove, 847/587-5512, www.dnr.state.il.us, 6 A.M.–9 P.M. daily in the summer, 8 A.M.–sunset in the winter), a few miles south of the state line, has about 3,000 acres of woods and prairie and nearly 6,500 acres of water. Most of that is freshwater bog over peat deposits. The state park offers access to some of these lakes, including Grass Lake, a 44-acre lake that was famous for its blooming lotuses (you can still see some in the backwater areas), plus Maria and Nippernik lakes. These lakes lead to the Fox River, which runs south through theeastern part of the park and connects to seven other lakes. You could spend a lot of time in your boat exploring these lakes. Fishing and boating is the thing to do for area residents and the lake can get a little loud as speedboats zoom by on sunny summer days.

Instead, take the quiet route. One of the most relaxing ways to see the park is by renting a canoe or rowboat from the park's concession stand and paddling out through some of the low-lying grassy areas of the lake, where you can listen to frogs and birds singing. Another great option is renting a horse from the park's stables and hitting the eight-mile-long equestrian trail on the west side of the park. Other trails include a 2.5-mile nature trail near the campgrounds and a bike (or in-line skating) trail throughout much of the park. You'll trek through oak and hickory and birch forests, restored prairie, and bogs. These trails, by the way, can be used for cross-country skiing in the winter.

Chain O' Lakes State Park offers what the department of natural resources calls "rent a tent." For a fee you camp in a tent or rent a cabin and the park supplies you with the necessary camping accessories (lanterns, etc.). Cabins come with bunk beds and a double bed and rent for about $45 per night. If you rent the tent, it'll cost $23, plus a $5 reservation fee. If you have your own tent, it'll cost $5. There are also electrical campsites for RVs. A word of caution: The park is open only to deer and waterfowl hunters early November–mid-December.

Volo Bog State Natural Area
South of Chain O' Lakes State Park is a treasure of a natural area, Volo Bog State Natural Area

(28478 W. Brandenburg Rd., Ingleside, 815/344-1294, www.dnr.state.il.us). A National Natural Landmark, Volo Bog is a quaking bog; it has a floating layer of moss at the edges and fresh water in the middle. Like the nearby lakes, the bog was formed when the Wisconsin glacier (the last glacier in the region) started melting and retreating, depositing sand, rocks, and blocks of ice. The ice eventually melted and formed marshes, ponds, and lakes. Volo Bog was originally a deep lake, but because of poor drainage several thousands of years ago vegetation such as sphagnum moss started growing in it, eventually forming a layer of peat around the edges. Eventually cattails, sedges, shrubs, and tamaracks grew around it. In the 1960s, the bog was almost plowed over for development, but area citizens rallied to protect it and helped the Illinois Department of Natural Resources buy the land.

The total site is about 1,100 acres; Volo Bog itself is a little less than 50 acres. There are also two smaller bogs nearby. A half-mile interpretive trail on a floating boardwalk has signs that explain how bogs form. The tamarack view trail, almost three miles long, weaves throughout the site, up and down sloping areas, through woods and wetlands. Because the bog's water is acidic (because of the presence of moss), rare plants thrive here. Look for orchids. You might also be able to spot some herons and sandhill cranes. Before you hit the trail, stop by the visitors center in a dairy barn to learn a little about the bog's history (natural and otherwise).

Farm Visit
While you're in the area, visit one of the few remaining farms in the Chicago region, the **The Glunz Berry Farm** (19655 W. Washington St., Grayslake, 847/548-6687) and **Glunz Family Winery** (888 E. Belvidere Rd., Grayslake, 847/548-9463, www.gfwc.com, 10 A.M.–6 P.M. Mon.–Sat., noon–5 P.M. Sun.). At the berry farm you can pick your own raspberries and blackberries (usually in July). And at the winery, sample wine made from raspberries, plus a few other concoctions such as sangria and mulled wine.

Events

Watch dogs perform tricks, listen to 1980s bands play music, and ride a camel. You can do all these things at the **Lake County Fair** (Lake County Fairgrounds, U.S. 45, north of Hwy. 20, Grayslake, www.lakecountyfairassoc.com, end of July, $7). The classic county fair has carnival rides, horse shows, a petting zoo, 4-H exhibits, and lots of fried food and sugar-laden food. Almost 200,000 people visit this weeklong fair.

Information

Check with the **Fox Waterway Agency** (5 S. Pistakee Lake Rd., Fox Lake, 847/587-8540, www.foxwaterway.state.il.us) for lake and river conditions, information about underwater fish cribs, and other hunting and fishing information.

LAKE MICHIGAN SITES

Illinois Beach State Park

Sandy beaches, nature and bike trails, marshland, campgrounds, and a resort—Illinois Beach State Park (main entrance at Sheridan and Wadsworth Rds., Zion, 847/662-4828 or 847/662-4811, www.dnr.state.il.us) seems to have it all. And it is a great park, but Illinois Beach has a past and some neighbors that it just cannot run away from. The park is divided into two sections, north and south, and between them is the Zion nuclear power plant. Towering nuclear reactors (the plant was shut down in 1998) are not exactly a pretty sight while you're sunbathing or on a nature walk. Then, to the south, is a federal Superfund site where asbestos was once manufactured. Asbestos has washed upon the shore in recent years. Oh, and the northern part of the park was a prisoner-of-war camp during the Civil War. If you can get past these things (and apparently many people have as it's the most-visited state park in Illinois), the park is quite beautiful. The 4,000-acre park has trails that weave through wetlands, dune habitat, and woodland areas, free sandy swimming beaches, fishing ponds, and more. In the northern section, between

7th and 21st Streets, you'll find North Point Marina, beaches, and picnic areas. The southern section, between just north of Greenwood Drive and 29th Street, contains more beaches, the resort, campground, interpretive center, and nature center. A bike trail connects the two sections. The campground has 224 electric sites, and some are wooded. Reservations are not required but this is a popular campground and sites fill up fast. Call the park office to reserve a place. As mentioned, chunks of asbestos have been known to wash upon the shore of the beaches, sometimes closing the beach. Just how this type of asbestos affects folks hiking and swimming in the area is up for debate. **Illinois Beach Resort and Conference Center** (Lake Front Dr., Zion, 847/625-7300 or 866/452-3224, www.ilresorts.com) is a modern hotel in the southern part of the park. If the beach is closed or it's cool outside you can swim in the Olympic-size swimming pool or warm up in the sauna. The restaurant, which has tables looking out onto the park, serves breakfast, lunch, and dinner daily. Dinner entrées such as fillets and seafood dishes are around $15.

North Point Marina

You can also swim or sun yourself at the beaches at North Point Marina (701 North Point Dr., Winthrop Harbor, 847/746-2845), a marina and park north of the state park. The marina has 1,500 boat slips, a fishing pier, fish-cleaning facilities, picnic tables and grills, plus two restaurants. Several fishing-boat charter tours depart from North Point Marina. (See *Fishing* in the *Know Illinois* chapter.)

GURNEE, LIBERTYVILLE, AND WADSWORTH

Six Flags Great America

What's a summer if you haven't spent at least one day riding roller coasters? At Six Flags Great America (Hwy. 134 and I-94, Gurnee, 847/249-4636, www.sixflags.com) you have your pick of 12 roller coasters, from the vintage Viper, a wooden coaster, to Raging Bull, a coaster that zips along at as much as 73 miles

THE GOLD PYRAMID HOUSE

As you drive on I-94 near Gurnee, look to the east just north of Great America. Off in the distance stands a statue of Ramses II. Yes, that's right. And there's more. Nearby is a massive replica of the Great Pyramid of Giza. The replica (built at a 1/100 scale) is covered in 24-karat gold, reportedly making it the largest structure in the world covered with 24-karat gold. What else? The six-story, 17,000-square-foot home (yes, it's a private home) has a re-creation of King Tut's tomb and is surrounded by a moat. Tours used to be offered of the home, but the owners have since stopped giving them. At least for now. Still, you can still drive by the home and check it out. It's at 37921 Dilleys Road, Wadsworth. More information is available on the couple's website (www.goldpyramid.com), an online shop that sells Egyptian rugs, papyrus, jewelry, and other items.

per hour and drops as much as 200 feet. And then there's Vertical Velocity, one of those terrifying, spiraling coasters on which riders' feet dangle in the air. Six Flags Great America has plenty of stuff for little kids too, low-to-the-ground coasters, carousels, and people dancing around dressed up like cartoon characters. The biggest change to the park in recent years has been the opening of a separate area called **Hurricane Harbor Water Park,** which opened in spring 2005. It's got the standard water-park features, such as a wave pool, water playground, flume rides, and mat slides.

The park is open May–October. Hours vary each year, but generally during the peak summer season, late June–mid-August, the park is open 10 A.M.–10 P.M. daily. Tickets are $45 and include admission into the theme park and water park. Early season tickets (for May) are a few bucks cheaper. Children under three are free. If you buy and print your tickets from the website you won't have to wait in line at the ticket counter. You can leave and come back the same day; just make sure you stop at the booth and get your hand stamped. There are bank machines in the park. No coolers, food, drink, or other picnic items are allowed. There are restaurants and concession stands in the park. You can rent strollers and wheelchairs.

Gurnee Mills

With more than 200 stores, restaurants, a movie theater, game arcade, and more, Gurnee Mills Mall (6170 W. Grand Ave., Gurnee, 847/263-

8500 or 800/937-7467, www.gurneemills-mall.com) is an exhaustingly large complex. Highlights include **Rink Side Sports** (6152 W. Grand Ave., Gurnee, 847/856-1064, www.rink-sidesports.com), where you can play with pretend guns (laser tag, video games) until the cows come home, and **Bass Pro Shops Outdoor World** (6112 W. Grand Ave., 847/856-1229, www.basspro.com), a 125,000-square-foot store where you can shop for real guns, stop by the archery range, check out fish in giant aquariums, and see how you look in blaze orange. The mall is open 10 A.M.–9 P.M. Monday–Friday, 10 A.M.–9:30 P.M. Saturday, 11 A.M.–7 P.M. Sunday. It's just off I-94 and Grand Ave.

Horse Show

Even if you're not a horse owner or horse admirer, the dressage shows at **Tempel Lipizzans** (17000 Wadsworth Rd., Wadsworth, 847/623-7272, www.tempelfarms.com, Sun. and Wed. during summers, $16) are amazing. A quick explanation: Lipizzans are a European breed of stallions (they're white horses, although they are born brown and gradually turn white) and dressage is a French style of riding or performing. After attending a performance where horses and riders demonstrate medieval battle techniques, jump, and dance, you can tour the stables and view antique carriages and other equestrian accessories.

Lamb's Farm

Families with young children should plan

a trip to Lamb's Farm (Hwy. 176 and I-94, 847/362-4636, www.lambsfarm.org, 10 A.M.– 5 P.M. daily late March–late Oct., $3), a petting zoo, pet shop, country restaurant, and game complex just off the interstate and not far from Great America. The whole project is to benefit children and adults with disabilities by providing them with places to live and opportunities for work. The petting zoo, called The Farmyard, has standard farm animals such as chickens and bunnies. Then there are a pet-supply shop, miniature golf course, miniature train ride around the 72-acre campus, and other games. The restaurant serves American country food such as fried chicken and mashed potatoes (in heaping portions). A country store and bakery sells fresh bread, jams, chocolates, and other goodies made by the staff. The farmyard, country shop, and pet shop are open 10 A.M.–5 P.M. daily and the restaurant is open for breakfast and lunch 7 A.M.–3 P.M. Tuesday–Friday, 8 A.M.–3 P.M. Sunday. Admission into the farmyard, where the animals are, is $3; however, you'll have to pay a few bucks extra for each minitrain ride, carousel ride, and other games. If you plan to do all these things, opt for the unlimited children's daily pass for $10 and adult pass for $5.

Cuneo Museum and Gardens

A Venetian-style mansion built for millionaire businessman John Cuneo, Cuneo Museum and Gardens (1350 N. Milwaukee Ave., Vernon Hills, 847/362-3042, www.cuneomuseum.org, tours at 11 A.M., 1 and 3 P.M. Tues.–Sat., self-guided tours 11 A.M.–3 P.M. Sun. Feb.–Dec., $10) is an extravagant estate hidden off Highway 21 (Milwaukee Avenue). The pink main house and its contents exude wealth. (It's like Italian Barbie's dream house.) Rich tapestries hang on the walls, a chapel has ornate stained-glass windows, and there are a greenhouse, an indoor swimming pool, and an amazing marble-floored ballroom that Cuneo's children actually used as a playroom. Outside are colorful rose gardens. Tours prices are a little steep, so if you're on a budget or don't want to spend much time inside the house, pay the $5 parking fee

and hang out in the lush gardens. Grounds are open 10 A.M.–5 P.M. Tuesday–Sunday.

Accommodations and Food

The rooms are not necessarily fancy at the 118-room **Best Western Hitch-Inn Post Motor Inn** (1765 N. Milwaukee Ave., Libertyville, 847/362-8700), but it is in a good spot: on the northeast edge of Libertyville, a few minutes from downtown, a few minutes from I-94, and about 10 minutes from Six Flags. Rooms are clean and come with coffeemakers in the rooms and continental breakfast. Some have views of the indoor pool. Rates are $50–70.

The Hollywood-style **M Adventure Inns** (3740 Grand Ave., Gurnee, 847/623-7777 or 800/373-5245, www.adventureinninc.com) is a hoot to stay in, with its themed rooms and indoor swimming pool. Choose from rooms decorated like an igloo, a bamboo shack, a Roman bathhouse, a carousel, and a variety of other interesting decor. Rates are $110–225.

If you'd rather spend your money shopping at the mall or at Six Flags Great America, book a room at the **Gurnee Grand Hotel and Suites** (5520 W. Grand Ave., Gurnee, 847/249-7777 or 866/874-7263, www.gurneegrandhotel.com), a budget hotel (rates are $50–110) with a few amusing fantasy suites of its own.

M Mickey Finn's (412 N. Milwaukee Ave., Libertyville, 847/362-6688, $7), a lively brew pub and restaurant on Main Street, is a great spot to fill up on big sandwiches such as stacked turkey clubs or classic burgers and fries. Or just have a seat at the 100-year-old bar and order a homemade beer such as oatmeal stout or root beer.

Events

Quaint, downtown Libertyville (along Milwaukee Ave.), with its city park, boutiques, and restaurants, transforms itself into a Norman Rockwell town at Christmas by organizing evening caroling events, offering horse-drawn carriages, and holding a tree-lighting ceremony. It's called **Dickens of a Holiday** and held from the end of November until a few days before Christmas.

Information

Downtown Libertyville (Milwaukee Ave., 847/680-0370, www.mainstreetlibertyville.org) organizes events, such as weekly food tastings in the park during the summer. For a list of shops and restaurants there, call or visit its website.

◼ HISTORIC VILLAGE OF LONG GROVE

Long Grove is a rarity in this part of Illinois. Surrounded by modern subdivisions, golf courses, and shopping centers, the village is a flashback to life more than 100 years ago, with whitewashed frame houses, a mill pond, and a covered bridge. First settled in the 1830s by immigrants from the Alsace-Lorraine region in Europe (between France and Germany), the village has preserved many of the original buildings, such as a community church and one-room schoolhouse. How much time you spend here depends on how much you love historic towns and shopping. Housed inside the vintage buildings are several boutiques where local residents sell imported French furniture, antiques, Scandinavian gifts, gourmet food, and more. The core business district is centered around Old McHenry Road and Robert Parker Coffin Road, near Highway 53 and 83. You have to drive to get here.

Shops

Buckets of molded chocolates and chocolate-dipped strawberries are sold at **Long Grove Confectionery Co.** (220 Robert Parker Coffin Rd., Long Grove, 847/634-0080, www.longgrove.com). When the company started years ago, the chocolate concoctions were actually made in the Long Grove schoolhouse. Now the schoolhouse is a retail shop and the cooking operations are housed in a factory to the south in Buffalo Grove. (You can tour the candy factory in Buffalo Grove. For tour information call 847/459-3100 or 888/459-3100. The one-hour tours are held during hours of production and cost $2 per person.)

Old-fashioned popcorn (meaning no artificial flavorings) is the specialty at **Long Grove**

Popcorn Shoppe (318 Old McHenry Rd., Long Grove, 847/921-9101, www.thelonggrovepopcornshoppe.com, 10 A.M.–5 P.M. Mon.–Sat., 11 A.M.–5 P.M. Sun.). See how good the stuff tastes with real butter and real caramel. Load up on bags or tins.

Coffee and tea are sold by the pound and the cup at **Beans and Leaves** (320 Old McHenry Rd., Long Grove, 847/844-9450, 7:30 A.M.–5 P.M. Mon.–Fri., 9:30 A.M.–5 P.M. Sat., 10:30 A.M.–5 P.M. Sun.), a bustling little coffee shop downtown.

Looking for some shiny accessories for your dinerlike kitchen? **Nifty 50s** (327 Old McHenry Rd., Long Grove, 847/821-7047) sells art deco and art nouveau decor (including neon items), jukeboxes, Betty Boop memorabilia, and lots of other imaginative pieces.

Nickelby's (219 Robert Parker Coffin Rd., Long Grove, 847/634-6552, 10:30 A.M.–5 P.M. Mon.–Sat., 11:30 A.M.–5 P.M. Sun.) sells fine stationary, greeting cards, stamps, and more.

Accommodations and Food

There's a wholesome, country-charm feel to the ◼ **Round Robin Inn** (231 E. Maple Ave., Mundelein, 847/566-7664, www.roundrobininn.com), south of Long Grove. Pick from seven rooms with names such as "Stars and Stripes Forever" and "Camelot." Rooms contain large beds covered with quilts and decorated with items such as a portrait of Abraham Lincoln. Rates are under $150.

Open since 1849, the ◼ **Village Tavern** (135 Old McHenry Rd., Long Grove, 847/634-3117, lunch and dinner daily, under $10) has a friendly publike atmosphere with American food entrées such as meatloaf and pizza. Its all-you-can-eat dinners throughout the week always attract a crowd.

Housed in a restored Victorian home, ◼ **Enzo and Lucia's Ristorante** (343 Old McHenry Rd., Long Grove, 847/478-8825, 11 A.M.–9:30 P.M. Mon.–Thurs., 11 A.M.–midnight Fri. and Sat., 11 A.M.–9 P.M. Sun.) is a white-tablecloth restaurant. Here it's all Italian all the time. Enjoy fresh homemade pasta, fresh calamari, and desserts while sitting outside.

Events

The Historic Village of Long Grove is a festi-val-happy village with several tourist-friendly events held throughout the year. The best ones are the **Strawberry Festival** at the end of June, at which you can eat as much strawberry short-cake and strawberry pie as you want. Another culinary extravaganza takes place at the end of May and beginning of June. At **Chocolate Fest,** chefs demonstrate all the fabulous dishes you can create with chocolate and you can nib-ble to your heart's content on samples and load your trunk with boxes of truffles. Both festivals are held in downtown Long Grove.

Information

The shops and restaurants within the **Village of Long Grove** (847/634-0888, www.longgrove-online.com) have put together a detailed bro-chure and website that contains information on the town's festivals, attractions, and more.

Lake County Discovery Museum and Curt Teich Postcard Archives

Not many people may recognize the name Curt Teich, but what about vintage postcards with "Greetings From..." written in large let-ters across a blue sky or street scene? The enor-mously popular postcards from the first half of the 20th century were created by the Curt Teich Postcard Company, formerly of Chicago. Hundreds of thousands of these postcards are stored and some of them are on view at the Lake County Discovery Museum and the Curt Teich Postcard Archives (27277 Forest Preserve Dr., Wauconda, 847/968-3400, www.lakecoun-tydiscoverymuseum.org, 11 A.M.–4:30 P.M. Sun.–Fri., 10 A.M.–4:30 P.M. Sat., $8 week-ends, $5.50 weekdays except on Tues. when it's $2.75), about 15 miles northwest of Long Grove in the Lakewood Forest Preserve. The museum's postcard exhibits detail the history

of postcards but also Teich's technique. After establishing a studio in Chicago in 1898, he traveled around snapping black-and-white pho-tographs of towns, monuments, and landscapes and jotting down notes about what colors ap-peared in them. Later, artists would draw in the colors and blot out anything unsightly in the images. In addition to the postcards on view and the historical exhibits, the Lake County Museum has a well-organized and educational exhibit about the history of the county, focusing on how the landscape has changed through the decades from residential and commercial de-velopment. It also has a gallery that showcases photography and works of area artists. Follow signs to the museum from Highway 176.

GETTING AROUND

Metra (312/322-6777, www.metrarail.com) op-erates several commuter train lines that service Lake County seven days a week. Times vary per line and day. Fees also vary, but you can buy a $5 weekend pass that's good on all trains for Saturday and Sunday. The Union Pacific North Line runs from Chicago's Ogilivie Transpor-tation Center to Kenosha with stops in Zion and Winthrop Harbor along Lake Michigan. The Milwaukee District Line connects Chica-go's Union Station to Fox Lake with stops in Grayslake, Libertyville, and other towns. And the North Central Service goes from Chicago's Union Station to Antioch (a town just south of the Wisconsin border), with stops in Round Lake Beach, Vernon Hills, and other towns.

INFORMATION

The main tourism bureau promoting the region is the **Lake County Convention and Visitors Bureau** (5455 W. Grand Ave., Gurnee, 847/662-2700, 800/525-3669, www.lakecounty.org).

The Grand Prairie

Back in Illinois's early days as a state, settlers initially avoided the central region which, back then, was covered by a vast prairie. Smoothed by ancient glaciers, the Grand Prairie was flat, muddy, and chock-full of insects, trees were few and far between (except along the rivers), and the winters were long and bitter, especially when the winds rushed in from the northwest. But under the tall prairie grasses was black soil loaded with nutrients. After Grand Detour blacksmith John Deere invented a plow that could cut through the thick soil, settlement took off. Immigrants carved out homesteads along rail lines and near towns, most of which were near wooded areas

along the rivers. Agriculture dominated the region in the 1800s, and it still is an economy driver. In the summer you don't have to drive far to find a white farmhouse and red barn surrounded by fields of tall corn stalks rustling in the wind. Lofty grain elevators dot the landscape and mark where the towns.

Much of what you see out your windshield while driving through the region are grain farms. But the landscape also features several rivers. The Sangamon River weaves a diagonal path through the central part of the state, from northwest of Champaign toward the southwest and eventually the Illinois River. The Middle

Must-Sees

Look for **M** to find the sights and activities you can't miss and **Ⅺ** for the best dining and lodging.

M Robert Allerton Park: The early 20th-century former estate of a grain baron, with its sunken garden, wooded trails, and reflection pond, is a jewel of the Illinois prairie. The mansion and surrounding gardens, now part of the University of Illinois, are in Monticello (page 159).

M Lincoln's New Salem: In 1831 Lincoln moved to the village of New Salem as a 22-year-old man and spent several years working here. The pioneer town, once long gone, has been recreated as a state historic site with log cabins and volunteers who demonstrate milling, weaving, and other chores (page 175).

M Lincoln Home National Historic Site: Before the 16th American president moved to Washington, D.C., Abraham Lincoln lived in a two-story home with his family in Springfield. The home and visitors center are surrounded by other historic homes near downtown (page 178).

M Kickapoo State Park and Middle Fork State Fish and Wildlife Area: Paddle down the Middle Fork, a National Scenic River that weaves through Vermilion County's former coal-mining region, past sandstone bluffs and hardwood forests. Along the river's shores are two great state parks with miles and miles of rugged trails for hiking and mountain biking (page 208).

© CHRISTINE DES GARENNES

One of the best Lincoln sites in Illinois is New Salem, his old stomping grounds near Petersburg.

THE GRAND PRAIRIE

Aurora
CHICAGO
Joliet
Chicago Heights
Mendota
Princeton
La Salle
Illinois River
Kewanee
Manteno
Momence
Bourbonnais
Bradley
Kankakee
Kankakee River State Park
Beaverville
Iroquois State Wildlife Area
Watseka
Pontiac
FURROW VINEYARD AND WINERY
El Paso
Gilman
Peoria
Illinois River
HARVEST MOON TWIN DRIVE-IN
UPPER LIMITS ROCK GYM
Normal
Gibson City
OCTAVE CHANUTE AEROSPACE MUSEUM
Bloomington
MILLER PARK ZOO
Middle Fork
Le Roy
MIDDLE FORK STATE FISH AND WILDLIFE AREA
Heyworth
Lake of the Woods Park
Rantoul
KICKAPOO STATE PARK
Farmer City
Mahomet
ALTO VINEYARDS
Urbana
Danville
PIG HIP RESTAURANT MUSEUM
Clinton
LINCOLN'S NEW SALEM
Lincoln
ROBERT ALLERTON PARK
Champaign
Vermilion
Westville
Broadwell
Monticello
Homer
Georgetown
Forest Glen Preserve
Petersburg
Elkhart
UNDER THE PRAIRIE FRONTIER ARCHAEOLOGICAL MUSEUM
Forsyth
Sangamon
Bement
LINCOLN HOME NATIONAL HISTORIC SITE
GOVERNOR OGLESBY MANSION
Decatur
Lake Decatur
Tuscola
Springfield
ROCK SPRINGS CENTER FOR ENVIRONMENTAL DISCOVERY
Scovill Park
Arthur
JOHNNY GRUELLE'S RAGGEDY ANN AND ANDY MUSEUM
Lake Springfield
GREAT PUMPKIN PATCH
ILLINOIS AMISH INTERPRETIVE CENTER
Divernon
Taylorville
Lake Shelbyville
Sullivan
Arcola
Paris
Eagle Creek SP
Mattoon
Charleston
Wolf Creek SP
Lerna
Pana
Shelbyville
LINCOLN LOG CABIN STATE HISTORIC SITE
Marshall
Litchfield
Greenup
To St Louis, MO
Effingham

INDIANA

The Grand Prairie

0   10 mi
0   10 km

© AVALON TRAVEL PUBLISHING, INC.

Fork National Scenic River snakes past sandstone outcroppings on the eastern side of the state. And the headwaters region of Champaign County is where six rivers, including the Sangamon, Kaskaskia, and Embarras (pronounced Embraw), begin their journeys.

Central Illinois is very much Lincoln land. During the quarter of a century that he lived in Illinois, Abraham Lincoln traveled much of the state practicing law, serving as a captain in the Black Hawk War and working on a steamboat. But it was in New Salem where Lincoln developed his business skills as a general store clerk. And it was in Springfield he matured as a politician and orator. And he was fond of the region and its people. Before leaving Springfield for Washington, D.C., Lincoln told a crowd gathered at the train station, "To this place, and the kindness of its people, I owe everything." Central Illinois towns, even the bigger ones such as the capital of Springfield, still manage to give off good Midwestern vibes. They are Main Street–kind of towns, with coffee shops frequented by regular groups of farmers, drive-ins where teens meet on Friday nights, and VFW halls where pancake breakfasts are served.

PLANNING YOUR TIME

While planning your itinerary through the Grand Prairie, ask yourself this question: How much do you love Abraham Lincoln? This being Abe land, you could easily spend several days traveling from one Lincoln sight to another, such as the **Abraham Lincoln Presidential Library and Museum** in Springfield or his old stomping grounds at **New Salem State Historic Site.** A week will allow you time to hit the main Lincoln sights in Springfield, the **University of Illinois** campus in Champaign and Urbana, put in some hiking time at **Kickapoo State Park** by Danville, antiquing in the town of **Lincoln,** or camping near **Lake Shelbyville.** Because the region is connected to Chicago by I-57 and I-55, it's easy to take off on a two- or three-day weekend jaunt to Grand Prairie towns from Chicago. If you're in the mood for small towns, drive **Route 66** from Chicago toward Springfield. Or

visit an **Amish family farm** near Arthur and Arcola and browse for handmade furniture or visit a pumpkin patch. All major metropolitan areas in the Grand Prairie region (Springfield, Bloomington-Normal, Champaign-Urbana, Decatur, Danville) are connected by interstates, making it easy to get to one from another.

Access

Aside from the occasional road-construction project, driving through central Illinois is usually free of any major hassles. Traffic jams are few and far between. The interstates and highways are in good shape and most of the cars and trucks clip along at a speedy pace. The main arteries through the Grand Prairie are the interstates 55, 57, and 72, and 74. I-55, the major northeast-to-southeast highway in the state, is the quickest route from Chicago to St. Louis, with stops around Bloomington-Normal and Springfield and other midsize towns along the way, such as Lincoln and Dwight. I-55 follows much of Historic Route 66, a good two-lane option if you need a break from interstate driving for a while. I-57 is a north-south highway primarily through the eastern part of the state, from Chicago and down to the south. U.S. 45 runs along most of I-57 through the central part of the state.

There are plenty of scenic two-lane options, Highway 10 from Champaign to Lincoln, Highway 133 through the Amish towns of Arcola and Arthur, and Illinois 1. Also known as the Dixie Highway, Illinois 1 was once the main route into Chicago from the south. It's a straight line along the eastern part of the state from Chicago to Danville, through Watseka, Momence, and more.

Resources

Most towns in central Illinois have convention and visitors bureaus or chambers of commerce with helpful, friendly residents working there. For information on the entire region, check with the **Central Illinois Tourism Development Office** (Hilton Hotel, 700 E. Adams St., Upper Mezzanine Level, Springfield, 217/525-7980, www.visitcentralillinois.com). Its territory covers much of the Grand Prairie region.

Kankakee and Iroquois River Valleys

HISTORY AND ORIENTATION

Before the white settlers arrived beginning in the mid-1830s, the land along the Kankakee River was used by the Miami and Pottawatomi Indians for hunting and fishing. Unlike parts of the prairie to the south, the land near the river was lush and full of native black walnut trees and oak and hickory forests. Because the area was teeming with game, eventually the French fur traders took notice and moved into the area also. The French founded the town of Bourbonnais (it actually came first, before Kankakee, which is now the larger of the two cities). And after the Illinois Central Railroad in 1855 established a stop in the area, along came settlers from the East Coast. In addition to the new white Yankees were African Americans who settled east of Kankakee in the Pembroke area. The historically black area and the city of Hopkins Park celebrate their heritage every year with Pembroke Days in August as well as the Thyrl Latting Rodeo Spectacular during Memorial Day weekend, which spotlights African-American achievements in the American West.

Kankakee and Iroquois counties were back then, as they are now, heavily into agriculture (including large- and small-scale farmers) and companies such as fertilizer and chemical manufacturers. Kankakee also prides itself on its connection to the Dairy Queen ice cream chain. In 1938 a man named Sherb Noble, who ran Sherb's, an ice-cream shop in Kankakee, offered customers for the first time soft-serve ice cream. He had recently partnered with an Iowan who had developed a new way of serving ice cream: soft. Later Noble would open the first Dairy Queen franchise in Joliet.

Kankakee is the largest city in the region with about 27,000 people. Immediately adjacent to the city's borders are Bourbonnais to the northwest and Bradley directly to the north. The entire county of Kankakee has about 100,000 people. Iroquois County to the south and east is a rural county with only about 30,000 people.

The largest town there is Watseka, about 12 miles east of I-57 with about 5,000 people. I-57 runs north-south through the region, skirting the west side of Kankakee. U.S. 45/52 slices through most of the east and center part of Bradley and Kankakee. The highlight of the region is **Kankakee River State Park** with its limestone bluffs, hiking trails, and campground northwest of the city of Kankakee.

KANKAKEE COUNTY SIGHTS AND ACTIVITIES

Kankakee River State Park

Stretching for 11 miles along the north and south sides of the river, the Kankakee River State Park (513 W. Hwy. 102, Bourbonnais, 815/933-1382, www.dnr.state.il.us) is a refreshing spot, topographically speaking, in an area dominated by corn- and soybean fields. The park is about 4,000 acres with spots for fishing, sitting on a rock and writing or reading, trails for walking, bicycling, cross-country skiing, or horseback riding. It's about six miles east of I-57 and if you've been on the road for a while, this is a good spot to stretch your legs. A good place to begin is the visitors center, where you can pick up trail maps and walk through the wildflower identification gardens outside or the prairie restoration area.

There's lots to do here. You can park your car at the Davis Creek Area on the far south end of the park (where the group campground is) and then hop on your bike and ride the 10.5-mile biking trail along the north side of the river. Or you can rent a horse (or bring your own) and explore the south side of the river by meandering along the 12-mile equestrian trail. In the winter you can go cross-country skiing on these trails. You can stroll along the bicycle trail, but there are several other nature trails and hiking trails, such as the two-mile Rock Creek Canyon trail near Rock Creek, which empties into the Kankakee. Here you can get a good look at the limestone canyons for which

The Grand Prairie

the park is famous. Walk along the Shaw-waw-nas-see nature trail north of the main entrance (off Deselm Road near the horse stables) and you can glimpse a waterfall. Or, walk across the river on a suspension bridge to explore the south side of the park, keeping an eye out for red-tailed hawks and wildflowers. The islands in the middle of the river are nature preserves where the Kankakee mallow, an endangered flower, grows.

There are two campgrounds here, Chippewa Campground to the north and Pottawatomi to the south. Both have sites near the river. Horseback riding is allowed 1 P.M.–sunset April–mid-May, sunrise–sunset mid-May–August 31 and in October, sunrise–11 P.M. in September. For more information on horseback riding at the park, call the stables at 815/939-0309. Hunting is allowed in the park in the fall, so use caution when hiking or horseback riding through the area during that time of the year. There is no swimming allowed in the river. The Kankakee River is notorious for its strong currents and people have drowned off the river's shores.

Scuba Diving

For about $20, you can explore a spring-fed quarry north of Highway 17, west of Bradley and Kankakee. **Haigh's Scuba Diving Quarry** (2738 E. 2000 North Rd., Kankakee, 815/932-7797, www.haighquarry.com, 7 A.M.–11 P.M. Mon.–Sat., 8 A.M.–11 P.M. Sun.) has observation platforms at different levels of the quarry down to 70 feet. Haigh's has sunk stuff like a dump truck and boat for you to explore. It costs $20 to dive for the day, more if you rent any equipment. A concession stand sells burgers, fries, sodas, and such. And you can also fish for bluegill, bass, and others.

Perry Farm Park

One of the first farmsteads in the area, established in the 1830s, the Perry family farm has been transformed into the Perry Farm Park (456 N. Kennedy Dr., Bourbonnais, 815/933-9905), a 170-acre complex with farm buildings, a petting zoo, children's museum, and

four miles of walking trails that lead along Bourbonnais Creek and to some caves. A popular spot for school groups, the park also has a pavilion where local musicians play on Tuesday nights in the summer, a rose garden, and orchard. At Exploration Station, the children's museum, visitors learn about arts and science through hands-on exhibits. The park and trails are free and open sunrise–sunset daily. Exploration Station is open 10 A.M.–5 P.M. Mon.–Thursday, noon–8 P.M. Friday, 10 A.M.–5 P.M. Saturday, 1–5 P.M. Sunday. Admission is $4 except on Tuesday, when it's free.

Museums

At the **Kankakee County Historical Society Museum** (801 S. 8th Ave., Kankakee, 815/932-5279, www.kankakeecountymuseum.com, 10 A.M.–4 P.M. Tues.–Sat., 1–4 P.M. Sun., $3, free Fri.) you can view permanent and rotating exhibits about the first 100 years of the county, 1853–1953. There are also exhibits on the area's Native American history and displays about the three Illinois governors hailed from the county (including most recently George Ryan, who was in office 1999–2003). Temporary exhibits have focused on the French influence in America and art deco buildings in the region. In addition to the main museum building, the grounds contain the boyhood home of Len Small, who was governor in the 1920s, and a one-room schoolhouse. For more glimpses of Kankakee's past, visit the **Kankakee Railroad Museum** (197 S. East Ave., Kankakee, 815/929-1889, 11 A.M.–4 P.M. Tues.–Sat., noon–4 P.M. Sun., donation) housed in a grand old train depot in downtown Kankakee. The local model-railroading club has several model-train displays on view that depict scenes from Kankakee's past. Outside there's a Pullman coach from the 1940s and a Union Pacific caboose. The museum is closed every fourth weekend of the month.

EVENTS

Every Memorial Day weekend in Hopkins Park, a historically black community west of Kankakee, folks come out and celebrate African Americans in the American West with the **Thyrl Latting Rodeo Spectacular,** complete with lassoing and other roping and riding demonstrations. The town also honors its heritage with **Pembroke Days** in August by showcasing blues, gospel, and jazz music. The Kankakee municipal band plays free at 7:30 P.M. Thursday nights at the riverside Bird Park first week of June through first week of August.

Free concerts are also held at the gazebo on the Perry farm Tuesday evenings in July and August, 7–8:30 P.M.

Markets

Kankakee hosts a farmers market 7 A.M.–1 P.M. on Saturdays May–October. It's at Merchant and Dearborn Streets.

ACCOMMODATIONS

The bulk of the hotels in the area are chain operations and they're all just off I-57 on exits in Bradley, Bourbonnais, and Kankakee. Rates are generally $80–100, although the Hilton has some suites that can reach $130.

The newer **Hilton Garden Inn** (455 Riverstone Pkwy., Kankakee, 815/932-4444, www.kankakee.gardeninn.com) is a business travelers hotel with rooms and suites with amenities such as coffeemakers, microwaves, minifridges, desks, and wireless Internet access. The hotel has a bar and restaurant, a whirlpool and indoor swimming pool, plus a laundry room with coin-operated machines for guests.

The 59-room **Hampton Inn** (60 Ken Hayes Dr., Bourbonnais, 815/932-8369, $89–120) has a 24-hour exercise room and offers guests continental breakfast. The **Fairfield Inn** (1550 North Highway 50, Bourbonnais, 815/935-1334, $85–95) has an indoor pool and exercise room and also offers guests a continental breakfast.has 59 rooms, a 24-hour exercise room, and a decent continental breakfast.

Fairfield Inn (1550 N. Hwy. 50, Bourbonnais, 815/935-1334) has an indoor pool and exercise room. Continental breakfast is included.

Camping

There are two campgrounds at **Kankakee River State Park** (513 W. Hwy. 102, Bourbonnais, 815/933-1382) with RV and tent sites available. Rates are $6–15 per night.

GETTING AROUND

Amtrak's City of New Orleans train (between Chicago and New Orleans) and the Illini train (between Chicago and Carbondale) stop daily at the Kankakee train depot (199 S. East Ave., Kankakee, 800/USA-RAIL or 800/872-7245).

Greyhound (815/939-2211 or 800/231-2222) buses come and go from the Kankakee Gas Depot at U.S. 45 and I-57.

INFORMATION

Contact the **Kankakee County Convention and Visitors Bureau** (1 Dearborn Sq., Ste. 521, Kankakee, 815/935-7390 or 800/74-RIVER—800/747-4837, www.visitkankakeecounty.com). The bureau operates a visitors information center at 1270 Larry Power Road, Bourbonnais. It's open 9 A.M.–5 P.M. Monday–Friday September–April, and 9 A.M.–5 P.M. daily May–August and the first week in September.

IROQUOIS COUNTY SIGHTS AND ACTIVITIES

Iroquois State Wildlife Area

Perhaps one of the state's quietest and least crowded parks, the Iroquois State Wildlife Area (2803 E. 3300 North Rd., Beaverville, 815/435-2218, www.dnr.state.il.us) is also quite a rare sight. Totaling about 2,480 acres, the wildlife area contains prairie and sedge meadow, and the 480-acre Hooper Branch Savanna Nature Preserve, the largest single track of native savanna left in Illinois. There you can find switch grass, June grass, some boggy areas with plants not common in the state (such as the sundew, which eats insects). Hiking and nature trails, including a .3-mile wheelchair-accessible trail, weave past sand dunes and marshy areas. The site is about 15 miles east of I-57 and a mile west of the Illinois-Indiana state line.

Heartland Health Spa

Called a "destination spa," Heartland Health Spa (1237 E. 1600 North Rd., Gilman, 815/683-2182 or 800/545-4853, www.heartlandspa.com) is a place where you retreat for the weekend, indulge in a few massages, practice a little yoga, eat fresh, healthy foods and get your hair done. The 32-acre estate in rural Iroquois County is a little oasis in the prairie. (Imagine a very, very upscale farmstead, if you can.) This is a place to go when you want to get away from work and far from a noisy, crowded city. (It's in Gilman, a city of about 2,000 people). Here guests essentially choose their objectives, such as reducing stress or to start exercising again, for their stay. Then they plan ways to meet that goal, such as signing up for group exercise classes, spending time in the weight room, swimming laps in the indoor pool, walking or cross-country skiing along the spa's trails. The spa also has adventure programs in which instructors teach you how to walk on a cable above the ground or fly down a zip-line. Meals here are the opposite of those served at the Bayern Stube in nearby Gibson City. They're light—fewer than 2,000 calories for guys and girls—although you can ask for more if you're not calorie-counting. Rates vary, but are definitely upscale. There are one-person and two-person rates, plus there's a two-night minimum stay. It's cheaper if you go with someone else. For example, rates are $730–800 for one person staying in a private room for two nights and $860–1,030 for two people staying two nights.

Onarga

If you can't afford to drop $700 a night to stay in a peaceful country retreat such as Heartland Spa, consider the **Onarga Bed and Breakfast** (1437 N. Hwy. 39, Onarga, 815/683-2774). There's no indoor pool, no massage room, but there are dairy cows you might hear peacefully baying in the distance. At this bed-and-break-

fast you'll stay with a family of grain and dairy farmers in a remodeled, clean white 1892 farmhouse. They rent three rooms for $50–60 per night. Continental breakfast is included.

If you can tear yourself off the farm for a night, head to downtown Onarga to catch a flick in a vintage storefront movie theater. The **Onarga Theater** (103 W. Seminary St., Onarga, 815/268-9862) shows recently released films for $5 a person.

GIBSON CITY

Activities, Accommodations, and Food

One of the best ways to spend a summer evening is catching a movie at the drive-in. **Harvest Moon Twin Drive-In** (Hwy. 47, Gibson City, 217/784-8770 or 877/54-MOVIE or 877/546-6843, weekends April, May, Sept., daily June–Aug., $5) is one of the few places in the state and the Midwest where you can see a flick under the stars (that is, if you choose to watch from the hood of your car or if you've got a sunroof or convertible). After opening in 1955, it had to be rebuilt a decade later after a tornado tore down the screen. Like many drive-in theaters, it closed when big movie theaters started cropping up and becoming more popular. It was closed for much of the 1980s before being reopened by a local drive-in devotee. Here the movies are shown even in the rain. All you need is an FM dial on your car radio and you can listen to the movie. Harvest Moon has two movie screens, picnic grounds, a concession stand, and it hosts events throughout the season, such as car shows and fireworks on the Fourth of July. The grounds open one hour before movies, which usually start around 7 P.M. You're welcome to bring a grill to cook out.

Run by Berlin natives, the **Bayern Stube** (209 N. Sangamon Ave., Gibson City, 217/784-8304, 4:30–9 P.M. Tues.–Sat., 11:30 A.M.–8 P.M. Sun., 11 A.M.–2 P.M. Thurs.) is a restaurant and bed-and-breakfast that, since opening in 1991, has developed a cultlike following among central Illinoisans who love

German beer and German food. The restaurant is decorated somewhat like a lodge, with no shortage of beer steins and taxidermy on the walls. And the food is oh so hearty, with plenty of sausage, sausage, sausage. And if sausage is not your thing there's beef tenderloin with portabella mushrooms and gorgonzola cheese, potato pancakes, frog legs, pickled herring, followed with some old-fashioned and homemade strudel. Or maybe you're not hungry enough for a meal. At least drop by for a pint of German beer and a stuffed pretzel. Throughout the year the owners organize food and drink fests, such as Octoberfest in late September and early October, a hunter's feast in mid- to late February, and May Fest in early to mid-May. There are two bed-and-breakfast rooms that come with kitchenettes (microwave, sink), whirlpool baths, and continental breakfast when you want it. Rates are $85–98 per night.

Gibson City offers visitors the use of four free **campsites** with electrical hookups. The sites, which are available on a first-come, first-served basis, have grills and fire pits. They're by South Park at Lott Boulevard and Highway 9, east of the intersections of highways 9, 47, and 54.

Information

Feel free to call the **Gibson City Area Chamber of Commerce** (126 N. Sangamon Ave., Gibson City, 217/784-5217) if you have any questions about the town or navigating through the area.

Bloomington-Normal

HISTORY AND ORIENTATION

Like Champaign-Urbana to the southeast, Bloomington-Normal was first settled by hunters and fisherman and eventually farm families as people realized the prairie was fertile ground. Yankees and immigrant families established homesteads, tamed the prairie, and started shipping their grain and livestock to Chicago on new train lines. Today the twin cities of Bloomington and Normal are fairly diverse communities with a mix of university students, academics, farmers, and white-collar and blue-collar workers. Illinois State University is here, agricultural and automotive manufacturers are here, and the headquarters for State Farm Insurance is here (a company that employs about 12,000 people in the area). Plus, Bloomington is the county seat for McLean, which means there's a fair amount of government activity going on also.

You'll notice the land rises slightly in this area. That's because about 15,000 years ago the last glacier in Illinois pushed and shoved enormous amounts of rocks and dirt around to create ridges, or moraines. There are four of these ridges in Illinois and one of the largest is the Bloomington moraine, which is covers an area from Elgin to the Illinois River and Saybrook, a tiny town east of Bloomington-Normal. Outside the cities the area mostly comprises grain farms and a few cattle or hog farms. In recent years the county has restricted residential and commercial development on prime farmland, and in McLean County there's a lot of that. The county is always among tops for corn and soybean production and yields.

Bloomington-Normal is also where several federal interstates intersect, meaning lots of travelers and truckers stop by overnight or for a meal. I-39 and U.S. 51 are the main north-south highways, with Business 51 (Main Street) slicing right through the center of the cities. I-74 runs diagonally through the region, from Champaign-Urbana and Indianapolis northwest to the Quad Cities, and it circumvents the cities to the south. Finally, I-55, the main drag between Chicago and St. Louis, also passes by Bloomington. Veteran's Parkway, Business 55, runs north-south on the east side of both towns. With that said, it's quick and easy to get around Bloomington; there are many highways you can hop on to go where you want. But in

© CHRISTINE DES GARENNES

Bloomington town square

the past it prompted many businesses to move away from the downtowns. However, in recent years restaurants, coffee shops, and boutiques are choosing to locate in the downtowns.

SIGHTS
Franklin Park Historic District

One of Bloomington's favorite sons was David Davis, a local politician who went on to become a U.S. Supreme Court justice 1862–1877. His grand home, the **David Davis Mansion State Historic Site** (1000 E. Monroe Dr., Bloomington, 309/828-1084, 9 A.M.–4 P.M. Wed.–Sun., $2) has been restored and filled with period furniture. When it was built in 1872, the home was quite fancy for the area. You can tour the interior and exterior (which includes a carriage house and gardens. Tours run every 30 minutes on the hour and half hour and last about an hour.

When you're done touring the Davis home, walk or drive through the Franklin Park Historic District (Chestnut, McLean, Prairie and Walnut Sts., bordering Franklin Park), once a posh Bloomington neighborhood. There are a number of rambling Victorian homes, brick streets, and antique streetlamps.

Another famous family that hails from Bloomington is the Stevenson family. **Adlai E. Stevenson,** born in 1835, moved to Bloomington in his late teens, attended Illinois Wesleyan University, worked as a postmaster, and then went on to serve in Congress and as a Grover Cleveland's vice president 1893–1897. Stevenson ran for president and Illinois governor unsuccessfully before retiring and returning to Bloomington. He's buried in Bloomington's Evergreen Cemetery (302 E. Miller St., Bloomington, 309/827-6950, dawn–dusk). His grandson, Adlai E. Stevenson II, had a distinguished political career and ended up becoming governor of Illinois. Born in 1900, he became governor of Illinois 1949–1953 and ran against Dwight D. Eisenhower in 1952 and 1956. (The Republican World War II general defeated him both times.) Former U.S. President John F. Kennedy picked him to be U.S. ambassador to the United Nations. Stevenson died in 1965 and is also buried in Evergreen Cemetery. Great-grandson Adlai E. Stevenson III, who is still alive, was also a politician, serving in the Illinois House of Representatives, as state treasurer, and as a Senator from Illinois during the 1970s. He ran unsuccessfully for the presidency in the 1980s.

Miller Park Zoo

One of the better small zoos in the region, Miller Park Zoo (1020 S. Morris Ave., Bloomington, 309/434-2250, $4) has an impressive rainforest exhibit with exotic animals such as leopards and tigers, plus a marine mammal section and petting zoo area for children. The park opens at 9:30 A.M. daily. The buildings close at 5:30 P.M. and the grounds close at 6 P.M. Memorial Day–Labor Day. During the fall, winter, and spring the buildings close at 4:30 P.M. and the grounds close at 5 P.M.

Museums

As far as regional museums go, the **McLean County Museum of History** (200 N. Main St., Bloomington, 309/827-0428, www.mchistory.org, 10 A.M.–5 P.M. Mon.–Sat., Tues. until 9 P.M., 1–5 P.M. Sun., $2, free on Tues.) is one of the better ones in the state, partly because of its venue. The museum is housed in the county's former courthouse, an American Renaissance–style building featuring mosaic tiles throughout and a marble staircase. Built in 1904, the courthouse is listed on the National Register of Historic Places and is in downtown Bloomington. You'll recognize it by the copper dome. Inside, museum volunteers have collected archives from the region, including exhibits on famous folks who lived or passed through town, including Adlai Stevenson and David Davis. There's a log cabin display, farming display with an old steel plow, and in one area visitors are asked to mimic chores of the pioneers such as hauling buckets of water. Other displays show photos of the town through the years, including one depicting the devastation caused by a fire in 1900. On Thursdays local women get together in one of the rooms and quilt.

The **McLean County Arts Center** (601 N. East St., Bloomington, 309/829-0011, www.mcac.org, 10 A.M.–7 P.M. Tues., 10 A.M.–

5 P.M. Wed.–Fri., noon–4 P.M. Sat., free) showcases regional artwork in its Spanish-style building in downtown Bloomington. You can view area landscape paintings, photographs, abstract art, and sculptures. Exhibits rotate throughout the year.

If you fly in or out of the Bloomington-Normal Airport (it's one of the best regional airports in Illinois) and find yourself with some extra time before your flight departs, or before you set off to explore after your flight, set aside some extra time to tour the **Prairie Aviation Museum** (Central Illinois Regional Airport, 2929 E. Empire St., Bloomington, 309/663-7632, www.prairieaviationmuseum.org, 11 A.M.–4 P.M. Tues.–Sat., noon–4 P.M. Sun., $2). Its collection includes vintage Cessnas, a restored Ozark Airlines DC-3, Marine Corps helicopter, and several airplane engines.

ENTERTAINMENT AND EVENTS
Theater

The **Normal Theater** (209 North St., Normal, 309/454-9722 or 309/454-9720, www.normaltheater.com, $5) is a 1937 renovated movie theater that shows new documentaries such as *The Fog of War* (about former Defense Secretary Robert McNamara), foreign films, and award-winning classics such as *From Here to Eternity*. The art deco–style theater features salmon- and silver-colored seats.

Theater and music students, visiting artists, and groups perform a variety of musicals, plays, operas, music concerts, and more at **Illinois State University's Center for the Performing Arts** (School and Beaufort Sts., Normal, 309/438-2535). The center has a recital hall, studio theater, and experimental theater within its walls.

Formerly a Scottish Rite temple, **The Bloomington Center for the Performing Arts** (110 E. Mulberry St., Bloomington, 309/829-3903 or 800/354-9640) is a 1,320-seat theater that dates to 1921 and once hosted jazz great Duke Ellington. By 2000 the temple was showing its age and a group of residents rallied to restore the building and revitalize the north side of

Bloomington's downtown. During the Easter season, the center is home to the oldest continually running passion play in the country.

Events

The **Illinois Shakespeare Festival** (Ewing Manor, Emerson St., east of Towanda Ave., Bloomington, day box office 309/438-8110, evening box office 309/828-9814, www.thefestival.org, $16–40) is one of the best summer events in central Illinois. Produced by Illinois State University on the beautiful grounds of the Ewing Manor, the festival's professional actors present about three different Shakespearean plays (usually a mix of comedy and drama) for a total of about 40 performances July–mid-August.

Arrive early to stake out a picnic spot on the lawn, bring your own basket or buy dinner from the concessionaire, stroll through the formal gardens, and listen to the madrigal singer. Then, take a peek inside the manor, where every summer staff prepare exhibits about Shakespeare, British theater, and other related subjects. Finally, take in a show under the stars.

Sponsored by the McLean County Arts Center, the **Sugar Creek Arts Festival,** held early–mid-July in downtown Normal, showcases the work of about 135 artists from the region and across the country. You'll find paintings, sculpture, jewelry, and other creations for sale, plus food and live music.

SHOPPING

Virginia Redskins, also known as **Beer Nuts,** are made in Bloomington. You can stock up on them at one of the company's stores in Bloomington (sale barn is at 2019 S. Main St./ U.S. 51 or plant and store at 103 N. Robinson St., Bloomington, 309/827-8580 or 309/829-8091, www.beernuts.com). The plant is open 8 A.M.–5 P.M. Monday–Friday; the sale barn is open 10 A.M.–6 P.M. Monday–Friday, 10 A.M.–4 P.M. Saturday, free admission.

You can pick up a bottle of California wine or accessory such as a wine stopper or corkscrew at **Villa di Vino** (413 N. Main St., Bloomington, 309/821-9463, 10 A.M.–6 P.M. Tues.–Fri., 9 A.M.–4 P.M. Sat.).

RECREATION
Climbing

Surrounded by miles and miles of corn- and soybean fields planted on low-lying land, Bloomington is not exactly a prime destination for rock climbers. But there is a growing and dedicated group of climbers in the state and one of their favorite places to climb is at **Upper Limits Rock Gym** (1304 W. Washington St., Bloomington, 309/829-TALL or 309/829-7255, $11.50–13.50 for climbing, plus $5 for initiation fee, $6 per rappel). Yes, you can scale the walls of a former grain silo. The 65-foot-tall silos have 20,000 square feet of indoor climbing surface, plus there's an outdoor, lighted wall. Outside is also a new "bouldering" area, for those interested in climbing without ropes in areas close to the ground. You can also rappel down the outside of the silos. (If you plan to rappel, call to make an appointment.) During the cold months the imaginative staff creates a frozen waterfall outside the silos with the sprinkler system. Regular two-hour classes for beginners run $30, and include equipment, instruction, and ability to use the gym all day. It's not far from Cargill's massive grain elevator complex. It's easy to confuse the two, but along the north end of one of the elevators the owners have painted the name Upper Limits. Summer hours: 4–10 P.M. Monday, noon–10 P.M. Tuesday–Friday, 10 A.M.–8 P.M. Saturday, 10 A.M.–6 P.M. Sunday. Winter hours: 4–10 P.M. Monday, Wednesday, Friday, noon–10 P.M. Tuesday and Thursday, 10 A.M.–10 P.M. Saturday, 10 A.M.–6 P.M. Sunday.

Hiking and Biking

If it's a nice day and you've got the time (and energy), see Bloomington's sights on your bike. Follow **Constitution Trail,** a 14-mile paved trail through the twin cities and you'll pass the David Davis mansion, Bloomington's historic districts, **Hidden Creek Nature Sanctuary**

(Sycamore St., between Fell and Linden), and other city parks, gardens, and residential and commercial areas. The trail runs largely from the north to south, but there is also an east-west branch. Along the way you'll find plenty of water fountains, picnic tables, and benches. The trail, by the way, was named the Constitution Trail because the towns started planning it in 1987 when the United States was celebrating the 200th anniversary of the signing of the constitution. The north-south trail runs from County Road 1850 North (just north of Normal) to Oakland Avenue in Bloomington. The east-west branch starts at Normal's parks and recreation office (611 S. Linden St., Normal, 309/454-9540) and ends at Towanda Barnes Road in Bloomington. The trail is accessible at several points along the trail. You can park at the Hugh Atwood wayside on Robinson and Jefferson Streets; at the parking lot adjacent to the Upper Limits climbing gym; or at Normal's parks and recreation department's office.

ACCOMMODATIONS

Because several interstates run through Bloomington-Normal, there is no shortage of national chain motels at the exits.

Under $50
There's a **Motel 6** (1600 N. Main St., Normal, 309/452-0422) on the north side of the twin cities, near I-55 and U.S. 51.

$50–100
Best Western University Inn (Six Traders Circle, Normal, 309/454-4070, $73) is easily accessible from all three interstates that run through Bloomington-Normal: I-74, I-55, and I-39. There's an indoor pool and pets are allowed. In Bloomington's Franklin Park Historic District, the **Burr House B&B** (210 E. Chestnut St., Bloomington, 309/828-7686 or 800/449-4182, $60–100) has six rooms for guests, some with private bathrooms and some with shared bathrooms. The stately brick home, built in 1864, is just across the street from Franklin Park. Rates are $60–100.

The **Hampton Inn West** (906 Maple Hill Rd., Bloomington, 309/829-3700 or 800/426-7866, $94) is close to Upper Limits gym and about three miles west of downtown Bloomington. The hotel has an indoor pool and fitness room, plus it offers a continental breakfast.

$100–$150
Ostensibly modeled after a French castle, **The Chateau Hotel and Conference Center** (1601 Jumer Ave., Bloomington, 309/662-2020 or 866/690-4006, www.chateauhotel.biz, $99–148) is a bit different from your standard chain hotels, with some antiques and decorative touches around the hotel and in the rooms, although it's still far from the real thing. But for folks looking for something a little different, this is a good option. There are 180 rooms here, including rooms with queen and king beds and some suites with fireplaces. The hotel has a restaurant and lounge on-site, but if you want to venture beyond the hotel, The Chateau offers free local transportation. The Constitution Trail is steps away from the hotel, so this is also a good option if you're planning to do some biking.

FOOD
American and Continental
One side of **Pumpernickel's Deli and Eatery** (113 N. Center St., Bloomington, 309/820-1200, 7:30 A.M.–9 P.M. Mon.–Thurs., 7:30 A.M.–11 P.M. Fri.–Sat.) is casual café or quick bite to eat or carry-out food. The other section is a bit more formal with a small dining room with white tablecloths and a sitting area with leather armchairs and low lights. The menu changes weekly, but you can expect such items as Jamaican jerk chicken wraps for $10 or a Reuben sandwich for about $6. Above the restaurant Abraham Lincoln delivered a speech to area residents after losing a campaign against Stephen Douglas for the Senate seat.

It's set back off Main Street just a bit, so you might miss **Crazy Planet Kitchen** (414 N. Main St., Bloomington, lunch 11 A.M.–2 P.M. Mon.–Sat., dinner 5 P.M.–Tues.–Sat., $8 lunch,

The Grand Prairie

$15 dinner) while walking by. What a pity. The small restaurant (the main dining room has about 10 tables) serves novel, mostly healthy sandwiches and entrées, such as garden burgers or dishes such as "Crazy Crepes," which are crepes filled with chicken and mushrooms and a cherry cream sauce.

The menu at the white-tablecloth **Ñ Lancaster's** (513 N. Main St., Bloomington, 309/827-3333, 5 P.M.–10 P.M. Mon.–Sat., $22) changes weekly, but you can always expect refreshing seafood and meat dishes, such as lobster cakes for appetizers, lamp chops, Tuscan chicken (with tomatoes, onions, bacon, and feta), and stuffed pork tenderloin. Fine dining is rare in these parts, and Lancaster's does a good job of keeping people coming back to this intimate storefront restaurant.

Pizza

Ñ Lucca Grill (116 E. Main St., Bloomington, 309/828-7521, www.luccagrill.com, 3–10 P.M. Sun., 10 A.M.–midnight Mon.–Wed., 10–1 A.M. Thurs.–Sat., $4–10) is one of those places where you can walk in as a stranger and feel at home. Lucca seems to attract quite a mix of clientele—professionals, students, and blue-collar workers. This casual restaurant and bar serves Italian-American food. Some of the food is what you would expect from an Italian restaurant—Italian beef sandwiches and fettuccine Alfredo. Then there are items such as deep-fried chicken livers (give 'em a try) and liverwurst sandwiches. You cannot beat the pasta, especially the fettuccine with spicy Italian sausage. Pizza is also a good bet, especially late in the evening.

Sweets

Here's your chance to be a kid in a candy shop once again. **The Chocolatier** (514 N. Main St., Bloomington, 9:30 A.M.–6 P.M. Mon.–Sat.) is an old-fashioned type of candy store: Counters are lined with dozens of glass jars filled with penny candy such as sweet tarts. It also has a selection of chocolate such as chocolate-covered strawberries and cherries, plus Italian ice.

Coffee Shop

While most of downtown Bloomington is closed on Sundays, **Main Street Expresso** (107 N. Main St., Bloomington, 309/829-4047) is a lively, cheery place where you can sip on hot and cold coffee and tea drinks, nibble on a scone or bagel, or check your email account on the computer.

Markets

The Common Ground Natural Foods (516 N. Main St., Bloomington, 309/829-2621, 9:30 A.M.–5:30 P.M. Mon.–Sat., during the summer it opens at 7:30 A.M. Sat.) stocks plenty of Paul Newman's line of foods, such as organic tortilla chips, plus a small selection of fruits and vegetables grown organically on regional farms.

The Bloomington **Farmers Market** and "artists' alley" is held 6:45–11 A.M. Saturdays at the courthouse square, mid-May–mid-October.

INFORMATION

The **Bloomington-Normal Area Convention and Visitors Bureau** (210 S. East St., Bloomington, 309/829-1641 or 800/433-8226, www.visitbn.org) has information on the region's many lodging and dining options and attractions. Give the staff a call or visit their website and they'll send you some brochures in the mail.

SERVICES

If the bike ride went awry or you just don't feel well, you can visit **OSF St. Joseph Medical Center** (2200 E. Washington St., Bloomington, 309/662-3311) or **BroMenn Regional Medical Center** (Virginia at Franklin Ave., Normal, 309/454-1400).

GETTING AROUND
Air

Fares are relatively inexpensive in and out of **Central Illinois Regional Airport** (Hwy. 9, two miles east of Veteran's Pkwy., Bloomington, 309/663-7383, www.cira.com), plus parking here is free. AirTran has flights to and from Orlando, Florida, and Atlanta, Georgia; Northwest flies to and from Detroit, Michigan; American Eagle and United Express fly planes back and forth between Bloomington and Chicago; and American Connection flies to and from St. Louis, Missouri.

Car

Several rental-car companies have offices at the airport, including Alamo (800/GO-ALAMO or 800/462-5266, www.alamo.com), Avis (800/230-4898, www.avis.com), Enterprise (800/261-7331, www.enterprise.com), and Hertz (800/654-3131, www.hertz.com).

FUNKS GROVE

Less than 10 miles south of Bloomington along old Route 66 is a historic farmstead surrounded by groves of sugar maples, big old white oak, trees and osage orange trees. This scenic corner of the world didn't belong to any old farmer. Lafayette Funk was a big-time cattle operator in Illinois, cofounder and director of the Union Stockyards in Chicago, and involved in many other successful agricultural business ventures. Today visitors can tour the old farmstead, take a look at the family's collection of minerals, and buy syrup made from the nearby trees.

Sights and Activities

Start your visit at the **Funk Prairie Home and Gem and Mineral Museum** (10875 Prairie Home Ln., Shirley, 309/827-6792, 9 A.M.–4 P.M. Tues.–Sat., Mar.–Dec., free). The home, built in 1864, has been restored and filled with antiques that once belonged to the Funks. On the grounds outside are formal gardens, a water fountain, and tennis court. Not exactly your typical farmstead. The gem and mineral collection also includes Native American artifacts, including arrowheads and other items found in the region. The gift shop stocks **Funks Grove Maple Syrup**

(309/827-3360, 9 A.M.–5 P.M. Mon.–Sat., 1–5 P.M. Sun. March–Aug. or by appointment, free) made from the sugar maple trees nearby. Guided tours in February and March show how the syrup is made from capturing the sap and boiling it down. The shop also sells Route 66 memorabilia.

Nearby is the **Funks Grove Nature Center** (off Route 66 on the county blacktop, follow signs, 309/827-2174), an 18-acre parcel that is one of the largest remnants of virgin forest in Illinois (now owned by the Illinois Department of Natural Resources). It was once dominated by native white and burr oaks, but in recent decades sugar maples have been moving in as the older trees start dying.

EL PASO

In the direction opposite of Funks Grove is El Paso, a village north of Bloomington. Just off I-39, El Paso makes for a nice detour for about an hour or two. Visit the local winery, then drop by downtown for a bite to eat at a tea room.

Sights

Just north of downtown El Paso is **Furrow Vineyard and Winery** (1131 Hwy. 251, El Paso, 309/527-8200, www.furrowwinery.com, 10 A.M.–5:30 P.M. Tues.–Sat., noon–5:30 P.M. Sun.), a winery and vineyard on a little slope overlooking the rural region. Established in 2001, this winery focuses on red, white, and blush wines made from French-American hybrid grapes such as chardonnel, plus traditional ones such as merlot and riesling. It offers tours of the winery and tastings. The shop stocks wines, plus accessories, gift baskets, cheeses, and other packaged food items.

A handful of antiques and second-hand shops lie along Front Street, which runs parallel to the railroad tracks in downtown El Paso.

Accommodations and Food

Close to the El Paso exit off I-39, **Days Inn** (630 W. Main St., El Paso, 309/527-7070 or 800/544-8313) is a newer hotel with an indoor pool. It also offers continental breakfast for guests.

The ladies will like **Front Street Gourmet** (31 W. Front St., El Paso, 309/527-3215, 10 A.M.–4 P.M. Tues.–Sat., $6), a café, tea room, and food shop with feminine touches such as flowers and antiques. (This is a popular spot for locals to hold bridesmaid luncheons or bridal showers.) The menu is not extensive, but you won't be disappointed by anything on it, such as warm spinach salad with hard-boiled eggs and red onions, a roast beef sandwich with cream cheese on marble rye bread. There's more: desserts, such as bread pudding, and beverages such strawberry lemonade. Lunch is served 11 A.M.–3 P.M.

PONTIAC

In a restored firehouse in downtown Pontiac, the **Route 66 Hall of Fame Museum** (110 W. Howard St., Pontiac, 815/844-5657 or 815/844-6937, www.il66assoc.org, noon–4 P.M. Mon., 10 A.M.–4 P.M. Tues.–Sat., by appointment Sun.) has an impressive collection of road memorabilia, including numerous old and new gas station signs, gas pumps, photographs of motels and restaurants along the road (some long gone, others still kickin'). For travelers who are actually driving Route 66, this is a must-stop. Volunteers with the museum (which is run by the Illinois Route 66 Association) can chat for hours about what to see and do along the road from Chicago to California.

I-74 to Champaign-Urbana

Agriculture is king here. See how many grain elevators you can count while driving the 45 minutes or so between Champaign-Urbana and Bloomington-Normal along I-74. It's easy to zip along on the highway and miss what's between the two regions. But take the slower route, Highway 150, which runs parallel to I-74. You find that in the shadow of these grain elevators are towns marked by red-brick buildings and town squares that date back 100 years. Shop for antiques in Farmer City or LeRoy. Pick up a pint of strawberries at a farm market. Hike through meadows or woods at Moraine View State Park or Lake of the Woods. The villages of Mahomet, Farmer City, and LeRoy were for many years autonomous towns home to farmers and people who worked in agribusiness. However, as the years have passed, more and more professionals from Bloomington and Champaign have settled there, particularly Mahomet.

LEROY

Moraine View State Park

At 1,700 acres, Moraine View State Park (27374 Moraine View Park Rd., Le Roy, 309/724-8032, www.dnr.state.il.us, sunrise–10 P.M. daily), five miles north of Le Roy, is not the largest state park in the state, but it offers a slew of activities. The center of activity is 158-acre Lake Dawson, which was created in the early 1960s when a dam was built on the North Fork, a tributary to Salt Creek, near U.S. 150 and Highway 9. Boats with engines higher than 10 horsepower need to run on an idle or no-wake speed on Lake Dawson. This means the lake is not overrun with large, loud boats zooming by, but mostly fisherman in 15-foot boats.

You can easily spend an afternoon or morning here. Start by renting a boat (you can rent rowboats, paddleboats, and canoes for $8–10 per hour) and fishing for bluegill, bass, walleye, northern pike, followed by a dip in the lake from the park's sandy beach and a meal at the restaurant near the boat ramp. Top it off with a walk along the nature trail that winds around part of the lake. During the fall, Moraine View is a popular spot for pheasant hunting. And during the winter, area residents go ice-skating and ice-fishing on the lake. In addition, park staff groom several miles of cross-country ski trails. The restaurant and concession stand operate seasonally. Swimming is allowed on the sandy beach Memorial Day–Labor Day. There is no admission fee to the park, but to swim you have to pay $1.

Camping

Moraine View State Park (27374 Moraine View Park Rd., Le Roy, 309/724-8032, www.dnr.state.il.us, $6–8 per night per site) has several different types of camping facilities. It has 137 campsites, plus 32 primitive sites accessible from the backpacking trail called Tall Timber. Class A sites have electricity with shower.

Folks traveling in an RV will feel welcome at **Tin Cup** (Mahomet), near Lake of the Woods Park and a couple of miles from I-74. There's also tent camping here, but the sites are not as private as those in Moraine View State Park.

Food

The motto of **M Steve's Silver Moon Restaurant** (200–202 E. Center St., LeRoy, 309/962-5751, 11 A.M.–1:30 P.M., 5–8:30 P.M. Tues.–Sat., 11 A.M.–2 P.M. Sun.) is that it's nestled at the base of Mt. Level. Get it? (The restaurant is owned by a former resident of New Hampshire.) This popular restaurant in downtown LeRoy serves American food. The big draws are the restaurant's buffets, which change nightly, and the ice-cream and soda fountain creations served by a soda jerk behind a massive bar that served visitors to the Chicago World's Fair. The brownie sundae, by the way, is stellar.

Except for the addition of televisions, a few video games, and tables, not much seems to have changed inside the **Old Bank Inn** (201 E. Center St., LeRoy, 309/962-9651, 11–1 A.M. Tues.–Sat., 11 A.M.–9 P.M. Sun.) since the days it operated as the LeRoy State Bank. The safe is still there (that's where the buffet is set up; same with a deposit box, marble flooring, and stained glass windows. You can order catfish, chicken, hamburgers, and other standard fare here.

A few area farmers set up flower, fruit, and vegetable stands for the **LeRoy farmers market,** held at the First Presbyterian Church, 101 E. Pine St., Saturday mornings in the summer.

FARMER CITY

Shopping

Farmer City's Main Street has a handful of antiques shops where you can spend hours getting lost looking at vintage jewelry, furniture, books, magazines, china, and more. Here's a sampling: **No Place Like Home** (320 S. Main St., Farmer City, 309/928-9696); **Salt Creek Emporium** (120 Main St., Farmer City, 309/928-2844); **Farmer City Antique Center** (201 S. Main St., Farmer City, 309/928-9210); and **Main Street Antiques** (115 S. Main St., Farmer City, 309/928-9208).

Events

The big to-do in Farmer City is its **Scarecrow and Pumpkin Festival** held in mid-October. Residents build scarecrows and display them throughout downtown. There are a petting zoo, art show, tractor show, live music (usually country), and plenty of food.

Accommodations

Try **Budget Motel** (825 E. Clinton Ave./Hwy. 54, Farmer City, 309/928-2157).

Information

Stop by the **Farmer City Visitors Center** (701 E. Clinton Ave./Hwy. 54, Farmer City, 309/928-2825, 6 A.M.–6 P.M. Fri.–Sun.) to pick up brochures and maps. To help set the mood as you drive through this region of the world, turn on the radio to **The Whip, WHHP 98.3 FM** (407 N. Main St., Farmer City, 309/928-9876). Disc jockeys play a blend of blues, bluegrass, and alt-country. You can hear Johnny Cash, Champaign native Alison Krauss, and blues musician Charlie Musselwhite.

MAHOMET

Sights and Activities

The 900-acre **Lake of the Woods Park** (109 S. Lake of the Woods Rd., Mahomet, 217/586-3360, www.ccfpd.org, free), run by the Champaign County Forest Preserve District, could be described as a suburban-style park. It's not

© CHRISTINE DES GARENNES

Lake of the Woods Park

right in town, but it's not exactly in the wilderness, either. (It's difficult to get lost here. You're never too far from a golf course, trailhead, or road.) There's a little bit for everyone here: a lake for bank fishing, a 3.3-mile multiuse trail along the Sangamon River, botanical gardens, an 18-hole golf course, a par-3, nine-hole golf course, a covered bridge, and a bell carillon for your listening pleasure.

There's lots of walking to be done in Lake of the Woods. A paved multipurpose trail follows the Sangamon River through the length of the park and extends west of Highway 47 for a little more than three miles. You can continue on the asphalt path or alongside on the gravel path. Or, throughout the 266 acres are mowed trails that weave up and down hills and near the river. Near the botanical gardens is a woodsy, winding nature trail in a section of the park called **Rayburn-Purnell Woods.** Finally, one of the nicest spots is the botanical gardens and the Miriam Davies Enabling Garden. This area was designed specifically for children and adults with disabilities, and it features raised beds (so people in wheelchairs can smell the flowers), and

plenty of patio space for relaxing by the little waterfall.

During the summer you can rent canoes, kayaks, rowboats, and paddleboats at Lake of the Woods Park 1–5 P.M. on Sundays for $3. The park is open 7 A.M.–10 P.M. daily. The gardens are open dawn–dusk.

Within Lake of the Woods park is the **Early American Museum** (600 N. Lombard St., Hwy. 47, Mahomet, 217/586-2612, www.earlyamericanmuseum.org, free), a first-rate local museum. Volunteers put together excellent rotating exhibits throughout the year. One recent exhibit highlighted how the Depression affected the region. In addition to the rotating shows, the museum's permanent collection tells the story of how the region was settled. Displays include agricultural equipment and a re-created blacksmith shop. On occasional Sundays, an artisan sets up shop in or outside the museum to demonstrate his or her art, such as woodcarving or quilting. During the summer the museum is open 10 A.M.–5 P.M. Monday–Saturday, 1–5 P.M. Sunday. March–May and September–December, it's open 1–5 P.M. daily.

Shopping

A handful of shops are along the 400 block of Main Street, such as **Earth Sight** (417 E. Main St., Mahomet, 217/586-2237, 10 A.M.–5 P.M. Tues.–Sat., noon–4 P.M. Sun.) and **Prairie Boatworks** (407 E. Main St., Mahomet, 217/352-1493, noon–5 P.M. Fri.–Sat., noon–4 P.M. Sun.). Earth Sight sells quite a few toys for children who have an interest in the natural world—kids who like to set up chemistry experiments in the garage and who need the right kit to catch butterflies and other insects. Natural guides and other books and other similarly themed decor is for sale for adults, too. Prairie Boatworks gallery features work of artists from the region, photographs that capture life here, pottery, and other fine art.

Accommodations and Food

Check out **Heritage Inn Motel** (801 Eastwood Dr., Mahomet, 217/586-4975).

Pickle Tree Farm (305 S. Prairieview Rd., Mahomet, 217/586-7003, www.pickletree farm.com, 10 A.M.–8 P.M. Mon.–Sat., 10 A.M.–6 P.M. Sun., $8) is just off I-74 in Mahomet, but it is hardly one of your run-of-the mill restaurants usually huddled near interstates. It's inside two warm, totally renovated barns, with an outdoor dining deck in the rear overlooking a pond. (You can still hear the cars rumbling down the highway, but it's as nice as you can get this close to the highway.) Food is wholesome and served in a warm atmosphere (friendly staff, plus in the wintertime, the dining room's fireplace is always welcoming). Food is basic, but good, with such items as a ham and Swiss cheese sandwich, or the garden veggie wrap, with cream cheese spread on a tortilla and layered with vegetables such as green peppers and tomatoes.

Farmers Markets

The Asbill family's farm stand, **First Fruits** (2272 County Rd. 350 E, Mahomet, 217/586-1333) is constantly expanding, it seems, and there's always a variety of fruits and vegetables. Throughout the spring there's asparagus and salad greens, and into the summer, strawberries, carrots, potatoes, and huge garlic bulbs. The Asbills also sell honey, jams, and meat from chickens and turkeys raised on pasture without hormones. (Meat availability is based on when they butcher.) Hours vary per season. They are generally open at 9 A.M., but are closed on Tuesdays and on Wednesday mornings when they sell at the farmers market in downtown Mahomet. In other words, call before you go.

Information

For more on restaurants and stuff to do in Mahomet you can contact the **Mahomet Chamber of Commerce** (202 N. East St., Mahomet, 217/586-3165, www.mahometchamberofcommerce.com).

The Grand Prairie

Champaign County

HISTORY AND ORIENTATION

Champaign-Urbana may lack the scenic overlooks common in hillier regions to the south and northwest, but the area is chock-full of recreational and cultural opportunities. This is in large part due to the presence of the University of Illinois, whose campus sits partly in Champaign and partly in Urbana. Known primarily for its engineering, physics, and computer science departments (the campus is home to the National Center for Supercomputing Applications), the UI attracts students from all across the state and the world. Its Krannert Center for the Performing Arts brings in top-notch musicians and shows, such as Ravi Shankar and the Julliard Quartet. And fans from all around come to cheer on the Fighting Illini at basketball and football games. The cities, which have a combined population of about 100,000 people, are home to a vibrant mix of musicians, actors, scientists, historic preservationists, and

more. There are a decent stock of Victorian and Craftsman-style homes, cobblestone streets in historic residential districts, plus revitalized downtown districts with a growing number of restaurants, coffee shops, and drinking spots.

Although designated a county in 1833, it wasn't until the 1850s that Champaign County started attracting settlers and begin to prosper. That was when the Illinois Central Railroad decided to lay tracks in the area and build a depot in Champaign County. The town of Urbana came first and people established homesteads around Boneyard Creek (now largely a drainage ditch through the towns). The county courthouse was built in Urbana in 1848, with the soon-to-be famous Abraham Lincoln occasionally arguing a few cases there. Most of the industry around Champaign and Urbana is still farm-related. You'll notice quite a few grain-processing plants and elevators on the outskirts of town, plus farm machinery retail stores. Of course, the University of Illinois,

© CHRISTINE DES GARENNES

An old cattle bank is now the Champaign County Historical Museum.

© AVALON TRAVEL PUBLISHING, INC.

initially the Illinois Industrial University when it was established in 1867, is a huge employer, as is Kraft Foods. When the wind is right, you can smell salad dressings and cheese powder brewing in the west Champaign plant. The town is still populated by many folks of German and Italian descent, but since the mid-20th century it has become home to a growing number of African Americans and immigrants from Central and Eastern Asia.

SIGHTS

The University of Illinois

Established in 1867, the University of Illinois was and is a focal point of culture and events in the two towns and it sits right between the two. The campus extends from 1st Street to the west and Lincoln Avenue to the east, University Avenue to the north and Windsor Road to the south. Take a stroll through the quad and the Illini Union, where you can grab a cup of coffee, view artwork by students, or go bowling. From the union, you can visit fine museums, among them the Krannert Art Museum and Spurlock Museum, parks such as the arboretum, and unique buildings such as Assembly Hall, all within about a 15-minute walk.

The **Krannert Art Museum** (500 E. Peabody Dr., Champaign, 217/333-1860, 9 A.M.–5 P.M. Tues.–Sat., until 9 P.M. Thurs.; 2–5 P.M. Sun., free) showcases a wide variety of artwork, from Latin America textiles to French lithographs to contemporary American drawings. The museum also frequently shows artwork by UI graduate students and faculty. Each gallery in the **Spurlock Museum** (600 S. Gregory Dr., Urbana, 217/333-2360, noon–5 P.M. Tues., 9 A.M.–5 P.M. Wed.–Fri, 10 A.M.–4 P.M. Sat., free) focuses on a different world culture, including those of Asia, Africa, the Middle East, Oceana, Europe, as well as Native American and ancient Mediterranean cultures. You'll see items such as brass engravings from 12th-century Europe, a Roman iron spearhead and sling bullets from 1,000 B.C., gongs from Ecuador, a replica of a Confucian home, Egyptian funerary masks from 1,000 B.C., and more.

Touted as the largest public university library in the world, the **University of Illinois Library** (1408 Gregory Dr., 217/333-2290, 8 A.M.–midnight Mon.–Thurs., 8 A.M.–6 P.M. Fri., 9 A.M.–6 P.M. Sat., and 1 P.M.–midnight. Sun., free) is a massive and impressive building for book lovers, with special and rare books collections that boast a first edition of John James Audubon's *Birds of America* and personal letters of Carl Sandburg, John Milton, and other notable authors. Free tours of the undergraduate library (built totally underground) and the main library are allowed. Pick up an audiocassette at the information desk.

That massive, white, spaceship-looking building on the southwest side of campus is **Assembly Hall** (1800 S. 1st St., Champaign, 217/333-5000, www.assembly.uiuc.edu), an indoor arena where the Illini basketball teams play and where big-name musicians play when in town.

The **University of Illinois Arboretum** (Lincoln Ave., between Florida Ave. and St. Mary's Rd., Urbana, 217/244-9934, free) is a fine spot to take a walk or pick up gardening ideas. The arboretum has rows of trees such as cypress and gardens of flowering plants, vegetables, and roses.

Museums

After years of fund-raising, soliciting artifacts, and extensive restoration efforts, the Champaign County Historical Society in 2001 opened the **Cattle Bank Museum** (102 E. University Ave., Champaign, 217/356-1010, 10 A.M.–5 P.M. Wed.–Sat, 1–4:30 P.M. Sun., free). Believed to be the oldest known commercial building in the Champaign-Urbana area, the Cattle Bank is an Italianate-style building that began life in 1857 as an actual cattle bank. For most of the years that the building was open and operating, it was as a grocery and drug store. Here you'll find exhibits on businesses that operated in town for decades, such as a shoe cobbler, displays on vintage clothing and accessories, and many photos of the towns. The front room has been re-created into a grocery store circa the turn of the 19th century, complete with an antique counting machine, paper dispenser, and twine ball.

The Orpheum (346 N. Neil St., Champaign, 217/352-5895, 9 A.M.–6 p.m. Tues., 1–6 P.M. Wed.–Sun., $2) is technically a hands-on children's museum, but because it is inside a former vaudeville theater built in 1916, architecture buffs and preservationists might want to stop by to take a look at the building's architectural features and check out the small exhibit on vaudeville theater. The building is a one-third-scale model of the La Salle de Spectacle, the opera house at Versailles, with French Renaissance and baroque friezes, among other intriguing accents.

Ship Model Museum

So the ocean is hundreds and hundreds of miles away but that doesn't mean little Sadorus, Illinois, can't have a **National Museum of Ship Models and Sea History** (201 S. Market St., Sadorus, 217/352-1672, 10 A.M.–4:30 P.M. Sat. and by appointment, $4) in it. About 15 miles southwest of Champaign in downtown Sadorus, a small farming community, is the rare and impressive museum. Housed in a beautifully restored storefront space (formerly a general store), the museum's collection includes ship models used in Hollywood films, paddlewheels, ocean liners, and more. Boats are on two floors, and there are nautical photographs and paintings hung around the building.

RECREATION

Meadowbrook Park, at Windsor Road and Race Street in Urbana, is a stunning park on the southeast edge of town. The park contains organic gardens tended by area residents, a paved path for inline skating and bicycling, a hiking trail along a creek and through a meadow, plus 80 outdoor sculptures throughout the park.

ACCOMMODATIONS

The vast majority of hotels and motels are north of I-74 by the Market Place Mall, between Prospect and Lincoln avenues. Here you'll find all the chain hotels and motels, from the economical Baymont to the more expensive Marriott Courtyard.

$50–100

The **Baymont Inn** (320 Anthony Dr., Champaign, 217/356-8900) has clean, no-frills rooms. Compared to the other economy hotels in the area, the Baymont is a newer building and has all the same basic amenities in the rooms, such as a coffeemaker and hair dryer.

A good bet in the moderate to high-end price range is **The Drury Inn** (905 W. Anthony Dr., Champaign, 217/398-0030 or 800/378-7946). Two great things about staying at the Drury Inn are the free evening cocktail hours during the week and the extensive continental breakfast, including fare such as steaming waffles and sausages. The hotel has 133 rooms, an indoor pool, fitness center, and high-speed Internet access in rooms.

Consider **The Lincoln Hotel** (209 S. Broadway Ave., Urbana, 217/384-9001) as an alternative to staying in a hotel room with views of the interstate. Built in 1924 in an English Tudor style, it's bedecked with lodge-type interior features (imagine lots of walnut woodwork and antler sets on the walls). The rooms don't feel like your run-of-the-mill hotel room; some have four-poster beds. Ownership and management turnover is high and the rooms are starting to show their age. The hotel could use a good renovation. However, this is an option if you want to stay in town.

Another alternative to staying by the mall is **The Illini Union Guest Rooms** (1401 W. Green St., Urbana, 217/333-3030) in the center of the campus. The 72 rooms are above the union, and all have private bathrooms. You don't need to be an alumnus or visiting scholar to stay here.

The Lindley House Bed and Breakfast (312 W. Green St., Urbana, 217/384-4800) is a Queen Anne house (complete with turrets and gables) in a historic district and within a short walk of downtown Urbana. The Lindley House has three rooms with queen-size beds, a loft suite with a king-size bed, plus a carriage house with a kitchenette.

FOOD

Cafés

Ⓜ Café Kopi (109 N. Walnut St., Champaign, 217/359-4266, 7 A.M.–midnight daily, $6), a thriving coffee shop in downtown Champaign, not only serves a gripping espresso, but also wholesome sandwiches and salads such as hummus plates, crab salad sandwiches, and spring greens. Expect the usual coffee-shop atmosphere: provocative art on the walls, newspapers scattered about on tables, and the freedom to lounge around for a while.

Caffé Paradiso (801 S. Lincoln Ave., Urbana, 217/384-6066) tends to attract more college students than Café does, since it is near the University of Illinois campus. The coffee menu is quite extensive, plus it has a variety of cookies, pastries, and sandwiches. Unlike in other coffee shops in town, you are allowed to smoke here. A few tables are set up for chess or backgammon.

Casual

Jerusalem Restaurant (601 S. Wright St., Champaign, 11 A.M.–9 P.M. daily, $4) is right in the middle of fast-food central, surrounded by burger and pizza joints. But at the Jerusalem Restaurant you can get items such as cucumber yogurt salad, falafel, and kebabs for the same price as a burger from a national chain and served in just about the same amount of time. Try the Arabian tea.

Li'l Porgy's (1917 W. Springfield Ave., Champaign, 217/398-8575; and 101 W. University Ave., Urbana, 217/367-1018, lunch and dinner daily, $6), serves the best 'cue in town (though Famous Dave's might dispute that) with all the fixings: corn on the cob, collard greens, and corn bread. It also has great pork sandwiches, ribs, and charbroiled chicken.

Open 24 hours, **Merry Ann's Diner** (1510 S. Neil St., Champaign, 217/352-5399; and 15 E. Main St., Champaign, 217/531-1160) attracts townies, farmers, and college students. There's

a reason the place is always packed. Speedy, adept, and friendly cooks and waitresses serve diner fare: eggs, pancakes, and sit-in-your-stomach biscuits and gravy. Try the genuine hot chocolate on a chilly day.

American

Inside a former lumber mill, **Ⓜ Silver Creek** (402 N. Race St., Urbana, 217/328-3402, 11 A.M.–10 P.M. Mon.–Thurs., 11 A.M.–11 P.M. Fri.–Sat., 10 A.M.–2:30 P.M. and 4–10 P.M. Sun.) is just a neat place to go eat. One of its dining rooms is in an enclosed greenhouse. With dishes such as London broil and veal cutlet, candles flickering on the tables, and soft music playing in the background, Silver Creek tends to attract couples and older crowds. Lunch dishes are around $6; dinner entrées run $12–22.

Another unique setting for a restaurant is the **Ⓜ Courier Café** (111 N. Race St., Urbana, 217/328-1811, 7 A.M.–11 P.M. Sun.–Thurs., 7 A.M.–midnight Fri.–Sat., $6) which is in a former newspaper office building and on the site of a cabin of an early settler in the mid-1800s. Antiques are placed throughout the restaurant: light fixtures in every booth, a massive gold-painted cash register, and stained glass windows. Food is basic and homey, such as BLTs and blueberry pancakes. The Courier serves breakfast, lunch, and dinner.

Eclectic

Fusing South American, Latin American, European, and African influences, **Ⓜ Radio Maria** (119 N. Walnut St., Champaign, 217/398-7729, lunch 11 A.M.–2:30 P.M. Tues.–Fri., dinner 5–10 P.M. Tues.–Sat., brunch 11 A.M.–2:30 P.M. Sun.), serves dinner dishes such as Caribbean jerk chicken, polenta, and other meals made with ingredients such as mangoes and bananas. Like the meals, the setting is aesthetically pleasing, with oil paintings by local artists hanging on the walls, tabletops designed with scenes from vintage postcards, and red, velvety curtains. Dinners are about $11. Also check out the impressive Sunday brunches from about $7.

Italian

Visitors have plenty of Italian restaurants to choose from in both towns. A standout is **M The Great Impasta** (114 W. Church St., Champaign, 217/359-7377, lunch and dinner daily, $6–18) Lasagnas are the popular dish here, from basic veggie to seafood lasagna with crabmeat and shrimp. Even the non-Italian dishes are outstanding, such as the beef stroganoff with its buttery egg noodles and tender meat. Portions are generous and served in a Tuscan café-type of environment with hand-painted murals on the walls.

Sweets

Chocolate aficionados need to head to **Moonstruck** (709 S. Wright St., Urbana, 217/367-7402), a chocolate bar where everything on the menu has chocolate as an ingredient. Choose from truffles, German chocolate cake slices, mocha lattes, and more. The atmosphere is soothing and relaxing with overstuffed chairs and occasional jazz musicians; you'll want to hang out for a while.

M Mirabelle's(124 W. Main St., Urbana, 217/384-6460) has such a fine reputation for its fine pastries and breads that many people are willing to stand in line at 7 A.M. on a Saturday morning to get their pick of fresh-baked brioche, baguettes, or fruit tarts. The line often stretches outside the shop and onto the sidewalk.

Markets

Being surrounded by farms definitely has its advantages. May–October, area farmers, including the Amish, set up booths in Champaign and Urbana. You can find everything from kohlrabi to zucchini, granola to free range turkey at the area's **farmers markets.** In Urbana they sell goods on Saturdays, 7 A.M.–noon in the Lincoln Square parking lot at the corner of Vine and Illinois streets. In Champaign, they sell on Wednesdays, 7 A.M.–1 P.M. in the Country Fair Shopping Center parking lot, by Springfield and Mattis avenues.

NIGHTLIFE

Live Music

Because Champaign-Urbana is home to thousands of undergraduate and graduate college students, it's no surprise that the towns have a thriving live music scene. Being not too far from Chicago, Champaign-Urbana is often a stop for bands coming or going to the Windy City, from blues musicians to popular bands. Venues range from the expansive Assembly Hall to the pub Mike 'n Molly's.

Mike 'n Molly's (105 N. Market St., Champaign, 217/355-1236), is a small bar with a large, always hopping beer garden. Beer connoisseurs, prepare to salivate over the number of beers from around the world on tap and available in the bottle. In the mood for a specialty imported beer such as a Lindeman's Frambois? Chances are, Mike 'n Molly's will have it. The pub hosts everything from spoken-word performances to comedy contests to the Prairie Jam music festival held there annually during Labor Day weekend.

On any given night, **The Highdive** (51 W. Main St., Champaign, 217/359-HIGH or 217/359-4444) could feature a Cajun band from Louisiana, DJs spinning club or hip hop music, or even a country swing band. The Highdive serves import and domestic beers, plus specialty drinks such as martinis. With two bars and plenty of bartenders, you don't have to wait long for a drink. Stop by for the popular jazz happy hour on weekday evenings.

Inside a former movie theater, **The Canopy** (708 S. Goodwin Ave., 217/344-BAND or 217/344-2263) is an intimate live music venue, with 1,000 seats and rainforest murals painted on the walls. The club, near the U of I campus, tends to attract the college crowd. Expect bands such as Frank Black and The Catholics or The String Cheese Experiment. The club also hosts the occasional Grateful Dead Night or Open Mic Night.

Bars

The beautiful **Boltini's** (211 N. Neil St.,

Champaign, 217/378-8001), in a renovated turn-of-the-20th-century storefront, has cool architectural features such as a silver-painted tin ceiling, intimate booths, and subdued lighting. You can order all kinds of specialty cocktails and imported and domestic beer here, as well as delectable munchies such as bruschetta. There's a small deck outside for summer evenings.

Farren's (308 N. Randolph St., Champaign, 217/359-6977) is part pub and part sandwich spot. Situated in a sunken room in a building accessible via an alley in downtown Champaign, Farren's features delicious but inexpensive drinks and sandwiches. Yes, you can get a basic burger here, but Farren's also serves a decent green chili burger and has quite a few veggie sandwiches, such as the spinach panini. Sandwiches start at $3.50.

Jupiter's Pizzeria and Pool (39 Main St., Champaign, 217/398-5988) is a pool hall that serves beer on tap and by the bottle, from Bell's Amber to Pabst Blue Ribbon. The kitchen serves thin-crust pizzas, such as pizza margherita and pizza pesto. A popular spot any time of the day, Jupiter's is in a turn-of-the-20th-century building with features such as high ceilings and hardwood floors.

The Office (214 W. Main St., 217/344-7608), housed in a vintage building in downtown Urbana, is a good place to chat with friends over a pint. It's not a full-blown sports bar with hundreds of TVs, but not yet a nightclub. With its many wooden booths, it's a place you can hang out for a while. You can order bar food such as nachos and burgers, and play a round of pool or a game of darts.

Theater and Film

You can see just about any kind of show at the **Virginia Theatre** (203 W. Park Ave., Champaign, 217/356-9053 or 217/356-9063), from films during the Roger Ebert Overlooked Film Festival to the local theater company's rendition of *The Sound of Music*. A former vaudeville playhouse and movie theater, the Virginia is an Italian Renaissance building on the exterior, with Spanish Renaissance features inside, including paintings of Spanish explorers.

The Champaign-Urbana Theater Company (203 W. Park Ave., Champaign, 217/356-9053) stages about three musical comedies per year in the Virginia Theatre.

The Celebration Company, a community theater group, produces original and traditional plays in the intimate Station Theatre (223 N. Broadway Ave., Urbana, 217/384-4000), a former train station.

Built in 1913 as the Park Theatre, a poor man's version of the more ornately decorated Virginia Theatre and Orpheum, **Boardman's New Art Theatre** (126 W. Church St., Champaign, 217/355-0068) presents foreign and art films, from Inuit movies to midnight showings of *The Rocky Horror Picture Show*.

The Krannert Center for the Performing Arts (500 S. Goodwin Ave., Urbana, 217/333-6280) brings in professional touring opera companies, renowned musicians such as Ravi Shankar, and University of Illinois string quartets.

SHOPPING

Although a bit of a renaissance is occurring in downtown Champaign, with a few more boutiques opening here and there, the region remains mall-focused. **The Market Place Mall,** on Market Street north of I-74, is anchored by the department store Famous Barr, and contains national chains such as Gap and Eddie Bauer. The mall is surrounded by numerous shopping centers that contain chain bookstores and home improvement stores.

You will find a few independently owned stores scattered throughout both towns. At **Champaign Surplus** (303 S. Neil St., Champaign, 217/356-4703) you can load up on camping supplies or field gear for your next bird walk or hiking trip.

Walnut Street Tea Company (115 S. Walnut St., Champaign, 217/351-6975) specializes in all kinds of imported teas and accessories.

It is possible to spend an afternoon exploring the three floors of **Jane Addams Book Shop,** 208 N. Neil St., Champaign, 217/356-

2555. This antiquarian shop specializes in out-of-print books and has quite the collection of cooking and art books.

Every Friday and Saturday, **The Corkscrew** (203 N. Vine St., Urbana, 217/337-7704, www.thecorkscrew.com) offers wine and beer samples at moderate prices (from $3 a person). In one afternoon you can try about 8–10 different wines of the Rhôone region in France and another day you can sample stout beers. Most of the wine bottles for sale have been reviewed (and extensively described) by savvy staff members.

EVENTS

Roger Ebert's Overlooked Film Festival in April keeps getting bigger every year. Films missed by most critics and audiences are shown in the classic Virginia Theatre. Area restaurants and artists set up booths at the **Taste of Champaign-Urbana** in West Side Park in Champaign in June. Teams of street ball players from the area compete in the annual **Slamma Jamma Basketball Tournament,** held in a different park in July each year. Corn is golden at Urbana's **Sweet Corn Festival** every July.

INFORMATION AND SERVICES

For more information about Champaign-Urbana contact **The Champaign County Convention and Tourism Bureau** (1817 S. Neil St., Champaign 217/351-4133 or 800/369-6151, www.cucvb.org). It stocks an information center in Market Square Mall on North Prospect Avenue.

The News-Gazette (www.news-gazette.com), the daily newspaper, serves both towns and the surrounding area. You can find it at gas stations and convenience stores, bookstores, and libraries.

Internet Access

Most cafés in downtown Champaign and Urbana offer free wireless access. You can also go online for a fee at **Kinko's Copies** (506 S. Mattis Ave., Champaign, 217/355-3400). Or you can log on for free at one of the public libraries: **The Champaign Public Library** (505 S. Randolph St., Champaign, 217/356-3980) or **The Urbana Free Library** (210 W. Green St., Urbana, 217/367-4069).

The two main hospitals are **Carle Foundation Hospital** (210 E. University Ave., Champaign, 217/337-3911) and **Provena Covenant Medical Center** (1400 W. Park Ave., Urbana, 217/337-2131).

The downtown **Champaign Post Office** is at 600 N. Neil Street. **The Urbana Post Office** is at 3104 E. Tatman Court.

GETTING THERE
Air
University of Illinois Willard Airport (U.S. 45 and Monticello Rd., Savoy, 217/244-8604, www.flycmi.com), about four miles south of Champaign, is serviced by four airlines: American Eagle, American Connection, Northwest Airlines, and Delta to and from Midwest hubs such as Chicago, St. Louis, Missouri, and Detroit, Michigan, but also Cincinnati, Ohio, and Dallas/Fort Worth, Texas.

Train
Amtrak's City of New Orleans train, which runs between Chicago and New Orleans, stops twice daily at Champaign's Illinois Terminal. The morning train is Chicago-bound; the evening train heads south. In addition to the City of New Orleans train, Amtrak's Illini train stops twice daily in Champaign. The Illini runs between Chicago and Carbondale, Illinois, the southern tip of the state. Round-trip fares from Chicago to Champaign range $32–64, depending on how far in advance you book your seat. The Amtrak ticket office is in the Illinois Terminal (45 E. University Ave., Champaign, 217/352-5905, 800/USA-RAIL or 800/872-7245).

Bus
Greyhound (Illini Terminal, 45 E. University Ave., Champaign, 217/352-4150 or 800/231-2222) has five buses that run between Chicago

The Grand Prairie

and Champaign every day. Four buses per day travel between Champaign and St. Louis. And two buses go to and from Indianapolis and Carbondale. **LEX-Lincolnland Express** (217/352-6682) offers vans rides to Chicago and Indianapolis airports.

GETTING AROUND
Bus
Champaign-Urbana Mass Transit District (217/384-8188, www.cumtd.com) runs routes seven days a week throughout both towns and to the southern suburb of Savoy, generally 6 A.M.–midnight. Buses depart every 10 minutes during peak hours and every hour on Sundays. Some routes around campus run until about 2:30 A.M. on the weekends. Buses do not run on major holidays: New Year's Day, Easter Sunday, Memorial Day, Fourth of July, Labor Day, and Christmas. Each ride costs $1; transfers are free. Exact change is required after 7 P.M. All routes are served by buses that are wheelchair-accessible and all buses are equipped with bike racks. Pick up a map and schedule at the Illini Terminal, (45 E. University Ave., Champaign).

Rental Cars
Most car-rental companies are at Willard Airport or within a few miles of the airport. **Avis** (407 S. Neil St., Champaign, 217/359-5441), can be found at Willard. **Enterprise** (1804 S. Neil St., Champaign, 217/351-1400 or 217/355-1300) is just south of the airport.

Taxi
You can catch a cab at the airport or Illini Terminal, but good luck trying to flag one down on a street corner or asking one to pick you up at a restaurant and take you to a bar. The towns' taxi companies stick to picking up and dropping off people at the airport. If you're coming into town at a later or early hour, you might want to call first to arrange a pickup. Try **Checker Cab** (217/355-0200), **Yellow Cab** (217/355-3553), or **Orange Taxi** (217/367-8888).

RANTOUL AND GIFFORD
Just north of Champaign-Urbana on U.S. 45 are the towns of Rantoul and Gifford. Rantoul was most well known for its connection to the air force; it was once home to the Chanute Air Force Base. Gifford is a small farm community and its claim to fame is Gordyville, an events center that hosts several major horse shows and auctions throughout the year.

Octave Chanute Aerospace Museum
When the air force closed Chanute Air Force Base in 1993, Rantoul was left with a huge site on the east side of town, with warehouses, barracks, and offices. One of the best things to happen to the space was the creation of the Octave Chanute Aerospace Museum (1011 Pacesetter Dr., Rantoul, 217/893-1613, www.aeromuseum.org, 10 A.M.–5 P.M. Mon.–Sat., noon–5 P.M. Sun., $7), which not only has extensive exhibits about the history of the base and life there (including an old food line), but the museum also has an amazing collection of airplanes. We're talking fighter jets, bombers, plus missiles. The museum also has exhibits on Rantoul area history. The former Chanute Air Force Base is east of U.S. 45 in Rantoul, south of U.S. 136.

Gordyville USA
West of Rantoul by about 10 minutes is Gordyville USA (U.S. 136, Gifford, 217/568-7117, www.gordyvilleusa.com, free), a vast complex in the middle of corn and soybean country where Amish farmers buy and sell horses and antique dealers sell everything you can imagine, books to tea kettles, china to farm equipment. Gordyville, by the way, is not an actual town, but the name of the complex, after the owner, long-time auctioneer Gordon Hannagan. Flea markets and auctions tend to be held on the second weekend of each month, 4–9 P.M. Friday, 9 A.M.–6 P.M. Saturday, 9 A.M.–4 P.M. Sunday.

Monticello and Piatt County

Robert Allerton Park is a grand estate in the middle of the prairie.

About 18 miles southwest of Champaign-Urbana, the town of Monticello is a growing community that keeps getting more intriguing every year, as artisans such as weavers, glass blowers, and potters move into town and open galleries. Because it is within a 30-minute drive of Champaign-Urbana, it has become somewhat more metropolitan than in years past, with more workers commuting to the twin cities and quite a few subdivisions popping up on the outskirts of town. But the town has not become just another suburb. The grocery store is still called Bill and Sandy's and the dinette serves factory workers alongside lawyers and doctors.

HISTORY AND ORIENTATION

From the 16th–19th century, the Monticello area was a hunting preserve for the Kickapoo and Potawatomi tribes of the Algonquin Indians. Eventually white settlers moved in and raised cattle here. After the railroads were built, the farmers switched to growing grain and shipped it to Chicago. (You can't miss the towering grain elevators, still in use, just west of the courthouse.) Throughout the mid-1800s, farmers around Monticello prospered. Cash crops such as corn and soy fared well in the area's rich soil. In 1841 it became the seat of Piatt County, a brand-new courthouse was built, and more businessmen from the region decided to build homes in Monticello.

In the 1890s the town became quite well known throughout the state when Dr. W. B. Caldwell invented a laxative that would bring him and his local business partners at the Pepsin Syrup Company loads of money. Mansions that once belonged to these medicine barons can by seen by taking a stroll or drive along North State Street, dubbed Millionaire's Row. A self-guided walking tour pamphlet, available from the Wabash Depot, highlights some of the most magnificent homes, and points out their neoclassical, Victorian, and Gothic-revival architectural features.

SIGHTS AND ACTIVITIES
◼ Robert Allerton Park
Situated among silver maple and sycamore woods, sprawling lawns, manicured gardens, and a reflection pond, Robert Allerton Park (515 Old Timber Rd., 217/762-2721, 8 A.M.–sunset daily) evokes the feel of a 19th-century European estate. Once a second home to Allerton, a Chicago banker, philanthropist, and art collector, the house, along with its gardens and farm fields, were deeded to the University of Illinois upon his death in 1946. The main

◼ The Grand Prairie

house tends to be closed to the public, unless you are attending a special event or conference sponsored by the university. But you can certainly explore the nearly 20 miles of trails and acres of gardens. (Go ahead and peek through the windows for a good look at the impressive library.) Favorite spots include the Fu Dog Garden, where lapis lazuli ceramic *Fu Dogs* hold court; the sunken garden, a local favorite spot for weddings; and the southwest field where the bronze *Sun Singer* raises his arms toward the sky. The visitors center is open 9 A.M.–5 P.M. daily during the summer, and 8:30 A.M.–4:30 P.M. during the winter. Call about special events, such as the Tuscan food and wine tasting weekend.

Museums

At the **Monticello Railroad Museum** (Iron Horse Pl., Monticello, 217/762-9011, rides are on weekends May–late-Oct., $6), you can catch a short train ride through the town, past the surrounding farms, and along the Sangamon River valley. Illinois is home to a lot of railroad museums; the Monticello museum is one of the best because of the sheer number of cars and equipment it has on display. At the museum's railroad park, check out a variety of vintage diesel and steam locomotives, freight and Pullman passenger train cars. The museum also offers special train rides geared toward kids, such as the Ghost Train and Haunted Box Car rides around Halloween and a Santa Train ride during the holiday season. The museum is off Iron Horse Place, a frontage road along I-72, off Monticello's Market Street exit. You can board the train there or at the Wabash Depot, at Center and State streets, downtown Monticello.

Like the Cattle Bank Museum in Champaign, the **Piatt County Museum** (315 W. Main St. and 315 W. Washington Ave., 217/762-4731, open by appointment, donations) is stocked with local artifacts, many of them related to farming. You'll also find photos taken of the town in the 19th and early 20th centuries.

A few miles south of Monticello the rural community of Bement lays claim to the fact

that it was here (or at least, on a road outside of town) that U.S. Senate candidates Abraham Lincoln and Stephen A. Douglas decided to hold a series of debates, debates that would later catapult Lincoln into the national spotlight. The story goes that Lincoln and Douglas passed each other on the road between Monticello and Bement in 1859. They later met at the home of Francis Bryant, now called the **Bryant Cottage State Historic Site** (146 E. Wilson St., Bement, 217/678-8184, 9 A.M.–5 P.M. Thurs.–Sun. March–Oct., 9 A.M.–4 P.M. Thurs.–Sun. Nov.–Nov.–Feb., donation). Douglas was staying with Bryant, who had been a state legislator with Douglas in the 1850s. At the home (a little white cottage with green shutters and cedar shingles) Lincoln and Douglas forged plans for the debate. Today the home is being restored, and it is adjacent to a city park with picnic tables, playground, and a veteran's memorial.

Recreation

Valentine Park, run by the Forest Preserve District of Piatt County, is a secluded little park on the outskirts of Monticello (on Cemetery Rd. east of Market St.). It's a great spot for a short walk or picnic; it's never crowded. In contrast to the open prairie nearby, Valentine Park sits among a dense grove of trees. The half-mile tree-identification walk takes you past hickory, black walnut, maple, and sycamore trees. Bird-lovers should bring their binoculars for a visit to the bird-viewing area.

Entertainment

For a look at local color, visit **Bement Country Opry** (117 S. Macon St./Hwy. 105, Bement, 217/877-6499, www.bementcountryopry.com), where you can put on your cowboy hat and boots for live country music and dancing every Friday at 8 P.M.

ACCOMMODATIONS

If you stay overnight in Monticello, check into the **Best Western Gateway Inn** (805 Iron Horse Pl., 217/762-9436). Rooms are clean and comfy in this new building. The hotel features an indoor heated pool and continental breakfast of bagels and juice. Rooms are from $60.

FOOD

You can't go wrong with any of the restaurants on the square. Two top picks are The Brown Bag Deli and Restaurant for casual food and Montgomery's on the Square for fine dining.

M The Brown Bag Deli and Restaurant (212 W. Washington St., Monticello, 217/762-9221, call for hours, $5) lunch counter and coffee shop serves homemade soups such as cream of asparagus and minestrone and a variety of deli sandwiches. The restaurant is well known for its pies, such as coconut cream and key lime.

Montgomery's on the Square (108 S. Charter St., Monticello, 217/762-3833, 5–9 P.M. Tues.–Sat., 8 A.M.–2:30 P.M. Sun.) is the white-tablecloth lunch and dinner spot with menu items such as grilled Asian salad, filet mignon with blue cheese and horseradish sauce, scalloped potatoes, and yellowfin tuna. It has an extensive wine and dessert list. Lunch entrées are from $5.50; dinner plates are from $7 for petite pastas, although the specials usually run around $20.

Down the street from the Opry in Bement is **Sweet Dreams** (201 S. Macon St./Hwy. 105, Bement, 217/678-2663, 11 A.M.–9 P.M. Mon.–Sat., 1–9:30 P.M. Sun.), a locally owned frozen custard joint with tables outside for eating the custard and watching the cars go by.

SHOPPING

Monticello has quite a few galleries and artisan shops, mostly clustered around the courthouse square. **Prairie Fire Glass** (217 W. Washington St., Monticello, 217/762-3332) sells hand-blown glass and custom stained glass, and offers workshops. **Gallery Virtu** (220 W. Washington St., Monticello, 217/762-7790) is a cooperative art gallery and education organization where you can buy everything from black-and-white photographic prints to hand-knit socks.

INFORMATION AND SERVICES

Stock up on travel brochures at the **Wabash Depot** (Center and State Sts.), a depot that houses a visitors center and offices of the **Monticello Chamber of Commerce** (217/762-7921 or 800/952-3396).

Clinton Lake Region

Built in the 1970s by the damming of Salt Creek, Clinton Lake is a popular spot for fishing and boating in central Illinois. A lot of regional folks head to Clinton Lake when they want to get some boating in but don't have time to drive down to southern Illinois or north to Wisconsin. The lake and much of the surrounding land may be a state recreation area, but the land is actually owned by the utility company Exelon, which leases some of the land to the state. The southern part of the lake is good for fishing and boating. The narrower north ends are more suitable for smaller watercraft such as canoes. Exelon operates a nuclear power plant on the shores of Clinton Lake. There's one plant at the site now, but the com-

pany may build another. A few miles west of the lake is Clinton, the county seat of DeWitt. With a population of 8,000 people, Clinton is the largest town in the county. Unlike the lake, Clinton has been around for a while. In fact, Abraham Lincoln once had a law office on the courthouse square, which locals now refer to as Mr. Lincoln's Square. To get to Clinton, follow Highway 10 from the east or west or U.S. 51 from the north or south.

SIGHTS

Clinton Lake State Recreation Area
Shaped a little like a right-leaning letter U, the 5,000-acre Clinton Lake (217/935-8722,

www.dnr.state.il.us) has two sides to it: motorized and nonmotorized sections. Powerboaters and water-skiers tend to stick to the south end. People canoeing or at the helm of sailboats are more likely to be found in the northern parts. If you have a canoe or kayak, launch it at the North Fork Canoe Access Area in the upper west part of the lake (off County Rd. 900 N). Here you might find osprey and other wildlife. On the northeast side by the Parnell Boat Access Area you have access to a 10-mile trail for hiking, horseback riding, or cross-country skiing in the winter (if the area receives enough snow). There are also more trails throughout the state recreation area, such as the 9.3-mile North Fork Trail, which winds through woods and past a restored prairie. You can fish all around the lake for just about every fish common in Illinois, including striped bass, walleye, and crappie. The lake reportedly has some of the best catfish fishing in the state. Some decent boat ramps are at the West Side Day Use and Mascoutin Access areas, both north of Highway 10. North of Mascoutin is a swimming beach and bathhouse. It's open Memorial Day–Labor Day and costs $1.

Weldon Springs State Recreation Area

A few miles south of Clinton Lake is Weldon Springs State Recreation Area (1159 County Rd. 500 N, Clinton, 217/935-2644, www.dnr.state.il.us), which was once home to a popular regional chautauqua at the turn of the 20th century. At 550 acres, it's a relatively small park. But it's accessible and there's lots of stuff to do for people with young children or for visitors who can't spend the entire day hiking up and down ravines. Choose from several trails, none of which are too exhausting. Two good trails are the 1.3-mile Schoolhouse Trail, which has several bluebird houses placed along this mainly prairie path, and the two-mile trail around the lake. Staff groom trails for cross-country skiing in the winter. Within the park is Lakeview Restaurant, a casual restaurant and concessionaire that rents rowboats and paddleboats, so you can paddle out

on the 30-acre spring-fed lake. The park also has a wheelchair-accessible fishing dock, campground, playground, and picnic areas.

EVENTS

One of the big to-do's in Clinton is the **Apple 'n Pork Festival** held annually at the end of September on the grounds of the **C. E. Moore Homestead** (219 E. Woodlawn St., Clinton, 217/935-6066, www.chmoorehomestead.org). If you don't want to eat the pig ears, you can dive into the pork sandwiches, apple fritters, apple pie, and then wash it all down with some apple cider. In addition to apple- and pork-related food, the festival features a flea market. The homestead, which includes an 1867 Italianate mansion, barn, and other outbuildings, has local-history and farm-machinery exhibits and hosts other traditional events throughout the year, such as classic car shows, quilt shows, and ice-cream socials. The homestead is open for tours 10–5 P.M. Tuesday–Saturday, 1–5 P.M. Sunday April–December. It's a block east of Business U.S. 51 on the north side of Clinton.

SHOPPING

Clinton has a handful of antiques shops in and around town. By far the largest is the **Clinton Antique Mall** (1439 W. Hwy. 54, 217/935-8846, 10 A.M.–5 P.M. Mon.–Sat., 11 A.M.–5 P.M. Sun.) on the west side of town with 15,000 square feet of furniture, china, books, magazines, silverware, jewelry, and everything else you can imagine. Downtown **Memories Past Antiques** (102 Eastside Sq., Clinton, 217/935-6569, 10 A.M.–5 P.M. Tues.–Sun.) is not nearly as large but still has several dealers set up booths inside its building, meaning there's quite a variety of china, quilts, toys, and furniture. Just around the block you'll find new home-decor items at **Loft 202** (202 Eastside Sq., Clinton, 217/935-8900, 9 A.M.–5 P.M. Mon.–Fri., 9 A.M.–4 P.M. Sat.), which not only sells things such as candles and soaps, but chocolates, penny candy, and gourmet dips.

ACCOMMODATIONS

Under $50

If you're looking for cheap accommodations, try the 26-room **Wye Motel** (721 E. Hwy. 54, Clinton, 217/935-3373). Rates are $30–40. Rooms are a tad outdated and not exactly sparkling, but if you need a place to crash, this fits the bill. Some come with kitchenettes. If you're hauling a boat, it's got parking spaces that can accommodate it.

$100–150

Sunset Inn and Suites (U.S. 51 at Kleeman Dr., Clinton, 217/935-4140, www.sunsetinnandsuites.com) is an amusing roadside hotel with 41 rooms, including so-called fantasy suites, i.e., imagine sleeping in a cave with faux torches flickering or in a spaceship. Other extras include massaging shower heads, microwaves, and minifridges.

FOOD

There's no shortage of classic American roadside eateries in Clinton. **Ted's Garage** (808 W. Van Buren St./Hwy. 54, Clinton, 217/935-8008, www.teds-garage.com, 4–10 P.M. Tues.–Thurs., 4–11 P.M. Fri.–Sat., $7–17), is a brand-new retro diner that serves dishes such as "the convertible" (barbecue pulled pork) and "the hot rod" (black Angus burger). Sure, it's got the usual sides of French fries, but also sweet potato fries and mac and cheese. Ted's also serves fountain drinks plus beer, wine, and mixed drinks.

In the same vein, **Mom's Diner** (603 Westside Sq., Clinton, 217/935-4772, 6:30 A.M.–7 P.M. Mon.–Fri., 6:30 A.M.–3 P.M. Sat., $5) on the square, serves breakfast classics (eggs, bacon, toast), sandwiches and fountain treats, but during the morning and lunch hour.

At **Rudy's Drive-In Restaurant** (308 S. Portland Pl., Clinton, 217/935-2011) you can fill up on hamburgers, hot dogs, corn dogs, and frozen custard at amazingly low prices. Ten corn dogs, for example, will set you back $7.

A gift shop that doubles as a tea room, **La Tea Da** (1100 S. Madison St., Clinton, 217/935-8855) serves tea and treats such as muffins along with a variety of teas 11 A.M.–2 P.M. Tuesday–Saturday.

INFORMATION

The Clinton Area Chamber of Commerce operates a **Clinton Visitor Center** (Hwy. 54 and U.S. 51, Clinton, 217/855-3364). Look for the white house a little larger than a toll booth, just by the antique mall.

Decatur

As you drive toward Decatur from virtually any direction, you can't miss seeing the smokestacks and grain elevators. Decatur is, for the most part, a blue-collar town home to agricultural processing plants and foundries. Many rail lines pass through here. The city has seen better days and seems to grab national attention only when something bad happens here, such as the closing of the Firestone tire plant or the racial clashes between black and white high-school students. But Decatur does have some great parks and gardens, and the people are welcoming. And there is something cool about being able to see industry up close. Corn and soybean processors Archer Daniels Midland and A. E. Staley are right there on Eldorado Street, crushing beans and shipping them across the world.

SIGHTS

Scovill Park

Every community should have a Scovill Park. Overlooking Lake Decatur, Scovill is a conglomeration of several museums, a zoo, and gardens. If you are traveling with children, this is a place you could spend the entire day. Start with **Scovill Zoo** (71 S. Country Club

Scovill Zoo in Decatur

Rd., Decatur, 217/421-7435, www.decatur-parks.org, 10 A.M.–4 P.M. Mon.–Fri., 10 A.M.–6 P.M. Sat.–Sun. April–Oct., $3.50), which has birds, reptiles, and mostly small animals housed on 10 acres. There are lots of winding sidewalks past the exhibits; some animals are in cages, some are in fenced-in areas. You'll pass by bald eagles, toucans, and flamingos. You can walk on a deck above the cheetah's playing ground or walk through a bird aviary where tropical birds preen themselves. Exhibits also include lemurs and prairie dogs. For a quick and easy visit, tour the zoo while riding a small train through the park. There's also a carousel near the entrance and exit featuring endangered animals.

Adjacent to the zoo are the **Oriental Gardens** (10 A.M.–dusk daily, free), an excellent area with shady areas, a waterfall, and Chinese Fu dog statues. Much of the gardens is wheelchair-accessible. Nearby is a large gazebo surrounded by colorful flowers such as salvia.

Inside the **Children's Museum** (55 S. Country Club Rd., Decatur, 217/423-5437, www.cmofil.com, 9:30 A.M.–4:30 P.M. Mon.–Fri., 10 A.M.–5 P.M. Sat., 1–5 P.M. Sun., $3.50) children are squealing, clapping, and lightbulbs are going off in their heads. As with most children's museum, this place is hands-on and educational. Kids can shop in a make-believe grocery store, blow giant bubbles, play with model trains, climb into a plane cockpit, or race boats. There's a picnic area outside with "whisper disks"—one person whispers into a satellite dish and the other person across the lawn can hear what he or she says.

Public engineers and contractors will probably best enjoy a trip through the **Hieronymus Mueller Museum** (61 S. Country Club Rd., Decatur, 217/423-6161, noon–5 P.M. Thurs.–Sun. Apr.–Sept., 1–4 P.M. Fri.–Sun. Oct.–Mar., $1). Mueller was an inventor of sorts and in one way or another influenced the designs of drinking-water fountains, fire hydrants, and roller skates.

Millikin University

West of downtown Decatur on West Main Street, Millikin University is a small liberal arts college where students study to be anything from musicians to medical technicians. It was founded in 1901 by local banker James

Millikin, whose house, near the picturesque campus, is open to the public. It is home to two fine museums.

Birks Museum (Gorin Hall, 1184 W. Main St., Decatur, 217/424-6337, www.millikin.edu, 1–4 P.M. daily during the school year, free) is known mostly for its decorative arts collection containing objects from around the world, including several objects from Asia. You will find Tiffany art glass, china vases, and handcrafted furniture on display here.

Kirkland Fine Arts Center and the Kirkland Galleries (1184 W. Main St., 217/424-6318, www.millikin.edu, 8 A.M.–5 P.M. Mon.–Fri., 10 A.M.–1 P.M. Sat., free) feature excellent work from established and up-and-coming regional and national artists and students. Stop by the studio gallery, where the photography exhibits tend to be held.

The **Millikin Homestead** (125 N. Pine St., Decatur, 217/422-9003, 2–4 P.M. Sat.–Sun. late-Mar.–late Oct., $2) was built in 1876 for the founder of Millikin University, James Millikin, quite an interesting figure in Decatur. He owned a lot of farmland and rented the land to livestock farmers, and then got into real-estate buildings and banking, and eventually became a city alderman. It's a gorgeous house that has been well maintained. The Italianate-style brick mansion features stained-glass windows, fancy moldings, paintings on the walls, and period furniture throughout. It's decorated as though the Millikins were still living there in the 1880s.

Historic Sights

Arguably Decatur's most famous resident, Richard J. Oglesby was a renaissance man. Among Illinois residents he is perhaps most well known as being a three-term governor in the 1870s and 1880s. But the man also was a gold miner in California, real-estate developer, state senator, U.S. senator, and a Civil War general. A friend to Ulysses S. Grant and Abraham Lincoln, he reportedly dubbed Lincoln the "rail splitter" candidate because of his days of chopping wood in New Salem, Illinois. Oglesby helped raise money for the con-

struction of Lincoln's tomb in Springfield. You can learn all about one of Decatur's favorite sons by touring the **Governor Oglesby Mansion** (421 W. William St., Decatur, 217/429-9422, 2–4 P.M. on the last Sun. of the month Mar.–Nov., free). The seven-room, two-story house built in 1874, is, like the Millikin mansion, Italianate. The original plans were drafted by architect William Le Baron Jenney, who is often called the father of the skyscraper. The mansion is not open often, but if you are in town when it is open for tours, it's worth a look. You won't be disappointed. It's a grand house with high ceilings, French doors, and several fireplaces with elaborate mantels. One of the mansion's finest rooms is the library, which is made of rich black walnut and features glass bookcases and a parquet floor.

The **Macon County Historical Museum Complex** (5580 North Fork Rd., Decatur, 217/422-4919, 1–4 P.M. Tues.–Sun., $2) is a mock village where several rescued historical buildings are arranged in a parklike setting. Prairie Village, as it is called, contains a gun and tackle shop, train depot, one-room schoolhouse, and log cabin, plus various modes of transportation from the past, including wagons, sleds, and a caboose. The log cabin was actually a courthouse in the 1830s and Abraham Lincoln practiced there while a young lawyer.

In downtown Decatur the **African American Cultural and Genealogical Society of Illinois** (314 N. Main St., Decatur, 217/429-7458, 11 A.M.–3 P.M. Mon., Wed., Fri., 11 A.M.–2 P.M. Sat., free) showcases African and African American artifacts, such as masks, ceremonial objects, musical instruments, and products, such as curling irons and mailboxes, that were developed by African Americans. You can also research slave genealogical records here. The society may be moving to a new location in late 2005, but their phone number will remain the same.

Farm Visit

Maribeth King, the owner of **Mari-Mann Herbs** (1405 Marimann Ln., St. Louis Bridge Rd. at Hwy. 48, Decatur, 217/429-1404 or

The Grand Prairie

Mari-Mann herb farm

800/779-4372, www.marimann.com, 9 A.M.–5 P.M. Mon.–Sat., noon–5 P.M. Sun.) credits homeopathic remedies and herbs for helping her beat cancer. Her herb farm and shop provide visitors with a little oasis on the outskirts of Decatur. You can stroll through rows of chamomile and *Echinacea* and then browse through her shop packed with everything from gourmet salsa to St. John's wort. There are vitamins, candles, books, jellies, and dried herbs. On Thursdays during the spring and summer King hosts teas in the greenhouse as well as homeopathy and cooking classes. Herb Fest, a well-attended local event, is held during Labor Day weekend. (For more information see *Entertainment and Events.*)

ENTERTAINMENT AND EVENTS
Theater
Built in 1916, the **Lincoln Square Theatre** (141 N. Main St., Decatur, 217/442-1711) is a Beaux Arts theater downtown that plays host to various music concerts and movie screenings.

Millikin University's **Kirkland Fine Arts Center** (1184 W. Main St., 217/424-6318,

www.millikin.edu) hosts dozens of dramas and comedy theater productions, classical and modern music concerts, and lectures. Performances are by visiting artists, faculty, and students. A recent season included visits by The Smothers Brothers and the Vienna Boys Choir.

Events
Naturalists will want to stop by Rock Springs in September for the annual **Prairie Celebration** (Brozio Ln. and Rock Springs Rd., Decatur, 217/423-7708, www.maconcountyconservation.org, free). You can go birding with other fellow amateur ornithologists, watch locals re-enact scenes from history at the center's homestead museum, or take in the sights of the park aboard a wagon.

Held during Labor Day, **Herb Fest** (Mari-Mann Herb Co., 1405 Marimann Ln., St. Louis Bridge Rd. at Hwy. 48, Decatur, 217/429-1404 or 800/779-4372, www.marimann.com) is a two-day event where doctors, herbalists, pharmacists, and aromatherapy specialists share information about the wonder and benefits of herbs. Food and beverage tastings are held throughout the weekend while music plays, and the owners offer tours of the herb farm. Admission is free.

SHOPPING

Forget about shopping at the mall off the interstate. **The Wabash Depot Antique Center** (780 E. Cerro Gordo St., Decatur, 217/233-0800, 10–5 Mon.–Sat., noon–5 P.M. Sun.) is an indoor antiques center housed in a former train depot that dates back more than a century. Vendors sell vintage toys, out-of-print books, pottery pieces such as bowls and pitchers, and salvaged architectural items.

SPORTS AND RECREATION
Rock Springs

At 1,300 acres, **Rock Springs Center for Environmental Discovery** (Brozio Ln. and Rock Springs Rd., Decatur, 217/423-7708, www.maconcountyconservation.org, free) is one of the largest parks in the region, and an excellent park for quiet hikes in the summer and cross-country skiing trips in the winter. This sprawling park has about six miles of well-groomed trails through various, but easy-to-navigate terrain such as rolling hills, flat prairie, and woodlands. The River Trail takes you past ponds (look for the turtles), through woods, and by the former site of a bottling plant for Rock Springs Water. (A company used to sell water from the springs here.) The park's other trails, such as the Big Oak Trail and Prairie Path, take you through quiet prairies and woods. The Lookout Trail, as the name implies, leads to a lookout tower over the river and prairie, past wildflowers and hopping bunny rabbits.

A short walk (less than five minutes) from the visitors center parking lot is the **Homestead Prairie Farm,** also known as the Trobaugh-Good home. Listed on the National Register of Historic Places, it was initially built as a one-room log home in 1850. Eventually other rooms were added (although it is still tiny by today's standards). The pale yellow house contains furniture and items that date to the 1860s, such as a stove and dish cupboard.

© CHRISTINE DES GARENNES

the bike trail at Rock Springs, one of the best public parks in central Illinois

Back at the visitors center you'll find several rooms with displays on Illinois geology, the prairie, wetlands, and wildlife. A large picture window in one room allows you to watch for birds such as downy woodpeckers and cardinals. You can shop for stuffed animals and items such as maple syrup made from the sap collected from trees at Sand Creek Recreation Area south of Decatur.

Another attraction in Rock Springs is the vintage baseball field at the northern part of the park. Throughout the year a group of locals plays on this grass field.

The Rock Spring visitors center is open 8 A.M.–5 P.M. Monday–Friday, 9 A.M.–4:30 P.M. Saturday, 1–4 P.M. Sunday. The trails are open 7 A.M.–dusk daily. The Homestead Prairie Farm is open 1–4 P.M. weekends June–October and by appointment. During the winter, you can rent cross-country skiing equipment 9 A.M.–2 P.M. for $6; trails open 8 A.M.–sunset, free, weather permitting.

The Grand Prairie

The Rock Springs/Fairview Bikeway (217/423-7708) is an easy, scenic 2.5-mile paved trail between Fairview and Kiwanis parks and Rock Springs. A good access point is at Rock Springs, where there is plenty of parking near the visitors center. The well-maintained trail jogs along Stevens Creek and over the Sangamon River.

Other Parks

About 10 miles southeast of Decatur, **Fort Daniel Conservation Area** (Fort Daniel Rd. and County Rd. 57, Mount Zion, 217/423-7708, free) has an intriguing history. It is named after area resident Rev. Daniel Traughber, who reportedly was a Southern sympathizer during the Civil War. He and his followers would ride on horseback through the night threatening pro-Union farmers. The area within and surrounding the park was first known as Whistleville and it was a community comprising mainly settlers from Kentucky who built log homes there. The 200-acre park has 4.5 miles of trails that follow the rambling Big Creek, past an old well and through restored prairie.

On the west side of town by Millikin University, **Fairview Park** (U.S. 36 and Hwy. 48, Eldorado and Fairview Sts., Decatur, 217/422-5911, www.decatur-parks.org) has quite a few spots alongside ponds and under trees that are good for picnicking. On the southeast side of town on Lake Decatur you can rent regattas for $1 per day at **Nelson Park** (Decatur Park District, just south of U.S. 36, 217/424-2837) on Saturdays mid-July to late August. Nelson Park also has boat ramps for visitors interested in exploring Lake Decatur and the Sangamon River.

Horseback Riding

One of the best places to bring your horse for a ride in the Decatur area is **Sand Creek Recreation Area** (S. Franklin St., Decatur, 217/423-7708, 8 A.M.–dusk, $2 for access to horseback trails). Part of the old Paris-Springfield Road runs through Sand Creek. A common thoroughfare from about the 1820s to 1850s, it was this road many homesteaders followed to find land. They included Abraham Lincoln and his family, which migrated to Illinois in 1830. South of Decatur on the Sangamon River, Sand Creek has 755 acres and 7.6 miles of trails for horseback riding or hiking. The park is quite accommodating to horses and their owners. There are hitch racks for horses at the entrances to trails and gravel picnic areas. Trails through oak and hickory woodlands and maple trees and along the creek are especially scenic.

Try to swing by in the early springtime, such as in March. This is when park staff tap the maple trees and catch the sap in buckets to produce maple syrup. (You can buy some syrup at the Rock Spring store.) Staff also have installed several bluebird houses throughout the park, and it is not uncommon to spot these birds during a walk or ride. (Because the park is in a floodplain, it can experience flooding in the springtime and does close some of its trails when this happens. If you plan to visit during a rainy spring, call first to inquire about the state of the trails.)

ACCOMMODATIONS

Staying overnight in Decatur will cost $70–90, with some suites at the Holiday Inn Select Conference Center ranging up to $130. There is a string of small motels near the grain processing plants on Decatur's east side that go for less than $70 per night, but they're not exactly in desirable locations.

Here's a sampling of national chain hotels. Near I-72 and U.S. 51 are **Wingate Inn** (5170 Wingate Dr., Decatur, 217/875-5500) and **Country Inn and Suites Hotel** (5150 Hickory Point Frontage Rd., Decatur, 217/872-2402), both of which offer indoor pools, exercise rooms, and continental breakfast for guests. The 370-room **Holiday Inn Select Conference Hotel** (U.S. 36 and Wyckles Rd., 217/422-8800) has a restaurant and lounge on-site.

There are two bed-and-breakfasts in town. Both are on the west side in historic districts. The **Younker House Bed and Breakfast** (500 W. Main St., Decatur, 217/429-9718), a large, brick home on a brick street, has three bedrooms, a screened-in porch, and fenced-in backyard with gardens. Just down the street, you'll find four rooms at **Victoriana** (640 W. Main St., Decatur, 217/428-0637) by Millikin University. The front porch looks out onto Main Street.

FOOD
Casual
The menu at **N Georgies** (1099 W. Main St., Decatur, 217/422-6740, 10 A.M.–10 P.M. Mon.–Thurs., Sun., 10 A.M.–midnight Fri.–Sat., $7) is extensive, and you really can't go wrong with anything on there. Billed as a Philadelphia joint, Georgies' specialties are Philly cheese steaks and hoagies. Then there are the countless Italian dishes such as pizzas, calzones, stromboli, plus traditional American meals of turkey sandwiches, wraps, wings, and salads. If you're traveling with a finicky eater or with a group of people with varied tastes, drop by Georgies for lunch or dinner.

Close to Millikin's campus, **Lock Stock and Barrel** (129 S. Oakland Ave., Decatur, 217/429-7411, www.lsb1.com, 11 A.M.–1 A.M. Mon.–Wed., 11 A.M.–2 A.M. Thurs.–Sat., 10 A.M.–10 P.M. Sun., $7) tends to attract the college crowd, especially on Sundays for the all-you-can-eat brunches. Food varies from healthy salads to the not-so-healthy horseshoe sandwiches. It has lots of hot and cold sandwiches plus sides such as twice-baked potatoes. Drop by for dinner on a Friday or Saturday and then stick around to hear a local rock or jazz band play.

Fine Dining
Some of the best fare in town is concocted within the kitchen at **N Marcia's Waterfront** (2301 E. Lake Shore Dr., Decatur, 217/422-7202, www.marciaswaterfront.com, lunch 11 A.M. Mon.–Fri., dinner at 5 P.M. Mon.–Sat., plus Sun. brunches on holidays). The cuisine is called continental and it includes plates such as pineapple bourbon brisket, shrimp-stuffed salmon, and pistachio pork loin. The atmo-

sphere is just as good as the food. In Nelson Park's former bathhouse, Marcia's has a deck for outdoor dining. It comes with a canopy, so you can sit outside even on misty or intensely sunny days. Average lunch entrée is $7.50; dinner entrées are around $20.

INFORMATION AND SERVICES
Information
The **Decatur Area Convention and Visitors Bureau** (202 E. North St., Decatur, 217/423-7000 or 800/331-4479, www.decaturcvb.com) publishes brochures and events information annually and maintains a listing of area lodging and dining options.

Post Office and Library
You'll find the main **Decatur Post Office** downtown at 200 North Franklin Street, Decatur, 217/428-4471. Nearby is the **Decatur Public Library** (130 N. Franklin St., Decatur, 217/424-2900).

Media
The Decatur Herald and Review is published daily and is available at all convenient stores, gas stations, and the library. Buy a copy of the bimonthly *Decatur Magazine* (www.decatur-magazine.com) at area grocery stores to get the scoop on any new restaurants, theater productions, or to read profiles about local residents. It costs $3.50 per issue.

Hospitals
There are two hospitals in town: **Decatur Memorial Hospital** (2300 N. Edward St., Decatur, 217/876-8121) and **St. Mary's Hospital** (1800 E. Lake Shore Dr., Decatur, 217/464-2966).

GETTING AROUND
Air
American Connection offers three daily round-trip flights between the **Decatur Airport** (910 S. Airport Rd., Decatur, 217/428-2423, www.decatur-airport.org) and Lambert-St. Louis International Airport. Parking is free.

Greyhound buses stop at Sandy's Motel (1675 E. Pershing Rd., Decatur, 217/877-6262).

Public Transportation

The **Decatur Public Transit System** (55 E. Wood St., Decatur, 217/424-2800, www.dpts.com) runs 14 buses through town from about 5:30 A.M.–7 P.M. Monday–Thursday and 5:30 A.M.–9 P.M. Friday–Saturday. Each ride costs $.60. On Saturdays you can buy an all-day pass to ride the buses for $1.

VICINITY OF DECATUR

Lincoln Homestead Site

Diehard fans of Lincoln will want to trek it on over to the **Lincoln Trail Homestead State Memorial and Lincoln Trail Homestead State Park** (705 Spitler Park Dr., Mount Zion, 217/864-3121, www.dnr.state.il.us). After arriving in Illinois, Lincoln and his father and stepmother chose a spot along the Sangamon River to build their first home. Lincoln lived there before moving on to New Salem. The actual log cabin is long gone; the state has placed a stone and plaque there.

Illiopolis

If you ever wanted to go country-western dancing, here's your chance. The **Prairie Land Dance Club** (650 Matilda St., Illiopolis, 217/428-1560, www.pldc.org) devotes several evenings a week to line dancing, square dancing, and other country moves. Plus, throughout the year it holds workshops on salsa dancing, the meringue, and more. The club is open for dancing 7–10 P.M. Wednesday, Friday, and Saturday nights. Admission is $5 for nonmembers.

I-55: Lincoln to Williamsville

If you dig road trips, small, historic downtowns, and vintage roadside attractions, one of the best legs along Route 66 in central Illinois is between Bloomington and Springfield. Drive the approximately 20-mile strip from Lincoln to Williamsville and you'll come across relics such as the Pig Hip in Broadwell, once a iconic restaurant and motel and now a museum with exhibits on its past and Route 66. You'll come upon Elkhart, a small town with a beautiful history museum, bakery, antiques shop, and pioneer cemetery. There's also no shortage of tributes to Abraham Lincoln. When he was a lawyer traveling on the Eighth Judicial Circuit, Lincoln tried cases at the Postville and Mount Pulaski courthouses. He also christened the town of Lincoln in 1853 by slicing open a watermelon.

LINCOLN

Downtown Lincoln

Park the car and take about an hour or so to walk around Lincoln's downtown and the courthouse square at Broadway, McLean, Pu-laski, and Kickapoo streets. Not far from the train tracks is a plaque that marks the probable spot where Lincoln broke open a watermelon, christening the town named after him. (It's at Broadway and Chicago streets). From there you can check out some colorful murals that have been painted on its buildings downtown around the courthouse. Not surprisingly, many feature a young Abe Lincoln. Throughout downtown are several antiques shops, including the multistory **Lincoln Antiques and Furniture Center** (112 S. McLean St., Lincoln, 217/732-2000) and some specialty shops, such as **Beans and Such** (115 S. Kickapoo St., Lincoln, 217/735-5520), where you can buy coffee beans by the pound and shop for dishware and other kitchen stuff.

Postville Courthouse State Historic Site

On the west side of town is a replica of the Postville Courthouse (5th Street/Route 66, between Madison and Union Sts., Lincoln, noon–5 P.M. Tues.–Sat., March–Oct., noon–4 P.M. Nov.–Feb., $2 donation), where Abraham Lincoln

Lincoln courthouse square

once tried cases back in the 1840s. The real one is in Dearborn, Michigan, where Henry Ford (yes, the car guy) moved it in 1929 after buying the building and the block on which it stood. (He had it dismantled and rebuilt in Greenfield Park.) The timber courthouse that visitors see today was rebuilt in the 1950s, although it was modeled after how it may have looked in 1840. Back then, the area was called Postville and it was the county seat of Logan before the seat was switched to Mount Pulaski to the south in 1848 and a few years after that to Lincoln, a few miles to the east. (Eventually Postville disappeared as a town and Lincoln expanded its boundaries.) When he was a lawyer on the circuit court in the 1840s, Abraham Lincoln, like many other lawyers and judges, traveled through the county and set up shop a few days before holding trials and taking care of business transactions. They'd come a few times a year. The courthouse, like many of its kind during that time, held offices for the county clerk, surveyor, sheriff, and others. And the replica is furnished much as it probably was back in the 1840s with separate offices and meeting space. Across the street from the courthouse is a VFW post on the site of Dekins Tavern, where lawyers such as Lincoln would stay while in town.

Edward R. Madigan State Park

Need a break from driving? Pull into Edward R. Madigan State Park (1366 1010th Ave., Lincoln, 217/735-2424, www.dnr.state.il.us) on the south side of Lincoln and just off Route 66. The 723-acre park along Salt Creek is divided into a north and south side. The north side, near the state correctional facility, has nature trails through meadows and the south side has a canoe launch on the creek. It's not the largest or most popular park in the state, but it certainly has a peaceful atmosphere. No crowds. No lines of RVs.

Accommodations

Most of the hotels and motels in Lincoln are at I-55 and Highway 10. Rates are usually around $50 per night. Here's a list: **Lincoln Inn** (1730 5th St., Lincoln, 217/732-9641); **Super 8** (2800 Woodlawn Rd./Hwy. 10, Lincoln, 217/732-8886); and **Comfort Inn of Lincoln** (2811 Woodlawn Rd./Hwy. 10, Lincoln, 217/735-3960).

the Postville State Historic Site

Food

The **Blue Dog Inn** (111 S. Sangamon St., Lincoln, 217/735-1743, www.bluedoginn.com, 11 A.M.–2 P.M. Mon., 11 A.M.–10 P.M. Tues.–Thurs., 11 A.M.–11 P.M. Fri.–Sat.) is an amusing, dog-friendly pub and restaurant. There's no shortage of photographs and paintings of dogs hanging on the walls. And some of the sandwiches, such as "the rare breed" (roast beef with cream cheese), have been named after dogs. Dinners include boneless pork loin and fried shrimp. Save room for a slice of chocolate or lemon cream pie.

A local gathering place of sorts in Lincoln is **Einstein's Louisiana Coffeehouse** (201 S. Sangamon St., Lincoln, 217/735-5282, 6:30 A.M.–10 P.M. Mon.–Wed., 6:30 A.M.–11 P.M. Thurs.–Fri., 8 A.M.–11 P.M. Sat., $5.25–7.25), near the Amtrak station in a beautifully renovated storefront space with tin ceilings, hardwood floors, and comfy chairs and tables. The walls are decorated with work by area artists, and local musicians occasionally perform here. The café also has wireless Internet access. The usual coffeehouse fare of cappuccinos, teas, and smoothies is available, but it also has quite an array of sandwiches, such as build-your-own sandwiches, Cuban-style sandwiches, panini, hot dogs, wraps, and salads. And of course, you can expect some Southern dishes such as gumbo and jambalaya.

Brandt's Arcade Café (513 Pulaski St., Lincoln, 217/735-1443, 6 A.M.–2 P.M. Mon.–Sat., $5) is a meat-and-potatoes kind of place. The breakfast and lunch spot, with its vintage counter and handful of tables, serves inexpensive comfort food, such as scalloped potatoes. It seems to be popular among the white-haired set.

Information and Transportation

For information, contact the **Abraham Lincoln Tourism Bureau of Logan County** (303 S. Kickapoo St., Lincoln, 217/732-TOUR or 217/732-8687, www.logancountytourism.org).

Several **Amtrak** (800/USA-RAIL or 800/872-7245, www.amtrak.com) trains stop at Lincoln's downtown train station, at Broadway and North Chicago Streets. The Texas Eagle, from Chicago to San Antonio, Texas, comes through three times a week, the Ann

Rutledge, between Chicago and St. Louis, Missouri, stops in Lincoln daily, as does the State House, between Chicago and Springfield.

BROADWELL

To get a sense of what traveling along Route 66 might have been like in the 1950s, drive to Broadwell, population 200. Here you'll come across a long-shuttered roadside motel, garage, and restaurant, which was recently reopened as a museum that venerates Route 66 and the restaurant's past. Oh, and pigs. The **Pig Hip Restaurant Museum** (Oak St. and Frontage Rd., Broadwell, 217/732-2337, free) is in a plain, one-story building that once housed the Pig Hip Restaurant, famous for its pig-hip sandwiches. Local residents Ernie and Frances Edwards ran this restaurant for more than 50 years—1937–1991. Inside you can view photographs of the restaurant through the decades, admire the Edwardses' collection of ceramic pigs, plus pick up brochures. Ernie and Frances are in their 80s now and are generally open 9 A.M.–5 P.M. daily, except when they have doctor appointments. Your best bet is to call Ernie ahead of time to let them know when you're coming and he'll try to meet you there.

ELKHART

From the highway you'd swear Elkhart is just another tiny rural village with a nondescript downtown. It's not. It's a real gem and a lot of that is due to its history and the folks who are preserving it. A little background: Many of the early settlers to Illinois and those who would continue west to St. Louis and beyond passed through this area, which used to be called Sangamo. They followed a trail known as Edwards' Trace, which weaved through Elkhart and connected the French towns to the south, near St. Louis, with those in the north by Lake Peoria.

Sights and Activities

East of town, overlooking the village and the region, is Elkhart Hill, one of the highest places in central Illinois. (Although you'd hardly know it, it tops out at 711 feet above sea level.) The hill belonged to rancher John Dean Gillett and his descendants still own land there. Governor Richard Oglesby, governor from the mid-1860s through the mid-1880s, married Gillett's daughter and is buried in the cemetery at the top of the hill. The **pioneer cemetery** is quite a sight. You enter through grand iron gates and in the center is St. John the Baptist, a little Gothic church made of limestone and with Tiffany stained-glass windows. To get to the cemetery follow Highway 10/Chapel Road north of downtown Elkhart.

But there's more to the town than the scenic cemetery on the hill. In fact, the best feature of the town is the **Under the Prairie Frontier Archaeological Museum** (109 Gov. Oglesby St., Elkhart, 217/947-2522, www.undertheprairie.com, 10 A.M.–4 P.M. Wed.–Sun., $3), a museum devoted to showing artifacts dating to years before the Civil War. All of them have been excavated from the area and belonged to settlers or the many people passing through. With crickets singing in the background (through the sound system), visitors walk through a dimly lit room where kettles, a tin cup, coins, and glass bottles are displayed in cases as though they were pieces of sculpture. Among some of the items you'll see are hand-forged nails from the years 1780–1820, part of an oxen shoe, and lots of kitchen items, such as dishes and utensils.

It's still a private residence, but the **Old Gillett Farm** (entrance off Gillett St., north of downtown by Hwy. 10, 217/947-2346, www.oldgillettfarm.com) is open occasionally (with notice) to visitors who are interested in hearing about the family and the estate's history. The chapel and 33-room main house are lovely spots for weddings or other formal events. Nearby is the 65-acre Elkhart Grove Forest Preserve, which has native trees and little blue bell flowers along its paths. You'll need permission from the house to walk the trails through here. If you're traveling with a group and you like to travel in style, you can stay at the farm's guesthouse, a three-bedroom, 2.5-bath brick house. It's called a guest house, but it's just like renting an entire house. (Except if you normally live in a 33-room mansion.) The guesthouse is beautifully restored and decorated with a mix of modern furniture and antiques. There's a full kitchen, formal dining room, and outside a pavilion and gardens.

Food

Adjacent to the Under the Prairie museum and sharing the same roof is **N Bluestem Bake Shop** (9 A.M.–4 P.M. Wed.–Sun., $5), which sells gourmet coffees and teas, sandwiches such as turkey clubs, and salads. Fresh bread, fresh lettuce, fresh tomatoes, it doesn't get any better. On Sundays it serves warm quiche.

WILLIAMSVILLE

Farther along Route 66 is another quiet rural town called Williamsville, where older men sit on stoops and front porches and kids roll down the sidewalks on tricycles ringing their bells. The highlight of this Mayberry-like town is **Die Cast Auto Sales** (117 N. Elm St., Williamsville, 217/566-3898), a 1930s-era service station along Route 66 that now displays an impressive collection of automobile and Route 66 memorabilia, including scale model cars and gas pumps. But the owner has not only amassed model cars and trucks, but a wide variety of toys— wind-up toys, vintage soda machines, and action figures from any given decade. The shop is open most afternoons Tuesday– Friday. On Saturday, it is open starting at around 9 A.M. Hours tend to vary, so it's best to call ahead.

The Williamsville Historical Society has stocked a boxcar full of local-history items such as farming tools, high school yearbooks, and old photographs of the town from decades ago. The result is the **Boxcar Museum** (Old Route 66/Elm St., just west of the train tracks, Williamsville, 217/566-2470, 10 A.M.–2 P.M. Wed., free).

Williamsville history is on view at the Boxcar Museum.

© CHRISTINE DES GARENNES

The Grand Prairie

New Salem and Vicinity

LINCOLN'S NEW SALEM

In 1831, when Abraham Lincoln was 22 years old, he left home to make a living for himself in New Salem, a pioneer town near the Sangamon River. The Illinois Historical Preservation Agency has recreated the town with a state historic site called **Lincoln's New Salem** (Hwy. 97, two miles south of Petersburg, 217/632-4000, www.lincolnsnewsalem.com, 8 A.M.–4 P.M. Wed.–Sun. Nov.–March, 9 A.M.–5 P.M. Wed.–Sun. Apr.–Nov., donation). Lincoln lived here for six years, although he left briefly to fight with a militia in the Black Hawk War. New Salem is, historians say, where Lincoln came of age, working as a store clerk, surveyor, and postmaster. He was a jack-of-all-trades here. During this time he began reading voraciously and learning about business, literature, and politics. This is also where Lincoln allegedly met Ann Rutledge, who, according to some folks, was the love of his life. While in New Salem, Lincoln was elected to serve as a state representative. He reported for duty in Vandalia, then the state capital, in 1834.

The town of New Salem has been reconstructed to appear as it did back in Lincoln's day. Staff achieved this by studying plat maps, surveys, and reading diaries. It's an impressive place, and except for the T-shirted tourists with cameras, it looks like a pioneer village with a dozen or so buildings lining roads. Women sit in log cabins sewing and men fiddle with the gristmill. The tour is a self-guided walking tour so you can take in the village at your own pace. There are 700 acres here and several miles of trails through the woods.

Also on the historic site is an outdoor amphitheater called **Theatre in the Park,** where locals dress in period clothing and share stores about pioneer life in Illinois or stage shows such as Mark Twain musicals. Productions are held Friday–Sunday evenings June–August.

Want to pick up some more Lincoln vibes? Camp overnight in the **Lincoln's New Salem**

One of the best Lincoln sites in Illinois is New Salem, his old stomping grounds near Petersburg.

Campground (Hwy. 97, two miles south of Petersburg, www.lincolnsnewsalem.com, $10–15 per night), which has 200 campsites. Half of those come with electricity. All of the sites are available on a first-come, first-served basis. It is open year-round; however, the water in the two shower buildings is not turned on December 1–March 15.

SIGHTS

While he was living and working in New Salem, Lincoln reportedly often stopped by the nearby town of Athens, about six miles to the east. He'd visit the post office and general store there and visit with the owner Colonel Matthew Rogers. After he was elected to the state legislature, Lincoln along with eight other men lobbied for the state capital to be moved from Vandalia to Springfield. After their colleagues approved the move, the "long nine" (they were all over six feet tall) celebrated at a dinner in a banquet room above the post office and general store. That building, which still very much looks like a general store and post office from the outside, is now the **Long Nine Museum** (200 S. Main St., Athens, 217/636-8755, 1–5 P.M. Tues.–Sat. June 1–Sept. 1, or by appointment, $2). Inside, the first floor has a hodgepodge collection of vintage items (dolls, pottery, etc.) and the second floor, where the dinner took place, has some dioramas about Lincoln's life, including a scene of him surveying in Athens.

Growing up in the small, rural towns of Petersburg and Lewistown in the 1880s, Edgar Lee Masters would encounter dozens of residents, from not-so-chaste ladies to bitter old men. Later on in his life, far away from these towns and the characters, Masters would be inspired to write honest collections of poems about small-town life. The result was the celebrated *Spoon River Anthology*. This book of poetry, along with other of Masters's works, are on view at his boyhood home in Petersburg, the **Edgar Lee Masters Home** (Jackson and 8th Sts., Petersburg, 10 A.M.–noon, 1–3 P.M. Tues., Thurs.–Sat. Memorial Day–Labor Day, free). For more information about the house or if you want to arrange a tour, call the Petersburg Chamber of Commerce at 217/632-7363. Masters is buried in Oakland Cemetery, west of Oakland Avenue on the southwest side of town.

ACCOMMODATIONS

Petersburg has two fine Italianate-style bed-and-breakfasts, both up on the hills overlooking Petersburg. **The Oaks** (510 W. Sheridan, Petersburg, 217/632-5444 or 888/724-6257, www.theoaksbandb.com) is a grand brick home on a 5.5-acre estate. The 1875 mansion once belonged to a state senator. There are five rooms available here, including the "maid's quarters," a gorgeous room with a private, screened-in porch. Rates are from $75 for a room with a queen bed, fireplace, and

private bath down the hall to $145 for a two-room suite with two fireplaces. Breakfast and afternoon wine and cheese included. The Oaks also offers lunches to the public 11 A.M.–2 P.M. Wednesday–Saturday and dinners by reservation for bed-and-breakfast guests.

A few blocks away in a historic neighborhood is the newer **Maple Crest** (319 S. 9th Ave., Petersburg, 217/632-0128 or 800/653-8012, www.maplecrest.us), an 1865 formal home with four rooms available, two of which come with private bathrooms. Rates are $70–110.

FOOD

In a neat old building across the street from the Long Nine Museum is the **Starlight Café** (201 S. Main St., Athens, 217/636-8511, breakfast and lunch daily, dinner Tues.–Sat., $5), a place where, amid the sound of clinking china, teens hang out, Rotarians hold meetings, and families come to eat. The menu is several pages long, with numerous sandwich options, most of them traditional, such as horseshoes, BLTs and, on Fridays, walleye or catfish sandwiches. Lots of the dishes, particularly those served during breakfast, bear old-school celebrity names: the Roy Rogers western omelet, the Cyd Charisse French toast. Breakfast is served until 2 P.M. The Starlight also has lunch and dinner buffets.

The best seats at **Fulgenzi's on the Hill** (Hwy. 97, across the street from the entrance to New Salem Historic Site, 217/632-4400, 5–8 P.M. Wed.–Thurs., 4:30–9 P.M. Fri.–Sat., brunch 10:30 A.M.–2 P.M. on Sun., $15) are in the back of the restaurant, past the buffet, in a round room with tall windows overlooking the Sangamon River valley. Wednesday features a fried-chicken buffet and Friday specials are walleye and catfish dinners. Other dinner entrées are typical Midwestern cuisine such as rib eye and grilled chicken.

Springfield

I hope you like Abraham Lincoln because Springfield is a virtual Lincoln-o-rama. It's impossible to tour the town without seeing his likeness (the stovepipe hat, the tall, bony frame) or seeing his words, usually excerpts from speeches, engraved or printed on plaques outside of buildings. As you'll see, many places you visit or walk by in Springfield play up a connection to Abraham Lincoln, who lived in this town 1831–1861. Sure you can see his home and tomb, but also on display are his bank ledger and a target board he used during shooting practice.

Springfield, especially the downtown and the Old Aristocracy Hill District surrounding it, has a historic feel to it. Some of the streets are brick-lined and the homes restored Victorians. With a population of about 111,000, Springfield is home to state bureaucrats, lobbyists, agribusiness employees, and people working in the service industry. It's a fairly quiet, provincial town compared with some other capital cities in other Midwestern states, such as Madison, Wisconsin. The skyline comprises mostly the Hilton hotel tower and the capitol building. Most shops and restaurants downtown are closed on Sundays. But it's a fun town, full of friendly people who like to eat (the hearty horseshoe sandwich was invented here) and who are proud of the city's history, whether because of its famous son, Lincoln, or its connection to Route 66, which slices through the center of the city.

ORIENTATION

Navigating through Springfield is fairly easy. The downtown streets that run east to west are numbered from 1st Street on up, ranging higher as you head east. Madison, Jefferson, and Washington streets are all downtown, and Capitol Avenue, not surprisingly, leads to the capitol. You'll find plenty of street signs

The Grand Prairie

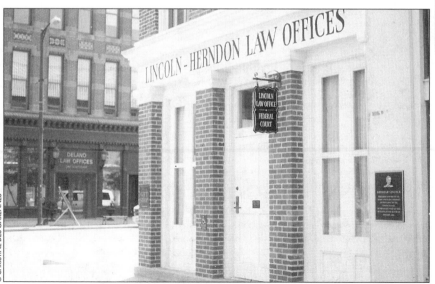

© CHRISTINE DES GARENNES

the office where Lincoln the lawyer made a living in Springfield throughout the city (not just downtown) that point visitors to Lincoln sights. The major Lincoln attractions, such as the Lincoln home, library, state museum, and capitol buildings are all within about a 10- to 15-minute walk of each other. You could stay downtown and not have to drive to any sights except to the Lincoln tomb, state fairgrounds, and some parks, which are generally on the north and northeast side of the city. I-72 runs east-west through town, and I-55 runs north-south, circumventing the city on the east to southeast. Route 66, or Business 55, cuts through the center of town from the northeast.

SIGHTS

Lincoln Home National Historic Site

The best place to start your visit is at Abraham Lincoln's former home (426 S. 7th St., Springfield, 217/492-4241, 8:30 A.M.–5 P.M. daily, free). The tours are free, but you need to get a ticket at the visitors center. (It limits the number of folks going

© CHRISTINE DES GARENNES

The Grand Prairie

the remarkably well-preserved neighborhood surrounding Lincoln's former home

through the home at a given time.) You might want to take a preview tour by watching the free film in the visitors center called *At Home with Mr. Lincoln.* It shows the inside of the rooms and shares a little history of how the house was built (in stages). You'll join a group of folks and listen to an interpreter share a little background on Lincoln's life and his activities in Springfield, where he worked as a lawyer and state legislator before being elected as 16th president of the United States. Your trip through the house may last about 20 minutes. It goes by quickly, especially in the summer when tours seem to run every five minutes. The home is not especially grand compared with some of the ornate Victorian homes south of the neighborhood. In fact, some of the furnishings are particularly dark. Literally, some of the furniture, such as a first-floor couch, is black. That's the way it was when Lincoln lived there.

What makes a visit to the Lincoln home so cool is the historic district that immediately surrounds it. You can amble down the street on plank sidewalks just like Abe used to do. (The planks are not original, however. Because of the volume of visitors who come here every year they actually have to be replaced about every

10 years. And the gravel road was dirt when Lincoln lived here.) Several homes have been restored to their mid-1800s appearance. Some of them now contain the offices of Illinois senators, some are being renovated, and others are open to the public. The Arnold house, across the street from the Lincoln home, has an excellent exhibit (preservationists will definitely want to see this) called *If These Walls Could Talk: Saving an Old House* It has photographs of the district's homes through the decades, before and after restoration, and explains the restoration processes used on the homes. There are also photographs and stories about Lincoln's neighbors. The Dean House, catercorner to the Lincoln home, has an exhibit called *What a Pleasant Home Abe Lincoln Has,* which provides background on the home's construction and the Lincoln family. From there, you can walk to other Lincoln sights.

Abraham Lincoln Presidential Library and Museum

The newest and grandest of them all is the multimillion dollar Abraham Lincoln Presidential Library and Museum (112 N. 6th St.,

Springfield, 217/785-0348, www.alincoln-library.com, 9 A.M.–5 P.M. Mon., Tues., Thurs.–Sun., Wed. until 8 P.M., $7.50). The complex, which encompasses several city blocks and almost 100,000 square feet, contains exhibits that chronicle Lincoln's life, his politics, and the state of the nation while he was president. After it opened to much fanfare (President George W. Bush dropped by for the grand opening), some scholars and visitors have criticized the design (and price tag) because the place has too many bells and whistles. One exhibit that has raised the ire of some people is the election section, where faux news anchors talk about Lincoln's chances of winning the 1860 presidential election and commercials for the candidates are aired. Umm, they didn't have television back then. It is all a bit splashy, but it certainly is a refreshing take on a presidential museum. Don't expect to spend hours walking down a quiet exhibit hall and peering down at papers displayed under a glass case. While the museum certainly has its fair share of artifacts, such as Lincoln's shaving kit, the place seems to be less about objects and more about exploring what might have been going on in his mind while he was drafting the Emancipation Proclamation.

Oak Ridge Cemetery and Lincoln's Tomb

As far as tombs and monuments go, the **Lincoln Tomb State Historic Site** (Oak Ridge Cemetery, North Grand Ave. to Monument Ave., Springfield, 217/782-2717, 9 A.M.–5 P.M. daily, free) is pretty magnificent. An obelisk towers above the cemetery's graves (the height of the entire tomb and monument is 117 feet). At the entrance is a bronze head of the president, with his nose showing some wear and tear; visitors rub it for good luck. Lincoln actually wasn't buried here immediately after his death. He was placed in vault in a nearby hillside. It wasn't until fans raised enough raised money that they built the huge granite monument. Completed in 1874, the tomb also would eventually contain Lincoln's wife, Mary Todd, and three

Lincoln Tomb State Historic Site in Springfield's Oak Ridge Cemetery

© CHRISTINE DES GARENNES

of their sons. (Robert Todd, the only one to survive through adulthood, is buried in Arlington National Cemetery).

The 365-acre cemetery on the north side of town is the largest in the state. Several governors are buried here, as well as poet Vachel Lindsay. Oak Ridge also contains an Illinois Vietnam Veteran's Memorial.

In a mausoleum-like building near the entrance of the cemetery, the **Museum of Funeral Customs** (Oak Ridge Cemetery, 1440 Monument Ave., Springfield, 217/544-3480, www.funeralmuseum.org, 10 A.M.–4 P.M. Tues.–Sat., 1–4 P.M. Sun., $3) takes a serious and artistic look at how caring for the dead has evolved throughout the decades. There are a re-creation of an embalming room (with an explanation of how embalming works), a scale model of Lincoln's tomb, and a variety of caskets. One of the neatest exhibits, which looks as if it is straight out of Victorian novel, is a black, horse-drawn hearse.

More Lincoln Sights

A few blocks north of the Lincoln home and just across the street from the Old State Capitol is the **Lincoln-Herndon Law Offices State Historic Site** (6th and Adams Sts., Springfield, 217/785-7960 or 217/785-7289, 9 A.M.–5 P.M. Tues.–Sat. Mar.–Oct., 9 A.M.–4 P.M. Tues.–Sat. Nov.–Feb., donation). Lincoln and his partner William Herndon practiced law on the third floor 1843–1852. Staff from the state historic preservation agency have recreated his office, complete with long tables, candlesticks, quill pens, and a portrait of George Washington hanging on the wall. Their office was nothing fancy. Exhibits explain the building's history; it was also used as a courtroom and judge's chamber.

Like most well-to-do families in town, the Lincolns had a pew reserved for them at the **First Presbyterian Church** (321 S. 7th St., Springfield, 217/528-4311, www.first-preschurch.org, 10 A.M.–4 P.M. Mon.–Fri. June–Sept.). The church in which the pew is now housed was actually built after Lincoln died. The old church is long gone. You can view the pew, but don't try to sit in it. Its seat is cordoned off by a rope. The Illinois Symphony Orchestra holds some concerts here.

Bank One has on view in its lobby the **Lincoln Ledger** (Washington and 6th Sts., Springfield, 217/527-3860, 8 A.M.–6 P.M. Mon.–Fri., 8 A.M.–noon Sat., free), the family's balance sheet managed by the Springfield Marine and Fire Insurance Company, where the Lincolns deposited their money.

When Abraham Lincoln left Springfield on February 11, 1861, for his inaugural trip to Washington, D.C., he said, "I now leave, not knowing when, or whether ever, I may return." You can visit the train depot where he addressed his supporters and said those words. It is now called the **Lincoln Depot** (10th and Monroe Sts., Springfield, 217/544-8695 or 217/788-1356, 10 A.M.–4 P.M., free). Fire damaged most of the building in the 1960s, but there are some things still intact, such as the same stairs Lincoln walked up to visit the depot manager's office. National Park Service history interpreters are on hand to recount Lincoln's last day in Springfield. Inside the building the depot's waiting room has been re-created, a video recounts Lincoln's train trip to D.C., and photographs show how the depot has changed structurally throughout the years.

State Capitol Buildings

A lot of state bills were debated and laws passed at the **Old State Capitol** (between 5th and 6th Sts., just south of Washington St. and north of the pedestrian walkway, 217/785-7961, 9 A.M.–5 P.M. Tues.–Sat. Mar.–Oct., 9 A.M.–4 P.M. Tues.–Sat. Nov.–Feb., donation), but this government building is probably most famous for Lincoln's House Divided speech, when he told his fellow state representatives that a house divided against itself cannot stand. You can visit the meeting room where he delivered this speech, the library, the Illinois State Supreme Court room, and wander through the hallways. The building's exterior, designed in a Greek-revival style, is rather simple, but inside you'll find a grand stairway, Grecian columns, and ornate rooms for the legislators and judges. Most of the furniture pieces you will see inside the building are reproductions. However, a few, such as a senate desk, are original. Interpreters present a "living history program" 10–noon and 2–4 P.M. Friday and Saturday January–April and June–December. Costumed volunteers hang out in different rooms in the capitol and assume the roles of clerks or businessmen. They tell stories about the building's history and the people who once walked its halls. Guided tours of the building are organized on a rolling basis throughout the day.

Because of Illinois's robust growth during its early days of statehood, politicians and judges and bureaucrats soon ran out of space in the Old State Capitol. In response they built the second capitol building, now called the **Illinois State Capitol** (2nd St. and Capitol Ave., Springfield, 217/782-2099, www.illinois.gov, 8 A.M.–4 P.M. Mon.–Fri., 9 A.M.–3 P.M. Sat.–Sun., free), which is still in use today. This is where the governor, lieutenant governor, secretary of state, attorney general, and others keep

CHASING ABE

Abraham Lincoln sure got around. During the two decades the surveyor, store clerk, lawyer, and politician lived and worked in Illinois, Lincoln visited dozens of towns and delivered countless speeches. Here's a roundup. For an even longer list of destinations in Illinois where Lincoln may have sat in desks or slept in beds, contact the **Looking for Lincoln Heritage Coalition** (1 Old State Capitol Plaza, Springfield, 217/782-6817, www.lookingforlincoln.com).

Springfield

Lincoln Home National Historic Site (426 S. 7th St., Springfield, 217/492-4241): This is where Lincoln lived with his family while he worked in Springfield as a lawyer and a politician.

Abraham Lincoln Presidential Museum and Library (112 N. 6th St., Springfield, 217/785-0348, www.alincoln-library.com): A huge complex, opened in 2005, with exhibits that illustrate Lincoln's life, politics, and the country during his presidential tenure.

Old State Capitol State Historic Site (between 5th and 6th Sts., just south of Washington St., Springfield, 217/785-7961): Lincoln delivered his House Divided speech here on June 16, 1858. It's also where he lay in state before his burial.

Lincoln Tomb (Oak Ridge Cemetery, N. Grand Ave. to Monument Ave., Springfield, 217/782-2717): The grand monument and tomb where Abraham Lincoln, Mary Todd Lincoln, and three of their children are buried.

Lincoln-Herndon Law Office State Historic Site: (6th and Adams Sts., Springfield, 217/785-7960 or 217/785-7289): Lincoln and his partner William Herndon practiced law on the third floor of this building in the 1840s and early 1850s.

Lincoln Depot (10th and Monroe Sts., Springfield, 217/544-8695 or 217/788-1356): Before departing Springfield for Washington, D.C., in 1861, Lincoln waved good-bye and gave a brief speech at the Great Western Railroad depot.

Petersburg

Lincoln's New Salem (Hwy. 17, two miles south of Petersburg, 217/632-4000, www.lincolnsnewsalem.com): A village modeled after the one in which Lincoln lived in the same area in the 1830s. In New Salem he worked as a sur-

offices (in addition to their Chicago offices). The most stunning feature of the capitol is the 400-foot-tall dome, which seems to glitter on sunny days. Built 1868–1888 and listed on the National Register of Historic Places, this capitol was designed in Renaissance-revival and Second Empire styles. When the legislature is in session, you can watch the representatives and senators debate, table, and vote on bills from the gallery above.

Illinois State Museum

The newest permanent exhibit at the Illinois State Museum (502 S. Spring St., Springfield, 217/782-7386, www.museum.state.il.us, 8:30 A.M.–5 P.M. Mon.–Sat., noon–5 P.M. Sun., free) is called *Changes: Dynamic Illinois Environments*. Most history or geography exhib-

its typically begin the story with the Ice Age, which dates to roughly 24,000 years ago. But the Illinois State Museum exhibit starts history way, way back in time—500 million years ago. The exhibit, which extends through several rooms on the first floor, is interactive without being too geared toward children.

Visitors learn about creatures that lived in the oceans millions of years ago, about Illinois's diverse environments and how they came to be, about floodplains along rivers, and more. On the second floor of the museum, exhibits called *Peoples of the Past* and *At Home in the Heartland* depict scenes from everyday life 1700s–1980s. (The 1980s exhibit is a re-creation of a teenager's bedroom. Note the vintage U2 poster.) Visiting and rotating exhibits are also on the second floor. On the lower level is veyor and store clerk and read about law and other issues.

Vandalia
Vandalia Courthouse State Historic Site (103 W. Gallatin St., Vandalia, 618/283-1161): Lincoln began his state legislative career in Illinois while serving as a representative beginning in 1834. He traveled often to Vandalia, which was the capital before Lincoln and other legislators lobbied for it to be moved to Springfield.

Lerna
Lincoln Log Cabin State Historic Site (County Rd. 1420E, Lerna, 217/345-1845, www.lincolnlogcabin.org): The reconstructed farmstead where Abraham Lincoln's father, Thomas, lived with his wife and Abe's stepmother, Sarah. Sarah and Thomas Lincoln moved to the area in 1840. Abe did not live at the site but he did visit.

Lincoln
Postville Courthouse (5th St./Route 66, between Madison and Union Sts., Lincoln, 217/732-8930 or 217/735-4977): A re-created courthouse where Lincoln tried cases in the 1840s.

Lincoln College Museum (McKinstry Bldg., near Keokuk and Ottawa Sts., Lincoln, 217/732-3155): Exhibits include a poem written by Lincoln, a ballot box used by Lincoln, and a campaign banner from 1860.

Mt. Pulaski
Mt. Pulaski Courthouse State Historic Site (Washington St. on the city's square, 217/792-3222 or 217/737-8500): An original courthouse where Lincoln tried cases as a lawyer traveling on the Eighth Judicial Circuit in Illinois.

Beardstown
Old City Hall and Courthouse (101 W. 3rd St., Beardstown, 217/323-3225): Lincoln successfully defended a murderer in the famous Almanac Trial here in 1858.

Danville
Vermilion County Museum and Fithian Home (116 N. Gilbert St., Danville, 217/442-2922): The museum contains a replica of the old courthouse where Lincoln once practiced law and an original desk used by Lincoln. The home contains a bed where Lincoln reportedly slept while visiting a friend in Danville.

The Grand Prairie

a hands-on discovery area for kids, plus a room full of stuffed birds that are native to Illinois. The museum store has a decent collection of artwork by Illinois residents, including pottery and jewelry, books, and the standard souvenirs, such as postcards and key chains.

More Museums
On the lighter side of things, **Shea's Gas Station Museum** (2075 Peoria Rd., Springfield, 217/522-0475, 7 A.M.–4 P.M. Tues.–Fri., 7 A.M.–noon Sat., donation) is an entertaining and nostalgic stop along Route 66. Bill Shea pumped gas at this Marathon gas station for decades before closing shop in the early 1980s. The museum consists of two former gas station buildings, one that dates to the 1920s and another from the late 1940s. The old gas pumps,

which have been restored and are shiny, always seem to draw the most attention from visitors, as do the photographs of Route 66 during its heyday.

Perhaps one of the more unusual museum collections in the state is at the **Illinois State Military Museum** (Camp Lincoln, 1301 N. MacArthur Blvd., Springfield, 1 P.M.–4:30 P.M. Tues.–Sat., free), which has on view the artificial leg of Mexican General Santa Anna. The museum, which focuses its exhibits on the national guard's history, also has a target board once used by Abraham Lincoln.

More military memorabilia is on view at the **Grand Army of the Republic Memorial Museum** (629 S. 7th St., Springfield, 217/522-4373, 11 A.M.–4 P.M. Tues.–Sat.), where the focus is on Union artifacts and photographs from that era. The museum has a flag that hung in the Ford Theatre in Washington, D.C., where Lincoln was assassinated.

A former telephone repairman for Illinois Bell, now SBC, Oliver Parks collected more than 100 telephones during his lifetime. Many of these are on display in the two-room **Oliver Parks Telephone Museum** (SBC/Ameritech Building, 529 S. 7th St., Springfield, 217/789-5303, 9 A.M.–4:30 P.M. Mon.–Fri., free). They include wooden wall phones, candlestick models, plus a picture phone from the 1960s, and an old switchboard.

Historic Homes

Unlike the other major homes in Illinois designed by Frank Lloyd Wright, the **Dana-Thomas State Historic Site** (301 E. Lawrence Ave., Springfield, 217/744-3598, 9 A.M.–4 P.M. Wed.–Sun., $3 suggested donation) is inexpensive to visit. (Others, such as his home and studio and the Robie house in the Chicago region, charge at least $10 per person.) Situated within the Old Aristocracy Hill Historic District in Springfield, less than a mile from Lincoln's home and a few blocks from the governor's mansion, this house is one of few Prairie-style homes in the neighborhood. (Many are Victorian and Italianate.) The primarily beige home was built 1902–1904 and features typical Wright characteristics such as low-pitched roofs, an open floor plan, and art glass. (Dozens of frames surround the house.) It is a house that flows horizontally. Note the entranceway on Lawrence Avenue with thin bricks lying horizontally and fanning out around the archway. Other than the state of Illinois (which now owns the home), there have been only two owners: the Dana family, which originally commissioned the house and where family lived until 1928; and the Thomases, who used the house as a business office. The inside has not been tampered with and is in great shape. It's one thing to admire a Wright home from the sidewalk, but another to wander through the hallways and rooms. What makes a trip through here worth it is that the house is filled with authentic, Wright-designed fur-

niture, most notably dozens of white-oak furniture pieces.

Just north of the Dana-Thomas home is another grand home, designed with an entirely different point of view. The **Governor's Executive Mansion** (410 E. Jackson St., Springfield, 217/782-6450, free) has a Georgian exterior and Greek-revival interior. Built 1853–1855, it is situated on a hill surrounded by lush gardens. On the tour you can see several parlors, the dining room, ballroom, and several bedrooms. The executive mansion is open 9:30–11 A.M. Tues., Thurs., and Sat., plus 2–3:30 P.M. Tues. and Thurs.

Across the street from the governor's mansion is the **Vachel Lindsey Home** (603 S. 5th St., Springfield, 217/524-0901, noon–4 P.M. Tues.–Sat., free). The frequent contributor to Chicago-based *Poetry* magazine was a well-known American poet at the turn of the 20th century. It was in this house that he was born in 1879 and where he would eventually return and commit suicide in 1931. In recent years the state spent $1 million restoring this quaint, gray home. Built in the 1840s, it was once home to Mary Todd Lincoln's sister and her family. Lincoln reportedly was a frequent guest in the home.

Parks

Designed by landscape architect Jens Jensen, **Lincoln Memorial Garden and Nature Center** (2301 E. Lake Dr., Springfield, 217/529-1111, www.lmgnc.com, free) has five miles of trails through prairie and woodlands along Lake Springfield. Developed in the 1930s as a memorial to Lincoln, the 100-acre site is one of the best places to go for a walk in central Illinois. Along the trails are wildlife-observation areas, benches, and bridges that stretch over ponds and streams. Throughout the park there are also council rings, circular stone benches where community groups meet and events are held. The trees planted throughout the park—such as oaks and hickories—are native to the Midwestern states where Lincoln lived, including Illinois, Indiana, and Kentucky. The park is open sunrise–sunset. The nature center is open 10 A.M.–4 P.M.

SPRINGFIELD AND THE NAACP

Despite being the former hometown of Abraham Lincoln, the "Great Emancipator," Springfield in its early years was not exactly a town where whites and blacks lived in harmony. After the turn of the 20th century, Springfield, like many growing industrial cities in Illinois, attracted European immigrants and Southern blacks. They moved to Springfield in hopes of landing jobs in the factories or starting businesses that would cater to the booming population. Eventually tensions began to build between the two communities, which were in separate areas of town.

In the summer of 1908, a white man named Clergy Ballard was murdered after chasing down an intruder to his house. Before he died, Ballard fingered a black man for the attack and reportedly said he had seen the intruder at his daughter's bedside. Not too long after that, a white woman named Mabel Hallam claimed she had been raped by a local black man. On August 14, while both black suspects were being held in jail, a mob of white residents gathered at the jail where the accused were being held. Fearing for the suspects' safety, the police transported them to another jail, which prompted the crowd to grow even more angry.

The mob then went on a violent rampage that lasted several days. People trashed a restaurant and car that belonged to a businessman whom they believed helped transport the suspects away from the jail. They smashed windows and set fire to homes and businesses that belonged to the city's black residents and threatened more violence if blacks didn't leave town. Eventually the mob killed a prominent black businessman named William Donovan, who was said to have been Abraham Lincoln's cobbler. After the National Guard swooped into Springfield and the dust cleared, about $200,000 worth of property had been damaged, and several blacks and whites were dead. Later, Mabel Hallam confessed she had never been raped.

Stunned at the violent outbreak, a group of white and black activists called for a meeting in New York City to discuss race and violence against blacks. Among those who came to the meeting: W. E. B. DuBois and Ida Wells-Barnett. This group, initially called the National Negro Committee, would become the National Association for the Advancement of Colored People.

Several historical markers about the riots have been placed throughout downtown Springfield. The self-guided tour starts at 7th and Jefferson streets. More information is available from the Springfield Convention and Visitors Bureau.

If you're in Springfield and need a quick relief from touring, **Adams Wildlife Sanctuary** (2315 E. Clear Lake Ave., Springfield, 217/544-5781, sunrise–sunset daily, free) is a good spot to take a break and stretch your legs by going for a short walk or sitting on a bench and watching for birds. The 30-acre site contains a restored prairie and an old fruit orchard. It's a few miles northeast of Lincoln's home.

Washington Park (1740 W. Fayette Ave., Springfield, 217/753-6228, free) has a botanical garden and impressive 132-foot-tall carillon bell tower. The domed conservatory contains tropical plants and flowers such as orchids.

Throughout the year the conservatory hosts several flower and plant shows, including one that highlights native Illinois plants around May, chrysanthemums in the fall, and poinsettias in the winter. Outside the dome are several gardens stocked with roses, irises, and cacti. The botanic garden is open noon–4 P.M. Monday–Friday, noon–5 P.M. Saturday–Sunday.

Also in Washington Park is the **Thomas Rees Memorial Carillon,** reportedly the third-largest bell tower in the world. You can climb up the tower (there are three different levels where you can stop and take in the view) or ride the elevator to the top. This is a good, cheap way to see Springfield from above. The carillon has 67 bronze bells. To give you an idea of how huge it is, and how impressive it is when you hear the music, the bells range from 22 pounds to a 7.5-ton G flat. It was installed in the park in 1962. You can listen to the bells on Sunday afternoons throughout the year and on Wednesday evenings in the summer. You can tour the tower noon–8 P.M. Tuesday–Sunday June–August, and on weekends only in the spring and fall. It is closed December–March.

The local zoo, **Henson Robinson Zoo** (1100 E. Lake Dr., Springfield, 217/753-6217, www.hensononrobinsonzoo.com, $3.25), has 300 animals from around the world, including cheetahs, monkeys, and bears. In addition there is a barn with farm animals and a butterfly garden. It's on the south side of Lake Springfield. Hours are 10 A.M.–5 P.M. Monday–Friday, 10 A.M.–6 P.M. Saturday–Sunday March–October, 10 A.M.–4 P.M. Monday–Friday November–February. It is open until 8 P.M. on Wednesdays June–August.

Camp Butler National Cemetery (5063 Camp Butler Rd., Springfield, 217/492-4070, 8 A.M.–sunset daily, free), northeast of town, is a veteran's cemetery where Union and Confederate soldiers are buried, as are soldiers who died during the World Wars and other conflicts throughout the decades. Before it was made a cemetery, the site held a Union training camp during the Civil War. Later in the war a Confederate prison was established and during the summer of 1862, 700 people died of a smallpox epidemic.

ENTERTAINMENT AND EVENTS
Theater

The restored **Route 66 Drive-In** (Knight's Action Park, 1700 Recreation Dr., Springfield, movie info 217/698-0066, park 217/546-8881, $5) is a twin drive-in adjacent to the adventure park. Movies are shown nightly Memorial Day–Labor Day, then on weekends only through October. The concessionaire sells corn dogs, cotton candy, ice cream, and other snacks.

Springfield Center for the Arts (420 S. 6th St., Springfield, 217/523-2787, www.scfta.org) is a community gathering place for visual artists, actors, musicians, and other performing artists. The 80,000-square-foot building (formerly a Masonic temple) houses three theaters, a gallery, and other reception areas. Something's cooking there every weekend, whether it's a local community theater production, a gospel concert, or photography exhibit reception.

The **Illinois Symphony Orchestra** (524 ½ E. Capital Ave., Springfield, 217/522-2838, www.ilsymphony.org) plays classics (Mozart, Rachmaninov), pops concerts, as well as matinees for children, chamber concerts, holiday shows, and more. Musicians perform at First Presbyterian Church in Springfield (321 S. 7th St.) and Sangamon Auditorium at the University of Illinois at Springfield campus (entrance off Shepherd Rd., south of I-72 and east of I-55).

Events

For more than 150 years, Illinois residents have been bringing their prized hogs, goats, and cattle to the **Illinois State Fair** (State Fairgrounds, Sangamon Ave. and Business U.S. 55, Springfield, 217/782-6661, 7 A.M.–midnight during fair days, $3 admission, $7 parking). While livestock shows are definitely a part of the fair, people do go for more than the animals. Homemade pies, jams, and wines are judged here. There are carnival rides, numerous food and drink vendors, and lots of bands performing country, classic rock, and some pop music. Inside the state fairgrounds is the Illinois Fire Museum (in Building 7) which houses antique fire equipment, photos, and patches. The fair runs for 10 days mid- to late-August every year. The 366-acre site is on the north side of town.

About 60,000 people make tracks to the **International Route 66 Mother Road Festival** (217/422-3733 or 866/783-6645, www.rte66fest.com) held in downtown Springfield every year in mid-September. Walk past hundreds of shiny, vintage cars, jitterbug in the street to a live band, and watch a parade go by. This festival, which started in 2001, expands every year.

SHOPPING

The main shopping areas in town are **Parkway Pointe** (Freedom Dr. and Veterans Pkwy.) where you can find big discount retailers such as Target and Wal-Mart; and the **Simon White Oaks Mall** (Veterans Pkwy. and Wabash Ave.), an enclosed mall with 115 stores, including the department store Famous Barr, Gap, and others. Near downtown **The Weber House** (925 S. 7th St., Springfield) is home to several boutiques, such as the gift shop Lily's, gourmet kitchen shop Thyme to Cook, and Incredibly Delicious, a bakery.

While you're downtown, satisfy your sweet tooth by dropping into **Del's Popcorn Shop** (213 S. 6th St., Springfield, 217/544-0037), which sells kettle corn, roasted nuts, ice cream, and candy. Also downtown, collectors will enjoy a walk through **Prairie Archives** (522 E. Adams St., Springfield, 217/522-9742), which specializes in antique books, rare books, and used books. Literary types can easily while away the afternoon here browsing through history books and literature. It also has a good collection of vintage children's and hobby books. Nearby **Recycled Records** (625 E. Adams St., Springfield, 217/522-5122) sells used CDs, records, and tapes.

RECREATION
Amusement and Water Park
Bumper boats, go-karts, volleyball. What'll you have? On the south side of Springfield, **Knight's Action Park** (1700 Recreation Dr., Springfield, 217/546-8881, www.knightsactionpark.com) is a combo amusement park and water park with water slides, miniature golf, batting cages, a driving range, arcade area, and Ferris wheel. Water park admission is $20 per person, $15 for kids under 48 inches and adults over 55 years. But admission into the regular amusement park is free. You just pay for the rides and the ac-

tivities as you choose them. Fees vary, such as $3–5 for activities such as miniature golf and hitting buckets of balls. The amusement park is open 9 A.M.–10 P.M. daily in the spring and until 11 P.M. mid-May–Labor Day weekend. The water park is open 10 A.M.–7 P.M. daily mid-May–Labor Day weekend. However, the water park is closed the Monday–Friday before Labor Day weekend. Next door to Knight's Action Park is the **Route 66 Drive-In.** (For more information see *Entertainment and Events.)*

Climbing
Rock-climbing options are limited in hill-challenged central Illinois. We have to make do with what we have and that is a lot of grain elevators. About five miles southeast of Springfield is an old grain elevator complex that some creative folks have converted into a climbing gym. **The Silo: Dare to Climb** (130 S. John St., Rochester, 217/498-9922, www.daretoclimb.com) has two 100-foot indoor climbing routes, plus several other routes throughout the complex. It's open 5 P.M.–9:30 P.M. Wednesday and Friday, noon–6 P.M. Saturday–Sunday. A day pass costs $11, plus if it's your first time there, you'll pay a $5 initiation fee. Equipment rental is extra.

ACCOMMODATIONS
$50–100
The affordable **Carpenter Street Hotel** (525 N. 6th St., Springfield, 217/789-9100 or 888/779-9100, www.carpenterstreethotel.com, $70) is north of downtown tourist sights, on the way to the state fairgrounds. Rooms in this newer building are sparse, but clean. The building has a coin-operated laundry and staff set up a continental breakfast in the morning. The entire building is smoke-free.

On the outskirts of southwest Springfield you'll find the economical, clean **Sleep Inn** (3470 Freedom Dr., Springfield, 217/787-6200 or 800/221-2222, www.sleepinn.com, $80–85). Hotel rooms come with one queen or two full-size beds, plus a few extra amenities such as in-room irons and ironing boards.

On the south side of town, along Route 66 and not far from the Cozy Dog Drive-In, is the **⚑ Route 66 Hotel and Conference Center** (615 E. St. Joseph St., Springfield, 217/529-6626 or 888/707-8366, www.rt66hotel.com, $55). This hotel has 108 rooms and six suites. Its slogan is "the museum you can sleep in" because it has several antique cars and motorcycles on display in the lobby. The rooms, however, resemble those found in most national chain motels, with big beds, televisions, tables, and coffeemakers. The hotel has RV parking available. Within the hotel is a casual, Route 66–themed restaurant called The Filling Station Bar and Grill. It serves regional and American food, such as horseshoe sandwiches, on red and white checkered tables. (See the sidebar, *The Horseshoe*, for more info on horseshoe sandwiches.)

Consider the **⚑ Mansion View Inn and Suites** (529 S. 4th St., Springfield, 217/544-7411, www.mansionview.com, $79), an upscale motor lodge. There are 93 rooms, some of them two-room suites and some with exterior entrances. The brick building fits in nicely with the historic downtown district surrounding it. You can walk to the Lincoln home, capitol buildings, and downtown restaurants and shops, and it's across the street from the governor's mansion.

Perhaps the closest place you can get to Lincoln is by staying overnight at the **The Henry Mischler House** (802 E. Edwards St., Springfield, 217/525-2660, www.mischlerhouse.com, $75–95), a bed-and-breakfast just down the street from the Lincoln home and across the street from the Lincoln historic district. The Queen Anne home, built in 1897, has five guest rooms, some with private bathrooms in the room and others down the hall from the room. (Those with bathrooms down the hall will receive bathrobes.) You can see the Lincoln home from a window in the Henry and Louise Suite. When you need a little R&R, there's a back patio with a garden and chairs. Wine and cheese is served in the evenings and a full breakfast in the morning.

Just down the block from the Lincoln home, within walking distance to the Old State Capitol and downtown restaurants, is the **Renaissance Springfield Hotel** (701 E. Adams St., 217/544-8800, www.renaissancehotels.com, $84–119), a popular spot for people in town doing business with the government. There are 316 rooms here, and the building contains an indoor swimming pool, tavern, and fine-dining restaurant.

$100–150

For a more pampered experience, try **⚑ The Inn at 835** (835 S. 2nd St., Springfield, 217/523-4466, www.innat835.com, $99–179), where you can lounge in a four-poster or sleigh bed, order a bottle of wine or scotch to your room, and draw a bath in a claw foot tub. The inn has a combination of rooms and several suites in the main building, a former luxury apartment building built at the turn of the 20th century and now listed on the National Register of Historic Places. The best rooms are those with large, brick private balconies facing south. Excellent spots to enjoy a morning cup of coffee or evening glass of wine. The building has high-speed Internet access, an elevator and is wheelchair accessible. The bungalow behind the inn contains two more suites.

FOOD

Cafés

Andiamoi (204 S. 6th St., Springfield, 217/523-3262, 7 A.M.–4 P.M. Mon.–Tues., 7 A.M.–8 P.M. Wed., 7 A.M.–midnight Thurs.–Fri., 8 A.M.–2 P.M. Sat., $6) has a little bit of everything—café au lait, bagels, and muffins for breakfast, salads and sandwiches for lunch and dinner, plus wine for the evening. All are served in a small storefront space with about 10 tables.

Just down the street is the cheery **⚑ Trout Lily Café** (218 S. 6th St., Springfield, 217/391-0101, www.troutlilycafe.com, 7 A.M.–4:30 P.M. Mon.–Fri., 9 A.M.–3 P.M. Sat., 9:30 A.M.–2 P.M., $6), which specializes in preparing quiche and gourmet coffee and tea drinks. It also has sandwiches such as ham and cheese and turkey. This is a good spot to sit at a table inside or on the sidewalk and strike up a conversation with

THE HORSESHOE

Dieters, cardiologists, and nutritionists beware. The horseshoe sandwich, for which Springfield is famous, is not only loaded with fat and calories, but it is so tasty, especially after a packed day of touring or partying.

The sandwich is believed to have been invented by a chef or chefs at the Leland Hotel in Springfield (now long gone). It was dubbed the horseshoe because it resembled one: The ham represents the shoe and the fries are like nails. Each horseshoe is different, but essentially the open-faced sandwich begins with two, maybe three pieces of toast, followed by your choice of meat (hamburger, ham steak, turkey, corned beef, you name it), French fries, and then a melted-cheese concoction. Sometimes the order of the cheese and the fries is reversed. Every sandwich is different, usually because everyone has a different recipe for the cheese sauce. Some make it with a cheddar and beer blend, with a touch of Worcestershire sauce. Others use white American cheese or Colby cheese with a dash of mustard. A lighter version of the horseshoe is the pony shoe, which (depending on the restaurant) will have one slice of toast, a smaller amount of meat, and fewer fries.

the owner or regulars about political or cultural activity in town.

American

A local favorite, the **Feed Store** (516 E. Adams St., Springfield, 217/528-3355, 11 A.M.–3 P.M. Mon.–Sat., $7) is popular among government employees for its homey, inexpensive food such as roast beef sandwiches, the veggie hero, and apple cake.

A Route 66 institution, the **Cozy Dog Drive In** (2935 S. 6th St., Springfield, 217/525-1992, www.cozydogdrivein.com, 8 A.M.–8 P.M. Mon.–Sat., $5) is most famous for creating the Cozy Dog, otherwise known as the corn dog. After you've scarfed down one or two of the signature dogs, take some time to look at photos of the highway and Springfield from decades ago. The restaurant has tons of Route 66 memorabilia plastered on the walls and on shelves and tables. There are some cool vintage road maps of Route 66 and the states it slices through.

On the lower level of one of Springfield's oldest buildings downtown, **Norb Andy's Tabarin** (518 E. Capitol Ave., Springfield, 217/523-7777, 11 A.M.–2 A.M. Tues.–Sat., $5–15) serves a mean horseshoe sandwich accompanied by live music. Norb Andy's also serves hamburgers and other filling pub fare.

Springfield is a long way from any ocean, but you'll be able to find some quality seafood at **Augie's** (2 W. Old State Capitol Plaza, 217/544-6974, lunch served 11 A.M.–4 P.M. Mon.–Fri., dinner served 5–10 P.M. Mon.–Sat., $15). Dishes may include an Asian-pesto red snapper or grouper. The restaurant also serves meat entrées such as roast duck.

People flock to **D'Arcy's Pint** (2413 S. MacArthur Blvd., Springfield, 217/492-8800, 11 A.M.–10 P.M. Mon.–Thurs., 11 A.M.–11 P.M. Fri.–Sat., $5–15) for its horseshoe sandwiches, which consist of toast, meat, French fries, and melted white American cheese on the top.

Middle Eastern

Greek and Lebanese food are served at the **Holy Land Diner** (518 E. Adams St., Springfield, 217/544-5786, 11 A.M.–7 P.M. Mon.–Fri., 11 A.M.–9 P.M. Fri.–Sat., $10). You can try gyros, kebabs, and falafel sandwiches here.

INFORMATION

Springfield Convention and Visitors Bureau (109 N. 7th St., Springfield, 217/789-2360 or 800/545-7300, www.visit-springfieldillinois.com) has lots of brochures and helpful, detailed maps of the city with the major points of interest, hotels, and restaurants marked on them. Unfortunately it is not open on the weekends. Hours are 8 A.M.–5 P.M. Monday–Friday. You can pick up regional maps and brochures at the **Central Illinois Tourism Development Office** (Hilton Hotel, 700 E. Adams St., Springfield, 217/525-7980, www.visitcentralillinois.com, 8:30 A.M.–5 P.M. Mon.–Fri.). It also has a collection of some state attractions, plus visitor magazines. The **Capitol Complex Visitors Center** (425 S. College St., Springfield, 217/524-6620, 9–3:30 Mon., 8–4:30 Tues.–Fri., 9–4 Sat.) has brochures, informational videos, and exhibits about the capitol.

GETTING AROUND
Airport
Several airlines offer flights to and from Springfield's **Capital Airport** (1200 Capitol Airport Dr., west of J. David Jones Pkwy., Springfield, 217/788-1060, www.flyspi.com), north of the city. American's commuter service, American Connection, flies to and from St. Louis, Missouri. ATA Express operates a shuttle to Chicago's Midway Airport and United Express flies to and from Chicago's O'Hare Airport. Parking is free. Avis (217/522-7228), Budget (217/523-9515), and Hertz (217/525-8820) have rental-car agencies at the airport.

Train
Amtrak has several trains that make stops at Springfield's Station (Washington and 3rd Sts., Springfield, 800/USA-RAIL—800/872-7245, www.amtrak.com). The Texas Eagle runs between Chicago and San Antonio, Texas, stopping in the Illinois towns of Joliet, Pontiac, Bloomington, Springfield, Lincoln, and Alton. The State House line operates daily between Chicago and St. Louis, with stops in Summit, Dwight, Joliet, Pontiac, Bloomington, Lincoln, Springfield, Carlinville, and Alton. The Ann Rutledge services Chicago, St. Louis, Kansas City, and some towns in between, including Springfield. A one-way ticket between Chicago and Springfield will cost about $40 and about $25 to and from St. Louis. The Springfield train station is staffed 6 A.M.–8:30 P.M. daily.

Bus or Trolley
Springfield Trolley (522 E. Monroe St., Springfield, 217/789-2360 or 800/545-7300) stops at most of the city's tourist attractions, including the Lincoln home.

Springfield Mass Transit (217/522-5531) buses run roughly 6 A.M.–6 P.M. Monday–Saturday. There are 12 different lines through the city. A one-way fare will cost $.75. Routes 1 and 2 take you to and from the fairgrounds. You can pick up a map and schedule at the convention and visitors bureau.

The **Greyhound** station is at 2351 South Dirksen Parkway, Springfield. You can contact the station at 217/544-8466.

Taxi
Several taxicab companies operate in Springfield. They include **Checker Radio Cab** (217/525-1630); **Lincoln Yellow Cab** (217/523-4545); and **United Taxi Cab** (217/585-8577).

Services
If you sprained an ankle or are feeling under the weather, you can visit one of the walk-in clinics in town, such as **Springfield Urgent Care Center** (1836 S. MacArthur Ave., Springfield, 217/789-1403) or **Prompt Care** (1025 S. 7th St., Springfield, 217/753-2273). For more serious matters, there is **St. John's Hospital** (800 E. Carpenter St., Springfield, 217/544-6464, www.st-johns.org).

Downtown there are two U.S. post offices. The downtown station is at 411 East Monroe Street, 217/753-3432, open 7:30 A.M.–5 P.M. Monday–Friday. The capital station is at 211 South Spring Street, 217/753-3543, open 9 A.M.–5 P.M. Monday–Friday.

DIVERNON
The roadside town of Divernon makes for a short, amusing detour while you're traveling down I-55 or Route 66 south of Springfield. Get off at Exit 82 and stop by the **giant covered wagon** (dubbed "the railsplitter") for a snapshot. At the front of the 40-foot-long wagon sits a 12-foot-tall Abe Lincoln dressed

THE MOTHER ROAD: ROUTE 66

If you really want to get a feel for Illinois, get off the interstate and take a drive down one of the historic two-lane highways that crisscross the state. The mother of all these is the legendary Route 66, which begins (or concludes) in Chicago.

Route 66 has been called the "Main Street Through America," and as you drive through the Illinois section, you'll see why that name fits. Aside from the Chicago and East St. Louis legs, a trip down Route 66 is largely rural in nature, past countless corn- and soybean fields and small towns home to grain elevators or former coal mines. Some of these towns have lively downtown districts complete with cozy luncheonettes and antiques shops, while others have empty storefronts and crumbling motels. Scattered along the way are signs of the old Route 66: vintage gas stations and Googie-style neon signs outside of businesses. This space-age type of design, with accents such as boomerangs and starbursts, can be still found in some sections along the historic highway.

The entire highway is about 2,400 miles long, with the Illinois section comprising about 300 miles. Construction started in the 1920s, although there were some non-contiguous roads along the route. For decades it was the main thoroughfare between Chicago and St. Louis and the way to go west. For the most part, the road follows I-55 on a southwest to northeast path. There are a few alternate routes through or around some cities such as Springfield. After I-55 was built in the 1970s, Route 66 essentially became a frontage road.

The highway begins at Jackson Boulevard and Lake Shore Drive along Chicago's lakefront. The route through Chicago and the suburbs can be nerve-wracking, time-consuming, and, in this traveler's opinion, not worth it if you specifically are out to drive the road. Neighborhoods and commercial districts along this section of the route have been so developed and redeveloped that it's often hard to imagine what it would have been like to drive the leg during the road's heyday. To avoid traffic headaches, you might want to start the journey near Joliet, which is about an hour or so southwest of the city. You'll pass through Wilmington, home to the Launching Pad Drive-In and several antiques shops; Pontiac and its Route 66 museum; Lincoln, with its courthouse square that's home to more antiques shops and a few cafés; Williamsville and Diecast Auto Sales, a vintage gas station and toy car museum. In Springfield, the top Route 66 attractions are Bill Shea's Gas Station Museum and the Cozy Dog Drive-In, followed by the Sky View Drive-In Theatre, which has been showing films since 1951 in nearby Litchfield. Finally, the iconic Brooks Catsup Bottle in Collinsville is a must-see for fans of roadside architecture.

Like to party with like-minded road warriors? Springfield hosts the **International Route 66 Mother Road Festival** (217/422-3733 or 866/783-6645, www.route66fest.com) every year in mid-September in downtown Springfield.

The Grand Prairie

in a black suit and stovepipe hat. Then, grab a bite to eat at the **Truckers Homestead Restaurant** (Hwy. 104, 217/628-3811, 5:30 A.M.– 9 P.M.), where not only can you chow down on some chicken, but you can take a look at the World Cowboy Gun-Spinning Hall of Fame, where photos of famous gun-spinning men line the walls.

COAL COUNTRY: PANA AND VICINITY

The town of Pana is in the heart of coal country, or at least, it was during the peak coal-mining years during the first half of the 20th century. At one time there were five mines operating in the area and several railroad lines running through town. Throughout downtown Pana are murals that offer glimpses at what life was like back then, with images of a marching band and people waiting to catch a train. You can also get a sense of the town's glory days by driving along Spruce, Locust, 2nd, and 3rd streets. You'll pass once-grand old homes where the coal barons used to live. Pana is also called the city of roses.

At the turn of the 20th century there were hundreds of greenhouses in the area and every year millions of roses grew inside them. You'll notice several homes are bedecked with rose gardens in the summer.

Sights and Activities

Managed by the local high school, **Anderson Prairie Park** (Chestnut St., just south of 9th St., Pana, 217/562-4240, www.andersonprairie.org, sunrise–sunset daily, free) is a quiet, natural park along an old railroad line. At the southern entrance off Chestnut Street you'll find an observation tower and a few benches. These are good spots to watch birds, such as cedar waxwings, indigo buntings, plus wild turkeys, owls, and a variety of butterflies. From there you can follow a narrow walking trail on a boardwalk past wildflowers. The north side of the park is a bit more wooded and easy to walk, as the main trail is wide and is made of gravel and dirt. It's good for hiking, biking, or jogging.

For a longer trip take to the **Lincoln Prairie Trail,** an asphalt trail that stretches for about 15 miles between Pana and Taylorville,

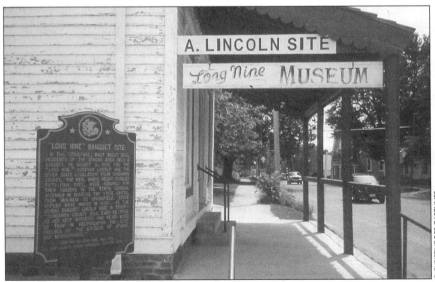

the Long Nine Museum in Pana, where Lincoln and friends once gathered to the northwest. It's a fairly level trail through woods, meadows, farm fields, and over creeks. The trail, which follows a former railroad bed and runs for the most part alongside Highway 29, opened in 2001 and is one of the state's newer rails-to-trails projects. You can reach it from Bear Creek Road in Pana.

Four genuine log cabins are open to the public at **Coal Creek Pioneer Village** (Pana Tri-County Fairgrounds, Pana, 217/562-4240, call for hours, free). The one-story cabins, built from the 1840s to the 1870s, all hail from throughout Illinois.

On the south side of town is **Kitchell Park** (U.S. 51 and 8th St., Pana, 6 A.M.–11 P.M. daily, free), a city park with an outdoor auditorium for band concerts, plus picnic tables, playgrounds, a little pond with a fountain, baseball diamonds, and a public swimming pool. The park was named after John Kitchell, a local resident who was a Civil War captain for Lincoln.

Accommodations

The **Lake Lawn Inn** (Hwy. 16 and U.S. 51, Pana, 217/562-2123) is a clean motor lodge on the outskirts of town. It's got an outdoor swimming pool and a casual restaurant on-site. Rates are around $45.

The **Oak Terrace Resort** (100 Beyers Lake Rd., Pana, 217/539-4477 or 800/577-7598, www.oakterraceresort.com) has a 37-room hotel with some rooms overlooking golf holes. In addition to the hotel and 18-hole golf course, the casual resort has an indoor pool, small exercise room, and a private lake for fishing or taking a pontoon boat out for a ride. It's also recently added a spa area where you can unwind with a massage or pedicure. Mulligans, a casual American restaurant, serves breakfast, lunch, and dinner daily. Rates are $60–100.

Information

The **Pana Chamber of Commerce** operates a visitors center in Karla's Kollectibles Antique Mall (Hwy. 16 and U.S. 51, Pana). For more information call the chamber at 217/562-4240 or visit www.panaillinois.com.

Moweaqua

The quiet mining town of Moweaqua was struck with tragedy on December 24, 1932, when methane gas in its coal mine exploded when the gas was exposed to carbide lights carried by the miners. As a result, 54 miners were killed. Two years later the mine closed. As a tribute to those who died during the accident and to educate folks about what it was like to be a coal miner in Illinois, local residents organized the **Moweaqua Coal Mine Museum** (129 S. Main St., Moweaqua, 217/768-3019, by appointment, free), a small museum on tiny Main Street where you can read newspaper clippings about the disaster, view photographs of the mine and the town, and see some mining artifacts and tools.

Nokomis

The town of Nokomis, population 2,300, has produced three national Hall of Fame baseball players (as well as several others who went on to play great baseball.) And boy, are the Nokomis residents proud of their connection to the sport. The **B-R-S Baseball Museum** (121 W. State St., Nokomis, 217/563-2516, 9–11 A.M. Mon.–Sat., free) in downtown Nokomis highlights the careers of "Sunny" Jim Bottomly, a first baseman for the St. Louis Cardinals, Cincinnati Reds, and St. Louis Browns in the 1920s; Charles "Red" Ruffing, who, despite losing four toes in a mining accident as a child went on to become a pitcher in the 1930s for the Boston Red Sox, New York Yankees, and Chicago White Sox; and Ray Schalk, a catcher for the New York Giants and Chicago White Sox in the 1910s known for his talent of stealing bases.

Taylorville

Taylorville is the self-proclaimed Christmas Capital of Illinois. And if you like twinkling light shows, this is one you've got to see. During the winter holiday season the town hosts a tour of homes, a Santa parade, cookie-baking events, and the festival of trees and "flight of angels," which are wire and light sculptures hanging in trees around the courthouse square. For information on Taylorville, contact the **Taylorville Tourism Council** at 217/824-2194 or the **Taylorville Chamber of Commerce** at 217/824-4919.

Litchfield

A must-do for Route 66 travelers, the **Sky View Drive-In Theatre** (Route 66, Litchfield, 217/324-4451, www.litchfieldskyview.com, $2) has been alive and kicking as

a drive-in along the historic road since 1951. New movies and classics are shown here. Pizza, chili dogs, popcorn, and drinks are sold at the concession stand. It's open the first or second weekend in April–late October, depending on the weather. Movies are shown daily except before Memorial Day and after Labor Day, when they're shown Friday, Saturday, and Sunday only. It's a half mile north of Highway 16 on Route 66.

Lake Shelbyville Region

After Congress passed the Flood Control Act of 1958, which authorized the Army Corps of Engineers to create Lake Shelbyville, central Illinois would never be the same. Water, water everywhere! People could buy boats, big boats, and they could lounge for hours on sandy beaches. The massive dam project (in size and cost) involved filling old mines, rerouting gas pipelines, moving graves and cemeteries, and building a 100-foot-tall, 3,000-foot-long dam on the Kaskaskia River. The result was an 11,000-acre lake with 250 miles of shoreline. The whole purpose was to control flooding, establish water supply for area towns, and spark development of the area as a recreation destination. Well, it's not Lake Powell, but for water-starved central Illinoisans it's an oasis. Two state parks are on its shores, one of them, Eagle Creek, with a resort and golf course. The town of Shelbyville on the south end of the lake has several restaurants and shops in its downtown, and there are countless modern campsites around the lake, making the area quite a gathering place for RVers.

ORIENTATION

The largest town in the area, Shelbyville is off Highway 16, just west of the dam and three of the Army Corps of Engineers recreation areas. Shelbyville is where you'll find the bulk of the dining and lodging options. Other area towns include Sullivan and Kirksville on the north end, Findlay on the west coast, and Windsor

on the east. Wolf Creek and Eagle Creek state parks are opposite each other on the lake (Wolf is on the east side, Eagle is on the west). It's rather difficult and time-consuming to drive around the lake. Lake Shelbyville is not shaped like a circle and there is no one road that follows the shoreline. There are dozens of parking areas and boat launches scattered around the lake.

SIGHTS
The Spillway and Dam East and West Recreation Areas

For a good overview of the lake, drop by the **Army Corps of Engineers Lake Shelbyville Visitors Center** (217/774-3951) one mile east of Shelbyville, just east of the dam from Highway 16. There you can pick up some maps and read about the history of the dam project. Visitors can walk along the spillway and through the picnic areas above the lake. Or you can take a tour of the dam with Army Corps staff at 11 A.M. Saturdays and 3 P.M. Sundays Memorial Day–Labor Day. On the other side of the lake from the visitors center, just off 16, is Dam West Recreation Area, with a sand beach and boat ramp. The beach is open 8 A.M.–sunset late May–mid-September. Beach access costs $1 per person. There are also boat-launching fees.

Eagle Creek State Recreation Area

One of the best places along the shores of Lake Shelbyville is Eagle Creek (south of the

© CHRISTINE DES GARENNES

The Grand Prairie

Lake Shelbyville

Bruce-Findlay Rd., east of Hwy. 128, Findlay, 217/756-8260, www.dnr.state.il.us), technically a state park, but probably more known for the resort there by the same name (800/876-EAGLE or 800/876-3245, www.eaglecreekresort.com). Its main attraction is the 6,900-yard golf course designed by Ken Killian. But the resort also has a slew of other stuff to do. Rent bikes and explore the park and the nearby country roads. Rent a paddleboat or pontoon boat and discover some of the lake's inlets. Take a dip in the outdoor swimming pool, take in a round of miniature golf, or play tennis. In addition, the park has a great 12-mile hiking trail that weaves along the woods and shoreline. If the area receives enough snow in the winter, you can cross-country ski on groomed trails in the park. Eagle Creek also has tent and RV campsites available. (For more information, see *Accommodations.*)

Wolf Creek State Park

Opposite Eagle Creek on the east side of the lake is Wolf Creek State Park (west of Hwy. 32, eight miles north of Windsor, 217/459-2831, www.dnr.state.il.us), a popular weekend get-away for families as well as horse owners. There are nearly 300 tent and RV campsites here, plus a swimming beach at the southwest part of the park, a boat ramp, playground, and picnic areas. A 12-mile horseback-riding trail (which you can also hike along) winds through the park.

More Hiking Trails

Bird-watchers will want to make tracks to the 1.2-mile **Okaw Bluff Trail** at Okaw Bluff Group Camp, on the east side of the lake north of the town of Bruce, off the Bruce-Findlay Road and east of Highway 32. Hike atop a bluff overlooking the lake and then past a 100-acre wetland area, stopping at the wildlife-viewing stands to look for herons and other waterfowl.

You can find the 11-mile **Chief Illini Trail** between Shelbyville and Eagle Creek Recreation Area at the Lone Point campground. Follow this invigorating trail up along the bluffs and down near the water and you'll be able to get a good sense of the Lake Shelbyville environment as you pass wildflowers and perhaps see fish jumping or catch a glimpse of a doe and her fawn walking through the woods or crossing a meadow. The shorter version of this trail, the **Little Chief Illini Trail,** is about two miles long and also accessible from the Lone Point campground.

Boating and Fishing

Lake Shelbyville has three marinas where visitors can rent boats, launch their own boats, stock up on snacks and drinks, bait and lures, and find out where the fish are biting. **Lithia Springs Marina** (217/744-4121 or 800/447-4121) is on the southeast side of the lake where Lithia Springs Creek enters the lake. The marina rents out houseboats and fishing boats. To get to Lithia Springs, follow County Road 2200E north from Highway 16, east of Shelbyville. East of Findlay, north of Eagle Creek and the Bruce-Findlay Road, is the **Findlay Marina** (217/756-8595) and to the northeast is **Sullivan Marina and Campground** (217/728-7338), just east of Highway 32. Several anglers in the area offer their expertise to visitors. For a complete list of fishing guides call or visit the Shelby County Office of Tourism (see *Information.*)

ENTERTAINMENT

The pet project of the local chamber of commerce and area automobile dealer Bob Boarman (his auto shop is just down the street), the **Roxy Theatre** (147 E. Main St., Shelbyville, 217/774-ROXY or 217/774-7699, www.boarmansroxytheatre.com, $3) is a cool, vintage movie theater in downtown Shelbyville. Classic, current, and kids' flicks are shown here.

Within Shelbyville's Forest Park is the **Chautauqua Auditorium** (N. 9th St., Forest Park, Shelbyville, 217774-5531), a historic round building that dates to 1903. Billy Sunday preached here. The John Philip Sousa Band performed here. Local and visiting musicians perform here throughout the summer. Contact the tourism office for a calendar of events.

The Little Theatre on the Square (16 E. Harrison St., Sullivan, 217/728-7375 or 888/261-9675, www.thelittletheatre.org) in downtown Sullivan is a professional theater

that presents about six musicals and plays throughout the year. It tends to produce classic Broadway shows such as *42nd Street, Fiddler on the Roof,* and children's shows such as *The Jungle Book.* Sullivan is on the north end of Lake Shelbyville.

SHOPPING

Downtown Shelbyville has a few antiques and gift shops, including the **The Wishing Well** (135 E. Main St., Shelbyville, 217/774-1321, 10 A.M.–5 P.M.Tues.–Sat., 1–5 P.M. Sun. during the summers, call for winter hours), which has a variety of vintage collectibles, antique furniture, and other items.

The Amish Warehouse (1501 S. Hickory St., Shelbyville, 217774-4210, www.theamishgallery.com, 10 A.M.–5 P.M. Tues.–Fri., 10 A.M.–2 P.M. Sat.) is chock-full of handmade oak furniture.

On the north side of the lake in the town of Sullivan is the **Old School Market** (208 W. Jackson St., Sullivan, 217/728-3166, 11 A.M.–7 P.M. Mon.–Thurs., 11 A.M.–8 P.M. Fri.–Sat.), a two-story, 14-store complex that has Amish furniture, antiques, primitives, and lots of tchotchkes your grandmother will like, such as candles, baskets, and stuffed animals. There's also a country buffet here.

ACCOMMODATIONS
$50–100

Folks on a budget can stay at the 21-room **Spillway Motel** (Hwy. 16, by the dam, east of Shelbyville, 800/845-0414, $50–54) for no-frills accommodations. It caters to boaters here with the large parking area, bait shop, and electrical hookups for recharging those boat batteries. Billed as a Victorian Inn, **The Shelby Inn** (816 W. Main St., Shelbyville, 800/342-9978, www.theshelbyinn.com, $59–$69) is actually a newer-construction inn with buildings that feature several porches. (Room registration is in the Tallman House, a restored 1905 home listed on the National Register of Historic Places). The 51 rooms come with double or king-size beds. The hotel is close to downtown and the lake.

The Deerfield Bed and Breakfast (Wolf Creek State Park Rd., Windsor, 217/459-2750 or 800/656-2750, www.deerfieldbb.com, $85–135) offers rooms in a rustic, log cabin setting, but with modern amenities such as air conditioning. Decor and furniture are modest here, not stylish or chic, but comfortable. One of the best features is the long front porch with its rockers and its location, adjacent to Wolf Creek State Park, where you can spend your days hiking and riding horses.

Eagle Creek Resort (217/756-3456 or 800/876-3245, www.eaglecreekresort.com, $89–109) has 138 guest rooms and 10 suites, decorated slightly different from your run-of-the-mill lakeshore resort, such as with Amish-made furniture. Rooms are nice and clean, but the main reason to stay here is the slew of activities available outdoors: swimming in the pool, playing tennis, playing golf or minigolf, hiking, boating, and fishing. There is a restaurant on-site. The resort has a two-night minimum on weekends in the summer.

$100–150

Lithia Resort (County Rd. 1500N, Shelbyville, 217/774-2882, www.lithiaresort.com) has two lodging options: 12 basic rooms in a motor lodge–type of building or newer log cabins. Several different layouts are available, but basically all include a kitchen. The resort has fishing ponds for bank fishing. Rates vary according to the season, but are generally $50–130 for the rooms and $90–150 for cabins.

For weekly accommodations, consider renting a single-family cottage or cabin in the area. (For a list of these options, contact the Shelby County Office of Tourism; see *Information.)*

Camping

Lake Shelbyville is a popular spot for visitors traveling with recreational vehicles. Wolf Creek State Park and Eagle Creek State Recreation Area both have campgrounds with tent and RV sites, but the Army Corps of Engineers has several campgrounds and there are a handful of private campgrounds situated around the lake. Here's a rundown on your options, in addition to the state parks.

The Army Corps of Engineers manages six campgrounds around the lake, including the 79-site **Forrest W. Bo Wood Recreation Area** (south of Sullivan on Hwy. 32); the 209-site **Coon Creek Recreation Area** (south of Findlay east of Hwy. 128 and south of County Rd. 1800N); the 114-site **Lithia Springs Recreation Area** (east of Shelbyville on Hwy. 16); the 98-site **Lone Point Recreation Area** (also south of County Rd. 1800N); the 79-site **Opossum Creek Recreation Area** (north of Shelbyville off Hwy. 128); and the 81-site **Whitely Creek Recreation Area** (east of Hwy. 32 and north of the Bruce-Findlay Rd.). Campgrounds are open April or May–September or October, depending on the site. Fees are $12–20 per night. To make a reservation for any of these campgrounds you'll have to go through the **National Recreation Reservation Service** (877/444-6777, www.reserveusa.com). Reserve anytime from 240 to four days in advance.

With about 200 campsites, most of them wooded, **Robin Hood Woods** (Hwy. 16, about three miles east of Shelbyville, 217/774-4222, www.robinhoodwoods.com, nightly fees $18.50–23 campsites; $70–130 cabin rentals) is one of the largest campgrounds in the area. It's popular among young families and the senior crowd because of its fishing pond, in-ground pool, horseshoe pits, and game room. Robin Hood Woods also has one-room cabins and two-bedroom cabins with air-conditioning and heating. There's a camp store on-site. For a comprehensive list of private campgrounds contact the Shelby County Office of Tourism (see *Information.*).

FOOD

You'll find many fast-food chain restaurants in and around Shelbyville, but you'll also find a few surprises in the family-owned restaurants in downtown Shelbyville. Your best option is to walk down Main Street, just west of the dam and by the Shelby County Courthouse.

American

When we say a dish is "just like Grandma used to make," we're not talking about baked potatoes with low-fat cheese, or salads hold the dressing; we're talking about dishes rich in butter and other good things. **Just Like Grandma's** (124 E. Main St., Shelbyville, 217/774-1721, 7 A.M.–1:30 P.M. Tues., Wed., Fri.–Sat., 11 A.M.–2 P.M. Sun., $5) is a homey place with antique kitchen utensils hanging on the walls and a menu that lives up to its claim, such as "chicken fried chicken," i.e., breaded and fried chicken. It ain't fancy, but it's clean and you certainly won't leave hungry.

A former grocery store in downtown Sullivan has been converted to **Two Sisters** (9 S. Main St., Sullivan, 217/728-2717, 11 A.M.– 2 P.M. and 5–8 P.M. Mon.–Sat., 11–2 Sun., $7 lunches, $15 dinners), an American restaurant that serves steaks, fish, barbecue ribs, and other comfort food. Make sure you try some of the potato chips made with sweet potatoes. This is a good place to eat dinner before taking in a show at the Little Theatre on the Square.

Bird-lovers will enjoy a trip to **⚑ The Timbers** (County Rd. 700N, Strasburg, 217/644-3130 or 217/644-3131, www.timberslodge.com, 11 A.M.–8 P.M. Tues.–Thurs., 11 A.M.–9 P.M. Sat., 11 A.M.–3 P.M. Sun., $7), a rural restaurant about 16 miles southeast of Shelbyville. Work up your appetite with a little stroll around the 30-acre property, near Hidden Spring State Forest and Richland Creek, and be on the lookout for woodpeckers, finches, and orioles. Take a seat in the casual dining room, which looks out onto woodlands and pastureland. A lot of what you eat is made fresh and by scratch in the kitchen: the bread, desserts, the staff even cut their own steaks.

After you've worked up an appetite hiking or spent the day boating, head to the casual pizza joint in town, **Joe's Pizza** (114 E. Main St., Shelbyville, 217/774-3535, 11 A.M.–1 P.M. Tues.–Fri., 4–10 P.M. Thurs., Sun., 4–11 P.M. Fri.–Sat., $9) which has everything from standard pepperoni to Hawaiian and taco-style pizzas.

Chicken, steaks, and pasta are the fare at **Longbranch Grill** (203 E. Main St., Shelbyville, 217/774-1700, 11 A.M.–2 P.M. Mon.–Fri., 4– 10 P.M. Mon.–Sat., $12), an American bar and grill in downtown Shelbyville.

Café

Hand-dipped ice cream and gourmet coffees are the specialties at **Big Sweeties** (157 E. Main St., Shelbyville, 217/774-4200, 11 A.M.–9 P.M. Mon.–Sat.). In case you're wondering, the "Big Sweetie" is an enormous sundae (12 scoops, hot fudge topping, whipped cream, and cherries). It costs about $17, but if you eat it by yourself in 30 minutes or less, it's free.

INFORMATION

The **Army Corps of Engineers Lake Shelbyville Visitors Center** (217/774-3951) is one mile east of Shelbyville, just east of the dam. Follow signs from Highway 16. The center is open noon–4 P.M. Saturday and Sunday early September–mid-October and early to mid-May. Starting in mid-May it's open 10 A.M.–4 P.M. daily through early September. More information is also available on the Corps' website, www.mvs.usace.army.mil.

The **Shelby County Office of Tourism** (315 E. Main St., Shelbyville, 217/774-2244 or 800/874-3529, www.lakeshelbyville.com) has comprehensive hotel, camping, and dining info. During the summers, the office is staffed on the weekends 10 A.M.–3 P.M.

VICINITY OF SHELBYVILLE
Covered Bridge

Well, it's not as picturesque as some of the barns featured in the film *The Bridges of Madison County* (declarations such as "LSD is for me" and "I love Carla" are carved and painted on the walls) but the **Thompson Mill Covered Bridge** is one of a handful of original covered bridges left in the state. Built in the late 1880s, the cedar-shingled bridge stretches over the Kaskaskia River south of Shelbyville and east of the little town of Cowden. You cannot drive on the bridge, but you can walk through it. To get to the bridge take Highway 128 into Cowden, and then follow signs to the covered bridge, about four miles to the east.

Vahling Vineyards

Tired of raising hogs full-time for a living, the Vahling family decided to give grape-growing a shot on their livestock and grain farm. After several years of testing different grape varieties, they developed several varieties that grew well on the relatively flat land in the Grand Prairie. Vahling Vineyards (County Rd. 400N, a quarter mile west of Hwy. 32, Stewardson, 217/682-5409, www.vahlingvineyards.com, 10 A.M.–5 P.M. Tues.–Sat., until 8 P.M. Fri.–Sat. June–Aug, 1–5 P.M. Sun.) sells sweet and semisweet wines, such as Prairie White, a semidry from the American hybrid cayuga grapes and Country Red made with fredonia grapes. Feel free to visit the nonpretentious wine-making operation south of Shelbyville.

Amish Country: Arthur and Arcola

Wide blue skies, long country roads, and the occasional horse-drawn black buggy and bicyclist—the area south of Champaign-Urbana and southeast of Decatur, where Coles, Moultrie, and Douglas counties come together, is Illinois Amish country. This bucolic region is home to several thousand Amish who make their livings on diversified farms, greenhouse operations, and carpentry shops. Drive through here and you may see an Amish farmer driving a set of Belgian horses through a field to cut hay or an Amish woman washing clothes with a wringer washer and then hanging the clothes out to dry. The main hubs are Arcola, just west of I-57, and Arthur, about 10 miles west of Arcola along Highway 133. Both are picturesque towns with small residential districts with brick-lined streets and well-cared-for homes and downtowns full of antiques and gift shops and casual American restaurants.

The Amish started settling in this area beginning in 1865 from places such as Indiana and Pennsylvania. Like others, they were seeking affordable land in a less crowded part of the country. The Amish work and socialize within their community; however, many of the children do attend public school with other area children and the people are quite receptive to polite, curious visitors. Some are willing to invite you into their homes to show you how they live (without electricity) and to talk about their customs. Not everyone in town is Amish. After the first farmers drained the

ground in the late 1800s and they discovered how rich the soil was, more pioneers from the south and east established homesteads next to the Amish. Today the region also has many large-scale corn and soybean farmers and businesses that cater to them.

ORIENTATION

If your main objective in the Arthur and Arcola area is to shop, it's a good idea to pick up a regional map from the Arthur visitor bureau. There are plenty of shops in downtown Arthur and Arcola; however, some of the best furniture stores and greenhouses are on the back roads. Many business owners have placed directional signs at intersections, making it easier to find their homesteads than if you were to drive around randomly. Still, if you're not familiar with the county road system, it can be a little confusing. (As you go north the road numbers increase. For example, you'll pass 1500N, then 1600N, 1700N, and so on. Sometimes you'll come upon a 1525N or 1650N, but not always and this is when it can get tricky.) At any rate, if you're ever lost, there's no shortage of friendly people around to help get you back on track. This is a close-knit community and everyone knows where everyone lives and the best route to get there. Because the Amish are religious and hold lengthy church services on Sundays, just about everything shuts down on Sundays. Shop and

The Grand Prairie

farm hours are generally 8 A.M.–4 P.M. Monday–Saturday. Some Amish businesses have phone numbers that connect callers with an answering service or answering machine. And some Amish carry cell phones (which run on batteries, after all, not electricity.)

This is beautiful country and a great way to explore it, as well as to meet some Amish folks as you pedal along the back roads, is by renting a bicycle. Visit **Schlabach's Bike Shop and Discount Store** (500N and 100E, Arthur, 217/543-3309, ext. 6075) on the northeast end of town and rent a bike for a few hours.

While visiting the area, remember that the Amish do not like to be photographed, although feel free to photograph an empty buggy or their horses. The back roads do have wide shoulders to accommodate the Amish buggies, but use caution when passing them in your car. Slow down. You'll notice while traveling through the area that the Amish speak German among themselves. The men grow beards (even in the summer) and the women wear little white prayer caps over their buns.

SIGHTS

To learn more about the Amish and Mennonite communities, stop by **The Illinois Amish Interpretive Center** (111 S. Locust St., Arcola, 888/45-AMISH or 888/452-6474, www.amishcenter.com, 9 A.M.–5 P.M. Mon.–Sat., March–Dec., Nov.–March by appointment). The center contains a lot of helpful historical information about how the Amish settled in this region. Inside visitors can see a vintage buggy, quilts, bibles, and a bedroom set displayed as if it were in an actual home. Here you'll be briefed about polite and not-so-polite behavior around the Amish.

Raggedy Ann and Andy creator Johnny Gruelle spent the first two years of his life in this region before moving to Indiana and the East Coast. Inspired by the quaint atmosphere of Arcola, his granddaughter Joni Gruelle Wannamaker decided to open the **Johnny Gruelle's Raggedy Ann and Andy Museum** (110 E. Main St., Arcola, 217/268-4908, www.rag-

gedyann-museum.org, 10 A.M.–5 P.M. Tues.–Sat., by appointment Jan. 1–Mar. 15, donation) here. This excellent little museum (which may impress people other than doll collectors) has a recreation of Gruelle's drawing studio, books, tea sets, and other toys inspired by the Raggedy dolls. And of course, there are plenty of Raggedy Ann and Andy dolls, with their button eyes, striped stockings, red hair, and freckles. In addition to showcasing the various styles of dolls through the years, the exhibits explore the path he took to creating the dolls and his other ventures, including creating the newspaper proverb series "Love is…" and painting murals. The story behind the dolls is that he found an old doll in an attic, painted a new face on it, and gave it to his daughter Marcella, who later died from a smallpox vaccination. (In the book series, the girl who cares for the dolls is named Marcella.) Gruelle patented the Raggedy Ann doll in 1915 and he started writing the books in 1918.

Between Arcola and Arthur **Rockome Gardens** (125 N. Country Rd. 125E, Arcola, 217/268-4106, www.rockome.com, $5, plus more for buggy and train rides) is somewhat of an Amish theme park for children and grandmas. On the grounds are several shops, including a furniture shop, doll shop, and general store that sells things such as homemade apple butter, honey, and noodles. For the kids, there's a petting zoo, train rides, buggy rides, one-room schoolhouse, and other buildings. Several music shows are held here throughout the summer and early fall, such as bluegrass and fiddling contests. A restaurant, open 11 A.M.–7 P.M. when the gardens are open, serves family-style meals such as fried chicken and homemade rolls. In 2005 Rockome's owners were trying to find a buyer for the attraction. However, the park was still open when this book went to print. Hours are 9 A.M.–5 P.M. weekdays and 9 A.M.–5:30 P.M. weekends in the summer. Call for hours during the rest of the year.

Farm Visits

Sure, **The Great Pumpkin Patch** (Springfield Rd., west of County Rd. 1800E, southwest of

BEYOND THE BUGGIES: ILLINOIS'S AMISH

With their plain dress, horse-drawn buggies, and religious lifestyle, the Amish are an intriguing bunch, especially to visitors. The central Illinois Amish community has a little more than 4,000 members. They live in integrated towns such as Arcola and Arthur, towns that are also home to non-Amish people, including Mexican immigrants and other nationalities. The Amish live simply. Essentially their lifestyles resemble those of families in America's rural communities before electricity arrived. Their homesteads are about 80 acres large with hay fields, vegetable gardens, fruit trees, horses, and a mix of livestock such as cattle, hogs, and chickens. There are the main house, several outbuildings, and usually a home for the grandparents. Inside the homes, refrigerators and stoves run on propane. Some appliances, such as sewing machines, are pedal and air-powered. You won't find any paintings or photographs on the walls. The Amish emphasize humility and don't believe in images (because preserving and showing off images could promote pride). That means they prefer not to have their photographs taken.

The Illinois Amish are considered House Amish because they hold religious services in their homes on Sundays. Among themselves they speak German. Families are large with several children. They attend school until they're in eighth grade and are baptized in their late teens and early 20s, before they're married. The Amish wear handmade clothes; women don dresses or skirts with white prayer caps and you'll often see men in suspenders. Women wear their hair long and pin it up in buns. Men wear helmet or bobbed styles. After men marry, they grow beards.

While they certainly do live much more simply than most modern-day people, the Amish are inventive, successful businesspeople. They read newspapers and follow local and world events. Some have cell phones. And as land prices continue to rise and it becomes more of a challenge for them to expand farmsteads, many Amish have increased their carpentry businesses, built greenhouses for growing plants, fruits, and vegetables, and launched other businesses.

Illinois has been home to the Amish since the mid-1800s; however, their roots are in the Anabaptist movement in Switzerland. In the late 1500s, a group of Protestants, led by a Dutchman named Menno Simons, believed people should be baptized as adults. About 100 years later a splinter group formed, named the Amish after their leader Jacob Amman. Fleeing harassment in Europe, the Amish immigrated to the United States throughout the 1700s, focusing mainly around Pennsylvania. In 1865 several families from Pennsylvania moved to present-day Arcola.

The Grand Prairie

Arthur, 9 A.M.–6 p.m. daily mid-Sept.–end of Oct.) has acres and acres of pumpkins, but it also sells hundreds of heirloom and rare squashes—we're talking delicious, edible squash from around the world. Pick your own or choose from among those already picked. The owners, the Condill family, also sell mums, Indian corn, and other fall goodies.

On the outskirts of Arthur, the friendly Graber family grows big, beautiful vine-ripened tomatoes at **Graber's Greenhouse** (Cadwell Rd./1500E, south of Hwy. 133, Cadwell, 217/543-5140). In addition to pro-

duce such as juicy cantaloupes, the Grabers, an Amish family, sell seeds and a variety of flowers, such as annual hanging baskets. Call the answering service for hours and to find out what's in season.

ENTERTAINMENT AND EVENTS

The annual **Raggedy Ann and Andy Festival** in downtown Arcola features look-alike contests, doll shows, storytelling, a parade, music, and food. It's held in mid- to late May and more information is available from the

Arcola Chamber of Commerce. Downtown Arcola is also host to the popular **Broomcorn Festival,** which celebrates the area's history as a broom-making capital. It's held annually in September. Over in Arthur, folks line up early for free cheese at the always well-attended **Arthur Cheese Festival** (www.arthurcheesefestival.com) held every year during Labor Day weekend. In addition to the free-cheese tent (hundreds of pounds of cheese are given away for free each year), there are tractor pulls, pancake breakfasts, live music, and a fun run.

SHOPPING

Downtown Arthur and Arcola are lined with Amish furniture and food shops. In addition, dozens of wood shops, spice shops, and produce farms are scattered throughout the countryside. For map of business locations, call or visit the area visitor bureaus. Most stores are closed Sunday.

ACCOMMODATIONS

Under $50

The **Arcola Inn** (238 S. Jacques St., Arcola, 888/729-9137) is a one-story brick motel with full, queen, and king beds. It's just off I-57. The **Arthur Country Inn** (785 E. Columbia St., Arthur, 217/543-3321) is a also a one-story, brick motel with entrances from the outside. It's on Highway 133 as you enter Arthur from the east.

$50–100

One of the best features of the **Heart and Home** (210 E. Illinois St., Arthur, 217/543-2910), a bed-and-breakfast within walking distance of downtown Arthur, is the big wrap-around porch. You could sit here for hours. Heart and Home has three rooms available, all with private bathrooms and decorated with antiques.

If you prefer to stay in a newer home, **Marsha's Vineyard** (212 Chaise Ln., Arthur, 217/543-4001) is a bed-and-breakfast in a recently built saltbox-style home. There are two

suites to choose from: The first-floor "garden room" comes with a queen- and twin-size bed and has direct access to the patio outside, and the loft room upstairs has a king- and full-size bed.

As the name suggests, the **Flower Patch B&B** (225 E. Jefferson St., Arcola, 217/268-4876) is surrounded by lots of colorful gardens and a charming little gazebo and front porch. The pale-pink house has five sunny rooms, three of them with private baths. The owner, a gardener, sells herbs and perennials.

The newer construction, two-story **Comfort Inn** (610 S. Ridge St., Arcola, 217/268-4000), just off I-57, has an outdoor pool and continental breakfast.

FOOD

Arthur and Arcola has several Amish families who open their homes to visitors and invite them to share a meal (for a fee), tour the home, and perhaps even go for a buggy ride. To arrange a dinner, call the visitors bureaus for more information. Otherwise, there are several other restaurants in the area that feature country-style cooking. And by that I mean freshly baked bread, meats from locally raised livestock, sweet corn grown in area fields, and more. Here's a sampling.

Dutch Kitchen (127 E. Main St., Arcola, 217/268-3518, 7:30 A.M.–7 P.M. daily, $8) in downtown Arcola serves meals such as fried chicken, Amish sausage, a variety of sandwiches, and homemade breads. It also has a salad bar.

If you're in the mood to eat, stake out a table at **Yoder's Kitchen** (1195 E. Columbia St./Hwy. 133, Arthur, 217/543-2714, www.yoderskitchen.com, 7 A.M.–8 P.M. Mon.–Sat., $5 lunches, $10 dinners), where the all-you-can-eat buffet features heaps of mashed potatoes, pork chops, bread, and real, creamy butter. If buffets aren't your thing, try a broasted chicken dinner, ham steak, or patty melt sandwich, followed by a slice of apple pie.

ℿ Dick's Pharmacy (118 S. Vine St., Arthur, 217/543-2913, 8 A.M.–6 P.M. Mon.–Fri.,

8 A.M.–5:30 P.M. Sat.) is a genuine soda fountain shop and pharmacy servicing phosphates, ice-cream sodas, and sundaes.

Food Markets
Clear out the cooler or run to the gas station and buy another one. **Dutch Valley Meats** (376 E. Hwy. 133, Arthur, 217/543-3354) is a great place to stock up on smoked sausages, homemade sausages, and butterfly pork chops. The folks here sell fresh and frozen meats, plus some items such as homemade noodles.

Garlic, basil, and other bulk herbs and spices are sold at bargain prices at the **Country Spice Shoppe** (661 N. County Rd. 100E, Arthur, 217/543-3664).

INFORMATION
Not only can you get tips on what to see and where to stay, the **Arcola Depot Welcome Center** (135 N. Oak St., Arcola, 217/268-4530 or 800/336-5456, www.arcola-il.org) contains an impressive collection of antique brooms and brushes manufactured in the area. You can pick up maps and brochures and use public restrooms at the **Arthur-Amish Country Visitors Center** (106 E. Progress St., Arthur, 217/543-2242 or 800/72-AMISH or 800/722-6474, www.illinoisamishcountry.com). It's in a little hut in downtown Arthur.

TUSCOLA AND ATWOOD
North of Arcola and Arthur by about six miles is Tuscola, another town with agricultural roots (a large grain-storage operation is here). But unlike the towns to the south, Tuscola is not home to nearly as many Amish. It's perhaps best known by travelers for its shopping opportunities, both at the outlet shops just off I-57 and downtown.

Sights and Activities
The **Tanger Outlet Center** (Tuscola Blvd., U.S. 36 and I-57, 217/253-2282, www.tanger-outlet.com) has around 45 stores, including Gap, Harry and David, and Rockport shoes.

Mall hours are 10 A.M.–9 P.M. Monday–Saturday, 11 A.M.–6 P.M. Sunday March 1–December 31; and 10 A.M.–6 P.M. Monday–Thursday, 10 A.M.–9 P.M. Friday–Saturday, 11 A.M.–6 P.M. Sunday January 1–February 28, plus extended hours around Christmas. Next to the outlet mall is **Amishland Red Barn** (1304 Tuscola Blvd., Tuscola, 217/253-9022, 11 A.M.–8 P.M. Mon.–Fri., 10 A.M.–9 P.M. Sat., 10 A.M.–8 P.M. Sun.) with several shops inside, including Amish furniture, antiques, a casual buffet restaurant that serves country-style meals (i.e., meat, potatoes, rolls).

Drive west to downtown Tuscola and you'll come upon a handful of antiques and collectibles stores in the **Sale Street District,** including **Prairie Sisters Antique Mall** (102 W. Sale St., Tuscola, 217/253-5211). On the town's main drag west of town is **Route 36 Antiques** (101 E. Southline Rd., Tuscola 217/253-9110).

Farther west a few miles of Tuscola is Atwood, a picturesque town of 1,000 people or so. Here you'll find the **Village Craftsman** (102 N. Main St., Atwood, 217/578-3834), where you can shop for finished handmade Amish furniture or special-order a table, rocking chair, or other piece of furniture. If you're in the area in mid-August, you must spend some time in downtown Atwood at the **Atwood Apple Dumpling Festival** to gobble some of the richest apple dumplings (topped with ice cream) you'll ever taste. Other typical fair food, such as kettle corn and pork sandwiches, are also sold at this food-laden festival.

Food
Ever hear of Krispy Kreme doughnuts? Well, dare I say it? **Dixie Cream Donuts** (211 N. Park St., Tuscola, 217/253-4561), Tuscola, are just as good, if not better—they're crispy and creamy.

In the shadow of the Tuscola grain elevator, **Lee's Specialty Bakery and Subs** (200 N. Park St., Tuscola, 217/253-9880, 7 A.M.–5 P.M. Mon.–Sat.) sells homemade baked goods such as the gooiest and sweetest pecan rolls ever and cheese Danish. Slices of pie are also on hand (if you're there in the early summer, you must try the strawberry pie). Plus, the folks here will put together a ham or turkey sandwich for you for a few bucks.

Accommodations

Simple Pleasures B&B (600 N. State St./ Hwy. 130, Tuscola, 217/253-3319, www.simplepleasuresbnb.com) is an 1870, robin's egg–blue home set on 11 acres, some of it wooded (yes, there are trees in the Grand Prairie region). The house has five decorative bedrooms available as well as several common areas that are quite unusual for a bed-and-breakfast in these parts, such as the whirlpool tub in the glass conservatory and the pool table in the house. Rates are $90–105.

Several national chain hotels sit off I-57 at the Tuscola U.S. 36 exit. Rates are generally $60–90. Two good options are the **Holiday Inn Express** (1201 Tuscola Blvd., Tuscola, 217/253-6363), an 82-room hotel with an indoor pool, a decent-size breakfast bar, in-room coffeemakers, and free wireless Internet. The 59-room **Amerihost** (1006 Southline Rd., Tuscola, 217/253-3500) also offers guests continental breakfast, an indoor pool, and it has two whirlpool suites.

Information

Both Atwood and Tuscola have visitors centers staffed with local residents who can help you with navigating through the area or let you know about any new restaurants or hotels. They are the **Tuscola Tourism and Visitors Center** (502 Southline Rd., Tuscola, 217/253-6240 or 800/441-9111, www.tuscola.org), and **Atwood Tourist and Information Center** (112 1/2 S. Main St., Atwood, 217/578-2734).

Coles and Edgar Counties

A quiet part of the state, Coles and Edgar counties are, like its neighboring counties, rural in nature. The terrain starts to change here, though, as there are more rolling hills and wooded areas. The scenic Embarras River curls through the eastern part of Coles County and several creeks meander through Edgar to the east. The largest towns in the region are Charleston in Coles County and Paris in Edgar. Both are courthouse-square towns and railroad towns. This is also Lincoln country. His father, Thomas, and his stepmother, Sarah, lived on a farm south of Charleston and he reportedly did visit with them there. Also, as a circuit lawyer he often passed through the towns offering legal services to residents several times a year. Highway 16 is the main east-west thoroughfare and Highway 1, otherwise known as the Dixie Highway, runs north and south on the eastern edge of the state.

COLES COUNTY

Lincoln Log Cabin State Historic Site

Living-history villages are a dime a dozen in the Midwest, but the Lincoln Log Cabin State Historic Site (County Rd. 1420E, Lerna, 217/345-1845, 8 A.M.–dusk daily, donation) is one of the best and perhaps one of the most underrated. It's not particularly easy to get to. It's not off an interstate, and it's about a 15-minute drive south of Charleston in a rural area. Essentially the 86-acre site consists of the reconstructed homestead, several outbuildings such as the homestead, plus vegetable and fruit gardens, and farm animals. This is the farmstead where Abe Lincoln's father, Thomas, lived with his wife (and Abe's stepmother) Sarah. Abe did not live at the site but he did visit. Sarah and Thomas Lincoln moved to the area in 1840 and Sarah, who outlived her husband, lived here until she died in 1869. Her grandson lived in the cabin until it was moved to the Chicago World's Fair in 1892 for display. What happened to the cabin after the show is a mystery.

Walking through the farm, you'd swear you were walking through an 1840s farm (minus the gravel walkways). Volunteers, dressed in 1840s clothing, are out and about hanging herbs to dry, dying or spinning wool, gathering peppers from the garden, and cooking over the cabin's hearth. A handful of horses, pigs, sheep, and chickens mill around in their fenced-in pens. Cucumber vines twist around twig contraptions. A wagon is off to the side as if someone had just pulled in for a visit, and piles of logs are common throughout the grounds. Throughout the year the park holds events to show visitors what life was like more than 150 years ago. It's had demonstrations on flax processing, gunsmithing, and cheese-making, and has even recreated weddings. The Harvest Frolic and Agricultural Fair, held in early October, includes activities such as music, a barn dance, and candlelight tours of the two farms.

Adjacent to the Lincoln farm is the Sargent Farm. A trail connects the two. Originally situated a few miles east of the Lincoln homestead, the Sargent Farm was larger—it had about 400 acres of cropland and 600 animals. The original buildings, including the white frame house (which is quite larger than the Lincoln log cabin), were moved to the site.

The visitors center has exhibits on the Lincoln family's migration, going back all the way to Samuel Lincoln, who was born in England in 1637. Displays include images of the cabin, including one taken in 1891, a chest said to have been made by Thomas Lincoln and a man named Reuben Moor, and other tools, dishes, and items from the 1840s. One revealing tidbit is information gathered about the Lincoln farm from the 1850 census. The Lincolns had 16 sheep, two cows, and 20 swine. There's also a 15-minute video about the site and the Lincoln family. The site also has shelters and picnic areas for visitors. To get to the park follow signs south from University Drive in Charleston for about seven miles.

Fox Ridge State Park

On a glacial moraine above the Embarras River, Fox Ridge State Park (seven miles south of Charleston, east off Hwy. 130, 217/345-6416, www.dnr.state.il.us) is a rustic park with a mix of wooded hills and some lowland grassy areas with shrubs and small trees. There are six miles of hiking trails through the park, most of them moderately easy to rugged and varying from three-quarters of a mile long to 1.5 miles long. The No Name Trail (that's actually the name) follows a section of the Embarras near the South Point canoe-launch area. There you can launch your canoe into the Embarras River for a peaceful ride. Chances are you'll see more turtles, birds, and fish than people. The Natural History Survey operates a research station here. Fishing is allowed but you'll need permission from the survey.

Entertainment

Eastern Illinois University's **Tarble Art Center** (S. 9th St., Charleston, 217/581-ARTS or 217/581-2787, 10 A.M.–5 P.M. Tues.–Fri., 10 A.M.–4 P.M. Sat., 1–4 P.M. Sun. during the school year, call for summer hours) hosts art shows, music concerts, and lectures throughout the year.

Just west of the courthouse square, **Charleston Alley Theatre** (718 Monroe Ave., Charleston, www.charlestonalleytheatre.com) is a small community theater that presents classic comedies, dramas, and musicals. For more information you can call the Lincoln Book Shop at 217/345-6070.

Accommodations and Food

There are two main hotels in Charleston, both with rates $50–70, depending on the day of the week and time of year. Both are near one another on the main drag through town, Lincoln Avenue, or Highway 16. The **Best Western Worthington Inn** (920 W. Lincoln Ave., Charleston, 217/348-8161) has 67 rooms, some with refrigerators and microwaves. The hotel has an outdoor pool and restaurant on-site. The 52-room **Days Inn** (810 W. Lincoln Ave., Charleston, 217/345-7689) is a newer hotel that also has some rooms that come with refrigerators and microwaves. Like the Best Western, standard rooms come with in-room coffeemakers. Continental breakfast is included.

How often do you get to stay in a genuine Civil War–era cabin? Set on a 50-acre country spread just west of Charleston, the **⋈ Osage Inn** (1344E County Rd. 720N, Charleston, 217/345-2622) is a restored hewn-log house that's more than 150 years old. There's a bedroom with a queen bed on the first floor and a full and twin in the bedroom on the second floor. Outside is a porch with rocking chairs, an arbor where you can eat breakfast or drink some wine, and a meadow for lounging or playing catch (kids are welcome here). Closed in January. Rates are $85–95.

Fox Ridge State Park (seven miles south of Charleston, just east off Hwy. 130, 217/345-6416, www.dnr.state.il.us) has tent and trailer camping available. Plus, it offers a cabin that can sleep six people, with bunk beds, a table, deck, and electricity, drinking water, showers, and dumping station. Rates are $6–12.

Marianne's (615 Monroe, Charleston, 217/348-7733, breakfast and lunch, $6) is a casual café with local art on the wall, magazines and newspapers scattered about, and a variety of sandwiches and desserts on the menu. Food is called "European" and there's no shortage of German type of fare, such as the grilled brat topped with sauerkraut on rye bread, or a lighter option, "Willems," a veggie sandwich on chewy, multigrain bread. The best part about Marianne's is the desserts: the Black Forest cake slices, apple kuchen, or thick cheesecake (there's have a vegan option made with tofu).

Information

The **Charleston Tourism Office** (520 Jackson Ave., Charleston, 217/348-0430, www.charlestontourism.org) publishes a visitors guide that you can order on the website or by calling the office during the week.

EDGAR COUNTY
Sights and Activities

The area in and around Paris is home to several small, innovative farms. Not everyone grows corn and soybeans. Explore the countryside and you'll find everything from strawberries to ostriches. The farms, while open to tourists, don't have set hours. Just call ahead. Most owners, you'll find, are willing to take you around. **Barkley Farms** (1300th Rd., Paris, 217/463-7003) specializes in perennials. **Indian Boundary Farm** (16132 E. 1950th St., Bloomfield, 217/269-2445) has a pick-your-own strawberry patch in the late spring and sweet corn and other veggies later in the summer. Fall is peak time for **Pumpkin Works** (21788 E. Terra Haute Rd., Elbridge, 217/275-3327), where owners sculpt several intricate corn mazes every year. They also offer hayrides and open their barn, where they sell pumpkins, corn, gourds, and other fall items. To the west of there is a similar operation, **Country Bumpkin Pumpkin Path** (5556 E. 150th Rd., Grandview, 217/273-4099), which also boasts a corn maze, wagon rides, and pumpkins.

Abraham Lincoln devotees can visit the **Edgar County Historical Society Complex** (408–414 N. Main St., Paris, 217/463-5305, call for hours, free) to view a desk and chair once used by Lincoln when he stopped by Paris to try cases. The museum also has exhibits on local history.

Information

For more information about the area contact the **Paris Area Chamber of Commerce** (105 N. Central Ave., Paris, 217/465-4179).

Danville and Vicinity

tubing on the Vermilion River in Kickapoo State Park

On the eastern end of the state, Vermilion County stands out among other counties in the Grand Prairie. For one thing, it's hilly and the topography resembles more of the eastern forests common in states such as Ohio than the flat, rich farmland and prairie to the west. And there's water: scenic rambling rivers such as the Vermilion and Little Vermilion and the Middle Fork, a National Scenic River. Its history, too, is not so deeply tied to agriculture as other towns in the central part of the state (although it is definitely a major industry here).

Founded in 1765, Danville was first known for its salt works. For hundreds of years Native American Indian tribes would live and hunt through the region, following the tracks of animals, such as buffalo and deer, as they made their way to the salt springs along the Salt Fork River. Settlers discovered these springs and set up saltworks where the brine was boiled in giant kettles. Eventually the supply diminished and the salt industry was eclipsed by another one: coal mining. Coal was king in the latter half of the 19th century and the first half of the 20th century. Strip-mining was a common practice in Vermilion County. And Kickapoo State Park north of Oakwood was once all strip-mining land. Eventually coal production also dwindled. Today Danville is, you might say, in a transition phase. After the town lost its major employer (General Motors) in the 1990s, residents and businesses packed up and left town. It's still a manufacturing center with grain-processing and distribution companies set up in town, but the Danville today is much different from the one 50 years ago when former famous residents such as Jerry and Dick Van Dyke and the late singer Bobby Short were growing up here. Downtown Danville is recovering. Residents are working to restore a historic downtown opera house. Welcoming businesses are setting up shop, such as the Java Hut. But the real reason to visit Vermilion County is to spend time hiking, biking through the parks, or canoeing down the Middle Fork.

The Danville area is home to several gorgeous parks. First is Kickapoo State Park on the Middle Fork River, and north of there are the Middle Fork State Fish and Wildlife Area and Kennekuk County Park. All of these are on the river and offer wooded, hilly hiking and biking trails. The state recently acquired more land between Kickapoo and Middle Fork and one day these two state parks may merge. Finally, there's Forest Glen south of Danville, with its stunning tallgrass prairie and pioneer homestead.

ORIENTATION

The major metropolitan area in the county is Danville, which has about 34,000 residents.

The Grand Prairie

It's just north of I-74, west of the Illinois-Indiana border. Navigating Danville can be tricky. The major state and U.S. highways don't stick to straight north-south or east-west routes in town. For example, Highway 150 runs north into Danville from south of I-74 and then shoots west through town. It's a good idea to review your map before driving through the area. The major parks are all west of town and north of I-74.

Kickapoo State Park and Middle Fork State Fish and Wildlife Area

Once strip-mine land, **Kickapoo State Park** (10906 Kickapoo Rd., Oakwood, 217/442-4915, www.dnr.state.il.us) is now one of the best parks in central Illinois. The 2,800-acre park, which borders the east and west side of the Middle Fork River, Kickapoo has challenging hiking and jogging trails, mountain-biking trails, horseback-riding trails, and canoeing, kayaking, and tubing opportunities. What more could you ask for?

First off, the water adventures. **Kickapoo Landing** (217/446-8399, www.kickapoolanding.com, 7 A.M.–Sun.–Thurs., 7 A.M.–9 P.M. Fri.–Sat.) inside the park organizes canoeing, kayaking, and tubing trips down the river. Float or paddle past bluffs, sandbars, and bottomland forests. The tubing loop is about two miles long and takes about an hour. Choose from eight-mile and 13-mile canoe/kayak trips, which can take 3–8 hours. Or you can rent by the hour and paddle around Clear Lake, a nearby inlet. Rates vary according to the day of the week you visit (prices are slightly higher on the weekends). Tubing costs $4–5. Canoing and kayaking is $12–30. Kickapoo Landing also serves food.

Next up, the trails. Kickapoo is one of the few places in the state where there are designated **mountain-biking trails.** And they're pretty fine. You've got about 12 miles of single-track trails along the river, up the hills, through the woods. Then, there's the 7.6-mile "out and back" trail for hiking or jogging. This narrow pathway also leads you through varied terrain, including some level areas along the river and

up steep hills. For a bit less physically stressful tour of the park, you can go **horseback riding** by renting horses at the park's stables (217/446-8575). Guided trail rides, which last 1–2 hours, are offered April–October.

Kickapoo State Park also has two campgrounds with a total of 184 sites, with a mix of electric, tent, and primitive.

A few miles upriver from Kickapoo State Park is the **Middle Fork State Fish and Wildlife Area** (same contact information as Kickapoo), a 2,700-acre site just loaded with trails for horseback riding, hiking, In total there are 35 miles of trails through this park. If you brought your own canoe or kayak, you can launch here. Middle Fork State Fish and Wildlife Area also has electric, tent, and backpack campsites.

Kennekuk County Park

East of the Middle Fork State Fish and Wildlife Area is **Kennekuk County Park** (22296 Henning Rd., Danville, 217/442-1691, www.vccd.org) and Lake Mingo, a deep pond created by strip-mining. Start your visit with a hike around some of the lake (it's 7.5 miles long), and then camp out on the beach and doze in the sun. Before you leave, tour the Bunker Hill Historic Area, a living history village with a pioneer chapel, school, train depot, and other buildings.

Kennekuk County Park is home to **Middle Fork Canoe Outfitters** (22296 Henning Rd., Danville, 217/442-4571 or 217/304-4240, www.middleforkcanoes.com), another company that rents boats and offers shuttle services to folks interested in canoeing the Middle Fork and other area rivers. It offers half-day, full-day, and overnight trips that launch from Lake Mingo, the Big Vermilion River at Forest Glen in Westville, or the Salt Fork from Ellsworth Park in Danville.

Forest Glen Preserve

Kickapoo and the other parks along the Middle Fork north of I-74 are certainly scenic, with their countless trails along rugged, wooded bluffs and rambling rivers, but there's another great park to the south. Set aside some time to explore the Forest Glen Preserve (2031 E. 900 Rd., Westville, 217/662-2142, www.vccd.org). Begin with a climb up the 72-foot-tall observation tower overlooking the Vermilion River Valley. Then choose your trail. As in the parks to the north, there's no shortage of trails here. About 25 miles of trails offer visitors views of tallgrass prairie, wetlands, and woods. Within the park is the Duffin Nature Preserve and Forest Glen Seep Nature Preserve, which protects a rare orchid, the twayblade orchid, that grows in bogs. Forest Glen also has an arboretum with more than 600 varieties of trees, with an emphasis on Illinois native trees. You'd be surprised to learn just how many varieties of oaks there are in the state. Finally, if you have your own canoe, you can launch it here for a quiet ride on the Vermilion River.

Museums

Veterans and historians will be impressed with the wide-ranging collections in the **Vermilion County War Museum** (307 N. Vermilion St., Danville, 217/431-0034 or 800/383-4386, noon–3 P.M. Tues.–Fri., 10 A.M.–4 P.M. Sat., 1–4 P.M. Sun., donation). Museum staff have filled two floors and almost 13,000 square feet of exhibit space with items from more than 200 years of American war history, including the Spanish-American War and Desert Storm. Mannequins are dressed in uniforms from different branches of service, medals from several wars are displayed in glass cases, and there's an array of newspaper clippings announcing deployments and major battles, flags, and more.

Here's another stop for travelers who are on quests to visit all the Lincoln sites in the state. The **Vermilion County Museum and Fithian Home** (116 N. Gilbert St., Danville, 217/442-2922, 10 A.M.–5 P.M. Tues.–Sat., 1–5 P.M. Sun., $2.50–4) consists of two main buildings: One is the Vermilion County Museum, which is a replica of the old courthouse where Lincoln once practiced law. (This building contains displays about the county's coal-mining history, its connection to the Dixie Highway, and a recreation of what Lincoln's law office may have looked like in Danville.) However, the must-see for Lincoln buffs is the Fithian Home, which is near the museum. Inside this brick 1855 home is a bed where Lincoln reportedly slept while visiting his friend, homeowner William Fithian.

ENTERTAINMENT

The **Danville Symphony Orchestra** (office 2917 N. Vermilion St., Danville, 217/443-5300, www.danvillesymphony.org), performs four concerts a year, plus a children's show and performance during Danville's Art in the Park festival in June. Concerts are held in Danville High School (202 E. Fairchild St., Danville). Tickets are available from the office or 90 minutes before the show. The box office is open 10 A.M.–4 P.M. Monday–Friday.

Performers with the **Danville Light Opera** (217/431-1660, Danville, www.danvillelightopera.com) present such musicals as *Chicago* throughout the year. They also stage productions in the high school.

EVENTS

Taking a cue from a *WKRP in Cincinnati* episode, members of the Balloon Association of Greater Illinois lift off from Turtle Run Golf Course (332 E. Liberty Ln., Danville, 217/442-3320) and drop rubber chickens from their balloons on the morning of Thanksgiving. Relax. They're not real. It's called the **Les Nessman Turkey Drop.**

Every June regional visual and performing artists participate in **Arts in the Park,** held in Danville's Lincoln Park on North Gilbert Street.

Hoopeston, which has declared itself the sweet-corn capital of the world, holds a **Sweet-corn Festival** every September, usually Labor Day weekend. There's a parade, sweet-corn sweetheart pageant, plus carnival rides, demolition derby, beer tent, you name it. Oh, and bushels and bushels of free sweet corn to festival attendees. For more information contact the Danville Area Convention and Visitors Bureau (see *Information*).

SPORTS

The real Babe Ruth didn't play baseball at **Danville Stadium** (Highland Blvd., east of Hwy. 150/Gilbert St., Danville, 217/431-2260), but the stadium was used as an on-site film location for *The Babe,* a movie about him. The stadium is somewhat of a historic site and reminiscent of what ballparks used to look like more than 50 years ago. Built in 1946, the 5,000-seat stadium was once a part of the farm team system for the Brooklyn Dodgers. Back then many of the players would go on to join the major leagues. Now the team, the Danville Dans, is part of the Central Illinois Collegiate League.

FOOD

Casual

The ⁊ **Java Hut** (15 N. Vermilion St., Danville, 217/443-6808, 6:30 A.M.–5 P.M. Mon.–Fri., 7:30 A.M.–1 P.M. Sat., $5) is a lively local coffee shop and sandwich place where you'll find it's easy to pass the afternoon reading a book while sipping a cappuccino. It's a community gathering place of sorts, a lively place in downtown. The Java Hut serves bagel sandwiches, quiches, pastries, and sandwiches such as turkey clubs and Italian beef. Local artwork hangs on the walls.

So the name may not be that appetizing, but **Gross's Burgers** (25 Henderson, Danville, 217/442-8848, 11 A.M.–8 P.M. Mon.–Sat., $3) has developed a loyal fan base of diners around town and the country for its burgers, which Gross's has been selling in Danville for two decades. Got an appetite? Order the triple cheeseburger. The fast-food restaurant is named after the family's last name, by the way.

Fine Dining

Chops, seafood, and ribs are the fare at the ⁊ **Possum Trot** (2918 Batestown Rd., Oakwood, 217/442-6066, 4–9 P.M. Mon.–Thurs., 4–10 P.M. Fri.–Sat.), a supper club west of Danville and south of Kickapoo State Park. Here you can watch the chef cook your steak on the giant grill, listen to a pianist perform, and sip some red wine or a glass of whiskey. If you're not in the mood for filet mignon or strip steak, choose from entrées such as fried grouper, baby back ribs, or grilled chicken.

In a historic renovated storefront in downtown Danville, **The Heron** (34 N. Vermilion St., Danville, 217/446-8330, www.danville-heron.com, 5:30–9:30 P.M. Wed.–Sat.) is a classy joint where you dine on tuna steaks or herbed chicken, followed by a slice of smooth tiramisu, and all the while a jazz musician sings in the background. Entrées are around $20.

ACCOMMODATIONS

Your lodging options in Danville are limited to chain hotels just off the interstate. Rates vary $50–100 depending on the type of room you choose and the day of the week you visit.

On the lower end of that range are **Super 8** (377 Lynch Dr., Danville, 217/443-4499), which has the standard free continental breakfast and choice of double or king beds; and just down the street from there is the **Comfort Inn** (383 Lynch Dr., Danville, 217/443-8004), which has an indoor heated pool and some suites with microwaves and fridges. Slightly more upscale accommodations (meaning there are usually coffeemakers in the rooms, hair dryers, and other amenities) include the **Fairfield Inn** (389 Lynch Dr., Danville, 217/443-3388), which has continental breakfast, indoor pool, and some suites with microwaves and fridges; **Sleep Inn and Suites** (361 Lynch Dr., Danville, 217/442-6600), which has an indoor pool and exercise room; and **Holiday Inn Express and Suites** (310 E. Gate Dr., Danville, 217/442-2500), another newer hotel with an indoor pool, exercise room, and high-speed Internet access.

If you prefer the bed-and-breakfast route, there's the **Lamp Post Inn** (420 N. Gilbert St., Danville, 217/446-9458) in a historical section of town. The Lamp Post is part of the Corner Victorian Shops, a group of home-decor shops and a tea room. There are five guest rooms here, two with private bathrooms.

INFORMATION

At some point during your trip, make a point to stop by the I-74 travel plaza just west of Danville. The **Salt Kettle Welcome Center** (at Exit 206) not only has a dozens of brochures for the taking, but an educational display about the region's history, including information about the salt springs and coal-mining industry. For more information on the area contact the **Danville Area Convention and Visitors Bureau** (100 W. Main St., Ste. 146, Danville, 217/442-2096 or 800/383-4386, www.danvillecvb.com) which publishes a guide listing area attractions, hotels, and restaurants.

SERVICES

The main hospital in the area is **Provena United Samaritans Medical Center** (812 N. Logan Ave., Danville, 217/443-5000, www.provenausmc.com) on the west side of town. The **U.S. post office** in Danville is at 303 North Hazel Street, Danville, 217/446-9440. It's north of Main Street and east of Gilbert Street.

The Grand Prairie

Great River Valleys

Packing list for western and west-central Illinois: a good pair of hiking shoes, jeans for horseback riding, binoculars, fishing pole, and a bicycle. With its limestone bluffs, prairies, savannas, and bottomland and upland forests, the Illinois and Mississippi River valleys offer quite the assortment of outdoor activities for visitors. As it flows southwest from Chicago, the Illinois River brushes past manufacturing centers such as Joliet, agricultural areas such as Marseilles, and wildlife preserves such as Chautauqua before it joins the Mississippi River, which runs along the western border of the state.

People have always been drawn to this region. Almost 1,000 years ago a Native American culture called the mound builders established thriving villages near present-day Lewistown and Collinsville. In the 1600s the French staked their claim on the area and protected it by building Fort de Chartres near

Must-Sees

Starved Rock State Park: Above the Illinois River near Utica, this popular state park was once the site of an early French fort and a battle between two Native American tribes. Hike the 125-foot-tall Starved Rock and watch barges chugging down the river and eagles searching for prey. Check into the historic lodge or one of the cabins (page 224).

M Bishop Hill Artisan Shops: In the 1840s Swedish religious leader Erik Jansson and his followers established a commune near the Edwards River, a tributary of the Mississippi. The commune eventually dissolved, but many descendants of the colony and Sweden remained in the area and transformed the village into a bustling community with restaurants and artisan shops (page 231).

M Joseph Smith Historic Site: Another remarkably well-preserved historic village is Nauvoo, perched above the Mississippi River. Smith and his fellow Mormons settled here in the 1840s and the town soon became a thriving city. A visit to the Smith site includes walking tours of about a dozen restored homes and shops, including Smith's homestead (page 266).

M Cahokia Mounds: Before the American pioneers, before the French and British, and even before the Illiniwek Indians, the Mississippi and Illinois River valleys were home to several mound-building cultures. The largest village, in existence roughly A.D. 700–1400, was near present-day Collinsville. Today the site includes several mounds, including the 100-foot-tall Monks Mound, and a comprehensive museum about Native American history (page 282).

M Fort de Chartres: To find out what it might have been like in the Illinois Territory during the 1700s, visit the remote, partially rebuilt French fort near Prairie du Rocher. The stone fort, which features musket ports, a powder magazine, and other structures, is near the Mississippi River (page 286).

M Illinois Caverns State Natural Area: The only cave open to the public in Illinois, Illinois Caverns near Red Bud is often called a wild cave. Guided by the light of flashlights and lanterns, visitors can expect to shimmy through narrow, cool (and oftentimes wet) passages and stand up in awe in expansive rooms filled with stalagmites (page 288).

THE TOURISM BUREAU SOUTHWEST ILLINOIS

Fort de Chartres, Prairie du Rocher

Great River Valleys

Great River Valleys

© AVALON TRAVEL PUBLISHING, INC.

Prairie du Rocher. When Joseph Smith arrived in 1839 he envisioned Nauvoo as an eden of sorts for himself and his fellow Mormons. In the same vein, the Swedish Janssonists prospered throughout the 1840s and 1850s at the Bishop Hill Colony. The region is steeped in history. Explorers Meriwether Lewis and William Clark set off on their journey westward from here. Abraham Lincoln debated with Stephen Douglas about slavery here. There's nothing like a drive along a historic river road or through a river town to remind you of the area's past and its connection to the development of Illinois. You can also get a feel for the richness of the region by hiking through one of the region's many natural areas, from the popular and majestic Starved Rock near Utica or the quiet Emiquon National Wildlife Refuge near Havana. And don't forget those binoculars. If there's an icon for this part of the state, it's the bald eagle.

PLANNING YOUR TIME

The Illinois and Middle-Mississippi River region covers a large part of the state, from the southwestern suburbs of Chicago to south of East St. Louis. Interstate 80 is a major east-west artery from the south side of Chicagoland to the Quad Cities (past Utica, Princeton, and other destinations); however, most of the other highways are two-lane, meaning travel can be slow going. In some spots, this is a good thing. The Great River Road, for example, is a scenic drive near Grafton and Nauvoo, although it's uninteresting near industrialized East St. Louis and East Moline. The Great River Road, you will find, does not always hug the Mississippi River. And it does not always follow one particular highway. Instead, follow the pilot wheel signs.

One way to explore the region is to set off from Chicago and follow the Illinois River southwest to the East St. Louis region and then head back north along the Great River Road through Alton, Quincy, Nauvoo, and up to the Quad Cities. If your time is limited, there are some places along this route that you

don't want to miss. They include **Starved Rock and Matthiessen state parks** near Utica and Collinsville's **Cahokia Mounds.** (If you can't get there, visit a similar site, **Dickson Mounds** near Havana along the Illinois River.) The **Bishop Hill** colony southeast of the Quad Cities is a must-see. A lot of travelers spend a day in Bishop Hill, but because of the cozy restaurants, growing number of artisan shops, and friendly residents, this author recommends staying the night in a bed-and-breakfast there. It's a long drive out to the remote **Fort de Chartres** near Prairie du Rocher and an even longer drive to Fort Kaskaskia, but for visitors who enjoy historic sites, these two are worth it. Naturalists also want to put in some **eagle-watching** time at Meredosia or one of the refuges along the rivers.

Resources

The **Western Illinois Tourism Development Office** (581 S. Deere Rd., Macomb, 309/837-7460, www.visitwesternillinois.info) is the umbrella organization for several regional convention and visitors bureaus, including Galesburg, the Quad Cities, Peoria, Jacksonville, Quincy, and others. The office maintains an online guide to **Illinois Great River Road National Scenic Byway** (www.greatriver-road-illinois.org). In addition, you may want to contact **The Tourism Bureau of Southwest Illinois** (10950 Lincoln Trail, Fairview Heights, 618/397-1488 or 800/442-1488, www.thetourismbureau.org), which has visitor information for the area in and around Collinsville and south to Prairie du Rocher.

There are several tourist information centers throughout this region along major highways: at eastbound I-80 at Rapid City, by Rock Island; northbound I-55 by Hamel, just northwest of Edwardsville; and eastbound I-64 at New Baden, east of O'Fallon.

A few **ferries** shuttle passengers or cars across the Mississippi and Illinois rivers. The Illinois Department of Transportation operates two free ferries in Calhoun County, where the Illinois and Mississippi rivers meet. There's the **Brussels Ferry** (618/786-3636) which connects Highway 100 between the Grafton and Pere Marquette State Park area with the town of Brussels; and the **Kampsville Ferry** (618/653-4518), which carries cars traveling along Highway 108 in Jersey County to Kampsville and Highway 100. In addition, there are several other toll ferries, such as the Modoc, Illinois-St. Genevieve, Missouri, ferry; the Golden Eagle, Illinois-St. Charles, Missouri, ferry; plus the Grafton Ferry Company between Grafton and St. Charles County Airport, Missouri, and the Canton, Missouri-Meyer, Illinois, toll ferry.

The **Spirit of Peoria** (309/636-6169 or 800/676-8988, www.spiritofpeoria.com) offers cruises along the Illinois River between Peoria and Pere Marquette State Park near Grafton. Choose from daylong cruises or overnights.

Upper I&M Canal Corridor

HISTORY AND ORIENTATION

While exploring the region in the late 1600s, Frenchman Louis Jolliet envisioned a grand canal that would connect Lake Michigan on the east with the Illinois and Mississippi rivers to the west. This canal would pave the way for commerce and settlement of the region. Two hundred years later construction of the Illinois and Michigan Canal, or I&M Canal, got under way. The process started in 1836 but stalled for several years because of lack of money. The expensive project, which cost an amazing $6.5 million, did indeed spark development of the region, but the canal ended up being eclipsed by the railroads and other waterway projects not long after it was finished. The building of the nearly 100-mile-long and 60-foot-wide canal, however, did open the area to settlers who otherwise would have traveled here on wagons and stagecoach. Building it also required a huge labor force and a heck of a lot of tools and material. Immigrant Germans and Irish came out to work on the project, and towns such as Lockport and Joliet popped up along the canal.

Joliet became known as the city of steel and stone after canal workers uncovered limestone there. Most downtowns, such as Lockport, have several buildings made from this limestone. Quarrying provided some jobs to workers after the canal was completed, but after a series of violent labor strikes in the 1880s and the discovery of limestone in Indiana, the industry started to decline. Stone is still quar-

© CHRISTINE DES GARENNES

Great River Valleys

I&M Canal trail near Ottawa

ried here, but it's mostly crushed limestone and gravel. Steel and iron works were also the big industries and eventually so were gas refineries, which are still operating today. Joliet is still very much a working-man and -woman's town. Driving through town and along I-80, you'll notice one warehouse or factory after the other. Today the upper canal corridor comprises towns from southwestern Cook County to Morris and toward Starved Rock, towns that were once shipping ports, manufacturing centers, and home to immigrant workers. The I&M Canal, the Des Plaines River, and the Chicago Sanitary and Ship Canal (which was built after the I&M Canal) all run southwest through here.

The Illinois River begins by Channahon, where the Des Plaines and Kankakee meet. The canal towns, many of them surrounded by hills and filled with historic limestone buildings and a growing number of restaurants, are great towns to visit for a day. Look for the yellow and orange signs depicting a boy and a mule. These signs will point you to the towns and any historic sites or parks along the way. For quick vehicle access through the area, I-80 is north of the canal and runs east-west through the region. U.S. 6 runs parallel to I-80 west of Joliet and is for the most part south of the canal. In the 1970s the Illinois Department of Natural Resources took control of the canal and started converting land along the canal into parks. In 1984 the federal government designated the 97-mile region as the I&M Canal National Heritage Corridor. A multipurpose trail follows the canal from Lockport to LaSalle with other spurs being developed in towns such as Lockport, Romeoville, and Lemont.

JOLIET
Sights
Instead of paving over the remains of an old iron factory, the Forest Preserve District of Will County saved a piece of Joliet's history by buying the land and turning it into a park. Visitors to the **Joliet Iron Works Historic Site** (Columbia and Scott Sts., Joliet, 815/727-8700, www.fpdwc.org, 8 A.M.–8 P.M. daily in the summer, 8 A.M.–5 P.M. in the winter, free) follow a one-mile-long walking trail past blast furnaces and stove ruins. Along the way are signs that explain how iron is produced and the history of the site, which was home to ironworks from roughly the 1860s to the 1930s. The park hooks up with the I&M Canal Trail, a paved or crushed limestone trail.

The star of downtown Joliet is the **Rialto Square Theatre** (102 N. Chicago St., Joliet, 815/726-6600, www.rialtosquare.com, box office open 9 A.M.–5 P.M. Mon.–Fri., 9 A.M.–noon Sat. and before shows) a restored 1926 theater. Once a vaudeville theater, it brings in national touring musical and dance troupes, comedians, and musicians from Wayne Newton to Carrot Top. Listed on the National Register of Historic Places, the theater features intricate plaster work, arched ceilings, and a historic pipe organ.

West of the theater along the Des Plaines River is **Bicentennial Park** (201 W. Jefferson St., Joliet, 815/740-2399, www.ci.joliet.il.us), a riverside park with a walkway along the river, views of the bridge, a fountain, and band shell.

Sports
Sports enthusiasts will want to put Joliet at the top of their lists. Here you can scale vertical walls, hunt down your friends in a game of paintball, or ride in a 600-horsepower race car.

First up is **Challenge Park Extreme** (2903 Schweitzer Rd., Joliet, 815/726-2800, www.challengepark.com, 10 A.M.–5 P.M. Wed.–Fri., 9 A.M.–5 P.M. Sat.–Sun.), an all-outdoors park southwest of Joliet near the Illinois River. The park boasts rough bike trails designed to rattle drivers with the many jumps and obstacles throughout the way. The skate park has everything from basic grind bars to a vertical wall and wedge ramps. Round up some friends and spend the morning or afternoon hunting each other down during a round of paintball. Don't worry about bringing any special equipment. You can rent all the goggles and pads you'll need. Admission to the skate park is $10, admission to the bike trails is $7. A combo ticket is $13. A day of paintball, including equipment and paint, will cost $50–60 per person.

For more thrills head to the **Chicagoland Speedway** or the adjacent **Route 66 Raceway** (500 Speedway Blvd., Joliet, 815/727-RACE or 815/727-7223, www.chicagolandspeedway.com, www.route66raceway.com, race times and ticket fees vary), both relatively new tracks south of Joliet. The Chicagoland Speedway is the larger of the two with a 75,000-seat arena. It hosts the ever-so-popular NASCAR speed races. The Route 66 Raceway, a dirt track, is for drag racing and other events. If you've got a lot of dough and fantasize about being a race-car driver you can ride or drive in a race car with an instructor at the Chicagoland Speedway. Prices vary from about $100 to more than $1,000, depending on whether or not you will get to drive the car yourself and how many laps you log on the track.

Gambling

Because it's situated on the Des Plaines River, perhaps it was no surprise when Joliet became the site of two casinos after riverboat gambling became legal in the state. The two casinos (Harrah's is downtown, Empress is southwest of downtown) certainly have brought more people to the town and the downtown has cleaned up quite a bit since they opened. But with thousands of slots, several restaurants, and lounge acts, these casinos make it nearly impossible for guests to want to leave their complexes and explore the rest of the area. Both offer a mix of slots and table games and charge a few dollars for admission. **Harrah's Joliet Casino** (151 N. Joliet St., Joliet, 815/740-7800, 800/HARRAHS or 800/427-7247, www.harrahs.com, 9 A.M.–5 A.M. Sun.–Thurs., 9 A.M.–6 A.M. Fri.–Sat.) has more than 1,000 slot machines, and table games such as blackjack, craps, roulette, three-card poker, and Caribbean stud poker. There are several restaurants, including a diner-type of restaurant, a fine-dining steak and seafood joint, buffet restaurant, coffee shop, and sports café. Adjacent to the casino is a 200-room hotel, which has rates from $60 (if you book in advance). The hotel offers standard and luxury rooms. And, yes, rooms come with blackout draperies so if you're up until 5 A.M. gambling, you should have no problem sleeping away the morning. Only people 21 years or older are allowed to stay in the hotel.

The 50,000-square-foot, Mediterranean-themed **Argosy's Empress Casino Joliet** (2300 Empress Dr., 815/744-9400, 800/4EMPRESS or 800/436-7737, www.argosycasinos.com, 9 A.M.–5 A.M. Sun.–Thurs., 9 A.M.–6 A.M. Fri.–Sat.) has about 1,000 slots and dozens of game tables, such as mini-baccarat, three-card poker, craps, and other games. Like Harrah's, this casino also has several dining options, including a steakhouse, café, buffet restaurant, and lounge that often features live music. The hotel also features an indoor pool, exercise room, and standard and luxury rooms that range in price depending on the day of week and time of year. Roughly for a weekend in the summer you can expect to pay about $89–99 for a room. Outside the hotel is an RV park that has shower facilities.

Accommodations and Food

Hotels in and around Joliet are primarily chain hotels centered around the I-80 exits. All are basically between $50–100 per night and offer two-double-bed rooms or king beds. Here's a roundup: the 62-room **Best Western** (4380 Enterprise Dr., Joliet, 815/730-7500); the 64-room **Comfort Inn North** (3235 Norman Ave., Joliet, 815/436-5141); the 67-room **Comfort Inn South** (135 S. Larkin Ave., Joliet, 815/744-1770); **Fairfield Inn North** (3239 Norman Ave., Joliet, 815/436-6577); and **Fairfield Inn South** (1501 Riverboat Center, Joliet, 815/741-3499). The casinos also have hotel accommodations.

A highlight of downtown Joliet is **Belle Amici's** (201 N. Ottawa St., Joliet, 815/722-0907, lunch Mon.–Fri., dinner Tues.–Sat.), an Italian restaurant with a welcoming dining room. The walls are painted in warm red and yellows and the windows look out onto the street. The white-tablecloth restaurant has casual lunchtime fare, such as hearty Italian meatball sandwiches, and fine dinners, including chicken, beef, and seafood dishes. Try the grilled tuna or gnocchi.

Al's Steak House (1990 W. Jefferson St., Joliet, 815/725-2388, 11 A.M.–midnight Mon.–Sat., 10 A.M.–midnight Sun., lunches $5–12, dinners $10–47) is an old-school lounge and steakhouse that specializes in charbroiled steaks. The menu is quite extensive and wide-ranging in selection and prices, from tenderloin sautéed with mushrooms and a wine sauce to fried calamari and lobster tail.

Information

The **Heritage Corridor Convention and Visitors Bureau** (81 N. Chicago St., Joliet, 815/727-2323, 800/926-CANAL or 800/926-2265, www.heritagecorridorcvb.com) has tourism information for towns along the canal from southern Cook County and into Will and Grundy counties, including cities such as Lockport, Joliet, and west to LaSalle. Another great resource is the **Canal Corridor Association** (Gaylord Bldg., 200 W. 8th St., Lockport, 815/588-1100, 800/926-CANAL or 800/926-2265, www.canalcor.org), a group that promotes the region as a historic and recreational destination. It publishes an excellent driving tour brochure that highlights historic places from Lemont westward. Call and the association will send you a free copy. Or pick one up at the Gaylord Building in downtown Lockport.

LOCKPORT

Once the headquarters for the I&M canal, Lockport is an increasingly picturesque town with several restored limestone buildings in its downtown. It's a must-see stop for travelers along the canal as it's home to a visitors center and museum that feature exhibits about the canal's history, plus some top-notch restaurants. All are near the intersections of Highways 7 and 71 near State Street, south of the canal.

Sights and Activities

A former limestone warehouse for storing construction material for the I&M Canal has been converted into a history and information center about the canal. The three floors of the Gaylord Building, owned by the National Trust for Historic Preservation, contain historical photographs, a mural, and displays about the building (which dates to 1838 and has housed a carpentry shop, brass foundry, and other businesses), the canal's history, and the towns along it. The **I&M Canal Visitors Center** (200 W. 8th St., Lockport, 815/588-1100, www.gaylordbuilding.org, 10 A.M.–6 P.M. Tues.–Sat., noon–6 P.M. Sun., free) also contains **Public Landing,** which serves regional cuisines such as lamb chops, steaks, and pasta. It's open for lunch 11:30 A.M.–2:30 P.M. and 5–9:30 P.M. Tuesday–Saturday and noon–7 P.M. Sunday. Dinner entrées range $16–50.

For more comprehensive historical information about the canal and the Illinois River, visit the **I&M Canal Museum** (803 S. State St., Lockport, 815/838-5080, call for hours, free). In the former canal commissioner's home and office, a white frame building from the 1830s, this museum contains furnishings from that time, plus photographs and more stories about the building of the canal. Behind the building is the Will County Historical Society's pioneer settlement, a group of various buildings moved here through the years to save them from demolition.

More historic photographs of the canal are on view in the **Gladys Fox Museum** (231 E. 9th St., Lockport, 815/838-1183, 1–4 P.M. Mon.–Fri.), another quick stop for folks who like old buildings. The museum is within an 1839 Old Congregational Church and run by the Lockport Park District.

In an old grain-storage building adjacent to the I&M Canal, the **Illinois State Museum Lockport Gallery** (201 W. 10th St., Lockport, 815/838-7400, www.museum.state.il.us, 10 A.M.–5 P.M. Tues.–Sat., noon–5 P.M. Sun., free) features the work of Illinois artists on three floors. The beautiful limestone building with hardwood floors has about 3,000 square feet of exhibit space for rotating exhibits of textiles, drawings, photographs, and other creations. Outside the building is a courtyard and nearby is the canal trail.

One of the best restaurants, if not the best one in the southwestern suburbs, **Tallgrass** (1006 S. State St., Lockport, 815/838-5566, dinner Wed.–Sun., $45–65) has been reaping praise from restaurants critics since it opened in a stone and brick building downtown Lockport in the 1980s. Diners choose from three-, four-, or five-course menus featuring locally and organically raised products when possible. The menu changes often, but here's an example of the alluring food served there: grilled bobwhite quail with toasted barley, pecans, prosciutto, and current sauce. Or how about this: grilled organic pork tenderloin with slow-roasted bacon, carrot loaf, pickled red grapes, dijon herb vinaigrette, and natural juices. The wines are mostly from France, Oregon, and Sonoma Valley, California. Tallgrass is an intimate classy place. You don't have to wear a suit and tie or an evening gown here, but leave the tennis shoes and jeans at the hotel. Reservations are required.

ROMEOVILLE

In the middle of the Des Plaines River between Lemont and Lockport is a small island, home to **Isle a la Cache Preserve and Museum** (501 Romeo Rd., Romeoville, 815/866-1467, www.fpdwc.org, 10 A.M.–Tues.–Sat., noon–4 P.M. Sun., free). The island's name refers to a local legend that a French fur trader stashed his goods on the island to hide it from other traders and potential looters. A kid-friendly museum on the island contains pelts (which visitors are encouraged to touch), a birch bark canoe, and other artifacts and recreations and exhibits about the fur trade in America. The park itself and a nearby lagoon provide habitat for egrets and waterfowl. If you've got a canoe, you can launch it here. And there's also a fishing pier and picnic area.

LEMONT

Surrounded by hills, Lemont is a scenic river town with a mix of antiques shops and two great restaurants, from the slightly upscale Stonecutters to the down-home White Fence Farm, famous for its fried chicken.

Popular among locals and hungry travelers along Route 66, **N White Fence Farm** (11700 Joliet Rd., Lemont 630/739-1720, www.white-fencefarm.com, 5–9 P.M. Tues.–Fri., 4–9 P.M. Sat., noon–8 P.M. Sun., $12) has been serving food like Grandma used to make ever since Grandma was a young girl. Established in the 1920s by an area coal baron, White Fence Farm was back then and still is a place for delicious comfort food. The signature meal is fried chicken made from fresh chicken, corn fritters, potatoes (mashed, baked, or fries), cole slaw, and other fixings. The dining rooms (there are several) are fairly basic, some with outdated wooden paneling. And it can get pretty busy, especially on weekends. But the chicken is so good, it's worth it. White Fence has also become quite the tourist attraction with a petting zoo for the kids and antique cars on display.

Like Tallgrass in Lockport, **Stonecutters** (103 Stephen St., Lemont, 630/243-7383, www.stonecuttersrestaurant.com, lunch Tues.–Sat., dinner Tues.–Sun., lunches $7–15, dinner entrées average $25) is housed in a beautiful and historic renovated limestone building. The food is American and definitely has an array of steaks and seafood; however, there are a number of creative options such as pork chops stuffed with apples and prosciutto. If you don't make it out to Stonecutters for dinner, at least drop by for a beer or glass of wine in its bar. Or, if dinners are too pricey, lunches can be affordable, especially if you go the sandwich route, such as a barbecued beef tenderloin sandwich or a veggie wrap.

MORRIS

Before Midewin National Tallgrass Prairie came onto the scene a few years ago, the 2,500-acre **Goose Lake Prairie State Natural Area** (5010 N. Jugtown Rd., Morris, 815/942-2899) was the best place to walk among a tallgrass prairie in northern Illinois. Though some may say it's been eclipsed by the sprawling Midewin to the south, Goose Lake is still worth a visit. The walking trails are certainly scenic, with towering cord grass (which can grow up to 12 feet tall) and other native grasses, but it's an interesting site historically and environmentally speaking. It's been through a lot in the last

150 years. Situated southeast of Morris, about a mile or so south of the confluence of the Des Plaines and Kankakee rivers, where the Illinois River begins, the site did indeed have a lake. Settlers drained the 1,000-acre lake to farm the area and to get at the clay. They dug out this clay and sent it to Joliet and other areas where it was made into bricks. Even though the area was drained it still was often wet, too wet to grow some crops. The area was also strip-mined for coal for many decades.

Today the site is made up of tallgrass prairie, ponds, and other wetland areas. There are several miles of trails of varying length up to 3.5 miles long. The Tall Grass Nature Trail is a beautiful trail showing you what the prairie may have looked like 200 years ago, with big blue stem grass and switch grass growing on all sides and the occasional sighting of a pheasant or fox. The marsh loop includes a boardwalk over a pond. Also on the site is a cabin built to resemble those that the pioneers built in the 1830s. Adjacent to the park's north end is Heidecke Lake, a 1,300-acre lake that provides cooling water for a nearby power plant. You can rent a rowboat and go fishing there.

On the west side of Morris is **Gebhard Woods State Park** (401 Ottawa St., Morris, 815/942-0796, www.dnr.state.il.us), a small state park that makes for a good launching point for a canoe trip down the I&M Canal or bicycling ride along the I&M Canal Trail. There's a canoe launch here and you can paddle up and down to Channahon State Park to the north. And the bike trail is also nearby, so you can start the bike ride here if you want. Also, if you're itching to put in some fishing time the 30-acre park has three fishing ponds. A backpack campground is one-third of a mile from the parking area.

Accommodations and Food

As in Joliet, lodging options around here are limited to national chain hotels near I-80, including a **Comfort Inn** (70 W. Gore Rd., Morris, 815/942-1433), which has an indoor pool and offers guests continental breakfast; and **Holiday Inn** (I-80 and Hwy. 47, Morris,

815/942-6600), which has an outdoor pool, restaurant, and cocktail lounge.

The vintage **Rockwell Inn** (2400 W. U.S. 6, Morris, 815/942-6224, lunch Mon.–Sat., dinner daily, brunch Sun., lunches $7–16, dinners $10–45) offers diners a hodgepodge of cuisine, from chicken picatta to Wiener schnitzel, plus sandwiches, steaks, and seafood. This family supper club–like restaurant contains several different dining rooms and a gallery of Norman Rockwell paintings. The coolest thing in the place is an opulent mahogany and red oak bar from the 1893 World's Fair in Chicago. It was used for the Anheuser-Busch display.

WILMINGTON

A popular stop along Route 66, the quiet town of Wilmington lies on the eastern shore of the Kankakee River, a few miles south of Goose Lake Prairie and about seven miles south of the I&M Canal and the Des Plaines River, and is surrounded by strip mines. Just north of the downtown is the huge Midewin National Tallgrass Prairie. Downtown Wilmington has a host of antiques shops and one of the icons of Route 66 in Illinois: the Launching Pad Drive-In.

Midewin National Tallgrass Prairie

Established in 1996 on the site of a former arsenal, Midewin National Tallgrass Prairie (30239 S. Hwy. 53, Wilmington, 815/423-6370, open one hour before sunrise–one hour after sunset daily, free) is the country's first national tallgrass prairie. For the most part, the area has been closed to visitors while the Army cleans the site of the explosive TNT, which was manufactured here (along with many other things). The entire site is about 19,000 acres; however, in 2004 about 6,300 acres on the east and west sides were opened to the public. One day the entire area, which is managed by the U.S. Department of Agriculture's Forest Service, will be open to the public. For now though, 6,300 is just fine. Begin your visit with a stop at the welcome center at Highway 53, two miles north of Wilmington. (This is the only place in the park with water and flush toilets.) There you can pick up some maps and some tips for exploring the region. You can explore Midewin by hiking, biking, or horseback riding along dirt roads or mowed grass trails. What makes Midewin so great is not only its enormous size, but that it's rustic. No paved roads. No fancy campgrounds. Just the sound of grassland birds singing and blades of grass swishing against each other in the wind. The tallgrass prairie once covered 60 percent of the state and a walk through Midewin, like the nearby Goose Lake Prairie, can give you a sense of what the region might have looked like when the pioneers came through in the 1800s. Where to go? You can park your car at the Hoff Road Trailhead and choose from 10 miles of trails for hiking, mountain biking, and horseback riding. Or the shorter, pedestrian-only trail off Explosives Road is another option. Another option is joining a guided tour. The park's staff offer hiking, biking, and horseback-riding tours throughout the year. Some tours focus on the birds of Midewin or the agricultural history of the area, and others highlight ongoing work to restore the prairie.

Shopping

Bargain hunters and treasure seekers could spend an entire weekend hopping from one antiques store to another. Shops can be found in downtown off Highway 53 or on its outskirts, along Highway 102. Here's a sampling of some of the shops. Most are open daily. **Mill Race Emporium** (110 N. Water St., Wilmington, 815/476-7660) is a two-story, multidealer shop with a wide range of antiques and collectibles from throughout the decades. Just down the street from the emporium is another multidealer shop, **Water Street Antique Mall** (121 N. Water St., Wilmington, 815/476-5900) with 15,000 square feet of antiques. **Mill Town Market** (508 N. Kankakee St., Wilmington, 815/476-0386) sells primitives and collectibles in a turn-of-the-20th-century lumberyard near downtown Wilmington. And in a century-old barn south of town, you'll find **Forked Creek**

Trading Company (1763 S. Water St., Wilmington, 815/476-1810), a gift shop with home-decor items, Amish furniture, gourmet food, and other items.

Food

With the 26-foot-tall iconic Gemini Giant standing guard outside, the **Launching Pad Drive-In** (810 E. Baltimore, Wilmington, 815/476-8535, www.launchingpadrt66.com, 9 A.M.–10:30 P.M. Sun.–Thurs., 9 A.M.–11 P.M. Fri.–Sat., $3.50) has been serving the Route 66 crowd since 1960, when it was called Dairy Delite. The attraction is the fiberglass space man (who looks a little like Superman with a helmet) grasping an eight-foot-long faux rocket, but the food, particularly the Italian beef sandwiches and ice-cream drinks, is another reason to stop by. It's fast food, such as barbecue ribs or grilled sandwiches, and it's cheap food, costing a few bucks a sandwich. Though the name might imply otherwise, the Launching Pad isn't a true drive-in, but an indoor restaurant with carry-out service and a drive-through.

Just a short drive southwest from Wilmington is the town of Braidwood and the **Polka Dot Drive-In** (222 N. Front St., Braidwood, 815/458-3377, www.polk-a-dot.com, 11 A.M.–9 P.M. daily, $5), another favorite stop for Route 66 travelers. A drive-in with an indoor restaurant and an outdoor eating area furnished with picnic tables, the Polka Dot (or "The Dot" as some call it) was initially a school bus with polka dots painted on it and a makeshift kitchen on wheels. But that was more than 50 years ago. The Dot today is a fun gathering place for roadies and foodies and Cruise Night, on the first Saturday in August every year, brings them all here. Inside you'll eat in a black and silver–themed dining area surrounded by walls covered with photographs of celebrities from the 1950s and '60s, and antique cars. The food is Midwestern drive-in food: corn dogs, pizza burgers, and French dip sandwiches. Don't leave without trying the signature dish, a heaping order of chili cheese fries.

Starved Rock State Park Area

Because it is about a 1.5-hour drive from Chicago, the Quad Cities, Bloomington, and Rockford, the Starved Rock region is a popular weekend getaway for residents of those metropolitan areas. It is not uncommon for the parking lot of area parks to be almost full on summer weekends.

The star of the region is Starved Rock State Park near Utica and it probably attracts such crowds because its topography is so sharply different from that of the prairie to the south and the slightly rolling hills to the north. When the glaciers receded thousands of years ago, the melting water surged through the region eroding the sandstone, which itself dates back several hundred millions of years. The result was several picturesque canyons.

Hopewellian Woodland and Mississippian Native American tribes lived in the region for thousands of years, perhaps as early as 8,000 B.C. And the Kaskaskian tribe of the Illiniwek lived along the river from the 1500s through the 1800s. Taken with the region's beauty and the potential to convert some of the Indians, Father Jacques Marquette established a mission at a village near where Starved Rock State Park is now. The French built a fort on top of Starved Rock, but later left it for Peoria. It's been a public park since 1911.

You've got lots of outdoor adventure here, from horseback riding to hiking, biking, camping. The Illinois River runs through here alongside towns such as Marseilles on the east, Ottawa, Utica, LaSalle, and Peru. Ottawa on the north side of the river has perhaps the best mix of restaurants and parks. Starved Rock is on the south side of the river and Matthiessen State Park south of it. Buffalo Rock, a small but scenic state park, is near Ottawa. The I&M Canal cuts a path through the region north of the Illinois River, with the bike trail along its side. U.S. 6 connects towns on the north side of the river.

SIGHTS

⋈ Starved Rock State Park

On the south side of the Illinois River near the town of Utica stands a 125-foot-tall sandstone bluff. It's a great lookout point. You can see up and down the river, the hills, and nearby farm fields. This bluff, after which Starved Rock State Park (Hwy. 178, Utica, 815/667-4726, free) is named, was the scene of a tragic event in local Native American history. The story goes that after the leader of an Ottawa Indian tribe, Pontiac, was killed in 1769 by a member of another tribe, the Illiniwek, a war broke out between the two tribes. Allies of the Ottawa Indians, the Potawatomi, reportedly drove a group of Illiniwek Indians to the bluff, where the Illiniwek stayed until they died of starvation. Before all this occurred, the area had been chosen as the site of a French fort, Fort St. Louis, in the late 1600s. The French would eventually abandon it in the 1700s.

It will take you about five minutes to climb to the top of Starved Rock. Half of the trail is paved concrete; the rest is up wooden stairs with a few decklike areas to rest along the way. You won't be the only one making the trek up the stairs (it's often crowded), but the view is worth it. Off the shoreline from the visitors center is Plum Island (no biological research is conducted here as there is on Plum Island near New York). And across the way is Lover's Leap Overlook, which also offers you great views and is sometimes not as crowded as the Starved Rock trail.

Hiking is the thing to do at Starved Rock State Park. All in all there are about 13 miles for hiking here. (Bicycling is not allowed.) They range in length from .3-mile Starved Rock trail to the 4.7-mile Illinois Canyon Trail. Pick any trail and you can expect to work out your calves; some will take you up to scenic overlooks, along canyons and cliffs. Springtime in the park is an especially beautiful time as the melting snow and spring rains prompt water to trickle and tumble down the sides of canyons.

The visitors center has exhibits on Illinois's geologic past, Native American Indian tribes, and the history of the park and the LaSalle fort. Staff is obliging to inquisitive visitors and armed with maps and brochures and recommendations on what to do in and outside the park. Stayed Rock State Park also holds guided tours in the park in October to highlight the fall foliage, as well as guided hikes in January. The **Bald Eagle Watch Weekend** in late January is a good one. You can take tours of the park and scout for the birds of prey, and watch videos about their habits in the lodge.

The park also has a lodge with hotel room accommodations, cabins, and a campground. The park is open 5 A.M.–10 P.M. daily. The visitors center is open 9 A.M.–6 P.M. daily.

Matthiessen State Park

About a mile or so south of Starved Rock State Park is the less-crowded Matthiessen State Park (Hwy. 178, Utica, 815/667-4868, www.dnr.state.il.us). The approximately 2,000-acre state park was originally a privately owned park developed by industrialist Frederick W. Matthiessen. The park is divided into two sections: the dells area to the north and the river area to the south, including land on the bluffs above the river and alongside an approximately one-mile-long canyon carved by the Vermilion River. If you travel to Matthiessen from the north, the first section you will come to is the dells part, where a little more than three miles of trails weave through wooded areas above the Vermilion River. This set of trails will take you past waterfalls, mineral springs, and over bridges. Along the way you will see butterflies, ferns, jacks-in-the-pulpit, and black-eyed Susans. This section has plenty of picnic tables and grills, a shelter, and bathrooms. The trails in the river section of the park can be a bit more tricky to navigate, especially after a heavy rain or in the spring when the dirt hiking trails can get muddy. They are also a bit more steep as they snake through wooded ravines.

In addition to the hiking trials, there are miles and miles of horse trails through here. Plus, the park has made plenty of accommodations for visitors with horses. There's trailer parking and, for those who want to stick around overnight with their horses, a horse campground. It is off Highway 178, south of Highway 71 and before the dells entrance.

During the winter, park staff groom about six miles of cross-country ski trails through the park. You can rent skis on weekends December–March at the dells area of the park. Also, the Vermilion River section has a model airplane–flying field open to anyone.

Buffalo Rock State Park

If you cannot hike up all those stairs at Starved Rock State Park, but you still want to take in views of the Illinois River from on high, drive to Buffalo Rock State Park (Dee Bennett Rd., between Utica and Ottawa, 815/433-2220, www.dnr.state.il.us, 8 A.M.–sunset daily). It is on the north side of the Illinois River, just south of Ottawa Street and the I&M Canal trail. Before becoming a state park, the area was used as, among other things, a retreat site for a religious group and the site of a sanatorium for sick employees of the Crane Company. At 300 acres, it's a nice little park, with a few unusual features, such as a handful of grazing buffalo, and an effigy *tumuli,* which is one artist's project to pay homage to the historic Native American practice of sculpting the earth into shapes of animals. In addition, the park has a scenic overlook, a few trails along bluffs above the river, and picnicking spots.

Historic Sights

It was in Ottawa's **Washington Square** that the first debate between Abraham Lincoln and Stephen A. Douglas took place. The date was August 21, 1858, and about 10,000 people gathered to hear the two Senate candidates address the issue of slavery. Lincoln's position was that slavery was morally wrong. Douglas took the stance that each state should decide whether or not it should legalize slavery. Statues and historical markers commemorate the spot. The park, which features well-tended gardens, is a nice little spot to take a break from bicycling or sightseeing.

Vintage mansions open to the public can be found in almost every major town or former industrial town in Illinois, but perhaps none is as enormous as the 16,000-square-foot **Hegeler Carus Mansion** (1307 7th St., La Salle, www.hegelercarus.org, free). The Second Empire–style home was built in 1874 by a businessman involved with an area zinc works. It stood on a full city block, complete with a greenhouse, pond, tennis courts, and gardens galore. Now undergoing a $12 million renovation, the mansion has had the slate roof and much of the exterior restored. Next up is the interior. Listed on the National Register of Historic Places, the mansion has some of the most amazing and intricate woodwork and plasterwork on its ceilings, floors, and other areas throughout the house. While it's quite fun to tour this estate and admire the architecture, it should also be noted that it housed an academic publishing company here for decades. Open Court Publishing specialized in translations of Asian manuscripts and is credited by some for introducing many Americans to Japanese and other cultures, as well as Buddhism. Until recently, a descendent of the family still lived in the home. Tours begin on the hour at noon, 1, 2, and 3 P.M. Wednesday–Sunday.

The **Ottawa Scouting Museum** (Ottawa, www.ottawascoutingmuseum.org, 10 A.M.–4 P.M. Thurs.–Mon., $3) is a tribute to Ottawa native W. D. Boyce, who founded the Boy Scouts of America, as well as to the history of the Boy Scouts, Girl Scouts, and Camp Fire girls. There are also displays on the I&M Canal and Native American history of the region.

RECREATION

Horseback Riding
Starved Rock Riding Stables (Hwy. 71, Oglesby, 815/667-3026, April–Nov.) offers one-hour guided trail rides and hayrides, bonfires, and other similar activities. Rides begin at noon, 2 P.M., and 4 P.M. Wednesday–Friday, and at 10 A.M., noon, 2 P.M., and 4 P.M. Saturday–Sunday.

Canoeing
For an adventure in canoeing, call **Ayers Land-**

hiking trail at Matthiessen State Park

© CHRISTINE DES GARENNES

ing (3494 E. 2089th Rd., Utica, 800/540-2394), which organizes canoe rentals and trips along the Fox River, which flows into the Illinois River near Ottawa from the north.

Water Park
Grand Bear Lodge near Starved Rock State Park opened a 24,000-square-foot indoor water park, **Grand Bear Falls,** in the summer of 2005. (For more information see *Accommodations.*)

ACCOMMODATIONS
$100–150
M Starved Rock Lodge and Conference Center (815/667-4227, 800/868-7625, www.starvedrocklodge.com, $105–115) has a mix of cabins and lodge rooms. The cabins, located 150 feet from the lodge, come with one king bed or two double beds. They're great cabins, but they're not exactly in a secluded area. The 72 lodge rooms are within a cozy

and rustic stone and log lodge. Rooms in the east wing are in the original part of the lodge that dates back to 1939. Other rooms are in the west wing, an addition to the lodge in 1989. All guests have use of a large indoor pool and children's pool.

$150–250

Set on a 14-acre homestead near Starved Rock and Matthiessen State Park, the **Brightwood Inn** (2407 N. Hwy. 178, Oglesby, 815/667-4600 or 888/667-0600, www.brightwood-inn.com, $115–190) is a country inn with bed-and-breakfast rooms and elegant evening dining. Built in 1996, the Brightwood is a modern farmhouse-type of building with eight rooms available, each with a private bathroom, gas fireplace, TV, and phone. One of the rooms is a 1,000-square-foot suite. Guests also are welcome to lounge in the library, which is stacked with books, unwind on the expansive veranda, or walk through the herb garden. Breakfast is included. Guests can also enjoy dinner at the inn Thursday–Sunday. The five-course meals, which feature contemporary pasta, seafood, and meat dishes, cost $20–30 per person.

Grand Bear Lodge (2643 N. Hwy. 178, Tonica, 866/399-FUNN or 866/399-3866, www.grandbearlodge.com, $169–189) rents a mix of lodge suites and what it calls "vacation villas," essentially townhouse and condolike accommodations. The decor is called rustic, meaning exposed logs, but the amenities are pretty high-end with whirlpool bathtubs, DVD players, and lots of television sets. If you like hiking in the outdoors, but you aren't thrilled about spending the night in a sleeping bag, you'll like this place. It's adjacent to Starved Rock State Park. The three-story lodge has 92 suites, some with bunk beds for vacationing families, others with whirlpool suites for couples. Deluxe suites can run up to $399 a night. All rooms include admission into the water park. Grand Bear also opened an indoor water park called Grand Bear Falls in the summer of 2005. The 24,000-square-foot indoor park has a wave pool, lazy river, and other rides.

Landers House (115 E. Church St., Utica, 815/667-5170, www.landershouse.com, $139), on the north side of the Illinois River, offers luxurious bed-and-breakfast rooms and cottages. If you're in town for a while and you're willing to spend a little mor than $300 per night, the cottages are the way to go. (Otherwise, the regular rooms are priced under $200.) The richly decorated cottages focus on one theme or another, such as the African-styled Serengeti cottage or upscale hunting lodge decor of the Caribou cottage. They feature fireplaces, whirlpool tubs, living rooms, loft bedrooms, and a lot more. They're cottages that will make you want to spend the entire day and evening inside.

If any of the above hotels or bed-and-breakfasts don't suit you or are not available, there's a slew of chain hotels near I-80 around Ottawa and the LaSalle/Peru area. They include the **Comfort Inn** (510 E. Etna Rd., Ottawa, 815/433-9600, and 5240 Trompeter Rd., Peru, 815/223-8585, $69–89); **Days Inn** (120 N. Lewis Ave., Oglesby, 815/883-9600, $60–65); **Hampton Inn** (4115 Holiday Ln., Ottawa, 815/434-6040, $99); **Holiday Inn Express** (900 Holiday St., Oglesby, 815/883-3535, and 120 W. Stevenson Rd., Ottawa, 815/433-0029, $76–85); and **La Quinta Inn** (4389 Venture Dr., Peru, 815/224-9000, $84).

Houseboating

Starved Rock Adventures (Starved Rock Marina, Dee Bennett Rd., Ottawa, 815/434-9200, www.srarock.com) rents houseboats for three-day trips up to seven-day trips. The boats sleep up to 10 people and feature sundecks, swimming platforms, kitchens, grills, ice chests, entertainment centers, phones, and radios. Houseboats rent for $800–1,800 and they're available April–mid-October. You'll need to bring along an electric motor boat for the ride, which will cost $49 per day, unless you bring your own boat. Starved Rock Adventures also rents one- and two-bedroom suites and villas for 3–7 days. Rates are from $495 for a three-day rental to $1,395 for a weeklong stay.

Camping

Starved Rock State Park (Hwy. 178, Utica,

815/667-4726, www.dnr.state.il.us) has 133 campsites with electric hookups, showers, flush toilets, and pit toilets. Because Starved Rock is a popular park, sites are snatched up quickly. The park takes reservations for about half of the sites. The others are available on a first-come, first-served basis. (Most of the wooded sites are ones that can be reserved.) You can find out which sites are available by stopping by the visitors center. Cost is $20 per site per night.

Matthiessen State Park has a campground for visitors with horses.

FOOD

Cheesy fries, pizza, burgers, and the excellent root-beer floats—the food at **Moore's Root Beer Stand** (225 N. Columbia Ave., Oglesby, 815/883-9254, 7 A.M.–about 10 P.M. daily, $4) is richly satisfying. Healthy? Probably not. Greasy? A little. But in the summertime, you can't beat a stop at a rare, bona fide drive-in such as Moore's, just off I-39. The stand tends to close earlier in the evenings during the winter.

On a hot summer evening, after a day of hiking, take a drive over to downtown Ottawa and the **Little Brown Cow** (600 Columbus St., Ottawa, 815/434-6422, 7 A.M.–9 P.M. Mon.–Thurs., 7 A.M.–10 P.M. Fri.–Sat., 1–9 P.M. Sun., $4.50) for some hand-dipped ice cream. The ice-cream parlor also serves sandwiches such as turkey, roast beef, and ham.

Thai Café (610 Columbus St., Ottawa, 815/431-8090, 11 A.M.–9 P.M. Mon.–Wed., 11 A.M.–10 P.M. Thurs.–Sat., 4–9 P.M. Sun., $8) is a storefront restaurant also near downtown Ottawa. The warm place (from the decor with its red-painted walls to its friendly wait staff) serves curry dishes, noodle soups, fried rice with vegetables, and beverages such as a delicious Thai ice tea, another good option on a hot summer day or evening.

Need a coffee fix? Head to **Planet Java** (203 W. Main St., Ottawa, 815/433-6030, 7 A.M.–6 P.M. daily) or **Jeremiah Joe Coffee** (807 LaSalle St., Ottawa, 815/434-3507, 7 A.M.–10 P.M. Mon.–Sat., 7 A.M.–5 P.M. Sun.).

Starved Rock Lodge (see *Accommodations*) also offers breakfast daily, lunch Monday–Saturday, dinner daily, plus a popular Sunday brunch. The lodge also has lounge that features live music. Outside is a veranda overlooking the valley. Various bands often perform here in the summer.

The **Brightwood Inn** (see *Accommodations*) serves multicourse dinners Thursday–Sunday. Reservations are recommended if you plan to eat dinner at either Starved Rock or the Brightwood.

INFORMATION

The **Heritage Corridor Convention and Visitors Bureau** maintains an office in Utica (801 E. U.S. 6, Utica, 815/667-4356 or 800/746-0550, www.heritagecorridor-cvb.com), where you can pick up brochures and maps of the region.

The **Ottawa Visitors Center** (815/434-2737, 888/OTTAWA-4 or 888/688-2924, www.visit-ottawa-il.com or www.experienceottawa.com, 9 A.M.–5 P.M. Mon.–Fri., 9 A.M.–4 P.M. Sat., 10 A.M.–2 P.M. Sun.) is in the Reddick Mansion (100 W. Lafayette St., Ottawa), just across the street from Washington Square, the Lincoln-Douglas debate site.

At the **Illinois Waterway Visitors Center** (Lock 14, Hwy. 351 and Canal Rd., near Utica, 815/433-2224, free) you can observe barges traveling along the river, learn about the history of water travel along the Illinois River, and how the whole locking process works. Call for hours; they vary according to the season.

Tours

If you're in a crunch or not up to hiking the park (it is hilly) you can see the park with **Starved Rock Trolley Tours** (815/667-4211 or 800/868-7625, $10). Tours run at 1:30 P.M. and 3 P.M. Wednesday and Thursday, and at noon, 1:30 P.M., and 3 P.M. Friday–Sunday. You can hop on the trolley at the lodge. This tour runs about 1.25 hours; you drive through the park, stopping at the visitors center, and over to the nearby lock and dam, where you can get out and walk around for a few minutes, followed by a drive through the town of Utica. Other trolley tours are offered throughout the year, such as a fall colors tour and a land-and-water tour package that includes a trolley tour, ride on the *Belle of the Rock* boat, and lunch at the park lodge. These special tours run higher, around $28.

For water-only tours, you can catch a ride on the **Belle of the Rock** (1 Dee Bennett Rd., Ottawa, 815/434-9200, $12) at Starved Rock State Park. Narrated tours aboard the *Belle* (a boat that looks like part paddlewheel and part pontoon) depart on the hour 10 A.M.–5 P.M. on weekends and 11 A.M.–4 P.M. weekdays May–October. The tours last slightly less than a hour. You'll cruise by Starved Rock, Lover's Leap, the lock and dam, Plum Island, and hear about the history of the region.

The Sherri Lynn (departs under the Hwy. 23 bridge, Ottawa, 815/228-5772, www.ottawariverboat.com, May–Oct., $18–27) offers longer tours at 1.5 hours that cover a bit more of the region's history. Ninety-minute river cruises aboard this paddlewheel depart at 2 P.M. and 4 P.M. Wednesday–Sunday plus there are 1.5-hour sunset cruises at 7 P.M. on the second and fourth Friday of the month; they include soda and beer. The lunch cruise leaves at 10:30 A.M. Wednesday–Sunday and lasts about 2.5–3 hours. It includes sandwiches and fries at a local marina. You'll need reservations for the sunset cruise.

Bishop Hill

Near the south branch of the Edwards River, a tributary of the Mississippi River, you'll find the extraordinary little village of Bishop Hill. With its artisan shops, Swedish restaurants, and local-history museum, Bishop Hill is a fascinating place to visit. A religious commune 1846–1861, the entire well-preserved village has been designated a National Historic Landmark. What makes Bishop Hill a great place to visit is that it's not a living history village, where old buildings have been brought in from around the state and assembled in a park, and where people dress up as if they were residents from the 1850s. This is an actual town with real residents. Former colony homes still stand and are home to gallery owners, gift shops, and restaurants.

HISTORY AND ORIENTATION

The village's story begins with Erik Jansson, a Swedish immigrant who walked all the way to this area from Chicago. He believed simplicity was the key to salvation. When he and his followers arrived in 1846, it was tough going. During the first winter, 96 people died, probably because of the lack of nutritional food and adequate housing. But Jansson's followers got to work building the colony. They put up almost two dozen buildings and started farming thousands of acres of land. They crafted furniture from the black walnut trees in the area. And they were among the first people in the area to adopt new technology, such as the mechanical reaper. Not exclusionists, they built a hotel and invited noncolony members to visit. After erecting a mill, colonists offered to grind grain for area farmers. (For every five bushels, the colony kept one.) It was a tough life. They worked 14–16 hours a day, but their work did pay off. At its peak, the colony owned about 14,000 acres.

The ride at the top didn't last very long, though. The first hit was the murder of Jansson in 1850, due to a dispute between him and the husband of one of the colony members who was also a relative of Jansson's. After he was shot and killed, Jansson lay in state for three days because his followers believed he was the second coming of Christ and that he would rise from the dead. That never happened. After some financial problems the colony dissolved in 1861 and many men left town to fight in the Civil War. Today about one-fifth of the town's 120 residents are descended from colony members.

Great River Valleys

Bishop, is north of U.S. 34, a few miles southwest of Kewanee and about a 10-minute drive east of I-74. Most likely you'll enter from the south on Bishop Hill Street. The state historic site museum is one of the first buildings you'll see on the west side of the road. This is a good place to begin your visit. From there continue downtown. Bishop Hill Park, surrounded by a white wooden fence, is in the center of town. Most historic buildings and restaurants are situated around the park and the side streets along Bishop Hill Street. All are within walking distance of each other.

SIGHTS

Bishop Hill Museum State Historic Site

The main feature of the Bishop Hill Museum State Historic Site (Bishop Hill St., Bishop Hill, 309/927-3345, 9 A.M.–5 P.M. Wed.–Sun., and until 4 P.M. during the winter) is Olof Krans, a folk artist who painted scenes of Bishop Hill. Krans moved here as a boy in 1850 and later painted images of the town from his memory. For example: a line of women sowing seeds in a field and a group of women driving piles into the ground to build a bridge. Many of the paintings on view in the museum are portraits of the town's blue-eyed, grim-faced residents dressed in black. Look closely and you'll notice Krans's paintings are not exactly flawless. Some bodies and objects are out of proportion. And he forgot to finish painting some lines. At the museum you can pick up a free brochures, a walking-tour guide, and other information. The museum also has a decent video about the history of the town, plus it has on view furniture made by colony members.

Colony Church State Historic Site

Colony Church State Historic Site (Bishop Hill St., Bishop Hill, 309/927-3345, 9 A.M.–5 P.M. Wed.–Sun. Mar.–Oct., 9 A.M.–4 P.M. Nov.–Feb., free) served as a church for the Christian colonists, but it also functioned like a dormitory. There were rooms here for

families plus a dining room. Rooms on the first floor are filled with a few straw beds, bare wooden tables, cradles, and other original colony furniture. Some rooms have other items salvaged from the town, such as the tin eagle that once stood outside the Bjorklund Hotel, and a collection of farm tools. Upstairs is where the men and women (on different sides of the church) listened to Jansson's sermons.

Other Sights

The **Colony Steeple Building Bishop Hill Heritage Association Museum** (Bishop Hill St., Bishop Hill, 309/927-3899, call for hours) is a large 1854 Greek-revival brick building downtown that colonists intended to be a hotel, but that ended up housing administrative offices, a school, and later a bank. Managed by the heritage association, the building today houses more historical exhibits and a video about the colony's past. The association also organizes guided tours of the town's sights. Tours last about 1.5 hours and cost $3.50 per person.

Undergoing renovation in 2004 and 2005, the **Colony Hotel** (309/927-3345, 9 A.M.–5 P.M. Wed.–Sun. Mar.–Oct., 9 A.M.–4 P.M. Nov.–Feb., free) stands on the southwest corner of Bishop Hill Park. The building was first used to house colonists and later opened as the Bjorklund Hotel. In the 1900s it was converted into an apartment building and then restored back to a hotel.

EVENTS

Bishop Hill hosts several Swedish heritage festivals throughout the year. They include the **Midsommar Music Festival** in mid-June, which features fiddlers, guitarists, and accordion players performing Swedish music concerts all day long, plus a barn dance. Feast on corn and apple dishes at **Jordbruksdagarna,** a harvest festival at the end of September. Finally, during **Lucia Nights,** the festival of lights in mid-December, area residents perform holiday choral music concerts.

ARTISAN SHOPS

Bishop Hill residents are a creative bunch. Area shops, inside historic and nontraditional buildings along Bishop Hill Street and nearby side streets, contain hand-crafted, artisan products, such as jewelry, pottery, quilts, and furniture. Shops hours vary, but most in town are open 10 A.M.–5 P.M. April–December. Some of the town's shopping highlights include **Bishop Hill Street Colony Peddlers** (110 S. Bishop Hill St., 309/927-3130), which is a little complex featuring work by several artists. There are an 1870 house filled with antiques, candles, and other home decor, a blacksmith shop, potting shed, and herb gardens. Just down the street is a red 1882 barn home to **Peasant Works** (Bishop Hill St., Bishop Hill, 309/927-3061), which sells handwoven baskets, herbs, and other items. Tucked off a side street, **Outsider Gallery** (409 Erickson St., Bishop Hill, 309/927-3314) is a little shop that sells jewelry and home-decor items made by regional and international artists. **Colony Store** (101 W. Main St., Bishop Hill, 309/927-3596) stocks smoked herring pâté, Swedish coffee, candy, drinks, books, and gift items such as Christmas ornaments.

ACCOMMODATIONS

If you want to stay in or near Bishop Hill, you'll have to stay in a bed-and-breakfast. You can't go wrong with either one of them.

The Colony Hospital Bed and Breakfast (110 N. Olson St., Bishop Hill, 309/927-3506, www.bishophilllodging.com) is in a yellow frame house that was once the town's hospital. There are five rooms, each with a queen-size bed, private bath, and a kitchenette that contains a little fridge, microwave, and coffeemaker. A library with a wood-burning stove is open for all guests to use. It's all a nice blend of old and new. The plank floors are original; the quilts on the bed are fresh and new. Rates are $80–120 per night.

For a stay in the country, really out in the country, check into **Indian Creek Vineyard B&B,** (County Rd. 550E, Toulon, 309/286-5302, www.indiancreekvineyard.com). About 20 miles southeast of Bishop Hill, the bed-and-breakfast looks out over corn- and soybean fields and rows and rows of grape vines. There are four rooms in the "chateau" (a pleasant, white frame house), including one room in which Lincoln reportedly stayed while campaigning in the area. Some rooms have shared baths. Rates are $55–100. While you're here, sample Illinois wines in the tasting room in a remodeled red barn. The tasting room and wine shop is open 9 A.M.–5 P.M. daily. Look for directional signs to the vineyard and bed-and-breakfast from state highways 17, 78, or 91.

FOOD

Try to spend a full day or a day plus one overnight in Bishop Hill. That way you can eat a meal at all the excellent restaurants. Begin at **Bishop Hill Colony Bakery** (103 S. Bishop Hill St., Bishop Hill, 309/927-3042, www.bishophillcolonybakery.com, 8 A.M.–5 P.M. Tues.–Sun.) for a cup of coffee and homemade granola or a cinnamon roll. Buy some Swedish rye or other Swedish specialty bread to take home with you.

For lunch, spend time in the cheery **The Red Oak** (106 Bishop Hill St., Bishop Hill, 309/927-3539, www.theredoak.com, 11 A.M.–2 P.M. daily, $6) dining room or outside at one of the tables on the deck. Scandinavian sandwiches are the specialty (such as open-faced sandwiches on rye bread). There's the Frikedellar, a meatloaf served with dill sauce and beets. Or The Biff, thinly sliced roast beef topped on rye with cucumbers and a light mustard sauce. House sauces, by the way, are for sale by the register.

Swedish sandwiches are also served grandly at **P. L. Johnson's Dining Room** (110 W. Bjorkland St., Bishop Hill, 309/927-3885, 11 A.M.–3 P.M. daily, dinners 5:30 P.M.–8:30 P.M. May–end of Aug., $5). Inside a former home near Bishop Hill Park, P. L. Johnson's is a restaurant-gift store combo. Named after a former colony member, the building has several antique bicycles hanging from its ceiling. Apparently P. L. Johnson (a blacksmith, farmer, and jack-of-all-trades) often cycled through town. Here you can dine on dishes such as Swedish meatballs or chicken salad sandwiches.

More fresh-brewed coffee, homemade sandwiches, and smiling faces can be found at **The Filling Station,** (303 N. Bishop Hill St., Bishop Hill, 309/927-3355, 11 A.M.–2 P.M. daily, dinner 5–8 P.M. Fri., breakfast, 7–10 A.M. Sat.–Sun.), an antique-laden café also on the main drag.

INFORMATION

The first stop you should make is the **Bishop Hill State Historic Site Bishop Hill Museum.** Watch the short video, check out Olof Kranz's paintings, pick up some maps, and then head into town. This is the first building you see when you drive into town on Bishop Hill Street heading north.

Several groups and businesses in town maintain a resourceful website, www.bishophill.com. It lists lodging, dining, and attraction information. Otherwise, regional information is available from the **Henry County Tourism Council** (308 W. Center St., Cambridge, 309/937-1255, www.visithenrycounty.com).

KEWANEE

A town of about 12,700 in southeastern Henry County, Kewanee began primarily as a railroad town. It wasn't until the mid-20th century however, that it garnered regional and some national attention by declaring itself the Hog Capital of the World. Henry County was a top county for pork production and after hearing the news, residents wanted to let everyone else know about how proud it was of this claim to fame. They organized a barbecue and now Hog Days, an annual festival on Labor Day weekend, is one of the county's top events for the year. Imagine a hog-calling contest, carnival, car show, live music, flea market, and more pork chops and pulled pork sandwiches

than you could possibly eat. If you're a barbecue fan, Kewanee should be on your list. And while you're in town for the eating, there are a few other places to check out.

Johnson-Sauk Trail State Park

Situated on a glacial moraine, Johnson-Sauk Trail State Park (27500 N. 1200 Ave., Kewanee, 309/852-0709, www.dnr.state.il.us), was once a marshy area home to diverse wildlife and frequented by Native American tribes who hunted for game here. It's along part of the Sauk Trail, which they followed while traveling from Lake Michigan to where the Rock River meets the Mississippi River. Eventually the pioneers drained the area for farming. The park itself is about 1,365 acres with more than 12 miles of trails. They're fairly easy, relaxing trails along a few rolling hills and around the 58-acre lake. You can rent a fishing boat with a trolling motor on it from the concessionaire on the lake. Or just bring a picnic and choose a table under a tall pine. Within the park is the huge **Ryan's Round Barn** (309/852-4262, $2). At 85 feet in diameter and 80 feet tall, it's one of the largest round barns remaining in the country. The barn, listed on the National Register of Historic Places, contains a collection of antique farm machinery and tools. It's typically open 1–4 P.M. on the first and third Saturdays of the month and sometimes on additional days May–October. Call ahead before you go.

The park, about three miles north of Kewanee just off Highway 78, also has a campground with RV and tent sites.

Good's Furniture

Downtown Kewanee is essentially centered around Good's Furniture (200–220 N. Main St./Hwy. 78, Kewanee, 309/852-5656, www.goodsfurniture.com, 9 A.M.–6 P.M. daily) a huge, mazelike furniture store in several connected buildings. Dozens of galleries showcase about 50 different furniture brands and styles, including leather couches, dining rooms, you name it.

A destination for serious furniture shoppers and daydreamers, Good's has started catering to visitors who hang around for more than an hour. It's added a gift and clothing shop, café, and bed-and-breakfast. The rooms within **Good's Bed and Breakfast,** which is in the store, feature fabulous furniture, as you might imagine, such as four-poster beds and sleigh beds. There are four rooms available (three with queen beds, one with a king bed), and continental breakfast is included. Rates are $95–145. **Good's Wine Cellar Bistro and Bakery** (9 A.M.–6 P.M. daily) serves a mix of salads, sandwiches, wine, and beer.

More Accommodations and Food

Right near the Amtrak station is the local hangout **Mr. K's Lunchbox** (300 W. 3rd St., Kewanee, 309/853-2414, 10:30 A.M.–2 P.M. Mon.–Sat., $4), a simple, red-checked-table-cloth kind of place. The specialty here is the butterfly pork chop sandwich, which will set you back about $3. Other options are barbecue sandwiches and hamburgers.

In addition to Good's Bed and Breakfast, other area lodging options include **Super 8** (901 S. Tenney St., Kewanee, 309/853-8800) and **Holiday Inn Express** (315 N. Canal St., Annawan, 309/935-6565), a town at Highway 78 and I-80 north of Kewanee.

Information

Folks at the **Kewanee Chamber of Commerce** (113 E. 2nd St., Kewanee, 309/852-2175, www.kewanee-il.com) can provide you with information about the Hog Days Celebration and the scoop on any local happenings or businesses.

Rock Island and Moline

Huddled together around the Mississippi and Rock rivers, the Quad Cities are an assortment of river towns in Iowa and Illinois. Rooted in agricultural manufacturing, iron and glass making, coal mining and other industry, the cities are solid Midwestern working towns. And the Mississippi River has always been the focus of activity here, economic and entertainment-wise. In the past tourists haven't exactly flocked here. But the cities are in riverfront revitalization mode and becoming much more diverse and vibrant, offering a surprisingly long list of things to do. The Rock Island entertainment district, with its nightclubs and watering holes, beckons on hot summer days and nights. Bicycle along the riverfront. Watch giant barges pass through the locks from Arsenal Island. Hop across the river to Iowa on a river taxi. Spend hours checking out the vintage collection of John Deere tractors. Order a malt at Lagomarcino's or cappuccino at Dead Poets Espresso. Stroll through the botanic gardens.

HISTORY

The area around Rock Island and Moline was originally home to the Sauk and Fox Indians. The Sauk, in fact, had a bustling village of sev-eral thousand residents near present-day Rock Island, where the Rock River meets the Mississippi. After the defeat of Sauk warrior Black Hawk (see *Know Illinois*), settlers pushed the Indians westward and more pioneers started moving into the region. Before the Army Corps of Engineers reconfigured the river, this section of the Mississippi was a notoriously dangerous area. The river was shallow and there were rapids for roughly 14 miles. Several businesses came about to service the steamboats and ferries as they pulled over while navigating the rapids. After John Deere opened his plow factory in Moline in 1848, many immigrants, particularly Germans, Belgians and Swedes, moved into the area. Soon the area was home to more and more agricultural equipment companies, lumber mills, rock quarries, breweries, and iron foundries. All these goods were shipped out along the river or on the railroads, which also prompted growth of the region.

ORIENTATION

The Quad Cities comprise Moline and Rock Island in Illinois (Moline is to the northeast

Great River Valleys

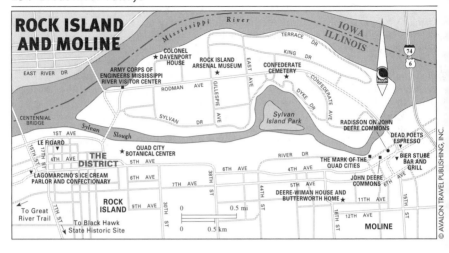

and Rock Island is south of it) and Davenport and Bettendorf across the Mississippi River in Iowa. Together the four cities have a population of about 400,000.

The Rock River comes in from the north and runs along the east end of Moline and south of Rock Island (just north of I-280) before it drains into the Mississippi River. In the middle of the river between the cities is Arsenal Island, which the U.S. government bought from Indians in 1804. It's been home to an American fort during the Black Hawk War, Confederate prison during the Civil War, as well as an armory. The John Deere sites are near Moline's riverfront. And The District in Rock Island, along with the riverboat casino and Quad City Botanical Center, are just south of the riverfront in northern Rock Island.

SIGHTS

Black Hawk State Historic Site

A good way to begin your visit to the Quad Cities is a tour of Black Hawk State Historic Site (1510 46th Ave., Rock Island, 309/788-9536, www.blackhawkpark.org) a small park and museum complex on a bluff above the Rock River in southwest Rock Island. Native Americans lived in this area for thousands of years, including the Sauk. During the 1700s it was the Sauk nation that was primarily living in the area. Its capital was Saukenuk, which historians believe was near this site. Before it became a state historic site, the area was actually home to a popular amusement park during the late 1800s and early 1900s. It was called the Watch Tower Park and there were vaudeville shows, boat rides, a roller coaster, and toboggan slide. (The toboggan was said to have been invented in Rock Island.) At about 200 acres, it's not a huge park, but there are quite a few interesting sites, especially for those interested in history. In the park is the **Hauberg Indian Museum** (309/788-0177, 9 A.M.–noon, 1–5 P.M. Wed.–Sun., donation), founded by John Hauberg, a Rock Island resident who collected Sauk baskets, jewelry, bowls, and other items. These types of artifacts are on view here as well as life-size dioramas of Indian homes. The museum is housed in **Watch Tower Lodge,** built by the Civilian Conservation Corps in 1939. Adjacent to the lodge is a picnic area and restored prairie and a trail leads to **Dickson Cemetery,** a two-ace pioneer cemetery.

John Deere Sights

On one end of the **John Deere Pavilion** (1400

Find that hard-to-find part for your vintage tractor at John Deere Collectors Center in Moline.

River Dr., Moline, 309/765-1000, www.john-deerepavilion.com, 9 A.M.–5 P.M. Mon.–Fri., 10 A.M.–5 P.M. Sat., noon–4 P.M. Sun., free) you'll see a corn planter from 1884 and a few steps away a mammoth combine that retails for more than $100,000. A brief history of the company is outlined for guests with an illustrated timeline on the wall. This documents the major events, such as Deere's development of the plow in Grand Detour, his decision to open a factory in Moline to be on a shipping route, and eventually the company's choice to branch out to computer-assisted farming in the 1990s. You can take a virtual tour of a tractor factory. And one enlightening exhibit for people who don't have an agricultural background is called *Cornucopia,* which attempts to demystify the whole seed-to-table concept and what happens in between. Adjacent to the pavilion is the **John Deere Store** (1300 River Dr., Moline, 309/765-1007) where a slew of Deere merchandise is for sale, including toy tractors, hats, and mugs. The store is open 10 A.M.–5 P.M. Monday–Saturday, noon–4 P.M. Sunday January–February. It's open 10 A.M.–6 P.M. Monday–Friday,

10 A.M.–5 P.M. Saturday, noon–4 P.M. Sunday March–December.

Just down the street is the **The John Deere Collectors Center** (320 16th St., Moline, 309/748-7944, www.johndeere collectorsctr.com, 9 A.M.–5 P.M. Mon.–Fri., 10 A.M.–5 P.M. Sat., noon–4 P.M. Sun., free), where the farm equipment on display is so shiny and new it all looks brand new. Housed in a beautiful 1885 Italianate brick building, the center contains mostly Deere tractors from the 1920s to the 1950s. The antique equipment is certainly fun to look at, but what might capture your attention even more is the area where workers are painting or tuning up the antique tractors. The center also has an area where you can buy old parts for your vintage tractor.

For those who want to hit everything Deere-related in Moline, you can also visit the company's **headquarters** (1 John Deere Rd., Moline, 309/765-8000, 9 A.M.–5 P.M. daily, free), which is off Highway 5, about 3–4 miles east of I-74. More new and old Deere equipment, including wagons, combines, and mowers, are on display in the lobby.

Great River Valleys

LOCKS AND DAMS

The Mississippi is often called a working river. To get an idea about just how it works (or rather, has been engineered) to handle heavy-duty traffic, such as barges loaded with corn or coal, pay a visit to one of the many locks and dams along the Mississippi River or its tributary, the Illinois. Boating today along the Mississippi River, you'll discover, is a vastly different experience from when Meriwether Lewis and William Clark paddled through its waters 200 years ago.

As the river flows from its starting point in Minnesota to its endpoint in Louisiana and the Gulf of Mexico, it drops several hundred feet in elevation. The Army Corps of Engineers has installed dozens of dams along the river that control the flow of water southward. From St. Paul, Minnesota, to St. Louis, Missouri, for example, there are 29 dams. These dams create what the corps calls a stairway of water, with the top stairs being on the northern section of the river. Essentially they help keep the water deep enough for the boats that need deep water to navigate. To go from one step or level of water to another, boats "lock through." It may sound baffling. But watch a barge or houseboat lock through and you should be able to grasp the gist of the process. Think of a lock as a water elevator. Say a boat is headed north. The driver steers it into the lock (which consists of gates in front of and behind the boat). The lock fills with water and slowly raises the boat to the level of the upper channel with the help of a series of valves and tunnels under the ground. The front gates open and the boat continues on its way north.

The Army Corps of Engineers has several visitors centers and lock and dams where you can watch the barges or even scout for eagles: the **Illinois Waterway Visitor Center** (950 N. 27th Rd., Ottawa, 815/667-4054); the **Mississippi River Visitor Center** (Rock Island Arsenal, Lock and Dam 15, Rock Island, 309/794-5338); and the **National Great Rivers Museum** at the Melvin Price Lock and Dam 26 (Hwy. 143, East Alton, 618/462-6979).

Sitting above the old Deere factories in the bluffs above the Mississippi River are two grand old homes, the **Deere-Wiman House** (817 11th Ave., Moline, 309/765-7970, open by appointment, free), where members of the Deere family once lived; and the **Butterworth Center** (1105 8th St., Moline, 309/765-7970, www.butterworthcenter.com, 8:30 A.M.–5 P.M. daily, free). Both were built by Charles Deere, John Deere's son, and are surrounded by acres of formal gardens. The Butterworth Center was actually a wedding president Charles Deere gave to his daughter. Not a bad gift.

Rock Island Arsenal
A long narrow island in the middle of the Mississippi, Arsenal Island, a National Historic Landmark, is quite a fascinating place. Start your visit on the northwestern side of

the island at the **Colonel Davenport House** (follow signs from Rodman Ave., www.davenporthouse.org, noon–4 P.M. Thurs.–Sun. May–mid-Oct., $3). The yellow two-story clapboard house was built in 1835, before the area became a boomtown for agricultural factories, coal mining, and other industries. It belonged to George Davenport, a fur trader and supplier for Fort Armstrong, which the government built shortly after the turn of the 17th century to control the waterway. Davenport earned the colonel title by volunteering as quartermaster at Fort Armstrong. Eventually, after the Black Hawk War, the government dismantled the fort.

Next, head to the site of a former prisoner-of-war camp and the **Confederate Cemetery,** a striking, somber cemetery on the south shore of the island. During the Civil War, Rock Island was chosen as a place to house Confederate prisoners of war. A plaque at Blunt and East avenues marks the spot of the 12-acre site on the northern part of the island. A little more than 12,000 prisoners were held here from December 1863 to July 1865. Of the 12,000, almost 2,000 died, many of them during the camp's first winter and from diseases such as smallpox. That first year the Army lacked supplies for all the prisoners and did not have a hospital yet. The cemetery is south of Rodman Avenue by Sylvan Island. Just east of the Confederate Cemetery is the **Rock Island Cemetery,** where Army veterans and their families are buried.

Eventually the Army established an armory on the island and by the Spanish-American War's end in 1898, employees were churning out things such as guns and gun holsters. The armory's peak was during World War II when as many as 18,000 people worked there manufacturing tanks, machine guns, and other weapons and defense items. Hundreds of guns and other weapons produced by the armory are on display at the **Rock Island Arsenal Museum** (North Ave., Rock Island Arsenal, 309/782-5021, www.ria.army.mil, 10 A.M.–4 P.M. daily, free). It's loaded with long arms, machine guns, pistols, and various experimental firearms developed at Rock Island decades ago. You'll learn how the M-9 pistol was developed, view rifles from the 1870s used by Native American warriors during the Battle of Little Bighorn, and sabers used by the U.S. military. Weapons themselves are no longer made here, but employees do assemble components, such as armored doors for Humvees and tool kits. In 2002, the arsenal employed 187 people.

From there, drive over to the **Army Corps of Engineers Mississippi River Visitor Center** (off the western tip of Rock Island Arsenal on Rodman Ave., 309/794-5338, daily 9 A.M.–5 P.M. free). Climb to the observation deck and you can watch barges travel down the river. Staff and exhibits explain how locking works, and why there are locks in the first place. Other displays discuss boating safety and similar issues. The center also has rest-rooms, a water fountain, and an information center stocked with area maps and brochures. Arsenal Island is about three miles long and three-quarters of a mile wide.

Quad City Botanical Center

A few blocks from the Mississippi Riverfront is the gorgeous Quad City Botanical Center (2525 4th Ave., Rock Island, 309/794-0991, www.qcgardens.com, 10 A.M.–5 P.M. Mon.–Sat., noon–5 P.M. Sun., $3.50), a complex of indoor and outdoor gardens. This is a must-see when you're traveling through the region in winter. Inside the main attraction is the center's "Sun Garden," a tropical garden with a nearly 15-foot-tall waterfall, little pools, and a variety of plants and flowers that thrive in the rainforest. Walk among huge palm trees, coconut trees, bird of paradise flowers, and orchids. Basically you can go any time of year and you won't be disappointed. Outside you'll find a spring bulb garden, perennial garden, fall mum garden, butterfly garden, and a conifer garden.

Niabi Zoo

Got kids? Haul them over to the Niabi Zoo (10908 Niabi Zoo Rd., Coal City, 309/799-3482, www.niabizoo.com, $4.50). Have a seat on a car pulled by a miniature steam engine train and travel the 40-acre site. The zoo is home to about 1,000 animals, including elephants, elk, bison, camels, zebras, reptiles, and ostriches. In addition to the animal exhibits, the zoo has a playground, carousel, and an education center. The center is focused on hands-on, kid-friendly activities. It's got an aquarium stocked with fish and exhibits that explain what animals need to survive and thrive. The zoo is in Coal City, just south of I-280 and Moline, east of the Quad City International Airport. The train ride costs $1.50. It's open 9:30 A.M.–5 P.M. daily spring and summer through Labor Day; noon–5 P.M. Monday–Friday, 9:30 A.M.–5 P.M. Saturday–Sunday in the fall (Labor Day–end of Sept.); and 11 A.M.–4 P.M. Saturday–Sunday in winter hours (end of Oct.–mid-Dec.).

Great River Valleys

ENTERTAINMENT

Every town needs an arts group like the one that runs the **Quad City Arts** (1715 2nd Ave., Rock Island, 309/793-1213, www.quadcityarts.com, 10 A.M.–6 P.M. Mon.–Sat., 10 A.M.–9 P.M. Fri., free). In addition to managing a gallery showcasing visual art (which may include photographs, paintings, sculpture, or mixed media), the group hosts regional, national, and internationally known visual and performing artists who read from their work, talk about their work, and/or perform. A recent guest was the playwright Edward Albee. If you're in town September–April, drop by for the free music concerts held 7–9 P.M. on Fridays.

The **Quad City Symphony Orchestra** (563/322-0931, www.qcsymphony.com) performs concerts throughout the year in venues around all cities, including Augustana College in Rock Island.

The **Mark of the Quad Cities** (1201 River Dr., Moline, 309/764-2054, www.themark.org) hosts visiting music guests from Neil Diamond to Green Day, arena football events,

Quad City Mallards hockey games, and theater productions.

In a renovated 1921 movie house, **Circa 21 Dinner Playhouse** (1828 3rd Ave., Rock Island, 309/786-7733, www.circa21.com) presents American musicals, children's shows, and concerts. It's hosted The Lettermen and produced musicals such as *Pump Boys and Dinettes*. Tickets are $34–39 per show and include a buffet dinner. Matinee and evening shows are scheduled throughout the year.

SPORTS AND RECREATION
Biking

The **Great River Trail** stretches for almost 63 miles from the Quad Cities to Savanna to the north. It's wide—about 10 feet—and primarily asphalt, so if you wanted to jog or in-line skate on it, you can. It starts at Sunset Park, on the river, south of downtown Rock Island, winds past the Quad City Botanical Center, the Rock Island Arsenal, several lock and dams, the John Deere headquarters, Campbell's Island in East Moline, and up to

riverboat gambling in Rock Island

Port Byron, where the residents hold a tug-of-war contest every year with their neighbors in Iowa across the river. A four-mile trail around **Arsenal Island** takes riders past the island's major sights such as the Colonel Davenport house and the cemeteries. April–November, the Quad Cities Convention and Visitors Bureau rents bicycles and helmets at its office in the Moline Depot, 2021 River Drive (as well as across the river in Davenport) for $7 an hour or $28 for the day. You can rent regular bikes, tandems, and kid trailers. They're available 8:30 A.M.–4:30 P.M. Monday–Friday and 10 A.M.–4 P.M. Saturday Memorial Day–end of September.

Skiing

One of the few places in Illinois where you can downhill ski is on the southern outskirts of Rock Island and Moline. **Ski Snowstar Winter Sports Park** (9500 N. 126th St., Taylor Ridge, 309/798-2666 or 800/383-4002, 9 A.M.–9 P.M. daily in winter, www.skisnowstar.com) is a 28-acre park atop a 790-foot hill. About half of the trails are labeled for advanced skiers and the other half are for beginners or intermediates. All hills are open to skiers or snowboarders. In addition to the ski or boarding trails there's a fun tubing hill. You can rent skis and boards here. There's also a restaurant on-site. Lift tickets range $21–29 for adults. Tubing costs $8 an hour and includes the tube.

Gambling

Docked on the Mississippi River on Rock Island's riverfront is **Jumer's Rock Island Casino** (18th St. and the riverfront, Rock Island 800/477-7747, www.jumerscri.com, 8 A.M.–3 A.M. daily), a genuine 200-foot paddlewheel boat. There are five stories of games and dining options here. Choose from around 700 slots (from penny to $25 machines), table games such as roulette, stud poker, and craps. The **Effie Afton Towboat Restaurant** (in a former towboat) serves buffets 11 A.M.–10 P.M. Monday–Thursday, 11 A.M.–11 P.M. Friday–Saturday, 10 A.M.–10 P.M. Sunday. Diners must be 21 years or older. Cost is $7–10.

ACCOMMODATIONS

$50–100

In the Broadway Historic District of Rock Island, a residential neighborhood lined with Queen Anne and Italianate homes, the **Victorian Inn Bed and Breakfast** (702 20th St., Rock Island, 309/788-7068 or 800/728-7068, www.victorianinnbandb.com, $70–90) is a large brick home that dates to 1876. There are six rooms here with king, queen, full, and twin beds. All come with private baths and are furnished with family antiques and touches of white lace. The Victorian Inn bed-and-breakfast, like Top O' the Morning, is not too far from the botanical center.

Top O' the Morning Bed and Breakfast Inn (1505 19th Ave., Rock Island, 309/786-3513, $65–80) is a brick, 1912 Prairie-style home across from Long View Park, a beautiful park that boasts several gardens and a greenhouse. There four rooms here. Three rooms cost $65–80; however, the bed-and-breakfast has a suite that rents for $120.

Because several interstates run through the Quad Cities, there's no shortage of national chain hotels along the exits. Here are a few. Contact the Quad Cities Convention and Visitors Bureau for a complete list. Near the airport you'll find **Comfort Inn** (2600 52nd Ave., Moline, 309/762-7000, $79–94); **Fairfield Inn** (2705 48th St., Moline, 309/762-9083, $75–90); and **La Quinta** (5450 27th St., Moline, 309/762-9008, $82).

$100 and up

The 175-room **Four Points Sheraton** (226 17th St., Rock Island, 309/794-1212, $109) is in Rock Island's entertainment district. It has a mix of rooms and suites, an indoor pool, and a bar and grill restaurant.

Right on the riverfront in downtown Moline, the newer **Radisson on John Deere Commons** (1415 River Dr., Moline, 309/764-1000, $99) is within walking distance of all the Deere sights and The Mark of the Quad Cities, which hosts concerts and sporting events. The hotel has rooms and suites, an indoor swimming pool, exercise room, and a restaurant.

Great River Valleys

FOOD

Coffee Shop

M Dead Poets Espresso (1525 3rd Ave., Moline, 309/736-7606, 7 A.M.–7 P.M. Mon.–Thurs., 7 A.M.–11 P.M. Fri., 7 A.M.–5 P.M. Sat., 8 A.M.– noon Sun., $6), within walking distance of Moline's riverfront, is a coffeehouse that serves healthy wraps, fruit smoothies, Italian sodas, pastries, and of course, some pretty good coffee drinks. Wander over here after you've toured the John Deere Commons. It's got great outdoor seating in wide, sunny alley.

Soda Fountains

M Lagomarcino's Ice Cream Parlor and Confectionary (1422 5th Ave. Moline, 309/764-1814, 9 A.M.–5 P.M. Mon.–Sat. www.lagomarcinos.com) is an institution in the Quad Cities. Founded in 1908 by an immigrant from Northern Italy, the shop and confectionary are now run by the fourth generation of Lagomarcinos. Slide into a walnut booth and order a phosphate or sundae topped with homemade fudge. Pick out a dozen or so homemade chocolates (the cream-filled ones are divine) for the ride home.

Mama Compton's (1706 3rd Ave., Rock Island, 309/786-MAMA or 309/786-6262, www.mamacomptons.com, 7 A.M.–8 P.M. Mon.–Thurs., 7 A.M.–11 P.M. Fri., 9 A.M.– 11 P.M. Sat., 10 A.M.–5 P.M. Sun., $4) is one of a kind. Part gourmet food and gift shop, part soda fountain, part deli, Mama Compton's is a friendly business in The District where you can buy a roast beef sandwich, a box of chocolates, a sundae, a pound of coffee, or a bottle of lotion. It's within a few blocks from the riverfront. After a day of biking along the riverfront, try a lemon shake-up.

Italian

In The District, **Huckleberry's** (223 18th St., Rock Island, 309/786-1122, 11 A.M.–3 P.M. Tues.–Fri., Mon. lunch buffet only) is best known for its cheesy pizza, of which there are many, many varieties beyond the tomato sauce, pepperoni, and mozzarella. Some come with pesto sauce, gorgonzola cheese, cheddar, and barbecued beef (but not all together). Carnivores will like the Mississippi pizza, which has pepperoni, salami, sausage, ground beef, mushrooms, onions, green peppers, and cheese. Dine inside the casual spot or out on the sidewalk to take in The District's scene. Lunches can cost from $2.99 for a slice of pizza to $8 for a platter of Italian, Polish, and andouille sausages. Dinners range from $8 for gourmet salads to $14 for a chicken and pasta bake.

French

In Rock Island's entertainment district, **Le Figaro** (1708 2nd Ave., Rock Island, 309/786-4944, dinner Tues.–Sat.) serves classic French food, such as chateaubriand (beef tenderloin) and escargot (snails).

Bars and Grills

As the name implies, the house specialties at the **M Bier Stube** (415 15th St., Moline, 309/797-3049, 11 A.M.–midnight Mon.–Wed., 11 A.M.–2 A.M. Fri.–Sat., noon–midnight Sun., $6–13) are German (and meat-laden) dishes, such as sauerbraten and rouladen. But the restaurant and bar also serves a variety of hamburgers and sandwiches. The Bier Stube is one of those places where you could spend an entire afternoon or evening swigging good beer and chatting with friends. Large windows, practically floor to ceiling, open onto the sidewalks and inside are vintage tin ceilings and exposed masonry. It's just a cool (and popular) place in downtown Moline. The beer and wine lists are extensive and feature quite the array of German and European beverages.

Finney's River House Bar and Grill (1510 River Dr., Moline, 309/797-1234, 11 A.M. daily until bar closes, $10) is a casual bar and grill that offers Cajun food (such as blackened catfish with rice and veggies) and some traditional American food such as burgers, wraps, and salads. Finney's has quite a few seafood options, from fried shrimp to swordfish. Local bands often play here on the weekends.

Live local bands also jam at **Rock Island Brewing Company** (1815 2nd Ave., Rock Island, 309/793-1999, www.ribco.com, 11 A.M.–

3 A.M. Mon.–Fri., 5 P.M.–3 A.M. Sat., $7). This is a casual joint that serves quesadillas, chicken salads, grilled and fried chicken sandwiches, and fish and chips.

GETTING THERE AND AROUND
Airport
The **Quad City International Airport** (2200 69th Ave., Moline, 309/764-9621, www.qcairport.com) is a few miles south of Moline and Rock Island, south of I-280 and between U.S. 57 and U.S. 150. Several carriers service the airport, including AirTran, American Eagle, Delta, Northwest Airlink, and United. Direct flights are available to and from Atlanta, GeorgiaChicago; Cincinnati, Ohio; Dallas/Fort Worth, Texas; Detroit, Michigan; Memphis, Tennessee; and Minneapolis, Minnesota.

Rental Car
Several rental car companies are at the airport. They include **Avis** (309/762-3605); **Budget** (309/762-7730); **Enterprise** (309/764-9611); **Hertz** (309/762-9429); and **National/Alamo** (309/764-4696).

River Taxi
The Rock Island Metropolitan Mass Transit District operates *Channel Cat* (309/788-3360, www.qcmetrolink.com), a 48-passenger, open-air pontoon boat that shuttles people between the Quad Cities. You can board it at the John Deere Commons and *Celebration Belle* in downtown Moline and the riverfront in East Moline. It carries passengers to the Isle of Capri Casino in Bettendorf, Iowa, and East Davenport, Iowa. Bikes are allowed on board. The taxi operates 11 A.M.–8 P.M. Monday–Thursday, 11 A.M. Friday, 9 A.M.–9 P.M. Saturday, and 9 A.M.–8 P.M. Sunday, Memorial Day–Labor Day. The shuttle operates on weekends only in September after Labor Day. As for the riverfront stop in East Moline, the shuttle stops there only on the weekends. Rides run every hour 11:30 A.M.–8:30 P.M. Fri., 9:30 A.M.–9:30 P.M. Sat., 9:30 A.M.–8:30 P.M. Sun. An all-day ticket on the Cat costs $5 per person.

Tours
The *Celebration Belle* (2501 River Dr., Moline, 309/764-1952 or 800/297-0034, www.celebrationbelle.com) offers lunch and dinner riverboat cruises aboard an 800-passenger excursion boat. Some cruises feature live music, such as brass bands; others are educational in focus and include commentaries on the history of the river and surrounding region. Tours cost $8–123.

INFORMATION
You can pick up brochures at the **Moline Depot** (2021 River Dr., Moline), at an information center on the north side of the terminal at **Quad City International Airport** or the **Mississippi Rapids Welcome Center,** just off the eastbound lane of I-80 in Rapids City, northeast of Moline and just before you cross the Mississippi River into Iowa.

To view a barge locking through or on its way down the river, stop by the **Mississippi River Visitor Center** (off the western tip of Rock Island Arsenal on Rodman Ave., 309/794-5338). Staff and exhibits explain how locking works, and why there are locks in the first place (see sidebar, *Locks and Dams*), in addition to displays on boating safety and the like. The center also has restrooms, a water fountain, and an information center stocked with area maps and brochures.

Otherwise, you can contact the Illinois office of the **Quad Cities Convention and Visitors Bureau** (2021 River Dr., Moline, 800/747-7800, www.visitquadcities.com).

Media
The two daily newspapers in town are the *Rock Island Argus* (www.qconline.com) and *Quad Cities Times* (www.qctimes.com). Both are available at most convenient stores and bookshops. The *River Cities Reader* (www.rcreader.com) is a free weekly with a blend of politics and entertainment. It's available at convenient stores, plus dozens of cafés and restaurants around the Quad Cities.

Great River Valleys

VICINITY OF QUAD CITIES

Aledo

About 25 miles southwest of the Quad Cities is an unusual bed-and-breakfast. Once the Mercer County Jail, **The Slammer Bed and Breakfast** (309 S. College Ave., Aledo, 309/582-5359, www.theslammer.net) is well, a bed-and-breakfast. Rooms are simple, modern, clean, and not tucked into jail cells. You will however, eat breakfast in cells on tables covered with black and white-striped cloths. The three-story 1909 building has nine guest rooms with king and queen beds. On the third floor is a sauna and whirlpool baths for all guests. Rooms are $65–85 per night.

Geneseo

Just north of I-80 and south of the Hennepin Canal, the quiet and picturesque town of Geneseo is known for its tree-lined streets and decorative Victorian homes. Downtown, **The Cellar** (137 S. State St., Geneseo, 309/944-2177) is in one of the many historic buildings lining State Street, in the basement of the Geneseo House. Steaks and seafood are cooked slowly over coals on the grill.

Recognizing the need for community theater, a creative bunch of area residents converted the top floor of a dairy barn into a performance space. The **Richmond Hill Players** (Robinson Dr., west of Oakwood Ave., Geneseo, 309/944-2244, www.rhplayers.com) now present six productions each year, May–October. They tend to include a mix of comedies, dramas, musicals, some well-known and others not-so-well known.

Along the Hennepin Canal, just north of town, the **Geneseo Campground** (22978 Hwy. 82, Geneseo, 309/944-6465) rents canoes and kayaks for use on the canal. It also has dozens of RV sites and a handful of rustic cabins clustered close to each other.

Warren and Henderson Counties

OQUAWKA REGION

Sights and Activities

North of Oquawka by about eight miles are two state parks near the Mississippi River offering hiking trails and bird-watching opportunities. Home to the oldest pine plantation in the state, the 2,900-acre **Big River State Forest** (East of County Rd. 1500E, between Keithsburg and Oquawka, 309/374-2496, www.dnr.state.il.us) has miles and miles of hiking or horseback riding trails on fire breaks (strips of cleared land to prevent the spread of fires). In the winter, these trails are great for some snowshoeing and cross-country skiing as you'll pass acres of stately red, white, and jack pines. The Riverview campground has about 50 sites for tents and RVs. Prime spots are those near the sandy beach. Camping costs $8–13 per day. South of Big River is **Delbar State Park** (follow signs from Hwy. 164 in Oquawka, 309/374-2496, www.dnr.state.il.us), a 89-acre park on the river. Trails about two miles long weave through the woods. The park also has boat launches and tent and RV camping. Anglers can also cast their lines in the 27-acre lake at nearby **Henderson County Conservation Area** (off U.S. 34, south of Gladstone, 309/374-2496), which has a boat ramp.

North of Gladstone on Highway 164 is a red covered bridge that dates to 1886. The bridge, about 100 feet long, is open to pedestrians only. Listed on the National Register of Historic Places, it has survived floods and two fires.

Love horses and horseback riding? Adjacent to the Big River State Forest, **Pine View Cabins** (County Rd. 2450N, four miles north of Hwy. 164, Keithsburg, 309/587-3217), with 3,000 acres and 70 miles of trails to explore nearby, is the place to go for serious horseback riding. Spend a day riding a Clydesdale, and then retire to an A-frame style pine cabin amid the pine trees. Unwind on the porch for a while, and then attend a bonfire. The log cabins have air-conditioning and heat, but they're not exactly luxurious. No marble shower stalls or whirlpool tubs. Horseback riding costs $15–20 per hour. Cabins go for $45–65 per night.

MONMOUTH

A quiet town of about 9,500 people, Monmouth has a scenic downtown square with historic eateries, shops, and an arts center.

Sights and Activities

A stagecoach driver, surveyor, and buffalo hunter, Wyatt Earp garnered fame as skilled gunfighter and frontier lawman who attempted to bring order to towns such as Dodge City, Deadwood, and Tombstone in the 1870s. This legendary figure was born in Monmouth, a quiet town west of Galesburg. The **Wyatt Earp Birthplace** (406 S. 3rd St., Monmouth, 309/734-6419, 1–4 P.M. Sun. Memorial Day–Labor Day weekend or by appointment, $1), a pale yellow home showing its age, has antique furniture in it and newspaper clippings about Monmouth's famous resident. Adjacent to the home is a little yard with a vintage wagon. Just down the street from the home near a lumberyard on 4th Avenue is a plaque marking the site of a **Lincoln-Douglas debate** that took place in Monmouth.

Buchanan Center for the Arts (64 Public Sq., Monmouth, 309/734-3033, bca@grics.net, 9 A.M.–5 P.M. Mon.–Fri., 10 A.M.–2 P.M. Sat., free) in downtown Monmouth hosts art shows spotlighting photography, sculpture, and you name it created by area artists.

On the north side of town is **Western Stoneware** (1201 N. Main St., 309/734-6809, www.westernstoneware.com), which has been in the region since 1890s, when a group of family-owned potteries banded together to sell their wares. At their outlet store you can shop for crocks, mugs, plates, and other kitchenware made from clay mined from south of Monmouth.

downtown Monmouth

© CHRISTINE DES GARENNES

ACCOMMODATIONS AND FOOD

If you're looking for a place to stay in Monmouth, there's a clean, newer **Hawthorn Inn and Suites** (1200 W. Broadway, Monmouth, 309/734-0909).

Before it was restored and converted to a soda fountain and lunch spot, **Monmouth Soda Works** (112 S. 1st St., Monmouth, 309/734-3221, $5) was a Plymouth car showroom, a billiard hall, millinery, and even a garage. Choose a booth along the wall, stool at the bar, or even out on the backyard patio and indulge in concoctions such as the huge banana-boat sundae. Follow the stairs and second-story walkway to check out an antique car collection. Typically it's open 10 A.M.–4 P.M. daily; however, sometimes during the week it closes at 3 P.M.

Maple City Candy Company (235 S. Main St., 309/734-3313) has grown from a one-room candy shop to a three-story, five-building complex with a coffee shop, gift shop, and restaurant. It's pure bliss for anyone with a sweet

Great River Valleys

NORMA JEAN, THE ELEPHANT

In July 1972, the Clark and Walters Circus, a small traveling circus, was in the Mississippi River town of Oquawka to perform for area residents. On the night of July 17, an animal trainer chained a 6,500-pound circus elephant named Norma Jean to a tall tree near the town square. A thunderstorm started brewing and as the trainer was trying to untie the elephant, lightning struck the tree, killing the elephant almost instantly and throwing the trainer several feet in the air. Rather than move the massive elephant, residents buried Norma Jean on the site. And one resident rallied to erect a memorial to the circus elephant. The fieldstone memorial, with a small elephant statue on top, is near the town square at 5th and Mercer Streets. More information is available from the Village of Oquawka (309/867-3481, www.oquawka.com).

tooth. Glass jars are filled to the brim with treats such as sweet tarts and licorice. Inside the complex is the colorful, parrot-themed **N Coconuts** (69 Public Sq., 309/734-8999, $6–12), a restaurant that serves such dishes as crab canapés, glazed apricot beef kebabs, and Cuban ham steak. Coconuts is open 11 A.M.–3 P.M. Sunday–Monday, 11 A.M. 9 P.M. Tuesday–Saturday during the summer. Winter hours vary.

The coffee shop is open 8 A.M.–9 P.M. Monday–Saturday, 11 A.M. Sunday, 9 A.M.–9 P.M. Tuesday–Saturday during the summer.

Information
You can pick up maps and other local information from the **Monmouth Area Chamber of Commerce** (68 Public Sq., Monmouth, 309/734-3181).

Galesburg

A bustling town of about 32,000 people, Galesburg is a historic town with quite the stock of historic, beautiful buildings and homes. Its downtown along Main and Seminary streets is packed with an eclectic mix of restaurants and shops. Galesburg got its start as a railroad town, and to some extent it still is. Amtrak stops here and freight trains roll by often. The comprehensive Galesburg Railroad Museum near the Amtrak station has several cars you can tour and exhibits about the town's railroading past. Galesburg is also a college town. The small liberal arts school Knox College, founded by abolitionists, is just south of downtown. It is on that campus that Abraham Lincoln debated Stephen A. Douglas in 1858. Perhaps the best site of all is the Carl Sandburg State Historic Site, a three-room cottage and complex of buildings south and east of the railroad yard where Sandburg's father worked. It's easy to get to Galesburg. The town is just east of I-74 and south of U.S. 34. The north-south U.S. 150 runs through town,

turning down Main Street for several blocks. The commercial district with hotels and shopping centers is along U.S. 150 and 34.

SIGHTS
Carl Sandburg State Historic Site
One of Illinois's (and America's) most beloved writers, Carl Sandburg was born in a tiny cottage in Galesburg. The Carl Sandburg State Historic Site (313 E. 3rd St., Galesburg, 309/342-2367, 9 A.M.–5 P.M. Weds.–Sun., donation) offers tours of that cottage as well as exhibits in nearby buildings that shed light on the author and his work. At 20 feet by 22 feet, Sandburg's childhood home is no bigger than a two-car garage. Inside are a few furniture pieces that did belong to the family, such as a bureau and a few shelves. It's a quick visit. You'll spend more time in the main visitors building, where there are exhibits that chronicle his life, activities, and his writings.

© CHRISTINE DES GARENNES

Carl Sandburg's boyhood home

Born in 1878 of Swedish immigrants, Sandburg spent the first few years of his life in a working-class neighborhood of Galesburg, not far from the railroad where his father worked repairing locomotives. As a young man, Sandburg enrolled in Lombard College in Galesburg, but he abandoned his studies to ride the rails and lead the life of a hobo. He traveled west through the Dakotas and upon his return worked several jobs, including selling stereoscopes. He wrote for the *Galesburg Evening Mail* and *System,* a business magazine. (One of Sandburg's articles, called "Training Eorkers to be Careful," is on view in the museum. He also worked for the *Chicago Daily News.*

It wasn't until 1914, when some of his poems were published in the Chicago-based journal *Poetry,* that Sandburg started to become better known as a writer. The collection of verse called *Chicago Poems* was published in 1916, followed by *Cornhuskers,* which would build his reputation as an American poet. Influenced by Walt Whitman, Sandburg was a regular man's poet. When Edward R. Murrow asked him what was the worst word in the English language, Sand-

burg replied, "exclusive." In addition to poetry, Sandburg wrote children's stories and nonfiction. One part of the multivolume Lincoln biography, *Abraham Lincoln: The War Years,* won him the Pulitzer Prize for literature. Several of his books are on display for visitors. Also on view are items such as a photograph of his confirmation class at the Lutheran high school, a pocket knife that once belonged to him, his reporter's pass from his days working for the *Chicago Daily News,* and clippings of his newspaper and magazine articles.

The building called "The Barn," which is behind the cottage and museum, contains more photos and displays on Sandburg, including several of him and Marilyn Monroe talking and practicing exercises together. Be sure to watch the 15-minute video. It shows Sandburg being interviewed by Edward R. Murrow and the author reading his poetry. Behind the tiny house is the Remembrance Rock, under which Sandburg's ashes were buried. Some of the stepping-stones that lead to the rock are engraved with lines of Sandburg's poetry, such as "Look at songs hidden in eggs" and "I am a brother of the cornhuskers."

Great River Valleys

Galesburg celebrates **Sandburg Days** in May with poetry readings, writing workshops, storytelling and music, antique car shows, and other exhibits.

Galesburg Railroad Museum

The Galesburg Railroad Museum (Seminary and Mulberry Sts., Galesburg, 309/342-9400, www.galesburgrailroadmuseum.org, 10 A.M.– 4 P.M. Tues.–Sat., noon–4 P.M. Sun. Memorial Day to Labor Day. After Labor Day and until mid-Oct., it is open noon–4 P.M. Sat. and Sun. The hours for Sept. through mid-Oct. tend to vary according to staffing, so it's best to call ahead of time if you plan to visit during that time) is one of the finest attractions in the region. For just a few bucks you can tour several rail cars, a locomotive, plus a new depot that contains railroad history displays. The center-piece of the collection is a hulking 1930 Baldwin locomotive, a shiny black engine with a coal bin attached to it.

Visitors also get to tour a rail car used by the Railway Mail Service, which was once a branch of the U.S. Postal Service. This car is set up as if it were still a working car, with letters ready to be delivered. The newly built depot and 1921 Pullman passenger car contain exhibits about railroading history and photographs of Galesburg depots from the past, plus old train schedules and telegraph equipment. The museum was planning to renovate the Pullman car's interior to make it look once again like a passenger car with a table, bed, and sitting area for travelers. The railcars and depot museum are adjacent to the Amtrak station. The museum hosts the annual Galesburg Railroad Days at the end of June, a two-day festival with model train shows, a carnival, and other events.

Old Main and Abraham Lincoln

The fifth of seven Abraham Lincoln and Stephen Douglas debates were held on a platform erected just east of Old Main on the campus of Knox College (2 E. South St., Galesburg 309/341-7000). The Gothic-style building, which dates to 1857, stands at the center of the college, with a lawn stretching out behind it. On October 8, 1857, Lincoln and Douglas

Knox College's Old Main building was the site of the Lincoln-Douglas debate.

met here. The building was renovated in the 1940s after it was designated a National Historic Landmark, and at the rededication ceremony Carl Sandburg read "Ode to Old Main," which he wrote for the occasion. At this time the college installed two bronze tablets of portraits of the speakers on the eastern wall of the building. "He is blowing out the moral lights around us when he contends that whoever wants slaves has a right to hold them."

Across the street from Old Main is the **Arboretum** (Cedar and South Sts., Galesburg), where dozens of mature trees, such as elm and hickory, tower almost as high as Old Main. There's a gazebo in the center of the small park, and a few benches if you need to rest for a little bit.

Other Galesburg Sights

Across the street from the railroad museum's locomotive is the **Discovery Depot Children's Museum** (128 S. Chambers St., Galesburg, 309/344-8876, call for hours, $3.50).

While you're downtown, take a few minutes to walk by the gorgeous **Central Congregational Church** (on the central square, Main and Cedar Sts., Galesburg, 309/343-5145), a solid red sandstone church with huge rose stained glass windows. It was built in 1898 and is now listed on the National Register of Historic Places.

Just off Main Street is the **Orpheum Theatre** (57 S. Kellogg St., Galesburg, 309/342-2299, www.theorpheum.org), a majestic theater (imagine theater boxes, a rich red curtain) boasting a melting pot of architectural styles, including Second Empire, Italian Renaissance, and French baroque. In the 1980s the community restored this 1916 vaudeville theater and it now hosts concerts by the Knox-Galesburg Symphony and performances by other area arts groups.

SHOPPING

The main shopping district is along **Seminary Street** (383 E. Simmons St., Galesburg, 309/342-1000, www.seminarystreet.com). More than a dozen shops lie along Seminary and Main streets, including the **Galesburg Antique Mall** (349 E. Main St., Galesburg, 309/342-8571); **Toys and Teachers** (53 S. Seminary St., Galesburg, 309/344-5547); and **Cooks and Company** (93 S. Seminary St., Galesburg, 309/342-3433), a gourmet food and kitchen accessory shop and espresso bar.

ACCOMMODATIONS

$50–100

A stay at **⚏ The Barn Bed and Breakfast** (1690 Kenny St., Dahinda, 309/639-4408, $60) is retreat to the country. Set on 200 acres, the newly constructed red barn (although you'd hardly know it; it looks quite rustic) contains a full kitchen, a hayloft where guests sleep, bathroom with a claw-foot tub, exposed beams, dried flowers hanging from the ceilings, and plenty of rocking chairs. The barn sleeps 8–10 people and guests have the entire barn to themselves. It's about 15 miles east of Galesburg.

Within the town of Galesburg there are plenty of chain hotels, including the **Best Western Prairie Inn** (I-74 at E. Main St., Galesburg, 309/343-7151, $69), a 109-room, one-story hotel with an indoor pool and exercise room; **Super 8** (260 W. Main St., 309/342-5174), a 48-room hotel that also has an indoor pool; and **Country Inn and Suites** (2284 Promenade Ct., Galesburg, 309/344-4444, $89), a 61-room hotel with indoor pool. For a complete list contact the visitor bureau.

$100–150

Located along a tree-lined street in Galesburg's historic residential district, the **The Fahnestock House** (591 N. Prairie St., Galesburg, 309/344-0270, $125) is somewhat of a unique bed-and-breakfast. Its two rooms are actually large suites. Both are quite impressive. The Victorian suite has a private balcony and the Empire suite has a large bow window and a Chippendale four-poster canopy bed. The Queen Anne home, which features a three-story turret tower, is a few blocks from Knox College and Seminary Street.

FOOD

Bakeries and Food Shops

The apple fritters at **М Swedough's Donuts and Deli** (7 A.M.–5 P.M. daily) are fresh and fluffy, bigger than your hand, and less than $1. They don't have dozens of doughnut types or sandwiches (such as a turkey club) to choose from, but those the chipper employees do dish up are fresh and so yummy. You can't go wrong by stopping here for a bite to eat. The dining area, with a handful of tables, is in a room that leads to an antiques store crowded with china, tables, glassware, and more.

Stock up on trail mix and other healthy goodies at **Cornucopia** (83 S. Seminary St., Galesburg, 309/342-6111, 7 A.M.–6 P.M. Mon.–Sat., 7 A.M.–Sun.), a health and natural food store. Adjacent to Cornucopia is **Uncle Billy's Bakery** (same contact information and hours), where you can indulge in fresh, warm bread, thick, rich brownies, and cookies.

American and Continental

Housed in a former meat-packing plant, the **Packinghouse Dining Co.** (441 Mulberry St., Galesburg, 309/342-6868, 11 A.M.–2 P.M., 5–9 P.M. Mon.–Thurs., 11 A.M.–2 P.M., 5–10 P.M. Fri.–Sat., noon–8 P.M. Sun.) is a popular spot during the lunch hour for its "Burger Bar." For about $7, it's all-you-can-eat burgers with French fries and unlimited toppings. But there's plenty more to this place than burgers. How about a rib-eye steak sandwich, catfish strips, or chicken walnut salad on a croissant? With an assortment of cheesecake desserts and hand-dipped ice cream, it's pretty much guaranteed you'll leave this place with a full stomach.

М Chez Willy's and Willy's Wines (41 S. Seminary St., Galesburg, 309/341-4141, 11 A.M.–2 P.M. Mon.–Fri., 4:30–9 P.M. Mon.–Sat., $10 lunches, $20 dinners) is an intimate storefront bistro with exposed brick walls that serves innovative and delicious food such as chicken with sherry mushroom sauce, coconut curried chicken, and vodka shrimp. Wines are available with dinner by the glass or bottle.

The **Landmark Café and Creperie** (62 Seminary St., Galesburg, 309/343-5376, 11 A.M.–9 P.M. Mon.–Thurs., 11 A.M.–10 P.M. Fri., 9 A.M.–10 P.M. Sat., 9 A.M.–9 P.M. Sun., $5–13), in the heart of the Seminary Street District, is a comfortable restaurant with a comprehensive menu, with breakfast perhaps offering the most tantalizing option: omelettes, crepes, Belgian waffles, and strawberry pancakes. On to lunch and dinner and you'll choose from standards such as quiche and grilled sandwiches but also some unusual (at least, for these parts) offerings, such as roasted duck quesadillas. In the summer, enjoy your meal on the patio.

INFORMATION

You can pick up brochures at the **Galesburg Area Convention and Visitors Center** (2163 E. Main St., Galesburg, 309/343-2485, www.visitgalesburg.com, 8:30 A.M.–5 P.M. Mon.–Fri.).

MACOMB

Home to Western Illinois University, Macomb is also county seat for McDonough County. Its courthouse square at Lafayette (U.S. 67) and East Jackson streets (U.S. 136) is packed with craft and antiques shops, hometown cafés and diners, and bars. It's in the center of western Illinois, between the Illinois and Mississippi rivers.

Accommodations and Food

Built in 1901, the **Inselhaus Bed and Breakfast** (538 N. Randolph St., Macomb, 309/833-5400, www.inselhausbb.com) is a large Victorian home with six bedrooms, all with private bathrooms. Rooms are quite beautiful and modern, not too frilly or dusty (as some bed-and-breakfasts can be).

Macomb also has several chain hotels along U.S. 67 and other major roads. For a list, contact the visitor bureau.

If you're craving breakfast and it's 4 in the afternoon, head to **Cookie's Diner** (118 S. Lafayette St., Macomb, 309/837-1180, 6 A.M.–8 P.M. Mon.–Sat., 8 A.M.–3 P.M. Sun., $6). You can get Swedish pancakes, large omelettes and other morning plates all day long, if you desire. Otherwise, your options are similar to what you would find at a Denny's: patty melts, turkey clubs, and other sandwiches. The food and service are not exactly top-notch, but the atmosphere is homey and the food will fill you up.

The Shoppes of the Taylor Block (119–125 S. Randolph St., Macomb) is a group of businesses in a historic block near the courthouse square. They include Sullivan Taylor Coffee Shop (309/836-7064, 7 A.M.–5:30 P.M. Mon.–Fri., 8 A.M.–5 P.M. Sat.), which sells bagels, sandwiches, and soups in addition to coffees; Your Wine Sellers (309/836-WINE or 309/836-9463), a gourmet food and wine and beer shop; and Jane's off Jackson (309/836-2909), which sells kitchen supplies.

Events

Watching dozens of balloons coasting through the air is quite a sight. And even more fascinating is watching them glow in the evening. Macomb's annual Balloon Rally takes place in September and includes balloon flights during the day, live music, food, and a classic car rally.

Information and Tours

For regional information, the place to call or visit is the Western Illinois Tourism Development Office (2900 E. Jackson St., Macomb, 309/837-7460, www.visitwesternillinois.info). Otherwise, the Macomb Area Convention and Visitors Bureau (201 S. Lafayette St., Macomb, 309/833-1315, www.makeitmacomb.com) can help you with any other questions about lodging, dining, or attractions in and around Macomb.

Haunted Macomb (309/836-5577, www.hauntedmacomb.com) organizes evening tours through the summer and holds special events the rest of the year.

Argyle Lake State Park

Less than 10 miles west of Macomb, Argyle Lake State Park (640 Argyle Park Rd., Colchester, 309/776-3422, www.dnr.state.il.us) is a heavily wooded park with about five miles of rugged hiking trails. The man-made 93-acre lake is stocked with fish and there's a concession stand where you can rent fishing boats.

Peoria

With about 125,000 people, Peoria is Illinois's largest city south of I-80. On the west side of the Illinois River, the city grew in the mid-1800s after meat-packing plants, distilleries, and machinery manufacturers set up shop here. A diverse workforce, comprising European immigrants and blacks from the South and Chicago, settled here to work in the factories. Then came the railroad boom in the 1850s and Peoria became a major transportation hub for the Midwest. Because of its mix of so-called regular folk, Peoria became somewhat of a testing ground for the performing arts community and for politicians. The expression "Will it play in Peoria?" essentially meant, how will regular Americans respond to the play or the policy proposal?

Although Peoria developed its identity as a meat-packing center and manufacturing and transportation hub in the 1800s, Peoria's history actually goes back even further. French explorer La Salle built Fort Crevecoeur on the east side of the river in 1680, making it the first European settlement in the state. A statue marks the spot in the present-day town of Creve Coeur, a middle-class city off Highway 116.

You'll spend most of your time in the city center, along the riverfront where there's a growing mix of restaurants and watering holes. It's also where the paddlewheel boat *Spirit of Peoria* is docked. To the north, the snakelike Grandview Drive offers some awe-inspiring views of the river valley. To the

Great River Valleys

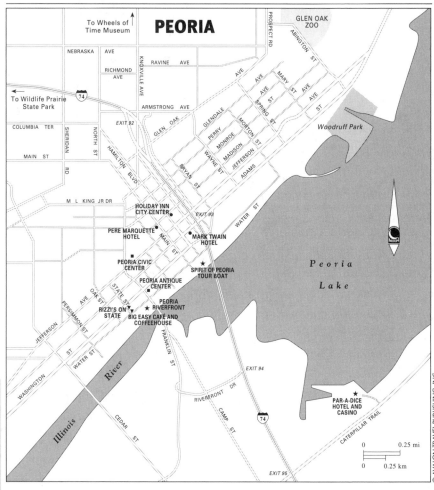

PEORIA

southeast is East Peoria, known for its riverboat casino.

SIGHTS
Riverfront

In recent years Peoria's riverfront has come alive with a 1.5-mile walkway lined with sculptures, visitors center, antiques mall, and restaurants. City officials and community groups, along with heavy-machinery equipment manufacturer Caterpillar (a major employer in the region), were planning to build a multimillion-dollar museum square that highlights the region's and Caterpillar's history. For now, though, the riverfront is also home to a farmers market in the summer and a paddlewheel boat. On summer evenings the Peoria Park District hosts outdoor music concerts on the landing by the riverfront. For more information about the riverfront, contact the **Peoria RiverFront Association** (309/671-5555, www.peoriariverfront.com).

One of the major draws to the riverfront is the ***Spirit of Peoria*** (100 N.E. Water St.,

© CHRISTINE DES GARENNES

The Spirit of Peoria, docked in Peoria on the Illinois River

309/636-6166 or 800/676-8988, www.spiritof-peoria.com), a paddlewheel boat docked at the landing. Choose from short sightseeing cruises during the day, dinner cruises, and overnight, themed excursions. The overnight rides may include storytellers, ragtime jazz bands, Mark Twain impersonators, and food and drinks. Often you'll catch glimpses of soaring eagles, pass through locks and dams, and stop to visit historic sites, such as Pere Marquette State Park near Grafton or Starved Rock State Park near Utica. It also organizes fall foliage trips during October, when the ship cruises south to Dickson Mounds and Havana. Sightseeing cruises, which last about 1.25 hours minutes, cost $12. Dinner cruises are $32. Longer trips range $89–415.

Museums

It's not a cavernous museum like The Art Institute of Chicago or Field Museum, but **Lakeview Museum of Arts and Sciences** (Lakeview Park, 1125 W. Lake Ave., Peoria, www.lakeview-museum.org, 309/686-7000, 10 A.M.–5 P.M. Thurs.–Sat., 10 A.M.–8 P.M. Wed., noon–5 P.M. Sun., $5) is a nice little museum with a few rare finds. One of the museum's highlights is a copper plate called the Peoria falcon. The plate, no larger than 10 inches high, is believed to have once been part of a warrior's headdress. It dates back to sometime between A.D. 1300–1450 and probably belonged to a warrior or chief from a Middle Mississippian tribe. A Peoria banker reportedly found the plate in 1859 near Lake Peoria, but later it ended up in the hands of John Wesley Powell, an Illinois State University geologist who would later join the Smithsonian staff.

In addition to the Peoria falcon, the museum has a small but impressive gallery of Illinois folk art. There's an oil portrait by Olof Krans, Anna pottery, and a collection of Illinois River duck and goose decoys from the turn of the 20th century. The museum also contains a dozen or so art glass specimens called American Brilliant cut glass. There are cologne bottles, vases, bowls, and a cool boudoir-type of lamp. Most of the pieces are from 1876–1916. Other finds include European lithographs and an armchair designed by Frank Lloyd Wright and a chair designed by Frank Gehry. The museum also has a gallery for rotating exhibits, plus a planetarium and children's center.

Great River Valleys

On the northern edge of town is a fun detour called the **Wheels O'Time Time Museum** (11923 N. Knoxville Ave., Peoria, 309/243-9020 or 309/243-5616, www.wheelsotime.org, noon–5 P.M. Wed.–Sun., May–Oct., $5). For a few bucks you could spend hours admiring the model airplanes and model trains, steam engines, music boxes, Packard automobiles, farm tractors and implements, and antique toys. Owned by dozens of collectors, this museum seems to get larger every year. As the name says, this place is all about things that go.

Parks
Wildlife Prairie State Park (3826 N. Taylor Rd., Peoria, 309/676-0998, www.wildlifeprairiestatepark.org, $5.50, $2 Tues.) is a 2,000-acre park modeled after what Illinois may have looked like when the first wave of pioneers came through here. The park is home to animals that were native to Illinois, such as timber wolves, bison, black bears, bison, elk, and deer, plus birds of prey. In one area staff have assembled a replica of a pioneer homestead and added some farm animals there. You can tour the park by riding a miniature train, but at least spend some time walking along the many trails. Climb a hill filled with wildflowers, pass a butterfly garden and several lakes, and stop at one of the viewing decks to look for wildlife and listen to songbirds. Pick up a map at the visitors center and staff will be able to tell you what animals you'll be able to see on certain trails that day. The park's schedule varies year to year, but generally it's open 9 A.M.–4:30 P.M. daily end of March–end of April and October–mid-December. It's also open 9 A.M.–6:30 P.M. throughout May and September, 8 A.M.–8 P.M. June–early September.

One of the park's best-kept secrets is its original lodging options. You can stay overnight in a caboose, stable, cottage, or cabin for $70–100. The cabin is a genuine, one-room cabin with a queen and two double beds, a kitchenette, and a front porch complete with a front porch swing. The cottages, which are along a lake, can sleep 3–8 people. They also come with small kitchenettes, heat, and air-condition-ing. The Prairie Stables building, which looks like a horse stable, is actually quite a modern building with two bedrooms. Some lodgings are available year-round; others are open only spring through summer.

On the west side of the river north of downtown, the **Glen Oak Zoo** (2218 N. Prospect Rd., Peoria, 309/686-3365, www.peoriaparks.org, 10 A.M.–5 P.M. daily) has about 250 animals from around the world, including lions, sea lions, and zebras. There's also a petting zoo of farm animals.

Go north on Highway 29 or Galena Road along the west side of the Illinois River until you get to **Grandview Drive** and the park by the same name. Follow this narrow winding road up along the bluffs, past mansions and manicured lawns for great views of the Illinois River valley below. After you've taken the drive, get ready for hiking some of these bluffs. Nearby, just off Prospect Road, a mile or two north of U.S. 150 is the **Forest Park Nature Center** (5809 Forest Park Dr., Peoria, 309/686-3360, nature center open 9 A.M.–Mon.–Sat., 1–5 P.M. Sun., trails open dawn–dusk). The nature center is great for children and the shop is great for naturalists—it's got everything from environmentally friendly cleaning products to wind chimes and greeting cards. But hikers, especially those in for a challenging hike, will salivate over the seven miles of rugged trails. The best time to go? Early morning just after the sun has started rising in the east and you can look out over the valley through the trees.

ENTERTAINMENT AND EVENTS
Performing Arts
Peoria has a vibrant arts community, with several dance, music, and theater companies staging productions throughout the year. The **Peoria Ballet** (8800 N. Industrial Rd., Peoria, 309/690-7990, www.peoriaballet.com) performs recitals and shows in Peoria's Scottish Rite Cathedral and the civic center. The **Illinois Ballet** (100 Walnut St., Peoria, 309/671-1222, www.illinoisballet.org) stages classic

ballets, such as *Swan Lake* and *The Nutcracker* at locations throughout the region. The **Peoria Civic Center** (201 S.W. Jefferson St., Peoria, 309/673-8900, www.peoriaciviccenter.com) in downtown Peoria brings in comedians and touring musicians such as Nelly, and hosts Bradley University sports, and other events. The **Peoria Symphony Orchestra** (203 Harrison St., Peoria, 309/637-2787, www.peoriasymphony.org) performs classical and pops music from around the world. Its shows are also in the civic center. For 50 years, the **Corn Stock Theatre** (309/676-2196, www.cornstocktheatre.com) has been staging summertime shows outside in the Peoria area. It showcases musicals and comedies in a tent at Upper Bradley Park (Farmington Rd. at W. Main St. and Park Rd.).

Events

Peoria is always partying, it seems. The River City Blues Society (www.rivercityblues.com) hosts a blues festival every summer on the riverfront. Tens of thousands of people flock to the Peoria Art Guild's **Fine Art Fair** at the end of September on the riverfront, where visual artists display their work for sale and musicians perform. **Jumbo Gumbo Mamba Combo** is a weekend of New Orleans jazz and zydeco and salsa music. During East Peoria's **Festival of Lights** in December, decorated floats cruise downtown East Peoria followed by a fireworks show.

SHOPPING

If you like antiques, especially antique furniture, jewelry, and prints, you might just spend hours at the **Illinois Antique Center** (311 S.W. Water St., Peoria, 309/673-3354, 9 A.M.–5 P.M. Mon.–Sat., 11 A.M.–5 P.M. Sun.). In an old warehouse on Peoria's riverfront, the center has hundreds of booths containing antiques from the 1800s up to the 1970s and '80s and styles from art deco to Victorian. Nearby are several other gift and home-decor shops.

Buy fruits and vegetables and local art at the outdoor **RiverFront Market** (309/671-5555, www.peoriariverfrontmarket.com, 7 A.M.–noon Sat. June–Oct.).

SPORTS AND RECREATION

An indoor recreation center, **inPlay** (316 W. Washington St., Peoria, 309/497-0090, www.inplaypeoria.com, 11 A.M.–midnight Mon.–Wed., 11 A.M.–2 A.M. Thurs.–Sat., 11 A.M.–10 P.M. Sun.) is loaded with pool tables, basketball courts, a climbing wall, skee-ball, and a bar and grill. It's a few blocks from the civic center near the riverfront.

Gambling

Par-A-Dice Hotel and Casino (21 E. Blackjack Blvd., East Peoria, 800/PARADICE or 800/727-2342, www.par-a-dice.com, 10 A.M.–6 A.M. daily) is a permanently docked riverboat casino on the east side of the river. It's got countless slot machines here that are coinless. Meaning, instead of cashing out coins, the machines prints out tickets. The casino also has dozens of blackjack, roulette, craps, stud poker, and other table games. A steakhouse, deli, and bar are on-site and a hotel is adjacent to the casino.

Minor League Baseball

The **Peoria Chiefs** (O'Brien Field, 730 S.W. Jefferson St., 309/688-1622) are a Class A minor league affiliate of the St. Louis Cardinals; season runs May–September.

ACCOMMODATIONS

The hotels listed here range widely in price, mostly because each hotel has standard rooms and luxury suites. Basically, in Peoria proper, you can expect to spend about $75 for a basic hotel room and up to $300 for a suite.

Listed on the National Register of Historic Places, the **Pere Marquette Hotel** (501 Main St., Peoria, 309/637-6500, www.hotelperemarquette.com) was built in 1927. This downtown Peoria hotel is an old-style hotel with rich dark colors and attentive staff. It's usually the first choice of conventioneers and brides. There are 253 rooms here—some whirl-pool-bath rooms, some suites, and some junior suites. Carnegie's is a classy dinner joint that serves items such as crab legs, grilled vegetables, veal, and duck.

In contrast to the old-school Pere Marquette is the **Mark Twain Hotel** (225 N.E. Adams St., Peoria, 309/676-3600, www.marktwain-hotels.com), a few blocks away and still within walking distance of the downtown riverfront district. This 110-room hotel was built in 1967 and does not exactly have the most appealing exterior (it's mustard yellow), but the deluxe rooms on the upper floors have been renovated into tasteful rooms with DVD players, luxury bath products, and other nice touches. Some rooms have views of the river. A hot breakfast buffet is included and a chain pizza parlor is in the building.

The 324-room **Holiday Inn City Center** (500 Hamilton Blvd., Peoria, 309/674-2500) in downtown Peoria is near the civic center and a short walk to the riverfront. The hotel features an indoor pool, whirlpool and sauna, game room, fitness center, and restaurant. It also has a mix of standard rooms and executive suites.

Stoney Creek Inn and Conference Center (101 Mariner's Way, East Peoria, 309/694-1300, www.stoneycreekinn.com) is about a mile from Par-A-Dice Casino. It's got 165 rooms, all with standard features such as cof-feemakers, high-speed Internet access, and hair dryers. The indoor pool is pretty large and is connected to another, outdoor pool so you can swim from one to the other.

Adjacent to the casino, **Par-A-Dice Hotel** (21 E. Blackjack Blvd., East Peoria, 309/699-7711, www.par-a-dice.com) has 208 rooms and suites, all with wireless Internet access and other basic features such as coffeemakers in the rooms.

In Peoria's Randolph-Roanoke Historic District just west of I-74 and near Hamilton Boulevard, **Randolph Terrace Historic Bed and Breakfast** (201 W. Columbia Terr., Peoria, 309/688-7858 or 877/264-8266, www.rthbb.com) has four rooms, all with pri-vate bathrooms. They're furnished with an-tique beds and armoires and come with comfy robes for guests.

Accommodations are also available at **Wildlife Prairie State Park.** (For more information, see *Sights*.)

FOOD

Cafés and Lunch Spots

The small, colorful **Big Easy Café and Cof-feehouse** (100 State St., Peoria, 309/637-9000, www.bigeasycoffee.com, 6 A.M.–4 P.M. Mon.–Fri., 10 A.M.–2 P.M. Sat.–Sun., $3.50–7) serves light breakfasts such as fruit wraps and lunches such as ham and cheddar wraps. As the name implies, the café has many nods to New Orleans, from the French-inspired art hanging on the walls to food such as beignets and muffu-letta sandwiches. This is a sunny and informal place that attracts everyone from antiquing re-tirees to young families and college students.

The sunny **Emerald Tea Room** (132 McKinley St., East Peoria, 309/694-1972, lunch Mon.–Sat.) in downtown East Peoria sells an array of sandwiches, soups, and teas from around the world.

Italian

Rizzi's on State (112 State St., 309/673-2500, 11 A.M.–10 P.M. Mon.–Thurs., 11 A.M.–11 P.M. Fri., 4–11 P.M. Sat.) is probably one of the best places to eat Italian food in Peoria. The res-taurant serves northern and southern Italian cuisine.

Bar and Grills

Kelleher's Irish Pub and Eatery (619 S.W. Water St., Peoria, 309/673-6000, lunch and dinner Mon.–Sat., under $10) is a festive bar and restaurant in downtown Peoria. It's espe-cially festive on Thursday and Friday nights when local bands play for free. It serves a mix of Irish and American food, and the free appetizer buffet on Thursdays always draws a crowd.

Roxy's (330 S.W. Water St., 309/676-7699) is probably as close as you'll get to the river while dining (unless you're riding on the *Spirit* *of Peoria* riverboat). It has the typical bar food (nachos, wings) with a few nice surprises such as walleye sandwiches. This place manages to be everything to everyone. It has a kids' menu, but after 10 P.M. the DJ starts spinning and it's a bit different scene. The bar is stocked with a fair amount of domestic and imported beers. It's open 11 A.M.–2 A.M. Sunday–Wednesday, 11 A.M.–4 A.M. Thursday–Saturday May 1–Memorial Day. It opens at 3 P.M. Monday–Tuesday, and opens at 11 A.M. Wednesday–Sunday after Labor Day. Closed Sunday in February and November.

Seafood
Jonah's Seafood and Oyster Bar (2601 N. Main St., East Peoria, 309/694-0946, lunch and dinner Mon.–Sat., $10) is another New Orleans–inspired restaurant. As you look out on the river, try some oysters on the half shell, a poor boy sandwich, or, the place's pride and joy, crawfish étouffee. This is another restaurant with a well-stocked bar.

GETTING THERE AND AROUND
Air
Several airlines service the **Greater Peoria Regional Airport** (6100 W. Everett McKinley Dirksen Pkwy., Peoria, 309/697-8272, www.flypia.com). They include American Connection to St. Louis, Missouri, American Eagle to Chicago and Dallas/Fort Worth, United Express to Chicago, Delta Connection to Atlanta, Georgia, Northwest Airlink to Minneapolis, Minnesota, and Allegiant Air to Las Vegas, Nevada, and Orlando, Florida. The airport is on the west side of town near I-474.

Car and Bus
Hertz (309/676-0650) and **Enterprise** (309/633-2200) have rental cars at the airport. In addition, there are **Avis Rent a Car** (500 Hamilton Blvd., 309/673-3081) and **Dollar Rent-A-Car** (200 N.E. Jefferson St., 309/674-2277).

For a taxicab, you can call **Peoria Yellow Checker Cab** (107 Cass St., Peoria, 309/676-0731).

Public transportation is provided by **Citylink** (309/676-4040, www.ridecitylink.org). A one-way bus ride costs $1.

INFORMATION
Your first stop for attractions, dining, or lodging information should be the **Riverfront Visitors Center** (110 N.E. Water St., Peoria, 309/672-2860 or 866/896-6853), just off I-74 and on the riverfront. Run by the **Peoria Convention and Visitors Bureau** (www.peoria.org), it's open 9 A.M.–5 P.M. Monday–Friday, 9 A.M.–4 P.M. Saturday, 1–5 P.M. Sunday May–September. It's open until 4 P.M. Saturday and occasionally on Sunday October–April,.

Media
The *Peoria Journal Star* (1 News Plaza, Peoria, 309/686-3000, www.pjstar.com) is published daily and sold throughout the region.

SERVICES
Tours
Carriage Classics (309/579-2833) offers horse-drawn carriage rides through downtown Peoria Tuesday–Saturday evenings. It'll pick up riders at Pere Marquette Hotel and on the riverfront landing. Cost is $20 per couple.

The Peoria Historical Society and Citylink take visitors on a narrated two-hour **trolley tour** (309/688-5668, www.ridecitylink.org) of the city on a renovated trolley. Tours run May–October. Cost is $8 per person.

The paddlewheel boat *Spirit of Peoria* (100 N.E. Water St., 309/636-6166), docked on the riverfront, offers a variety of tours for visitors. (For more information see *Sights.*)

NORTH OF PEORIA
Peoria Heights
At the tail end of Grandview Drive you'll come out onto Prospect Road and downtown Peoria Heights, a quiet, well-to-do suburb. Downtown the main attraction is **Tower Park,** just off Prospect Road. A 170-foot-tall water tower

has been outfitted as an observational tower. Take the elevator up to several decks and peek through the telescope for more views of Peoria and the Illinois River valley.

In a cottage just off the main drag, Prospect Road, **Leaves and Beans Roasting Co.** (4800 N. Prospect Rd., Peoria Heights, 309/688-7685, www.leavesnbeans.com, 7 A.M.–5 P.M. Mon.–Fri., 7 A.M.–3 P.M. Sat., $7) is a welcoming café where the staff roast their own beans. As a result, the coffee is just spectacularly fresh. Although you'll be quite pleased with a regular cup of coffee, Leaves and Beans also offers a ton of flavored and blended coffee drinks, plus milk shakes. A few sandwiches, such as smoked turkey panini and chicken salad, are also available.

Wine Country and French Toast (4600 N. Prospect Rd., Peoria Heights, 309/686-0234, 5–10 P.M. Tues.–Thurs., 5–11 P.M. Fri.–Sat., $15) is an upscale French restaurant and gourmet food and wine shop in downtown Peoria Heights. With its subdued lighting, white tablecloths, gourmet foods, and impressive wine selection, the restaurant is the place to go to celebrate an event or if you like to treat yourselves to fine French food, such as imported cheeses, rack of lamb, pork loin, and homemade ice cream.

Rock Island State Trail

One of many rails-to-trails projects in the state, the Rock Island State Trail follows the path of the former Peoria and Rock Island Railroad. From Alta in Peoria County to Toulon in Stark County, the trail etches a path through prairie and woods for 26 miles. Pedal along past creeks, over the Spoon River, and through small towns such as Wyoming, Princeville, and Dunlap, where you'll come upon Green View Nursery, an extensive nursery, and north of Alta off Fox Road is the Kickapoo Creek Recreation Area, home to a restored prairie. The trail is accessible in several places, including near the Williams Street Depot in Wyoming off Highway 17, by Parks School Road in Dunlap, and at the Peoria-Stark county line at North Cedar Bluff Road. The trail headquarters is at 311 East Williams Street, Wyoming, 309/695-2228, www.dnr.state.il.us.

Chillicothe

About 10 miles north of Peoria is the small riverfront town of Chillicothe. **Three Sisters Park** (17189 Hwy. 29, south side of Chillicothe, across from the Illinois River, 866/278-8837) is a 400-acre park donated to the city from three sisters. The site includes a white vintage farmhouse, a big red barn made to resemble barns built in the early 1900s, a butterfly garden with a gazebo, and a handful of fruit trees. The park hosts a bluegrass festival in early June.

EAST OF PEORIA
Morton

At the hilarious **Punkin Chuckin'** in Morton at the end of October, participants see how far they can shoot pumpkins using slingshot-type of contraptions and heavy-duty air cannons. Their targets? Stuff rescued from junkyards: beat-up cars, old refrigerators. All the while visitors dine on pumpkin doughnuts and pumpkin pie. There's usually an admission fee of a few bucks per car. Morton, by the way, calls itself the pumpkin capital of the world because 85 percent of the world's pumpkins are processed here. The town also holds a more traditional pumpkin festival in September with food tents, carnival rides, a parade, and other activities. For more information about the festival or Punkin Chuckin,' contact the Morton Chamber of Commerce (888/765-6588, www.pumpkincapital.com).

WEST OF PEORIA
Canton

Once home to plow manufacturers, a cigar factory, and coal mines, the Canton area is now a comfortable suburb of Peoria, about 30 miles southwest of the city. Make the trip out here to visit the Palm Café.

Accommodations and Food

The two best lodging options in Canton are the **Heritage Grand Inn Hotel** (1150 E. Linn St.,

Canton, 309/647-9675 or 800/338-6050), a locally owned modern hotel that features hotel rooms containing non–cookie-cutter furniture. We're talking pine headboards and cabinets. The rooms aren't fancy (no in-room coffeemakers), but they are clean and the staff there is friendly. Free continental breakfast is included. Rooms are $52–119.

The **Landmark Inn** (1060 N. Main St., Canton, www.landmarkinnofcanton.com), a bed-and-breakfast on the north end of Canton, has four rooms available, each decorated with a different theme, from the seashore-themed Cape Cod and Florida rooms to the Southwest room. Two have private baths; the other two share a bathroom. Rooms are $69–82 per night.

The **Palm Café** (101 E. Elm St., Canton, 309/647-2233, dinner Wed.–Sat., $15) is one of those places that makes you willing to travel great distances to enjoy a meal there. Transplants from the Northwest, chef

Heidi Wilner and her husband, Gary Leese, the host, opened this intimate restaurant in the late 1990s within the restored Canton House Hotel. With its slate floors, windows looking out on the Canton street scene (not much, but mood-setting nonetheless), and subdued lighting, it's a beautiful restaurant with great food. The menu changes often, but you can expect such entrées as pan-seared duck breast with apricot sauce or grilled pork chops with bourbon mustard glaze. Don't skip desserts. Previously served dishes have included the jaw-dropping mocha pot and apple bread pudding with rum butter sauces.

The casual, family-friendly **Geppetto's** (47 S. Main St., Canton, 309/649-0240, www.cantongeppettos.com, $7) serves toasty meatball sandwiches, thin and pan pizza, plus the usual Italian pasta fare such as linguine with clam sauce and tortellini. The food is good and prices are reasonable, plus it features imported Italian beer.

The Imperial Valley and Vicinity

With the Spoon River to the northwest, the Sangamon River to the east, and the Illinois River in between, the Imperial Valley region, as it is often referred to, is home to many fruit and vegetable farms where crops such as pumpkins and watermelon are grown. The towns along this stretch of the Illinois River are small, quiet, rural. And in between are large, primarily rustic, local, state, and national wildlife areas, home to eagles, herons, and other waterfowl and animals. The roads that run through here are wandering, two-lane highways. Highway 100 and U.S. 24 follow the west side of the river connecting Beardstown to Havana. On the east side is Highway 78.

LEWISTOWN AND HAVANA
Dickson Mounds
On a bluff overlooking the Illinois River, Dickson Mounds (10956 N. Dickson Mounds Rd., Lewistown, 309/547-3721, www.museum.state.il.us, 8:30 A.M.–5 P.M. daily, free) is a 230-acre site where a Native American mound-building culture lived about 1,500 years ago. Unlike the Cahokia Mounds near Collinsville and East St. Louis, these mounds are in a more rural area. They were discovered in 1927 when the area was a farm. Landowner Don Dickson removed the dirt of the mounds, left the bones there, covered the area with a tent (and later a building), and then charged people admission to visit the archaeological site. Eventually he sold the land to the state of Illinois, which later added more buildings and a museum. The museum has several floors of exhibits about the Illinois River valley geography and its history going back thousands of years. There are extensive displays about the Native Americans who lived in the Illinois River valley and the Mississippi River mounds culture. Don't forget to walk out onto the third-floor observation deck. From there you can see the Larson site, the site of another mound village that's

Great River Valleys

Chautauqua National Wildlife Refuge on the Illinois River

now a picnic area. The Eveland Village site, also on the grounds, shows excavated remains of a village. And the Ogden-Fettie site, on the south end of the park, has more mounds.

Another Native American historical site, the **Rockwell Mound** (N. Orange and Franklin Sts., Havana, 309/543-6240) is near the town of Havana. At about 14 feet high and two acres in size, it's one of the largest in the area. The Rockwell Mound dates to about A.D. 200.

Chautauqua National Wildlife Refuge

Eight miles north of Havana on the Illinois River is the beautiful Chautauqua National Wildlife Refuge (19031 E. County Rd. 2110N, Havana, 309/535-2290, free), home to about 250,000 waterfowl and 10,000 shorebirds. With that said, it's a great, great spot for bird-watching. It's in the middle of the Mississippi River Flyway, and migratory birds such as Canada geese and trumpeter swans drop by often for a visit, especially in the backwater lakes. Bald eagles nest here from late fall to early spring. What else can you see? Great blue herons, egrets, and wood ducks. The entire site is about 6,200 acres with backwater

lakes, wetlands, and bottomland forest. If you want to take a boat out onto one of the backwater lakes, you can launch it from the ramps at Eagle Bluff Access Area. You can also park your car there and explore 12 miles of levee roads on the back of your bike. Otherwise, the refuge headquarters (on County Rd. 2110N) has a short wheelchair-accessible nature trail, where you may also see more wildlife.

Nearby, just east of Highway 78 and north of Havana, is **Emiquon** and the Merwin Preserve at **Spunky Bottoms,** sites owned and managed by The Nature Conservancy. Most of Emiquon is farmland, created by draining wetlands and clearing woodlands. However, the conservancy along with governmental agencies is working to restore the area to wetlands and build a diverse habitat. Access is prohibited because of the restoration work ongoing there.

Sand Ridge State Forest

North of Chautauqua is Sand Ridge State Forest (accessible from County Rd. 2300N or 2500N, Forest City, 309/597-2212), another huge park on the east side of the river. The 7,200-acre park is full of sandy prairies and native oak-hickory forest and pine plantations. The pines were planted by members of the Civilian Conservation Corps to control erosion. This is a working forest; pine trees are still felled here. In the sand prairie areas you'll come across plants normally found in the American Southwest such as prickly pear cactus. (Yes, cacti grow in Illinois.) The sandy areas were created thousand of years ago when the Kankakee torrent flooded the region as a glacier melted. The flood was followed by a long dry and windy period when 100-foot-high dunes formed at the base of ridges in the park.

The park has a staggering 44 miles of hiking trails, ranging about 1.5–17 miles. There are also numerous fire lanes, which are rustic roads that you can drive or bike along. Pine Campground has 27 sites with pit toilets. Plus there are 12 sites scattered throughout the park near the hiking trails for people interested in backpack campsites. You'll need a permit to camp in the primitive sites. Also, there's a huge fish hatchery on the north side of the forest. It stocks many of the lakes in the state.

downtown Havana

© CHRISTINE DES GARENNES

Downtown Havana and Lewistown

While you're in the area, take a few minutes to stroll downtown Havana and Lewistown, small river towns with a few craft stores, antiques shops, and bar and grills.

Information

The **Fulton County Tourism Council** (700 E. Oak St., Canton, 309/647-6074, www.fultoncountytourism.org) publishes a brochure listing annual events and lodging and dining options.

Camp Ellis

After the Japanese attacked Pearl Harbor on December 7, 1941, and the United States entered World War II, the Army bought 17,500 acres in southwestern Fulton County to build a Army service unit training camp. The Army demolished farm buildings, built a railroad, landing strip, and dozens of buildings. Before closing in 1945, about 125,000 Army personnel trained at Camp Ellis. It also served as a prison

for prisoners of war. This is a place in Illinois you don't hear about often. The buildings are now piles of bricks and concrete blocks and most of the area has been returned to farmland. But it may interest historians, particularly World War II buffs. The area is north of U.S. 136 near the tiny towns of Ipava and Table Grove. Along the route you'll see Dobbins Cemetery, where some German prisoners were buried, and old baseball diamonds. More information is available from the Dickson Mounds Museum or Fulton County Tourism Council.

BEARDSTOWN

Beardstown lies along a bend in the Illinois River. That bend, Mascouten Bay, was once quite popular for boating and fishing and the town was often a stopping point for steamers and other river boats. But silt deposits, erosion, and other problems have caused sediment to build up and slow river traffic. Once famous

Great River Valleys

© CHRISTINE DES GARENNES

site of Lincoln's "Almanac Trial" in Beardstown

for its duck hunting and fishing opportunities, Beardstown is now probably known more for the Beardstown Ladies Investment Club, whose members garnered national attention in the 1990s because of their profitable stock picks on Wall Street. (They have three meetings per year that members of the public can attend in February, June, and October.) But Beardstown is also a stopping point for travelers following in the steps of Abraham Lincoln.

Sights and Activities

Old City Hall and Courthouse (101 W. 3rd St., Beardstown, 217/323-3225, 10 A.M.–4 P.M. Mon.–Sat., donation) is where Lincoln defended a murderer in the famous Almanac Trial in 1858. In addition to a room set up like it may have been organized in 1858, the old courthouse building also contains a collection of Civil War guns, arrowheads, antique tools, and models of paddlewheel boats.

More model riverboats are on display at the **Beardstown River Museum** (101 W. 3rd St., Beardstown, 217/323-3271, www.beards townil.org), a small museum housed in the Beardstown Chamber of Commerce and Visi-

tors Center. Exhibits illustrate life and work in a river town such as Beardstown. (Check out the big ice-cutting saws.) Plus, there are displays about the Beardstown Ladies. You can buy copies of their investment guide-books here.

Take in the sights of the river at the Beardstown River Look, an observation platform, at State Street near the river.

Information

Got questions about Beardstown lodging or dining? Contact the **Beardstown Chamber of Commerce** (121 S. State St., Beardstown, 217/323-3271, www.beardstownil.org).

CHANDLERVILLE

Sanganois Conservation Area

The Illinois River floodplain between Peoria and Beardstown is marshy, with a lot of sloughs and bottomland forests. North of Beardstown, the **Sanganois Conservation Area** (3594 County Rd. 200 N, Chandlerville, 309/546-2628, www.dnr.state.il.us, free), on the east side of the Illinois River and west of the Sangamon River, is a huge, 11,000-acre site. Like Chautauqua National Wildlife Area, this area is rustic and loaded with hiking and bird-watching opportunities. Walk, bike, or drive along the 18.5 miles of levee roads, past willow and black walnut trees, and creatures such as ducks, beavers, turtles, osprey, and bald eagles. Once a private duck-hunting club, the Sanganois Conservation Area is still often visited by waterfowl hunters. It's also prone to flooding. If you visit in the winter or spring, call to check if any access roads are closed because of flooding.

Jim Edgar Panther Creek State Fish and Wildlife Area

The parks in the Illinois River valley just seem to get bigger and bigger. At 16,500 acres and 26 square miles, Jim Edgar Panther Creek State Fish and Wildlife Area (10149 County Hwy. 11, Chandlerville, 217/452-7741, www.dnr.state.il.us, free) is one of the largest in the state. Formerly called Site M (in reference to utility company and former landowner Commonwealth Edison's name for it), the area was once targeted to be the location for a coal power plant. That never happened and the state eventually bought the land. The site has all kinds of land, from farms to meadows to forests. Deer and pheasant are common sights. The park is also home to hawks, bluebirds, frogs, and turtles. The lady's slipper orchid, an Illinois endangered species, has been found here. Because the park was purchased and developed in the 1990s, buildings and trails are fairly new. About 24 miles of rough trails carve paths through woody ravines, hilly prairie, and past sunflower and wheat fields. There are three main hiking loops. The Governor's Trail, the northernmost trail, and the middle trail, the Yellow Trail, have several scenic overlooks above Panther Creek. You can get to either the Red or Yellow Trail at the South Trailhead off South Reed Road. A three-mile hiking, walking, or jogging trail winds around Gridley Lake. There are three lakes—Gridley Lake, Prairie Lake, and Drake Lake—where you can launch a fishing boat, canoe, or sailboat. Prairie Lake is the largest at 210 acres.

If you dig quiet, rustic campsites, the park has walk-in sites about one-quarter of a mile from a parking lot. Dozens of other sites with modern shower facilities and electrical hookups are also available. If you didn't pack along any camping gear, you can rent a tent for $8–12. The rent-a-tent package actually includes much more than a tent, but also a camp light, broom and dust pan, and fire extinguisher. The tent fee is in addition to a $5 utility fee. The park also has nine cabins available for rent for $40 per night. Accommodations are rustic (no bathroom or air-conditioning), with two bunk beds and a full bed. But they do have ceiling fans and an electric heater for chilly nights. Outside are decks and picnic tables. You will need to make reservations for the tents and.

MEREDOSIA

On the banks of the Illinois River, the quiet river town of Meredosia is a good spot for eagle-scouting in the winter. The town hosts an eagle-watching festival in mid-January. During the event you can watch a live raptor show in the local high school, attend a workshop about eagles, tour the river museum, and of course scout for eagles.

One of the best spots to look for eagles is in or near the **Meredosia National Fish and Wildlife Refuge** (309/535-2290), a 3,000-plus-acre refuge north of town along the river and Lake Meredosia. In and around Meredosia, you'll notice that the Illinois is a working river. There are grain elevators and shipping points, and coal and oil-fired power stations. But this refuge offers a relief from that scene. Just north of the town is an observation platform off Beach Road, where you can look for eagles. A short trail through some pine trees leads you to a wooden deck tucked into the bottomland forests of the river and Lake Meredosia. Follow signs to the trail and viewing platform from Highway 104 from downtown Meredosia.

While you're in town, stop by the small **Meredosia River Museum** (305 Main St., Meredosia, 217/584-1356, donations), which has a few display cases of arrowheads, videos

Great River Valleys

Meredosia National Fish and Wildlife Refuge, on the Illinois River

and books about eagles, plus a tiny but eye-opening display about the fur-trading business, including traps and stretch boards for furs. It's open 1–4 P.M. Friday in summer; noon–4 P.M. Saturday in winter.

Meredosia saved its old 1882 train depot from demolition and you can drive by to take a look at it. It's on the south side of the river off Montgomery Street.

Jacksonville

Jacksonville is a town for history and architecture buffs. It's not a booming metropolis, but it once was and it has a number of surprises, such as the excellent coffee shop Due Gatti and the restaurant Mugsy's. If you love big old homes, brick streets, and towering oak and elm trees, take a drive through the historic neighborhoods in Jacksonville. Meander down State Street and East College Avenue. You'll notice this is a town focused on education. Illinois College was established in 1829 in part by Harriet Beecher Stowe's brother, Edward Beecher, who was the college's first president. (The college was considered a center for abolitionism.) On the east side of town is MacMurray College, founded in 1846 as the Illinois Conference Female Academy. But wait, there's more. The Illinois School for the Deaf, Illinois School for the Visually Impaired, and Jacksonville Mental Health and Developmental Center were all built here. During the Civil War, Ulysses S. Grant and his Illinois division of troops camped in an area of Jacksonville that is now part of the Morgan County Fairgrounds. And William Jennings Bryan and Stephen Douglas practiced law here.

SIGHTS

Underground Railroad

The town of Jacksonville was a stop along the Underground Railroad for many blacks escaping from the South. Several families in the area provided shelter, food, and other necessities for

A Jacksonville man developed the modern-day Ferris wheel; here's one of his first creations.

Ave.) is Big Eli No. 17, the 17th Ferris wheel built by the Eli Bridge Company in 1907. The company is credited with building the first portable Ferris wheel in 1900, which made its debut in Jacksonville. (The original Ferris wheel, introduced to the world at the World's Fair in Chicago in 1893, was much, much larger at 264 feet tall.) W. E. Sullivan wanted to scale it down. Townspeople moved the wheel to the park in the late 1950s. Eli Bridge still is in the business of building wheels and other carnival rides. Ever taken a spin on the Scrambler? That's an Eli Bridge Company invention.

In addition to the wheel, in the middle of the park you'll find two ornate, Victorian-style bandstands that are more than 130 years old. Nearby are a few picnic benches if you want to take a break.

Art Gallery

Donated to the city's arts association, this stately brick mansion houses the **David Strawn Art Gallery** (331 W. College Ave., Jacksonville, 217/243-9390, Sept.–May). It showcases local and nationally known artists, plus a permanent collection of antique dolls and Native American pottery.

ACCOMMODATIONS

Basically, if you're going to stay in Jacksonville, you're going to stay in a chain hotel near I-72 and U.S. 67. Your best bet is the 72-room **Comfort Inn** (200 Comfort Dr., South Jacksonville, 217/245-8372) or the 41-room **Super 8** (1003 W. Morton Ave., Jacksonville, 217/479-0303), which is on the west side of town.

FOOD

American

Imagine an antique unicycle hanging on a brick wall, a vintage model airplane dangling from the ceiling, and photos of Elvis Presley. Throw in a few local ladies celebrating a birthday in the back and a couple of guys watching an Illini basketball game at the bar. That's the scene at **M Mugsy's** (230 Mauvaisterre, Jacksonville,

escaped slaves as they made their way north from the 1830s through the Civil War. You can drive by or tour the inside of some of these homes. Perhaps the best Underground Railroad site is the Woodlawn Farm east of town, recently purchased by the Morgan County Historical Society. It plans to convert it to a living-history museum and now hosts tours and events throughout the year. You can also drive by other homes in the area said to have been stops along the railroad, including the Talcott Home (859 Grove St., Jacksonville); Gillett Home (1005 Grove St., Jacksonville); and Clay Home (1019 W. State St., Jacksonville). For a tour, contact the Morgan County Historical Society's Underground Railroad Committee (217/243-3755, www.woodlawnfarm.com) or the Jacksonville Area Convention and Visitors Bureau.

Community Park

In the northeast corner of Jacksonville's **Community Park** (U.S. 67/Main St. and Morton

217/245-0641, 11 A.M.–9 P.M. Tues.–Thurs.,
11 A.M.–10 P.M. Fri.–Sat.), a cozy restaurant
just off Jacksonville's town square. From outside, the place looks a little fancy, but inside
it's casual and upbeat. The food is comforting,
with beer cheese soup, pub pickles (breaded
and fried pickle spears), and entrées such as
blackened chicken, catfish fillet, and the favorite horseshoe sandwich. Prices range from
about $7 for sandwiches, $10–20 for entrées.
Mugsy's has a little patio out back.

Quick Eats

At the **Classic Diner** (100 Comfort Dr., South
Jacksonville, 217/243-9962, 6 A.M.–10 P.M.
daily) you can fill up on steak and egg com-
bos, omelettes, biscuits and gravy, and pigs in
a blanket (sausage links rolled up in pancakes).
Mmm. The restaurant is right on U.S. 67, just
north of I-72. It's not a bona fide diner, but it
certainly looks like one with shiny red, white,
and black decor and images from *Life* magazine
circa 1950. It also serves lunch and dinner.

Popular among truckers, **CR's Drive In**
(403 E. Morton Ave., Jacksonville, 217/243-
2100, call for hours, $5) has burgers for about
$3, horseshoe sandwiches, chili dogs, and apple
pie. Walk up or drive up to place your order.

Coffee and Doughnuts

Due Gatti (27 S. Central Park Plaza, Jacksonville, 217/243-9788, www.duegatticoffee.com,
8 A.M.–10 P.M. Tues.–Fri., 10 A.M.–10 P.M.
Sat., $3) is on the Jacksonville square within a
two-story building filled with vintage wooden
booths, tables, and an ornate wooden bar salvaged from an old confectionary. A few photographs of early Jacksonville street scenes
hang on the walls. Due Gatti serves smooth
cappuccinos, lattes, and other drinks. A variety of pastries and panini sandwiches are
also available.

For a quick cup of coffee and giant glazed
bear claw, drop by **The Donut Shoppe** (218
W. Morton Ave., Jacksonville, 217/243-0000),
a bare bones–type of establishment off Jacksonville's main drag of Morton Avenue.

INFORMATION

The **Jacksonville Area Convention and Visitors Bureau** (155 W. Morton St., Jacksonville,
217/243-5678 or 800/593-5678, www.jackson-
villeil.org) is in Community Park. It's open
Monday–Friday, but if you visit on a weekend,
a sign outside has a map of Jacksonville with all
the major sights highlighted on it.

Nauvoo

Standing near the gardens in front of the rebuilt Mormon Temple, you'll soon realize why
Joseph Smith and his Mormon followers chose
this area as their home in 1839. At a bend on
the east bank of the Mississippi River, the historic town of Nauvoo sits on a bluff looking
out over the river and the valley. It's a beautiful sight, and perhaps that's why Smith christened the town Nauvoo, which may or may
not mean beautiful place in Hebrew (the topic
is subject to debate). The Joseph Smith Historic Site, where Smith's home is situated along
with a dozen or so other historic homes, is in
the lower part of the town, closer to the river.
The downtown commerce area with shops,
restaurants, and lodging options, is up on the

hill near the temple. Although it's certainly
rich in Mormon history, Nauvoo also has a
past linked to wine-making and cheese-making. After you visit Mormon temple and other
sights, be sure to drive east of town to Baxter's
Vineyards and Winery. One way to see Nauvoo
is to take a horse-drawn carriage ride. You can
catch a ride 9 A.M.–4:30 P.M. Monday–Saturday year-round at the northwest corner of the
Latter-Day Saints Visitor Center.

HISTORY

Nauvoo was actually a Native American village before the Smith family and his followers
arrived in 1839. Between 1839 and 1846 the

Mormons built more than 2,000 homes here and Nauvoo became the center for the church. They started building a temple in 1841 and established the Nauvoo Legion, a state militia. Nauvoo grew into quite a thriving town, eventually attracting the attention of other Illinois towns as well as politicians. At the helm of this prosperous city was Smith, who acted as mayor, lieutenant general of the legion, justice of the peace, and several other local leadership positions.

Eventually some members grew dissatisfied and they started publishing a newspaper that was critical of Smith. The city council, under the direction of Smith, of course, called the publication a nuisance and ordered the press be demolished. Not surprisingly, the publishers filed a complaint against Smith and other members of the city council, including Joseph's brother Hyrum. Smith and the others traveled to Carthage, the county seat several miles east of Nauvoo, to respond to the claims filed against them in which the publishers stated Smith violated their Constitutional right of freedom of the press. Some of the accused posted bail and simply went home. Smith stayed at the jail to wait and talk to the governor about the situation. Later he and the others were charged with treason and citing a riot. On June 27, 1844, a group of men came to jail and shot and killed Joseph and his brother Hyrum. With their leader dead, many Mormons eventually left in the year or two that followed. Most went to Utah, some headed to Texas and Michigan. A few stayed.

Hearing that the town was nearly empty a Frenchman named Etienne Cabet decided to establish his own colony here. He and his followers, called Icarians, settled here in 1849. The colonists, mostly French and German immigrants, found the sunny hills were well suited for grape growing and they introduced wine-making into the region. But communal living didn't suit the residents and the colony disbanded a few years after they arrived. Several decades after that, residents discovered the cellars that used to store wine bottles could also be used to age cheese, and Nauvoo became somewhat of a center for cheese-making.

Joseph Smith Historic Site in Nauvoo

SIGHTS

Joseph Smith Historic Site

A good place to begin your visit in Nauvoo is by dropping by the Historic Nauvoo Visitors Center on the grounds of the Joseph Smith Historic Site (149 Water St., Nauvoo, 217/453-2246, 9 A.M.–5 P.M. Mon.–Sat., 1–5 P.M. Sun.). Here staff will be able to tell you when the next guided walking tour of the sites begins. And while waiting for the next to start, you can view a few exhibits about the history of Nauvoo and the Mormons. The center has 20-minute video that provides a good overview of the site, plus a few original Smith family pieces, including washstand and Nauvoo temple chair. Feel free to walk around the historic site yourself, but the walking tours are wonderfully narrated by members. They know their stuff and can talk endlessly about Smith and Nauvoo. On your walking tour, you'll visit Joseph Smith's homestead and the mansion house he and his family moved into after the town began to prosper. The mansion house has its original pillars and stoop. And the bedroom of Joseph and his wife, Emma, contains a bureau and mirror that belonged to them, plus a trunk with a secret compartment where Emma stored Joseph's translation of the Bible. After Joseph and his brother were killed in Carthage, their bodies were on display in the mansion and about 10,000 people came through to view them.

Next to the homestead is the **Smith Family Cemetery.** After the funeral, the coffins were actually emptied and the empty coffins were buried in a tomb near the temple. The bodies were secretly buried near the Nauvoo House, then reburied under a small building by the homestead house. Later, the construction on the Nauvoo House forced them to move the bodies. In 1928, the grandson of the Smiths hired a surveyor to find the graves and they then moved the bodies a few feet and also buried Joseph's parents in the cemetery. They're expected to stay put near the homestead house.

Throughout the site are several other beautifully restored, original brick buildings where Mormons lived and worked: Scovil Bakery, Lyon Drug Store, the post office and dry goods

The Nauvoo Illinois Temple was built on the site of the former Mormon temple.

store, Stoddard Tin Shop, a boot shop, and a gun shop. Inside these shops church members, dressed in period costumes, talk about the proprietors of the shops and explain how people used to make tin pans and candleholders, how boots were made, and so on. These stops are quite revealing about not only the early Mormons, but pioneer life in general. For example, people would write lengthwise and widthwise on the same side of a piece of paper to save money. The Red Brick Store is the only building that is a reconstruction of the original. You can barely tell. Here you can buy journals, pens, candy, and other items. It's organized just as it was more than 150 years ago, based on an old ledger that detailed what was bought and sold here.

Nauvoo Illinois Temple

In 1848, after the Mormons left town and had sold the temple, someone set the building on fire and eventually it crumbled to the ground. About 150 years later the church decided to rebuild it and the Nauvoo Illinois Temple (Mulholland and Wells Sts., Nauvoo, 217/453-6252, free) was dedicated in June 2002. This huge, 54,000-square-foot limestone building stands on the western edge of downtown Nauvoo looking west. On the site of the former temple, this temple is a working one. The church performs baptisms here and holds other church-related activities. You won't be able to tour the inside of the temple, but you can view a video and pictures of it in the visitors center. Only members of the church who receive a recommendation to visit can see the inner sanctum. The center is open 9 A.M.–6 P.M. Monday–Saturday, 11 A.M.–5 P.M. Sunday May–August, 9 A.M.–5 P.M. Monday–Saturday 12:30–5 P.M. Sunday September–April.

Nauvoo State Park

East of the Joseph Smith Historic Site and south of the downtown is the 150-acre Nauvoo State Park (Hwy. 96 and Parley St., Nauvoo, 217/453-2512, www.dnr.state.il.us). In the center is a brick home built by a Mormon family in the 1840s, later occupied by a French Icarian family. This building now houses the Nauvoo State Park Museum, which has exhibits about the area's wine-making past. In 1880 there were about 40 wine cellars and 600 acres of grapevines in the area. The oldest vine still around (it's a Concord grapevine) was planted in 1851 and it is just behind the house. It's still producing grapes. A tour of the house and environs includes a visit to a room where the Icarians pressed grapes and a cellar where wine was stored. You can see the exhibits and tour the home, including the wine cellar 1–5 P.M. daily May 15–October 15.

There is one trail through the park about 1.5 miles in length. Most of it follows the shoreline of Lake Horton, a 13-acre, man-made lake. It's a quiet lake; only boats with electric trolling motors are allowed. You can fish from the shores for catfish, bass, and bluegill. The park also has a campground.

Held during Labor Day weekend, when the grapes are ripening, the **Nauvoo Grape Festival** (Nauvoo State Park, 217/453-6648) is a three-day festival celebrating the region's wine heritage. The festival's main event is called the "Wedding of the Wine and Cheese," modeled after a traditional French pageant. As expected there are wine tastings, a grape stomp, and plenty of food tents. Other activities include a car show, carnival, arts and craft show, and the tradition of almost every Midwestern festival: pancake breakfasts.

Baxter's Vineyards and Winery

Less than a mile east of the state park on a bucolic country road are more vineyards. Baxter's Vineyards and Winery (2010 E. Parley St., Nauvoo, 217/453-2528 or 800/854-1396, www.nauvoowinery.com, 9 A.M.–5 P.M. Mon.–Sat.) is the oldest winery in Illinois. It was founded by Emile Baxter, who was part of the Icarian colony. He and his family remained in the area after the colony disbanded. Eventually his sons joined him in the wine-making business and his descendents are still involved in the venture. Here they make wine and juice from Concord grapes, plus wines from several other grape varieties. They offer free tours and wine tastings and sell accessories such as wine racks, wine glasses, and wine-making supplies for people interested in starting a new hobby. They also sell homemade pies and other baked goods in the main winery building.

ACCOMMODATIONS

$50–100

N Ellis Sanders (1285 Sidney St., Nauvoo, 888/253-2444, www.ellissandershouse.com) is a circa-1844 red brick Federalist home on a hill above Nauvoo State Park and the Joseph Smith Historic Site. One of the owners' great-grandfather was a Mormon who lived in Nauvoo before moving out west. The owners offer evening dessert served by candlelight and serve a four-course breakfast at 9 A.M., but you can have a continental breakfast earlier if you request it. Drinking alcohol is not permitted. There are two bedrooms available.

As the name implies, **Nauvoo Family Inn and Suites** (1875 Mulholland St./Hwy. 96, Nauvoo, 217/453-6527, 800/416-4470, www.nauvoonet.com) is geared toward large families that travel, and you'll find plenty of extended families staying here while touring through Nauvoo. (If you want to avoid children, this is not the place to go.) It's a newer hotel with a faux historic facade that fits well with the brick, Federalist-style architecture common in the area. The 136-room hotel has family suites that contain one, two, or three bedrooms. Rooms are big, and some contain extras such as minirefrigerators and microwaves. The extra large "Family 7 and Family 12" units come with full-size refrigerators and kitchenettes if you're planning to stay in town for a long time or are with a group of seven or 12 people.

Built in 1841, the slate-blue **N Hotel Nauvoo** (1290 Mulholland St., Nauvoo, 217/453-2211, www.hotelnauvoo.com) is considered a Mormon Prairie-style building. The front porch and second-story balcony overlook Nauvoo's main drag of Mulholland Street. The hotel has eight rooms, most of them with one queen bed. Prices can range from $50 for a

room with a full bed to $109 for a family suite that sleeps eight people. All come with private baths and are decorated with country touches such as quilts. It's attached to a restaurant.

Just down the street is the **Motel Nauvoo** (1610 Mulholland St., Nauvoo, 217/453-2219) which has similar, but cheaper accommodations on the lower end of this price category. It also has a mix of room styles, from one queen to two queens.

Riverview Guest Home (1981 Hwy. 96, Nauvoo, 217/453-6556 night or 217/453-9980 day) is about five miles south of downtown Nauvoo on the Great River Road. Choose from two lodging options. The Riverview Guest Home, a white renovated cottage, has two full beds, plus one queen, a sitting area, loft area, and kitchen. It can sleep up to six people. Nearby, the carriage house, which is above a garage, sleeps 4–6 people. It's smaller but has views of the river.

Camping

Nauvoo State Park has 150 sites for tent and RV camping. The best sites are those near the shore of Lake Horton. There's a small boat launch, picnic areas, playgrounds, and a 1.5-mile walking trail. Fees are $13–15 per night.

FOOD

There are several rooms where diners can eat at the **Hotel Nauvoo** (1290 Mulholland St., Nauvoo, 217/453-2211, www.hotelnauvoo.com, dinner Mon.–Sat., brunch Sun., $12), which is much like a big, historic home. The dinner buffet, a popular option, features carved roast beef, catfish, steamed vegetables, muffins, and homemade bread. The buffet runs about $12 per person. Other options include sugar-glazed ham and fried shrimp. There is a small bar that serves wine, beer, and mixed drinks. Spirited hot and cold drinks are also a good way to finish a meal. The staff can whip up grasshoppers (creme de menthe and creme de cocoa) or Irish coffees. The restaurant is closed in the winter.

Downtown Nauvoo is lined with several casual restaurants. Each serves standard American sandwiches such as turkey clubs and hamburger and french-fry meals for under $10. You can't go wrong with any of these for lunch spots: **Nauvoo Mill and Bakery** (1530 Mulholland St., Nauvoo, 217/453-6734, 8 A.M.–5 P.M. Mon.–Sat., 11 A.M.–5 P.M. Sun.); **Past Times** (1390 Mulholland St., 217/453-2050, 7–10 P.M. daily); and **Grandpa John's Café** (1255 Mulholland St., Nauvoo, 217/453-2310 breakfast, lunch, and dinner Mon.–Sat., brunch Sun.).

INFORMATION

The **Historic Nauvoo Visitor Center** on the grounds of the Joseph Smith Historic Site (Young and Hubbard Sts., Nauvoo, 888/453-6434) is run by the Community of Christ, an offshoot of the Church of Jesus Christ of Latter-day Saints. It's open 8 A.M.–9 P.M. Monday–Saturday May–August, 10:30 A.M.–6 P.M. Sunday May–August; 9 A.M.–6 P.M. Monday–Saturday, noon–6 P.M. Sunday September–April.

The **Nauvoo Temple Visitors Center** (on Wells St., between Mulholland and Young Sts., Nauvoo, 217/453-6844) is run by the Church of Jesus Christ of Latter-day Saints and open 9 A.M.–6 P.M. Monday–Saturday 11 A.M.–5 P.M. Sunday, May–August, 9 A.M.–5 P.M. Monday–Saturday 12:30–5 P.M. Sunday September–April.

In addition, the **Nauvoo Tourism Office** (877/NAUVOO-1 or 877/628-8661, www.beautifulnauvoo.com) has comprehensive information about attractions, lodging, dining, and events.

CARTHAGE

About 25 miles southeast of Nauvoo is the town of Carthage, a plain small town off U.S. 136. Visitors interested in learning more about the murder of Mormon founder Joseph Smith and his brother Hyrum can tour the **Carthage Jail** (Marion and Walnut Sts., Carthage, 217/357-2989, free), where, after being charged with treason, they were gunned down by a group of men on June 27, 1844. A tour of the restored jail includes a visit to the room where Joseph was killed and a look at the bed, writing desk, and rocking chair that Joseph used during his stay in the jail. Outside the jail is a garden with a statue of the two brothers. Hours are 8 A.M.–9 P.M. Monday–Saturday, 11 A.M.–6 P.M. Sunday in summer; 9 A.M.–5 P.M. Monday–Saturday, 12:30–5 P.M. Sunday in winter.

Quincy and Vicinity

Perched on bluffs above the Mississippi River, Quincy is a quintessential river town with a historic downtown and city square surrounded by tall brick and sandstone buildings and tree-lined residential neighborhoods with brick-lined streets. Originally a Sauk Indian village, Quincy was a boomtown in the 19th century after it became a decent-size port on the river. It attracted European immigrants and Americans from the Northeast, including abolitionists. In 1858 Lincoln and Douglas met in Quincy to debate the subject of slavery, quite the controversial topic because just on the other side of the river was Missouri, which allowed slavery. Today Quincy is a midsized town of about 40,000 people, a small liberal arts school, Quincy University, and a number of architecturally interesting sites, including a Moorish villa and grand Romanesque home, and a museum entirely devoted to river-town architecture.

SIGHTS
Museums
The **Gardner Museum of Architecture and Design** (332 Maine St., Quincy, 217/224-6873, www.gardnermuseumarchitecture.org) has been open since 1977, but the building itself, an awesome limestone

view of the Mississippi River from Quincy

Richardson Romanesque building, was built 1888–1889 and was home to the Quincy Public Library. The museum's focus is on the architecture and design characteristics of Mississippi River towns such as Quincy. Permanent exhibits highlight historic buildings that once stood or are still standing in Quincy and there are useful displays that explain, to novices, the different types of building materials and styles. The library's former reading room is a must-see. The room, which has a vaulted ceiling more than 20 feet high, has a beautiful stained-glass exhibit showcasing glass pieces salvaged from churches long gone. Galleries are open 1–4 P.M. Wednesday–Sunday, store and library are open 9 A.M.–5 P.M. Monday–Friday.

Illinois Veterans Home and All Wars Museum (1701 N. 12th St., Quincy, 9 A.M.–noon, 1–4 P.M. Tues.–Sat., 1–4 P.M. Sun., donation) has thousands of military artifacts, including uniforms, medals, patches, and some artillery from as far back as the Civil War to the current war in Iraq.

In a huge 1891 Romanesque stone mansion, the **Quincy Museum** (1601 Maine St., Quincy, 217/224-7669, www.thequincymu-seum.com, 1–5 P.M. Tues.–Sun., $2) has several floors of local-history displays and exhibits for children, including a *Tyrannosaurus rex* and other dinosaur replicas and an Indian village. You'll also be able to tour some of the mansion's grand rooms, including the den and parlor, where you'll be able to glimpse some of the intricate woodwork and other details.

The Jesus Tree

You know how sometimes oak trees have protruding growths from their trunks? That look like humps or giant tree warts? Well, a big old oak tree in the middle of a Quincy cemetery happens to have one of these growths, along with some discolored bark. It's known as the Jesus Tree or Apparition Tree (Calvary Cemetery, 1730 N. 18th St., Quincy). Some believe the image of Jesus Christ is on that tree. If you step back and turn your head just so, and squint your eyes, it does look a little like a man with a beard in a robe. Unfortunately, as the years go by, the hump continues to grow and as one resident put it, "It doesn't look so much so anymore since the growth has gotten bigger." The tree is in the

COURTESY OF QUINCY AREA CONVENTION AND VISITOR'S BUREAU

The famous "Jesus in a tree," or just another big bump in a tree?

middle of the cemetery; it's one of the biggest ones.

Parks

While they were both campaigning for the U.S. Senate, Abraham Lincoln and Stephen A. Douglas met in Quincy's **Washington Park** (bordered by 4th, 5th, Main, and Hampshire streets) on October 13, 1858, to debate slavery, among many other topics. A Laredo Taft sculpture marks the site.

Looking for a place to picnic? North of downtown Quincy in the Mississippi River is **Quinsippi Island** (Front and Cedar streets). To get there you'll have to cross a one-lane plank bridge. The island has several picnic areas, a playground, and log cabins moved here from around Adams County.

Historic Homes

Villa Katherine (532 Gardner Expy./3rd St., Quincy, 217/224-3688, by appointment, free)

looks as if it would fit in Morocco, not Quincy. This majestic-looking estate is on a bluff overlooking the Mississippi. Quincy native George Metz built it in 1900 and based the design on places he had visited around the world.

The **John Wood Mansion** (425 S. 12th St., Quincy, 217/222-1835, 1–4 P.M. weekends Jan.–June and Sept.–Dec., 1–4 P.M. daily June–Aug., $3) is a good example of Greek-revival mansion, painted white and featuring several tall columns and a second-story balcony in the front. It was built for Quincy's founder, John Wood, who served as the city's mayor several terms. While he was lieutenant governor, the governor died and Wood acted as governor for 10 months in 1860. Wood did not seek the governorship after the term ran out; he chose to stay in Quincy. Also on the mansion grounds are an 1835 log cabin and a parsonage containing local-history exhibits.

ACCOMMODATIONS

Under $50

The **Ν Althoff Motel** (3511 N. 24th St., Quincy, 217/228-2460, $43) is a medium-size brick motel in a suburban area north of town. It has an indoor pool, hot tub, and offers continental breakfasts.

In Quincy's historic residential district east of downtown, the **Kaufmann House** (1641 Hampshire St., Quincy, 217/223-2502, $70) is an 1875 Queen Anne home. The bed-and-breakfast has three rooms with private baths.

The **Days Inn** (200 Maine St., Quincy, 217/223-6610, $63), a motor lodge, and the **Hampton Inn** (4th and York Sts., Quincy, 217/224-8378, $84) are within walking distance of downtown Quincy and its shops and restaurants. Both overlook the Mississippi River.

Over $50

The location may not be so great (it's in a nondescript commercial corridor east of downtown), but the **Ν Stoney Creek Inn** (217/223-2255 or 800/659-2220, www.stoneycreekinn.com, $89) has outstanding accommodations. With

Great River Valleys

THE RETURN OF THE BALD EAGLE

Illinois is somewhat of a magnet for bird-watchers, particularly people who enjoy watching birds of prey in action. Why? The Mississippi River borders the western part of the state, meaning Illinois is part of the Mississippi River Flyway. Think of it as I-95 on the Eastern Seaboard when residents of New York, Pennsylvania, and elsewhere head south to Florida for the winter. Well, eagles, ducks, snow geese, and many other birds travel along the Mississippi River during the fall and spring migrations. Some of the birds are headed south to the Gulf of Mexico or beyond. Others, such as the eagles, come down from the north and settle in Illinois for several months before heading back north when the weather warms.

For decades, bald-eagle sightings along the Mississippi River and its tributaries such as the Illinois River were rare. Thanks to hunting, pesticides such as DDT and other chemicals, populations took a nosedive. Bald eagles were placed on the endangered species list and they're making a comeback. Today you can visit parks such as Pere Marquette State Park in Grafton in the winter, stake out a spot with a view of the river, and chances are you won't have to sit long before seeing an eagle. Bald eagles tend to show up in Illinois beginning in November and will stay through late March. The peak eagle-watching time is January and February. They roost in groups, with giant nests (as big as 10 feet in diameter) high in trees. Eagles, which can weigh up to 14 pounds, have wingspans of up to almost eight feet. They're birds of prey. They hunt fish, which is why they stick to the river shores, although they will pluck up small animals to eat, too.

A few choice eagle-watching spots are the Chautauqua and Meredosia national wildlife refuges south of Peoria on the Illinois River, Mississippi Palisades State Park in Savanna, Starved Rock State Park in Utica, and Pere Marquette State Park in Grafton. Several towns and state parks host bald eagle–watching events in January in February, including Meredosia, Pere Marquette, and Starved Rock. If you don't spot an eagle on your visit, maybe you'll be able to see other birds that frequent the river and its backwaters, such as the great blue heron.

fieldstone and pine log accents throughout the building, the decor here is lodge-style. The regional chain hotel has a variety of rooms available, from the basic double to corporate suites with whirlpool tubs and family-style suites with bunk beds. The building has an exercise room and pool.

Several other bed-and-breakfasts and chain hotels are in and around Quincy. For a complete list contact the Quincy Convention and Visitors Bureau (see *Information*).

FOOD

Quick Bites

The regional fast-food chain called **Maid Rite** (507 N. 12th St., Quincy, 217/222-9767, 11 A.M.–7:30 P.M. daily, $3) got its start in Quincy in 1928. A visit here is a bit like stepping back into the past. Employees still don hair nets and white paper hats and the decor looks as if it hasn't been updated in a few decades. That's the, umm, charm of this place, along with the ground-beef sandwiches and slew of cheap food options such as fried-egg sandwiches and hot ham and cheese sandwiches. Maid Rite is reportedly the country's second-oldest franchise.

American

The **M SkyRide Inn** (236 N. Front St., Quincy, 217/222-9703, call for hours, $10) is just about the closest restaurant you can get to the river. Drop by this local hangout in the summertime for a catfish dinner and a cold beer. Then walk across the street to the riverside park and watch the barges chug by.

Italian

The divine 🍷 **Tiramisu** (137 N. 3rd St., Quincy, 217/222-9560, www.tiramisuquincy.com, 11 A.M.–2 P.M. Mon.–Fri., 5–9:30 P.M. Mon.–Sat., $12), a white-tablecloth Italian restaurant, is in a vintage building near the riverfront. The staff do everything well here, from simple sautéed spinach salad to the pastas and entrées, such as the surprisingly fresh *spaghetti arlecchino,* which is spaghetti topped with shrimp, calamari, sea scallops, mussels, clams, and tossed with olive oil, garlic, and cherry tomatoes. Individual pizzas are available at lunchtime.

Mexican

In a small strip mall, behind an auto parts store, **El Rancherito** (307 N. 36th St., Quincy, 217/228-2182, $8) may not be in a choice location, but that doesn't keep the locals from coming. The food here is billed as authentic Mexican, and it is delicious and served in hefty portions. Take your pick from fajitas, enchiladas, or burritos accompanied by fresh chips and salsa and "monster margaritas." Finally, top off the meal with a dish of deep-fried ice cream.

Chinese

The lunch and dinner buffets are popular choices at **Golden China** (1139 Broadway, Quincy, 217/224-5501, 11 A.M.–9 P.M. Sun.–Thurs., 11 A.M.–10 P.M. Fri.–Sat., $8), a semicasual restaurant on the main strip leading to downtown Quincy. Chicken, pork, beef, and tofu dishes are available, including traditional meals such as General Tso's Chicken (chicken coated with water-chestnut flour and served with hot ginger sauce), pot stickers, and wontons.

GETTING THERE AND AROUND
Air

Quincy Regional Airport (1645 Hwy. 104, Quincy, 217/885-3241, www.quincyregionalairport.com) has daily, round-trip flights aboard American Connection (the regional airline owned by American Airlines) to St. Louis International Airport.

Car

You can rent a car or truck from **Hertz** (217/885-3994) or **Budget** (217/224-7253) while in the Quincy region.

Train

Amtrak's Illinois Zephyr train travels between Quincy and Chicago daily. The station is at 30th Street and Wismann Lane, Quincy, 800/872-7245, www.amtrak.com.

INFORMATION

The **Quincy Convention and Visitors Bureau** (300 Civic Center Plaza, Quincy, 217/223-1000 or 800/987-4748, www.quincy-cvb.org) can help with any questions you have about lodging, dining, or recreational opportunities in and around Quincy.

Villa Katherine also serves as a **tourist information center.** You can pick up brochures and maps when the mansion is open. During all other times, you can park in the lot and walk to view the river from the bluff. There's a Great River Road way-finder sign with a map of the routes along the river.

Media

The daily *Quincy Herald-Whig* (130 S. 5th St., Quincy, 217/223-5100 or 800/373-9444, www.whig.com) newspaper is available at most gas stations and grocery stores.

GOLDEN

Settled mainly by German immigrants, the rural town of Golden, about 30 miles northeast of Quincy, is home to an 1873 windmill once used by the town's residents to grind corn. At one time there were several mills operating in the area, but the **Prairie Mills Windmill** (902 Prairie Mills Rd., Golden, 217/696-2360, 217/696-4678, or 217/696-2622, weekends May–Sept.) is the only one that remains. It was operational until the 1920s. Inside is a local-history museum that contains information about the windmill, farm tools, and a gift shop.

BARRY

Near a cement factory and just off I-72, the **Collver Family Winery** (2 Rooster Way, just off Hwy. 106, Barry, 217/335-3279, 10 A.M.– 5 P.M. Mon.–Wed., noon–5:30 P.M. Sun.) may not be in the most scenic of spots, but the wine is pretty good. It's known for its sweet wines, such as the Red Rooster, which has hints of plum in it. It also makes a dry red, Ramaja, which has a black-cherry flavor. There's a shop

with accessories such as glasses and wine-chilling bags, plus books on wine and cookbooks.

At **Good Scents Perfumery** (722 Bainbridge, Barry, 217/335-3244 or 800/305-4515, 10 A.M.–5 P.M. Mon.–Sat.), you can request a custom-blended perfume or order one that smells similar to a famous perfume such as Chanel No. 5. Also in the shop are candles, talcum powder, bath salts, rose hips, bath oil beads, and glycerin soap. A two-ounce bottle of cologne will cost about $18.

From Quincy to Grafton

PITTSFIELD

Accommodations and Food

Red Dome Inn and Wine Nook (109 N. Madison St., Pittsfield, 217/285-6502) is in a renovated former department store building that dates to the 1880s. With restored tin ceilings and gleaming original woodwork, it's a beautiful place to dine, something you would expect to see in Springfield, not Pittsfield, a town of about 4,500. Food is primarily American and varies from the inexpensive $3 roast beef sandwich to a $17 prime rib dinner. The Domeburger special consists of two four-ounce hamburger patties on a bun with potatoes. Try the onion rings; they're hand-cut and batter-fried. Adjacent to the restaurant is the Wine Nook, which stocks about 70 different kinds of wine, from Illinois wine (such as Collver Winery in Barry) to those from Chile and France.

Typically, small towns in Illinois have two lodging options for travelers: little bed-and-breakfasts in homes or older motel rooms off Main Street. Open since 2004, **Monroe Street Suites** (221 S. Monroe St., Pittsfield, 217/285-6129) is a real find. Rooms are immaculate and originally designed (each is different), similar to those in a bed-and-breakfast. However, the six rooms are in a renovated engraving building a few blocks from the courthouse square. It's not exactly a motel and not exactly a bed-and-breakfast. (There is no breakfast.) But

the rooms are comfortable and decorated in a lightly African theme with muted browns, maroons, tans, and yellows. Guests have use of lockers outside in the rear of the building if they come bearing fishing or hunting gear.

Harpole's Heartland Lodge

Harpole's Heartland Lodge (rural Nebo, 217/734-2526 or 800/717-4868, www.heartlandlodge.com, open Jan.–Sept.), south of Pittsfield, is, if you can imagine it, a bed-and-breakfast, hunting lodge, horseback-riding farm, and all-around country retreat. The whole place has an Up North atmosphere and attitude. It's laid-back, and people are friendly and ruddy, probably because everyone here is busy enjoying the outdoors, whether it's setting off on a guided trip to hunt for waterfowl, upland game, or deer; horseback riding, riding all-terrain vehicles, mountain biking, or, in the winter, cross-country skiing. You don't have to stay at the lodge to take a horseback ride here. Rent a horse by the hour and take off on some of the trails (there are about 40 miles of horseback-riding trails to explore.) But do think about staying here. The main lodge has several rooms with twin beds and bathrooms, plus several more luxury suites tailored to couples. These come with things such as fireplaces, decks, whirlpool tubs, and four-poster beds made of rustic pine. An overnight package typically includes dinner, a hayride, bonfire, and brunch.

Room rates are $125–250 with meals, $62.50–138 without meals. If you stay Sunday–Thursday, deduct $10 per night. Mountain bikes rent for $5 per hour; ATVs are $30 per hour; and horseback rides are $20 per hour. Hayrides are free. Fishing and hunting fees vary. If you have your own horse, you can board it here.

GRIGGSVILLE

In the center of Griggsville, a small town just off I-72, towers the 40-foot-tall "Empire State Building of the Bird World," a complex of about 600 different compartments that house up to 1,200 purple martins. Residents of Griggsville, the Purple Martin Capital of the World, just love these mosquito-eating birds. They've erected birdhouses all along Quincy Street (otherwise known as Purple Martin Boulevard) and just about everyone has a purple martin house in the front or back yard. Visit

© CHRISTINE DES GARENNES

Griggsville is the purple martin capital of the world

Griggsville April–August and you're bound to see these little birds all over the place.

Sights and Activities

Back in the 1960s, the purple martin, a member of the swallow family, was nearing the endangered species list. Birders got together and started building and buying shelters for these little guys. (The males are deep blue and black with forked tails and their heads and the tops of their wings have a purple iridescence to them. The females are light-bellied.) One of the largest manufacturers of purple martin homes is in Griggsville. At the **Nature House Showroom and Store** (Hwy. 107, Griggsville, 217/833-2323, 8 A.M.–5 P.M. Mon.–Fri.) you can buy your very own purple martin house.

The **Ray Norbut Fish and Wildlife Area** (south of County Hwy. 2, east of Griggsville, 217/833-2811, www.dnr.state.il.us), is a 1,140-acre site along the Illinois River with wetlands, fields, ravines, hills, and woodlands filled with stocky oak trees, wildflowers, and ferns. Eagles seek refuge in the bluffs in the winter. A Native American village was here around 2,000 years ago and there are some burial mounds around the park.

Food

The **Purple Martin Inn** (5:30 A.M.–8:30 P.M. Tues.–Sat., 5:30 A.M.–2 P.M. Sun.–Mon., $1.50–6.50) is the kind of place where, when you walk in and you're an out-of-towner, everyone will stop what he or she is doing and take a look at you. It's a no-frills place where food is served cheaply and quickly. An order of a short stack of pancakes costs about $2.50. Or you can load up on "Daddy Jim's Special" (two eggs, a five-ounce rib eye, potatoes, toast, and coffee), and not have to eat for the rest of the day.

KAMPSVILLE

This region's history goes way back beyond the French traders and the pioneers. And there's an excellent center where you can learn about that history.

Great River Valleys

The **Center for American Archeology** (in the Kamp General Store building, Hwy. 100, downtown Kampsville, 618/653-4316, www.caa-archeology.org, 10 A.M.–5 P.M. Tues.–Sat., noon–5 P.M. Sun., free) may be a bit off the beaten track (it's about an hour's drive from any interstate highway), but it is a gem and well worth the ride for students of history. The center dates to the 1950s. Since then archaeology students from the University of New Mexico and Northwestern University have spent their summers digging and researching and learning about the people who lived in this part of the state several thousands of years ago.

Inside a former general store (a building listed on the National Register of Historic Places and beautifully renovated), the center consists of a museum about Native American culture, a museum store, and clearinghouse of sorts for several archaeology workshops. Staff conduct a variety of workshops, from one-day to four-week programs, such as a "family dig it weekend," when parents and children visit excavation sites and learn about prehistoric culture, crafts, and more. If you don't participate in a dig, a visit to the museum is still worth it. Exhibits illustrate the history of this region (where the Illinois and Mississippi rivers meet), which the center refers to as the "Nile of North America," as well as the people who inhabited this land thousands of years ago.

Need a ride across the Illinois River? The free **Kampsville Ferry,** which operates 24 hours a day, weather permitting, shuttles cars to and from Highway 108 in Calhoun County on the east side of the river with Highway 96/100 at Kampsville on the west side.

Alton, Grafton, and Vicinity

To be honest, the East St. Louis area is not very charming. Refineries, factories, and other industrial sights line the Mississippi River and most major highways. But hang in there; head northwest toward Alton and beyond that, Grafton, and you'll be pleasantly surprised. Along the towns' main streets (often lined with Victorian and Federalist architecture), you'll discover an ice cream shop here and an antiques shop there, followed by a historic hotel, and small-scale wineries. The two-lane scenic highway Highway 100 connects Alton and Grafton with the Mississippi on one side and sandstone bluffs on the other. This is where the Mississippi River takes a turn to the east before going south again. And it's also where the Illinois River meets the Big Muddy.

Alton and Grafton are old river towns with colorful histories. French explorers Marquette and Jolliet landed here while exploring the region in the late 1600s. Lewis and Clark spent the winter of 1803–1804 south of Alton near Hartford before setting off on their journey westward. Their populations grew because of the steamboat traffic coming through here and as steel mills, glass-making factories, and quarries kick-started their operations. In the years leading up to the Civil War, Alton drew national attention after an abolitionist was killed. Just across the river from the slave state of Missouri, Alton became a common stop on the Underground Railroad for slaves escaping to the North. In 1837 Elijah Lovejoy, publisher of an antislavery newspaper in Alton, was killed defending his press from a mob that had destroyed several other presses. Later, Lincoln and Douglas squared off in a debate about slavery in the town in 1858. And during the Civil War, Alton housed thousands of Confederate prisoners of war.

Alton is the larger of the two towns, with about 30,000 people. Grafton, which is lower and closer to the river, is the more touristy of the two. Motorcyclists and RVers often stop by for a fish sandwich and ice-cream cone, and then drive or walk through nearby Pere Marquette State Park. The park, high in the hills above the river, is just north of Grafton. Book a room or campsite at this park or at least visit for the Sunday brunch.

downtown Alton

ORIENTATION

The main road through this region is Highway 100. It's part of the Great River Road, although this leg has been dubbed the Meeting of the Great Rivers Road because the Mississippi, Illinois, and Missouri converge near here. It's about 15 miles between Pere Marquette and Alton, and you can travel between the two by way of Highway 100 or the Sam Vadalabene bike trail, which follows the Mississippi. Another option is to take Highway 3 north of Grafton to Godfrey and then enter Alton from the north. Around the Grafton area there are several ferries that shuttle cars and passengers between Illinois and Missouri. They include the **Grafton Ferry Company** (618/786-3373), which goes between Grafton and the St. Charles County Airport, Missouri, the **Winfield and Golden Eagle Ferries** (618/396-2447 or 618/396-2535), which go to St. Charles County, Missouri; and the **Brussels Ferry,** which connects Highway 100 between the Grafton and Pere Marquette State Park area with the town of Brussels. St. Louis is just across the Mississippi and Missouri rivers

from Alton. That huge cable-stay bridge (part of U.S. 67) in Alton is called the Clark Bridge and it's 4,000 feet long.

SIGHTS

Lewis and Clark Interpretive Center

Before they launched their historic exploration of America's west, Meriwether Lewis and William Clark camped out near the confluence of the Illinois and Missouri rivers, called Camp River DuBois, to gather supplies, train men, and basically prepare for the trip. Before the bicentennial celebration of their journey got under way across the country, the state opened the Lewis and Clark Interpretive Center (New Poag Rd., just off Hwy. 3, Hartford, www.campdubois.com, 9 A.M.–5 P.M. Wed.–Sun., free), a few miles south of Alton. It's an impressive, 14,000-square-foot center with museum exhibits and a reproduction of the camp, complete with a wooden stockade. The most impressive item in the museum is a 55-foot keelboat replica, designed to resemble the original one used on the trip. Other exhibits explain what the

COURTESY OF THE TOURISM BUREAU SOUTHWEST ILLINOIS

at the Lewis and Clark Interpretive Center in Hartford

men and their team did while in Illinois, plus highlights from the trip. Reproductions of their journals and the drawings within them are included throughout the museum as well as highlights about the tools they used and maps they brought with them. The exhibits don't just discuss what they saw and did, but they discuss the significance of the West and what it meant to the country that Lewis and Clark went to check it all out. In addition to the museum, gift shop, bookstore, and stockade, the site has some walking trails through woods and prairie.

National Great Rivers Museum

What's the story behind the Mississippi River? How did it evolve into one of the most important rivers if not the most important river in the country? At the National Great Rivers Museum (at the Melvin Price Lock and Dam 26 off Hwy. 143, East Alton, 618/462-6979, 9 A.M.–5 P.M. daily, free), run by the Army

Corps of Engineers, visitors learn about the river's natural history and the river's connection to the development of the country. The new, 12,000-square-foot museum and Illinois Esplanade, an adjacent park, are right on the river and offer great barge-watching opportunities. It's also got some hands-on, kid-friendly exhibits, such as the simulation of driving a boat through the locks.

Monuments and Historical Markers

A monument to newspaper publisher **Elijah Lovejoy** is on the Monument Avenue in the Alton Cemetery, north of Broadway. One of the presses dug up from the river is on display at the offices of *The Telegraph,* 111 East Broadway, Alton.

In October 1858, while campaigning for the U.S. Senate, politicians and orators Lincoln and Douglas met in front of Alton's city hall (no longer standing) to debate the current issues, including slavery. Two bronze statues of the men are at what is now called **Lincoln-Douglas Square** at Broadway and Market, Alton.

During the Civil War, a closed prison in Alton was reopened to house prisoners of War from the Confederacy. During the war years about 11,000 soldiers passed through the prison. More than 1,000 of them died because of a smallpox outbreak, malnutrition, and other diseases. The long-gone Confederate prison near the riverfront was at Broadway and Williams Street in Alton and a monument stands on Rozier Street where they were buried (go north on State Street from town. It's south of Highway 3.)

When Alton native Robert Wadlow died in 1940 at 22 years old, he measured eight feet 11.1 inches long. Wadlow, who earned the nickname "the gentle giant" for his demeanor, was the tallest man in the world. A life-size statue of him is on College Avenue (also Highway 140) above the river.

With a painted human face, long, sharp teeth, scales like a fish, and horns like a deer, the mythical **Piasa Bird** was a mysterious creature from Native American lore. Hundreds and

Great River Valleys

hundreds of years ago the image of this frightening-looking bird-man-animal was carved high on the side of a cliff. Jolliet and Marquette wrote about it during their journey down the river in the 1670s. A recreation of that image has been painted on a rock face, closer to a driver's eye level, between Alton and Grafton. It's on the east side of Great River Road.

Gambling

Argosy's Alton Belle Casino (Alton riverfront, 800/711-GAME or 800/711-4263, www.argosy.com, 9 A.M.–5 A.M. daily) is a gambling and restaurant complex near the Clark Bridge on Alton's riverfront. Inside are a variety of table games and about 1,000 slot machines, several restaurants, and a stage where national touring musical acts often perform.

ACCOMMODATIONS

The **⛰ Beall Mansion** (407 E. 12th St., Alton, 866/THE-BEALL or 866/843-2325, www.beallmansion.com) is a renovated 1903 home in one of Alton's historic, turn-of-the-20th-century residential neighborhoods. There are five guest rooms (four rooms, one suite) available, each outfitted with private bathrooms, feather beds, and other comforts. The mansion offers a lot of extras here, such as in-room massages, robes, and nightly turn-down service. Choose to have breakfast in bed or in the dining room. Rates are $100–200.

Other options in town include the **Comfort Inn** (11 Cross Roads Ct., Alton, 618/465-9999); **Holiday Inn** (3800 Homer M. Adams Pkwy., Alton, 618/462-1220); and **Super 8** (1800 Homer M. Adams Pkwy., Alton, 618/465-8858).

FOOD

The menu changes often at **The Cane Bottom/My Just Desserts** (31 E. Broadway, Alton, 618/462-5881, 11 A.M.–3 P.M. daily, $6), a popular lunch and dessert place in downtown Alton, but basically you can expect sandwiches such as chicken salad and roast beef and

an array of desserts. Don't even think about leaving without slicing your fork into a divine piece of pie or buying one whole and bringing it home for later. Two favorites: blackberry cobbler and caramel apple.

The friendly **Italia Bakehouse** (104 W. 3rd St., Alton, 618/462-8384, lunch Mon.–Sat., $7) serves hearty sandwiches with sides such as slaw, chips, or pasta. Options include meatball sandwiches, hot ham and cheese, or hand-breaded grouper fillets. You can also get pizza here.

Fried tacos are the specialty at **Morales Tacos** (121 W. 3rd St., Alton, 618/465-6033, lunch and dinner daily, $8), a sit-down Mexican restaurant that also serves heaping plates full of nachos, tostadas, and giant burritos.

Market

Local vendors pitch tents and tables to sell fruit, vegetables, and arts and crafts at Alton's **Farmers and Artisans Market** held 8 A.M.–noon Saturdays June–October in the parking lot off 3rd Street in downtown Alton.

INFORMATION

The Tourism Bureau Southwest Illinois (10950 Lincoln Trail, Fairview Heights, 618/297-1488, www.thetourismbureau.org) publishes brochures on attractions, lodging, and dining information for the Metro East Louis region.

Alton Regional Convention and Visitors Bureau (618/465-6676 or 800/ALTON-IL or 800/258-6645, www.visitalton.com, 8:30 A.M.–5 P.M. Mon.–Fri., 9 A.M.–3 P.M. Sat.–Sun., www.visitalton.com), operates a visitors center at 200 Piasa Street, between downtown and the riverfront.

Tours

The site of a former Confederate prison, a stop along the Underground Railroad, and an all-around old river town, perhaps it's not surprising that Alton has been called one of the most haunted small cities in America. Two groups have organized evening tours of the city's more notoriously haunted places, such as a church and a cemetery. Choose from **Antoinette's Alton Haunted History Tours** (618/462-4009, www.hauntedalton.com) or **History and Hauntings Tours of Alton** (618/465-1086).

How about a cruise on the Mississippi or Illinois River aboard a 120-passenger yacht? The Alabama-based *Grampa Woo III River Excursion Boat* (251/421-4211, www.grampawoo.com) offers full-day or overnight tours focusing on everything from fall color to lock-and-dam trips departing from Alton and Grafton.

GETTING THERE AND AROUND
Airport
St. Louis Lambert International Airport (1071 Lambert International Blvd., St. Louis, Missouri, www.lambert-st.louis.com) is just across the river from Alton. Just follow U.S. 67 south to I-270. All the major airlines fly in and out of Lambert.

An alternative to Lambert is **MidAmerica St. Louis Airport** (9768 Airport Blvd., Mascoutah, www.flymidamerica.com), south of I-64, just off Highway 4. From this airport, TransMeridian flies to Orlando, Florida, and Allegiant Air flies to Las Vegas, Nevada.

Train
Several of **Amtrak's** (3400 College Ave., Alton, 618/462-1879, 800/USA-RAIL or 800/872-7245, www.amtrak.com) train lines stop in Alton daily, including the Texas Eagle, which goes to San Antonio, Texas, and Los Angeles, California; the State House between St. Louis and Chicago; and the Ann Rutledge between Chicago and Kansas City.

Metrolink (618/271-2345, www.metrostlouis.org) is the St. Louis regional light-rail line that stops daily in some Illinois towns, such as East St. Louis, Fairview Heights, and Belleville.

Car
You can rent a car from **Enterprise** (590 Lewis and Clark Blvd., East Alton, 618/254-0638) or **Premier Auto Rental** (18 Terminal Dr., East Alton, 618/259-3230).

GRAFTON
With a string of antiques shops on Main Street, two wineries, a kitschy fish restaurant, and a magnificent state park, Grafton has become quite the weekend destination for area residents and people driving along the Great River Road.

Pere Marquette State Park
Next to Starved Rock, Pere Marquette State Park (Hwy. 100, Grafton, 618/786-3323, www.dnr.state.il.us) is one of the most popular parks in Illinois. You can't get a better location. The 8,000-acre park is on a bluff overlooking the Illinois and Mississippi rivers and just north of the Great River Road. It's hard to pinpoint the park's best feature. It could be the 12 miles of hiking trails, many of which offer awesome views of the river valley. Or is it the scenic drive through the park's wooded hills and even more scenic overlooks, which are perfect for watching eagles swoop to catch fish? Instead of hiking, you can explore the park by horseback. Rides are offered April–October and by appointment November–April. For more information contact Pere Marquette Riding Stables at 618/786-2156.

One of the stars of the park is the stone- and slate-colored timber lodge built by the Civilian Conservation Corps in the 1930s. Inside are a 50-foot-high stone fireplace and 50 guest rooms. Nearby are 22 stone cabins. Before you hit the trails or head to the lodge, stop by the park's visitors center, which contains a 300-gallon aquarium. Here you can pick up trail maps, learn about the park's natural history, and take a look at the calendar of events. A popular spot for watching bald eagles, Pere Marquette hosts **Bald Eagle Days** in December and January, when park interpreters lead people on eagle-watching expeditions. Pere Marquette's campground has sites for tents and electric hookup sites for RVers. You can rent tents and tent equipment at the park.

Biking and Canoeing
You've seen the Illinois and Mississippi rivers

from the car window. Now park that car and get a little closer to the waterways. **Grafton Canoe and Kayak Rentals** (618/786-2192 or 618/786-3632, www.graftonoutdooractivities.com, sunrise–sunset daily) rents personal watercraft, water-skiing boats, pontoon boats, kayaks, and bicycles. Take your pick. You can also rent canoes, kayaks, and bicycles from **Riverside Recreation** (618/786-2455). If you plan to bicycle, one popular route is the approximately 15-mile-long **Sam Vadalabene Bicycle Trail,** which runs between Pere Marquette State Park and Alton along the Great River Road and just about as close to the Mississippi River as you can get. As far as kayaking goes, just north of Grafton is where the two rivers meet and there are several backwater lakes.

Wineries and Farm Visit

At the **Piasa Winery** (211 W. Main St., Grafton, 618/786-WINE or 618/786-9463, www.piasawinery.com, open daily) you can sip wine while sitting at a table outdoors with the Mississippi River in front of you. The winery, housed in a stone cottage along the Great River Road, features sweet whites to dry reds, sausages, cheese, and other goodies and wine accessories. The newest addition to the winery is the adjacent Piasa Pub, an English-style pub with import beers and sandwiches.

Up the hill from the Piasa Winery is the newer **Aerie's Riverview Winery** (Grafton, 618/786-VIEW or 618/786-8439, www.graftonwinery.com, 1–8 P.M. Wed., Thurs., Fri., 1–10 P.M. Sat., noon–8 P.M. Sun.), another scenic spot to drink Illinois wines. Munch on cheese and crackers and order a glass while sitting on a deck above the river. To get to the winery follow Mulberry Street north from Main Street in Grafton.

Traveling with kids? They'll love **Eckert's Farm** (20995 Eckert Orchard Rd., Grafton, 618/786-3445, 9 A.M.–6 P.M. daily July–Oct.). The Eckerts grow and sell peaches, apples, and pumpkins, but in recent years the place has become much more than a farm and evolved into a place where you can spend

hours letting the kids run around. There are a petting zoo, miniature golf course, and outdoor concert venue. They've even added a few inflatable rides for the kids. To get to the farm from Grafton drive north of Highway 3 and then west on Otterville Road and look for the signs.

Accommodations and Food

If you want to be within walking distance of the river, Grafton's antiques markets, and the handful of restaurants on Main Street, book a room at the **Ruebel Hotel** (Main St., Grafton, 618/786-2315, www.ruebelhotel.com), a historic 22-room hotel. The original 1884 hotel and restaurant, which served steamboat traffic, was damaged by a fire. It was later rebuilt after the turn of the 20th century and then remodeled in the late 1990s by the current set of owners. Accommodations include 22 standard hotel rooms above the restaurant, plus cottages and lodge rooms on a hillside above town. Hotel rooms are $59–129, the cottages rent for $119–149 per night, and lodge rooms are $99–199. The bar and restaurant, or saloon as the owners call it, also serves walleye, catfish, and buffalo-fish platters. Food is available 11–9 P.M. daily, although the bar is open later. In front of the hotel you can catch a 15-minute horse-drawn stagecoach ride through Grafton. Cost is $4 per person.

The **Pere Marquette State Park lodge** (618/786-2331) has 50 guest rooms, plus an indoor pool and dining room. The park also rents 22 stone cottages. Rates are $88–113 including tax.

Fish, fish, and more fish. The **Fin Inn** (100 W. Main St., Grafton, 618/786-2030, www.fininn.com, 11 A.M.–9 P.M. daily in the summer and until 8 P.M. in the winter, $7) batters and fries up catfish, buffalo fish, grouper, and other kinds of fish in a kitschy restaurant and gift shop north of the Great River Road. The decor may be dated, but it's a fun place. Two dozen booths have aquariums right next to them in the wall. The aquariums, which contain a total of about 8,000 gallons of water, are stocked with common Mississippi River fish, turtles, and other critters. The menu also lists items such as hamburgers, hotdogs, shrimp, and frog legs.

If you want a fish sandwich to go, drop by **O'Jan's Fish Stand** (101 W. Main St., Grafton, 618/786-2229), a market that also cooks fresh fish sandwiches. Another quick spot is **Grafton Ice Cream Company** (224 E. Main St., Grafton, 618/786-2663) where you can order a hand-dipped ice-cream cone.

American Bottoms: Cahokia to Chester

You never know what you'll stumble upon in the region east and south of East St. Louis. At one intersection you may see a sign advertising a winery. On another corner you'll see a sign pointing to the local taxidermy shop. It's a diverse area, rural and industrial, home to the historic Cahokia Mounds, an ancient Native American Indian village, a French-Catholic church built by missionaries in 1699, and iconic roadside architecture such as the Brooks catsup bottle. Towns close to St. Louis such as Collinsville, which is about 14 miles from the city, are busy, commercial towns with middle-class residents. South of Belleville, the countryside is dotted with horse stables and livestock farms.

This is where Illinois began: in settlements along the low-lying Mississippi River floodplains. Called the American Bottoms, this region has rich, rich soil and a past that goes back thousands of years. Before the industrialists opened refineries and factories, before the American colonists took control of the area from the British, before the French fur traders and missionaries established outposts, and even before a mound-building culture built a great city near present-day Collinsville, this area had attracted travelers. On a quiet highway south of Prairie du Rocher is an indentation of sorts in the side of a rock cliff. It's called the Modoc shelter and archaeologists have determined that humans sought shelter there as far back as 9,000 years ago. Perhaps the people were on a hunt and following the buffalo. Perhaps they were merely stopping by on a journey elsewhere.

SIGHTS

Ⓜ Cahokia Mounds

Even if it's a hot summer day, tough it out. Grab a water bottle and climb to the top of Monks Mound, a 100-foot-tall earthen mound east of the Mississippi River. Atop the mound you'll be able to see dozens of mounds rising from the land and imagine a Native American village that thrived about A.D. 700–1400. The Cahokia Mounds (Collinsville Rd. and Ramey St., Collinsville, 618/346-5160, www.cahokiamounds.com, donation), are an impressive sight. As you can imagine the landscape has changed drastically since Cahokia was inhabited by Native American tribes. You can still find cornfields in this fertile area, but the residential and commercial districts directly surrounding the mounds are not exactly picturesque. It's not uncommon to drive past pawn shops and empty storefronts. Nevertheless, this is one of the rarest finds in North America, and well worth a visit. You might want to start your visit at the visitors center, on the south side of Collinsville Road. Monks Mound is on the north side of the road, across from the center. Woodhenge, a calendar made of wooden posts, is just west of Monks Mound, also on the north side of the road. Walking trails are accessible from the visitors center and wind past several smaller mounds and borrow pits.

The area is called Cahokia (after an Illinois Indian tribe that lived in the same region in the 1600s), but we don't know the real name of the Indians who lived there when it was a bustling city. When it was a city, Cahokia stretched six square miles and 10,000–20,000 people lived there. People lived there A.D. 700–1400. First came the Woodland Indians and then the Mississippian Indians. Peak prosperity was probably around A.D. 1100. Originally there were about 120 mounds of various sizes. Today 69 mounds have been documented within the park (it's a 2,200-acre site). The other mounds

© CHRISTINE DES GARENNES

Cahokia Mounds, near Collinsville

were plowed over decades ago through development or farming. The tribes built the mounds with dirt dug from nearby pits called borrow pits. Some of these empty holes would become dumping grounds. Others would fill with water and become ponds. Some mounds were used to bury important people in the city. Others were used as sites for religious ceremonies, and some mounds were reserved for rulers and priests.

As you walk through the grounds, you can see parts of a reconstructed wall made of timber. Residents erected this wall around the city's center three times, requiring 15,000 logs each time. Historians do not know the true purpose of the wall but have theorized that it was built for defense or to separate residents from the outside world. No one is quite sure what happened to the city after about A.D. 1200 or 1400, but many believe the city may have deteriorated or been abandoned because of overpopulation, overuse of the area's natural resources, disease, or war.

You can easily spend several hours at Cahokia, visiting the center, walking the grounds, climbing Monks Mound, and checking out Woodhenge, a calendar made of wooden posts.

(It's next to a cement factory and along the busy Collinsville Road.) The center has numerous exhibits about the Native Americans who lived there, what they ate (corn, berries, fish, deer), how they lived (in grass huts), rituals, and what they made. Researchers believe Cahokia was a trade center. In their excavations they've found objects such as sea shells, which are not native to this area.

The grandest mound is Monks Mound. With a base of 14 acres and a height of 100 feet, it is the largest Indian mound north of Mexico. This is where the ruler lived and some ceremonies were conducted. You will have to climb 154 steps to get to the top of Monks Mound, but it's worth it. You can get a better sense of the city from above as you watch tourists strolling about. Monks Mound was named after the French monks who lived in the area at the turn of the 17th century. They did not live on the mound.

The grounds are open 8 A.M.–dusk; the interpretive center is open 9 A.M.–5 P.M. Wednesday–Sunday. The center is closed November–February. You can get a free self-guided taped tour from the visitors center,

Great River Valleys

which describes the mounds you see along three hiking trails. The tour takes about 30–45 minutes, depending on your pace. Free guided tours are held at 10:30 A.M. and 1:30 P.M. Wednesday–Saturday, and at 12:30 P.M. and 2:30 P.M. on Sunday June, July, and August. Tours are at 1:30 P.M. Saturday and Sunday in April, May, and September. Cahokia Mounds is a state and National Historic Landmark as well as a UNESCO (the United Nations Educational, Scientific, and Cultural Organization) World Heritage Site.

Brooks Catsup Bottle

The iconic Brooks Catsup Bottle (800 S. Morrison Ave./Hwy. 159, Collinsville, 618/345-5598, catsupbottle.com) stands 170 feet tall off the National Road in Collinsville. Built in 1949, the tower stored water for the city and the catsup factory. Eventually the factory closed and the tower fell into disrepair. In the 1990s a local resident noticed its sorry state, rallied the troops, and they saved it from demolition. The restored tower is now a beloved symbol of revitalized roadside architecture.

Town of Cahokia Sights

Sometimes Illinoisans forget that the first explorers and settlers to Illinois were the French. Perhaps it is because a lot of them chose to leave when the British took over the territory, leaving few buildings behind. However, the town of Cahokia, just south of East St. Louis, has two buildings built by the state's first white residents. More than three centuries ago French missionaries founded the Holy Family Parish. They built the **Holy Family Church** (1st and Church Sts., Cahokia, 618/337-4548, call for a tour, free) in 1799. It's believed to be the oldest church west of the Allegheny Mountains. Like the nearby Cahokia Courthouse, it was built in typical French outpost style: hewn logs placed upright with the spaces filled in with mortar and stone. Part of the Belleville Diocese, it's still a functioning church. Masses are held there on Saturday evenings and Sunday mornings. Call the parish to make an appointment to tour the church.

About two blocks from the church is another building from the same period. The **Cahokia Courthouse** (1st and Elm Sts., Cahokia, 618/332-1782, 9 A.M.–5 P.M. Wed.–Sun., free), a state historic site, was built in 1740. Back then only about a dozen Frenchmen lived in the area, and they got along well with the Indian tribes nearby. Within a few years the area became a trading post and more people moved into the area. When Illinois became a state, Cahokia was chosen as the county seat for St. Clair. However, because it was near the river, the town was often flooded and the county seat was moved to Belleville. The courthouse was dismantled and shown in St. Louis World's Fair in 1904, later dismantled again and moved to Jackson Park in Chicago. It wasn't until 1939 that it was returned to Cahokia. Today the four-room building contains a courtroom, schoolroom, and offices.

EVENTS

Collinsville is not only home to the world's largest catsup bottle, it's the Horseradish Capital of the World. (About 65 percent of the world's horseradish is grown in the region.) The much-loved root is honored annually at the **International Horseradish Festival** held the first weekend in June in Collinsville's Woodland Park. Events include cooking contests, root tosses, and food vendors selling dishes made with horseradish.

Cahokia Mounds hosts several solstice and equinox events throughout the year. In addition, Cahokia often sponsors artisan workshops and performing arts concerts on the grounds. You can listen to flutists, learn how Native Americans stored food to keep it from spoiling, how to make moccasins, and how to carve gourds.

ACCOMMODATIONS

If you want to stay in or around Collinsville, chances are you're going to stay in a hotel room off I-55. About a dozen midsize and midpriced hotels ($50–100) are here, including the 73-room **Hampton Inn** (7 Commerce Dr., Collinsville, 618/346-4400), which has an indoor pool and exercise room; the **Drury Inn** (602 N. Bluff Rd., Collinsville, 618/345-7700) has an indoor pool and allows pets. Cheaper options include the 86-room **Motel 6** (295-A N. Bluff Rd., Collinsville, 618/345-2100), where pets are allowed; and **Howard Johnson's Express Inn** (301 N. Bluff Rd., Collinsville, 618/345-1530), which has an outdoor pool and lounge.

INFORMATION

More info on lodging, dining, or attractions is available from the **Collinsville Convention and Visitors Bureau** (1 Gateway Dr., Collinsville, 800/289-2388, www.discovercollinsville.com).

THE OLD FRENCH FORTS: KASKASKIA AND FORT DE CHARTRES
Fort Kaskaskia State Historic Site

You'd hardly know it today but the area in and around the Fort Kaskaskia State Historic Site (8 A.M.–4 P.M. Wed.–Sun.) was one of the more important forts and towns in Illinois's early years. The state historic site itself is a small park of about 200 acres high above the river. It was here that Fort Kaskaskia once stood. It was originally a French fort, but the British took over after 1763. And a few years after that, Virginian George Rogers Clark secured the fort for the American colonists during the Revolutionary War. There's not much left of the fort, except for some earthen mounds at the top of the bluffs. What else is long gone? The town of Kaskaskia, the second European settlement in the state and the first capital. Established near the confluence of the Kaskaskia and Mississippi rivers, the town was often flooded. Drive through the park to the scenic overlook of the valley. Nearby, at the shelter, there's a poignant photograph of a house barely standing after one of the many floods. Also nearby is the remarkable Garrison Hill Cemetery on a steep hill overlooking the river. These are graves of people who had been buried in Kaskaskia but because of the floods had to be moved in 1881. In the spring locals reenact Revolutionary

a renactment at Fort de Chartres, Prairie du Rocher

COURTESY OF THE TOURISM BUREAU SOUTHWEST ILLINOIS

Great River Valleys

War camp life in the park. And there is a small campground on-site.

Just across the river from the old fort is the **Kaskaskia Bell** (4372 Park Rd., Ellis Grove). It's on a 14,000-acre island on the western side of the Mississippi River and it's quite the drive to get there. The area is remote and barely inhabited. After George Rogers Clark claimed Kaskaskia for the Americans in 1778, France's King Louis XV presented this bell to the residents.

Ⓜ Fort de Chartres

A remote and sometimes overlooked site in southwest Illinois is Fort de Chartres (Prairie du Rocher, 618/284-7230, 9 A.M.–5 P.M. Wed.–Sun.), a partially rebuilt French fort near the Mississippi River. Far from any major town, the fort is situated in the river's floodplain. And that's one of the reasons why eventually the fort was abandoned. It flooded a lot. The remarkable feature of the fort is its sheer size. It's not just a wall of logs. The stone fort had walls 15 feet high and several feet thick. There are musket ports, a powder magazine, barracks, chapel, and other rooms and buildings. What visitors see today is actually based on the third fort that stood on this site. The first one was made of logs and assembled rather hastily. It didn't last long. A second one was built in 1725. It was larger and builders added the powder magazine, prison, and other components. The third and final fort was the largest and most expensive to build. It served as a fort in the French territory roughly 1753–1763, when the French ceded the Illinois Territory to the British as a result of losing the French and Indian War. After the Brits took possession of the fort, they called it Fort Cavendish. But they didn't stick around for long and ordered it closed in 1771.

Through time the stone walls started to crumble and people hauled away the stones. The only structure to survive was the powder magazine. The rest has been rebuilt. But you'd hardly know the difference. It looks pretty authentic. Feel free to stroll around the grounds and through the rooms (the chapel, the priest's room, a grain-storage area). Be sure to tour the museum inside the storehouse building. It has several items on display, such as weapons, that date to when Illinois was part of France. If you're wondering when to visit, think about June. The fort hosts a popular two-day rendezvous then when people dress up in French military uniforms and fur trader outfits and dance, cook out, and compete in shooting contests. To get to the fort, follow signs from Highway 154 near Prairie du Rocher.

Modoc Rock Shelter

Beginning around 9,000 years ago Native American people used the Modoc Rock Shelter (County Rd. 7, two miles south of Prairie du Rocher) to seek shelter from storms or to camp while passing through the area in search of animals to hunt. Because of changes in topography during the last several thousands of years, the shelter gradually filled with sediment. Today, driving by it, you'll see it's a small indentation on the side of a rock cliff. The site is listed on the National Register of Historic Places.

Pierre Menard State Historic Site

Tucked into the side of a hill in a beautiful, remote part of the county, a few miles south of the Fort Kaskaskia State Historic Site is an old French colonial home built for Pierre Menard, a French-Canadian who was a successful fur trader in the area and later went on to become lieutenant governor of Illinois in 1818. The Pierre Menard State Historic Site (Fort Kaskaskia Rd., Ellis Grove, 9 A.M.–5 P.M. Wed.–Sun. March–Oct., 9 A.M.–4 P.M. Wed.–Sun. Nov.–Feb., free) comprises the 1802 home, with its long front porch that faces the Mississippi River, and a few outbuildings such as Menard's smokehouse, plus an herb garden.

Wineries

This region is home to a handful of boutique wineries. Both offer free tastings and tours. **Lau-Nae Winery** (1522 Hwy. 3, Red Bud, 618/282-WINE or 618/282-9463, www.lau-naewinery.com, 10 A.M.–5 P.M. Fri.–Sat., noon–5 P.M. Sun.) crafts wine from French hybrid another sign of French roots in Illinois: the Pierre Menard home north of Chester

© CHRISTINE DES GARENNES

Great River Valleys

grapes, Concord grapes, and other fruit grown on-site. You can drink the wines while sitting on the front porch or inside by the fireplace. **Waterloo Winery** (725 N. Market St., Waterloo, 618/939-5743, noon–5 P.M. Wed.–Sun.) is on an 18th-century farmstead where the wines are aged in caves under the home. Unwind with a glass while sitting on the patio overlooking the vineyard.

CHESTER AND RED BUD
Sights and Activities

Popeye creator Elzie Segar was born in Chester, a quiet river town south of Fort de Chartres and the Pierre Menard home. To honor his memory, the town erected a Popeye statue at **Elzie Segar Memorial Park,** a small park on Highway 3, just before you cross the Chester Bridge to go to Missouri. Other residents have paid tribute by amassing hundreds of pieces of Popeye memorabilia. At the **Spinach Can Collectibles** (1001 State St., Chester, 618/826-4567, www.popeyethesailor.com, 9:30 A.M.–4:30 P.M. Mon.–Fri., 9 A.M.–4 P.M. Sat., free) vintage figurines, lunch boxes, toys,

and other Popeye paraphernalia are for show and some are for sale. The museum is in the back of the store.

If you're in the mood for a scenic country drive, follow Highway 150 northwest of Chester to see the **Mary's River Covered Bridge,** an 1854 oak timber bridge. Once part of a regional toll road, the bridge was used by car travelers up until 1930. Visitors can walk across it.

Accommodations

Red Bud is a picturesque little town with brick sidewalks and old-fashioned lamp posts just off Highway 3, a rolling two-lane highway near the Mississippi River. Along Main Street is ⋈ **Magnolia Place Bed and Breakfast** (317 S. Main St., Red Bud, 618/282-4141, www.magnoliaplace.com), a brick Victorian mansion with three rooms. One of the best features of this bed-and-breakfast is its garden, where couples often wed in the gazebo surrounded by flowerbeds. Unlike some bed-and-breakfasts in Victorian homes, you're not expected to forgo modern devices such as televisions in your room. Also, you pick the time of your breakfast in the morning. Rates are $75–160 per night.

Two other options where rooms are usually under $60 are **Red Bud Country Inn** (1617 S. Main St., Red Bud, 618/282-4444), a new, clean 12-room motel just off Red Bud's Main Street where continental breakfast is included; or **Reid's Best Western Inn** (2150 State St., Chester, 618/826-3034), a 46-room motel with an outdoor pool.

Also, **Fort Kaskaskia State Historic Site** has 23 electrical hookups for RV campers.

ILLINOIS CAVERNS STATE NATURAL AREA

What's awesome (and to some, terrifying) about Illinois Caverns State Natural Area (south of Waterloo near Redbud, 618/458-6699 or 618/785-2555, www.dnr.state.il.us, free) is the darkness. You will not explore the cave while sitting on a tram or following a group of 30 people along a lighted passage. Instead you explore the miles of passages guided by the light of your waterproof flashlight. The only cave open to the public in the state, Illinois Caverns is owned and managed by the Illinois Department of Natural Resources. Although this is the state's only cave open to the public, Illinois has several hundred caves. They're found in the driftless area in the northwest, throughout the Shawnee Hills, and along much of the Mississippi River in Illinois in what geologists call karst areas, which are marked by sinkholes and shallow depressions in the land. Hundreds of millions of years ago shallow seas covered much of Illinois. The seas deposited organic and carbonate sediment, which would become limestone and dolomite bedrock. Through time rainwater and groundwater dripped through the cracks of these rocks, causing a chemical reaction and the rocks gradually dis-

solved. Streams meandered through the rock and formed caverns.

The experience here is, as the brochure bills it, wild. Lace up your boots, and then pick up a map of the cave from the entrance. There are a total of about six miles of paths to explore, and about three of those miles where you can stand up. You will come upon areas called Cascade Canyon (a pleasant sight) and Marvin's Misery, where you'll crouch and crawl through slippery mudlike material (not as pleasant). Along the way you may see bats, salamanders, and the endangered amphipod, tiny shrimplike creature. You'll also see stalagmites and stalactites. (When mineral-rich water drips down, the minerals, calcium carbonate, pile up.)

The cave is on a 120-acre preserve on a former farm. The whole site is pretty rustic; there's no running water. But there is a half-mile walking trail through a meadow prairie if you want to take a walk above ground. Before you go, a few things to know: Visitors must explore the cave in groups of four or more, wear boots and a hard hat, and carry three sources of light per person (waterproof flashlights, lanterns, etc.). To get to the cave follow Highway 3, a few miles south of Waterloo, go right on Kaskaskia Road, left on County KK, and then right on County G. It's open 8 A.M.–3:30 P.M. Wednesday–Sunday April 15–September 15, 8 A.M.–3:30 P.M. Thursday–Saturday September 16–April 14. No one is allowed to enter the cave past 2:30 P.M.

INFORMATION

Staff at **The Tourism Bureau of Southwest Illinois** (10950 Lincoln Trail, Fairview Heights, 618/397-1488 or 800/442-1488, www.thetourismbureau.org) will be able to help you plan your itinerary through this region.

Northern Hill Country

Every time I visit northern Illinois, particularly in and around towns such as Galena and Savanna, I find myself saying, as I look out over the rolling hills or drive through the lively downtowns, "Yup. I could live here." It's a fetching region of the state (and one of the best places to choose a road and follow it through the country). Galena, in the far northwest corner, is the state's tourism gem, a place every small town's tourism office would love its town to become. Situated along the Galena River and a few miles from the Mississippi, the former mining town and steamboat hub was once home to Ulysses S. Grant. It's filled with historic sites and museums and home to artisans, performing artists, and engaging entrepreneurs who run restaurants or antiques or gift shops. South of Galena by about 25 miles is one of the best state parks, Mississippi Palisades, in Savanna. Drive or hike up the steep bluffs, and then pick a spot at one of the many scenic overlooks to scout for eagles. In addition to Mississippi Palisades State Park, the region has the small but scenic Apple River Canyon State Park near the Wisconsin border, where visitors are treated to an excellent example of driftless

![M]ust-Sees

Look for **M** to find the sights and activities you can't miss and **N** for the best dining and lodging.

M Ulysses S. Grant Home State Historic Site: Grateful for General Ulysses S. Grant's role in defeating the Confederate Army, residents of Galena presented him a brick Italianate home upon his return to Galena, a lead-mining and steamboat town where Grant had lived before the war. Today Galena is still chock-full of historic homes such as Grant's (page 293).

M Apple River Canyon State Park: Just below the Wisconsin border this state park, with its river canyons and rocky hilltops, offers visitors a good look at the geology of the driftless region, an area untouched by the glaciers (page 305).

M Mississippi Palisades State Park: Another top-notch park with several endurance-building hiking trails through steep, wooded bluffs. This Savanna-area park is perched atop a bluff overlooking the Mississippi River and it boasts several lookout points with awesome views of the river and the many eagles that call the area home in the winter (page 305).

M Castle Rock State Park: This 2,000-acre park south of Oregon is perhaps best known for the sandstone bluff and viewing platform above the rambling Rock River, but it also has several miles of excellent hiking trails that wind through quiet native forest and prairie west of the river (page 309).

M John Deere Historic Site: After Grand Detour blacksmith John Deere in 1837 invented a plow that could handle the thick prairie soil, farming in Illinois, and the Midwest, would never be the same. The Rock River historical complex, comprising an archaeological site, recreated (and working) blacksmith shop, and Deere family home, highlight the significance of that discovery, not to mention the art of blacksmithing (page 312).

© CHRISTINE DES GARENNES

Castle Rock State Park

WISCONSIN

Galena

M Apple River Canyon State Park

Ulysses S Grant Home SHS

Rockford

M Mississippi Palisades State Park

Castle Rock State Park **M**

MISSOURI

M

John Deere Historic Site

NORTHERN HILL COUNTRY

Northern Hill Country

© AVALON TRAVEL PUBLISHING, INC.

geology. The glaciers bypassed this part of the state, and as you'll see when driving through here, it can be a rugged, rolling land. This part of the world is rural, with dairy farms nested in and among the valleys and a fruit orchard here and there. Spend an afternoon picking apples or pumpkins or sampling wine.

As you drive along the old stagecoach road east of Galena, you'll understand why Black Hawk did not want to give it up so easily to the United States. It's a beautiful part of the world. The Sauk and Fox Indian tribes lived in this region until 1730, when they were forced to move westward. Years later the Sauk leader Black Hawk tried to reclaim parts of the land and despite a few victorious battles with U.S. militia, his tribe was eventually forced west of the Mississippi River for good.

PLANNING YOUR TIME

Visiting Galena should be at the top of your to-do list. A three-day weekend is fine for hitting the town's major sights, such as Grant's home and a few other historic homes, plus allowing time for shopping downtown, strolling along the river, and visiting the small towns on the outskirts. A week, however, is definitely doable with all the vacation homes available on a weekly basis. In fact, you could base your vacation in Galena, and then explore towns beyond Galena, such as Scales Mound and Apple River, basically following the Old Stagecoach Trail northeast of Galena or U.S 20 eastward. Plus, you can also drive south to Savanna for a day. The only downside is that staying in Galena will drain your checking or credit card account faster than if you choose to stay in some of the smaller, outlying towns.

Another road trip option is to start near Chicago's southwestern suburbs and spend a three-day weekend visiting towns near or along U.S. 34. You can begin with Plano and Mies van der Rohe's Farnsworth House, followed by a visit to Sandwich's huge flea market. Then it's on to the town of Princeton, near the Hennepin Canal. Spend a day or part of a day biking along the supremely quiet and not-at-all crowded bicycle trail that follows the canal. One more scenic route to follow is the Rock River from southwest of Rockford to Dixon. Drive along Highway 2 through towns such as Oregon, visiting Castle Rock State Park near the river and the John Deere State Historic Site in Grand Detour where the blacksmith forged the plow that would make him a famous and rich man. Finally, this is Ronald Reagan country. Begin with a visit to the apartment where he was born in Tampico and continue to his boyhood home in Dixon.

Resources

The umbrella tourism organization for the region is the **Northern Illinois Tourism Development Office** (200 S. State St., Belvidere, 815/547-3740, www.visitnorthernillinois.com). Its territory includes a bulk of the towns and counties covered in this chapter.

In addition, the **Blackhawk Waterways Convention and Visitors Bureau** (201 N. Franklin Ave., Polo, 815/946-2108 or 800/678-2108, www.blackhawkwaterwayscvb.org) covers Carroll, Lee, Ogle, and Whiteside counties in the northwestern part of the state, including towns such as Savanna, Morrison, and Dixon.

Most towns featured in the chapter have local convention and visitors bureaus or chambers of commerce that publish maps and guides to their towns.

Galena

In this author's opinion, Galena is Illinois's most picturesque town. Driving into the town from the east or west on U.S. 20, you'll see white church steeples poking out among tall oak trees, a Main Street lined with historic and beautifully preserved brick buildings, and dotted about the hills above the Galena River are the steamboat captains' Italianate mansions, many of which have been converted into bed-and-breakfasts.

Galena can thank two industries for its growth in the early–mid-1800s: river travel and lead mining. The town was actually named after the type of lead ore that was mined in the region: Galena lead ore. The area's lead-mining era lasted from about the early 1820s until the 1850s, when many miners left town after learning that gold had been discovered in California. Today you can visit the Vinegar Lead Mine north of town to learn more about lead mining and Galena's mining past. A port to the Mississippi River, Galena was also home to steamboat captains and businesses that serviced boats and barges. The Galena River, you see, leads directly to the Mississippi River. In the 1840s there were 14,000 people living in Galena. Today the year-round residents number around 3,500.

Galena today is a popular weekend destination for Chicago-area residents (it's about 150 miles from the city). Potters, painters, weavers, and other artists have shops in and around the town. Ulysses S. Grant's former home is open to the public, as well as the town's old market house and several other historic mansions and museums. And don't forget to pack your clubs. Eagle Ridge Resort, east of town in The Galena Territory, has 63 holes set amid rolling fairways, near woodlands, ravines, and bunkers.

ORIENTATION

Most likely you'll enter Galena off U.S. 20. This will take you directly through the center of town. The Galena River runs diagonally through downtown. Most of the shops and restaurants are on the west side of the river along Main Street. Ulysses S. Grant's home is on the east side of the river, just off Bouthillier Street, which also leads to the river, but does not cross it. Historic homes and bed-and-breakfasts are scattered all throughout town. The mansions tend to be up on the hills overlooking the town. Even though downtown Galena has well-marked public parking lots, spaces can be hard to come by, especially on sunny summer weekends. Your best bet is to find a space several blocks away and then walk to downtown. The visitors bureau operates a **free shuttle** between its two information centers at the Old Train Depot on the east side of the river and Old Market House on the west side. It runs on weekends May–October. About six miles east of town is a 6,800-acre resort community called **The Galena Territory.** This is where the famed Eagle Ridge Resort is located as well as dozens of condominiums, townhouses, cottages, and mansions tucked into the woods, in valleys and on the side of hills.

SIGHTS
Ulysses S. Grant Home State Historic Site

Before he went off to fight in the Civil War, Ulysses S. Grant (who had decided to leave the Army and enter civilian life again) moved his family to Galena, where he had planned to work in one of his family's leather shops. They moved here in 1860 and rented a home. Then the Confederates fired at Fort Sumter in South Carolina in 1861. He left his job and family and was appointed colonel of the Illinois Volunteer Infantry Regiment. He was credited with organizing the successful victory at the battle of Vicksburg, Mississippi, in 1863, was promoted and later led the U.S. Army to defeat the Confederacy and General Robert E. Lee. When he returned to Galena, the city was just

Northern Hill Country

Northern Hill Country

plain thrilled and presented him a brand-new house, a big brick Italianate home.

A few years later, in 1868, Grant was elected president and he and his family visited Galena only occasionally after that. In 1904 his children returned the home to the city of Galena, which later sold it to the state. The Ulysses St. Grant Home State Historic Site (500 Bouthillier St., Galena, 815/777-3310, www.granthome.com, 9 A.M.–5 P.M. Wed.–Sun. Apr.–Oct., and until 4 P.M. Nov.–Ap., $3) appears much like it may have been back

in the 1860s and 1870s as much of the furniture placed throughout the house once belonged to the Grant family and was original to the house.

Historic Sites

A few blocks west of Grant's home is the former estate of one of his pals, Elihu Washburne. At the **Washburne House State Historic Site** (908 3rd St., Galena, 815/777-9406, 10 A.M.–4 P.M. Fri. May–Oct., free) you can tour a grand 1843 Greek-revival home and learn a

COURTESY OF GALENA AREA CONVENTION AND VISITORS BUREAU

Ulysses S. Grant Home State Historic Site in Galena

little about the local attorney and U.S. congressman who would become a friend and political adviser to Abraham Lincoln and Grant. Grant appointed him ambassador to France. Washburne, by the way, didn't speak too fondly of Galena, calling its residents litigious and the town itself dull.

Just west of the Galena River is the **Old Market House State Historic Site** (123 N. Commerce St., Galena, 815/777-3310, 9 A.M.–5 P.M. Wed.–Sun. Apr.–Oct., 10 A.M.–4 P.M. Wed.–Sun. Nov.–Apr., free). Opened in 1846, the building was somewhat of an early mall. The first floor contained several different stalls where vendors sold food and goods. Later it housed jail cells and some city offices, including the town's surveyor. The Market House today often features local-history exhibits, including a long-running one about Grant. One of the highlights of that exhibit is a buggy used by Grant's family. During Old Market Days, held throughout the year, locals sell flowers, bread, and other food.

Housed in an 1858 Italianate mansion on a hill just west of Main Street, the **Galena/Jo Daviess County History Museum** (211 S.

Bench St., Galena, 815/777-9129, www.galenahistorymuseum.org, 9 A.M.–4:30 P.M. daily, $4) has an impressive and wide-ranging collection of historical artifacts and exhibits about the town and county's past. One of the oddest items may be a cigar butt that Grant reportedly threw into the gutter after learning he didn't win the 1880 presidential nomination. The museum has plenty of guns, earthenware pottery made in the area during the second half of the 19th century, quite a lot of clothes from the 19th century, and some portraits of Galena's residents from the past, including one of Grant's wife. Visit the gift shop to browse for books about Grant, the Civil War, lead mining, plus maps and other souvenirs. The historical society leads walking tours through downtown Galena May–October. (For more information see *Tours.)*

The historical society also runs the **Blacksmith Shop** (254 Commerce St., Galena, 815/777-9129, www.galenahistorymuseum.org, 10 A.M.–4 P.M. Fri.–Mon. May–Oct., $2), a blacksmithing museum in a former blacksmith shop. It rebuilt the forge and occasionally the shop holds demonstrations. Hanging on the walls of this 1897 building are dozens of tools used to make iron products as well as tools made during the process. At the gift shop you can buy items made by the resident blacksmith.

If you can't get enough of touring old homes, here are two other old homes to visit. **The Belvedere** (1008 Park Ave., Galena, 815/777-0747) is, like many other homes in town, a brick Italianate mansion from the 1850s. It's filled with antique furniture and some unusual collectibles, such as the green drapes from the set of *Gone with the Wind*. The **Dowling House** (220 Diagonal St., Galena, 815/777-1250), an old stone house near downtown that dates to 1826, is the oldest home in the city. Dress up in 19th century garb and have your photo taken here.

Arts

Galena is home to many visual artists and artisans. Galleries and gift shops along Main Street and its side streets sell everything from landscape oil paintings to jewelry and pottery. If you're feeling inspired, visit the **The Galena Art Center** (601 S. Prospect Rd., Galena, 815/777-9040, www.galenaschoolofart.com) to attend a one-day workshop while you're in town. Past topics have included papermaking, painting, and pottery and jewelry making. The center also has a gallery (where you can buy art), outdoor sculpture garden, and studios.

One of the most recent additions to Galena's art scene is the **Chicago Athenaeum Museum of Architecture and Design** (122 S. Bench St., Galena, 815/777-4444, call for hours, $4), which showcases contemporary design (including industrial and product), photography, sculpture, and other media. The museum has headquarters in Chicago and has a branch in Schaumburg also.

Other Sights and Activities

In addition to Grant's home and the DeSoto House Hotel, a visit to the **Galena Cellars and Winery and Vineyard** (515 S. Main St. and 4746 N. Ford Rd., Galena, 815/777-

3300, 800/397-WINE or 800/397-9463, www.galenacellars.com) should be high up on your tour itinerary. It has two locations, a shop housed in an renovated granary barn in downtown Galena, and the actual vineyard with its own shop and tasting room about six miles northeast of Galena. The vineyard is in a bucolic setting north of The Galena Territory. It's worth the short drive. Before you go out there, call and find out when it's offering tours of the winery. That way you can see how it all comes together, in addition to sampling some of the wines while sitting on a deck overlooking the vineyard. You can't beat it. Want to stick around for a while? The winery rents a one-bedroom suite above the tasting room. It's open 9 A.M.–5 P.M. Monday–Thursday, 9 A.M.– 8 P.M. Friday–Saturday, 9 A.M.–6 P.M. Sunday January–May; 9 A.M.– 8 P.M. Monday–Saturday, 9 A.M.–6 P.M. Sunday Memorial Day–Labor Day.

Linmar Gardens (504 S. Prospect Rd., Galena, 815/777-1177, open 10 A.M.–4 P.M. daily May–Sept., but call ahead, $4) is a privately owned 3.5-acre garden on a hill overlooking downtown Galena. Pick a gazebo or bench, preferably near one of the waterfalls and flower beds, and then catch up on writing in your travel journal or writing postcards.

ENTERTAINMENT AND EVENTS

Theater

Two local community theaters present several productions each year at locations around town. To find out what's on tap for the season contact the **Main Street Players Theatre Company** (815/777-2787), **Galena Art Theatre** (815/777-3288), or check the local newspaper entertainment listings.

Events

Galena is home to many artists, so perhaps it's not surprising that it has several art-related events throughout the year. The **Galena Art Festival,** held in Grant Park on the river usually in late July, showcases the work of 100 juried artists along with food and live music. Grant Park also hosts the **Galena Country Fair** in

October, where more than 100 nonjuried artists sell arts and crafts (paintings, photography, jewelry, you name it). Come mid-June, hot-air balloonists race across the sky and area gardeners open up their gates and allow visitors to take a peek at their projects. During Galena's **Festival of the Performing Arts** in mid-July, area musicians perform in the Galena Public Library and area churches. On select weekends in the fall, visitors are invited to tour Grant's home by lamplight. For more information on any of these events, contact the Galena and Jo Daviess County Convention and Visitors Bureau (see *Information*).

RECREATION
Horseback Riding
Tucked into the rolling hills of The Galena Territory east of town, the **Shenandoah Riding Center** (200 N. Brodrecht Rd., Galena, 815/777-2373, www.shenandoahridingcenter.com) offers Territory and non-Territory guests guided trail rides. (The Territory has about 40 miles of trails through green hills,

woods, and along creeks.) The one-hour rides are offered daily. Call to make a reservation.

Canoeing and Kayaking
Sometimes visitors to Galena get so caught up with all the town's historic sites that they forget that running through town is not only a scenic, rambling river, but one that is navigable and friendly to canoeists and kayakers. **Fever River Outfitters** (525 S. Main St., Galena, 815/776-9425, www.feverriveroutfitters.com) takes people out on guided canoe or kayak adventures on the Galena River. Trips can last 2–4.5 hours on the Galena River and cost around $40. If you prefer to canoe or kayak at your own pace and navigate your own way, you can just rent the canoe or kayak. The sports store also rents bicycles and snowshoes.

Golf
One of the finest places to golf in northern Illinois is **Eagle Ridge Inn and Resort** (800/892-2269, www.eagleridge.com), just off U.S. 20 east of downtown Galena. The resort's golfing options include three 18-hole courses plus

summertime at Chestnut Mountain, south of Galena

Northern Hill Country

a nine-hole course, 63 holes in all. The resort's pride and joy is The General course (109 Eagle Ridge, 815/777-4525). Other options include the North course (400 Eagle Ridge Dr., 815/777-2500); South course (10 Clubhouse Dr., 815/777-2280); and the nine-hole East course (100 E. Point Dr., 815/777-5200).

The surrounding region (up to about a 20-mile radius) is home to about a dozen more courses. Here are a few: **Galena Golf Club** (11557 U.S. 20, Galena, 815/777-3599), a par-71 course with yardages 5,339–6,623; **Woodbine Bend** (3500 E. Center Rd., Stockton, 815/858-3939, www.woodbinebend.com), a par-72 course with yardages 5,280–6,755; and **Blackhawk Run Golf Course** (3501 S. Golf Rd., Stockton, 815/947-3011), a par-72 and 76 course with yardages 5,591–6,378.

Chestnut Mountain Resort: Skiing and Other Activities

For Illinois, **Chestnut Mountain Resort** (8700 W. Chestnut Rd., Galena, info and ski conditions 800/798-0098, reservations 800/397-1320, www.chestnutmtn.com), which is south

of downtown Galena, has some of the best skiing around. The "mountain," with its 475-foot drop, overlooks the Mississippi River. You can downhill ski or snowboard down the 17 trails, some of which are labeled for advanced skiers and others for novices. The resort has set aside an area for beginners (called Beginner's Bowl and Rookies Ridge) where, if you're new to the whole skiing thing, you don't have to worry about looking ridiculous as you fall down over and over. A magic carpet, like a moving sidewalk, shuttles you from one area to another as you stand.

The resort has a cafeteria, game room, and lounge. The resort rents not only equipment for downhill skiing but snowboarding, too. Fees vary depending on time and day you visit. It's cheaper to ski in the evenings during the week. Ski passes are $20–40 and equipment runs $20–50. The ski shop is open 9 A.M.–9 P.M. Monday–Thursday, 9 A.M.–10 P.M. Friday–Saturday, 9 A.M.–midnight Friday in January and February.

In the summertime, the resort doesn't shut down but instead opens what's called an al-

an overlook at Chestnut Mountain Ski Resort

pine slide, an open-air tube slide that you fly down. There's also an 18-hole miniature golf course. And you can also rent mountain bikes for $25 per day.

ACCOMMODATIONS

Galena has an enormous number of bed-and-breakfasts, inns, condominiums, and vacation homes available to guests. Outside of Chicago, this is probably the most expensive town to stay in Illinois. Some homes are in downtown Galena, a block or three from shops, and others are a few miles from town, on private estates amid gardens, hills, and wooded areas. This is a popular town to visit, especially from spring to fall. It's a good idea to make your reservation as soon as you know when you'll be visiting Galena.

Two businesses in town offer help in sorting through the sheer number of bed-and-breakfasts in the region. They include **A Bed and Breakfast Sampler of Galena** (11410 U.S. 20, Galena, 815/777-1334, www.galena-bnb.com); and **Galena's B&Bs** (513 Bouthillier St., Galena, 815/777-8097 or 866/777-1484, www.galenainns.com).

In addition, several companies and private families offer small to large vacation homes for long-term rental (a week or more) in the area. For a list, contact the visitor bureau.

$50–100

The **Grant Hills Motel** (9372 U.S. 20, Galena, 815/777-2116, www.granthills.com) is a clean, comfortable 34-room motel a mile or so east of downtown Galena. The motel, which overlooks the hills and valleys of the driftless region, has an outdoor pool.

One of the best things about **Ann's Snoop Sisters Inn** (1000 3rd St., Galena, 815/777-3062, www.snoopsisters.com, $65–103) is its location. The 1858 brick home is within a few blocks from Main Street's shops and restaurants and a block from Grant's home. The friendly inn has three feminine rooms for rent. Most go for under $100; however, there is a suite option that will cost about $140 per night.

Similar to the Snoop Sisters Inn, the **Bielenda's Mars Avenue Guest Home** (515 Mars Ave., Galena, 815/777-2808, www.bmarsave.com, $90–110) is a historic brick home within walking distance of downtown Galena. The Mars home sits on a hill above town, surrounded by a white picket fence and a few gardens. There are three cozy rooms available here.

If you prefer to be where the action is, you can't get any closer to downtown than the **Main Street Inn** (404 S. Main St., Galena, 815/777-3454, www.mainstinn.com, $85–130). The 1850s-era inn is right smack in the heart of Galena's shopping and restaurant district. There are six rooms available, and all come with private baths and continental breakfast.

On the east side of the Galena River, across the street from Grant's home, is **The Stillman Inn** (513 Bouthillier St., Galena, 866/777-0557, www.stillmaninn.com, $80–140), an 1858 brick mansion with seven guest rooms, some standard with mini-fridges, CD players, and televisions, plus some suites with fireplaces and whirlpool tubs. The suites can cost up to $260 on a summer weekend. Rooms contain fireplaces, minifridges, CD players, and televisions. Outside the house are gardens and plenty of places to sit. Rates vary according to the season—some go down to $80 in the off-season (Jan.–May) and as high as $260 in the high season.

Over $100

Stay overnight in a hotel where Abraham Lincoln, Mark Twain, and Teddy Roosevelt have all stayed. The **◐ DeSoto House Hotel** (230 S. Main St., Galena, 815/777-0090 or 800/343-6562, www.desotohouse.com, $141), a grand, brick hotel built in 1855, is in the center of downtown Galena, steps from shops, restaurants, historic sites such as the Old Market House, and the Galena River. Named after Hernando DeSoto, reportedly the first European who discovered the Mississippi River, this hotel has quite a past. Lincoln delivered a speech from a balcony inside the hotel on July 23, 1856. And Ulysses S. Grant

COURTESY OF GALENA AREA CONVENTION AND VISITORS BUREAU

DeSoto House Hotel in Galena

had his presidential campaign headquarters here. A range of rooms are available, from a standard room with one double bed to two doubles, kings, and a parlor suite which comes with a private parlor or sitting room with a fireplace, plus a suite with a king bed. Some rooms overlook the inner courtyard. Rates are $156 and up in summer.

If you're visiting the region during the winter, and skiing is on your agenda, book a room at the **Chestnut Mountain Resort** (8700 W. Chestnut Rd., Galena, 800/397-1320, www.chestnutmtn.com), a ski resort that has a 120-room lodge. Lodge rates vary ($84–200, plus more for suites) according to the day of the week you visit and the season. Winter, of course, is when rooms are on the pricey side. Consider this lodge during the summer if you're looking for some good deals, or if you want to stay near the Mississippi River.

South of Galena a few miles, overlooking the Mississippi River is **The Goldmoor Inn** (9001 Sand Hill Rd., Galena, 815/777-3925 or 800/255-3925, www.goldmoorinn.com, $135–345), an inn with four suites, two rooms, cottages, and a cabin. Each one is decorated a little

bit differently (French country, Irish cottage, etc.). They come with amenities such as fireplaces, microwaves and minifridges, stereos, and more. In some you can soak in a hot tub and look out a window at the Mississippi River. Guests have use of bicycles.

Also on the outskirts of town are **Allen's Log Cabin Guest Houses** (11661 W. Chetlain Ln., Galena, 815/777-2043 or 866/847-4637, www.victorianpineslodging.com, $159–225) a cluster of five log cabins from the 1830s. They've all been renovated with modern decor and amenities such as double whirlpool tubs and minifridges. The cabins range in size, from one that sleeps two people to a larger model that can sleep six people. Rates are $159–225.

Many people, when they visit Galena, tend to stick around the town or maybe venture east for a drive along the Stagecoach Trail. Unless they're headed to Iowa, many don't drive through East Dubuque, a small Illinois town about 15 minutes west of Galena on the Mississippi River. Rates at the **N Captain Merry Guest House and Fine Dining** (399 Sinsinawa, East Dubuque, 815/747-3644, www.captainmerry.com, $164–274) may seem steep for a small town such as East Dubuque, but the rooms are huge, absolutely gorgeous, and the food divine. The 1867 Italianate mansion, once home to a successful ferry captain, has five suites (one has 800 square feet). Each has been exquisitely and tastefully designed in muted, earthy colors, and according to a different theme (Mediterranean, Egyptian, etc.) Owners have added some great amenities to the guesthouse, such as a fine-dining restaurant and a movie room with oversized armchairs (for guests only). They were also planning to add a spa to the house.

About six miles east of Galena, at the edge of the resort community The Galena Territory, is **Eagle Ridge Inn and Resort** (444 Eagle Ridge Dr., Galena, 815/777-2444 or 800/892-2269, $199–309). The resort, just off U.S. 20, has 80 rooms, plus it also rents an array of one- to eight-bedroom homes, town houses, and condominiums. Homes rent for $249–1,129 per day. Nearby are four golf courses, exercise and dining facilities, a spa, and horseback-riding center. Consider this resort for longer stays.

FOOD
American
In the mood for some fine chops? **Backstreet Steak and Chophouse** (216 S. Commerce St., Galena, 815/777-4800, www.backstreet-galena.com, open for dinner daily), in the old Galena State Bank, serves everything from grilled lamb chops to pepper-crusted fillets or salmon and other seafood items. Try the New York strip with a crawfish cream sauce. Choose your steak for about $30, and then pick sides such as grilled mushrooms for about $5 more. Most entrées are $15–30; however, the restaurant also offers a few large high-end dishes such as a 28-ounce New Zealand lobster tail and Kansas City strip for more than $100.

The historic **M DeSoto House Hotel** (230 S. Main St., Galena, 815/777-0090, www.desotohouse.com) has three places where you can dine. The Green Street Tavern is a bar and grill that serves lunch and dinner daily. Its brats and burgers will run you about $7. The Courtyard

restaurant in the atrium serves breakfast and lunch daily. If you're looking for a place to indulge in breakfast, put The Courtyard on your list. Its raspberry pancakes, stuffed omelettes, and skillet breakfast will make you want to skip lunch. If you come by during lunchtime, try a Cornish pasty. Breakfasts and lunches are around $8. The General's Restaurant is the hotel's fine-dining operation with a range of steak, seafood, and chicken options. It's open for dinner daily.

Italian
Another great place to eat because of its location (and tasty dishes) is **M Fried Green Tomatoes** (213 N. Main St., Galena, 815/777-3938, www.friedgreen.com, 5–9:30 P.M. Mon.–Thurs., 11:30 A.M.–10 P.M. Fri.–Sun., $15–30). The intimate dining room in downtown Galena, with its exposed brick and stone walls, is in a building that has seen just about every possible use, including a theater, courthouse, and shop. The food is primarily traditional

Fried Green Tomatoes restaurant in Galena

Italian, such as fettuccine Alfredo and lasagna, lots of pasta dishes, plus seafood, veal, beef, and chicken dinners. You must save room for dessert. The restaurant's resident pastry chef prepares the treats daily. The lunch menu has other options for diners, such as grilled vegetable and meatball sandwiches for around $10. On Sundays, singers meander around the room crooning jazz and cabaret tunes.

Vinny Vanucchi's Little Italy (201 S. Main St., Galena, 815/777-8100 or 815/777-8140, www.vinnyvanucchis.com, lunch and dinner daily, $7 lunches, $15 dinners) also cooks traditional hearty Italian fare, such as chicken cacciatore and veal marsala. For lunch, go for the Italian beef or Italian sausage sandwich. With its hardwood floors, checked tablecloths, and outdoor dining deck, this restaurant is comfortable and you might want to prolong your lunch or dinner as you drink some red wine or a glass of beer. If you're traveling with a group, Vinny's is an option. In addition to preparing single-plate servings, the restaurant can serve meals family-style.

Bar and Grill

Benjamin's (103 N. Main St., Galena, 815/777-0467, www.benjaminsgalena.com, lunch and dinner daily, $7 lunches, $15 dinners) is a lively pub and grill on the corner of Hill and Main Street housed in two buildings that date to the 1850s. You'll find standard pub fare here, such as pizza and pita sandwiches, but also quite a surprising selection of not-so-standard tavern food, such as apple pork chops, fried tilapia, and lemon pepper chicken. On some weekend evenings a band strikes it up in the bar.

Coffee Shop

Kaladi's .925 Coffee Bar (309 S. Main St., Galena, 815/776-0723, www.kaladis.com, 7 A.M.–9 P.M. Mon.–Sat., 7 A.M.–7 P.M. Sun.) is the perfect place to go for your morning espresso or cappuccino and plan the day's itinerary or simply read the newspaper. Return in the afternoon for panini sandwiches and gelato. Kaladi's is quite the hotspot on the weekends and the counter line can get long, but usu-

ally everyone, including the staff, is in cheery moods. Sandwiches are around $7.

Wine Bar

The chichi **Grape Escape** (233 S. Main St., Galena, 815/776-WINE or 815/776-9463, www.grapeescapegalena.com, 5–11 P.M. Tues.–Thurs. 5 P.M.–1 A.M. Fri., noon–1 A.M. Sat.) is a wine and martini lounge in downtown Galena that also offers accompaniments such as appetizers and cheese spreads and often features live music (the smooth jazz kind) on the weekends.

Food Markets and Farm Markets

For gourmet food, walk down Main Street to **Galena River Wine and Cheese** (420 S. Main St., Galena, 815/777-9430), which stocks domestic and imported cheese, sausage, beer, and wine. Another option is **The Great Galena Cookery** (in the Galena Art Center's Artists' Annex, 412 Spring St., Galena, 815/777-1556), which sells soapstone cookware and holds cooking classes, and its sister shop, **The Great Galena Peddlery** (116 N. Main St., Galena, 815/777-2307), where you can browse the collection of herbs and teas from around the world.

For fresh produce, head on over to the **Old Market House Square** (123 N. Commerce St., Galena, 7 A.M.–noon May–Oct.), where area farmers sell freshly picked tomatoes, beans, and other items.

On the outskirts of town is **Wooded Wonderland** (610 Devil's Ladder Rd., Galena, 815/777-1223, mid-July–late Aug.), a pick-your-own blueberry farm southeast of Galena and just off U.S. 20; and **Murphy's Gardens** (12550 W. Norris Ln., Galena, 815/777-1177, weekends Aug.–Sept.), which grows raspberries, flowers, and produce. Murphy's is northwest of town, south of U.S. 20.

INFORMATION

The **Galena and Jo Daviess County Convention and Visitors Bureau** (720 Park Ave., Galena, 877/GO-GALENA or 877/464-2536, www.galena.org) has two visitor information centers in Galena. One is in the Old Train Depot (101 Bouthillier St., 815/777-4390) on the east side of the river and the other is at the Old Market House (121 N. Commerce St., 815/777-1448) on the west side of the river in downtown Galena.

Tours

A popular way to tour Galena is on a renovated trolley. Two companies in town offer trolley tours through town and past the major sights, such as Grant's home. They include **Brill's Trolley Tours** (102 N. Main St., Galena, 815/777-3121) and **Galena Trolley Tours** (314 S. Main St., Galena, 815/777-1248, 877-GALENA1, 877/425-3621 www.galenatrolleys.com). Choose from day or evening tours that last an hour or more. Prices can vary from about $10 to $25.

The Jo Daviess County Historical Society leads one-hour walking tours of downtown Galena on Saturdays May–October. Cost is $5 per person. Tours depart from the DeSoto House Hotel.

Set off at sunrise or sunset and take in the awesome views of the Galena River valley aboard a hot-air balloon and thousands of feet up in the air. **Galena on the Fly** (815/777-

2747, www.buyaballoonride.com) organizes one-hour flights for visitors by reservation only. Flyers meet at Eagle Ridge Resort, then head to a departure point, which can vary.

For the paranormal perspective on Galena, join the **Annie Wiggins Ghost Tour** (1004 Park Ave., Galena, 815/777-0336, www.anniewiggins.com), a 1.5-hour walking tour of the village. They're offered on weekend afternoons and evenings May–October and cost $10 per person.

Iowa-based **Mississippi Explorer Cruises** offers scheduled trips along the Upper Mississippi River. It recently started offering 1.5-hour-long river tours that depart from Chestnut Mountain Resort, south of Galena. For more information contact the cruise company at 563/586-4444, www.mississippiexplorer.com or Chestnut Mountain Resort at 800/397-1320, www.chestnutmtn.com. Cost is $20 per person.

Media

The weekly community newspaper is the *Galena Gazette* (716 S. Bench St., Galena, 815/777-0019, www.galenagazette.com), a good source for event listings. Its offices are in downtown Galena, just south of U.S. 20 on the west side of the river.

The Apple River Valley

Believe it or not, there's more to Jo Daviess County than Galena. In fact, when the summer crowds swell in downtown Galena, escape for a day or afternoon by driving along a rolling two-lane highway, through towns where the populations are well below 1,000. Southeast of Galena by about 15 miles is Elizabeth, home to the Apple River Fort State Historic Site, where Sauk leader Black Hawk battled with early miners in 1832. Elizabeth is also a Main Street town where a few artists have opened galleries and on the hilly outskirts is Massbach Winery. The Old Stagecoach Trail northeast of Galena leads to tiny border towns such as Apple River and to the scenic Apple

River Canyon State Park, where you can hike through canyons.

ELIZABETH
Apple River Fort State Historic Site
In 1804 the Sauk Indians sold millions of acres of land to the United States, including land in northwestern Illinois, where they had lived and hunted for many years. Under the agreement, the Sauk could continue to hunt on the land until the government sold it to settlers. Several years later, after returning from the west, Sauk Indians returned to northwestern Illinois and encountered lead miners, who had built a camp

on the Apple River. The Indians were ordered to go west of the Mississippi River. But the leader Black Hawk wanted to return to his native land and led a group of Sauk up the Rock River to reclaim the land. After hearing about Black Hawk's arrival in the state and about the tribe's skirmishes with white settlers, the miners erected a wall of timber around their settlement, now called the Apple River Fort State Historic Site and Interpretive Center (311 E. Myrtle St., Elizabeth, 815/858-2028, 9 A.M.– 5 P.M. Wed.–Sun. Mar.–Oct., 9 A.M.–4 P.M. Wed.–Sun. Oct.–Feb., free). On June 24, 1832, Black Hawk and his warriors attacked the fort. The settlers managed to keep them at bay and Black Hawk moved on. Eventually, however, the tribe was defeated in the brutal Battle of Bad Axe in Wisconsin.

The original Apple River Fort didn't last for more than a dozen years. What you see when you visit is all reconstructed—the log cabins and the firing stations. The whole site, which is actually quite small (around 3,500 square feet) was built in the mid-1990s based on excavations and historical documents. An interpretive center has exhibits on the background of the Sauk Indians, the area's mining history, and the Black Hawk War. If you want to understand more about the region's history, this is a great place to do it. And it shouldn't take you more than an hour to tour the site.

Other Sights and Activities

While in the area, history buffs might want to pay a visit to the **Great Western Railroad Museum** (815/858-2098, 1–4 P.M. Sat.–Sun., May–Oct. or by appointment, free). In an old depot on one of the earliest rail lines in the state—the Chicago Great Western Railroad—the museum highlights the railroad's history and the development of Elizabeth and other area towns.

Downtown Elizabeth (along Main St./ U.S. 20) is home to a handful of galleries and antiques and gift shops. Here's a sampling. **Studio Work** (130 N. Main St., Elizabeth, 815/858-3588) shows pottery, paintings, and

other works of art by locals. **Eshelman Pottery** (238 N. Main St., Elizabeth, 815/858-2327, www.eshelmanpottery.com) features red stoneware creations such as mugs, teapots, and bottles. And the folks at **Harms Cabinetry** (130 N. Main St., Elizabeth, 815/858-3863) restore old furniture and design and build new furniture by hand.

One of the newer wineries in the state, **Massbach Ridge Winery** (8837 S. Massbach Ridge Rd., Elizabeth, 815/291-6700, www.massbachridge.com, noon–6 P.M. Fri.– Sun. Apr.–Oct., noon–5 P.M. Sat.–Sun. Nov.– Apr.) is tucked among 20 acres of hills south of town. It produces more than a dozen wines— red, white, and some fruit wines, such as apple wine. It has a tasting room and gift shop. Winery tours are available.

Just off U.S. 20, about a 10-minute drive east of Galena, is the **Long Hollow Tower** by the town of Elizabeth. Climb the tower for splendid views of the surrounding valleys, farmland, and small towns. Actually, you don't even need to climb the tower to admire the pastoral views. Just pull off into the parking lot and look north and leaf-peepers should be satisfied.

Accommodations

Marcotte's Family Motel (2156 U.S. 20, Elizabeth, 815/858-2217) is not a luxurious hotel (no marble shower stalls here), but the rooms are clean, with comfy touches such as quilts. It has just about every type of room: one king bed, one queen and a double, or two doubles in a room, plus two- or three-room units with kitchens. Rates are $55–85.

If you're planning to visit the region for a three-day weekend or longer, check out **The Home Place** (344 E. Menzemer Rd., Elizabeth, 815/845-9050, www.homeplacegalena.com). It has seven restored log homes from the 1850s surrounded by lush flower and vegetable gardens. All are outfitted with full kitchens, wood-burning fireplaces, and air-conditioning. Other extras? Whirlpool tubs, an outdoor shower, outdoor hot tub, porches. The list goes on and on. Rates are from $150.

Information

The **Elizabeth Chamber of Commerce** (P.O. Box 371, Elizabeth, 815/858-2221, www.elizabeth-il.com) can help with any questions about what to see and do in the area.

MILLVILLE

�ⁿ Apple River Canyon State Park

At about 300 acres, Apple River Canyon State Park (8763 E. Canyon Rd., Millville, 815/492-2477, www.dnr.state.il.us) is one of the smaller state parks in Illinois, but it's definitely one of the most scenic. The rambling Apple River runs through here, past 250-foot-high limestone cliffs, bottomland, and upland forests. Thousands of years ago the Illinois glacier stopped short of this region. While much of Illinois was scraped over by the glacier, the driftless region in far northwest Illinois remained relatively unscathed. The Illinois glacier actu-

ally halted its advance a few miles from the state park and ended up blocking water flow in the Apple River, causing the water to rise and the river to change direction. This high water gradually eroded the limestone and dolomite and created the canyon visitors see today. The park is just off the old stagecoach route and a little town called Millville used to be here; you can see remains of a gristmill and sawmills. Five hiking trails through the park will take you along the river, through the canyon, and atop the bluffs. Along the way are ferns, the rare woodland white violets, and other wildflowers, and trees such as birch, aspen, and chestnut. The park has a campground with tent sites.

While you're in the area, give the folks at **Stage Coach Trails Livery** (5656 Stagecoach Trail, Apple River, 815/595-2423) a call. They organize stagecoach rides pulled by draft horses, plus sleigh rides in the winter.

South of Galena

Follow Highway 84, the Great River Road, south of Galena. Here the land turns a bit more dramatic the closer you get to the Mississippi River. For outstanding views of the river, not to mention some excellent hiking, head to Mississippi Palisades State Park, one of the best parks we've got in the state. The towns here are small (no bigger than 4,000 people), and the restaurants homey. The focus is on outdoor activities: biking, fishing, hiking, and watching birds, particularly eagles in the winter. Fulton, a historically Dutch village about 15 miles south of Savanna, is right on the Great River Road Bike Trail. It's also got a genuine working windmill on the riverfront. South of there is the even smaller town of Albany, which was once home to an ancient mound-building Indian tribe.

SAVANNA

ⓝ Mississippi Palisades State Park

One of the best state parks in the state, Mississippi Palisades State Park (16327 Hwy. 84,

Savanna, 815/273-2731, www.dnr.state.il.us) is a hiker's delight, especially for hikers who love steep hills and wooded bluffs. The 13-mile trail system is essentially divided into two areas: the northern section and the southern section. The southern trails are more rugged and steep than those on the northern side. Novice hikers or hikers who want a more relaxing walk will enjoy the Aspen and Deer trails in the north by the primitive campsites. In the south, Sunset Trail will test your calf muscles, but you'll be rewarded with an awesome view of the Mississippi River at Lookout Point at the top. The Sentinel Trail takes you around a giant, 200-foot-tall column of dolomite. So you're not up for a challenging hike? Drive the roads and pull off at one or all of the scenic overlooks. The sheer number of vistas in Palisades is amazing. Some are quite accessible, even for those who have trouble walking. Handicapped parking spaces for those are close to some vistas with benches, such as Oak Point. Because of the many overlooks, benches, and views of the river, this is a

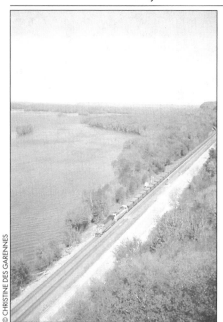

Mississippi Palisades State Park in Savanna

good park for eagle-watching in January and February. Throughout the 2,500-acre park are small caves (including one called Bat Cave), sinkholes, steep cliffs, rock outcroppings, and wildflowers such as trilliums and lady's slippers. The park has several campgrounds. (See *Accommodations* for more information.)

Boating

To cruise the Mighty Mississippi or embark on a fishing expedition, you'll want to launch your boat at the public launch across from the state park's northern entrance. Chances are you'll hook a catfish, bluegill, carp, or bass. There's a boat launch on the Mississippi River on Highway 84, just across from Mississippi Palisades State Park's northern entrance. And there's one on Spring Lake, a backwater lake that's part of the **Upper Mississippi River National Fish and Wildlife Refuge,** just off Highway 84, south of Savanna.

Didn't bring the boat along or you don't own one? You can still see how the fish are biting on the Mississippi River by calling **Captain Ron's Airboat Tours** (630/531-1172, Savanna, www.captainronsadventures.com), which will arrange a fishing charter for you. Don't like fishing? That's fine. You choose what you want to do and it'll arrange the tour. Because you'll be riding in a 20-foot airboat, consider riding through the river's backwaters to scout for eagles and other wildlife. The company will also take you on guided rock-climbing adventures in Mississippi Palisades State Park.

Other Sights and Activities

Spend an hour or so browsing **Pulford Opera House Antique Mall** (324 and 330 Main St., Savanna, 815/273-2661, 9:30 A.M.–5:30 P.M. Mon.–Thurs.), a downtown Savanna antiques shop where several dealers showcase their wares.

The fertile soil in and around Savanna has been great for growing melons. Savanna, which calls itself the Watermelon Capital of the World, celebrates its melon growers and melon-producing history with **Melon Days.** The festival is held annually during Labor Day weekend and features watermelon-eating contests and plenty of watermelons to eat.

For those of you traveling on the back of a Harley-Davidson or other motorcycle, Savanna has two biker-friendly bars: The **Iron Horse Social Club** (314 Main St., Savanna, 815/273-2600), which has a collection of motorcycle memorabilia inside; and **Poopy's** (417 Main St., Savanna, 815/273-4307).

Accommodations

Adjacent to Mississippi Palisades State Park, **M The Nest at Palisades Cabins** (Scenic Ridge Rd., Savanna, 815/273-7824, www.thenestatpalisades.com) rents cabins with kitchens (fridges, microwave ovens), wood-burning stoves, whirlpool tubs, porches, and pluses such as satellite television if the mosquitoes are biting and you'd rather not sit outside. The location can't be beat if you're in town for some serious hiking. A trail leads directly to the park. The owners also provide bicycles for guests. Rates are $138–158 per night.

© CHRISTINE DES GARENNES

For standard hotel or motel accommodations around $50 per night, try the **Thomson House Village Lodge** (800 1 Mile Rd./Hwy. 84, Thomson, 877/675-3233, www.thomson-houselodge.com), a motor lodge between Fulton and Savanna. Otherwise, **Super 8** (101 Valley View Dr., Savanna, 815/273-2288) is a newer hotel with an indoor pool.

Whatever your fancy, if it's private, wooded campsites, or sites large enough to accommodate your new RV, **Mississippi Palisades State Park** has got it. There are more than 240 campsites for RVs (105 sites have electrical hookups), tent campers, and people who want to pack into a primitive site. Some sites are well-manicured and lawnlike. Others are more rustic. Pack-in sites are about a half-mile hike from the parking area. Latrines are scattered throughout the campgrounds. In addition, there are three shower buildings that have running water May–October. A camp store that sells food, snacks, and camping tools can be found near the northern entrance to the park. It's open May–mid-September. The campgrounds, at the northern end of the park, fill up quickly in summertime, especially on holiday weekends. If you plan to camp then, stake your claim early. Campsites are first-come, first-served. Camping is $13–15 per day.

Food
The simple **Café Blue** (321 Main St., Savanna, 815/273-3797, 7 A.M.–3 P.M. daily, $5) in downtown Savanna serves American standards for breakfast and lunch such as biscuits and gravy, French toast, and grilled-cheese sandwiches. Have a seat at the lunch counter or one of the tables. The Blue Burger is a good option for lunch. It's a burger topped with ham and Swiss cheese on sourdough bread.

Similar to a supper club in northern Wisconsin, the **Riverside Supper Club** (Hwy. 84, Savanna, 815/273-5014, 5–9 P.M. Wed., Thurs., 5–10 P.M. Fri., Sat., 10 A.M.–8 P.M. Sun., $12) serves a variety of freshwater fish. Try the all-you-can-eat walleye buffet on Friday evenings or a brunch buffet on Sundays. The restaurant is next to the boat launch across the highway

from Mississippi Palisades State Park's northern entrance by the campground.

Information and Services
The **Savanna Chamber of Commerce** has a tourist information center next to its offices on Main Street. You can't miss it. The offices are in an old train car, and the brochures and maps are at a center next to the car. You can park your car at the lot there and hop on the Great River Trail from there, if you like.

Mount Carroll: Raven's Grin Inn
After working as a plumber, the eccentric Jim Warfield decided he was ready for a career change. He bought a creepy, 1870 Italianate mansion in Mount Carroll (less than 10 miles east of Savanna) and transformed it into the enormously popular Raven's Grin Inn (411 N. Carroll St., Mount Carroll, 815/244-4746, www.hauntedravensgrin.com, open year-round, call for hours, $10). The tour, which usually lasts 1.5 hours, can vary according to who you are (curious child, fearless teen, skeptical adult). Gather some strength and ride the "bad dream bed slide." Strapped to a mattress, you'll drop four stories into the wine cellar, also known as the freaky torture chamber. If you're going to visit during October, call ahead to reserve a spot. The entrance line can wind down the sidewalk.

FULTON
Christened "De Immigrant," **Fulton's Dutch Windmill** (10th and 1st Sts., Fulton, 815/589-4545, www.cityoffulton.us, free) is the city's pride and joy (and biggest attraction). Many immigrants settled here in the late 1800s and this is a tribute to the city's Dutch heritage. The windmill sits atop a flood-control dike overlooking the Mississippi River and is adjacent to flower gardens. The site, with its river views and benches, makes for a good resting stop if you're traveling along the Great River Road. The windmill is authentic (built in the Netherlands), but it's not exactly historic. The 90-foot-tall windmill dates back a few years,

the re-created Dutch windmill at Fulton

rather than centuries. Still, it's fully operational and there are grinding stones inside. (Stone-ground flour is for sale in the gift shop.) You can check out the exterior any time of year. But if you want to tour the welcome center or climb into the windmill to see how it works, you'll have to visit in the spring through the fall. Hours are 10 A.M.–5 P.M. Saturday, 1–5 P.M. Sunday in May and October; 10 A.M.–3 P.M. Monday–Friday, 10 A.M.–5 P.M. Saturday, 1–5 P.M. Sunday in September.; 10 A.M.–5 P.M. Monday–Saturday, 1–5 P.M. Sunday June–August.

At the top of the dike where the windmill is runs the **Great River Bike Trail,** a path that follows the river for more than 60 miles from the Quad Cities on the south to the northern town of Savanna. There's a parking lot here if you want to start your bike ride from here.

The other main attraction in Fulton is **Heritage Canyon** (515 N. 4th St., Fulton, 815/589-2838, 9 A.M.–5 P.M. daily, weather permitting, Apr.–mid-Dec., $2), a limestone quarry that one local couple transformed into a little historical village. It's within steps of the Mississippi River in a residential neighborhood. Visitors

take a self-guided walking tour through the 12-acre site, past buildings mainly from the mid-1800s. They include a log cabin, one-room schoolhouse, church, and other buildings.

Vendors sell kitchen gadgets, tools, glassware, and an assortment of tchotchkes at **Great River Road Antiques** (23080 Hwy. 84, Fulton, 815/589-3355, 10 A.M.–6 P.M. daily Apr.–Oct.). Outside are sale tables, inside are more antiques plus some food and drink for sale.

ALBANY

Another example of the ingenuity of ancient Native Americans can be found at **Albany Mounds State Historic Site** (Cherry St. and 12th Ave., Albany, 309/887-4335, sunrise-sunset daily, free), one of several sites in Illinois where a mound-building village was situated. The inhabitants were from the Middle Woodland Period (about 2,000 years ago) and they built nearly 100 mounds overlooking the Mississippi River. In some of them they buried their dead along with their possessions. Previous excavations of the mounds have turned up items such as obsidian, copper, and sea shells, suggesting the villagers traded with people from the western United States, south to Mexico, and north to the Great Lakes. The present-day site, now listed on the National Register of Historic Places, is about 200 acres and you can see the remaining mounds (ranging in height from a few feet to 15 feet) by walking along a mowed grass path. You can also get to the Great River bike trail from the parking lot.

HANOVER

Old Blanding Tavern and Campground (6848 S. River Rd., Hanover, 815/591-3346) has a 24-foot aluminum flat-bottom boat available for fishing charters on the Mississippi River. A five-hour charter costs $275 for four people. The campground, about a mile or so from the Mississippi River, has 20 sites and seems to attract mostly RVers who plan to stay in the area for a while. RV camping costs $25 for the first week of camping (cheaper thereafter), and $5 per night for tent camping.

It has two trailers available for rent if you're traveling sans RV. A casual bar and restaurant serves burgers, ribs, walleye, and other American food.

The Artful Lodger (500 Washington St., Hanover, 815/591-2365, www.the-artful-lodger.com), a six-bedroom Victorian bed-and-breakfast, is also somewhat of a local arts center. The owners host low-key music concerts, such as Irish dance music, in the parlor, hang local art on the walls, and offer music workshops. The parlor, by the way, is also home to **Koffie met Gebak,** where the owners serve baked goods and vegetarian-friendly lunches. A full breakfast is included. A wheelchair-accessible guest room is available on the first floor. Rooms have a light and airy feel to them (must be the white lace and white bedcovers) and feature some antiques such as iron beds. Rates are $70–100. If you're traveling with a pet, **Hanover Antiques** (201 Jefferson St., Hanover, 815/591-3339) rents a pooch-friendly queen suite, called Schatzi's, for $95 per night.

Along the Rock River

The Mississippi and Illinois rivers garner quite a lot of attention in Illinois because of the bluffs that often jut above their shorelines and because of the fishing and wildlife-viewing opportunities in the parks that border the rivers. Sometimes residents forget about the Rock River, which runs south from Wisconsin, through Rockford and southwesterly to the Mississippi River. It's a river just as scenic as the other two, with its own bluffs and parks here and there. Highway 2 follows much of the river from Rockford south through towns such as Oregon, where you can board a paddlewheel boat for a cruise of the river. Just south of Oregon brake for some hiking or picnicking at Castle Rock State Park, where a sandstone bluff rises above the river's west bank. From there, it's on to the even smaller town of Grand Detour, where blacksmith John Deere forged a plow that would make farming the thick prairie soil a much more manageable chore. And

beyond Grand Detour you'll come to Dixon, a river town known for the thousands of petunias residents plant each year, as well as a local boy who went on to become a Hollywood actor and U.S. president, Ronald Reagan.

OREGON
ⓜ Castle Rock State Park

Right smack in the middle of the Rock River hills region, the 2,000-acre Castle Rock State Park (1365 W. Castle Rd., Oregon, 815/732-7329, www.dnr.state.il.us) is a riverside park with land right along the river as well as up on the hills west of Highway 2. Castle Rock, after which the park is named, is a sandstone bluff east of Highway 2. You can climb up a few sets of stairs to a platform that looks eastward over the river. Near the rock are a few picnic tables and areas for bank fishing. The trails—there are six miles through prairie and native

ALONG THE ROCK RIVER

© AVALON TRAVEL PUBLISHING, INC.

forest—are in the west side of the park, west of Highway 2. Part of this area is set aside as a nature preserve. A layer of glacial till blankets the area, making it a hospitable region for diverse species of flora and fauna. Castle Rock is three miles south of Oregon.

White Pines State Park

If you're tired of staying in hotels or bed-and-breakfasts and prefer a more rustic experience, but are not exactly ready or willing for full-fledged tent camping, make tracks to **White Pines State Park** (6712 White Pines Rd., Mount Morris, 815/946-3717, www.dnr.state.il.us, www.whitepinesinn.com), a 385-acre park west of Oregon. The Civilian Conservation Corps in the 1930s built the log lodge that now houses a restaurant and the 25 cabins near it. The log cabins come with a queen-size, hand-hewn log

bed with a trundle underneath, a private bathroom, air-conditioning, and heat. Rates are $78–98 per night. If you prefer camping, the park does have a 110-site campground with tent and RV sites. The **White Pines Inn Restaurant** (815/946-3817, lunch and dinner Mon.–Sat., brunch Sun., $10) serves steak, seafood, and chicken dishes. The restaurant also often hosts dinner theater productions.

The park, as the names suggests, is home to native pine forest. A little more than five miles of trails, ranging in length up to 1.4 miles, wind through the forest and along creeks. (Try the lookout trail, which takes you along Pine Creek.) The park is about six miles east of U.S. 52, off County Highway 6.

Other Sights and Activities

While you're in the area take a quick detour to

Northern Hill Country

THE GRAND ILLINOIS TRAIL

The Grand Illinois Trail is a series of bicycle trails and street routes that loops around the northern section of the state. The 535-mile trail begins in Chicago and moves northwest and then westward to the Mississippi River, parallel to the Wisconsin border. It then turns south along the Mississippi before heading back east along the Hennepin and I&M canals to Chicago again. The idea for such a trail was floated around for several years. But only since 2003, after more trails were linked to each other and an annual weeklong ride was launched, has the idea of traveling the trail really taken hold with bicyclists.

The trail essentially allows you to bike from downtown Chicago through the rolling hills around Rockford and Freeport to Rock Island, with side trips to some of the state's best state parks, such as Mississippi Palisades, Starved Rock, and Kankakee River state parks. Depending on where you begin your ride, you could be peddling on crushed limestone along rails-to-trails paths or on paved road routes (with directional signs that guide riders). Some of the trails along the way include the Old Plank Road Trail southwest of Chicago, the Illinois Prairie Path in the western Chicago suburbs, the Great River Trail along the Mississippi, and the east-west–running I&M and Hennepin Canal state trails, which are just north of I-80.

More information is available from the **Illinois Department of Natural Resources** (www.dnr.state.il.us) or the **League of Illinois Bicyclists** (www.bikelib.org). Most visitor bureaus in northern Illinois have pamphlets on the trail. Or you can request a copy of the detailed user's guide to the trail from the DNR or League of Illinois Bicyclists. The guide divides the trail into 10 different segments and lists bike repair shops, lodging options, including campsites, and other tips on riding the trail. Both organizations also have information on the annual Grand Illinois Trail and Parks Ride in June.

visit **Lowden State Park** (1411 N. River Rd., Oregon, 815/732-6828, www.dnr.state.il.us), a small park just north of Oregon on the east side of the Rock River. The park contains a nearly 50-foot-tall statue of Black Hawk. The concrete statue, sculpted by Illinois artist Loredo Taft after the turn of the 20th century, looks out over the river valley. The statue is actually hollow, but visitors are not allowed inside.

Docked at Maxon Riverside Restaurant north of Oregon, the *Pride of Oregon* (Hwy. 2, north of Oregon, 815/732-6761 or 800/468-4222, www.maxonrestaurant.com, Apr.–mid-Nov.) is a 100-foot-long paddlewheel boat. It offers lunch and dinner cruises and Sunday brunch rides, plus sightseeing-only rides. Tickets cost $12–30 per person. The restaurant serves lunch and dinner daily.

An old piano factory has been converted into a series of shops called the **Conover Square**

Mall (201 N. 3rd St., Oregon, 815/732-3950, www.conoversquare.com, 9:30 A.M.–5:30 P.M. Mon.–Fri., 9:30 A.M.–5 P.M. Sat., 1–5 P.M. Sun.) Among the businesses are a bookstore, cheese shop, bakery, and pottery store.

Accommodations and Food

The recently remodeled **Patchwork Inn** (122 N. 3rd St., Oregon, 815/732-4114) is a two-story brick inn in downtown Oregon. The inn, more than 150 years old, has been a hotel for most of its years. Abraham Lincoln reportedly slept here. Today there are 10 rooms modestly decorated with homemade quilts. Continental breakfast is served in a sun room. Rates are $75–115.

As noted, the White Pines Inn in White Pines State Park has cabins available for rent plus a campground with tent and RV sites.

A bona fide drive-in with teenage carhops, **Jay's Drive-In** (107 W. Washington

St., Oregon, 815/732-2396) is an old-school drive-in near the Rock River. The menu is extensive, varying from plain hamburgers for under $2 to chicken dinners for $8, gyros, grilled chicken sandwiches, and chicken wings. The main attraction is the drive-in's grilled butter burgers and fries (zesty, twisty fries or cheddar fries). Cones and shakes are also available.

GRAND DETOUR

Named for the bend in the Rock River nearby, Grand Detour is a tiny town with a smattering of white frame houses and flower beds, a place where you'll see older folks on walks. More than 160 years ago an entrepreneurial man came into town, established a blacksmith shop, and would invent an item that would change how farming was done in Illinois and other Midwest states.

John Deere Historic Site

The John Deere Historic Site (8393 S. Main St., Grand Detour, 815/652-4551, www.deere.com, 9 A.M.–5 P.M. daily April–Nov., $3), just west of Highway 2 and the Rock River, comprises an archaeological site, re-created blacksmith shop, and the Deere family home. Deere arrived in town in 1836 and developed the plow in 1837. The original is in the Smithsonian, but there are plenty of other old plows and blacksmith tools on view throughout the site. What was so remarkable about Deere's invention is that it was a self-scouring plow. Farmers could drive it through the thick prairie soil and instead of sticking to the blade, the soil would brush off. This meant farmers could cut down on the amount of time they'd spend in the field scraping the soil off their plows. Farmers loved it, of course, and it was such a success that eventually Deere moved his operation closer to the Mississippi River and Moline, where he could easily ship the plows across the country.

You can see the foundations of Deere's original blacksmith shop by touring a building that was constructed around the excavation site. After walking through there, visitors are treated to a demonstration of the art (by the site's engaging resident blacksmith) at a re-created, but fully functioning, blacksmith shop. The shop was modeled after Deere's shop. (You can buy items made by the blacksmith in the gift shop, where, incidentally, there's also no shortage of green and yellow Deere collectibles.) Also on the site is the six-room, two-story white frame house where Deere lived with his family. Staff have set it up as though the Deere family were still living there. Throughout the summer the site often hosts vintage tractor shows.

DIXON, ROCK FALLS, STERLING
Sights and Activities

Former Hollywood actor and late U.S. President Ronald Reagan grew up in northern Illinois, including Tampico and Dixon. It was in Dixon where he spent his so-called formative years attending school and spending the summers working as a lifeguard at a Rock River park.

The family moved to Dixon from Tampico

Ronald Reagan's boyhood home, Dixon

"DUTCH": THE PRE-HOLLYWOOD AND WASHINGTON, D.C., YEARS

Even before Ronald Reagan died in 2004, it was not uncommon for Illinois folks to wax nostalgic about the former president's time here—from birth to college. In fact, stories about Reagan, such as his days as a lifeguard at a Rock River beach, sound almost mythical. For example, during the summers he worked at the beach in Dixon, the hunky lifeguard reportedly saved 77 lives. (And how many of them were teenage girls who wanted to attract his attention?)

When he was a child, Reagan's family moved around a lot, beginning in Tampico, where he was born, and continuing through Galesburg, Monmouth, and Dixon. From there Reagan was off to college in Eureka, east of Peoria. Not only did the family live in several towns, but they lived in different houses, too. There's no shortage of Reagan destinations in the state. The state has placed a series of highway signs featuring his silhouette throughout the region. They direct travelers to Reagan sites. More information is available from the state-sponsored website, www.ronaldreagantrail.net, which offers lodging and dining suggestions in towns where Reagan once lived or passed through.

Reagan was born on February 6, 1911, in a simple apartment above a bakery in Tampico, where his father worked as a store clerk. The restored **Ronald Reagan Birthplace** (111 S. Main St., Tampico, 815/438-2130), which is open to visitors, is decorated as though it were still 1911. From there, the Reagans moved to Galesburg when Ron was five years old. Ironically, Nancy Davis, whom Ron would later meet in Hollywood and marry, also often spent time in Galesburg visiting relatives there. After Galesburg came Monmouth and finally, Dixon in 1920.

It was in Dixon, a medium-size Rock River town, where Dutch developed into an all-star football player, got the acting bug with the school's drama club, and worked as a lifeguard at Lowell Park. The family lived in what is now the **Ronald Reagan Boyhood Home and Visitors Center** (816 Hennepin Ave., Dixon, 815/288-5176) for only several years before moving into another one, but no matter. Like the Tampico apartment, it's been restored to reflect the years when the Reagans lived there and is filled with 1920s-era furnishings and photographs of Dutch from his years in Dixon and his visits back to the area. The town of Dixon was planning to renovate South Side School, which Reagan attended, and install displays on Reagan and local-history exhibits.

Before eventually leaving for Hollywood, Reagan studied economics and sociology at Eureka College, near the Illinois River to the south. There he also played every sport imaginable (football, track, swimming) and all the while continued to hone his acting skills. Exhibits in Eureka College's **Ronald Reagan Museum** (Donald B. Cerf Center, 300 E. Peoria Ave., Eureka, 309/467-3721, www.eureka.edu) highlight his years here, plus events from throughout his movie and political career. A large room is filled with about 2,000 items, such as photographs of him in his football uniform and books about his life and politics. Nearby is the peace garden with a piece of the Berlin Wall.

in 1920 when Reagan was nine years old. The **Ronald Reagan Boyhood Home and Visitors Center** (816 Hennepin Ave., Dixon, 815/288-5176, 10 A.M.–4 P.M. Mon.–Sat., 1–4 P.M. Sun. Apr.–Nov., 10 A.M.–4 P.M. Sat., 1–4 P.M. Sun. Feb.–Mar., or by appoinment, free) has been restored to a 1920s-era home, complete with all the furnishings. Next to the home is a small garden with a statue of Reagan and a few benches. (Reagan and his pals used to play football in the side yard). Also on Hennepin Avenue is the former South Side School, now undergoing renovation. Ultimately it will house the Dixon Historic Center and contain exhibits about Dixon's favorite son.

For about 50 years, residents of Dixon have been planting thousands and thousands of flowers in beds along roads and in boxes, earning the nickname the Petunia Capital of the World. The town's popular **Petunia Festival** (www.petuniafestival.org), held for several days in late June through early July, is the quintessential Midwestern festival, complete with a parade, the coronation of the petunia queen, country music concerts, a pancake breakfast, fishing derby, and craft show.

The **Midway Drive-In Movie Theater** (Prairieville Rd., Sterling, 815/625-4099) has been showing films for about five decades. All you need is an FM radio in your car to be able to listen.

Drop by **Selmi's Farm Market and Greenhouse** (1206 Dixon Ave., Rock Falls, 815/626-3830, 7 A.M.–7 P.M. daily May–Oct.) for some fresh vegetables, such as sweet corn and pumpkins. There is also a playground area and activities for children.

Accommodations and Food

There are several national chain hotels in Dixon and Rock Falls. Prices here range about $50–75 per night. In Dixon, there's the **Comfort Inn** (136 Plaza Dr., Dixon, 815/284-0500) and **Best Western** (443 Hwy. 2, Dixon, 815/284-1890); and in Rock Falls you'll find **Country Inn and Suites** (2106 1st Ave., Rock Falls, 815/625-3200) and **Holiday Inn** (2105 S. 1st Ave., Rock Falls, 815/626-5500).

In addition, up the hill from Dixon's downtown in a residential area above the Rock River you'll find the **Crawford House Inn** (204 E. 3rd St., Dixon, 815/288-3351, www.crawfordhouseinn.com), an 1869 Italianate brick home. There are three bedrooms, two with king beds, one with queen. All three have feather beds. The decor is Victorian with period antiques (dark wood, floral patterns). The stay includes a full breakfast. Guests share two full bathrooms; there's one bath on each floor. Common sitting areas include the library, parlor, and an expansive porch looking out over the town. Prices here are competitive with those at the chain hotels, up to about to about $85 a night.

If you like a little kick to your food, try the **Salamandra Restaurant** (105 W. 1st St., Dixon, 815/285-0874, $9), an authentic Mexican restaurant in downtown Dixon. The colorful family-run restaurant features dishes from all regions of Mexico, including traditional fare such as *carne asada,* burritos, sandwiches, salads, but also specialties such as the excellent potato and chorizo *sincronizada* (flour tortillas filled with chorizo, potatoes, jalapeño, cheese, and other ingredients).

A few feet away is another find, **Baker Street** (111 W. 1st St., Dixon, 815/285-2253, 7 A.M.–5:30 P.M. Mon.–Fri., 7 A.M.–2 P.M. Sat.), a coffeehouse and *boulangerie* (French for bakery).

Information

For more info about the region, contact the **Rock Falls Visitors Bureau and Chamber of Commerce** (601 W. 10th St., Rock Falls, 815/625-4500, www.rockfallsil.com).

MORRISON

Just off U.S. 30, the Lincoln Highway, the town of Morrison has a surprisingly thriving downtown, where the casual restaurants are especially busy on Friday nights serving families and teens. North of town, take a quick detour to drive through a new covered bridge, and then drop a fishing line in the lake at Morrison-Rockwood State Park for some R&R.

Morrison-Rockwood State Park

In the summer the focal point of the 1,100-acre Morrison-Rockwood State Park (18750 Lake Rd., Morrison, 815/772-4708, www.dnr.state.il.us) is Lake Carlton, a spring-fed reservoir stocked with a variety of fish. If you have a boat you can launch it from a ramp here, or have a go at bank fishing. In the winter, this is a great place to go for some serious cross-country skiing or snowshoeing. Follow the 14-mile horse trail through the woods and along the rambling Rock Creek, a tributary to the Rock River. The park also has a campground.

On the way to Morrison-Rockwood State Park, look for signs to the **Covered Bridge** (Crosby Rd., follow signs north of Morrison, 815/772-5175). It's actually a new bridge that stretches almost 150 feet in length. Feel free to drive through it. It's full of light because dozens of spaces or windows line both sides of the bridge.

Food

Blue Goose Run (14609 Blue Goose Rd., Sterling, 815/772-7200, www.bluegooserun.com) is a country farm that has become home to a fine-dining, white-tablecloth restaurant and wine bar, banquet hall, corn maze, huge chess and checkers set, and 3.5-acre gardens. Lunches are served beginning at 11 A.M. Monday–Friday, dinners 5 P.M.–10 P.M. Friday–Saturday, brunches 10 A.M.–2 P.M. Sunday. It's halfway between Sterling and Morrison, just north of U.S. 30.

At the casual and kid-friendly **Isle of Rhodes** (Main St., Morrison, 815/772-7431), you can try the regional specialty called Chicken George. A plate of Chicken George usually consists of white chicken strips deep-fried in a slightly sweet batter. (Some say the batter tastes like funnel cakes or elephant ears.) It's open 11 A.M.–9 P.M. Monday–Thursday, 6:30 A.M.–10 P.M. Friday, 6 A.M.–10 P.M. Saturday, 7 A.M.–9 P.M. Sunday.

SOUTH OF I-88 AND THE ROCK RIVER

Tampico

An apartment where Ronald Reagan was born has been restored and fans of the 40th president of the United States are welcome to tour the place. The **Ronald Reagan Birthplace** (111 S. Main St., Tampico, 815/438-2130, 10 A.M.–4 P.M. Mon.–Sat., 1–4 P.M. Sun. Apr.–Dec., donation) also has a souvenir shop.

The Dutch Diner Family Restaurant (105 S. Main St., Tampico, 815/438-2096) serves good old American standards such as casseroles and homemade pies.

Amboy

If you're feeling nostalgic, drive south on U.S. 52 to the town of Amboy and pay a visit to the **Amboy Pharmacy** (202 E. Main St., Amboy, 815/857-2323, 8 A.M.–5 P.M. Mon.–Fri., 8 A.M.–10 P.M. Sat., 8 A.M.–2 P.M. Sun.), an actual pharmacy and soda fountain shop. A soda jerk mixes phosphates, milk shakes, and whips up sundaes. And if you're out of aspirin or bug spray, well, you can stock up on some of those too while you're here.

© CHRISTINE DES GARENNES

Amboy Depot

Northern Hill Country

Rockford and Vicinity

The largest city in Illinois outside of Chicago, Rockford is a diverse city of more than 152,000 people on the Rock River. Founded by a group of Galena residents in the 1830s, Rockford, halfway between Chicago and Galena, was once called Midway. For years travelers tended to think of Rockford as exactly that—a halfway point, a place to fill up your tank of gas while traveling to Galena or north to Madison, Wisconsin. Those travelers, when they think of Rockford, tend to think of the traffic backups that can occur near the toll plaza south of town at I-90 and U.S. 20.

But a visit to Rockford can yield surprises, especially for people interested in regional history and art. Because the city was quite a hub for manufacturing, thousands of immigrants migrated to the area, attracted by the hope of landing jobs at agricultural equipment factories, furniture makers, knitting mills, and other businesses. Swedes, Irish, and Eastern Europeans, followed by Southern blacks, all made Rockford their home. Several homes and buildings around town showcase photographs, furniture, and other items left behind by many of the city's early residents. One of the finest is the Tinker Swiss Cottage, a home that looks as if it belongs in the Swiss Alps, not northern Illinois. On the west bank of the river is a museum park, home to, among other art organizations, the Rockford Art Museum, which contains an impressive collection of American art; and the Burpee Museum of Natural History, a must-see for anyone curious about how Illinois is shaped the way it is and what kind of cultures lived here before the white settlers arrived.

Finally, Rockford should be on your list if you're a gardener or interested in horticulture. The town has an amazing collection of parks. Stroll through Anderson Gardens (formal Japanese gardens), Klehm Arboretum and Botanic Garden, plus riverside parks with walking and biking paths.

SIGHTS

Museums

Outside of Chicago's Field Museum, the place to learn about prehistoric life in Illinois is Rockford's **Burpee Museum of Natural History** (737 N. Main St., Rockford, 815/965-3433, www.burpee.org, 10 A.M.–5 P.M. Mon.–Sat., noon–5 P.M. Sun., $5, free Wed.). The most recent addition to the museum is a skeletal cast of a *Tyrannosaurus rex,* dubbed Jane. (Jane is Rockford's answer to the Field Museum's Sue, another famed *T. rex.*) Near the 10-foot-high and 40-foot-long skeleton is a reproduction of a wooly mammoth. A reminder: Things were big millions of years ago. The museum also has a cool recreation of what a coal forest may have looked like 300 million years ago, exhibits about glaciers and how they shaped the land, plus displays about Native American life in the region before the white settlers arrived.

How does air move? How does an airplane work? What's the best way to swing a bat or toss a football? The kid-friendly **Discovery Center Museum** (711 N. Main St., Rockford, 815/963-6769, www.discoverycentermuseum.org, 10 A.M.–5 P.M. Mon.–Sat., noon–5 P.M. Sun., Thurs. until 7 P.M. in the summer, $5), also at the riverfront park, attempts to demystify science and explain theories to youth and the nonscientific set. In addition to the applied-science exhibits, the museum has a planetarium and an outdoor playground called WaterWorks where kids can race boats and engage in other water play.

Adjacent to the Discovery Museum is the **Rockford Art Museum** (711 N. Main St., Rockford, 815/968-2787, www.rockfordartmuseum.org, 10 A.M.–5 P.M. Mon.–Wed., Fri.–Sat., 10 A.M.–7 P.M. Thurs., noon–5 P.M. Sun., $3, free Thurs.). It showcases 19th- and 20th-century American art by organizing rotating exhibits and highlighting pieces from its permanent collection. Expect everything from realism landscape paintings and portraits to

ROCKFORD

To Rock Cut
State Park

CREEK RD

To Rock Cut
State Park

Charlie Woodward
Martin Memorial Park

CLIFFBREAKERS
RIVERVIEW SUITES

MAIN ST

RIVERSIDE BLVD

KILBURN AVE

CENTRAL AVE

AUBURN ST

WHITMAN

CHURCH ST

MAIN ST

BURPEE MUSEUM

CORONADO THEATRE

MARIA'S
ITALIAN CAFÉ

PARAGON ON STATE

DISCOVERY CENTER

ROCKFORD ART MUSEUM

TINKER PARK/TINKER
SWISS COTTAGE

CHESTNUT

WALNUT ST

MORGAN ST

MONTAGUE RD

JEFFERSON ST

2ND

E STATE ST

ETHNIC
HERITAGE
MUSEUM

KLEHM ARBORETUM
AND BOTANICAL
GARDEN

MAIN ST

15TH AVE

KISHWAUKEE ST

BROADWAY

HARRISON AVE

ROCKFORD AVE

CHARLES ST

ANDERSON
JAPANESE GARDENS

PARKVIEW AVE

WELTY AVE

SPRING

HIGHCREST RD

RURAL ST

FOREST HILLS RD

2ND ST

Sinissippi
Park

Rock River

ALPINE RD

GUILFORD RD

MULFORD RD

CREEK RD

MIDWAY VILLAGE
AND MUSEUM
CENTER

E STATE ST

PERRYVILLE RD

PERRYVILLE RD

NEWBURG RD

BELL SCHOOL RD

NORTHWEST TOLLWAY

BEST
WESTERN
CLOCK TOWER
RESORT

MAGIC WATERS
AMUSEMENT PARK

90 39

251

251

20 39

1 mi

1 km

0

0

Northern Hill Country

© AVALON TRAVEL PUBLISHING, INC.

abstract sculpture. Among the highlights: a Loredo Taft sculpture, painting by Rudolph Ingerle, and an Ed Ruscha lithograph.

You'll find the **Tinker Swiss Cottage** (411 Kent St., Rockford, 815/964-2566, www.tinkercottage.com, tours at 1, 2, and 3 P.M. Tues.–Sun., $4) in Rockford's historic west bank district. On the National Register of Historic Places, the cottage (it's more like a miniestate) was built in 1864. Rockford businessman Robert Tinker modeled it after homes he saw while traveling through Europe. (Tinker, by the way, was not born in Switzerland, but in Hawaii). The home, which features intricate woodwork and plasterwork, also contains a conservatory and a rose garden. Inside the house is furnished with period items and on the walls hang portraits of the Tinker family's relatives.

If you enjoy touring old homes and want to learn more about Rockford's past, walk a block south from the Tinker Cottage to the **Ethnic Heritage Museum** (1115 S. Main St./Hwy. 2, Rockford, 815/968-6044, 2–4 P.M. Sun., $2). Each room in the 1850s-era home is devoted to a different ethnic group that helped build Rockford: African Americans, Hispanics, Irish, Italians, Lithuanians, and Poles.

The folks behind the **Midway Village and Museum Center** (6799 Guilford Rd., Rockford, 815/397-9112, www.midwayvillage.com, 11 A.M.–4 P.M. Tues.–Sun. June–Sept., 11 A.M.–4 P.M. Thurs.–Sun. May and Oct., $4–5) have amassed quite the collection of historic and re-created buildings from the turn of the 20th century. Two dozen buildings are clustered around the 137-acre site to make visitors think they're visiting a town circa 1900. Walk into an old-time barbershop, general store, hotel, fire station, and other buildings. It looks pretty real except here the grass is kept nicely trimmed and some of the structures were rebuilt at three-quarter scale. Speaking of small scale, there's a doll museum on the grounds.

Parks and Gardens

Though some of its downtown buildings could use some rehabbing, Rockford's parks are in tip-top shape. **Klehm Arboretum and Botanic Garden** (2701 Clifton Ave., Rockford, 815/965-8146, www.klehm.org, 9 A.M.–8 P.M. Memorial Day–Labor Day, $2) is a 150-acre park south of downtown where lots of trails curl past blooming flowers and trees. Walk among flowering dogwoods and crabapple trees and a 12-acre bur oak grove. Have a seat under a pergola and listen to the water fountain. Gather ideas for your own garden by visiting the demonstration garden, and check out the ornamental grasses, hostas, and daylilies.

One of the best parks in the county is **Anderson Gardens** (318 Spring Creek Rd., Rockford, 815/229-9390, www.andersongardens.org, 10 A.M.–5 P.M. Mon.–Fri., 10 A.M.–4 P.M. Sat., noon–4 P.M. Sun. May–late Oct., $5), formal Japanese gardens along the riverfront that feature trickling waterfalls, a tea-house replica, and some sculpture. Nearby are two more riverside parks. **Sinnissippi Park** (1300 N. 2nd St., Rockford, 815/987-8858, www.rockfordparkdistrict.com) is a good place to unwind, soak in the sun, or read a book or magazine. Pick a bench looking out onto the river, a spot under the trees, or near the lagoons. Here you have access to the **Rock River Recreation Path,** a paved trail that follows the river for seven miles from downtown Rockford north to Loves Park. Sinnissippi also has a lagoon (home to mute swans) and a greenhouse that is open 9 A.M.–4 P.M. daily spring–fall. To the north is **Charlie Woodward Martin Memorial Park** (5600 Park Ridge, Loves Park), which is also on the Rock River Recreation Path. Here you'll find a pavilion, playground, and boat ramp.

Farther north of town, **Rock Cut State Park** (7318 Harlem Rd., Loves Park, 815/885-3311, www.dnr.state.il.us) is a 3,000-acre park just off I-90. (I-90 actually divides the park into two sections, sections that are connected by an overpass road). Fat-tire riders, rejoice. The park has 23 miles of designated mountain-biking trails that wind around lakes, oak and hickory forest, and prairie. Park your bike for a while and choose from more than 40 miles of hiking trails, and, in the winter, go cross-country skiing and snowshoeing. The park also has a campground, wheelchair-accessible fishing piers, and a swimming beach on Olson Lake, which is on the east side of the park. The beach is open noon–7 P.M. daily, Memorial Day–Labor Day. Beach access costs $1 per person.

ENTERTAINMENT

More than a dozen performing arts groups call Rockford and the surrounding towns home. Some of the highlights include the baroque, gilded, and just plain opulent **Coronado Theatre** (314 N. Main St., Rockford, 815/966-2100, www.coronadotheatre.com), a renovated 1927 vaudeville house that hosts concerts and Broadway plays and musicals; and the **Metro-Centre** (300 Elm St., Rockford, 815/968-5222, www.centreevents.com), a modern 10,000-seat venue that hosts music concerts and sporting events. Organizations include (but are certainly not limited to the **Rockford Dance Company** (815/963-3341, www.rockforddance-company.com) and the **Rockford Symphony Orchestra** (815/965-0049, www.rockfordsymphony.com). Both are both in the riverside museum park at 711 N. Main St., Rockford.

For a change of pace, head to **Octane Interlounge** (124 N. Main St., Rockford, 815/965-4012, www.octane.net), part coffee joint, Internet café, and nightclub. Sink into a blue velvet couch with a newspaper, coffee, and muffin in the morning. At night, sip on a martini.

ACCOMMODATIONS
$50–100
Sweden House Lodge (4605 E. State St., Rockford, 815/398-4130 or 800/886-4138, www.swedenhouselodge.com, $60) is a 105-room Swedish motor lodge halfway between downtown Rockford and I-90. The cheery hotel has a mix of standard motel rooms and suites that come with kitchenettes. The lodge also has an indoor pool.

Rockford also has a dozen or so chain hotels off I-39 and U.S. 20 exits. A sampling: **Comfort Inn** (7392 Argus Dr., Rockford,

815/398-7061, $105); **Hampton Inn** (615 Clark Dr., Rockford, 815/229-0404, $109–119); **Red Roof Inn** (7434 E. State St., Rockford, 815/398-9750, $54); and **Sleep Inn** (725 Clark Dr., Rockford, 815/398-8900). For a complete list, contact the visitor bureau.

$100–150
Overlooking the Rock River and a few hundred feet from the Rock River Recreation Path, **Ⅶ Cliffbreakers Riverview Suites Hotel** (700 W. Riverside Blvd., Rockford, 815/282-3033 or 800/478-9395, www.cliffbreakers.com, $129) is the best place to stay if you want to keep driving to a minimum. Bring your bikes along, and then ride across the bridge and head south to town and the parks and museums. The hotel has a restaurant and indoor pool on-site.

For more of a retreatlike setting, try the **Ⅶ Best Western Clock Tower Resort** (7801 E. State St., Rockford, 815/398-6000, www.clocktowerresort.com, $119–129), just off I-90 and State Street (U.S. 20). The 247-room hotel complex has just about everything travelers could ask for: a large indoor pool playland for the kids, fitness center with tennis and racquetball courts for the adults, plus a restaurant and lounge and high speed Internet access.

FOOD

The usually busy **Maria's Italian Café** (828 Cunningham St., Rockford, 815/968-6781, dinner Tues.–Sat.) serves northern Italian dishes, heaping portions of pasta, polenta, and steak dinners. People keep going back to Maria's for the homemade pasta and sauces, which taste amazingly fresh. Most entrées are less than $10.

Another popular eatery is the **Stockholm Inn** (2420 Charles St., Rockford, 815/397-3534, www.thestockholminn.com, 6 A.M.–8 P.M. Mon.–Fri., 6 A.M.–12:30 P.M. Sat., 7 A.M.–1:30 P.M. Sun.). The sunny Swedish restaurant and gift shop churns out traditional meals such as Swedish pancakes and meatballs, and some seafood dishes.

Housed in a refurbished brick building in Rockford's downtown river district, **Paragon on State** (205 W. State St., Rockford, 815/963-1660, lunch Tues.–Fri., dinner Tues.–Sun, $5–12 lunches, $19–32 dinners) is a modern restaurant and sushi bar with modular decor (cherry chairs and purple-painted walls). Dishes are creative here, such as shiitake mushroom salad, chicken bruschetta sandwich, New Zealand rib chop.

INFORMATION

The **Rockford Area Convention and Visitors Bureau** (102 N. Main St., Rockford, 815/963-8111 or 800/521-0849, www.gorockford.com) has comprehensive lodging, dining, and tour information for visitors.

Tours

The Rockford Park District operates open-air **trolley tours** departing from Riverview Park (324 N. Madison St., Rockford, 815/987-8894). A ride, about 45 minutes long, will cost $4 per adult. From the same location the park district launches **riverboat rides** on the Rock River aboard the *Forest City Queen*. Call for hours.

Media

The daily newspaper is the ***Rockford Register Star*** (99 E. State St., Rockford, 815/987-1200, www.rrstar.com), available in most grocery stores and convenient stores.

GETTING THERE AND AROUND

Air

Rockford Airport (Airport Dr., Hwy. 2, south of U.S. 20, Rockford, 815/969-4000, www.rockfordairport.com) is a full-service airport south of town. (Technically, it's called Northwest Chicagoland International Airport—International because some companies fly to the Caribbean Islands.) The airlines that service the airport include Northwest Airlines (to and from Detroit, Michigan), TransMeridian (Orlando/Sanford, Las Vegas,

Nevada, and San Juan, Puerto Rico); Vacation Express (Aruba, Bahamas, Cancún, and several other Caribbean destinations); Hooters Air (Atlanta, Georgia, Denver, Colorado, Myrtle Beach, South Carolina, Las Vegas, Nevada); and SunShip1 Airlines (Cancún and Puerto Vallarta, Mexico).

Car

Rental-car companies **Avis** (815/962-8447), **Hertz** (815/963-5318), and **National/Alamo** (815/965-4466) are all at the Rockford Airport.

Rockford has several taxicab services. They include **Caravan** (815/633-8461), **Reliable Cab** (815/968-2227), **Spee-Dee Taxi Cab Service** (815/963-3322), **Latino's Service** (815/765-0294), **Trans A Town** (815/962-8253), and **Yellow Line Cab** (815/962-5511).

Mass Transit

Rockford Mass Transit District (520 Mulberry St., Rockford, 815/961-9000, www.rmtd.org) buses run daily. Rides cost $1 per person.

DAY TRIPS FROM ROCKFORD

Cedarville and Vicinity

In honor of Cedarville native and humanitarian Jane Addams, founder of Chicago Hull House, the community helped develop the **Jane Addams Trail** (www.janeaddamstrail.com), a 13-mile crushed-limestone trail from north of Freeport to the Illinois-Wisconsin state line. A rails-to-trails project, the trail follows part of the Galena and Chicago Union Railroad line, past oak groves, corn and soybean fields, and prairie. A section of the trail passes Cedarville Cemetery on Mill Street, where Addams is buried. In the winter it's open for snowmobiling and cross-country skiing. You can get to the trail north of Freeport, off Fairview Road, which is south of U.S. 20. Other places to park your car and hit the trail are at the Richland Creek Trailhead on High Street, north of Orangeville; off Red Oak Road in Red Oak; and off McConnell Road in Buena Vista.

Chomp on a sweet, crunchy apple or slice into a warm apple fritter at **Honey Hill Orchard** (7469 W. McConnell Rd., McConnell, 815/369-5119, daily Sept.–Nov.). Pick out your pumpkins, shops for mums, and come hungry. The folks here bake cider doughnuts, apple pies and breads, and just about every other type of apple concoction you can dream up.

Rockton

One of the area's first white settlers was a man named Stephen Mack, a fur trader. His humble 1834 home, now listed in the National Register of Historic Places, is straight north of Rockford on the Pecatonica River. The **Stephen Mack Home and Whitman Trading Post** (Macktown Forest Preserve, 2221 Freeport Rd., Rockton, 815/877-6100, call for hours, $1) contains a few tools and pieces of furniture from the early 1800s, plus some Native American artifacts.

Information

For lodging, dining, and recreational options in towns west of Rockford, contact the **Freeport-Stevenson County Convention and Visitors Bureau** (2047 Ayp Rd./U.S. 20, Freeport, 815/233-1358 or 800/369-2955, www.stephensoncounty-il.org).

U.S. 34 Corridor: Plano to Princeton

PLANO

The Farnsworth House

Far from the steel skyscrapers he designed for Chicago, Mies van der Rohe's **The Farnsworth House** (14520 River Rd., Plano, 630/552-8622, 10 A.M.–3 P.M. Tues.–Sat. March–Nov., $20) is planted in a patch of woods along the Fox River. The white steel and glass home, built in 1951 for Chicago doctor Edith Farnsworth, is something else. It's a completely unadorned house that directs visitors to look at the river instead of paintings on a wall. It's transparent; many of the walls are windows. A must-see for architecture and design buffs. To others, it's just a modern house that could use some drapes in it.

SANDWICH

Sights and Activities

Every year about 65,000 people wander up and down the aisle of the **Sandwich Antiques Market** (Sandwich Fairgrounds, 1401 Suydam Rd., Sandwich, 815/786-3337, www.sandwich-il.org, 8 A.M.–4 P.M., third or fourth Sun. of the month, May–Oct., $5 admission) to hunt for 19th- and 20th-century antiques. About 500 dealers set up tables and tents (some inside buildings and some outside) here.

Built in 1878, the **Sandwich Opera House** (140 E. Railroad St., Sandwich, 815/786-2555, 8:30–noon, 1:30–4:30 P.M. Mon.–Fri., and during performances, www.sanwichoperahouse.com) once housed city hall on the first floor and a vaudeville theater on the second floor. Today the renovated performance space showcases everything from bluegrass to gospel music.

Information

Any questions about the area? Call the **Sandwich Chamber of Commerce** (128 E. Railroad St., Sandwich, 815/786-9075).

PRINCETON

A picturesque town south of the Hennepin Canal and I-80, Princeton in recent years has emerged to become a nice little detour for drivers along U.S. 6, the Grand Army Highway, and U.S. 34. Its downtown is lined with antiques and gift shops. The residential neighborhoods along Euclid Avenue and Church Street boast many restored turn-of-the-20th-century homes. And north of town is a red covered bridge.

Princeton is a railroad town literally (the tracks are just north of U.S. 6) and figuratively. Slaves escaping to the north were said

Northern Hill Country

downtown Princeton

to have traveled through here. The **Owen Lovejoy Homestead** (E. Peru St., Princeton, 815/879-9151, 1–4 P.M. Fri.–Sun. May–Sept.), was a stop on the Underground Railroad. It was home to an abolitionist preacher. Near the home is a one-room schoolhouse also open to visitors. While you're in downtown Princeton, visit **Hoffman's** (513 S. Main St., Princeton, 815/875-1944), an antiques shop with a vast collection of discontinued china. And for some refreshment, there's **Jaya Juice Bar** (509 S. Main St., Princeton, 815/875-1751) which specializes in herbal teas, juices, and herbal and nutritional supplements. A few doors down is **Eco Espresso** (529 S. Main St., Princeton, 815/872-6246), where servers whip up smoothies and coffee drinks. The 1863 **covered bridge** is a few miles northwest of Princeton off Highway 26. Signs will point you to the bridge.

Information

You can gather more traveling tips about the region from the **Bureau County Tourism Council** (Princeton, 800/664-4420 or 815/454-2502) or the **Princeton Chamber of Commerce** (815/875-2616, www.princeton-il.com).

North of Princeton

One of the state's newest multiuse recreational trails runs alongside the **Hennepin Canal,** a nearly 100-year-old canal that connects the Illinois River with the Mississippi River near Moline. The canal, now listed on the National Register of Historic Places, was mainly used as a shipping canal throughout the first half of the 20th century. In the 1950s it opened to boat traffic. In recent years the state developed a trail on one side and opened up the old tow path on the other side (which, because it's mostly grass, is good for hiking and fat-tire riding). Depending on where you go, the canal itself spans through five counties through Bureau, Henry, Lee, and Whiteside, mostly through farmland and prairie, past locks and dams, some aqueducts, an old boat-repair yard, and parks. On some legs the trail is paved with oil and chip, and in other areas there's crushed limestone. All told, there are about 95 miles of trails. A visitors center is one mile south of I-80, just west of U.S. 34, Sheffield, 815/454-2328.

Because of erosion and overgrazing, what was once cattle pasture is now a 200-acre park with dunes, prickly pear cactuses, and tall, willowy prairie grasses such as big blue stem. The **McCune Sand Prairie** (5.5 miles north of Mineral on County Rd. AA, Mineral, 815/875-8732, ext. 3) is transforming itself back to a prairie. It's a peaceful place, miles from any major highway, where several narrow walking paths crisscross over rolling hills and dunes. Managed by the local soil and water conservation district, it's open sunrise–sunset daily.

McHenry County

WOODSTOCK

In the center of McHenry County, Woodstock (population 21,000) is a picturesque town surrounded by rolling hills and horse farms. Its courthouse square, home to a Dick Tracy museum, opera house, park, and antiques and gift shops, is a postcard-perfect Midwestern town. Remember the Bill Murray movie *Groundhog Day?* That was filmed in downtown Woodstock.

Sights and Activities

Chester Gould, the man who invented the comic strip about a plainclothes detective named Dick Tracy, spent the last 50 years of his life in Woodstock. The **Chester Gould and Dick Tracy Museum** (in the Old Courthouse Arts Center, 101 N. Johnson St., Woodstock, 815/338-8281, www.chestergould.org, 11 A.M.–5 P.M. Thurs.–Sat., 1–5 P.M. Sun., donation) on the square contains exhibits about Gould's life and art. Gould grew up in Oklahoma and moved to Chicago in 1921 specifically to become a cartoonist. It wasn't easy. His cartoons were often rejected, and you can see some of those rejection slips (which he saved) in the museum. Also on view are Gould's drawing table and memorabilia from the 1990 movie starring Warren Beatty as the detective with the chiseled jaw. And of course, there are many images of Tracy and the criminals he battled, such as Pruneface and Wormy, and some of the technological gadgets Tracy was famous for using, such as the two-way wrist radio and the spaceship powered by magnetism. In a side room, kids get to play detective with some interactive exhibits.

Down the street from the museum is the

1889 **Woodstock Opera House and Performing Arts Center** (121 Van Buren St., Woodstock, 815/338-5300, www.woodstockoperahouse.com), a gorgeous steamboat Gothic building that has had everyone from Orson Welles to Paul Newman perform here. It hosts city band concerts, an opera festival, and other events. Visual art is also displayed here.

Unlike other areas of the state where large bodies of water were created by men, the northeastern corner of Illinois is full of naturally formed lakes. Thousands of years ago when the last glacier was retreating from Illinois, a giant block of it broke off and melted. Thus we have Lake Defiance in **Moraine Hills State Park** (914 S. River Rd., McHenry, 815/385-1624, www.dnr.state.il.us). Moraine Hills, in the northeastern part of the county, has 1,690 acres, half of which is lakes or wetland areas. It's also home to a few nature preserves, such as Leatherleaf Bog and Pike Marsh. Follow the Leatherleaf Bog Trail to view the floating layer of sphagnum moss growing on the water's surface, and walk past willows, ferns, marsh marigolds, and other wetland plants.

Otherwise, the Fox River Trail, which takes visitors to the river on the west side of the park, has some wildlife-viewing platforms so you can take a break from walking and watch ducks, beavers, and other animals. Finally, visit the nature center on Lake Defiance to learn more about how bogs develop. The park also has concession stands at the McHenry Dam and Lake Defiance, where you can rent fishing boats and buy some bait. In the winter you can rent cross-country skis at the Lake Defiance building.

UNION, ALGONQUIN, BARRINGTON

Sights and Activities

Hulking locomotives, sleek streamliners, and dozens of other railcars are open to the public at the **Union Illinois Railway Museum** (7000 Olson Rd., Union, 815/923-4000, www.irm.org, open April–Oct., call for times, $6–12). The 50-acre site is packed with steamers, diesels, and a variety of different railcars. Visitors take a 10-mile ride on an old intraurban line on a steam locomotive or diesel passenger train. The museum hosts special events throughout the year for Mother's Day, Father's Day, and other holiday weekends. In a similar vein, but on a much smaller scale, the **Valley View Model Railroad Museum** (17108 Highbridge Rd., Union, 815/923-3135, Memorial Day–Labor Day, call for hours) features miniature locomotives and railcars.

You don't have to drive down to Branson, Missouri, if you want to take in a country music show or wander around a faux pioneer town. Rally up the kids for a day at **Donley's Wild West Town** (8512 S. Union Rd., Union, 815/923-9000, www.wildwesttown.com, 10 A.M.–6 P.M. daily Memorial Day–Labor Day, and weekends only Apr., May, Sept., Oct., $12.50), a Wild West playland of sorts. Ride through the park on a scale-model locomotive train, watch a dramatized shootout, country music shows, belly up to the bar at a re-created saloon, and pan for gold. But wait, there's more: pony rides, a blacksmith shop, ice-cream parlor, steakhouse, and cowboy museum.

Raging Buffalo (Hwy. 31 at the McHenry/Kane County Line, Algonquin, 847/846-RAGE or 847/846-7243, www.ragingbuffalo.com) is a winter park specifically for snowboarding. During the season (generally Nov.–Mar.) it's open 4–10 P.M. Monday–Thursday, 4–11 P.M. Friday, 9 A.M.–11 P.M. Saturday, 9 A.M.–Sunday. Admission costs $28–38; rentals are $15–40.

If you've got shopping on the brain, this area has several shopping centers, from **Prime Out-** lets (I-90 at Hwy. 47, Huntley, 847/669-9100 or 888/545-7222, www.primeoutlets.com), which contains a mix of name-brand clothing, sporting goods, and houseware stores such as London Fog, Pfaltzgraff, and Reebok. You'll find designer clothing, jewelry, and other specialty shops in **Barrington's Ice House Village** (200 Applebee St., Barrington, 847/381-6661), a 1904 former icehouse in downtown Barrington. Finally, near the Fox River you can shop for neoclassic and country-style ceramic items at **The Haeger Potteries Museum and Shop** (7 Maiden Ln., East Dundee, 847/783-5420, www.haegerpotteries.com, 10 A.M.–6 P.M. Mon., Thurs., Fri., 11 A.M.–5 P.M. Sat., Sun.). The family-owned business has been creating artistic vases, pitchers, plates, and sculptures since the 1800s.

Food

One of the best restaurants near the Fox River, **M Emmett's Tavern and Brewing Co.** (128 W. Main St., West Dundee, 847/428-4500, www.emmettstavern.com, lunch and dinner daily, lunches $5–13, dinners $13–25) is a slightly upscale tavern in West Dundee's historic district. It serves gourmet comfort food, from the freshly baked pretzels, hand-crafted beer (made in the copper tanks on view in the restaurant), to the whitefish sandwiches and homemade bread. Other options include peppercorn sirloin and buffalo burgers. Emmett's is one of those places that you could never grow tired of.

A fixture on the Fox for decades, the **Port Edward** (20 W. Algonquin Rd., Algonquin, 847/658-5441, www.portedward.com, lunch Mon.–Fri., dinner daily, seafood brunch) is probably known best for its seafood buffet on Friday or the Sunday champagne brunch. Menu items here include mussels (always a good bet), oysters, trout, stuffed mushrooms, and baked artichokes. The restaurant has some amusing seating areas for couples: a booth tucked into a windmill or a table inside the cabin of a 25-foot-long sailboat, a sailboat that is actually floating on water inside the restaurant.

Part country-style restaurant and part entertainment complex, **The Milk Pail** (Hwy. 25, just north of I-90, Dundee, 847/742-5040, www.themilkpail.com) always seems to be hosting some kind of event, whether it's a business meeting, wedding, murder mystery dinner, or flea market. One of the best times to dine at The Milk Pail is during the Sunday jazz brunch, when you can dive into some pancakes while a brass band plays some ditties. The restaurant is open for lunch Tuesday–Thursday, lunch and dinner Friday, breakfast lunch and dinner Saturday, and for brunch and dinner Sunday.

Southern Illinois

The first settlers to Illinois did not make a bee-line toward the Chicago region. Instead they headed to the hills of southern Illinois. With its green valleys, wooded ravines, and rivers teeming with fish, southern Illinois reminded the early settlers of where they came from—Kentucky and Tennessee. There was enough timber to build homes, and after coal, salt, and fluorspar were discovered, plenty of jobs. This is where Illinois got its start—in former mining towns such as Shawneetown and Elizabethtown and river towns such as Cairo and Metropolis, where steamboats carried passengers, grain, and coal to other parts of the country. There's a lot of history here—remains of American Indian villages, re-created French and British forts, river pirate caves, and memorials to Meriwether Lewis and William Clark, who recruited men and gathered supplies before embarking on their great westward journey.

The southern tip of Illinois escaped the glaciers' advances and as a result the land is rugged and gorgeous. Its boundaries are three great rivers: the Wabash to the east, the flood-prone Ohio to the southeast and south, and the Mississippi River to the west. In addition, the Saline River charts a course about 45 miles long, southeasterly from McLeansboro to the Ohio River near Cave-in-Rock. The Cache weaves through the center part of the region, leaving cypress and tupelo swamps behind. In the midst of it all are the grand Shawnee Hills, an extension of the Ozark range, and the Shawnee National Forest. At 270,000 acres with countless miles of trails, the forest is a splendid sight any time of year. Wildlife, such as deer, turkeys, and ducks, are abundant, making the region a favorite weekend spot for hunters from the area. Boaters cruise the Ohio River, anglers stake out spots on quiet ponds, and hikers take to the countless hills. Southern Illinois, you will find, is about driving scenic two-lane roads, spending hours hiking, biking, or canoeing, and then filling up on juicy peaches, sipping wine, and indulging in barbecue.

PLANNING YOUR TIME

Ahh. If only you had an entire month to hike through southern Illinois. With 1,250 miles of trails for not only hiking, but horseback riding and mountain biking, the **Shawnee National Forest** (not to mention all the parks and natural areas outside the forest boundaries) has almost unlimited opportunities for outdoor adventure. You could pack the major sites into a week, beginning with hiking and a night or two's stay in the lodge at **Giant City State Park** south of Carbondale, followed by a walk through the cypress swamps or a canoe ride in the **Cache River State Natural Area** near Belknap, a quick exploration into the former home of bandits at **Cave-in-Rock State Park** by Elizabethtown, and finally more hiking to see the rock formations at **Garden of the Gods** south of Harrisburg. If all you have is a weekend, pick one of the regions above, and stay in a cabin, bed-and-breakfast or campsite.

Access

Southern Illinois is road-tripping country; it's full of two-lane highways that cut through the Shawnee Hills or follow rivers such as the grand Ohio. It's also got several interstates running north and south and east and west, making it somewhat of an easy area to navigate. The major highways in southern Illinois are heading elsewhere, to cities such as St. Louis, Memphis, or Nashville, Tennessee. Interstate 57 slices through the center of the southern part of the state, jogging along Rend Lake and other fishing and boating areas. Just as it enters the Shawnee National Forest, south of Marion, there's a Y in the road. I-24 begins here and pushes to the southeast to Paducah, Kentucky, Nashville, Tennessee, and onward. I-57 turns slightly southwest and then straight south to Memphis, Tennessee. An alternative to I-57 is U.S. 51, which for most of southern Illinois follows a route parallel to I-57 about 10 miles to the west. The east-west I-64 shuttles drivers from St. Louis to Mount Vernon in the middle of southern Illinois, and then eastward to Evansville, Indiana, and over to Louisville, Kentucky. I-70 divides central Illinois from the southern region by running diagonally across the region, with St. Louis on the west, Vandalia and Effingham in the middle, and Greenup and Marshall on the eastern side.

Most of the two-lane highways and back roads in southern Illinois wind past horse farms, orchards, wooded hills, corn- and soybean fields, and through one-stoplight towns. Tourism agencies have compiled road maps to the region's orchards, wineries, and art galleries and antiques shops. Maps to the **Orchard Trail, Wine Trail, and Art Trail** are available at most visitors bureaus. The **Ohio River National Scenic Byway** trails the river for 70 miles in Illinois, from Cairo on the southern tip of the state to the tiny Grand Chain in the southeast. Illinois Highway 127 between Anna-Jonesboro and Murphysboro is quite the scenic route, as is Highway 146 from Dixon Springs State Park to Golconda and then on to Elizabethtown. If you plan to discover the back roads, buy a copy of DeLorme's *Illinois*

Must-Sees

M **Giant City State Park:** This popular 4,000-acre park south of Carbondale is loaded with outdoor adventure possibilities: climbing or rappelling off sandstone bluffs, hiking through ravines, and horseback riding through hardwood forests and prairie. Make it an overnight trip and stake out one of the campsites or cabins (page 335).

M **Little Grand Canyon Trail:** Take off on one of the best hiking trails in the state. This steep and winding trail in the heart of the Shawnee National Forest rewards hikers with views of the Big Muddy River valley, Mississippi River floodplain, waterfalls, and the occasional bobcat or snake (page 342).

M **Cache River State Natural Area:** In this 13,000-acre natural area, visitors can explore cypress swamps by walking on a floating boardwalk or canoeing along the quiet Cache River. Plus, learn about wetland wildlife at a visitors center or hike through bottomland forests (page 356).

M **Garden of the Gods Wilderness:** Millions of years of wind and rain have eroded the rocky land southwest of Shawneetown and south of Harrisburg to create startling formations. An easy .25-mile trail takes hikers past formations such as Devil's Smokestack and Camel Rock (page 365).

M **Cave-in-Rock State Park:** Once a hideout for gangs of violent thieves in the 1800s, the cave within this state park, which is right on the Ohio River, is now a tourist-friendly destination with walking trails and picnic tables (page 367).

© CHRISTINE DES GARENNES

Cave-in-Rock State Park on the Ohio River

Southern Illinois

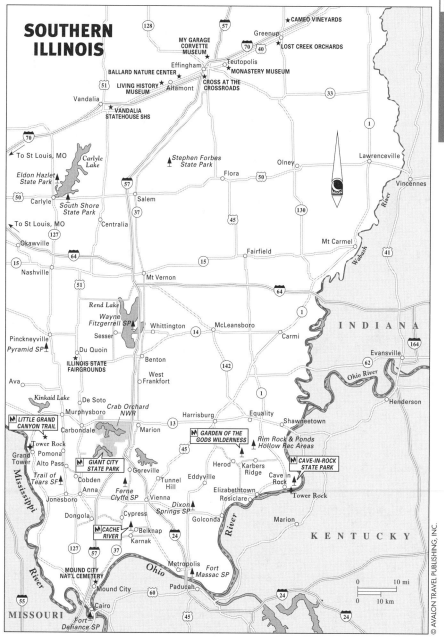

SOUTHERN ILLINOIS

★ CAMEO VINEYARDS
Greenup
★ LOST CREEK ORCHARDS

MY GARAGE
CORVETTE
MUSEUM

Teutopolis
MONASTERY MUSEUM

Effingham

BALLARD NATURE CENTER

CROSS AT THE
CROSSROADS

LIVING HISTORY
MUSEUM   Altamont

Vandalia

VANDALIA
STATEHOUSE SHS

To St Louis, MO

Carlyle
Lake

Eldon Hazlet
State Park

Carlyle

South Shore
State Park

Stephen Forbes
State Park

Flora

Olney

Lawrenceville

Vincennes

Centralia

To St Louis, MO

Okawville

Salem

Fairfield

Mt Carmel

Nashville

Mt Vernon

Rend Lake
Wayne
Fitzgerrell SP

Whittington   McLeansboro

INDIANA

Pinckneyville
Pyramid SP

Sesser

Du Quoin

ILLINOIS STATE
FAIRGROUNDS

Ava

Kinkaid Lake

Benton

West
Frankfort

Carmi

Evansville

Ohio River

Henderson

Little Grand
Canyon Trail

De Soto

Murphysboro

Crab Orchard
NWR

Carbondale

Tower Rock

Grand   Pomona
Tower   Alto Pass

Trail of
Tears SF

Jonesboro

Cobden

Anna

GIANT CITY
STATE PARK

Ferne
Clyffe SP

Harrisburg   Equality

Marion

Goreville

Tunnel
Hill

Vienna

Cypress

Dongola

CACHE
RIVER

Belknap

Karnak

GARDEN OF THE
GODS WILDERNESS

Herod

Eddyville

Karbers
Ridge

Shawneetown

Rim Rock & Ponds
Hollow Rec Areas

CAVE-IN-ROCK
STATE PARK

Cave in
Rock

Tower Rock

Elizabethtown
Rosiclare

Dixon
Springs SP

Golconda

Marion

KENTUCKY

MOUND CITY
NAT'L CEMETERY

Mound City

Cairo

Metropolis

Fort
Massac SP

Paducah

Fort
Defiance SP

MISSOURI

Mississippi River

Ohio River

Wabash River

0   10 mi
0   10 km

© AVALON TRAVEL PUBLISHING, INC.

Gazetteer, which has detailed information on the rural roads.

Resources

The main source of tourism information for the southern tip of the state is the **Southern Illinois Tourism Development Office** (501 W. DeYoung/Hwy. 13, Ste. 2, Marion, 618/998-9397 or 888/998-9397, www.adventureillinois.com), which is like an umbrella organization for all the other smaller, regional visitors bureaus and chambers of commerce. There are two other bureaus that cover larger areas. The **Southernmost Illinois Convention and Tourism Bureau** (Shawnee College Bldg., 1000 N. Main St., Anna, 618/833-9928 or 800/248-4373, www.southernmostillinois.com) is a clearinghouse for information on the six southernmost counties in the state (Pope, Alexander, Massac, Union, Pulaski, and Johnson). This includes everything from the Trail of Tears region by Jonesboro-Anna to Cairo and Metropolis. The **Southeastern Illinois Convention and Visitors Bureau** (1707 E. Main St., Ste. 5, Olney, 618/392-0925 or 877/273-4554, www.southeastillinois.com) covers seven primarily rural counties: Crawford, Jasper, Richland, Lawrence, Edwards, Wabash, and White. These are the counties north of the Garden of the Gods area that primarily border Indiana.

The **Shawnee National Forest** is divided into two districts: Hidden Springs (Vienna and Elizabethtown area) to the east and Mississippi Bluffs (Jonesboro and Murphysboro) to the west. The headquarters is in Harrisburg (50 Hwy. 145, Harrisburg, 618/253-7114 800/MY-WOODS or 800/699-6637, www.fs.fed.us/r9/forests/shawnee), and ranger stations are in Jonesboro (521 N. Main St., Jonesboro, 618/833-8576), Murphysboro (221 Walnut St., Murphysboro, 618/687-1731), Vienna (602 N. 1st St./U.S. 45, Vienna, 618/658-2111), and Elizabethtown (618/287-2201). The stations are staffed 8 A.M.–4:30 P.M. Monday–Friday, but sometimes you can find rangers on hand during the weekends.

Carbondale and Vicinity

HISTORY

The town of Carbondale was first established and settled in the 1850s, but the region had been home to human beings for thousands of years. As indicated by the blackened ceilings within rock shelters at Giant City State Park, just south of Carbondale, Indian tribes hunted and camped in the region for many years. The first white people in the area were French fur traders, followed by the British and eventually American colonists. The permanent settlers arrived from Kentucky and Tennessee, and they planted fruit trees along the hills and worked in the coal mines. Like many towns in Illinois, Carbondale grew as a city after entrepreneurs bought land along the Illinois Central Railroad. After Carbondale was designated a stop along the rail line, it became a transportation center for shipping fruit grown in the nearby hills and coal mined from the region. In 1866 educators founded Carbondale College, which eventually became Southern Illinois University. In its early years it was a teacher training institution. SIU was back then and still is today a large employer for the region's residents. Carbondale is home to about 26,000 people.

ORIENTATION

Carbondale is a jumping-off point to the Shawnee National Forest, just a few miles to the south, west, and east. The north-south U.S. 51 slices straight through the city and intersects with Highway 13. Hotels and motels are clustered along Highway 13 just east of downtown. Interstate 57 is about 15 miles to the east. Several large lakes surround Carbondale, including Cedar Lake to the south, Crab Orchard Lake to the east, and Kinkaid Lake to the

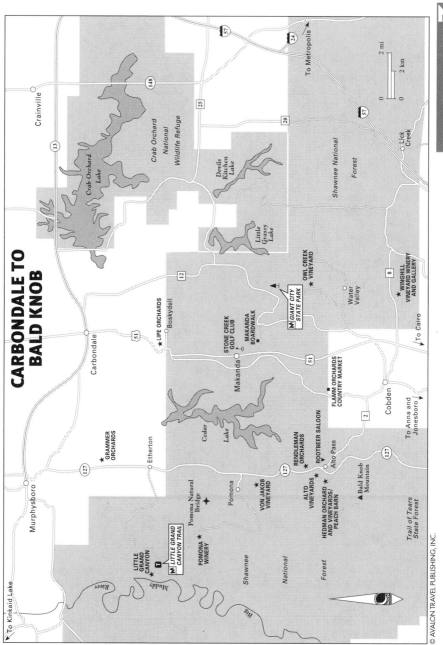

Southern Illinois

CARBONDALE TO BALD KNOB

2 mi
2 km

To Metropolis

57

24

148

25

20

57

13

Crainville

Crab Orchard
National
Wildlife Refuge

Crab Orchard
Lake

Devils
Kitchen
Lake

Shawnee National
Forest

Lick
Creek

Little
Grassy
Lake

12

8

LIPE ORCHARDS

Boskydell

Carbondale

51

OWL CREEK
VINEYARD

WINGHILL
VINEYARD WINERY
AND GALLERY

GIANT CITY
STATE PARK

Water
Valley

To Cairo

STONE CREEK
GOLF CLUB

MAKANDA
BOARDWALK

Makanda

51

GRAMMER
ORCHARDS

Etherton

127

Cedar
Lake

FLAMM ORCHARDS
COUNTRY MARKET

Cobden

2

RENDLEMAN
ORCHARDS

ROOTBEER SALOON

To Anna and
Jonesboro

Murphysboro

Pomona Natural
Bridge

Pomona

VON JAKOB
VINEYARD

Alto Pass

127

ALTO
VINEYARDS

HEDMAN ORCHARD
AND VINEYARDS/
PEACH BARN

Bald Knob
Mountain

127

LITTLE GRAND
CANYON

LITTLE GRAND
CANYON TRAIL

POMONA
WINERY

Muddy

Shawnee

National

Forest

Trail of Tears
State Forest

Big

River

To Kinkaid Lake

© AVALON TRAVEL PUBLISHING, INC.

northwest, and Little Grassy Lake and Devils Kitchen Lake to the southeast.

SIGHTS

Southern Illinois University

The best way to spend a rainy day or learn about the region before setting off on a hike is to pay a visit to the **Southern Illinois University Museum** (Faner Hall, 618/453-5388, 9 A.M.–3 P.M. Tues.–Sat., 1:30–4:30 P.M. Sun., closed university holidays, free). The museum is divided into North Hall and South Hall, which contain several galleries of rotating and permanent exhibits. Two permanent shows are *Life Through Time,* a geology exhibit, and several dioramas of pioneer life. The atrium gallery contains modern sculptures and rotating exhibits. The SIU museum has an impressive collection of prehistoric items (about 50,000 geological and anthropological objects) from southern Illinois and regions around the world, including Central and South America and Africa. It has everything from ancient Melanesian masks (from the Papua New Guinea and Fiji areas), Civil War weapons, and Anna pottery. Anna pottery, also known as Kirkpatrick pottery, was made by a pair of brothers in Anna during the second half of the 19th century. Their folk art creations (frogs, pigs, fair jugs) are a favorite among collectors. In addition, the museum has paintings, metal sculptures, and photographs. Outside the museum is a modern sculpture garden with a Japanese garden and koi pond. To get to the museum follow signs from Lincoln Drive.

After your visit to the museum, take a stroll through the campus to admire some of the architecture. Built in 1898, **Altgeld Hall** (1000 S. Normal Ave., Carbondale) is the oldest building on campus. The Gothic-revival, castlelike building comes complete with a tower and turrets. Initially a science building, it now houses the music department. **Wheeler Hall** is a Romanesque red-brick and sandstone building that dates to the turn-of the 20th century. Originally the school's library, it now contains administrative offices.

Southern Illinois University (618/453-2121, www.siuc.edu) is in southwest Carbondale. Enter from U.S. 51 and follow Lincoln Drive through the campus.

Woodlawn Cemetery

One of Carbondale's claims to fame is that the first Memorial Day service was held here. On April 29, 1866, area residents met at a church and organized a procession to the **Woodlawn Cemetery** (405 E. Main St., Carbondale), a small cemetery on a hill within the city limits. Civil War General John A. Logan, a southern Illinois native, spoke at the service commemorating area soldiers who died during the Civil War. Logan was later elected national commander of the veterans group Grand Army of the Republic, and he spearheaded efforts to establish a national Memorial Day observance, which took place May 30, 1868. Memorial Day services are held in the cemetery, now listed on the National Register of Historic Places, every year. About 400 people were buried in Woodlawn from the mid-1800s to mid-1900s. In addition to the bodies of Civil War soldiers and other veterans, the cemetery is the final resting place for 30 slaves who died of smallpox. The freed slaves died in Carbondale shortly after arriving in the city in 1864.

Orchards

The warm, sunny hills of southern Illinois are great for growing peaches, not to mention apples and other fruit. You'll find several orchards within a short driving distance of Carbondale. **Grammer Orchards** (144 Peach Rd., follow Grammer Rd. from Hwy. 127, Carbondale, 618/684-2471) is between Carbondale and Murphysboro. It grows peaches and apples, and because bushels of apples are kept in cold storage, you can snack on crispy apples months after the apple season has wrapped up. Run by the Lipe family since the 1880s, **Lipe Orchards** (3925 Illinois Ave./Old U.S. 51, Carbondale, 618/549-1263, 9 A.M.–5 P.M. Mon.–Sat. mid-June–early Dec., extended hours during peach season) is just south of Carbondale by Giant City State Park. You can stock up on fruit such as peaches and apples, but also plums, nectarines, cider, and pumpkins.

SPORTS

Catch competitive bike racing at **Evergreen Park BMX Raceway** (2175 McLafferty Rd., Carbondale, 618/924-6862 or 618/568-1076, May–Oct.), a National Bike League–sanctioned track, on Sunday afternoons in the summer and fall. You can also watch bikers practice on Tuesday and Thursday evenings. Novice and experienced bow hunters can fine-tune their skills at **Archery International** (3002 Airport Rd., Carbondale, 618/351-1510), a national training center for archers. You can rent equipment here and hunt for game via interactive video programs.

ENTERTAINMENT

Southern Illinois University at Carbondale boasts several performance spaces. Student-produced plays, performance art, and other productions are presented at SIU's **Kleinau Theatre** (Communications Bldg., Lincoln Dr., Carbondale, 618/453-2291, tickets 618/453-5618, www.siuc.edu), a 100-seat theater in the Communications Building. The box office is open one hour before performances.

McLeod Theatre (Communications Bldg., Lincoln Dr., Carbondale, 618/453-5741, box office open noon–4:30 P.M. Mon.–Fri. and one hour before shows) is the SIU theater department's 488-seat main stage. Everything from elaborate Greek drama to modern musicals has been staged in McLeod. The theater also has a small laboratory theater space. The next size up as far as theaters go is the university's **Shryock Auditorium** (618/453-ARTS or 618/453-2787, www.siuc.edu). Built in 1918, the renovated 1,200-seat theater hosts lectures, visiting dance troupes, musicals, and other events. (It is here where the late former U.S. Senator Paul Simon announced he was running for president in 1988.) The beautiful, Roman-style theater is also the home for the **Southern Illinois Symphony Orchestra,** comprising university professors and students. Tickets for Shryock events can be purchased from Ticketmaster at 866/646-8849 or in person at the box office (open 9 A.M.–4 P.M. Mon.–Fri.) Phone orders for special tickets, such as groups or for patrons with disabilities, can be made by calling 618/453-2000.

The Stage Company (101 N. Washington St., Carbondale, 618/549-5466) is the local community theater group in downtown Carbondale. It presents four productions a year, plus a children's play in June.

ACCOMMODATIONS
$50–100
Several national chain hotels are on or adjacent to Highway 13, the main east-west road through Carbondale. They include the **Hampton Inn** (2175 Reed Station Pkwy., Carbondale, 618/549-6900, $86), which has 70 rooms, an indoor pool, plus a full free breakfast; and the **Ramada Inn** (801 N. Giant City Rd., Carbondale, 618/351-6611, $89), a 65-room hotel which also has an indoor pool and offers free breakfast to guests.

$100–150
Southeast of town, on a hill above a small farm and near the scenic Crab Orchard Lake, are two cabins available for rent. The newer-construction homes at **Cabin on the Hill** (2751 Dogwood Rd., Carbondale, 618/529-5667, www.cabinonthehill.com, $95–125) feature exposed knotty-pine decor, modern kitchens (stocked with coffee, coffee pots, plus cooking pans), living areas with board games and satellite televisions, and comfortable, clean bedrooms. Down the hill the owners live on a small farm with horses, donkeys, and other animals.

FOOD
American
The Bald Knob dining room at **Giant City Lodge** (460 Giant City Lodge Rd., Makanda, 618/457-4921, www.dnr.state.il.us, breakfast,

lunch, and dinner Mon.–Sat., chicken dinners only on Sun.) serves traditional dishes, such as prime rib, steaks, and a variety of seafood in a hunt-club atmosphere. It's almost worth a dinner here just to take everything in—the brick and fieldstone walls, white oak accents. The lodge also has a cocktail lounge. On Sundays folks come from all around for the all-you-can eat, family-style chicken dinners.

Asian

Run by a friendly Laotian and American couple, **Hunan** (710 E. Main St., Carbondale, 618/529-1108 or 618/529-1109, 11 A.M.–9:30 P.M. Mon.–Thurs., 11 A.M.–10 P.M. Fri., 11:30 A.M.–10 P.M. Sat., 11:30 A.M.–9:30 P.M. Sun.) offers a wide range of Chinese food— dishes from Peking, Canton, Shanghai, you name it. Hunan is a local favorite (and has been for years). Why? You can't go wrong with any of its meals (chicken, pork, duck, beef, plus plenty of vegetarian options), all under $13 and averaging about $10. It also stocks imported and domestic beer and wine and whips up lovely tropical drinks that you'll savor on a hot southern Illinois summer evening.

A little bit Thai, a little bit Japanese and Korean, **Ŋ Kaya** (817 S. Illinois Ave., Carbondale, 618/457-0968, 11 A.M.–9:30 P.M. daily) is a small locally owned restaurant that serves wonderful, fresh sushi, noodle dishes, and steak entrées. Most dishes are under $10.

Middle Eastern

The name means house of peace and **Ŋ Dar Salaam** (218 N. Illinois Ave./U.S. 51, Carbondale, 618/351-9191) is a relaxing environment, where soft music plays in the background and you can sit cross-legged on cushioned seating. (It also has plenty of tables.) The cuisine here is Middle Eastern, with dishes from Lebanon, Iraq, Israel and Palestine, and Egypt. Some examples? Saffron stew with chickpeas, shish kebabs, *halal* chicken, plus a few items such as grilled fillet of grouper. You can go the expensive route with filet mignon with a mushroom

sauce or casual with a falafel sandwich. After the meal, stay a while and sip some Arabic coffee. Hookahs are available during the last hour the restaurant is open. It's open for lunch 11:30 A.M.–2:30 P.M. Monday–Friday, dinner 5:30–9:30 P.M. Monday–Saturday in summer. Call for hours during the rest of year. Entrées are $9–20, averaging about $12.

Mexican

The lively **Tres Hombres** (119 N. Washington St., Carbondale, 618/457-3308, daily lunch and dinner) in downtown Carbondale offers standard Mexican and Southwestern fare such as *chiles rellenos,* tostadas, huge burritos and enchiladas, and large combination platters. On some evenings, local bands kick it in gear and the margaritas start flowing. Entrées are $6–10.50.

Café

The **Longbranch Coffee House** (100 E. Jackson St., Carbondale, 618/529-4488) is one of those places where you can settle in and stay for a while reading a book, paper, or talking with a friend. The outdoor patio is especially inviting, especially on evenings when a local band starts jamming. Beverages are the specialty— coffee, tea, smoothies, and juice—but it also has baked goods, toasty panini sandwiches, salads, and some light, Southwestern-style food such as enchiladas.

Markets

Before you spend a day hiking or biking through the Shawnee hills, load up on nutritional bars, juice, fruit, and other healthy snacks at **Neighborhood Co-op Grocery** (104 E. Jackson St., Carbondale, 618/529-3533, www.neighborhoodco-op.com, 10 A.M.–8 P.M. daily). The co-op also bakes bread daily, so you can pick up some bread, cheese, and a fresh tomato to make sandwiches for the ride.

Carbondale hosts a farmers market on the town square (Jackson and Washington Sts. at Hwy. 13) 4–6 P.M. Wednesdays May–October.

TRANSPORTATION

Getting There and Away

American Connection offers several flights daily between St. Louis and **Williamson County Regional Airport** (10400 Terminal Dr., Marion, 618/993-3353, www.wilcoairport.com). The airport is at Highways 13 and 148, about 10 miles east of Carbondale, between Carbondale and Marion.

The Illini and City of New Orleans **Amtrak** (401 S. Illinois Ave., Carbondale, 618/457-3388 or 800/872-7245, www.amtrak.com) trains stop daily in downtown Carbondale. The Illini runs between Chicago and Carbondale; the City of New Orleans links Chicago and New Orleans.

Bart Transportation (800/284-2278) shuttles riders to and from Carbondale and Lambert International Airport in St. Louis (about two hours away).

Greyhound (618/549-3495, www.greyhound.com) buses arrive and depart from 404 South Illinois Avenue. If you're in town and need a lift, call **Yellow Cab** (618/457-8121).

INFORMATION

For the scoop on hotels, hiking trails, or events, contact the **Carbondale Convention and Tourism Bureau** (Old Passenger Depot, 111 S. Illinois Ave./U.S. 51, Carbondale, 618/529-4451 or 800/526-1500, www.cctb.org).

SERVICES

Hospital

If you need medical care, go to **Memorial Hospital of Carbondale** (400 W. Jackson St., Carbondale, 618/549-0721 or 866/744-2468, www.memorialhosptialofcarbondale.org).

Newspapers

The daily newspaper for all of southern Illinois is *The Southern Illinoisan* (www.southernillinoisan.com), available at most convenient stores, coffee shops, and the like. The Thursday paper includes an entertainment guide supplement. Also, *The Daily Egyptian* (www.dailyegyptian.com), a publication of Southern Illinois University, is published Monday–Friday and sold throughout the Carbondale area.

GIANT CITY STATE PARK

Giant City State Park is one of those places where you can return every year and never tire of it, where everywhere you turn you see a trail you want to explore. One of (if not the most) scenic parks in Illinois, Giant City is best known for its towering sandstone bluffs, some as high as 70 to 80 feet, and its excellent hiking trails. Bluffs that high may not be rare out West, but in Illinois, they're few and far between. As a result, they always attract a crowd, especially the climbing and rappelling crowd. Giant City is one of the few places in Illinois where you can go rock climbing and rappelling.

Hiking

The 4,000-acre park got its name when early settlers through the area walked among the rock formations and said the experience was like walking through a giant city. To see what they were talking about, wander down (or rather, up) the one-mile-long Giant City Nature Trail. The park boasts several short (about one-third of a mile) but steep trails, including Devil's Standtable Trail, a trail you climb to take a look at a towerlike sandstone formation, and the Stone Fort Nature Trail, which highlights the remains of a wall built sometime between A.D. 600 and 800 by Indians during the Late Woodland Period. A solid hiking trail is the two-mile Trillium Trail, named after the many wildflowers growing along its path during the spring. The Post Oak Trail, one-third of a mile long, is wheelchair-accessible and also an excellent option if you're pushing any children in strollers. If you're here for the long haul, strap on the hiking boots and backpack and hit the challenging 12-mile Red Cedar Hiking Trail, which covers the entire park. You'll come upon a primitive campsite about eight miles into the trail. If your time is limited, climb to

© CHRISTINE DES GARENNES

Little Grand Canyon, south of Carbondale, has great hiking.

the top of an 82-foot-tall water tower near the lodge. The water tower has an observation platform that offers astounding views of the area.

You can't go wrong with any trail in Giant City. All are scenic, winding through dark wooded areas lush with ferns and moss growing on trees, past small ponds, scenic overlooks of the Shawnee Hills, and past rock shelters used by camping hunters for thousands of years. (During the Civil War soldiers were said to have camped in some of these shelters).

You can pick up detailed maps of the trails at the park's newer 4,000-square-foot **visitors center** (618/457-4836, open 8 A.M.–4 P.M. daily). The center has exhibits on the region's geology, a gift shop, a "discovery corner" for children, plus it shows a short film about the park's history. Pick up all your maps and brochures here.

Climbing and Horseback Riding

Other activities in the park are climbing and horseback riding. If your feet need a break from all the hiking, see the rest of the park on horseback. At the park's **Giant City Stables** (618/529-4110, 9 A.M.–5 P.M. Wed.–Mon.,

March 15–Nov. 1) you can rent horses and take a one-, two-, or three-hour guided tour of the park. If you bring your own horse, there's an equestrian campground and 12-mile horse trail in the park. Rock climbers can head to Devil's Standtable rock and Shelter 1 bluff. No need to pay a fee or register; just bring your own equipment and be the lookout for poisonous copperhead snakes that like to sun themselves on the ledges. Maps to the rocks are available from the visitors center.

Lodging and Camping

At the top of the park sits the impressive **Giant City State Park Lodge** (460 Giant City Lodge Rd., Makanda, 618/457-4921, www.dnr.state.il.us), built by the Civilian Conservation Corps in the 1930s. The lodge contains the Bald Knob Dining Room restaurant, a cocktail lounge, and gift shop. Nearby are 34 cabins for rent. All are near the lodge high up in the hills. Take your pick from 12 one-room cabins, 18 two-room cabins, or four large bluff cabins that can sleep up to six people. They come with bathrooms, tables and chairs, and televisions, but no kitchens (although the bluff cabins have minifridges.) Guests have use of an outdoor swimming pool. Cabins are closed mid-December–February. Rates are $60–115.

The **campsites** at Giant City State Park (235 Giant City Rd., Makanda, 618/457-4836) are tucked away in the northeast corner of the park near Little Grassy Lake. The 85 electric sites with showers are in one area; 14 sites for tent camping in another, plus several walk-in sites for folks carrying backpacks. (The walk-in sites have pit toilets.) There's also an equestrian campground with electrical hookups in the southwestern part of the park.

MAKANDA

A tiny town easy to miss, Makanda is a treasured community of artists just outside the secondary entrance to Giant City State Park. To get to Makanda from U.S. 51 south of Carbondale, follow Makanda Road east. The main attraction in this 400-person town is the **Makanda Boardwalk,** a string of shops built in the 1890s, connected by plank boards. At 530 Makanda Road, you'll find a handful of boutiques and galleries including **Rainmaker Art Studio** (618/457-6282, 11 A.M.–6 P.M. daily), where you can browse for stone and metal creations, such as bronze and copper sculptures, jewelry, and water fountains; **Visions** (10 A.M.–5 P.M. Mon., Wed.–Sat., noon–5 P.M. Sun.), which showcases glassware, photographs, and woodcarvings created by southern Illinois artists; and **Makanda Trading Company** (618/351-0201, www.makandatradingcompany.com, 10 A.M.–5 P.M. daily), which sells fair-trade clothing, musical instruments, jewelry, and more from Asia, Africa, and other far corners of the world.

Finally, nearby you can hunt for vintage furniture, glassware, and other collectibles at **Spider Web Antiques and Used Furniture** (4588 Old U.S. 51, Makanda, 618/457-0227, 12:30–5 P.M. Mon., Thurs.–Sat.).

Recreation

One of the most scenic courses in the state,

Stone Creek Golf Club (503 Stone Creek Dr., Makanda, 618/351-GOLF or 618/351-4653, www.stonecreekgolf.com) is an 18-hole public golf course within the Shawnee Hills, a few miles from Giant City State Park. Golfing here (course is 6,875 yards, par 72) is not only pleasant and challenging, but affordable. A round will cost you about $30 (including use of a golf cart.)

Accommodations

Set up somewhat like a duplex, the **Toolshed Corner B&B** (1420 Hall Church Rd., Makanda, 618/893-4063 or 866/300-4063, www.tscbb.com) has two rooms available for guests, divided by a common area. Each room comes with its own queen-size bed, private bathroom, deck, and gas fireplace. The common area has a full kitchen and laundry area. Rates are $85–100 per night and include breakfast.

Stone Creek Golf Club has 11 one- and two-bedroom log cabins available for rent on a nightly basis, in a residential area of the club. The newer-construction cabins come with fieldstone fireplaces, small kitchens (microwave and fridge), lounge chairs, and private decks. Rates are $89–109 per night. If you plan to golf, ask about its overnight golf packages.

CRAB ORCHARD NATIONAL WILDLIFE REFUGE

Developed as a refuge for waterfowl migrating along the Mississippi River Flyway, Crab Orchard National Wildlife Refuge (8588 Hwy. 148, Marion, 618/997-3344, www.fws.gov/midwest/craborchard) is an interesting site ecologically speaking (it's home to more 200 species of birds), but also historically. The area it encompasses is believed to have once been prime hunting ground for Native American tribes. As white settlers moved into the area they were also attracted to the region's vast number of waterfowl, upland game, and other animals. After years of hunting and logging altered the landscape, the U.S. government, through the Works Progress Administration, built Crab Orchard Lake in 1939 as a way to entice boaters and fisherman to the area and build up water supply. Plus, it planted thousands of trees. Along came World War II and plans to build two more man-made lakes for the area were put on hold as the area became the site of the Illinois Ordnance Plant, one of the Army's largest munitions plants. After the war, the other two lakes were eventually created and the area is now being restored to more of a natural state.

The entire site is more than 43,000 acres. About half of the refuge, much of it on the eastern side, is closed to the public as a wildlife sanctuary. The three lakes—**Crab Orchard, Little Grassy, and Devils Kitchen**—together are 8,300 acres. The largest is Crab Orchard Lake, popular among boaters. The other two are smaller and tend to be quiet. All three are stocked with crappie, bass, bluegill, and catfish. You can rent fishing boats at Little Grassy and canoes and fishing boats at Devils Kitchen. Because the refuge is a haven for birds along the flyway, it's a prime bird-watching area, especially during the winter. The winter population of Canada geese alone can peak at 200,000. Several hiking trails wind around the lakes, wetlands, and forests. Nearby on some of the land cattle graze and farmers harvest hay. All three lakes have boat docks and campgrounds: **Devils Kitchen Boat Dock and Marina** (1625 Tacoma Lake Rd., 618/457-5004); **Crab Orchard Campground** (10067 Campground Rd., 618/985-4953); and **Little Grassy Boat Dock, Marina, and Campground** (Grassy Rd., 618/457-6655).

To get to the refuge, enter from Highway 13, about 3.5 miles west of Marion. Follow High-

way 148 south to the visitors center for a few miles. The center (open 8 A.M.–5 P.M. daily) has a few trails that lead to the lake. There is a $2 daily entrance fee assessed per vehicle, or you can pay $5 for a five-day pass.

Marion

Just off I-57 at Highway 13, not far from U.S. 51 and I-24, Marion is at the crossroads for southern Illinois and is packed with lodging options, the majority of which are situated at I-57 and Highway 13. Depending on the season and day of the week, rates at these hotels range $50–100 per night. Here's a sampling of some of the many chain hotels in Marion: **Drury Inn** (2706 W. DeYoung, Marion, 618/997-9600); **Holiday Inn Express** (400 Comfort Dr., Marion, 618/998-1220); and **Comfort Suites** (2608 W. Main St., Marion, 618/997-9133).

One of the more original lodging options in southern Illinois is the **Olde Squat Inn** (14160 Liberty School Rd., Marion, 618/982-2916 or 618/922-2637, www.oldesquatinn.com), comprising genuine log cabins from 1825 to 1874. The owners have moved the cabins from spots throughout the region to their Marion farm, restored them, added to them, and outfitted them with modern amenities, most notably air-conditioning (a must in southern Illinois in July). Choose from five cabins. All come with private bathrooms, porches, and full breakfasts for guests. The farm has a walking trail through the property. Rates are $75–85.

For more information on the area, contact the **Williamson County Tourism Bureau** (Marion, 618/997-3690, 800/GEESE-99 or 800/433-7399, www.wctb.org).

Murphysboro and Kincaid Lake

SIGHTS AND ACTIVITIES

Kincaid Lake State Fish and Wildlife Area

Most folks headed to Kincaid Lake (52 Cinder Hill Dr., Murphysboro, 618/684-2867, www.dnr.state.il.us), about five miles northwest of Murphysboro, are on expeditions. Fishing expeditions. This expansive man-made lake, at 2,650 acres, offers prime muskie fishing. From Highway 149, follow the signs to one of the many boat launches and try your luck. Created in 1958, the lake, as deep as 80 feet in some spots, has an average depth of 30 feet. The lake also has plenty of walleye, bluegill, and other fish common in Illinois. On the northwest corner of the lake is **Johnson Creek Recreation Area,** accessible from Highway 3 and Highway 151 North. The area has a boat launch, swimming area, and 20-site campground geared toward groups. Camping fees are $5–12. The beach is open 6 A.M.–10 P.M. May–September. In this area you'll also find **Kincaid Lake Trail,** a hiking and horse trail that snakes around the woods and lake for 16 miles. To get to the trail, also follow Highway 3 to Highway 151 North.

If you prefer smaller, quieter lakes, spend the day fishing at **Murphysboro State Park** (Hwy. 149, Murphysboro, 618/684-2867, www.dnr.state.il.us), just east of Kincaid Lake and west of Murphysboro. This man-made lake, about 140 acres, is also stocked with bass, catfish, and other fish. Speaking of quiet, the park is in an oak-hickory forest and naturalists should hike along the three-mile lakeside and forest trail at Murphysboro State Park, where you can spot wild orchids and wildflowers such as lady's slipper. The park also has a campground. There are 20 tent campsites and 54 electrical sites for RVs, plus a shower building.

Orchard and Winery

If you've never had a white peach or a sweet Mutsu apple, drop by **Mileur Orchard** (172 Mileur Orchard Rd., 1.5 miles west of Murphysboro on Hwy. 149, 618/687-3663, 9 A.M.–5 P.M. Mon.–Sat., noon–5 P.M. Sun., July–Oct.) while driving through the area. The orchard sells white peaches and white nectarines and some rarer varieties of apples, in addition to the standard regional favorites such as Jonagold.

About halfway between Murphysboro and Carbondale, **Kite Hill Winery** (83 Kite Hill Rd., Murphysboro, 618/684-5072 or 877/648-8725, www.kitehillvineyards.com, 11 A.M.–5 P.M. Mon.–Sat.) is one of the newer wineries in the region. It grows French-American hybrid grapes and specializes in producing white and red grape wines such as those from chambourcin and chardonel grapes. A tasting room is open to the public.

John A. Logan Museum

The local hero in Murphysboro is a man by the name of John Logan, a Civil War general credited with starting Memorial Day. The John A. Logan Museum (1613 Edith St., Murphysboro, 618/684-3455, www.loganmuseum.org, $2) has exhibits on his life as a lawyer, congressman, senate and vice presidential candidate, orator, and lecturer, as well as displays about and artifacts from the Civil War. A walking trail from the house museum leads to the site of the home where Logan was actually born (it was in the process of being excavated) and the home of Samuel Dalton, a freed slave who fought in the Civil War and later moved to Murphysboro. It's open 10 A.M.–4 P.M. Saturday, 1–4 P.M. Sunday March–May and September–November, 10–4 P.M. Monday, Wednesday–Saturday, June–August, or by appointment.

EVENTS

If you're looking to attend a down-home, slice-of-Americana kind of festival, then this is it. Murphysboro's **Apple Festival,** held every year in mid-September, is an extravaganza.

There's a reason (actually several) it is the longest-running festival in southern Illinois. There is absolutely no dull moment at the festival. Residents square off in the apple pie–eating and apple–peeling contests, bid on apple baked goods, watch area firefighters hose each other down, cheer on weekend warriors as they race lawnmowers, and get together and show off their vintage cars and motorcycles. More information about the festival is available from the Murphysboro Chamber of Commerce at 618/684-6421.

SHOPPING

If antiquing is your thing, then stopping in Murphysboro is a must. Start with a visit to **Joseph Redleggs Antiques** (1517 Walnut St., Murphysboro, 618/687-5360, 11 A.M.–5 P.M. Fri., 10 A.M.–5 P.M. Sat. or by appointment), where a bevy of antiques for sale are displayed within an Italianate Victorian home. After you've spent hours there, go treasure-hunting down the street at **George's Resale** (1324 Walnut St., Murphysboro, 618/687-1337) or **Phoebe Jane's Antiques and Collectibles** (1330 Walnut St., Murphysboro, 618/684-5546).

ACCOMMODATIONS

The quaint roadside motel, **Apple Tree Inn** (200 N. 2nd St., Murphysboro, 618/687-2345 or 800/626-4356, www.1appletree.com) has several room-size options for guests (such as rooms with one queen-size bed or rooms with three double beds). All come with handy extras such as minifridges, coffeemakers, and ironing boards. Adjacent to the hotel is an indoor pool complex with an indoor pool, sauna, and hot tub. Rates are around $50.

For more of a private getaway, book a room or cottage at **Kite Hill Vineyard B&B** (83 Kite Hill Rd., Murphysboro, 618/684-5072 or 877/648-8725, www.kitehillvineyards.com), a winery and bed-and-breakfast in rural Murphysboro. On a serene, 30-acre estate with views of the grapevines, the bed-and-breakfast offers two rooms in the main house, plus a little cottage set back from the house near a private pond. All have private baths. The cottage comes with a kitchen and amenities such as a claw-foot bathtub. Rates are $95–110 per night.

FOOD

You know it's a good sign when a barbecue joint has trophies proudly displayed throughout the restaurant. These trophies weren't awarded for softball playing, but for Mike Mills's mouth-watering barbecue. In southern Illinois, where barbecue stands are a dime a dozen, **N 17th Street Bar and Grill** (32 N. 17th St., Murphysboro, 618/684-3722, 10 A.M.–11 P.M. Mon.–Sat.) is a standout. Mmm. Barbecued ribs, barbecued pork, beef brisket, walleye fish sandwiches, baked beans, coleslaw. Diet? Who's dieting? Top off that sandwich with a slice of cheesecake or apple pie. Sandwiches will run you about $6, a rack of ribs with two sides is $20.

The Old Depot (1701 Walnut St., Murphysboro, 618/565-1904, 11 A.M.–9 P.M. Tues.–Thurs., 11 A.M.–11 P.M. Fri.–Sat., 11 A.M.–8 P.M. Sun.) is a steakhouse that serves chopped steak, chicken dinners, sandwiches, and other hearty American fare. It's in the former Mobile and Ohio Railroad Depot, which dates to the 1880s. Sandwiches start around $5, steaks are priced up to $19.

INFORMATION AND SERVICES

Contact the **Murphysboro Chamber of Commerce** (203 S. 13th St., Murphysboro, 618/684-6421) for questions about attractions and lodging. For information on the Shawnee National Forest stop by or call the ranger's office in Murphysboro (221 Walnut St., Murphysboro, 618/687-1731). If you need a ride while in town, there's **Crosstown Cab** (618/684-3506).

VICINITY OF MURPHYSBORO
Ava

About 20 miles or so northwest of Murphysboro is another small artists community. At the

Ava Craft Center (Main St., across from the bank, Ava, 618/426-3547 or 618/426-3054, generally Tues.–Sat., call for hours), visitors can have a seat in front of one of several antique looms and learn how to weave for free. Braided rugs and other home-decor items are for sale. At the **Old Bank Gallery** (Main and Oak Sts., Ava, 618/426-3466, by appointment) you can admire a variety of artwork—oil and watercolor paintings and much more by local artists.

De Soto

Northeast of Murphysboro and north of Carbondale is the small rural community of De Soto, just off U.S. 51. Stop by **Ken's Reproductions and Judy's Antiques** (Hwy. 127, DeSoto, 618/867-2932, 9 A.M.–5 P.M. Mon.–Sat.) to browse thousands of imported items and local antiques. Then have a slice of pie and cup of coffee across the street at the homey **Chestnut Café** (Hwy. 127, De Soto, 618/867-2244), where you can look at photographs of favorite customers placed under plastic tablecloths. The Chestnut serves what's called "heartland country cooking"—in other words, butter-rich waffles and thick slices of bacon strips. Meals are about $4.

The Big Muddy River Watershed

SIGHTS AND ACTIVITIES

Grand Tower

The town of Grand Tower, or more appropriately, the rocks and ridges nearby, have a storied history. If you believe local legends (and there are many of them), the place is haunted. The stories go back hundreds of years and all revolve around the giant limestone formation jutting more than 60 feet from among the rushing waters of the Mississippi River and other similar rock formations along the river. The rock in the river is called Tower Rock. The rocky ridge along the northern end of Grand Tower is Devil's Backbone and Devil's Bake Oven is the funky formation at the end of the Backbone ridge. For centuries, the rapids and whirlpools around Tower Rock have sabotaged ships as they traveled down the Mississippi. According to Native American folklore, a pair of Indian lovers jumped to their deaths here because they could not marry. Explorers Louis Jolliet and Father Pere Marquette wrote about their encounter with Tower Rock on their adventure in the late 1600s. They managed to maneuver around it safely. After them a group of French missionaries erected a wooden cross on top of it. The place was evil, they had heard. Bad stuff continued to happen. A tribe of Indians reportedly killed several white travelers as they came

through the area in the late 1700s, prompting the lone survivor to embark on a lifelong mission to kill any Indians who were involved with the murders. River pirates often hid behind the rocks in its shelters and caves and attacked boats, until the U.S. Calvary pushed them out. Later, the town grew into a shipping center and hub for iron manufacturing. Local legend says the ghost of a girl who died either from grief or illness after a man she loved left town (at the request of her father) still lingers among the Devil's Backbone area, where she and her father lived. Another version goes that she jumped off the ridge after learning the man she loved had drowned in a boating accident.

Grand Tower is no longer the shipping port or manufacturing center it once was. Visitors can see remains of the iron furnaces near the Devil's Backbone and crumbling pieces of the home where the girl supposedly makes an appearance. You can view the tower any time from the levee road. To get there follow Highway 3 to Grand Tower and follow the signs. The **River-to-River Trail** (www.rivertorivertrail.com), part of the American Discovery Trail, ends or begins here (and continues to Cave-in-Rock, clear across the state on the Ohio River).

As a short side trip from Grand Tower, drive north along Highway 3 to Gorham Road and the tiny town of Gorham. Continue to Lake Street and follow the gravel road to **Fountain Bluff** (watch for signs; it's about a mile or so southwest of Gorham). The site has several rock shelters with drawings of animals such as birds (possibly eagles or turkeys), wolves, and deer. They are believed to have been carved by the Mississippian Indians who lived in the region around A.D. 850–1200. To find the animal drawings you'll have to sort through other symbols and declarations of love carved by people in more recent decades.

Oakwood Bottoms

During the fall, tens of thousands of mallard ducks stop by Oakwood Bottoms and the **Greentree Reservoir,** a bottomland forest flooded annually for the sole purpose of providing habitat for migrating waterfowl. Walk along the one-third-mile wheelchair-accessible trail and boardwalk, have a seat in one of the bird blinds, and scout for not only ducks, but great horned owls, pileated woodpeckers, and hawks. To get to the reservoir, follow Highway 149 west from Murphysboro to Highway 3. Drive south on Highway 3 for about six miles. There will be signs for Oakwood Bottoms; the entrance is south of Gorham.

LaRue/Pine Hills Research Natural Area

A National Natural Heritage landmark, the LaRue/Pine Hills region of the Shawnee National Forest overlooks the Mississippi River and abounds in diverse wildlife. The 2,500-acre site is gorgeous and includes pine hills to the east and the low, level Mississippi River floodplain to the west. It's another favorite among the region's hikers. But you don't even have to get out of your car to take in the splendor (although it's highly recommended). The main road through the area, called the LaRue/Pine Hills Road, climbs along the 350-foot-tall bluffs, offering several places along the way to pull off and take in views of the mighty Mississippi River.

One of the reasons people love it so is because of the wildlife. In the swampy areas, search for blooming lotus flowers, listen to singing frogs, and look out for muskrats. In the hills, listen for woodpeckers and look for bobcats and timber rattlesnakes. The LaRue/Pine Hills area is probably most known for its snakes. In the spring and fall, forest rangers limit car and truck traffic to allow cottonmouth snakes (also known as water moccasins) and other amphibians to migrate from their winter homes in the limestone bluffs to the swampy areas by the river.

As far as hiking opportunities go, try **Inspiration Point Trail,** a .75-mile trail that begins on the bluffs and has awesome views of the Big Muddy River and, on clear days, the Mississippi. As the name suggests, this is a great trail to watch the sun set, write in your travel journal, and be inspired. But remember, snakes like this area, too, so keep an eye out for them. The area has picnic sites and a campground. **The Pine Hills campground** has 12 primitive sites and is open mid-March–mid-December. Camping costs $5 per night. The two-mile **White Pine Trail** is accessible from here. It can be used for hiking and horseback riding. LaRue/Pine Hills is just east of Highway 3, about eight miles south of Grand Tower and 15 miles northwest of Jonesboro. More information is available from the **Shawnee National Forest ranger station** in Jonesboro (521 N. Main St., Jonesboro, 618/833-8576) or Murphysboro (221 Walnut St., Murphysboro, 618/687-1731).

Little Grand Canyon Trail

One of the best hiking trails in the state (it's challenging, remote, and scenic), the Little Grand Canyon Trail in the heart of the Shawnee National Forest offers views of the Big Muddy River valley, Mississippi River floodplain, waterfalls, and thick vegetation. The loop is almost four miles long and pretty steep; you'll work your calves while hiking down and back up. But there are some stops along the way to take in the scenes and a few overlooks. Mink, fox, or deer might skirt across the trail in front of you. Bobcats also live among the hills, as do cottonmouth, copperhead, and timber rattlesnakes.

The snakes make their winter dens in here and migrate between the canyon and nearby Turkey Bayou. For hiking, you have several options. The shortest option is to hike one mile to the canyon overlook and turn around. It can take you about 30 minutes back and forth, depending on how much time you spend staring out across at the maple, oak, and beech trees and at the hawks soaring through the sky. To view the Mississippi River valley will take you about an hour to hike 2.1 miles. You can hike to the cool canyon floor and return to the parking lot in about an hour. Of course, you can also hike the entire loop to view all the scenic overlooks and hike through the canyon floor. The trail starts at the top of a ridge and goes down to the canyon and along the Big Muddy River, then back up again, making a loop. The entire loop is 3.6 miles long, however there are several different options for hiking it. The three best options (if you don't want to hike the entire loop) include 1: going down to the canyon and coming back (1.5 miles), 2: going to an overlook of the canyon and coming back (1 mile), and 3: going down to the canyon and then to an overlook of the Mississippi River and coming back (2.1 miles). They all start from the same place (the parking lot at the top of a bluff), but length/sights vary according to how far you along the loop you go.

To get to the trail, watch for signs to the Little Grand Canyon from Highway 127, south of Murphysboro. From Murphysboro, you'll want to go south on 127 for about 5–6 miles to Etherton Road. Follow Etherton for another five miles or so. More information is available from the Shawnee National Forest's Murphysboro Ranger District at 618/687-1731.

Pomona Natural Bridge

Shaped during the course of millions of years, the Pomona Natural Bridge is a sandstone arch over a creek in a rural, wooded and hilly region south of Murphysboro. A steep, sometimes slippery trail takes you over hills and down into the ravine to the bridge. The trail is about one-third of a mile and has a little lookout area over the bridge if you need a break from climbing up

Pomona Natural Bridge

© CHRISTINE DES GARENNES

or down the incline. It also leads down to the creek so you can get a look at the bridge from below. The bridge spans about 90 feet and is made of soft bedrock that has eroded through the years from water and wind.

It's a pretty cool sight, but if you're pressed for time, you might want to think twice. It takes a long time to get there along sometimes unmarked, serpentine gravel roads. On the map, it looks as if it'll take about 20 minutes from Murphysboro, but in reality it's more like 45 minutes to an hour. Signs posted along the way will point you in the right direction, but still, it's easy to get lost. If you're not rushed, no matter. The drive, along rolling hills, past oak and hickory forests and farmsteads set in the valleys, is beautiful. To get to the bridge from Highway 127, go west on Pomona Road, about nine miles south of Murphysboro and four miles north of Alto Pass. Then follow signs to the site. For more information you can contact the Shawnee National Forest's Murphysboro Ranger District at 618/687-1731.

Shawnee Saltpetre Cave

Local blues, bluegrass, and other concerts are often held in this cave's natural amphitheater. About seven miles south of Murphysboro, Shawnee Saltpetre Cave (3747 Hwy. 127, halfway between Murphysboro and Alto Pass, 618/687-9663, $5) is an approximately 50-acre park with the amphitheater, walking trails, picnic tables, and, after a string of rainy days, waterfalls streaming down from the rocks. Hours vary; call ahead to make sure the owners will be there. You can camp there for a fee during weekend events.

Wineries

Take a break from hiking in the forest and spend an afternoon tasting wines at two wineries not too far from the Little Grand Canyon and Pomona Natural Bridge trails. **Pomona Winery** (2865 Hickory Ridge Rd., 618/893-2623, 10 A.M.–5 P.M. Mon., Tues., Fri., Sat., 1–5 P.M. Sun.), hidden in a woodsy area of the forest, specializes in wine made from fruit such as peaches, apples, and blueberries. Set in a sunny valley, **Von Jakob Vineyards** (1309 Sadler Rd., Pomona, 618/893-4500, www.vonjakobvineyard.com, 10 A.M.–5 P.M. Thurs.–Sat., noon–5 P.M. Sun., plus extended hours in the summer) offers an awe-inspiring place to taste its wines with an expansive deck that overlooks the vineyard. Von Jakob makes red, white, and blush wines, plus mead and port wines. Von Jakob was preparing to open a second winery on Highway 127 between Murphysboro and Alto Pass.

The Bald Knob Area

SIGHTS AND ACTIVITIES

Bald Knob Mountain and Cross

One of the highest hills in the Shawnee region, Bald Knob Mountain rises 700 feet above the valley floor southeast of the town of Alto Pass (about 1,000 feet above sea level). It is part of the Bald Knob Wilderness Area within the Shawnee National Forest and neighboring mountains range 400–900 feet tall. Bald Knob, however, stands out thanks to the 100-foot-tall steel and marble cross erected on the top. The cross's story began back in the 1930s when locals began holding Easter sunrise services on the mountain's summit. The idea for the cross hatched in the '50s and it took about 10 years for organizers to raise money. (One of the most well-known fund-raisers was a poor widow farmer named Myrtle Cutts who raised pigs for the cause.) It was finally completed in 1963. Easter sunrise services are still held there every year along with events such as the blessing of the bikes and barbecue fund-raisers. A welcome center, with a gift shop and restrooms, has been added in recent years. To get to the cross, follow signs from Highway 127 in Alto Pass. Head west on Chestnut Street to Bald Knob Road for about 4–5 miles, winding up and around the mountain. For more information, call 618/893-2344. Free admission, but donations are accepted.

Parks

If you need a few moments to stretch your legs, there are two choices in Alto Pass. The **Quetil Trail** is a short nature trail along the old Cairo-St. Louis Narrow Gauge railroad in downtown Alto Pass (just off Main Street). Then, one mile east of Highway 127 and just south of downtown Alto Pass is **Cliff View Park,** a small but definitely scenic overlook on Skyline Drive. Have a seat at a picnic table, bite into a fresh peach or apple, and look out onto the horizon for Bald Knob Cross.

Horseback Riding

Southern Illinois is jam-packed with trails for horseback riding. Alto Pass is no exception. East of town **Kosmic Acres Stables and Rentals** (Hwy. 127 and Prospect Rd., Alto Pass, 618/893-2347) offers year-round riding through the Shawnee Hills and along the Lit-

© CHRISTINE DES GARENNES

view of Bald Knob Cross from an overlook by Alto Pass

tle Cedar Lake spillway. Take your pick from two-, three-, or four-hour rides or daylong regional tours. Pack a lunch and tuck it into the saddlebag and you'll be set. The owner, a zoologist, will point out wildlife or signs of wildlife as you ride through the woods. Beginners are welcome, but reservations are required.

Wineries

Perhaps the most well known of southern Illinois wineries, **Alto Vineyards** (8515 Hwy. 127, Alto Pass, 618/893-4898, www.altovineyards.net, 10 A.M.–5 P.M. Mon.–Sat., noon–5 P.M. Sun.) has been growing grapes and producing wine since 1988. Its award-winning wines vary from dry to sweet and are mostly made from grapes grown in its 10-acre vineyard. However, it also makes specialty wines such as sparkling raspberry. The tasting room and winery is just off 127 north of Alto Pass. Another winery that has won awards is **Owl Creek Vineyard** (2655 Water Valley Rd., Cobden, 618/893-2557, www.owlcreekvineyard.com, noon–5 P.M. Sat.–Sun. Jan.–Apr., noon–5 P.M. Wed.–Sun. May–Dec.), a small winery in rural Cobden. You can sample wines

for free in the tasting room and gift shop or spend some time outside relaxing on a picnic bench near the vineyard. In addition to selling excellent wines, **Winghill Vineyard Winery and Gallery** (5100 Winghill Rd., 618/893-WINE or 618/893-9463, www.winghillwinery.com, noon–5 P.M. Fri.–Sun.) showcases work of regional artists, such as handmade jewelry, ceramics, and paintings. Open since 2003, **Inheritance Valley Vineyards** (5490 Hwy. 127, Cobden, 618/893-6141, noon–5 P.M. Sat.–Sun. Jan.–March, noon–5 P.M. Wed.–Sun. Apr.–Dec.) is, like Alto Pass, easy to get to, just off Highway 127.

EVENTS

Several wineries in and around Alto Pass and Cobden hold spring tasting festivals in May and grape-stomping events in the fall. Check with the wineries or the **Shawnee Hill Wine Trail** website (www.shawneehillwinetrail.com) for dates and activities. Cobden celebrates its fruit heritage with the **Peach Festival** in mid- to late August with plenty of peach treats for sale, carnival rides, and coronation of the peach queen. Alto Pass's Dog Days of Summer **Root Beer Festival** is also in mid- to late August.

SHOPPING
Orchards and Fruit Markets
This is fruit country. And here it is so easy to spend an entire day hopping from one farm market to another, filling up on luscious peaches and crispy apples. Here's a sampling of the markets, farm stands, and u-pick farms in and around Alto Pass and its neighboring town to the south, Cobden.

Pick some of the freshest strawberries, blackberries, and blueberries you can imagine at **Blueberry Hill Farm** (67 Wrights Crossing Rd., just north of Cobden off U.S. 51, 618/893-2397, open May–July), a u-pick berry farm just north of Cobden off U.S. 51. This author's favorite orchard is just outside Alto Pass on the way to Bald Knob Mountain. **Hedman Orchard and Vineyards** (560 Chestnut St., Alto Pass, 618/893-4923, www.peachbarn.com, July–mid-Sept.) sells peaches, nectarines, grapes, and apples from a

big white barn overlooking a valley. The owners plan to start making wine also from grapes grown on their hillside. **Flamm Orchards Country Market** (8760 Old Hwy. 51, Cobden, 618/893-4241, 9 A.M.–6 P.M. daily May–Nov., after daylight saving time ends, the store closes at 5 P.M.) sells fruits and vegetables, plus take-home treats such as strawberry shortcake, peach cobbler, jams, and honey. At **Rendleman Orchards Farm Market** (9680 Hwy. 127, Alto Pass, 618/893-2771, www.rendlemanorchards.com), you can load your car with crates full of peaches, sweet corn, and other produce, plus gourmet food items such as prepackaged soup mixes and jams.

Shops
Austin's of Alto Pass (595 Main St., Alto Pass, 618/893-2206, 10 A.M.–4 P.M. Sat., 1–4 P.M. Sun. or by appointment, open by chance or appointment Jan. and Feb.) is a 3,500-square-foot antiques store filled with furniture, ceramics, and other collectibles. A few miles south of Alto Pass you can gather ideas for your yard while strolling through **Fernwood Gardens**

Fruit trees can be found throughout Southern Illinois.

(2395 Hwy. 127, Cobden, 618/833-2162, 9 A.M.–6 P.M. Mon.–Sat., noon–5 P.M. Sun.), which has display gardens for you to admire. Fernwood sells a variety of herbs, medicinal plants, perennials, and native plants.

ACCOMMODATIONS

Your lodging options in and around Alto Pass are limited to bed-and-breakfasts. Gorgeous, refreshingly affordable bed-and-breakfasts nestled among the Shawnee Hills. You'll never want to stay in a hotel overlooking the interstate again.

Windy Hill Acres Inn (830 Bell Hill Rd., Cobden, 618/893-4065, www.windyhillacresinn.com) is a renovated stone house that once stored farmers' sweet potatoes (back in the 1800s). Renovated into a two-bedroom inn, the house features a living room with fireplace, kitchen stocked with pots and pans, and beautiful touches such as queen-size sleigh beds in the bedrooms, and hardwood floors. Rates are $65 for one bedroom; $130 for two bedrooms.

Shawnee Hill Bed and Breakfast (U.S. 51 and Upper Cobden Rd., 209 Water Valley Rd., Cobden, 618/893-2211, www.shawneehillbb.com) is a retreatlike bed-and-breakfast with fishing pond, hiking trails to a nearby cave (where Daniel Boone reportedly signed his name in 1766), an outdoor hot tub, and antiques shopping at the owners' nearby Shawnee Hill Barn Antiques. Rooms are decorated in country style with antiques. You have the option of choosing a continental or a full breakfast. Rates are $60–150.

The **Peach Barn B&B** (560 Chestnut St., Alto Pass, 618/893-4923, www.peachbarn.com) at Hedman's Orchard and Vineyards by Alto Pass offers guests a suite in its renovated barn overlooking grapevines and fruit orchards. The two-room suite has a queen bed plus a sleeper sofa in the living room. Decorated in Swedish blue and white decor, the barn suite has nice touches such as a down comforter, robes, and radiant floor heating, which visitors will appreciate during winter visits. Rates are $80–115.

FOOD
Cafés
You can spend hours looking at all the stuff at the **Northwest Passage Root Beer Saloon** (Alto Pass, 618/893-1634, 11:30 A.M.–4 P.M. Mon.–Fri., 11 A.M.–6 P.M. Sat., 11 A.M.–5 P.M. Sun.). And we're not just talking about the stuff for sale (coffee, tea, spices, gourmet foods), but also the taxidermy. A staggering, impressive number of fish and stuffed waterfowl and the occasional pair of snowshoes are mounted on the walls. Have a seat at one of the tables throughout the store/saloon or at the vintage bar. (Root beer is on tap.) You can order gourmet sandwiches here such as heaping turkey clubs, but also full seafood plates featuring salmon and other fish. Dishes are about $8.

Another local institution is **Grammer's Market** (10 W. Pine St., Alto Pass, 618/893-2490, 7 A.M.–5 P.M. Mon.–Fri., 7 A.M.–4 P.M. Sat.) a general store that sells deli sandwiches

the famous Northwest Passsage Root Beer Saloon in Alto Pass.

(the local favorite is the "flying pig" pork sandwich). You can also stock up on drinks, groceries, and a variety of hardware tools here.

The festive **Yellowmoon Café** (110 Front St., Cobden, 618/893-2394, 7:30 A.M.–10 A.M. Mon.–Wed., 7:30 A.M.–2:30 P.M. Thurs., 7:30 A.M.–midnight Fri.–Sat., 11 A.M.–5 P.M. Sun., www.yellowmooncafe.com) is somewhat of a community gathering place. In a renovated storefront in little downtown Cobden, the café features live, local music on the weekends and hangs local artwork on its walls. It sells coffee, beer, wine, Italian sodas, milk shakes, and other beverages along with some sweet treats such as hand-dipped ice cream and light sandwiches. The café has wireless Internet access.

Swedish cuisine is the specialty of **Peach Barn Café** (at Hedman Orchard and Vineyards, 560 Chestnut St., Alto Pass, 618/893-4923, www.peachbarn.com, 11 A.M.–6 P.M. July–mid-Sept), and that means warm open-faced sandwiches and lingonberry desserts as well as dishes made with peaches and other fruit grown at the orchard.

INFORMATION

The Union County Chamber of Commerce (330 S. Main St., Anna, 618/833-6311, www.shawneeheartland.com) has loads of info about the county's orchards, events, bed-and-breakfasts, and attractions.

The Trail of Tears: Anna and Jonesboro

RECREATION
Trail of Tears State Forest

The history of southern Illinois is unfortunately tied to one of the saddest chapters in the history of the United States. In 1838 the U.S. Army ordered the Cherokee, Creek, and Chickasaw Indians off their lands in the southeastern United States. They were to settle in the Oklahoma Territory, about 1,000 miles to the west, and they headed west in wagons, on horses, but mostly on foot. During the winter 1838–1839, unable to cross the Mississippi River because of floating ice blocks, they camped in an area about four miles south of the forest. During this brutal winter hundreds died from cold, starvation, and disease. Today the forest is a quiet area with hilly forests and some prairie and low-lying areas. It comprises a total of about 5,000 acres a few miles south of Jonesboro. A walk through here will take you past oak trees, sugar maples, wild blueberry shrubs, wood violets, and possibly deer and foxes. Several miles of remote trails wind through the hills and valleys. You can bike or hike along these interior gravel roads, accessible from Highway 127 or Highway 3. The Oak Hills Nature Preserve, in the middle of the forest (and also accessible from Highway 127 or 3),

has a lookout tower. There's tent camping south of the preserve. Stop by the forest headquarters (3240 State Forest Rd., Jonesboro, 618/833-4910, www.dnr.state.il.us) for maps.

Hunting and Fishing

Whether it's hunting for pheasants, shooting clays, or practicing your shot at the gun range or archery range, the privately owned **Trail of Tears Lodge and Sports Resort** (1575 Fair City Rd., Jonesboro, 618/833-8697, www.trailoftears.com) has a slew of outdoor activities for day and overnight guests. If you're not into hiking, you can rent horses for $25 an hour and explore the Shawnee Hills.

Didn't bring along your fishing rod, but have the urge to fish? No license either? Fishing is easy at **Bob's Shrimp and Trout Farm** (1.5 miles west of Jonesboro on Hwy. 146, 618/833-6409), where you can rent poles and buy bait. Drop by Bob's for rainbow trout fishing in March and April. You won't need a license because it's on a private fish farm.

Orchard

Southern Illinois is famous for its sweet peaches and apples. Sample a few fruits and stock up

Southern Illinois

© CHRISTINE DES GARENNES

Trail of Tears State Forest

for pies at **Boyds Orchards** (675 Sadler Rd., Anna, 618/833-5533, 9 A.M.–6 P.M. Mon.–Sat., noon–6 P.M. Sun. Sept. 1–Oct. 31). With the rope swing, barn slide, petting zoo, and maze, Boyds has become quite the tourist destination, especially in the fall during pumpkin season. You can also shop for flowers, honey, jams, and cookbooks.

EVENTS

Most of the festivals that take place in Union County, not surprisingly, have to do with outdoor activities. During the **Trail of Tears Rendezvous** (618/833-3129) held in the Trail of Tears State Forest in mid-May, men and women camp out in the forest and reenact the Civil War and demonstrate life back in the 1800s. The forest is also the site of an early August **hummingbird festival** (618/833-4910) sponsored by the Illinois Audubon Society. During the **Union County Colorfest** (618/833-6311, www.shawneeheartland.com), farm markets and shops around the county celebrate the harvest season with fun runs, music, cooking demonstrations, and more.

SHOPPING

Back in the late 1800s, the Kirkpatrick brothers manufactured pottery in Anna. Also known as Anna pottery, their work included traditional pieces such as jugs and jars, but also animal shapes that have been called everything from bizarre to whimsical. To check out some of this stoneware, buy a piece or two, or browse for other antiques, drop by **Isom's Antiques** (107 N. Main St., Anna, 618/833-3516, call ahead for hours).

ACCOMMODATIONS

Your best bet for accommodations in this area is a bed-and-breakfast or lodge, of which there are plenty.

Hunters and other outdoor enthusiasts will feel at home at **Trail of Tears Lodge and Sports Resort** (1575 Fair City Rd., Jonesboro, 618/833-8697, www.trailoftears.com), about nine miles south of Jonesboro on a 425-acre site adjacent to the Shawnee National Forest. The lodge itself has seven rooms, plus there's a two-bedroom cabin that sleeps four adults, and a campground. Rooms don't have telephones or televisions. But

MUSHROOM HUNTING

Every spring, usually around the time the mayapples start poking up above the forest floor and the redbud trees start blooming, a small but devoted group of Illinoisans hit the woods in search of morel mushrooms. The mushrooms, which can range in size from a quarter inch to 14 inches tall, feature an oval, honeycombed cap that looks like a sponge. They're delicious and taste best simply pan-fried with butter, perhaps rolled in a little flour. A cup of smooth and mild morel mushroom soup is also a good bet.

Morel-hunting season in Illinois is mid- to late April–beginning of May. You can find morels in all regions of the state, although many people believe they are most plentiful in bottomland forests. And many mushroom hunters swear morels are most plentiful near dead elm trees, especially trees that have bark peeling off them. One of the Midwest's most popular mushroom-related festivals is the **Illinois State Morel Mushroom Hunting Championship and Spongy Fungi Festival** in Magnolia, a small town about 25 miles southwest of LaSalle and Peru. Held annually on the first weekend in May, the contest attracts hundreds of mushroom hunters. On the day of the hunting contest they board buses and are dropped off at a top-secret location. They then take off in search of morels. Prizes are awarded to hunters who find the most number of mushrooms, plus the largest and smallest mushroom. The Trail of Tears Lodge near Jonesboro in southern Illinois also hosts a morel festival. The **Mid-America Morel Mushroom Festival** is in mid-April.

For more information about morels in Illinois, check with the Magnolia company **Morel Mania** (800/438-8213, www.morelmania.com), which sells hunting supplies such as sacks and walking sticks.

there is a gathering room with a television in it if you really want to watch something on the tube. The barn has a game room and laundry for guests, and there are showers for campers. Fees are $10 per night for tent camping, $25 for RV camping, $65–80 for a room in the lodge, and $125 for the cabin. The resort has a slew of activities for overnight and day visitors, such as horseback riding, shooting clays, and practicing your shot at the gun range.

Ⓜ Hidden Lake B&B (433 Cook Ave., Jonesboro, 618/833-5252, www.hidden-lakebb.com) exudes relaxation. This is a place where you just might abandon the trip itinerary and spend the days reading a book and looking out over the lawn. The 12-acre site has a private two-acre lake with a paddle boat and a little pier for catch-and-release fishing. There are flower gardens, walking paths, and a sunroom. Some of the rooms come with fireplaces, whirlpool baths, and private balconies. There are five rooms total; three are in a guest house, and two are in the main house where the owners live. Rates are $95–160.

If some hotel and bed-and-breakfast rooms make you feel claustrophobic, you'll love the **Davie School Inn Banquet Center** (300 Freeman St., Anna, 618/833-2377, www.daviecenter.com), where a 1910 school building has been transformed into a bed-and-breakfast and banquet center. The eight rooms are spacious, about 850 square feet. Each one comes with a king-size bed, private bath and whirlpool tub, and sitting area. Antiques fill the rooms and hallways. (You'll also notice in places such as the hallway that a few fixtures from the school's past remain, such as the tiny water fountains.) Room rates start at $100.

FOOD
Barbecue
Leather-clad Harley-Davidson motorcyclists mingle with white-haired locals and visitors

at **Dixie Barbecue** (205 W. Broad, Jones-boro, 618/833-6437, 10 A.M.–8 P.M. Mon.–Sat., $4), a popular lunch and dinner spot along Highway 127. The little white building is a classic roadside restaurant. Food is cheap, simple, and comforting, such as hamburgers, ham and cheese, and the famous barbecue sandwiches. Wash down your meal with a lemonade.

American

Found next door to the Anna-Union Art Guild is **Alexcine's at the Guild** (308 S. Main St., Jonesboro, 618/833-5443, $9), a storefront restaurant that resembles the interior of someone's living and dining rooms, complete with a fireplace and blue-checked tablecloths. Food is standard Midwestern, such as pork chops and applesauce cake, but there are also a few untraditional items (especially for a small town such as Jonesboro), such as tilapia.

The name of **The Potato Barn** (169 E. Vienna St., Anna, 618/833-7827, 10:30 A.M.–2 P.M. Tues.–Wed., 10:30 A.M.–8 P.M. Thurs.–Sat., 11 A.M.–2 P.M. Sun., call for winter hours, $3–10) was not just picked out of a hat by the restaurateurs. The maroon barn, which dates to 1921 and is near downtown Anna, was actually the place where the local sweet potato crop was stored. Through the years it's housed many agriculturally related businesses. Now it's a countrified restaurant with a few gifts for sale such as candles and stuffed animals. The food is reminiscent of a Sunday dinner at Grandma's house: meat loaf, country-fried steak (breaded and deep-fried steak), fried chicken. There are some low-fat options for dieters.

For more homemade food, but in a rural setting, head to the restaurant at the **Trail of Tears Lodge and Sports Resort** (1575 Fair City Rd., Jonesboro, 618/833-8697, www.trailoftears.com, 5–8 P.M. Fri.–Sat., $8). It has traditional American fare, plus Cajun cooking and dishes such as catfish

and even some more exotic items such as frog legs.

INFORMATION

For visitor information, turn to **The Union County Chamber of Commerce** (330 S. Main St., Anna, 618/833-6311, www.shawneeheartland.com) or the **Southernmost Illinois Tourism Bureau** (Shawnee College Bldg., 1000 N. Main St., Anna, 618/833-9928 or 800/248-4373, www.southernmostillinois.com), which has information on the six southernmost counties in the state, including Union County. You can also stock up on brochures at the **Trail of Tears Welcome Center** (I-57 and Hwy. 146, Mount Pleasant, 618/833-4809), a rest area boasting a little memorial to the prized pig known as King Neptune, a Navy mascot auctioned for $19 million in war bonds during World War II.

SERVICES

If you're feeling ill or sprained an ankle during a hike in the Anna-Jonesboro area, contact the **Union County Hospital** (517 N. Main St., Anna, 618/833-4511, www.unioncountyhospital.com).

DONGOLA

Between Jonesboro and Cairo is the popular roadside eatery and garden center **Fragrant Fields and Mule Barn Café** (102 S. Garden St., Dongola, 800/635-0282, www.fragrantfields.com, 10 A.M.–5 P.M. Tues.–Sat., lunch served 11 A.M.–3 P.M.). First and foremost a garden center (with beautiful display gardens of perennials, herbs, and other plants), the complex has become a bit of a tourist attraction with its café housed in an old mule barn, its gift shop of local art, and events (such as the herb festival in May) and occasional concert.

Cairo

HISTORY AND ORIENTATION

Cairo (pronounced Caro, like the syrup), is not exactly a tourist destination. Its downtown is crumbling, as are many of the grand old homes that once belonged to the river men. Good jobs are scarce, and utilities are expensive. Not many young people live here. Cairo, however, is a fascinating place for people interested in river towns and history. First a French colony, the city eventually grew into an industrial and agricultural trade center for shipping grain and dairy products down to New Orleans. During the Civil War Ulysses S. Grant had his troop's headquarters just outside of Cairo at Fort Defiance. When the Illinois Central Railroad chose Cairo as its southern terminus, the city thrived for a while as goods were traded with Chicago. But it wouldn't last long. The population dwindled, manufacturing eventually left for other towns, and in the mid-20th century, racial tensions prompted even more residents to leave town. To get a sense

of the town's past, you can visit several historic buildings in town and drive over to Fort Defiance State Park, a small park where the Mississippi and Ohio rivers meet.

SIGHTS
Historic Homes

To get a sense of the town's former glory days, drive down Washington Avenue to view some of the grand old homes. You can visit two of them, which are across the street from each other. Both homes are decked out for the holidays in December.

Magnolia Manor (2700 Washington Ave., Cairo, 618/734-0201, 9 A.M.–5 P.M. Mon.–Sat., 1–5 P.M. Sun., closed Christmas Eve–Jan. 2, free) is a red brick Italianate mansion with 14 rooms. The home was built in 1869 for a friend of Grant's. It's now listed on the National Register of Historic Places and is dressed up with holiday decorations in November and December.

Riverlore is one of many old mansions in Cairo

© CHRISTINE DES GARENNES

Riverlore (2723 Washington Ave., Cairo, 618/734-0177 or 618/734-1840, $5) French Second empire–style mansion, was built in 1865 for William Parker Halliday, a steamboater turned banker. It features a captain's walk on the third story and gardens. Later William Wolter, a vivacious, some say obnoxious, riverman owned the house. Hours vary, but generally the house is open 10 A.M.–noon and 1–4 P.M. Wednesday–Saturday.

U.S. Custom House Museum

If you're an admirer of Ulysses S. Grant, visit the U.S. Custom House Museum (14th and Washington Ave., Cairo, 618/734-1019, 10 A.M.–noon, 1–3 P.M. Mon.–Fri., weekend hours vary, call ahead, $2 donation). Listed on the National Register of Historic Places, the building, once a customs house, post office, police department headquarters, and you name it, is now a local-history museum. Among the highlights are a desk used by Grant while he was stationed in Cairo,

exhibits on Meriwether Lewis and William Clark, who stopped by Cairo before setting up camp in Wood River, an arrowhead collection, plus plenty of photographs from the town's beginnings and some recent years, including photographs of a campaign stop by former President Bill Clinton.

Fort Defiance State Park

It's been called the ugliest state park, the park no one wanted, and many other things, but Fort Defiance State Park (U.S. 51, two miles south of Cairo), is a park of historical significance. Again, if you're a fan of General Ulysses S. Grant, you will want to stop by. Found at the southernmost tip of Illinois, the park is at the confluence of the Mississippi and Ohio rivers. At one point during the Civil War, this area was the site of a fort under Grant's command. He and his men had the job of supplying Union troops. So although it's in need of a makeover (or at least a good afternoon of weed-whacking), the park is a good spot to watch barges as they chug down the rivers.

THE OHIO RIVER SCENIC BYWAY

A great way to organize your visit to southern Illinois is by following the Ohio River Scenic Byway. The 967-mile route through Ohio, Indiana, and Illinois trails the river's shoreline, passing through river towns, historic state parks, kitschy museums, and scenic overlooks. In Illinois the byway winds along the river for about 200 miles from roughly Shawneetown to Cairo. You can easily spend three days driving the stretch. Begin in Cairo on the southern tip of the state, with a tour of one of the handful of old river baron mansions there. Then take a short drive to the confluence of the Ohio and Mississippi rivers at Fort Defiance State Park, where Ulysses S. Grant was stationed with his Union troops during the Civil War. Spend a few quiet moments at the Mound City National Cemetery north of Cairo. Then take a short detour to the Cache River State Natural Area for a hike through a cypress swamp. After that, it's off to Metropolis, with its Superman Museum and Fort Massac State Park, which has a re-creation of an 1802 fort. Stay overnight in the restored lock and dam houses in Golconda or in Elizabethtown, a scenic little river town. Try the Rose Hotel or River Rose Inn, both overlooking the river. Both towns are good bases for side trips of hiking in the Shawnee National Forest, such as those in the Garden of the Gods Wilderness Area, known for its sandstone bluffs and rock formations. From there you can also spend time at Cave-in-Rock State Park, which is just off the byway route. Visitors are allowed to explore the immense cave there that was once home to bands of thieves. Throughout the scenic byway, you'll drive on several county, state, and U.S. highways (such as Highway 13, Highway 146, and U.S. 51). But there are plenty of signposts along the way. More information is available from the regional tourism bureaus or www.ohioriverscenicbyway.com.

FOOD

The Shemwell family of **Shemwell's Barbecue** (1102 Washington Ave., Cairo, 618/734-0165, 7 A.M.–8 P.M. Mon.–Sat., and 9 A.M.–8 P.M. Sun., under $10) has been barbecuing in southern Illinois and Cairo since the 1930s. The decor is nothing special, with just a few tables and a countertop, but the barbecue is sweet and tangy with a little kick. It has fans who drive hours just to eat here. Try the sliced barbecue pork sandwich or beef brisket.

INFORMATION

For tips on visiting the area call the **Cairo Chamber of Commerce** (220 8th St., Cairo, 618/734-2737).

MOUND CITY

Mound City National Monument and Cemetery (U.S. 51 and Hwy. 37, Mound City) is a solemn reminder that Illinois did not remain unscathed from the Civil War. Battles were not fought here, but gunboats were built near Cairo and military hospitals were set up in Cairo and Mound City. The cemetery, listed on the National Register of Historic Places, is about a five-minute drive north of Cairo. It contains the graves of thousands of Union and Confederate soldiers, many of whom were from Illinois, Wisconsin, Indiana, and other Midwestern states. Verses from the "Bivouac of the Dead" poem have been printed onto markers placed throughout the cemetery.

Civil War soldiers are buried in the Mound City National Monument and Cemetery.

Lower Cache River

HISTORY

What makes the Cache River region such a fascinating and beautiful place is that it's at a biological midpoint in North America (one of six such places in America) where physiographic regions overlap. What this means is that as the regions (defined by terrain, soils, and wildlife) meet, they all bring a set of diverse animal, plant, and tree species. The Cache River basin is surrounded by the Shawnee Hills physiographic region (an extension of the Ozark mountain range) to the west, the Central Plateau to the north, the Interior Lowland to the east, and the Gulf Coastal Plain to the south. A dizzying array of amphibians (such as tree frogs, salamanders), mammals (beavers, mink), plants (floating emerald duckweed, buttonbush), trees (red oaks, cypress) and birds (egrets, eagles) live in the basin. As a result, it is and has been a prime fishing and hunting region. Native American tribes fished, trapped, and hunted seasonally here long before the white settlers from Kentucky, Tennessee, Ohio, and other states moved into Illinois. Back then the swamp was about 250,000 acres.

When the settlers arrived in the late 1700s and early 1800s, they focused on harvesting the thousands of mature tupelo, oak, and black gum trees in the area for timber. Lumber mills in Cairo and other towns churned out railroad ties, shipping crates, and other products. Some pioneers established farms and grew tobacco, cotton, wheat, and other crops. They dammed streams to create ponds for their livestock. Settlement in the basin area, however, was limited. The swamps and bottomland forests were ideal mosquito-breeding areas, and residents often became ill from malaria and other diseases. The threat of disease and the prospect of turning the area into more of an agricultural region prompted people to drain many of the wetlands in the early 1900s. Corn and soybeans were planted, but yields still didn't match those found in the central part of the state.

Today the Cache River region is still a stunning site, though agriculture, erosion, and development have taken their toll on the river and its inhabitants. The Cache River State Natural Area was established in 1970 to preserve and manage the region, plus several other national and regional groups have been working to acquire land and restore wetlands, control stream-bank erosion, and address other environmental problems. The Cypress Creek National Wildlife Refuge comprises about 15,000 acres, and let's hope it will also expand in coming years.

ORIENTATION

The Cache River can be divided into an upper region and lower region. The northern, more narrow, section of the river flows through hills and bluffs. The lower Cache River, where the Cache River State Natural Area is, has a wider floodplain with plenty of swampy areas, sloughs, and small oxbow lakes. It's between I-57 and I-24, south of Highway 146 and north of Highway 169, east of Highway 37 and west of U.S. 45.

The lower section is loaded with nature preserves and trails. If you're coming from the north a good starting point is the Wildcat Bluff Access Area southwest of Vienna, which has a lookout and trail to the swamps and huge championship cherrybark oak tree. If you're coming from the south, a good place to learn about the region is the Henry Barkhausen Wetlands Centera few miles north of Karnak. Some trails in the region are more than a mile long, but most are easy, as they are through bottomland swamps and forest. Tunnel Hill State Trail skirts the southern part of the state natural area; you can reach Heron Pond, Barkhausen Center, Section 8 Woods Nature Preserve, and other natural areas from the trail. Regional roads have plenty of signs that mark popular destinations (such as Heron Pond) and driving distances.

CACHE RIVER STATE NATURAL AREA

With about 13,000 acres stretching into Johnson and Pulaski counties, the Cache River State Natural Area (headquarters 930 Sunflower Ln., Belknap, 618/634-9678, www.dnr.state.il.us) should be your first destination while visiting the Cache River basin region. The area boasts several nature preserves, accessible boardwalks, scenic overlooks, giant trees, and tiny plants (perhaps the tiniest are duckweed, little plants that float on water). Plus, more than 20 miles of trails wind through dark bottomland forests, low ridges, barrens, meadows, and other areas. You can't go wrong with any of the trails.

Heron Pond

This 75-acre nature preserve has three trails along the Cache River and to and along Heron Pond (it looks more like a swamp, actually). There are three trails: a half-mile hike to the Heron Pond boardwalk; .75-mile hike to the cherrybark oak; and one just over two miles to the Little Black Slough, an adjacent nature preserve. The Heron Pond boardwalk trail is a must-see. There you have the chance to walk into the swamp (well, above the water on the boardwalk) and get close to some several 100-year-old cypress trees and look for river otters, snowy egrets, and other animals. Along the mostly woodchip trail to Heron Pond are educational signs that point out plants, such as bloodroot, and explain their significance (Native Americans used it for dye). The cherry-bark oak tree stands about 100 feet tall with a circumference of more than 22 feet. It's pretty big. But if you're in town visiting from Oregon or Washington, you could probably skip the walk to this tree. The area is accessible from the Belknap blacktop, just west of U.S. 45.

Little Black Slough and Wildcat Bluff

The total length of the Little Black Slough Trail is 5.5 miles. It connects with Heron Pond, Marshall Ridge, and the Wildcat Bluff. Some parts of it may challenge infrequent hikers. This trail lets you see it all. You'll climb sandstone bluffs that are a common sight in Illinois, trudge through wooded floodplain areas and

cypress and tupelo swamp at Heron Pond

through cypress and tupelo swamps, cross the Cache River on a rock ford, and hike to Boss Island. The one-mile long lookout trail, accessible from the Wildcat Bluff access area south of Highway 146, is a hillside and hilltop trail with overviews of the river valley.

Section 8 Woods Nature Preserve

In the southwestern corner of the Cache River State Natural Area, just east of the town of Perks (and about four miles south of the town of Cypress) is the Section 8 preserve. This site also has a 475-foot-long, wheelchair-accessible boardwalk into the cypress and tupelo swamp. It leads to the state champion water tupelo tree that boasts a buttress circumference of 22.5 feet.

Wetlands Center

The excellent new **Henry N. Barkhausen Cache River Wetlands Center** (Hwy. 37 and Perks Rd., White Hill, 618/634-9678, www.dnr.state.il.us, free) is another must-see stop for new visitors to the Cache River region. A short film and several interactive exhibits explain the geologic, natural, and cultural history of the Cache River region. Take a "photo safari" and test your plant and animal identification skills. Head outside and take a stroll along a half-mile wheelchair-accessible trail along a newly created wetland. Have a seat on a bench and look for shorebirds and waterfowl. Adjacent to the center is the Tunnel Hill State Trail's western terminus, so after your visit you can hop on your bike and ride to the swamps. The Wetlands Center is open 9 A.M.–4 P.M. Fri. and Sat.

Canoeing

The **Lower Cache River Canoe Trail,** is a section of the Cache River designated for canoeing. Paddle northeast to the state championship tupelo tree, past cypress and gum trees, and the occasional river otter and egret. You can launch your canoe or kayak at the Lower Cache River Access Area, where Cypress Creek meets the Cache River. The trail, up to six miles long, has signposts with arrows and other markings

that point you in the right direction, but you might want to pick up a map from the state natural headquarters office in Belknap, just in case you get lost. The canoe trail is just west of Highway 37 and north of Highway 169. (Follow signs from Highway 37.) You can rent canoes at **Cache Core Canoes** (237 Dean Ln., Ullin, 618/845-3817).

SIGHTS AND ACTIVITIES

Tunnel Hill State Trail

Johnson County's nickname is the biking capital of the state, and that's largely because of the 45-mile-long Tunnel Hill State Trail (618/658-2168, www.dnr.state.il.us or www.il-bikecap.org), which carves a path through the county. It begins at U.S. 45 and Highway 13 in Harrisburg (where there are bathrooms, parking, and a bike rack) and continues to the Henry Barkhausen Wetlands Center west of Karnak. You'll find there are several places where you can start your ride, including Community Park in Vienna and the wetlands center. The crushed-limestone and gravel trail follows part of the old Norfolk Southern Railroad line, through fairly flat farmland, up and down the hills of the Shawnee National Forest, the bottomlands of the Cache River basin, along creeks, past ghost towns, and atop trestle bridges (one that is more than 90 feet high south of the town of Tunnel Hill). The trail's highlight is a 500-foot-long, sandstone and shale tunnel built in 1872, also near the town of Tunnel Hill. **Morris Acres** (1645 Tunnel Hill Rd., Tunnel Hill, 618/658-4022) offers shuttle service on the tunnel trail for a fee.

The nine-mile section between the towns of Tunnel Hill and Vienna intersects with the **River-to-River Trail,** a 175-mile trail that connects the Mississippi and Ohio rivers (www.rivertorivertrail.org) between Cave-in-Rock and Grand Tower.

Scenic Overlook

The Nature Conservancy's **Grassy Slough Preserve** (off the Belknap blacktop, a few miles north of Karnak, 618/634-2524) has an overlook, the Jean Campbell Farwell Overlook, that offers views of an ongoing wetland restoration project. More than 2,500 acres of land damaged by drainage, farming, and logging will one day look like a cypress-tupelo swamp again.

Wineries

Just down the road from Heron Pond, **Cache River Basin Vineyard and Winery** (315 Forman Ln., Belknap, 618/658-7023 or 618/658-2274, www.crbwinery.com, 10 A.M.–6 P.M. Mon.–Sat., 1–5 P.M. Sun.) offers wine tastings and tours of its winery. Its wines include red and white brands such as Hawk Tail Red and Cottonmouth White, named after Cache River wildlife. The winery holds events throughout the year—the wine and arts festival in July, grape stomp in July, plus barbecue dinners and murder mystery dinners. Opened in 2004, **Shawnee Winery** (200 Commercial Dr., Vienna, 618/658-8400, www.shawneewinery.com) is a cooperative of small regional wineries. Its shop is just off I-24 in Vienna.

ACCOMMODATIONS

$50–100

Two decent national chain hotels are on the eastern edge of Vienna, just off I-24. There's the **Ramada Inn** (Hwy. 146 and I-24, Vienna, 618/658-6300) with an indoor pool and continental breakfast; and the **Budget Inn** (Hwy. 146 and I-24, Vienna, 618/658-2802).

Camping

Cedar Lake Ranch (2090 Gillead Church Rd., Vienna, 618/695-2900, www.cedarlakeranchllc.com) has more than 200 camp sites with access to electricity, water, and a shower house. Plus there are four basic, one-bedroom cottages with small kitchens (minifridges, microwaves). The bedrooms have two full beds and are air-conditioned. Camping costs $12–20. Cottages are $60. There's also camping at Ferne Clyffe State Park to the north.

FOOD

The locally famous **Little Shop of Pastries** (U.S. 45, Country Garden Shopping Center, Vienna, 618/658-2087, 8 A.M.–5 P.M. Mon.–Fri., 8–2 P.M. Sat.) is a good, inexpensive lunch spot for enjoying a turkey sandwich and soup or hamburger and French fries. Leave room for dessert. The pies and sweet treats are homemade. Sandwiches are less than $4.

Farm Markets

You can pick up some fresh fruits, veggies, and flowers at **Trover Produce** (992 Gilead Church Rd., Vienna, 618/658-5100, open seasonally) or **Eastman Orchard and Fruit Market** (Hwy. 37, two miles north of Goreville, 618/995-2118, 8 A.M.–5 P.M. daily Sept.–Nov.).

INFORMATION

The **Johnson County Chamber of Commerce** (Vienna, 618/658-2063, www.johnsoncountyilchamber.org, 9 A.M.–3 P.M. Tues.–Sat.) operates a visitors center within a renovated train depot at Vienna Community Park, on the north side of Highway 146 just as you drive west into town. Friendly staff have brochures on nearby attractions, maps, and photographs of the old train depot that once stood in the area. They also sell a few gifts such as train whistles. The depot is on the Tunnel Hill Trail and there's plenty of parking if you want to make this the launching point of your bike trip through the region.

For a regional overview, contact the **Southernmost Illinois Convention and Tourism Bureau** (Shawnee College Bldg., 1000 N. Main St., Anna, 618/833-9928 or 800/248-4373, www.southernmostillinois.com), which has lodging and attractions info for the Cache River area as well as surrounding counties. Another good resource is the **Shawnee National Forest's** ranger station in Vienna (602 N. 1st St./U.S. 45, Vienna, 618/658-2111, 8 A.M.–4:30 P.M. Mon.–Fri.). And for more information about the Cache River basin, you can contact staff at the **Cypress Creek National**

Wildlife Refuge (Cypress Creek National Wildlife Refuge, Rustic Campus Dr., Ullin, 618/634-2231, 7:30 A.M.–4 P.M. Mon.–Fri., www.fws.gov/midwest/cypresscreek).

FERNE CLYFFE STATE PARK

As the name implies, Ferne Clyffe State Park (one mile south of Goreville on Hwy. 37, 618/995-2411, www.dnr.state.il.us) is in a rich, forested area at the southern edge of the Shawnee National Forest. Ferns abound, but so do trilliums, lilies, flowering dogwoods, and redbud trees, making this place a beautiful sight in the spring. It's also interesting on a historical level. Revolutionary War hero George Rogers Clark was said to have hiked through here with his men after securing the British Fort Massac and on his way to Fort Kaskaskia. Speaking of hiking, the park, at almost 2,500 acres, has great hiking—a total of 18 trails, from the easy one-mile loop around Ferne Clyffe Lake to the steep, five-mile-long Happy Hollow Trail. (You won't be happy if you forget to bring along enough water, especially in the summer.) One of the coolest sights in the park is Hawks' Cave, a rock shelter about 150 feet long. To get there follow the half-mile Hawk Cave Trail in the northern part of the park. Follow Rebman Trail to the climbing and rappelling area. If you want to keep your visit low-key drop a line into the Ferne Clyffe Lake for bank fishing or picnic at one of the spots overlooking the hills.

The park has several campgrounds, each geared toward a different camper. Deer Ridge has modern sites with electricity and gravel pads. Turkey Ridge is a walk-in campground with tent pads, picnic tables, and showers. The backpack campground is a half-mile hike through the woods from Turkey Ridge. There's also an equestrian campground. Camping costs $8–15 per night.

Climbing

Learn how to rock climb at **Drapers Bluff and Vertical Heartland Climbing School** (618/995-1427, www.verticalheartland.com, open daily year-round) just south of Ferne Clyffe State Park.

Metropolis

Reportedly the only city named Metropolis in the United States, Metropolis, Illinois, has capitalized on its connection to the man of steel. Decades ago the Illinois legislature declared Metropolis, Illinois, as Superman's hometown. The town celebrates with a Superman festival every summer, and Jim Hambrick's Super Museum is arguably one of the best roadside attractions in the region. In addition to the Superman sights, Metropolis has the oldest state park in the state, Fort Massac, a place once visited by legendary figures such as Revolutionary War hero George Rogers Clark and explorers William Clark and Meriwether Lewis.

SIGHTS
Fort Massac State Park
Almost hidden at the eastern end of Metropolis near an industrial site and shopping center is Fort Massac State Park (1308 E. 5th St., Metropolis, 618/524-9321, www.dnr.state.il.us, visitors center open 9:30 A.M.–4:30 P.M. daily), a park with quite a history. Shortly after you enter the park you'll see on a hill above the Ohio River a replica of an 1802 timber fort. The version you see is one of many forts that once stood guard in the area. Back in 1702 the French established a trading post in the area and as the French took control of the area, they built a fort to protect their growing territory. (They initially called it Fort Ascension.) After France and Great Britain signed the Treaty of Paris in 1763 to end the Seven Years War (or French and Indian War), the French surrendered territory, including the areas in and around the fort. A few years later the Brits failed to adequately supply the fort and in June

1778 George Rogers Clark, with fewer than 200 men, was able to secure it for the American colonies in 1778. General George Washington ordered it rebuilt in 1794. In the early 1800s it was mostly a point of entry for pioneers and explorers and used as a customs office in the 19th century. Explorers William Clark (younger brother to George Rogers Clark) and Meriwether Lewis stopped by here to recruit some men for their Corps of Discovery.

Eventually the fort was dismantled. In 1866 a man named J. C. Blair, later the dean of the University of Illinois College of Agriculture, rode by the park on horseback and thought the area would make a nice park. The Daughters of the American Revolution bought land there in 1908 and it became the first state park.

Today the park, almost 2,000 acres, has a new fort modeled after how it may have looked when Washington ordered it rebuilt. A visitors center has exhibits on the fort's history, and there are picnic spots and hiking trails. A one-mile loop wanders through the woods and a

© CHRISTINE DES GARENNES

Fort Massac State Park, Metropolis

2.5-mile trail follows part of the Ohio River. The park also has a campground.

Superman Sights

The **Super Museum** (Metropolis, 618/524-5518, www.supermancollectors.com, 9 A.M.–5 P.M. daily, $3) is a maze of a museum with constantly changing exhibits that run the gamut. The owner has hundreds of thousands of pieces of Superman paraphernalia: action figures, costumes worn by television and movie actors, lunch boxes, posters, inflatables, you name it. The museum has a large shop with plenty of T-shirts and Superman and comic book ephemera. A few feet from the Super Museum is a bronze statue of Superman in the town square. You can't miss it.

Birdman of Alcatraz

Made famous by Burt Lancaster in a movie about life in Alcatraz, Robert Stroud was known as the birdman of Alcatraz. Stroud, convicted for murdering a bartender, was not exactly a model prisoner in his youth. But after being transferred to Alcatraz Island in the San Francisco Bay, he grew to love tending to birds. He raised hundreds of them while there and even wrote books about bird diseases. He's buried in Metropolis in the Masonic Cemetery on North Avenue in Metropolis.

ENTERTAINMENT AND EVENTS

Parked on the bank of the Ohio River, **Harrah's Casino** (100 E. Front St., Metropolis, 800/929-5905, www.harrahs.com, 9 A.M.–7 P.M. daily) is one of Illinois's several riverboat casinos. (It's not really a boat moving along the river, though.) This place is hopping, especially on weekend nights. There are 1,100 slot machines, 25 tables with games such as blackjack, plus three restaurants (a diner, steakhouse, and a buffet restaurant). Harrah's was building a new hotel and event center adjacent to the casino, expected to open in Spring 2006.

The big to-do in the summer is the annual **Superman festival** held in June. In addition to the standard carnival rides and fried food, the festival has Superman-themed games and usually former stars of Superman movies and television shows show up. Over at **Fort Massac** several re-enactments and encampments are held throughout the year, including French and Indian War reenactments in mid-May and a "living history" weekend in mid-August, when participants live as if they were inhabitants of the fort.

ACCOMMODATIONS
$50–100
The **Amerihost Inn** (203 E. Front St., Metropolis, 800/434-8500) overlooks the Ohio River and is just across the street from the riverboat casino. It has an indoor pool, and rooms come with wireless Internet access and coffeemakers. Continental breakfast is included. The **Holiday Inn Express** (2179 E. 5th St., Metropolis, 618/524-8899) and **Comfort Inn** (2118 E. 5th St., Metropolis, 618/524-7227) are both on U.S. 45 on the east side of town by Fort Massac State Park. Each has an indoor pool and offers continental breakfast.

$100 and Up
The beautiful **Old Bethlehem Schoolhouse Cottage** (6512 Old Marion Rd., Metropolis, 618/524-4922, www.bethlehemschool.com) is a one-room schoolhouse renovated into a three-bedroom cottage with an eat-in kitchen and one bathroom. Tastefully decorated with antiques, the cottage can sleep up to six people (one queen, one double, and two twin beds). Outside the windows are views of cornfields and the Shawnee Hills.

Standing guard on a hill overlooking the Ohio River, the **Isle of View Bed and Breakfast** (205 Metropolis St., Metropolis, 618/524-5838, www.isle-of-view.net) is an 1889 brick Victorian home converted into a bed-and-breakfast. There are five rooms total, all with private bathrooms and richly decorated with Victorian-style antiques and decor. Extras, such as the two-person tubs and canopy beds, make it a good choice for couples on romantic getaways. A full breakfast is included. The hosts also offer extensive in-room dinners if you give them notice.

Items on the menu could be Cornish game hens, sherried shrimp, and other dishes.

Camping
Fort Massac State Park (1308 E. 5th St., Metropolis, 618/524-9321, www.dnr.state.il.us) has campsites for RVs and tents. Fees are $8–15 per night.

FOOD
In downtown Metropolis, a block from the Super Museum, you'll find a rare sight: a cafeteria. It's not a school or retirement center, but an old-fashioned storefront restaurant cafeteria. **Farley's Cafeteria** (613 Market St., Metropolis, 618/524-7226, 3:30–7 P.M. Wed.–Sat., $7) features smiling, older ladies serving big spoonfuls of green beans, creamed corn, and slices of roast beef and steaming pork. The crowd definitely leans toward the white-haired. It's a good people-watching spot.

Stock up on groceries at **Big John's** supermarket (1200 E. 5th St., Metropolis, 618/524-4096). Look for the giant fiberglass "Big John" (who, like Superman, boasts a brawny figure) grasping a bag of groceries at the parking lot entrance.

Farm Market
Faughn Farms (3059 Old Marion Rd., Metropolis, 618/524-8383, 10 A.M.–2 P.M. Tues., Thurs., Sat.) specializes in organic herbs for culinary or medicinal use.

INFORMATION
You can get lodging information from the **Metropolis Chamber of Commerce** (607 Market St., Metropolis, 618/524-2714, www.metropolischamber.com).

DIXON SPRINGS AND GLENDALE LAKE
Dixon Springs State Park
Named for the mineral springs in the area, Dixon Springs State Park (618/949-3394) is

© CHRISTINE DES GARENNES

Dixon Springs State Park

tiful in the spring, when the oak and hickory trees have pale green buds and dogwood trees bloom cream-colored flowers. There are about 40 campsites here with electricity, plus 10 rustic sites for tents. The swimming pool is open to the public Memorial Day–Labor Day.

After your rigorous hike atop bluffs and along canyon walls, treat yourself to a hand-dipped ice-cream cone at **The Chocolate Factory** (Hwy. 146, 618/949-3829 or 877/949-3829, www.thechocolatefactory.net, 9 A.M.–5 P.M. Mon.–Sat.) across the highway from the park. Then, pack some fudge or peanut brittle in the cooler for the ride home.

Lake Glendale

If you need to cool off, you can take a dip in the 80-acre Lake Glendale (Hwy. 145, north of Dixon Springs, 618/658-2111), a few miles north of Dixon Springs State Park and part of the U.S. Forest Service. The lake has a sandy beach, concession stand, shower house, and paddleboats for rent.

In the Shawnee National Forest near Lake Glendale, **Lake Glendale Stables** (201 Lake Glendale Rd., Golconda, 618/949-3737, www.lakeglendalestables.com, rides available daily, year-round, call for times) offers horseback rides by the hour or entire day, plus overnight camping trips, or lunch and dinner trips. The main attraction is horseback riding, but the owners also have a private lake for bank fishing, a zip line swing (where you grab onto a bar, zoom down the line and jump into the lake), and a rustic campground. In addition, there's a lodge that sleeps up to four people. Nothing fancy—just air-conditioning, a wood-burning stove, and a kitchen stocked with dishes. Camping costs $20 per night. The lodge is $95 per night.

tucked off Highway 146 west of Golconda and easy to miss. It could use some updating (the roads are a little bumpy) but that doesn't matter; the park's best attraction is its geology (and for the kids, it's the swimming pool). Park your car and spend some time hiking one or both of the two trails here. Hike them both and they'll add up to less than three miles. (The park is about 800 acres.) Ghost Dance Canyon, which can get a little slippery and follows along the side of a canyon for a section of the trail, takes you past canyon walls that stretch about 50 feet high. On rainy days and some of the days thereafter, little waterfalls and rivulets come rushing down the hillsides and rocks. The wooded park is beau-

Golconda

This little town on the Ohio River makes for a great base for your trip through the Shawnee National Forest. It has a short but reemerging Main Street with a few alternative lodging options, friendly restaurants, and a marina for boaters.

SIGHTS AND ACTIVITIES

Rauchfuss Hill is a small recreation area on a bluff above the Ohio River and is connected to Golconda marina below by a walking trail. The selling point of this state-owned park is the view of the river. It used to be called Steamboat Hill because you could watch the steamboats pass by. Now you can count the barges. There are two short trails through the area, a few picnic tables, and a few campsites. To get to the park, follow signs to the marina from Highway 146.

For a peaceful hike through river bottomland, past oak trees, ferns, and through meadows, visit **War Bluff Valley Wildlife Sanctuary** just north of Golconda. The 500-acre site, owned by the Illinois Audubon Society, boasts several mowed grass trails and hiking trails by several ponds and along Simmons Creek. (To get to the site, drive 3.5 miles north of Golconda on Highway 146, take a left on Bushwack Road, and follow a gravel road for a few more miles, open dawn–dusk daily, free.)

Fishing and Boating

Golconda is near the Smithland Pool, a 23,000-acre area created by the lock and dam near Smithland, Kentucky. The fishing there is, well, famous. Bass? They're there. Bluegill? Yup. Catfish? You bet. If you want to give it a shot, you can rent a boat or launch your boat at the **Golconda Marina** (just off Hwy. 146, Golconda, 618/683-5875, www.golcondamarina.com, open March–Nov., call for hours). Rent a fishing boat or pontoon boat here, buy some snacks, and learn about where the fish are

biting. You can walk to the marina from downtown via a highway bridge, or vice versa.

EVENTS

In the fall, farmers harvest not only corn and soybeans, but prawns, otherwise known as shrimp. Prawns are freshwater shrimp. And every year it seems more farmers in southern Illinois are raising them in ponds behind their houses. (It's called aquaculture.) In mid-September Golconda celebrates the shrimp harvest with the **Shrimp Festival.** As you listen to live music, nibble on fresh shrimp, watch shrimp being prepared in the great shrimp cook-off, and then take home some frozen shrimp to eat later.

ACCOMMODATIONS

How often do you get to stay in the house of a former lock keeper? You can at **Lock and Dam 51 houses** (Levy Rd., Golconda, 618/683-6702, www.mainstreetgolconda.org). After they fell into disrepair from disuse, the city of Golconda bought the four buildings and restored them. Opened in 2002, the homes are decorated with 1920s antiques, plus a few modern amenities such as whirlpool tubs and pull-out couches. There are four houses, two different styles. Both have porches and offer great views of the river. And both have full kitchens that contain dishes and pots and pans. The wooden frame houses have one bedroom with a queen bed, plus a pull-out in the living room, and a bathroom with a whirlpool tub. The brick homes have three bedrooms, plus a pull-out sofa in the living room. Rates are $85–185.

There are two bed-and-breakfasts in town. The **Main Street Bed and Breakfast** (Main St. between Monroe and Market Sts., Golconda) is in downtown Golconda and is a one-bedroom apartment with private bath. It rents for $100 a night. For information call the True Value hardware store at 618/683-2551.

The Mansion of Golconda (222 S. Columbus Ave., Golconda, 618/683-4400) is tucked safely behind the levee. It has four rooms decorated Victorian style, plus some gathering rooms for all guests, such as an enclosed porch off the back and a dining room. The innkeeper, who has cookbooks with her recipes, whips up elegant American and French dishes. Rates are $75–110.

FOOD

Continental

The European-styled �ⁿ Café Bella Mia (217 E. Main St., Golconda, 618/683-2094, 11 A.M.–2 P.M. Tues.–Thurs., Fri.–Sat., 5–9 P.M. Fri.–Sat., $10) in downtown Golconda is a little bit of everything: bakery, restaurant, and wine bar. You can visit the intimate cream and black-decorated storefront café for a panini sandwich and café latte or seafood dinner entrée accompanied by a glass of wine.

American

Dari-Barr (209 W. Main St., Golconda, 618/683-4878, 6 A.M.–8 P.M. daily, call for winter hours) is the kind of place where local farmers eat their meals of biscuits and gravy and regulars sit and drink coffee for most of the morning (and make wisecracks to the waitress). Food is cheap and good. An egg, two pieces of toast, and sausage costs about $3. Dishes also include catfish sandwiches, hot dogs, and chicken dinners.

Farm Market

For fresh-picked peaches, tomatoes, and salad mix, drop by the Golconda Farmers Market, held on Saturdays mid- to late April–September, on the courthouse lawn on Main Street. Vendors sell 8 A.M.–noon.

INFORMATION

Before you visit, give the folks a call at Main Street Golconda (618/683-6246 or 888/490-2850, www.mainstreetgolconda.org) to get the scoop on any new lodgings, driving tips, or other information.

GETTING AROUND

A great and inexpensive way to see the Ohio River and some of the Ohio River towns is on the *Shawnee Queen River Taxi* (618/285-3342 or 877/667-6123, www.ridesmtd.com), which rolls along the Ohio River with stops in Golconda, Rosiclare, Elizabethtown, and Cave-in-Rock. It's managed by the Rides Mass Transit District and operates Tuesday–Saturday, second Tuesday in May–November 1. The river taxi seats 48 people and has bike racks. You can reserve a seat online.

MERMET SPRINGS

Illinois is hundreds of miles from any ocean, sea, or gulf. But that doesn't mean you can't scuba dive and explore the underwater world. About halfway between Metropolis and Vienna is an abandoned stone quarry that has been transformed into a scuba school and scuba adventure spot for more experienced divers. Visitors to Mermet Springs (west side of U.S. 45 between Vienna and Metropolis, 618/527-DIVE or 618/527-3483, www.mermet-springs.com) can dive down to depths of 10, 15, 20, and even more than 100 feet. The owners have placed things such as an old school bus and airplane down there for visitors to explore. There's a $15 entry fee for divers, plus more if you rent equipment. Lessons are available. If scuba diving is not your thing and you're still interested in checking out a spring-fed quarry, rent a kayak from the scuba center for $10 per hour. There's a two-hour minimum.

While you're in the area, drive through the Mermet Lake State Conservation Area (618/524-5577), also on U.S. 45 between Metropolis and Vienna. This area was once a cypress swamp and is now used primarily for waterfowl hunting.

Hardin and Saline Counties

HISTORY

One of the first regions to be settled in Illinois, the Hardin and Saline counties region was one rich place, rich in natural resources (salt, coal, fluorite) and therefore rich with business opportunities for entrepreneurs. In Saline County, early settlers had heard from the Native Americans about the salt springs along the Saline River and set up operations to extract the brine out of the water. This involved importing slaves from the South and ordering them to chop wood used for the process. The salt was later sold as a food preservative and an ingredient for hide tanning. To the south, towns such as Rosiclare and Elizabethtown cropped up as settlers and later immigrants from Germany, Ireland, and other European countries moved in after hearing that coal and fluorspar mines were being established. Ironworks were also constructed in the outlying areas. With the Ohio River nearby and all the steamboat traffic, perhaps it was only natural for outlaws to show up. A large, dark cave now at present-day Cave-in-Rock State Park was the perfect hiding place for them. After the river gangs were kicked out, along came the bootleggers in the early 1900s. By the turn of the 20th century the region was churning out hundreds of thousands of pounds of coal.

Today the salt mines and fluorspar mines are closed. Coal mining is still going on, but not at the levels it was 30 years ago. Most folks in the area are here for a hike through the Shawnee National Forest, namely the Garden of the Gods, an area where eroded sandstone and limestone formations resemble people and creatures.

ORIENTATION

Part of the Ohio River Scenic Byway, Highway 146 follows the river along the southeastern part of the region. There are plenty of signs along the way to point you in the right direction and a few spurs along back roads and through small towns. The north-south Highway 1 hooks up with 146 and will lead you to the town of Cave-in-Rock and the state park by the same name. Highway 13 runs east-west from Old Shawneetown on the Ohio River toward Harrisburg and beyond. It's a quick, smooth road. The county and forest roads are sometimes paved, sometimes gravel, and it's not uncommon for some to be unmarked. With that said, when you drive to places such as the Illinois Iron Furnace and Garden of the Gods, allow some extra time to get lost. Even navigating with a county map can be a challenge.

GARDEN OF THE GODS WILDERNESS

More than 300 million years ago, Illinois was covered by an inland sea. Through time, sand and soil washed into the sea from rivers that flowed into it. The sand and mud settled along the shores, building up layer by layer, year after year, becoming bedrock. At one point there was a great tectonic uplift and these bedrock formations pushed up out of the water, exposing them to wind, rain, sand, and other elements. What you see during your visit to the Garden of the Gods country is the result of all that erosion: pretty cool-looking rock formations. The Garden of the Gods Wilderness is a 3,300-acre site southwest of Shawneetown and south of Harrisburg where a cluster of these formations are viewable from a short hiking trail. The .25-mile Observation Trail takes you past rocks called Mushroom Rock, Camel Rock, and Devil's Smokestack. The trail is steep, but short. Nearby Pharaoh Campground has 12 tent campsites available year-round. To get to the site follow Highway 34 south to Karbers Ridge Road (there will be signs to the Garden of the Gods Wilderness). Head east for 2.5 miles to Garden of the Gods Road.

Rim Rock/Pounds Hollow Recreation Area

Rim Rock National Recreation Trail is a .75-mile loop on top of a bluff called the Rim Rock Escarpment. Hike through an upland forest and past a cedar plantation and then down a set of stairs into the valley. There you'll find remains of a Native American wall and a shelter bluff called Ox Lot cave, where pioneers used to keep their oxen. From there it's on to "fat man's misery," a narrow passageway through boulders. Rim Rock and Pounds Hollow Recreation Areas are connected by Beaver Trail. On the northwestern part of the site are remains of a wall believed to have been built by Native Americans. In the southeast at Pounds Hollow Recreation Area is a 25-acre man-made lake with a beach, picnic area, and campground. You can rent rowboats and paddleboats. The area is about four miles east of Karbers Ridge along the Karbers Ridge Road.

Scenic Overlooks

Overlooking the Ohio River, **Tower Rock** (not to be confused with the Tower Rock in the Mississippi River near Grand Tower) is a small park with trail about one-eighth of a mile. The Shawnee National Forest manages a 25-site campground there. It is four miles south of Highway 146 between the historic river towns of Elizabethtown and Cave-in-Rock. You can drive to the top of High Knob, which has overlooks of the Garden of the Gods country. Park here and explore about five miles of trail through wilderness. The trails here are part of the River-to-River Trail. To get there follow Highway 34 to Karbers Ridge Road. Head east a few miles to a gravel road. There will be signs for High Knob. At 1,064 feet high, **Williams Hill** is the second-highest point in southern Illinois, after Bald Knob. It's off Williams Tower Road a few miles west of the town of Herod and Highway 34.

LUSK CREEK AND BELL SMITH SPRINGS

Lusk Creek Wilderness

With 80- to 100-foot-high bluffs, the Lusk Creek Wilderness is an amazing site with challenging hiking trails and glimpses of an old Native American stone wall. Perhaps Lush Creek is a better name. An array of plants such as moss and ferns and wildflowers thrive throughout the canyon. And as one of the least polluted waterways in the state, Lusk Creek is home to more than 20 species of fish. The creek begins just south of Delwood and zigzags toward the Ohio River near Golconda. At Lusk Creek Wilderness it carves through a 100-foot-high gorge which you can see by hiking along a two-mile trail. Along the trail you'll find remains of a Native American stone wall, thought to have been built sometime between A.D. 600–900 by Indians of the Late Woodland Period. The wall may have been built for defense, ceremony, or hunting purposes. (Charging buffalo would have stumbled over the wall and down the cliff.) A footpath leads to a rock shelter called **Indian Kitchen,** 70 feet above the canyon. Views are unbeatable from here. Lusk Creek Wilderness is a few miles northeast of Eddyville and Highway 145. Watch for signs.

Bell Smith Springs

Another gorgeous wilderness site, Bell Smith Springs has the distinction of being a U.S. Park Service National Natural Landmark. Four creeks meet in the canyon here where hundreds of species of plants and animals live. Walk among beech and tupelo trees. Listen for pileated woodpeckers and tanagers. Several trails ranging in length 1.5–3.2 miles meander through the area, atop canyons and down in the canyons. They are all interconnected so you can hike a total of eight miles if you want. A highlight is a natural stone bridge that spans 125 feet and has a 30-foot-high arch. Other discoveries are rock formations such as the Devil's Backbone (not to be confused with the Devil's Backbone in Grand Tower on the Mississippi River) and remains of an old gristmill. There is a campground here, called Redbud, which has 21 tent sites available for $5 per night. Drinking water is available.

To get to the site from Harrisburg follow Highway 145 south to Delwood about nine miles. Then take Forest Road 402 for four miles to Forest Road 447 and continue to Forest Road 848. Go southwest on Forest Road 848 for a few more miles. If you're coming from Vienna follow U.S. 45 toward Ozark. Signs will point you east on forest roads to the recreation area.

SALINE COUNTY STATE FISH AND WILDLIFE AREA

West of the tiny town of Equality and southeast of Harrisburg is a hidden, peaceful park on a quiet lake, the Saline County State Fish and Wildlife Area (85 Glen O. Jones Rd., Equality, 618/276-4405, www.dnr.state.il.us). This is a good spot for bank fishing. The lake is stocked with bluegill, bass, and other fish. You can rent fishing boats from the concession building and there are two boat docks. (The lake has a 10-horsepower engine limit.) In addition, the park has several scenic picnic spots and plenty of lakeside campsites. The park is about four miles south of Highway 13. Four trails totaling seven miles wind around the 1,270-acre site.

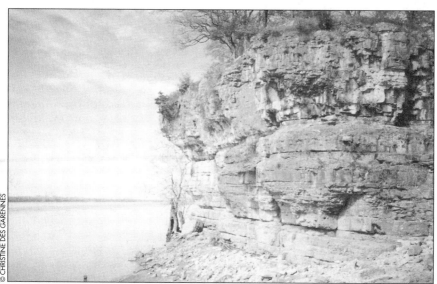 CAVE-IN-ROCK STATE PARK

Like most caves, Cave-in-Rock was an ideal hiding place for outlaws. This large cave on the Ohio River has had quite a chilling history. Samuel Mason, once a soldier for George Washington during the Revolutionary War, was one of the more notorious inhabitants of the cave. He and his gang in the late 1790s were said to have lured unsuspecting travelers to the cave, then rob them, beat them, and maybe even murder a few. After Mason's gang disbanded, the Harpe brothers, who were convicted of murder in Kentucky (and somehow escaped execution) took refuge in the cave and used it as their headquarters for more murder and mayhem. Now the worst activities that occur in the cave are visitors writing their names into its walls. The cave and surrounding area are part of Cave-in-Rock State Park (1 New State Park Rd., Cave-in-Rock, 618/289-4325, www.dnr.state.il.us). A set of stone stairs leads down to the cave and a small beach. There are also two trails that follow the river and cut through the woods. Several picnic

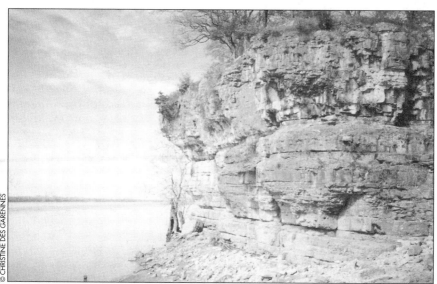

© CHRISTINE DES GARENNES

Cave-in-Rock State Park, on the Ohio River

tables are throughout the nearby wooded valley. And there are tent and RV campsites.

ACCOMMODATIONS
$50–100
Perched on a high bluff within **Cave-in-Rock State Park** (618/289-4545, open Mar.–Nov., $69) are four lodges, each with two units. Each suite has a private bathroom, private deck, and living room area. You cannot beat the view from up here. Rates start at $69.

$100 and up
In the heart of the Garden of the Gods region, **Rim Rocks Dogwood Cabins** (Pounds Hollow Blacktop, 618/264-6036, www.rimrocks-dogwoodcabins.com) offers two rustic cabins. Each cedar cabin comes with a screened-in porch, a loft sleeping area, bathroom and full kitchen (stove, fridge, microwave), and some extras such as DVD players. Outside each one is a fire ring, picnic table, and flower gardens. It's one of the best spots to stay if you're doing some serious hiking in the region and do not want to camp.

Built in 1812 and listed on the National Register of Historic Places, the **M Grand Rose Hotel Bed and Breakfast** (10 Main St., Elizabethtown, 618/287-2872, www.rosehotelbb.com, $95) is one of the oldest, if not the oldest hotel in Illinois. Facing the Ohio River, the white-painted hotel with its porches and gazebo offers incredible views of the river valley. Perched on a limestone bluff, the hotel has five rooms, outfitted with classic bed-and-breakfast furniture (four-poster beds, sleigh beds), and some modern touches such as flat-screen televisions. If you don't stay here, at least drop by and take in the view from the gazebo on a rock above the river.

Across the street and also overlooking the river is the **River Rose Inn** (1 Main St., Elizabethtown, 618/287-8811, $69–99), another bed-and-breakfast with a large front porch accented with hanging flower baskets. The 1914 Greek Gothic home has four guest rooms in the house, plus a little cottage adjacent to the main house. Rooms come with private bathrooms.

Camping
Cave-in-Rock State Park (Hwy. 1, Cave-in-Rock, 618/289-4325, www.dnr.state.il.us) has 25 tent campsites and 34 electrical sites for RVs. Fees are $8–15 per night.

The Shawnee National Forest has several campgrounds in its eastern district. Most are unbeatable private, wooded tent sites with drinking water, fire pits, and vault toilets. Fees are $5 per night for tent camping. Area campgrounds include **Rim Rock Recreation Area**, which has 76 campsites available April–mid-December; Redbud campground in **Bell Smith Springs Recreation Area** with 21 tent sites; Pharaoh Campground in the **Garden of the Gods Wilderness Area** with 12 tent campsites available year-round. For more information on camping in the forest call the Hidden Springs Ranger District at 618/658-2111.

FOOD
During the winter, dining options are limited. But once the trees start flowering and the weather warms, two great seasonally operated restaurants open for business. They include **M Kaylor's Restaurant** (in Cave-in-Rock State Park, 618/289-4545, open 8 A.M.–9 P.M. daily March–Nov.), which specializes in Southern-style cooking such as fried chicken and catfish. And there's **Rebecca's Dairy Delights** (Main St., Elizabethtown, 618/287-2322), where you can indulge in some thick, hand-dipped ice cream. Otherwise, when you're in town November–March, drop by the casual local joint **Gee Jays** (7:30 A.M.–8 P.M. Mon.–Thurs., 7:30 A.M.–9 P.M. Fri.), where you can fill up on a cheeseburger and fries or a chicken sandwich for a few bucks.

INFORMATION
For information on exploring the **Shawnee National Forest** in the Elizabethtown region, you can call the regional ranger at 618/287-2201.

ROSICLARE

American Fluorite Museum

Rosiclare, now a town of about 1,200 people at the edge of Shawnee National Forest, was once a major mining town in the region. Calcium fluoride, barite, and calcite were all at one time mined here. (The peak was 1910–1945.) An excellent museum about that mining history is the American Fluorite Museum (Hwy. 34 and Main St., Rosiclare, 618/285-3513, 1–4 P.M. Thurs.–Fri., Sun., 10 A.M.–4 P.M. Sat., $3). Open since 1997, it's housed in the former office building of the Rosiclare Lead and Fluorspar Mining Company and run by former miners and volunteers. The focus of the museum is fluorspar or fluorite, the state mineral. Made of calcium fluoride, the brittle mineral comes in a variety of colors, such as purple, blue, yellow, green, and white. In ultraviolet light the mineral is fluorescent. There's plenty of fluorite in the museum, including a giant hunk placed in the middle of the room. When the sun shines on the various angles, it's quite a dazzling sight. The museum also has petrified wood, galena lead, calcite needles, and other gems and minerals on view. Visitors can pick through the ore piles near the museum and buy some fluorite for about $1 per pound.

Illinois Iron Furnace

Northeast of Rosiclare is another example of the region's industrial past. The Illinois Iron Furnace is a re-created furnace modeled after the one that stood in the same spot in the mid-1800s. The original stone one was built in 1837 and production started two years later. Workers burned about 1,800 bushels of charcoal (gathered from area hills) each day to fuel the furnace. Then, iron ore from the area was smelted with limestone to draw out the slag or impurities. The end product was something called pig iron, oblong pieces of iron shipped to manufacturers. The furnace could produce nine tons of pig iron each day. Eventually, as iron production shifted elsewhere, locals blasted the furnace to get the stones. It was

Illinois Iron Furnace

© CHRISTINE DES GARENNES

declared beyond repair in the mid-1960s, but locals raised some money and rebuilt it. The 42-foot-high stone furnace is tucked away in the hills off a scenic back road near the babbling Big Creek. To get to the site follow signs north from Highway 146 in Rosiclare or Elizabethtown.

HARRISBURG

Harrisburg is billed as the gateway to the Shawnee National Forest. It's a good place to stock up on food supplies, film or other gear at the several grocery and department stores in town. They're all clustered along Highway 13 and U.S. 45. Chain hotels include **Comfort Inn** (100A E. Seright St., Harrisburg, 618/252-2442) and the **Super 8** (100 E. Seright St., Harrisburg, 618/253-8081). There's also an inexpensive bed-and-breakfast in town. The **White Lace B&B** (202-204 W. Poplar St., Harrisburg, 618/252-7599), which is just off Highway 13 near downtown.

Southern Illinois

Southern Illinois

Rend Lake Region

HISTORY AND ORIENTATION

Stretching for about 19,000 acres, Rend Lake is one big lake. But it's not a giant circle of a lake. Instead, it's shaped somewhat like a hand holding fingers up in a peace sign. It's got plenty of quiet little bay areas for fishing or snoozing in the sun in the back of your boat. Built by the U.S. Army Corps of Engineers in 1970, the lake (formed by damming the Muddy River) acts as a reservoir for the area. The whole construction project was envisioned after a drought in the 1950s. Most of the people who gravitate to Rend Lake are boaters and anglers. This is definitely fishing country. Some would say it offers the best crappie fishing in the state, not to mention, bass, catfish, and bluegill fishing.

Before you visit, drop by the **visitors center** on the main Rend Lake Dam Road on the south side of the lake. It's accessible from I-57 and Highway 14. You can pick up lake maps, get directions to campsites, and recommendations for best times to fish, and more. Plus there's an aquarium stocked with fish found in the lake and a terrarium with snakes. It's open 10 A.M.–5 P.M. Saturday and Sunday April–end of May and mid-August–end of October. It's open 10 A.M.–5 P.M. daily from the end of May–mid-August.

SPORTS AND RECREATION

There are two major sites for recreation at Rend Lake: **Wayne Fitzgerrell State Park** (11094 Ranger Rd., Whittington, 618/629-2230, www.dnr.state.il.us) on the east side of the lake and **Rend Lake Recreation Complex** (south of Hwy. 154, look for the giant water tower masquerading as a golf ball and tee, Golf Course Dr., Whittington, 618/629-2600, www.rendlake.org), also on the east side of the lake. In addition, throughout the lake the Army Corps of Engineers has day-use parks, campgrounds, and boat launches.

Rend Lake

© CHRISTINE DES GARENNES

Boating and Fishing

As mentioned, Rend Lake is teeming with bass (there's a white bass fishery at Rend Lake), bowfin, white and black crappie, channel catfish, and bluegill fish. As you drive around the lake, you'll see one turnoff after the other for boat ramps or a day-use area where you can pick a spot along the edge of the lake and cast a line. If you're not hauling your own boat along on this trip, you can rent fishing boats and pontoon boats at the **Rend Lake Marina** (Rend City Rd., 618/724-7651), in the southwest corner of the lake in the Sandusky Creek Day Use Area. The area is accessible from Highway 154 or Rend Lake Dam Road. Or if you have your own boat, you can rent a slip. To use the boat ramp will cost $3. Remember, you'll need to buy a fishing license.

Hunting and Shooting

Most of the hunters in the Rend Lake region are there for the upland game (pheasants, quail, and the like.) The **Rend Lake Conservancy District** maintains a prairie and wooded hunting preserve on the south side of the lake for such game open to members of the public with the proper permits. Over in **Wayne Fitzgerrell State Park,** a controlled pheasant hunt is held each fall. Enthusiasts might be interested in the dog field trials also held in the state park, where you can watch or enter your dog in hunting contests.

Otherwise, if you want to practice your shot or if you don't want to go after an actual animal, the Rend Lake Recreation Complex has skeet and sporting clay stations near the clubhouse. No traipsing through mud or tall grass; the paths are paved and guided by lights. The district can help you get the right license, pair you up with a hunting dog or dogs, and even outfit you in some camouflage clothing.

Golfing

On the southeast side of the lake you'll find the **Rend Lake Golf Course** (Golf Course Dr., Whittington, 618/629-2353), a 27-hole public course. There's also a lighted driving range and pro shop.

Swimming

You can sun yourself, get your toes wet, or practice handstands under water at two public swimming beaches on Rend Lake. **North Marcum Beach** is on the east side of the lake off Highway 37 by Benton. The **South Sandusky Beach** is on the west side of the lake off Rend City Road. There's a $1 per person swimming fee or $4 per car. Kids 12 and under are free. Beaches close at 10 P.M.

Hiking

Because this is primarily a boating, fishing, and hunting area, your hiking options are limited to a handful of trails in Wayne Fitzgerrell State Park and a few in the Army Corps of Engineers' day-use areas. The trails are fairly easy and short, not more than a mile long. Two options are the Blackberry Nature Trail, a .75-mile trail by the Sandusky Day Use Area, and the Rend Lake Hiking Trail, also a .75-mile wheelchair-accessible concrete trail that connects the South Sandusky Trail with the Sandusky Day Use Area.

ENTERTAINMENT AND SHOPPING

Art

Set on a 90-acre site, the **Cedarhurst Center for the Arts** (Richview Rd., Mount Vernon, 618/242-1236, www.cedarhurst.org, 10 A.M.– 5 P.M. Tues.–Sat., 1–5 P.M. Sun., free) has an outdoor sculpture park with a walking trail, a collection of American paintings (including works by John Singer Sargent and Mary Cassatt), and a performing arts center. In addition to the permanent painting collection, the center organizes rotating exhibits, indoor and outdoor musical concerts, a craft fair, lectures, and more.

Run by the Illinois State Museum and just off I-57, the **Southern Illinois Artisan Shop and Visitors Center** (14967 Gun Creek Trail, Whittington, 618/629-2220, www.museum.state.il.us, 9 A.M.–5 P.M. daily Apr.–Dec., Tues.–Sat. Dec.–Mar., free) is a great find with rotating exhibits of glasswork, sculptures, paintings, and photography, all by regional artists. It's not strictly a museum though. There's lots of original artwork for sale. The center often holds workshops and demonstrations.

Winery

Focusing mainly on red and white grape wines, but also selling some rose and apple, **GenKota Winery** (301 N. 44th St., Mount Vernon, 618/246-WINE or 618/246-9463, www.genkotawine.com) has a gift shop and deck that overlooks the vineyard. Open 10 A.M.–6 P.M. Monday–Thursday, 10 A.M.–7 P.M. Friday–Saturday, and noon–6 P.M. Sunday April–December 31; and 10 A.M.–6 P.M. Monday–Saturday, noon–4 P.M. Sunday January–March. GenKota Winery is near the intersection of I-57 and I-64, just east of Mount Vernon.

ACCOMMODATIONS

Under $100

Louise Harrison, sister of the late great Beatle George Harrison, used to live in Benton. Back in 1963 he visited her while she was living with her husband in a 1930s cottage-style house. Louise no longer lives in Benton, but the current owner has transformed the house into a little Beatle-o-rama, saving it from being demolished for a parking lot. The result was the comfy **Hard Days Nite B&B** (113 McCann, Benton, 618/438-2328, www.harddaysnitebnb.com). There are four rooms, each one named after one member of the band. As you might expect, there are a few photographs and posters of the band and its members hanging in the rooms.

$100–150

At **Rend Lake Resort** (11712 E. Windy Ln., Whittington, 62897, 618/629-2211 or 800/633-3341, www.rendlakeresort.net) you have your pick of more than 100 cabins. (They're called cabins, but they are really modern, clean cottages.) The resort is in Wayne Fitzgerrell State Park and all units are within a short walking distance of the lake, a swimming pool, two resort restaurants, a fishing and boating pier,

tennis courts, and horse-riding stables. Some rooms have fireplaces and whirlpool tubs. Others are wheelchair-accessible.

Seasons Lodge (Rend Lake Recreation Complex, Golf Course Dr., Whittington, 800/999-0977, www.rendlake.org) looks and feels more like a large modern country home than an actual hotel. There's also an outdoor swimming pool. Depending on what day of week you stay and whether or not you opt for features such as a fireplace in your room, room rates vary. Winter rates are cheaper, $59–89.

$150 and Up

Plan on staying around for a three-day weekend or a week and money is not an obstacle? The more luxurious **Fairway Suites** (Rend Lake Recreation Complex, Golf Course Dr., Whittington, 800/999-0977, www.rendlake.org) building in the Rend Lake Recreation Complex includes two- and three-bedroom suites. Each has amenities such as a kitchen, private balconies, and bathrooms with whirlpool tubs.

Camping

If you're traveling in an RV, you're in luck. Around the lake there are hundreds of sites with electrical hookups. The Army Corps of Engineers has campsites in North Sandusky, South Sandusky, and South Marcum. Fees range from $12 for a walk-in tent site to $40 for a double family site with electrical hookup. Camping is allowed May 1–October 31. To make a reservation, you'll need to call Reserve America reservation service at 877/444-6777 or www.reserveusa.com.

A cheaper option is staying at **Wayne Fitzgerrell State Park** (11094 Ranger Rd., Whittington, 618/629-2230, www.dnr.state.il.us), where there are 243 electric sites and 40 tent sites. Fees range $6–15 per night. Only 31 of the sites can be reserved. The others are available on a first-come, first-served basis.

FOOD

As the sun sets over the lake, sip some wine and sink your teeth into a lobster tail at **Rend**

Lake Resort (11712 E. Windy Ln., Whittington, 62897, 618/629-2211 or 800/633-3341, www.rendlakeresort.net, 7 A.M.–9 P.M. Sun.–Thurs., and until 10 P.M. Fri.–Sat.). The resort in Wayne Fitzgerrell State Park has two restaurants with extensive menus. Reilley's Lounge is more casual. Windows is the more fancy restaurant with lake views. It serves breakfast foods, sandwiches, ribs, fried chicken, you name it. Windows's buffets always draw a crowd. A seafood buffet is on Friday nights and a prime rib and pasta buffet is on Saturday nights. Average entrée is $15.

At **Seasons Lodge and Restaurant** (Golf Course Dr., Whittington, 618/629-2454, www.rendlake.org, breakfast, lunch and dinner daily) you can order traditional American meals such as bacon and eggs and pancakes for breakfast, an Italian beef or fried-cod sandwich for lunch, and for dinner beef tips or rainbow trout. Sandwiches are around $5; dinner entrées are about $10–20.

Perry County

Although Perry County has had salt mined there, been home to successful meat-packing plants, creameries, and plenty of farms, its history is linked to coal. Situated above coal veins, Perry County started seeing coal mines and coal-related businesses established beginning in the mid- to late-1800s. They thrived through the first half of the 20th century, but activity slowed down significantly in the '70s through the '90s after the Clean Air Act modified pollution rules and the high-carbon coal of Illinois was no longer in demand. And anyone in town will tell you the local economy took a hit. Today Perry County is a largely rural county with livestock and grain farms. The hidden gem of the area is Pyramid State Park, a vast park with dozens of trails for mountain biking, hiking, and horseback riding.

RECREATION AND SIGHTS
Pyramid State Park
The beauty of Pyramid State Park (1562 Pyramid Park Rd., Pinckneyville, 618/357-2574, www.dnr.state.il.us) is that it's one of the state's underdeveloped parks. At 19,000 acres, it's also one of the largest. Most of the roads are gravel and the campsites are pretty rustic (meaning no electrical hookups). Almost 17 miles of hiking and horseback-riding trails encircle lakes, wrap around hills, and extend into the woods. A rarity in Illinois, there's a rough 12-mile trail that mountain bikers are welcome to explore. For a change of pace, the park has several areas where you can just sit at a picnic table or at the edge of a little lake and watch deer come out to eat in the evening or beavers as they build a dam. Several little lakes, such as Reed Lake, Heron Lake, and Marsh Lake, are scattered throughout the park, as are boat launches. Lakes have a 10-horsepower engine limit, but who needs an engine? Bring your canoe and slip into one of the lakes (Lost Lake, maybe?) and count how many times you see a fish jump. Park entrances are off Galum-Church Road and Pyatt-Cutler Road, about a mile west of Highway 127 and 13.

Horseback Riding
You can also explore Pyramid Park while on a horseback riding trip with a horse and guide from **James' Outback Stables** (7230 Hwy. 152, Du Quoin, 618/542-3560 or 618/559-7443, 11 A.M.–8 P.M. Wed.–Fri., 7 A.M.–8 P.M. Sat., 7 A.M.–3 P.M. Sun.). You take a 45-minute ride through the owner's property or longer trips to Pyramid State Park or Giant City State Park. Kids will get a kick out of the pony rides and pumpkin patch in the fall. A restaurant is also on-site.

Perry County Jail Museum
Ostensibly a jail museum, the Perry County Jail Museum (108 W. Jackson St., Pinckneyville, 618/357-2225, 8 A.M.–4 P.M. Mon., 8 A.M.–noon Wed., 10 A.M.–3 P.M. Sat., closed

Sat. Jan.–Mar., donation) is also a depository of sorts for local-history artifacts and a community center. (On Mondays quilters come and work in one of the front rooms.) Built in 1871, the building was initially a county jail building, one of many throughout the state where the sheriff lived adjacent to the jail and the sheriff's wife cooked for the prisoners. It remained a jail for more than 100 years, until 1987. During your tour you'll walk through the jail, inspect the drawings of cartoon characters and weapons on the walls, check out all the drug paraphernalia seized through the years, and investigate a part of the old shower area where a man did escape once by digging a hole. (He was captured.) The other rooms of the building, former offices and bedrooms, are stocked with local-history items. One room has been converted into a one-room country schoolhouse, another highlights the area's coal history, and another features posters from old county fairs and packages from the old Blue Bell packing plant. (As tour host Eunice said, if you've never tasted a Blue Bell wiener you've never tasted a wiener.)

Antiquing

Downtown Pinckneyville and Du Quoin have several antiques shops. Here's a sampling: **Pinckneyville Antique Mall** (7 E. Jackson St., Pinckneyville, 618/357-8963); **White Rabbit** (10 N. Main St., Pinckneyville, 618/357-2543); and **Mulberry Tree** (24 S. Mulberry St., Du Quoin, 618/542-6621).

EVENTS
Du Quoin State Fair

Even if you're not in town during the Du Quoin State Fair (U.S. 51, just north of Hwy. 14, Du Quoin, 618/542-1515, www.dnr.state.il.us, fairgrounds open at 10 A.M. daily), which takes place at the end of August and early September, if you love art deco, take a tour of the fairgrounds, first established in the 1920s. The grounds include livestock barns, a grandstand, concession stands, and other outbuildings. About 400,000 people come to the fair every year for its agricultural events, food, music concerts, and races. One of the main events of the fair is the World Trotting Derby, a horse-racing event.

Du Quoin State Fairgrounds

Farm Festival

Ever see an antique steam thresher perform its magic? It's a sight to see. The **The American Thresherman Association** (Pinckneyville Fairgrounds, Hwy. 154, 127, and 13, 618/329-5573, www.americanthresherman.com) sets up camp for a show during the third weekend in August. The fest includes demonstrations of these magnificent (loud, smoky) machines harvesting wheat and other crops. Admire the vintage steam- and gas-powered plows and tractors, chat with some of the collectors (who can talk for hours about their machines), and watch other demos such as a blacksmithing workshop. There's also a good old parade through Pinckneyville.

ACCOMMODATIONS

Under $50

The **Mainstreet Inn** (112 S. Main St., Pinckneyville, 618/357-2128 or 800/455-7378) is a good bargain. The motel has 27 single or double rooms. Each comes with a desk, chair, alarm clock, and television. There is no continental breakfast, but coffee is always brewing at the front desk.

$50–100

If you don't have any plans to visit Du Quoin, you should at least come to the town for a stay at **M Francie's Bed and Breakfast Inn** (104 S. Line St., Du Quoin, 618/542-6686 or 877/877-2657, www.franciesinnonline.com), a real treasure of an inn. The five rooms are gorgeous, but there are two spots to relax that make this inn stand out: an expansive front porch looking out onto an equally expansive front lawn, and a back deck overlooking gardens and more green lawn. The house, which sits on three acres, was built in 1908 as a home for orphaned children. But don't imagine any kind of sparse, white-washed accommodations. Extras include free wine in the evening and wireless Internet access throughout the house.

Another inn with plenty of room to wander is the **Oxbow B&B** (3967 Hwy. 13/127, Pinckneyville, 618/357-9839 or 800/929-

6888), which is situated on a 10-acre site with gardens and several sitting areas. A remodeled barn contains a hot tub and pool. Yes, a pool in a barn. The bed-and-breakfast has five rooms and one barn suite in a separate building. A full country breakfast is included.

Camping

Pyramid State Park (1562 Pyramid Park Rd., 618/357-2574, www.dnr.state.il.us) has several rustic campgrounds (no electricity) for tent camping, backpack camping, and people traveling with their horses. Some sites are hike-in, and others have tent pads with car or truck access. Fees are $6–8 per night.

FOOD

A southern Illinois tradition, **Alongi's** (18 W. Main St., Du Quoin, 618/542-2468, www.alongis.com, 11 A.M.–10 P.M. Mon.–Thurs., 11 A.M.–11 P.M. Fri.–Sat., 11 A.M.–9 P.M. Sun.,) is an old-school Italian restaurant with quite the following among locals. It's been run by a local Italian family for decades. The menu is impressive, with panini sandwiches for under $6, pastas around $10, and an a surprising array of seafood dishes, including a lovely tilapia with artichokes, tomatoes, and olives in a white wine and butter sauce.

James' Outback Stables (7230 Hwy. 152, Du Quoin, 618/542-3560 or 618/559-7443, A.M.–8 P.M. Wed.–Fri., 7 A.M.–8 P.M. Sat., 7 A.M.–3 P.M. Sun., $7) serves country-style cooking, such as chicken and dumplings, and yes, even liver and onions.

The bright and cheery **Malachi's** (14 N. Main St., Pinckneyville, 618/357-2902, 7 A.M.–2 P.M. Mon.–Sat., entrées under $10) is a small American restaurant (with only about six tables) on the Pinckneyville town square. Traditional dishes such as chicken fingers and rib eye are the specialty. Try the key lime pie.

INFORMATION

Du Quoin and Pinckneyville have chambers of commerce where you can find out more information about lodging or attractions: **Pinck-neyville Chamber of Commerce** (2 S. Main St., Pinckneyville, 618/357-3243, www.pinck- neyville.com) and **Du Quoin Chamber of Commerce** (20 N. Chestnut St., Du Quoin, 800/445-9570, www.duquoin.org).

Carlyle Lake Region

HISTORY AND ORIENTATION

Topping out around 26,000 acres, Carlyle Lake is just humongous. Like many of the state's big lakes, Carlyle is man-made. (In fact, it's the largest reservoir in the state). Thousands of years ago and up until about 50 years ago, the region looked quite different. The Kaskaskia River flows southwest through here and Native American tribes often traveled along its shores and in canoes from villages upriver south toward the town of Kaskaskia, where the river meets the Mississippi. An old buffalo trace passed through here, which the Indians and eventually pioneers followed. The trail ran from the salt mines near Shawneetown by the Ohio River to present-day Edwardsville. It became a popular trail because there was a nat- ural rock ford in the river by the present-day town of Carlyle and eventually a bridge was built over it to accommodate more traffic. (The General Dean Bridge, as it is now called, is a suspension bridge listed on the National Register of Historic Places. It's just north of U.S. 50 at the Kaskaskia River, before you enter the town of Carlyle. You can walk over it.)

This area was great for hunting and fishing, but the river often flooded, which became a problem as farmers started growing corn, wheat, and other crops. After a series of floods from the 1920s to 1940s, a local attorney named Eldon Hazlet proposed a major damming project to control the river. After several years of raising money and soliciting Congress for the funds, the project was completed in 1967.

Carlyle's historic General Dean Bridge

© CHRISTINE DES GARENNES

Carlyle Lake is shaped like a right-leaning kidney bean. The town of Carlyle, where you'll find grocery stores, hotels, and a few restaurants, is on the southern tip of the lake, just south of the dam. The Army Corps of Engineers has several recreation areas around the lake where there are boat launches and picnic tables. In addition, the Illinois Department of Natural Resources has two state parks here. Eldon Hazlet State Park on the southwest shore, the larger and more developed of the two parks, has cottages for rent, a campground, outdoor swimming pool, and several trails. South Shore State Park is across the lake from Eldon Hazlet in the southeast corner. It also has boat launches and camping but tends to be a little less crowded. Something to keep in mind: The Eastern Massasauga rattlesnake, an Illinois endangered species, lives in the Carlyle Lake area. This reclusive snake with black and brown spots on it tends to stick to the marshy areas around the lake. It's poisonous. If you get bitten, you probably won't die from it, but you should seek medical attention.

The **Carlyle Lake Visitor Center** (Dam West Recreation Area, Lake Rd., Carlyle, 618/594-LAKE or 618/594-5253) has displays on the dam's history, info on what kind of fish and animals are in the area, plus plenty of brochures and maps. It's open 10 A.M.–6 P.M. Saturday–Sunday April–May and in the month of September except Labor Day weekend. It is open daily 10 A.M.–6 P.M. June–early September. The visitors center occasionally offers walking tours of the dam during the summer. The Carlyle Lake 24-hour information line is 618/594-4637.

CARLYLE LAKE FISH AND WILDLIFE AREA

Dam West Recreation Area

Just north of the town of Carlyle, off Highway 127 and County Road 1430N, is Dam West Recreation Area, where you'll find the visitors center, a large sandy swimming beach, boat launches, and nature trails. The Little Prairie Nature Trail is a .75-mile trail through woods

and prairie adjacent to the dam area. You'll walk among such prairie grasses as little and big blue dtem, and Indian and switch grass. The wood-chip and grass trail is an easy, quiet walk. There's also a short hiking trail, the Willow Pond Nature Trail, near the visitors center. The beach is big and faces northeast so it's a good place to soak up some morning sun. Bank anglers tend to stake out spots early in the Dam West area to fish for walleye, largemouth bass, bluegill, white bass, and crappie. It costs $1 to use the beaches, which close at sunset. There is also a $3 boat-launching fee. The Army Corps of Engineers manages several other recreation areas on the lake, including **Keyesport Recreation Area** in the middle of the lake on the west side (east of Highway 127). It also has a marina, boat ramp, beach, and picnic area. It tends to be a bit less crowded than Eldon State Park and Dam West Recreation Area.

Eldon Hazlet State Park

Eldon Hazlet State Park (20100 Hazlet Park Rd., Carlyle, 618/594-3015, www.dnr.state.il.us) is one of the state's most popular parks. And why not? It's a family-friendly kind of place with activities for people of any age and level, with large campgrounds for groups, Rvers, and tent campers, modern cottages, an outdoor swimming pool, several trails, boat launches, picnic areas, and playgrounds. The 3,000-acre park has tallgrass prairie, hardwood forest, and low brush areas. Throughout the park grow wildflowers, such as purple coneflowers, and several bluebird boxes have been installed near the trails in an effort to attract the songbirds back to the area. There are nine miles of trails through here, many of them winding through wooded areas of the park and along the shore. The Cherokee Trail is one of the best. You'll walk under tall oaks and hickory trees, by a little cemetery with graves more than 150 years old, and by the lakeshore. Some trails are off-limits during pheasant-hunting season. Check with the ranger before you go hiking during the fall.

Boating is the big thing to do at Carlyle Lake. Within Eldon Hazlet State Park are three wildlife viewing at Eldon Hazlet State Park

© CHRISTINE DES GARENNES

free boat ramps. The Peppenhorst Branch small boat launch is just south of the camp store and swimming pool in a more quiet area of the park. (It's easy to miss.) If you have a small canoe or sailboat, this is a good spot to launch it. You can also come here to watch herons fishing or look for waterfowl that stop by the backwaters of the lake during the spring and fall. Hunting for deer, pheasants, doves, and some waterfowl is allowed in some areas of the park during the season, which runs typically early November–mid-January. Permits are required from the office. The park is on the west side of the lake, about three miles north of the town of Carlyle, east of Highway 127.

South Shore State Park and Coles Creek Recreation Area

Across the lake from Eldon Hazlet Park is South Shore State Park (County Rd. 2200E, north of U.S. 50, Carlyle, 618/594-3015, www.dnr.state.il.us), an 800-acre narrow park in the southeast corner of the lake. It's a good spot for a short picnic on the shore or a walk around the .75-mile walking trail. As with many parks and areas near Carlyle Lake, blue-

bird boxes have been mounted here. There's a boat ramp for smaller fishing boats and canoes, and spots for bank fishing. Hickory Hollow Camping Area has 33 sites. North of South Shore State Park is the Army Corps of Engineers' Coles Creek Recreation Area, which has a beach on one of the lake's little bays, a boat ramp, plus camping with showers. It is just off County Road 1500N.

Carlyle Lake State Wildlife Management Area

On the northern tip of the lake is Carlyle Lake State Wildlife Management Area (618/425-3533), an area of about 9,600 acres, including woods, wetlands, grasslands, and farmland. A good spot for bird-watching, the northern region is home to ducks, eagles, herons, turkeys, and doves. Up here there are several boat ramps for canoes and smaller fishing boats. The northernmost ramp, called the Hitogi Access Area, is on the Kaskaskia River off County Road 700N. There is parking for the wildlife area off County Road 450N, a few miles east of Highway 127; and off 450N, 500N, and 525N, a few miles west of U.S. 51.

SPORTS AND RECREATION

Boating

At **Carlyle Lake Rentals** (West Access Marina, 1422 Lake Rd., Carlyle, 618/594-4480) you can rent pontoon boats and houseboats. Pontoon boats costs $40 per hour and houseboats cost $150 per hour. Plus, you will pay for gas. The houseboats come with extras such as grills, dishes, CD players, microwaves, and have an upper deck with a slide.

Carlyle Lake Wet Bike Rentals (Dam West Recreation Area, 618/594-8680, www.clwetbikes.com, sunrise–sunset daily May 1–Sept. 30) rents personal watercraft. Rates range $50–60 per hour depending on how long you rent. You pay for gas.

Amusement Park

Practice your batting and minigolfing skills at **Fisherman's Cove** (4211 N. 12th St., Carlyle, 618/594-2972), which also has bumper boats, go-karts, and other games. It's just off Highway 127 north of Carlyle.

ACCOMMODATIONS

$50–100

Microtel Inn and Suites Mariner's Village (1 Resort Dr., Carlyle, 618/594-7666, www.carlylemarinersvillage.com) is within a short walk from the Dam West Recreation Area and the beach, marina, and trails. Take your pick from one of 65 rooms (singles, doubles, or one-room suites) in the hotel or rent a log cabin. (See the *$100–150* category for more information about the cottages.) Guests have use of an outdoor swimming pool.

The cottages at **Eldon Hazlet State Park** (two miles east of Hwy. 127, Carlyle, 877/342-8862, www.carlylelakecottages.com) are surprisingly affordable and pleasant. The 20 lakefront cottages, set in a less crowded area of the park, come with private boat docks and fish-cleaning stations. Inside the living is pretty easy, with satellite televisions, gas fireplaces, and minikitchens with stoves, microwaves, and refrigerators. A short distance down the road

the state park also has an outdoor swimming pool and campground store with groceries. Three cottages are wheelchair-accessible. And there's parking outside the cottages if you bring your own boat.

The **Super 8** (1371 William Rd., U.S. 50 and Hwy. 127, Carlyle, 618/594-8888 or 800/800-8888) in Carlyle is a newer building with an indoor swimming pool. No fancy soaps or lotions here, but rooms are clean and the hotel is a short drive from the lake.

$100–150

The five cabins for rent at **Microtel Inn and Suites Mariner's Village** (1 Resort Dr., Carlyle, 618/594-7666, www.carlylemarinersvillage.com) are steps from the lake and the Dam West Recreation Area, meaning you can walk to the beach, dam, marina, and trail. The cabins come in two different styles: two-level lofts and one-level ranch-style cabins. Both styles can sleep up to six adults, and include a gas fireplace, porch, bathroom, and heating and air-conditioning. They're not in a secluded area, but behind the hotel and near the marina. So if you're looking for privacy, you're probably better off renting a cottage at Eldon Hazlet. Still, they offer a nice alternative to standard hotel rooms. There is a five-night minimum for cabin rentals Memorial Day–Labor Day.

On the northwest side of the lake, about six miles from the Dam West Recreation Area, is **Hickory Shores Resort** (21925 Dove Ln., Carlyle, 618/749-5288, www.hickoryshoresresort.com), which has 148 campsites, more than 12 cabins that sleep four people, and a few others that sleep up to 10. This is a recreation complex, complete with swimming pools, fishing ponds, tennis courts, miniature golf, and a recreation building with table tennis. Cabins have full kitchens, porches, fire pits, and picnic tables, and they come with air-conditioning.

Camping

The Carlyle Lake region has more than 600 campsites, about half of which are in the Eldon Hazlet and South Shore state parks. **Eldon Hazlet State Park** (two miles east of Hwy. 127, cottages at Eldon Hazlet State Park, Carlyle Lake.

2100 Hazlet Park Rd., Carlyle, 618/594-3015, www.dnr.state.il.us.) has 328 camp sites. You can reserve sites 1–65. The others are available on a first-come, first-served basis. Fees range from $7 for tent camping only to $11 for those with electrical hookups. A majority of the sites are occupied by RVs. Tent campers can park by the RVers, but there are plenty of walk-in tent camping areas. This means you park your car in a lot and then carry your stuff to sites about 100 yards away. In the middle of the park is a camp store. Scattered throughout are playgrounds.

Hickory Hollow Camping Area at **South Shore State Park** (618/594-3015, www.dnr.state.il.us) has 33 sites near the lakeshore. No electrical hookups or showers here, but you could probably run to Eldon Hazlet if you need to shower. Fees are $7 per night. The park has a boat ramp for smaller fishing boats and canoes.

FOOD

American

A little red shack off the side of the road, **The Pit BBQ** (Hwy. 127, Carlyle, 618/594-3207) serves barbecue sandwiches, fresh catfish, and sides such as baked beans for about $5.

Near, but not on the lake, the **Dockside Diner** (on Lake Rd., at the entrance to the Dam West Recreation Area, Carlyle, 6 A.M.–9 P.M. Sun.–Thurs., 6 A.M.–10 P.M. Fri.–Sat.) has a solid array of Midwestern cuisine: omelettes and pancakes, Reuben sandwiches, fried walleye, and hot dogs. Sandwiches are around $6; dinner entrées such as ribs or fried walleye fillets with sides range $7–18. It serves breakfasts, lunches, and dinners. If you plan to spend a day on the lake, staff can prepare picnic baskets for you.

The black-and-white–themed **Fifties Cruisers Diner** (911 Fairfax St., Courthouse Sq., Carlyle, 618/594-5940, 10:30 A.M.–8 P.M. Mon.–Thurs., 10:30 A.M.–9 P.M. Fri., 7 A.M.–9 P.M. Sat., 7 A.M.–8 P.M. Sun.,) in downtown Carlyle is a fun local gathering place also with solid American eats: BLT, ham and cheese, and meatball sandwiches, plus basic breakfasts of eggs, meat, and toast. Breakfast and lunches cost around $5. Most dinners are around $8; however, a handful of entrées cost more, such as a 12-ounce rib eye for $15.

Markets

Stock up on water and other essentials at **Carlyle IGA** (1110 S. 12th St., Carlyle, 618/594-3415) or **Super Valu** (U.S. 50 and Hwy. 127, Carlyle, 618/594-3522); both are full-service grocery stores.

CENTRALIA

A town rooted in oil and coal production and home to a state prison, Centralia is not exactly one of the top tourist destinations in the state. But it does have a great balloon festival every year, nice parks, and friendly restaurants that serve satisfying food.

Sights and Activities

For an admission fee of about $2, cheer on hot air balloon races or watch balloons glow in the evening as brass or bluegrass bands play. The **Centralia Balloonfest** (Foundation Park, Pleasant and McCord Sts., Centralia, 618/352-6789, www.centraliail.com), held in mid- to late August, features a car show, fireworks display, cardboard boat races, and other fun events.

At the 235-acre **Foundation Park** (McCord St./Hwy. 161 and Pleasant Ave., Centralia, sunrise to 11 P.M. daily, free) you can hike through restored prairie, visit a little chapel in the woods, or stop by a memorial to a 1947 mining accident in the area that killed more than 100 miners.

Food

Centralia's streets are dominated by casual national chain restaurants. But here are two good places to go to if you're looking for local color and you're in the mood to eat food that will fill you up. Load up your tray with napkins when you go to **Burger Haven** (U.S. 51, Centralia, 11 A.M.–8:30 P.M. Mon.–Thurs., 11 A.M.–9 P.M. Fri.–Sat., $4), where the cheese oozes down the sides of hamburgers and the chili is piled on top of cheese fries. This locally owned drive-through and sit-down restaurant offers burgers, hot dogs, fries, and ice cream.

The fare at **Centralia House Restaurant** (Centralia, 11 A.M.–2 p.m., 4–10 P.M. Mon.–Fri., dinner only Sat., $8–20) tends to have a New Orleans touch to it, such as a Creole shrimp entrée. Although many of the dinners cost around $20, you can still find a sandwich (try the andouille sausage sandwich) for about $8. Dress is casual in this historic restaurant facing the railroad tracks. Atmosphere is dark and clubby, with big booths and stained glass windows.

SALEM

Most visitors to Salem, a town of about 8,000 people, don't venture beyond the gas stations or hotel rooms. Situated where I-57, U.S. 51, and Highway 37 meet, Salem is often dubbed the "Gateway to Little Egypt." Folks stop by here on their way down south. But it's worth your time to take an hour or so out of your schedule to hang out here, order a latte at the Courtyard Coffee House or pork chop at the McMackin House, and learn a little about William Jennings Bryan.

William Jennings Bryan Sights

The orator is perhaps most famous for his role as one of the prosecutors in the John Scopes Trial, or the so-called Monkey Trial of 1925, in which teacher John T. Scopes was taken to task for teaching evolution in a Tennessee school. (Scopes, in an interesting twist, was also a Salem native.) Bryan, a three-times nominated presidential candidate, was born in a modest house in Salem, now the **William Jennings Bryan Birthplace Home** (408 S. Broadway, Salem, 618/548-2222, noon–4:30 P.M. Mon., Wed., Sat., free). Bryan was born in the white clapboard house in 1860. His father, Silas, was a lawyer, judge, school superintendent, and state senator. Later Bryan would become a lawyer himself, U.S. secretary of state, and crusader against evolution theory. About a mile or so away is a statue honoring Bryan at **Bryan Memorial Park** (North Broadway and Millett Dr., 618/548-2222). Created by Mt. Rushmore sculptor Gutzon Borglum, the statue was dedicated by former U.S. President Teddy Roosevelt in 1934.

© CHRISTINE DES GARENNES

statue of Salem native William Jennings Bryan, by Gutzon Borglum

Stephen Forbes State Park

The highlight of the 3,100-acre Stephen Forbes State Park (6924 Omega Rd., Kinmundy, 618/547-3381, www.dnr.state.il.us) is its 200-foot-long beach, a rarity in central and southern Illinois. The 500-plus-acre lake is stocked with a variety of fish and is a popular destination for fishing. (There's a relatively new marina with bait shop and restaurant.) The campground offers a "rent-a-camp," where you pay a few bucks to use the park's eight-person tents (along with cots, lights, and other camping tools), or you can stay in a two-room cabin with bunk beds. Otherwise, the park has 115 campsites with electrical hookup and 10 walk-in tent campsites for visitors wanting more rustic accommodations. The park is 14 miles northeast of Salem.

Shopping

South of town in the middle of an industrial and agribusiness district is the **Rusty Nail** (1101 S. Broadway, 618/548-3034, Salem, 10 A.M.–6 P.M. Tues.–Sat., 1–4 P.M. Sun.), a gift shop and antiques shop where you can find new and vintage garden accessories, from the practical such as watering cans to the not-so-practical such as lawn ornaments.

Accommodations and Food

Because it is situated where U.S. 50 meets I-57, Salem has a number of national chain hotels in its town, all of which are near these main thoroughfares. They include the **Comfort Inn** (1800 W. Main St., Salem, 618/548-2177 or 800/221-2222), which has an indoor swimming pool and continental breakfast; and **Super 8** (118 Woods Ln., Salem, 618/548-5882 or 800/800-8000, www.super8.com), which also has continental breakfast. The Super 8 will accept pets.

In a restored house just south of downtown, in a primarily residential neighborhood, **McMackin House** (413 N. Broadway, Salem, 618/548-2006, $9–25) bills itself as a fine-dining establishment. But it's not too fancy for travelers coming off the dusty road. The best seats in the house are in the front of the house in front of all the windows. Food is for the most part American, with a selection of beef, pork, chicken, and seafood dishes. A few traditional plates, such as rib eye with a baked potato and vegetable and a pork chop with mashed potatoes, line the menu. Plus there are a few for the brave: pan-seared chicken livers mixed with fettuccine noodles and a garlic cream sauce. Vegetarians will find their options limited to salads.

Staff at the unpretentious **Courtyard Coffee House** (107 E. Main St., Salem, 618/548-8600) are friendly and unhurried, lending an easygoing feel to this storefront coffeehouse in Salem's downtown district. They serve coffee, teas, and desserts (mammoth carrot cake slices) here for about $3 each.

Washington County

Once a posh destination for the wealthy and even a gangster or two, Okawville (pronounced Okaville) is now a quiet rural community. Like many other towns in Washington County, about an hour drive southeast of St. Louis, Okawville and nearby Nashville have German and Polish roots. In the late 1800s Okawville sprang up from relative obscurity after mineral springs there were reportedly found to possess curative powers for people suffering from arthritis and other ailments. The Original Springs bathhouse, listed on the National Register of Historic Places, still stands as a main attraction in the county (albeit it's a little fading and in need of the remodeling it was undergoing). In addition to the bathhouse, the towns have a few small local-history museums and antiques shops.

SIGHTS AND ACTIVITIES

Original Springs Bathhouse

Saddle and harness shop owner Rudolph Plegge needed water for his business so he dug a well, as most business owners would do. But his kettles were leaking and he wondered if something in the water were causing the corrosion. He hired a firm to test the water and discovered it had lots of potassium, zinc, iron, iodine, calcium, magnesium, and other minerals. He shifted entrepreneurial gears and partnered with a local farmer who had worked in mineral baths in Europe. In 1868 they opened a bathhouse, now called The Original Springs (506 N. Hanover St., Okawville, 618/243-5458). They spread the word that folks suffering from arthritis and other rheumatoid conditions could alleviate their symptoms by soaking in their waters. Soon other hotels and bathhouses popped up in the area and Washington County became bathhouse central. In 1893 a fire destroyed Plegge's building, but it was rebuilt in 1893. This building still stands, although it has been remodeled several times throughout the decades. And another phased-

in renovation was planned by the current owners. (A good idea, too because the hotel was showing its age with peeling paint and sagging floors.) Today the hotel still offers pampering services (massages, manicures, pedicures, body wraps) at nonexclusive prices. Spa admission is $10 for hotel guests and $15 for those not staying at the hotel. The hotel has a swimming pool, steam rooms, game room, restaurant, and 33 guest rooms. Stop by the restaurant if you're interested in seeing the building, but not a massage or mineral bath soak.

Museums

Okawville has two museum complexes. The **Schlosser Home, Harness Shop, and Laundry** (114 W. Walnut, Okawville, 618/243-5694, noon–4 P.M. Sat.–Sun., and most afternoons Mon., Wed., Fri., $2 donation) is a collection of several buildings (a home, laundry building, outhouse) set up as if they were operating in the turn of the 20th century. The house is nice enough, but how often do you get to see what a laundry shop used to look like 100 years ago? It's like an earlier version of today's dry cleaners. Ironing boards are set up and several irons (made of real iron) are placed nearby, as if a worker had just taken it off the stove to cool. A few blocks away is the **Dr. Poos Home** (202 N. Front St., Okawville, 618/243-5694, open by appointment, donation) a pink Second Empire building once home to the local medical doctor. Built in 1888, it was actually originally designed to be a bathhouse. For a glimpse of Okawville's intriguing past, call the Okawville Chamber of Commerce and arrange a tour. The home has plenty of photographs of Okawville back when it was the place to be.

Rainbow Ranch

Yes, zoos are fun, but at the Rainbow Ranch (9906 Hwy. 15, nine miles west of Nashville, 618/424-7979, 9 A.M.–6 P.M. Wed.–Sat., noon–6 P.M. Sun., $3) you can get up close and personal with the animals—llamas, sheep, cows, peacocks, a pot-bellied pig, and "Simon, the Kissing Camel." Bring shoes or boots that you can get muddy (and put in a plastic bag and put in the trunk of the car) after your visit to this petting zoo and exotic animal farm.

Log Chapel

Reportedly the smallest chapel in the world at about 96 square feet, the log chapel at the Little Nashville Truck Stop (I-64 and Hwy. 127, 618/327-3700) was built in the 1980s as a place for weary travelers to take a break from the road and read Bible passages carved into wood. Supposedly you can fit about 10–18 people inside; someone did get married here. It's open all the time.

Washington County Conservation Area

A 1,440-acre retreat south of Nashville and I-64, the Washington County Conservation Area (18500 Conservation Dr., Nashville, 618/327-3137, www.dnr.state.il.us) has a great seven-mile hiking trail around the 248-acre Washington Lake and through hardwood and pine woods. It's also a great park for fishing if you prefer quiet lakes. Rent a fishing boat with a trolling motor or drop a line from the fishing pier. Boats rent for $20 for a six-hour period or $36 for 12 hours. A few private, wooded RV and tent campsites overlook the lake. The park is just east of Highway 127 between Nashville and Pinckneyville.

ACCOMMODATIONS

Within walking distance of downtown, the **Nashville Motel** (346 E. St. Louis St., Nashville, 618/327-4472) is a small white motor lodge with clean rooms. Rooms are under $50. Over by I-64, the newer **U.S. Inn Best Western** (11640 Hwy. 127, Nashville, 618/478-5341 or 800/528-1234, www.bestwestern.com) has an outdoor swimming pool, laundry room for guests, free high-speed Internet access, and offers guests a continental breakfast. Rooms are about $50 per night.

Camping

Washington County Conservation Area (18500 Conservation Dr., Nashville, 618/327-

Washington County Conservation Area, Nashville

© CHRISTINE DES GARENNES

3137, www.dnr.state.il.us) has tent and RV camping, rustic sites with pit toilets, and a modern shower building. Some overlook the lake. Rates are $8–15.

FOOD

In downtown Nashville, **Mugs Coffee Shop** (221 E. St. Louis St., Nashville, 618/327-4262) is a small, bright, and cheery café offering hot and cold coffee drinks and desserts. Adjacent is a gift shop selling home-decor items. Northwest of Nashville, it seems the entire town of Addieville (which has a population of less than 300) hangs out at the **Eagle's Nest** (120 W. Front St., Addieville, 618/424-7777, kitchen open 11 A.M.–10 P.M. daily, bar is open later).

Given its proximity to St. Louis, perhaps it's not surprising that Addieville residents are fans of St. Louis sports teams. The walls of the Eagle's Nest are plastered with St. Louis Cardinals and Blues paraphernalia. The food here is solid, too, focusing on seafood (the walleye platter is a good bet) and red meat, such as prime rib.

INFORMATION

Staff at the **Nashville Chamber of Commerce** (247 E. St. Louis St., Nashville, 618/327-3700) or **Okawville Chamber of Commerce** (P.O. Box 345, Okawville, 618/243-5694) are eager to talk with visitors coming into the area, so give them a call before you swing by.

Vandalia

Home to the oldest surviving Illinois capitol building, Vandalia is a good place for amateur historians and Lincoln fans to visit. So the town lacks the quaint shops, galleries, and restaurants of other historic towns in Illinois, such as Galena, but the building is remarkably well preserved. You can easily imagine newly elected state representative Abraham Lincoln walking the halls and sitting at the desks taking notes.

SIGHTS
Vandalia Statehouse State Historic Site
Springfield has not always been the capital of Illinois. Before Abraham Lincoln and a group of legislators dubbed the "Long Nine" lobbied to move the capital to Springfield, it was in Vandalia, a bustling town on the Kaskaskia River. (And before Vandalia, it was the town of Kaskaskia on the Mississippi River.) Dominating downtown, the Vandalia Statehouse State Historic Site (103 W. Gallatin St., Vandalia, 618/283-1161, 9 A.M.–5 P.M. Wed.–Sun. Mar.–Nov., 9 A.M.–4 P.M. Wed.–Sun. Nov.–Feb.) is a large white, federal-style building. It's the oldest surviving Il-

linois capitol building. State government was headquartered here 1820–1839.

The first capitol building was a plain, two-story frame house. State officials met here but conducted the bulk of their work in their homes or other buildings. After this building burnt down, they hurried to build another one in 1824. Ten years later the quickly built structure had sagging floors and other construction defects. So they planned for another building. What visitors see today is the third building, finished in 1836. This one, while built much more solidly, as you will see, would not serve as the capitol for long, though. Three years later the capitol was moved to Springfield, thanks in part to Lincoln, who did serve here as a young legislator.

The building has been wonderfully preserved and it does look the way you might imagine it would have looked while legislators were in town. The secretary of state's office and treasurer's office contain period furnishings of large desks lined with tall, half-burnt candles, ledgers and books, and quill pens. The second floor, featuring original hardwood flooring, contains the state senate and house of representatives chambers. If you're in the area during December, stop by for the candlelight tour.

© CHRISTINE DES GARENNES

Before Springfield, the capital of Illinois was Vandalia.

Fayette County Museum

More local historic photographs and documents on Vandalia can be found at the Fayette County Museum (U.S. 51 and Main St., Vandalia, 618/283-4866, 9:30 A.M.–4 P.M. Mon.–Sat. year-round, 1–4 P.M. Sun. Apr.–Dec., donation), less than a block north of the capitol building in a former Presbyterian church. The collection includes a printing press used in the Vandalia capitol building and Civil War uniforms.

SPORTS AND RECREATION

Skydiving

About 12,000 people jump each year out of the Cessna planes run by **Archway Skydiving** (Vandalia City Airport, Airport Rd., I-70 Exit 61, Vandalia, 618/283-4973, www.archwayskydiving.com), a local skydiving school where an episode of MTV's adventure reality show *Road Rules* was once filmed. After spending about 15 minutes in the plane, you'll jump out of an airplane at 4,000–14,000 feet. The trip down takes about six minutes. You can jump with someone in a tandem setup or by yourself. Dives for beginners range $159–189.

If you're a licensed skydiver it can cost $10–20. There's a little area set aside on the ground for travelers who would rather watch their friends than do it themselves.

Hunting and Fishing

Ramsey Lake State Park (one mile west of U.S. 51 on County Rd. 2900 N, Ramsey, 618/936-2469, www.dnr.state.il.us) is a 2,000-acre park that appears geared toward sportsmen. Long before it became a state park, the area was popular among hunters of raccoons and fox. Today, during the fall, you can hunt for deer, pheasant, and, believe it or not, squirrels. For the most part though, most of the park's attraction is its lake and the fishing opportunities. Drop a line for bluegill, largemouth bass, and other Illinois fish. What's great about Ramsey is it's one of the more quiet lakes; gas motors are not allowed. (Although anglers are allowed to troll for fish using an electric motor.) Park staff maintain a boat ramp and dock and rent rowboats for a few dollars. In addition to fishing, you can ride horses or hike along a 13-mile horse trail that winds through the park. There is also a campground with 95 sites.

If you're interested in speedboating, head to **Vandalia Lake** (Hwy. 185, four miles northwest of Vandalia, 618/283-4770). You'll have to buy a $10–15 day pass from Vandalia's city hall (219 S. 5th St.) or at the marina. The marina also sells bait. The lake is stocked with bass, catfish, and bluegill. There's a wheelchair-accessible fishing pier near the marina, which is just inside the main entrance from the highway. To the left of the lake's entrance is **Jaycees Beach,** where everyone goes swimming. There's a bathhouse with showers and plenty of picnic tables in the area. A lifeguard is on duty during the day. The beach is open noon–5:30 P.M. Monday–Friday, 10 A.M.–6:30 P.M. Saturday, 11 A.M.–6 P.M. Sunday. The marina is open 4–6 P.M. Monday–Friday, 10 A.M.–7 P.M. Saturday, 11 A.M.–6 P.M. Sunday.

ACCOMMODATIONS
Camping
Ramsey Lake State Park (one mile west of U.S. 51 on County Rd. 2900 N, Ramsey, 618/936-2469, www.dnr.state.il.us) has a total of 95 campsites. Half of those are in an area called Hickory Grove, where the sites are more rustic (no running water or electricity), but more quiet, secluded, and in a wooded area. The other sites have electricity, a bathhouse with showers, and tend to be frequented by RVs. Nightly camping fees range $6–15.

INFORMATION AND SERVICES
The Vandalia Tourist Information Center (1408 N. 5th St., just off I-70 and U.S. 51, 618/283-2728), staffed by cheery locals, has tons of brochures and magazines about regional attractions as well as some from throughout the state. There are restrooms, too.

Feeling ill? The **Fayette County Hospital** (7th and Taylor Sts., Vandalia, 618/283-1231) serves the region surrounding Vandalia.

The National Road: Altamont to Greenup

EFFINGHAM

Who and what you'll find in Effingham are 100 percent Midwestern: a museum devoted to Corvettes, a giant cross on the side of the highway, and anglers spending a Saturday on the lake. At the intersection of I-57 and I-70, Effingham is a crossroads town and the majority of the economic activity is at the exits of these interstates, focused around hotels and chain restaurants. Around 12,000 people live here. They work in manufacturing (printing or painting), agriculture (either on the farm or for an ag-related business), or the service industry. The town was established and grew in the mid- to late 1800s after several rail lines sliced through town. Effingham is still a railroad town; freight trains pass daily and two Amtrak lines stop by each day. Thousands and thousands of travelers, truckers, and other people zip by Effingham daily, one of the reasons why a group of folks chose the city as the site of a massive cross.

Sights and Activities
Situated at the edge of an industrial park, just off I-57/70, **The Cross at the Crossroads** (Exit 159, I-57/70, 217/347-2846, www.crossusa.org, 10 A.M.–7 P.M. daily, free) is a towering, glaring white structure that attracts everyone from truck drivers to minivans full of families. The cross itself is nearly 200 feet tall and 113 feet wide and was completed in 2001. You can't actually go inside the cross or climb to the top, but you can stand below it or sit at one of the many benches arranged in a circle at its bottom. Surrounding the cross are polished granite stones with the Ten Commandments carved into them. During your visit, orchestral music booms out of speakers (speakers made to look

like granite rocks). At the visitors center (a trailer just below the cross), you can watch a short film about how the regional foundation built the cross. A visitors center on the site sells religious items.

The motto of **MY Garage Corvette Museum** (at Mid America Motorworks, 1 Mid America Pl., just off U.S. 45, Effingham, 217/347-5591 or 800/500-8388, www.mamotorworks.com, 8 A.M.–5 P.M. Mon.–Sat., free) should be "all Corvettes, all the time." (Heaven forbid the collection become tainted and a car other than a Corvette be featured here.) You've got rare racecars and show cars so polished they look brand new—as if they have never been driven before. Detailed displays accompany the cars, complete with mannequins dressed in attire appropriate to when the car was developed. Plans call for building a drag strip for races and car shows. The shop stocks parts and accessories for collectors. Mid America Motorworks hosts several car shows throughout the year, including a Corvette fest in mid-September and Beetle FunFest in early June.

Got an urge to fish? Launch your boat at **Lake Sara** on Effingham's northwest side. You can park your truck and slide the boat into the lake at **J&J Marina** (8641 E. Marine Dr., follow Beach Rd. from 1600th Rd., rural Effingham, 217/868-2791). A launch will cost you $4. Near the marina is a public beach, south of Moccasin Road and off Beach Road.

Classic and art films are showcased at the historic **Heart** (133 E. Jefferson St., Effingham, 217/342-6161, www.effinghamheart.com, $5), a movie theater in downtown Effingham. The theater shows a wide range of films, from *The Seven Year Itch* to *Super Size Me* and *Shrek*. On Saturday mornings it shows cartoons for free.

After you visit the Heart theater, walk a few steps to **Langes News and Books** (129 E. Jefferson Ave., Effingham, 217/342-6066, 6:30 A.M.–7 P.M. Mon.–Fri., 6:30 A.M.–5 P.M. Sat., 6:30 A.M.–3 P.M. Sun.). Space in this narrow storefront bookshop is a bit tight, but the staff are friendly and eager. They'll place special orders for customers for no extra charge and have made Internet access available to visitors on two computers in the rear of the store. Langes has a good selection of regional newspapers and magazines. Also on Jefferson Street is **Baseball Card Collection** (123 E. Jefferson St., Effingham, noon–5 P.M. Mon., 10 A.M.–5 P.M. Tues.–Fri., 10 A.M.–3 P.M. Sat.), a must-stop for any collector or baseball fan.

Accommodations and Food

A cluster of national chain hotels and motels is near the I-57 and I-70 exits in Effingham. One good option is **Comfort Suites** (1310 W. Lafayette Ave., Effingham, 217/342-3151, $50–100), which has an indoor pool, offers continental breakfast, and allows pets. Closer to downtown Effingham is the **Paradise Inn** (1000 W. Lafayette Ave., Effingham, 217/342-2165), a small, independent motel/inn. Rooms are sparse but cheap (less than $50). There are no alarm clocks, but you can request a wake-up

© CHRISTINE DES GARENNES

A cross competes with other billboards, Effingham

U.S. 40: THE NATIONAL ROAD

In 1806 Congress authorized money to build a road that would extend from Cumberland, Maryland, to the Northwest Territory. The first federal highway, the National Road would become the route most pioneers followed to the west, earning the nickname "the road that built a nation." Until the steamboat and railroad era in the 1850s, the National Road was the major east-west thoroughfare for stagecoaches and covered wagons. With the development of the automobile, the National Road became U.S. 40, a two-lane highway. In Illinois, U.S. 40 stretches for about 150 miles from the state line to East St. Louis. The highway still exists, but now it's overshadowed by I-70, which also moves at a southwest diagonal across the state.

The National Road in Illinois does not pass any mountains or canyons. But it's still an awesome drive. It's a nostalgic route through the core of middle America. You'll drive through towns such as Marshall on the east, home to an old stagecoach inn; Greenup, dubbed the "city of porches," with its antiques stores, soda fountain shop, and winery; quiet Teutopolis, site of an old monastery; Altamont, with its homespun farm museum; Vandalia, where Abraham Lincoln served as a state legislator; and finally, Collinsville, home of the giant Brooks Catsup bottle (a water tower). Travel the road by yourself or with a group of other two-lane road enthusiasts. The National Road Association of Illinois (217/849-3188, www.nationalroad.org) organizes the **National Road Festival** every year in mid-June. Several communities along the road host ice cream socials, garage sales, music concerts, and car shows.

phone call. On the outskirts of town are two cottage and campground options. **Anthony Acres Resort** (15286 N. Resort Rd., Effingham, 217/868-2950, www.anthonyacres.com, $50–125), a fishing resort, has motel rooms near Lake Sara. (Request a room in the newer motel building.) It has a boat dock and a little sandy beach for guests. **Camp Lakewood** (1217 W. Rickelman Ave., Effingham, 217/342-6233, www.camplakewoodcampground.com, open Mar.–Nov.), has sites above 33-acre Lake Pauline, also a fishing lake. There's no sandy beach, but there is a boat ramp, which campers are free to use. The woodsy campground is mostly populated by people staying in RVs, although there are some tent sites. The campground rents rowboats.

Slide into a pea-green booth at **Betty's Café** (125 E. Jefferson St., Effingham, 217/342-3584, 6 A.M.–2 P.M. Mon.–Fri., $4) and you'll swear you were being transported back several years (maybe even decades). At this mom-and-pop coffee shop a plate of eggs, potatoes, and toast will set you back by about $2.50. A noontime meal of meatloaf? About $4.

Information and Services

If you have any questions about the area, the staff at **Effingham Chamber of Commerce or Convention and Visitors Bureau** (508 W. Fayette Ave., Effingham, 217/342-5310, www.effinghamchamber.org) should be able to help.

Effingham has an **Amtrak** station downtown (401 W. National Ave., Effingham, 800/USA-RAIL or 800/872-7245, www.amtrak.com). The City of New Orleans train stops here once daily between New Orleans and Chicago as does the Illini line, which also operates daily between Chicago and Carbondale. **Greyhound** (2500 N. 3rd St./U.S. 45, 217/342-4075) buses stop at the McDonald's on U.S. 45.

ALTAMONT

A small but dynamic farming community, Altamont (population 2,283) is just north of I-70 and west of Effingham on U.S. 40, the National Road. It's a delightful town with a few surprises: an old church that hosts lively bluegrass concerts every week, an amusing barn museum, a nature center with beautiful, quiet walking trails, and a hometown café.

Sights and Activities

Ballard Nature Center (5253 Hwy. 40, Altamont 618/483-6856, free) is a real gem, especially if you are looking for an easy, peaceful hike. No bicycles, all-terrain vehicles, or horses are allowed on these trails. There's no hunting ever and pets must be leashed. Sure, there are a lot of rules, but when you walk along the trails—through restored prairie, past wildflowers, a wetland, woods, or above a creek—you'll hear only the sound of your feet crunching on wood chips or stepping on the occasional twig. (OK, and maybe some woodpeckers, some squirrels, and the wind rustling through wheat.) Because of the quietness of this place, birding is big here. You can look for birds while walking on one of the trails or have a seat in the newer nature center and watch as the birds feed outside the picture windows. Staff have placed several binoculars near the window for

© CHRISTINE DES GARENNES

a hidden gem near I-64: Ballard Nature Center

guests to use. Along the trails are several signposts that illustrate which creatures, plants, or flowers you might encounter on your walks. All in all, it's a welcoming place, with a few treasures, such as a tiny cemetery that dates to the 1800s. The trails are open dawn–dusk daily. The visitors center is open 8 A.M.–4 P.M. Monday–Friday, noon–4 P.M. Saturday, 1–4 P.M. Sunday.

For the most part, the **Ben Winter Museum** (1815 E. 900th Ave., Altamont, 618/483-6665, donation), in a barn not far from I-57, is a museum of heavy equipment, particularly engines. He's got a Buffalo Springfield steamroller from 1923 and a generator from a milk company that dates to 1910. But Winter's barn is chock-full of other items, especially antique farm equipment, such as threshing machines, and lots of model trains. Then, there's a wall covered with thousands of bullet pencils. (Winter inherited the collection from an area schoolteacher.) This place is dusty, but quite a hoot, and so is Mr. Winter, who has plenty of stories about growing up in a small, rural community. Open 8 A.M.–6 P.M. Monday–Saturday, 1–4 P.M. Sunday mid-April–mid-June, and 10 A.M.–5 P.M. Monday–Saturday mid-June–mid-October.

It's called the **Altamont Living Museum** (102 S. Main St., Altamont, 618/483-3333, www.altamontlivingmuseum.org), but basically it's a community center. The 1912 church (with dazzling Tiffany stained-glass windows) hosts bluegrass concerts every Tuesday evening, plays and musicals by local actors, lectures or discussions about topics such as World War II, local art shows, and other concerts by area musicians.

Food

The cheery **Railroad Street Coffee Shop** (120 N. Main St., Altamont, 618/483-6411, 6 A.M.–2 P.M. Mon.–Fri., 6 A.M.–1 P.M. Sat.) features traditional country dishes such as biscuits and gravy and oatmeal. Like Betty's in Effingham, this coffee shop is a blast from the past, complete with a lunch counter and tables covered with oilcloth. (It's popular with the older set.)

Breakfast or lunch is also affordable here and will cost about $5. Get your road-trip food—creamy ice cream and crispy French fries—at the **Dairy Bar** (600 S. Main St., Altamont, 618/483-5656), a red and white–striped building just south of the National Road.

TEUTOPOLIS
Sights
The monks are long gone, but you can learn about their presence in Teutopolis, a town of about 1,600 people, just east of Effingham at the **Monastery Museum** (adjacent to St. Francis church, 110 S. Garrett St., Teutopolis, 217/857-3586, open first Sun. of the month Apr.–Nov. and by appt., $3). Exhibits highlight the history of the Franciscan monastery that was built 1858–1904. Items on view include vintage bibles, clothes the monks wore, and furniture from the monastery. Additional museum displays are about the region's agricultural history. Behind the museum is a park with a few religious statues, grotto, playground, and basketball courts.

Along the old National Road, cheery staff at **Dutch Treat** (600 W. Main St./U.S. 40, Teutopolis, 217/857-1661, 9 A.M.–10 P.M. Mon.–Sat., 10 A.M.–9 P.M. Sun., $3) serve hand-dipped ice cream to walk-up and drive-through customers. Other don't-miss items on the menu: corn dogs and curly fries.

GREENUP
Billed as the "village of porches," Greenup has become somewhat of a burgeoning tourist destination. Just off the National Road, south of I-70, and along the rambling Embarras River, the town boasts a winery, covered bridge, restored train depot, and a handful of antiques shops and restaurants. It also claims a Lincoln connection. On their journey from Indiana into Illinois, Lincoln's family reportedly camped for a few nights in Greenup.

Sights and Activities
The tasting room at **Cameo Vineyards** (400 Mill Rd., Greenup, 217/923-9963, www.cameowine.com, 10 A.M.–5 P.M. Tues.–Sat., noon–5 P.M.

© CHRISTINE DES GARENNES

downtown Greenup, the "village of porches"

OLNEY'S WHITE SQUIRRELS

An oil-drilling town in the state's quiet (sparsely populated) southeastern corner, the town of Olney continues to attract curious visitors every year for its high population of white squirrels. In this town the white squirrels (technically they're albino gray squirrels) have the right of way. A badge with an image of the white squirrel is featured on the City of Olney uniforms. And white-squirrel crossing signs are dotted throughout town. The squirrels have been in town at least since 1902, when according to local lore one or two area farmers reportedly caught albino squirrels and then displayed them for visitors to see. Later they were released in town, and one thing led to another. Today the white squirrel population is estimated at around 120.

The squirrels are all over town, but the most common place to see them is at Olney City Park, just off Highway 130. More information is available from the City of Olney (300 S. Whittle Ave., Olney, 618/395-7302) or Olney and the Greater Richland County Chamber of Commerce (201 E. Chestnut St., Olney, 618/392-2241, www.olneychamber.com).

Sun.) could be one of the best Illinois wineries has to offer. In a turn-of-the-20th-century barn, it overlooks a vineyard and has cozy chairs and a roaring fireplace. The wines are pretty grand, too.

On your way out to the winery, drive through the **Cumberland County Covered Bridge** (Cumberland St., one mile west of Greenup, 217/923-9322). This 200-foot-long bridge over the Embarras River was built recently to resemble bridges that were once common throughout the region.

Continuing the rural theme, stop by **Grissom Lost Creek Orchards** (Hwy. 130, 1.5 miles north of Greenup, 217/923-3736, 9 A.M.–6 P.M. daily spring–fall) to stock up on apples, peaches, plums, nectarines, and melons. At Lost Creek Orchards you can find about 100 different varieties of apples (including heirloom varieties) beginning in August and continuing through November. The store also sells cider, homemade jams, and crafts. During the fall, **Earthborne Farm** (754 County Rd. 1625E, Greenup, 217/923-3035, 5–10 P.M. Fri., noon–10 P.M. Sat., noon–8 P.M. Sun. in Oct.) opens its gates to the public for its pumpkin patch, petting zoos, and straw maze. The farm is a half mile west of Greenup off Highway 121.

The Greenup Depot (204 W. Cumberland St., Greenup, 217/923-9306, noon–4 P.M.

Sun., free), which dates back to the 1870s, is currently being restored to reflect its past. It is open during restoration and visitors can tour the waiting room and view model trains and displays of antique railroad tools.

Antiques

Stroll through downtown Greenup on Cumberland Road and peek inside some of the antiques shops. **Neat Stuff** (113 S. Kentucky St., Greenup, 217/932-9233) has stockpiles of toys from the 1950s–1980s, including tin toys, toys from the movie *Star Wars,* and a hodgepodge of other antiques and collectibles such as soda bottles, Hot Wheels miniature cars, and lunch boxes. The mazelike **Greenup Antiques Mall** (15 E. Illinois St., Greenup, 217/923-9322, 9 A.M.–5 P.M. Mon.–Sat., 11 A.M.–5 P.M. Sun.) is musty old shoe factory packed with furniture, including pie safes and bedroom bureaus, antique kitchen utensils and farm tools, records, dolls, and glassware. **Cumberland Road Collectibles** (100 W. Cumberland St., Greenup, 217/923-5260, 9 A.M.–5 P.M. Wed.–Sat., noon–5 P.M. Sun.) has posters, magazines, books, advertisements, china, and an assortment of collectibles. **The Tin Ceiling** (101 W. Cumberland St., Greenup, 217/923-3877) sells a variety of antiques, from affordable to high-end, including primitives, furniture, and garden supplies.

Accommodations and Food

The **Daisy Inn** (315 E. Illinois St., Greenup, 217/923-3050), a big white farmhouse, is within walking distance of downtown Greenup's shops and restaurants. It has three guest rooms in the main house, plus a one-bedroom cottage. Rates are $100–130. The 29-room **Budget Host** (716 E. Elizabeth St., Greenup, 217/923-3176) has rooms for about $40–65.

Decades before becoming a candy shop, soda fountain, and diner, **The Candy Kitchen** (123 W. Cumberland St., Greenup, 10 A.M.–9 P.M. daily in the summer, call for winter hours) actually housed a soda fountain and candy shop back in the 1920s. Much of what's available at the shop is reminiscent of an earlier time: homemade fudge, hand-dipped ice-cream sundaes, and awesome banana splits. It also has sandwiches such as steakburgers and grilled chicken accompanied by baskets of french fries. Down the street you'll find fare that's also traditional, but geared toward the dinner crowd. **The Stockyards** (119 S. Kentucky St., Greenup, 217/923-9367) cooks up black Angus steaks and dishes such as beef and noodles and ham loaf. Food is served 4:30–9 P.M. Tuesday–Thursday, 11 –9 P.M. Friday–Sunday. The lounge is open later.

Information

The village of Greenup maintains a helpful website, www.villageofgreenup.com, that lists area attractions and contact information for area lodging and dining.

Moonshine

After receiving national attention for its out-of-this-world burgers on television shows such as *Sunday Morning CBS,* Moonshine (6017 E. 300th Rd., Martinsville, 217/569-9200, lunch daily) has been transformed from a local secret to tourist destination. You may even see a tour bus parked outside. No matter how popular it gets or how many people they feed, the owners, Roy Lee and Helen Tuttle, are still cooking up thick, juicy Moonburgers and cold-cut sandwiches for a few bucks. Once a country store, Moonshine has antiques scattered about among benches and picnic tables. This is a rural community and people eat early here. Order by 12:30 P.M. or you might not get a burger.

Marshall

Just off the Dixie Highway, not far from the Illinois-Indiana border, is a great old hotel, or should I say, stagecoach stop. The **Archer House** (717 Archer Ave., Hwy. 1 and U.S. 40, Marshall, 217/826-8023, www.thearcherhouse.com), built by town founder William Archer in 1841, is far from what you might expect from a stagecoach stop. Walk up the marble steps to a lobby filled with antiques, unwind in a solarium, and then head up to a room where perhaps Abraham Lincoln once stayed. (He reportedly stayed here while traveling on the circuit court as a lawyer.) There are nine rooms here with private baths. Rates are $75–225.

Know
Illinois

The Land

Right smack in the middle of the Midwest, Illinois is considered part of a transitional region, the land between the eastern forests and the treeless central plains. It's not as hilly and woodsy as Ohio, not yet level and expansive as the Nebraskan plains. Most folks, when they think of Illinois, think of the central region: cornfield followed by soybean field, followed by a slight slope in the land, followed by grain elevator. Illinois's nickname, after all, is the prairie state.

Much of the state's midsection is flat, but there's so much more than level farmland in Illinois. There are savannahs, grasslands, wetlands, upland and bottomland forests, craggy ravines, sandy dunes, lofty sandstone bluffs, waterfalls, sinkholes, and limestone caves. Rivers, such as the Illinois, Sangamon, and Rock, crisscross the state with woods clustered along their sides. The grand Mississippi River lines the western border. To the southeast are the Ohio and Wabash rivers. And let's not forget

Lake Michigan, which plays prominently in the northeastern part of the state.

Much of Illinois's topography—the rich farmland in the central region, the myriad lakes in the northeast, the sandy dune region along parts of the Illinois River—was sculpted by glaciers thousands of years ago. The only regions spared from advancing and retreating glaciers were the far northwest corner of the state by Galena (called the Driftless Area), the far southern tip of the state in the Shawnee National Forest, and Calhoun County in west-central Illinois. These areas are hilly, full of caverns, ravines, eroded sandstone bluffs, and other stunning geological markers.

FORMATION

Rewind time to 150,000 years ago and most of Illinois was covered by ice. The glaciation was massive. It stretched across 85 percent of the state, in some places as thick as 2,000 feet.

This restored prairie in Meadowbrook Park, Urbana is how much of Illinois looked back in the late 1700s and early 1800s, before farmers drained the land to grow crops.

This glacier, called the Illinois, pushed as far south as the northern edge of the Ozark Range, or just north of Carbondale.

The second glacier that shaped the state's topography was the Wisconsin glacier about 12,000–18,000 years ago. It reached across the northern and east-central part of the state and is credited with creating Lake Chicago (later Lake Michigan) and the Chain O' Lakes in Lake County. The Wisconsin glacier also had a significant influence on shaping the Illinois River valley. About 12,000 years ago, massive amounts of melting glacial water poured down the valley, eroding the surface and river channels. Westerly winds blew sand and soil throughout the region and formed dunes around modern-day Havana and surrounding areas. As a result of the flood, water filled deep lakes around the Illinois River. And over time, these lakes slowly filled up with sediment and became shallow lakes.

After the Wisconsin glacier retreated, the state looked much like a boreal forest found now in northern Canada. Through time the climate warmed and the forests gradually retreated to the rivers and the prairies expanded. Up until the 1800s when the white pioneers started moving in, the state was chock-full of oak groves and prairies, and native forests in the north and south. Gradually settlers cut the trees for timber and drained the wet prairies for farming. Forests, which once covered 42 percent of the state, now comprise about 5 percent of the terrain. When French explorers arrived in the late 1670s, the prairie covered about 23 million acres of the upper two-thirds of the state. Now you'll find about 2,300 acres of prairie. Most of the remaining native prairie is near the Mississippi and Illinois rivers.

GEOGRAPHY

Stretching about 385 miles from north to south and 218 miles wide in the center of the state, Illinois is diverse, not only in topography, but also climate and flora and fauna. It's a fascinating state to tour. Based on the state's geology, glacial history, soil compositions, and animal and plant habitat, there are 14 natural divisions. They include the Driftless Area in the northwest, the Rock River hill country near Freeport and Oregon, the Northeast Moraine surrounding Chicagoland, the Grand Prairie in the central part of the state, the Southern Till Plain in the south-central part of the state, and Wabash Border division along the eastern part of the state. In the far southern region of Illinois are the Shawnee Hills and the Coastal Plain division. West from the Shawnee Hills is the Ozark division, just east of the Mississippi River. The Mississippi River runs through four natural divisions in Illinois: the Upper Mississippi River and Illinois River bottomlands, Illinois River and Mississippi River Sands, Middle Mississippi Border division, and Lower Mississippi River Bottomlands east of St. Louis. Finally, there's also the Western Forest near Galesburg and Carlinville.

The **Driftless Area** is a small corner in the northwest near Galena, often cited as one of the most scenic areas in the state. The glaciers skirted around this region and as a result the area is much more rugged. The highest point in the state, Charles Mound, is here (not in the Shawnee Hills to the south, as one might think). For a good look at the geology of this area, hike through **Apple River Canyon State Park** near Millville to admire the cliffs and flora such as wood violets and ferns. East of the Driftless Area is the **Rock River Hill Country** near the towns of Freeport and Oregon. The scenic Rock River rolls through this area, through hills, limestone, and sandstone bedrock, pines and more ferns.

The **Northeast Moraine** division around Chicago consists of the dune habitat along Lake Michigan (visit **Illinois Beach State Park** to see this), the scrub oak forests and marshes surrounding Chicago, moraines formed by glaciers piling up rock and debris, and lakes and bogs formed by retreating glaciers. (Don't miss **Volo Bog** near Ingleside.) The northeast is home to many lakes created by the glaciers. The Chain O' Lakes region, just south of the Wisconsin border, is a prime example and popular for boating and fishing.

Know Illinois

Illinois is more than corn and soybeans: an actual sand prairie north of Mineral.

As you move south, the **Grand Prairie** includes the flat, rich farmland areas in central Illinois, with some marshes, scrub oak forest, and the Shelbyville and Bloomington moraines (yes, there are some hills!). As you continue south through the center of the state, you come to what is called the **Southern Till Plain,** which includes the farmland around Effingham, but also the Mount Vernon hill country, which has upland forests and rolling, wooded hills. The landscape of both these rural regions is dominated by farm fields.

Bordering the eastern part of the state from Danville and south to the Shawnee Hills is the **Wabash Border division,** which includes the magnificent and sometimes underrated Vermilion River system. To the south are the Wabash and Ohio River valleys. This region is marked by thick deciduous forests, sandstone ravines, more marshes, and river floodplains. Take a canoe ride down the Middle Fork River while you're along the eastern edge of the state.

Farther south is the **Shawnee Hills** region, which teems with outdoor opportunities. Hikers and bikers, get ready to salivate; you'll see one bluff, ravine, and stream after the other.

The fall brings out many apple pickers and leaf peepers. Next door to the Shawnee Hills (and often lumped together with the region) is the **Coastal Plain,** famous for its bottomland forests of cypress and tupelo tree swamps in the Cache River area. Although untouched by the glaciers, this region was still affected as flood waters surged in the area creating swamps. Believe it or not, this is the northernmost extension of the Gulf Coastal Plain. Moving north and west from the Cache River is a thin strip of the state called the **Ozark division.** It has steep bluffs and Mississippi River floodplains. For a look at the awesome bluffs, swampy areas as well as perhaps a few migrating snakes, head to **LaRue/Pine Hills,** a national natural landmark near Wolf Lake.

The Mississippi River and Illinois River corridors are divided into several sections. The Upper Mississippi River and Illinois River bottomlands near Alton and Pere Marquette State Park have bottomland forests, bogs, backwater lakes, and bluffs. The Illinois River and Mississippi River Sands division has, as the name implies, sandy areas. Then we have the Middle Mississippi Border section and Lower Mississippi River Bottomlands Division, also referred to as the American Bottoms. This low-lying area is east of St. Louis, near Cahokia, and frequently floods. It has rich farmland, wet prairies, marshes, and few trees. The area around Galesburg, north of the Illinois River valley, is called the **Western Forest,** but that may be a tad misleading. There are definitely patches of woods here, but not like a pine forest found in Illinois's neighbor to the north, Wisconsin, or like the mountainous forests southeast of Illinois, such as in Tennessee.

Rivers

With the exception of the northeastern part of the state, Illinois does not have many natural lakes, compared with Wisconsin or Minnesota. But we do have rivers, from major commercial riverways such as the Illinois to scenic rivers such as the Vermilion, perfect for canoeing. The major river basins in the state include the Illinois, Rock, Kaskaskia, Big Muddy (a tributary to the Mississippi River), Wabash, and Ohio rivers. The Illinois drains an area 250 miles long and 100 miles wide—quite a large part of the state. The Wabash River, about 475 miles long, moves in a southwesterly direction across Indiana and along part of Illinois's eastern border. It leads into the Ohio River, which also borders Indiana in the southeast corner of the state. The flooding-prone Ohio has several shallow sloughs where people harvest mussels for pearls. Also on the eastern edge of the state near Danville is the Middle Fork, a National Scenic Waterway popular among canoeists. South of that is the Saline River, which runs about 45 miles southeasterly from the Ohio River near Cave-in-Rock to McLeansboro. The Sangamon River dominates much of the central region of the state. It's about 225 miles long and flows south and west from McLean County in the central part of the state to the Illinois River. The Fox River is in the northern part of the state and flows south from southern Wisconsin to the Illinois River. It's a good river for fishing and has many multiuse recreation trails along its banks and towns such as Elgin, Batavia, Geneva, and St. Charles. Other important rivers include the Kankakee, Chicago, Du Page, and Des Plaines.

Natural Resources

Coal is a dominant natural resource in Illinois and for many years drove the state's economy. Illinois coal, which has a lot of carbon in it, has been mined in the south and along the upper Illinois River valley. Most of the state's coal dates to the Paleozoic Era, around 250 million years ago, when Illinois and most of the United States was covered by a tropical sea. Through time the sea advanced, retreated, advanced, retreated, and so on. These cycles went on for many, many years. Coal occurs in layers or seams underground that vary in width from three-quarters of an inch to 15 feet thick. Each layer represents a swamp at the edge of the ancient shallow sea where the water levels rose and fell.

Other fossil fuels include, oil, lead, and fluorspar. Commercial oil production dates back to the turn of the 20th century, but really kicked into high gear in the 1950s and '60s, when the state produced about 80 million barrels a day. Today that figure is closer to 10 million–12 million barrels per day. Most of the oil wells are in the south-central and southern part of the state.

The Sac and Fox Indians were believed to be the first to mine lead near Galena. Galena dolomite in the northwest part of the state contains lead, which was mined. The town of Galena really came into being in the 1820s and mining occurred for about 30 years until the discovery of gold in California lured miners westward.

Fluorite, or fluorspar, the state mineral, was mined in the south near Rosiclare. Made of calcium fluoride, fluorite is brittle and comes in a variety of colors such as purple, yellow, green, and white. In ultraviolet light, it's fluorescent. Fluorite production peaked about 1900–1945, when it was in demand for processing steel, aluminum, and other materials because it helped to remove impurities during steel smelting. Most of those mining operations have since shut down.

Earthquakes

No, this isn't California, but don't be surprised if you feel the ground shake while traveling through southern Illinois. Earthquakes are rare here, but not unheard of. Southern Illinois is part of the New Madrid seismic zone, which snakes through the area from northwest of Memphis, Tennessee. The region hasn't had any significant earthquakes in decades. The most recent quake of any significance was in 1987, when a quake registering a 5.0 on the Richter scale struck. Based on research at the U.S. Geological Survey, there's a 25–40 percent chance an earthquake of 6.0 or higher will occur in the next 50 years. In December 1811 and January 1812, Illinois, Arkansas, and Missouri were rattled by a series of quakes estimated to be 7.5–8.0 in magnitude. The chance that will happen in the next 50 years is about 7 percent–12 percent, according to the survey.

CLIMATE

The beauty (or frustrating thing) about Illinois climate and weather is its variability. Take a recent week in January. One day the temperature climbed to a near-record high of 50°F; the next day it dived 20 degrees to near-normal temperatures. Sure, the state does see sunny, 70 degree days similar to those found in San Diego (Illinois has about 220 sunny days a year). But the next day it could be cold and rainy. This phenomenon is fairly common throughout the Midwestern states, and Illinois has standard Midwestern climate: four distinct seasons with winters that can get pretty wet and cold and summers that can turn hot and humid.

Temperatures and Precipitation

The state's average spring temperature is 51.6°F, summer is 73.4°F, fall is 53.8°F, and the winter state average is 28.1°F. These numbers can give you a pretty good idea of what to expect, but account for some variability depending on your location in the state. Winter is shorter and warmer in southern Illinois than in the north. And summer in the south can be more sticky than in Chicago. Remember, Illinois is nearly

400 miles long from north to south. In April and October, highs can be in the low 60s in northern Illinois and in the low 70s in southern Illinois. In Chicago, the mean temperature in January is 22°F. In Champaign-Urbana, in east central Illinois, the mean temperature is 24°F, and in Carbondale, near the Shawnee Hills in the south, it's 30.1°F. Northern Illinois will have about 10 days below zero in a typical winter, whereas southern Illinois will have one day below zero.

Summers in the southern part of the state can get pretty humid, but the north is certainly not immune from heat waves. Warm temperatures can get not only uncomfortable, but dangerous. A heat wave in 1995 claimed the lives of about 739 people in Chicago. Since then, whenever temperatures rise and humidity clamps down, cities open "cooling centers," such as libraries and schools, and invite the public to chill out there. When traveling through Chicago, remember it's a few degrees cooler by Lake Michigan in the summer and a few degrees warmer in the winter.

Illinois receives about 39–40 inches of precipitation in a year, about seven inches of which is snow or sleet in the winter. The wettest months are in the spring and summer. Floods, caused by heavy spring rains and melting snow, occur throughout the state, particularly along the Illinois and Sangamon rivers. When you visit parks in the floodplains after a string of rainy days, it's a good idea to call the rangers ahead of time to check on road conditions. One of the more destructive floods in Illinois was in 1993, when the Mississippi River flooded because of not only major spring rains but heavy rains through the summer. Illinois and several other states were hit hard as levees failed. Towns and farm fields were not just soaked, but completely buried in water. In Grafton, for example, flood stage was 18 feet, but a record was set at 38 feet. Then, in late spring 2004, the Des Plaines River, which flows through the western and northwestern suburbs of Chicago and drains into the Illinois River, rose above its banks, flooding basements and causing street closures in Gurnee and other towns.

Thunderstorms and Tornadoes

Watching a thunderstorm roll across the prairie is an awesome sight. A tornado is another story. Illinois averages 28 tornadoes each year, so it's a good idea to learn a little about them and recognize the signs of a developing tornado. In Illinois the tornado season generally runs March–May, but technically, tornadoes can pop up at any time of the year. Most form 3–7 P.M. All areas of the state are susceptible to tornados. From 1995 to 2003, Illinois had 561 tornadoes and 10 deaths due to tornadoes. In 2003 a record 120 tornadoes were reported in the state.

Thunderstorms in Illinois usually form in warm, humid conditions as an eastern cold front moves in. A storm that produces a tornado will often be accompanied by hail and high winds. Tornadoes are essentially windstorms with twisting funnel clouds, formed when cool air moves above a layer of warm air. Think of them as rotating columns of air that reach down from the thunderstorm to the ground. Tornado watches are issued when conditions are favorable for the development of a tornado. If you're traveling through the state in the spring and the skies turn stormy, turn on the radio or television to keep tabs on the weather alerts.

When a tornado watch is issued, that might be a good time to think about where you are, and find out if there is a basement nearby and how to get there. A tornado warning is issued when a funnel cloud has been sighted or detected by radar. Usually the air becomes very calm before a tornado hits. Sometimes you won't see a tornado, but flying clouds of debris. When a tornado warning is issued (you'll hear the sirens in towns or hear a warning on the radio), move to a basement or the lowest floor. If you are not in a building with a basement, move to one of the interior rooms, away from windows. According to the Federal Emergency Management Agency you should avoid being in buildings with wide-span roofs; that includes auditoriums and shopping malls. If you're in a car and in the path of a tornado, get out of the car. A tornado, in which winds can reach 300 miles per hour, can pick up your car and flip it through the air. If you don't have time to get to a building, move away from the car and to the closest low-lying area you can find. Tornadoes often shift direction; they don't always move in a straight path.

FLORA AND FAUNA

Because of Illinois's location near several biomes—the eastern deciduous forest, the southern coastal plains, western great plains, Ozark uplift, and the boreal forest—many animal and plant species thrive in the state. Discover songbirds and migratory birds, snakes, white-tailed deer, prairie chickens, native wildflowers, oak and hickory forests, and bald cypress swamps, and more.

Flora

In 1820, Illinois had 22 million acres of prairie. How much native prairie exists now? About one-tenth of 1 percent, or 2,200 acres. In recent years, however, residents have grown more fond of native prairie grasses and wildflowers. Rehabilitated prairies now dot the Illinois landscape, from large projects such as the **Midewin National Tallgrass Prairie** near Wilmington and many local, in-town prairie plots. Prairies are amazing communities home to hundreds of plant species, including tall grasses such as big and little blue stem, switch grass, prairie dropseed, and Indian grass, which can grow 3–7 feet tall, flowers such as purple and yellow coneflower, rough blazing star, and butterfly weed.

When hiking through the woods in state forests and parks, you'll likely spot the petite state flower, the wood violet, growing on the forest floor. Trilliums and blood root flowers are also common across the state.

The state tree is the towering white oak, which can shoot up 80–100 feet tall and grow several feet wide. It's a strong tree; the pioneers used it to build furniture and fences. Common in many state parks, such as **Starved Rock State Park,** the white oak's leaves turn a brilliant red in the autumn (check out **Morton Arboretum** in Lisle to witness this display.)

Black-eyed Susans are native wildflowers.

Other native trees found throughout the state in parks and towns are hickory trees, sycamores, white cedars, walnuts, and redbuds. The bald cypress is most often found in the southern part of the state, but since it grows in swampy areas, you can find it in wet pockets across the state. It's most common in the Cache River State Natural Area in the far south. Tupelo is also common in the far southern tip of the state in the Cache River basin. The gingko, which is actually native to China, is common throughout Illinois, particularly in urban areas of the state because it can tolerate dust and insects. A ginkgo tree has fan-shaped leaves. The sugar maple, native to the eastern United States, is common in the northern part of the state. Its sap is collected in the spring and used to make syrup.

Fauna

About 600 different species of vertebrate animals and almost 300 species of birds can be found in Illinois. Because the state is situated along the **Mississippi Flyway,** a migration route millions of birds follow twice a year, birders can catch sight of species that don't nor-

mally make their homes in Illinois, plus plenty of geese and swans. In river valleys and creeks, look for the little blue heron, wood duck, loon, and the tern, which can be found along sandbars near rivers. The great egret hides out in the state's wetlands from spring through fall. The gray falcon, a large white raptor with brown specks on its wings, makes its home in Illinois during the winter.

The prairies teem with meadowlarks, woodchucks, box turtles, monarch butterflies, and red-winged blackbirds. The rare metalmark butterfly lives in wetland areas. Upland game such as the prairie chicken, grouse, and wild turkeys roam the prairies and grasslands. Throughout the state look for Baltimore orioles, the common blue jay, robin, and cardinal, the state bird. The male cardinal is a deep red and the female is a light reddish-brown. You can see cardinals throughout the year. Robins migrate, but some stick it out during the winter and survive by eating berries. The great horned owl is a common owl in the state. The short-eared owl, much more rare, tends to stick to the grassland areas of the state.

The white-tailed deer is common in every county, even Cook County, where Chicago is. Be on the lookout for deer while driving in rural areas (they like to eat the grasses along the highways), but especially during the fall hunting season when they might be fleeing hunters. Also prevalent in all regions is the eastern cottontail rabbit, a brown short-eared rabbit known for its fluffy little tail.

Now, a few words about snakes. Illinois has 39 different species of snakes; 10 are on the state's endangered or threatened list and four are venomous. The poisonous ones include the northern/southern copperhead, the cottonmouth water moccasin, timber rattlesnake, and Masasauga rattlesnake. The copperhead is found in the bottom one-third of the state and along the southern tip of the Illinois River. For the most part the timber rattlesnake is in the bottom third of the state, along parts of the Mississippi River in Illinois. The water moccasin is in the very southern tip of the state. As for the eastern Masasauga rattlesnake, it usually hides out in the middle part of the state, plus around the Chicagoland region. All of the poisonous snakes in Illinois have elliptical pupils, a pit on each side of the head (this helps them sense heat), and a row of scales under their tails. None are aggressive. Most bites occur when a person steps on the snake, picks it up, or forces it into a corner. Snakes can bite when they feel threatened. If you see a poisonous snake, leave it alone.

There are about 200 fish species in Illinois. The state fish is the bluegill, but you will also find many other kinds in the rivers and streams of Illinois, many of which are also common in other Midwestern states. They include the large and smallmouth bass, walleye, sauger, yellow perch, yellow, white and striped bass, a variety of catfish and trout, carp, muskie, northern pike, green sunfish, white and black crappie, and salmon.

History

EARLY NATIVE AMERICANS

The first people to live in Illinois, or at least spend part of the year hunting or gathering here, are believed to be descendents of the folks who hiked across the Bering Strait. The original explorers made the trek about 15,000–20,000 years ago when waters receded and revealed a land bridge connecting Asia and North America or modern-day Russia with Alaska. By the time their descendents arrived in Illinois it was around 10,000 years ago. These early tribes followed herds of animals, such as bison, stopping in places such as the **Modoc Rock Shelter,** a sandstone bluff near Prairie du Rocher in southwest Illinois. A National Historic Landmark, the shelter was used by hunters beginning around 8,000 years ago.

As the years passed, the climate warmed and the native hunters may have cut down on the amount of traveling they did, perhaps migrating twice a year in the fall and spring. As they lived in more permanent locations they started cultivating plants such as squash for food, and making tools and bowls that they could keep since they didn't have to move around so much.

The early inhabitants of Illinois were **Woodland Indians.** The Woodland Period can be divided into the Early, Middle, and Late Periods, ranging from about 2,500 B.C. to A.D. 200. The Early and Middle Woodland Indians were hunters and foragers and grew corn, pumpkins, and other vegetables. They also built small animal-shaped burial mounds. By the Late Woodland Period, people had begun to settle in larger villages in the Illinois and Mississippi River valleys. And by A.D. 700, a new group emerged called the Mound Builders.

The **Mound Builders,** such as those who lived near Cahokia, were the main people living in Illinois from A.D. 700 or 900–1400. This is considered the Mississippian Period. These villages, which in some cases had as many as

10,000–20,000 people living in them, were mainly in the Mississippi and Illinois River valleys. The villages comprised open plazas, farm fields, plus several earthen mounds built for village religious and governmental leaders. Residents raised crops, hunted, gathered, and honed their pottery, weaving, and tool-making skills. Based on items excavated from some mounds, historians believe the Mound Builders traded with other tribes in North America. When residents died, they buried them in mounds. It's not clear where the Mound Builders came from, or whether they were related to Maya or Aztec Indians, or any other tribe. These cultures eventually disappeared around 1500, probably because of disease, war, overcrowding, or other reasons. Although many of their mounds were eventually plowed over for farming and developments, thousands of mounds can still be spotted throughout the state, namely **Cahokia Mounds** east of St. Louis near Collinsville, and Dickson Mounds by Havana.

By 1500, about 8,000 Native Americans were living in Illinois, the majority of whom were members of the **Illini** or Illinois Nation. The Illinois, who spoke the Algonquin language, were divided into 6–12 tribes, the main ones being the Cahokia, Kaskaskia, Michigamea, Moingwena, Peoria, and Tamoroa. They lived throughout the state but were centered around the Peoria area. Illiniwek, as they were called, were, for the most part, peaceful and friendly to the early white explorers. They worshiped a great spirit called Manitou and hunted and grew corn, squash, and other crops.

In the mid-1600s, the Iroquois Indians made their way west from the eastern United States, such as New York. They moved into the northern part of Illinois and clashed with the tribes living there. The Iroquois were said to be strong warriors and often allied with other tribes to fight against the white men. In 1680 the Iroquois attacked Illinois Indians living in villages along the Illinois River and toward the Mississippi River.

The Illinois had to not only contend with the Iroquois encroaching upon their territory, but the Sauk and Fox Indians who came from the north (such as Wisconsin) and claimed territory between the Mississippi and Rock rivers. (Before living in Wisconsin, the Sauk hailed from regions along the St. Lawrence River but were pushed out of there by the Iroquois.) The Sauk eventually allied with the Potowatomi Indians and pushed the Illinois Indians farther south in the state.

Other early Indians included the Shawnee, who lived in southern part of the state, and the Miami, who lived for a time around Chicago.

THE FRENCH ARRIVE

The land in and around Illinois became French territory in 1671 thanks to a declaration made in the French trading-post town of Sault Sainte Marie in modern-day Michigan's Upper Peninsula. That is when the governor of New France (territory that included the Great Lakes region and other parts of Canada) claimed that all the interior land of North America was property of France. With that said, the first white men to explore the Illinois region were the French— French fur traders, missionaries, explorers, and soldiers. The French, who came from French Canada via the Great Lakes and rivers, had a hold on things in Illinois for about 100 years, beginning from the late 1600s.

One famous pair of French explorers was missionary **Father Jacques Marquette** and fur trader **Louis Jolliet,** who traveled through Illinois in 1673. They came down from St. Ignace in the Upper Peninsula, journeyed through Wisconsin and down the Mississippi River. From there, they made it as far as the mouth of the Arkansas River before heading back north and east on the Illinois and Des Plaines rivers, eventually to Lake Michigan.

Meanwhile, traveling French fur traders were busy trapping and trading with Indians. Once the fur traders set up posts, settlements cropped up around the trading posts. And along with the settlements came missionaries. One of the earliest missions and settlements was Cahokia and the **Church of the Holy Family** mission, founded in 1699. Another in Kaskaskia was founded by Father Marquette after he finished exploring the region.

Another important pair of explorers were Rene Robert Cavelier Sieur de la Salle and Henri de Tonti, who voyaged down the Illinois River and built Fort St. Louis (near present-day Utica, now called Starved Rock) and Fort Crevecoeur near Peoria (in present-day Creve Coeur) in 1680. LaSalle promised the Illinois Indians in both areas that the French would help protect them from the Iroquois. While Tonti was on a trip to visit the Kaskakian Illinois Indians at Starved Rock, some Frenchmen ransacked Fort Crevecoeur, stealing ammunition and other supplies, before taking off. After hearing about what happened, Tonti decided to bring whatever was left at Fort Crevecoeur to Starved Rock. Both the Iroquois and Illinois Indians were fuming mad with Tonti, who they saw as a traitor. A fight ensued, the Kaskaskian village was burned, and the Iroquois took over. Tonti managed to escape.

Illinois officially became part of the French colony of Louisiana in 1717 and almost 14 years later was named a province of the kingdom of France in 1731. After the city of New Orleans was established in 1718, trade picked up along the Mississippi River, and more French people, traders, farmers, and land speculators started trickling into the region. To protect their territory, in 1720 the French erected **Fort de Chartres** on the banks of the Mississippi River, about an hour south of present day Collinsville. Fort de Chartres would become the seat of French government in the Illinois country for a while.

Into the late 1740s and early 1750s, the British began expanding their territory in the New World. The Ohio Land Company, comprising a group of Virginia land speculators, planned to establish villages in the Ohio River valley. And the French felt threatened. In response, the French built more forts and revamped their current ones. As more Brits moved west, it was inevitable the two countries would clash over land. The **French and Indian War** lasted 1754–1763. The Illinois Indians allied with the French and the Iroquois partnered with the British. After seven years of war, France ended up ceding its land east of the Mississippi to Great Britain in 1763 in the Treaty of Paris. Illinois now belonged to the king of England.

At the time France was handing over some of its land to Great Britain, Ottawa Indian Chief Pontiac from Michigan led several attacks against white settlers, particularly the British. Pontiac and his Indians later settled in Illinois near the Illinois River and claimed they would make peace with the Brits. But then in 1769 Pontiac was killed near Cahokia by a Peoria Indian (Peorias were part of the Illini nation, who allied with the French). Seeking revenge, tribes loyal to Pontiac, including the Ottawa, Chippewa, and Potawatomi, streamed into the area and drove a band of Illinois Indians to the top of a rock above the Illinois River near La Salle's fort. The Illinois ran out of water and food, and many eventually died. The rock is now called **Starved Rock** and is home to a popular state park.

REVOLUTIONARY WAR, LEWIS AND CLARK, AND BLACK HAWK

In the years after the French and Indian War, Illinois was still considered a wild, desolate place, deep in the interior of the continent. Only a few thousand Frenchmen and women lived here, and many of them ended up crossing the Mississippi into Missouri after the territory was ceded to the Brits. Meanwhile tension was brewing out east. The American colonists had had it with British attempts to control and tax them and declared independence in 1776.

While most of the Revolutionary War battles were in the east, Illinois did see some action. Virginian **George Rogers Clark,** stationed in Kentucky, learned from spies that the British had not bothered to safeguard some of the Illinois forts where they stored military supplies. Patrick Henry, then governor of Virginia, delegated Clark to be leader of the colonists' efforts to wrestle control of the west from the Brits. In 1778 Clark and about 200 of his comrades set off and took control first of Fort Massac, near present-day Metropolis, and marched on northwestward to Kaskaskia, Cahokia, Prairie du Rocher, and back east to Vincennes (on the Illinois and Indiana border), and others. Of these forts, Vincennes was later recaptured by the British. And in the winter of 1780, Clark led another scraggy group of fewer than 200 men to reclaim Vincennes. For 22 days he and his men trudged through the cold and wet Little Wabash River Valley before tricking the British into surrendering. That hike across Illinois became known as The Impossible March.

After the American colonists won the war, Illinois settlements became part of Virginia. And in 1784 Virginia ceded Illinois to the U.S. government. Illinois, along with Wisconsin, Michigan, Indiana, and Ohio, officially became part of the **Northwest Territory.** Surveying of the territory began. A few adventurous souls started moving into Illinois, most of them into the southern towns of Cairo, Shawneetown, Cahokia, and Kaskaskia. It wasn't until **Jean Baptiste Point Du Sable** arrived in Chicago that the region started to grow as a settlement. Du Sable was a black trader from the Caribbean who traded with the Indians in the area about 1779–1800.

In 1795, probably a few years before Du Sable left Chicago for other business opportunities farther west, a group of Indian tribes signed the **Treaty of Greenville** with the United States. In the treaty, and many other treaties that followed, the tribes gave up much of their territory to the United States. One parcel transferred to the government was six square miles near the mouth of the Chicago River. Later, it would become the city of Chicago. By 1800 only a few hundred Illinois Indians remained in the region; most had sold their holdings and moved west of the Mississippi River. In 1803, the U.S. Army built **Fort Dearborn** near the mouth of the Chicago River to protect the new territory, a region that was becoming more of a trading and transportation center.

When Thomas Jefferson became president of the United States in 1801, much of the west was still uncharted territory, explored largely by French fur traders and Spanish explorers. He thought it was about time a team of Ameri-

cans hit the road, so to speak, and write home about it. The chosen men? **Captain Meriwether Lewis and William Clark** (George Rogers Clark's younger brother). Before setting out on their famous journey westward, Lewis and Clark spent about six months in Illinois recruiting men and stocking supplies. In November 1803 they arrived at Fort Massac, then went on to Fort Kaskaskia, Cahokia, and finally Wood River. At Wood River they established **Camp River DuBois,** believed to be north of the present-day town of Hartford. (Hartford, north of East St. Louis, has an extensive interpretive center about the men and their travels.) It was from this camp that they embarked on their trip westward.

Not long after Lewis and Clark completed their expedition, the United States found itself edging closer to war with Britain again. In 1812 the relationship between the two countries was strained as they butted heads over maritime trade rights, the Canadian territory, and many other issues. At the same time, the Americans' relationship with Native Americans in Illinois was also strained as some tribes allied with the British. After the British captured the American post at Mackinac, Michigan, the U.S. government ordered soldiers and their families at Fort Dearborn in Chicago to leave. As soldiers and their families left town, they were attacked by Indians (which tribe it was is up for debate). About 60 Americans were killed during the incident, called the **Fort Dearborn Massacre.** The Indians burned the fort, which the Americans later rebuilt in 1816 and the Army used until the mid-1830s. Around that same time, the Potawatomi signed away their land in northern Illinois and were forced west.

In the spring of 1832, under the leadership of **Chief Black Hawk,** the Sauk Indians crossed the Mississippi River and moved into northwestern Illinois. The Sauk had lived in the region and in southwestern Wisconsin several decades earlier, but were forced into Iowa because of an 1804 treaty (a treaty Black Hawk disputed) in which they gave up some territory east of the river. The Sauks' return made settlers jittery, and white residents formed militias.

(Abraham Lincoln was one who signed up.) Black Hawk's route in Illinois roughly followed the Rock River northeastward. Early on in the journey, he realized the Sauks could not live peacefully with the white settlers and decided to go back across the Mississippi. However, several skirmishes occurred and before they knew it they were at war with the United States.

One episode that stands out in Illinois history took place in May 1832 south of Rockford at a place now called **Stillman's Run.** Black Hawk reportedly sent some scouts to Major Isaiah Stillman's militia to make peace, but none of Stillman's men spoke Sauk. They ended up attacking the Sauks. Black Hawk's men retaliated, frightening the militia and prompting them to flee. It was a short-lived victory. More militia and eventually U.S. troops pursued Black Hawk and his tribe into Wisconsin, where they were defeated in the Battle of Bad Axe. Not long afterward, other Indian tribes, such as the Winnebago, Potawatomi, Ottawa, and Chippewa ceded their land to the U.S. government and agreed to move west of the Mississippi River.

STATEHOOD AND SETTLEMENTS

Illinois became a state in 1818; however it was still quite small, population-wise. It was actually the smallest state to be admitted into the union. In 1820 there were about 55,000 people living here. New residents initially came from the southern states such as Kentucky, Tennessee, and the Carolinas. Most settled in the southern third part of the state because the hills reminded them of home. They chose towns such as Shawneetown in the southeast near the salt mines and Kaskaskia to the southwest along the Mississippi River. (Kaskaskia, the first capital, would eventually be washed away from frequent floods.) It was easier to live in the south than in the prairie or northern region. The ground was not as wet as in the prairies to the north, where people often got sick from living near mosquito-infested wetlands. There was plenty of timber to harvest, animals to hunt, farmland to plant corn, and

opportunities to make whiskey. Early residents of Illinois were frontiersmen, subsistence farmers, veterans, miners, and land surveyors.

When the Erie Canal was finished in 1825, people from the East Coast could travel westward from the Hudson River at Albany to Lake Erie and to the Great Lakes. The opening of the canal spurred the development of Midwestern states such as Illinois and cities such as Chicago and Milwaukee. Chicago went from a sleepy trading post to a bustling center of commerce. People began to flock to Illinois. In the mid-1800s, several ethnic and religious groups arrived in Illinois with grand hopes that they could prosper here free from prejudice. These groups included the Mormons, who settled in Nauvoo on the west, and shortly after them, the French Icarians who also settled in Nauvoo; and the Swedish immigrants known as Janssonists who established Bishop Hill also in the west.

As steam travel continued to develop, talk surfaced about connecting via canals the Great Lakes to the Illinois and Mississippi rivers. Real-estate developers poured into Chicago and other towns. During this time Galena and JoDaviess County in the northwest of the state started prospering as a hub for lead ore mining, farming, and steamboating. By 1830 about 157,000 people were living in the state. Another boom to development was the opening of the **Illinois and Michigan Canal** in 1848, which would link the Great Lakes to the Mississippi River. The massive capital improvement project cost about $6 million at the time.

Then the first railroad—the Galena and Chicago Union—was built, connecting Chicago with the lead mines in Galena. As the canals sparked development in the northern part of the state, the railroads were responsible for jumpstarting hundreds of towns throughout Illinois. The **Illinois Central,** begun in 1851, set off a development boom. Towns such as Champaign, Rantoul, Pana, Mattoon, and many others sprung up around the depots. Once the railroads were in place, farmers realized they didn't have to be subsistence farmers, but they could sell their grain and livestock

Know Illinois

at the Chicago markets. Travel also was much more of a speedy and pleasant experience. People didn't have to travel great distances on stagecoaches, which often became stuck in the thick, deep prairie soil.

LINCOLN, SLAVERY, AND THE CIVIL WAR

One of the many families who moved to Illinois in hopes of seeking good, affordable farmland were the Lincolns. In 1830, 21-year-old **Abraham Lincoln** moved into the state from Kentucky, along with his father, Thomas, and stepmother, Sarah. Lincoln eventually set out on his own, working as a flatboat pilot, surveyor, merchant, and eventually politician. He spent quite a bit of time in New Salem, a town along the Sangamon River, just northwest of Springfield. There he toyed with several jobs, among them postmaster and clerk at a general store. But it was there he read books (including law books) and toyed with the idea of becoming involved in politics.

He was elected as a state representative in 1834 and spent time between New Salem and Vandalia, the second capital. He passed the bar exam and received a license to practice law. He had an office in Springfield but also traveled on the Eighth Judicial Circuit court and tried cases in county courthouses throughout the state. Lincoln then went on to serve a term in the U.S. House of Representatives beginning in 1847. He didn't run for a second term and instead chose to return to practicing law in Springfield.

During the next 10 years slavery would become more of a contentious issue not only in Illinois, but throughout the country. Illinois was torn. Many northern Illinois residents came from the northeastern United States and were antislavery. Illinois's southern neighbors of Kentucky and Missouri permitted slavery. Based on the fact that many southern residents of Illinois hailed from the Southern states, perhaps it was not surprising that many residents of southern Illinois supported slavery. (Southerners op-

Lincoln's Tomb, sculpture by Gutzon Borglum

posed to Lincoln and the Civil War were called Copperheads.)

While some French settlers brought slaves with them to Illinois and there were slaves working in the state, such as at the salt mines in Gallatin County, slavery was not common in Illinois. The Northwest Ordinance prohibited slavery in the territory; however, once Illinois became a state, the ordinance's governing laws were not pertinent. The **Missouri Compromise** in 1820, which allowed slavery in Missouri, banned it in Illinois and other states from the Louisiana Purchase. Just because slavery was illegal in Illinois, the living was definitely not easy for its black residents. They could serve in militias and testify in court, but they had no right to vote. Slaves who had escaped from the South tried to escape through Illinois to Canada, but risked being kidnapped. In 1853 the state legislature passed a law that forbade free slaves from entering the state. Abolitionists also didn't have it easy. **Elijah Lovejoy,** who published an antislavery newspaper in Alton, had his printing presses destroyed several times by mobs. Eventually he was murdered in 1847. Lovejoy's death shocked and incited other abolitionists in the state to stand up against the slavery opponents and try to free as many slaves as possible. **Underground Railroad** stops were established throughout the state, particularly in and around Jacksonville.

In 1850 a U.S. senator from Illinois, **Stephen A. Douglas** (also known as the "little giant"), proposed a solution to the question of slavery in the country. In the Compromise of 1850, Douglas said states should decide themselves whether or not slavery was legal or illegal. The proposal didn't move forward, but a few years later the **Kansas-Nebraska Act** did. The 1854 act left it up to the two territories (Kansas and Nebraska) to decide if slavery would be allowed or not. The act outraged slavery opponents, the Republican Party was born, and Lincoln readied himself for a return to politics.

After Republicans nominated Lincoln as a candidate for U.S. Senate, he and his opponent, Douglas, decided to tour the state during the summer and fall of 1858 and debate the issue of slavery and other topics. The **Lincoln-Douglas debates** were held in Ottawa, Freeport, Jonesboro, Charleston, Galesburg, Quincy, and Alton. Lincoln lost the race, but his performance at the debates brought him national attention. Republicans later nominated him as their presidential candidate and he was elected president of the United States in 1860.

Not long after Lincoln took office, the Civil War began. No Civil War battles were fought in Illinois, but there were several prisons here that held Confederate soldiers, among them Rock Island in the Quad Cities and Fort Douglas in Chicago, as well as hospitals, such as one near Cairo. About 250,000 men and boys from Illinois fought in the war, among them Galena resident Ulysses S. Grant, who would become general and eventually U.S. president. About 34,000 Illinois soldiers died in battle or from disease.

INDUSTRIALIZATION AND MODERNIZATION

The latter part of the 19th century was a busy one for Illinois. New settlers drained wetlands and established farmsteads. In 1865 the Union Stock Yards opened on the southwest side of Chicago and trading grain futures at the Chicago Board of Trade became more formalized. Manufacturing—steel, glass, farm tools, pearl buttons, lumber—was big. Textiles and food-processing businesses boomed. Gas, oil, and minerals were discovered and mined throughout the state. Steel rail lines were developed in the city, and more rail lines were added throughout the state. **Cyrus McCormick** built his mechanical reaper factory in Chicago. **George Pullman** launched his Pullman Palace Car company.

The **Chicago Fire** in October 1871 destroyed much of downtown Chicago and the north side. But Chicagoans pulled themselves up by the bootstraps and architects such as Daniel Burnham, Louis Sullivan, Jens Jensen, and Frank Lloyd Wright swooped in and redesigned the city. Chicago, not to mention the entire state, was proud of itself, especially in 1893 when the city hosted the world's fair, the **Columbia Exposition.**

In response to the growth of factories and the influx of workers, worker's rights became a hot-button issue around the state. Strikes, protests, and riots were not unheard of. During **The Haymarket Riot** in 1886, several police officers were killed when a person or group of people threw a bomb during a protest against police violence. While employees were striking at the McCormick reaper factory, demanding an eight-hour workday, police shot several workers. Workers at Pullman's factory went on strike in 1894 after Pullman reduced wages but did not reduce rent on the company-owned houses. Skirmishes between protesting miners and managers and scabs were also common in southern Illinois. Some progress was made. Mother Jones rallied miners, seamstresses, and others and fought for workers rights. Jane Addams founded the **Hull House** in 1889 in

Chicago to help the poor and uneducated. The state shortened the women's work day to eight hours, passed laws limiting child labor, and organized schools.

As the businesses climate ballooned, so did Illinois's population. Yankees flooded Chicago, as did European immigrants such as Germans, Irish, and Scandinavians, followed by immigrants from southern and eastern Europe. By 1900, the state's population swelled to about 4.8 million people. Along with the immigrants who came to Illinois looking for good jobs, came Southern blacks. In the early 20th century many more riots erupted because of racial strife. The 1908 Springfield race riots, brought on after a white woman said a black man assaulted her (a statement she later retracted), several black and white people were killed and many shops and homes burned. Stunned and urged to act, several people met in New York to discuss what happened, eventually forming the **National Association for the Advancement of Colored People.** In the 1917 race riot in East St. Louis, sparked after factories invited blacks to move to town and work there, 48 blacks and nine whites were killed. Chicago was also fast becoming a tense, segregated city. From 1910 to 1920, the city's black population doubled to 109,000. Most blacks settled together in the city's south side neighborhoods. In 1919 a black boy drifted into the white swimming area on the lakefront and drowned after a white youth threw a stone at him. The murder sparked days of riots throughout the city and elsewhere in the United States.

The first few decades of the 21st century were quite violent. Shortly after Prohibition, a man named Alphonse Capone joined Chicago mob's bootlegging, gambling, and brothel businesses. When Capone's boss was shot and killed, he took the helm of the organization, known as **The Syndicate.** Capone ran speakeasies, racetracks, and dance clubs. Capone was responsible for the St. Valentine's Day Massacre in 1929, when his strong-arm men killed off rival gang lord Bugs Moran. Eventually he was sent to prison on Alcatraz Island in California for income tax evasion.

Later Chicago and many other towns became preoccupied with World War II, sending hundreds of thousands of young men to fight there and modifying factories to produce supplies and help with the cause. One of the biggest contributions to indirectly ending the war happened in 1942 beneath the University of Chicago's Stagg Field. It was there that Enrico Fermi and other scientists conducted the first nuclear chain reaction.

MID- TO LATE-20TH CENTURY AND CONTEMPORARY TIMES

Following a trend that occurred throughout the country from the 1950s onward, rural residents moved to the cities, and the populations of the rural counties aged and dwindled. The federal highway system rendered two-lane highways such as Route 66 obsolete. Chicago became even more of a transportation hub for the Midwest as semitrailers roared along the highways and more freight train lines came in and out of the city. Richard J. Daley was elected mayor of Chicago in 1955 and became known as a builder mayor, approving and overseeing dozens of modernization projects, including the high-rise housing projects on the west and south side now being torn down.

Segregation occurred somewhat reluctantly around the state and clashes between blacks and whites were not uncommon. In the town of Cairo, for example, many white businessmen closed up shop and left town rather than have blacks as customers. Cairo and many other towns, such as East St. Louis, Peoria, Rockford, and Elgin were the scenes of race riots in 1966 and 1967. In April 1968, after Dr. Martin Luther King was assassinated, National Guardsmen flew in after more riots exploded in Joliet, Alton, Maywood, Carbondale, and other areas.

Despite the racial tension, the state was a melting pot of people, art, and ideas. Architect Mies Van der Rohe's glass and steel skyscrapers changed the look of Chicago. Carl Sandburg and Gwendolyn Brooks penned moving prose and poetry. Blues musicians such as Buddy Guy made Chicago a destination for budding musicians. Toward the mid-'70s, though, things began to change. After six terms in office, in December 1976 Daley died of a heart attack. The oil embargo and inflation put a damper on the economy. New regulations from the Clean Air Act prompted many coal mines and plants to shutter. Farmland prices crashed in the mid-1980s, causing many farmers to file bankruptcy and sell their farms.

Like many other states, Illinois, for the most part, recovered. While many coal-mining towns continue to struggle and people look elsewhere to find jobs in manufacturing, tourism, or in prisons, most of the state's towns and residents thrived in the 1990s. New businesses were launched, everyone's stock portfolios were in the black, and everyone rallied around Michael Jordan and the Chicago Bulls. The economic downturn in recent years has caused a few folks to suffer. State spending for education and research is not at the level teachers or parents would like, tuition at most universities is up, some capital improvement projects have been delayed, and Illinois has lost quite a few soldiers in the war in Iraq.

Government

In 2005 Illinois had a Democrat in the governor's house and a Democrat-controlled general assembly. During the 2004 presidential election, Illinois rarely hosted a presidential candidate visit. The state was, and is, solidly Democratic. This is largely because of the power of Chicago. The Dems dominate metropolitan areas, but many suburbs, particularly those in Du Page County, are solidly Republican, as are plenty of rural counties. Even though the capital is Springfield, many state bureaus and departments have offices in Springfield and Chicago. Governor Rod Blagojevich, who is from Chicago, has been criticized for not spending enough time in Springfield. It's not uncommon for downstate residents (generally anyone living below I-80) to complain that Chicago politicians run the state.

Illinois voters are a tough crowd, quite a bit cynical and mistrusting of state and local government. Maybe it has to do with the scandals, the allegations of patronage, the embezzlements, and the bribes that have plagued the state since its early days. During the Prohibition era there was Big Bill Thompson, Chicago's mayor, who unabashedly hung out with Al Capone and his buddies. In the 1950s, the state auditor and several others pleaded guilty to embezzling money from the state. In the 1980s the U.S. attorney's office was busy investigating voter fraud. In the 1990s the FBI's Operation Silver Shovel uncovered widespread political corruption in Chicago's city hall. And recently, the U.S. attorney's office has been handing out indictments in the licenses for bribes scandal in which staffers of the secretary of state's office reportedly issued commercial truck licenses to people in exchange for political contributions. Former Republican governor George Ryan was heading to court in late 2005 in a federal corruption trial for essentially steering state contracts to friends.

But there have been some bright spots in the state's political history. The late, bow tie–wearing U.S. Sen. Paul Simon, a newspaper publisher turned politician, had admirers from both sides of the aisles. The late former President Ronald Reagan, who was born in Tampico and raised in Dixon, is beloved here. Republican Governor Jim Thompson, who served 1977–1991, was criticized for his pork barrel politics, but his terms in office were relatively free from scandals. U.S. Sen. Barack Obama, an enthusiastic politician from Chicago, is also adored by Democrats and even has impressed a few Republicans.

Practically speaking, the governor is Illinois's chief executive officer, elected for a four-year term. The lieutenant governor, and other constitutional officers, such as the attorney general, secretary of state, treasurer, and comptroller are also elected to four-year terms. The Illinois Supreme Court has seven justices who serve 10-year terms. Three of the justices hail from Cook County, which is the first district, plus four others come from four districts across the state. Appellate and circuit court judges are elected for 10- and four-year terms respectively.

The Illinois General Assembly has 59 senators and 118 representatives, a majority of whom are from Chicago and its collar counties. Across the country in 2003, Republicans gained more seats than Democrats in state and national elected offices. Not so in Illinois. That year Illinois voters elected a Democrat to the governor's office and enough Democrats into the state senate and house that both chambers would be controlled by the Democrats, the first time in almost three decades. A few years later, folks are grumbling about the current administration. A slew of Republicans have lined up to challenge current Democratic Governor Rod Blagojevich.

Two senators represent Illinois in the U.S. Senate and 20 representatives are in the U.S. House of Representatives.

Economy

Illinois's gross state product is about $475 billion, ranking it fifth among other U.S. states. Using that statistic, if Illinois were a country it would rank 12th in terms of gross domestic product. The three main drivers of Illinois's economy are manufacturing, agriculture, and industrial production. Chicago is a hub for the transportation industry (including truck, train, airline, and bus companies), as well as insurance and consulting companies. Peoria is known for equipment manufacturing, Decatur for grain processing, Bloomington for general manufacturing and health-care jobs, Champaign-Urbana for University of Illinois jobs and health-care employment. East St. Louis is home to a lot of iron and steel production.

About 16 percent of the state's workforce is employed in manufacturing. Companies in

Illinois cornfields

© CHRISTINE DES GARENNES

Illinois build tractors, electronic equipment, computer chips, and more. The major names in manufacturing are Caterpillar, General Electric, Illinois Tool Works, and John Deere. Other large private employers in the state are Motorola, Lucent Technologies, Abbott Laboratories, and Kraft Foods. In recent years, the state's manufacturing sector has dampened somewhat as tire manufacturer Firestone closed shop in Decatur, Maytag closed a plant in Galesburg, and Mitsubishi scaled back its workforce in Bloomington.

Illinois is a big agricultural state. Corn and soybeans are grown across the state, and it is a top producer of both crops. Dairy farms are in the northern, hilly part of the state, particularly near the Wisconsin border. Fruit orchards are concentrated in the southern third of the state. But Illinois is not just big in terms of crop output. It's huge in corn processing and soybean milling, largely because of Archer Daniels Midland in Decatur and Bunge in Danville. The grains processed there are made into everything from corn syrup for sodas to soy protein for vegetarian burgers.

In the southern part of the state, coal mines have dominated the economies of several local towns for many years. (A quick look at a map of this region yields names such as Coalton, Coal Valley, Carbondale, and Carbon Cliff.) However, the economic climate for coal in Illinois has changed dramatically in the last 15 years. The Clean Air Act amendments passed in 1990 had quite an affect on the industry in Illinois. In fact, the state estimates coal production and industry sales in Illinois dropped by one-third because of price competition and the move from high-sulfur coal to low-sulfur coal. You

see, Illinois coal is butimous and has a lot of carbon in it. After the act, many mining companies in Illinois shifted their attention to coal beds out west where the coal does not have such a high sulfur content. But the coal industry in Illinois is not dead. About one-eighth of the country's coal reserves are under Illinois and underground coal beds cover about 65 percent of the state. About 33.5 million tons of coal is still mined each year in Illinois. (Much of it goes to produce electricity for Illinois utilities.) And in recent years, researchers have unveiled promising technologies that could reduce the harmful pollutants emitted when high-sulfur coal is burned. In addition to coal, Illinois has oil reserves and is home to four oil refineries. These refineries produce more gasoline than any other Midwest state. (Their production levels however, do not nearly meet the state's demands.)

The State of Illinois employs the most people in the state, followed by the federal government (including postal workers), the Chicago Public School District, and the city of Chicago. The state's largest private employer is Wal-Mart, which has about 40,000 employees in Illinois. Other top employers include Jewel-Osco (a grocery chain), Caterpillar, United Parcel Service, Advocate Health Care (an HMO or health maintenance organization), and State Farm Insurance. The state's unemployment rate was around 4.5 percent during the late 1990s and climbed gradually to about 6.5 percent in 2002. By early 2005 it had dipped to 5.9 percent. Unemployment rates are higher in downstate counties where mining and manufacturing jobs have dwindled.

The People

SETTLEMENT AND IMMIGRATION PATTERNS

In the biased opinion of this writer, Illinois has the most fascinating mix of residents compared with any other Midwest state. We have people from every ethnic background and racial makeup in towns across the state, not just in Chicago. We have Nobel Prize–winning scientists, internationally known artists, cunning developers, smart and some might say, smarmy politicians, homespun country folk, wealthy businessmen, migrant workers, inventors, copycats, do-gooders, poets, curmudgeons, conservatives, liberals, independents, and everyone in between. On a tour of the state you could meet a couple who has farmed on the same land for five generations, an immigrant couple from Southeast Asia who runs a hotel in a small southern town, an East Coast transplant who never planned on staying in Illinois for more than a few years, but found himself making a home in the state for several decades. We make up quite a collage.

From its early beginnings, Illinois never really belonged to one particular group of people. Settlement started with the French, followed by the Brits and the American colonists. The early arrivals were explorers, fur trappers, farmers, land speculators, and people seeking religious freedom. After the Native Americans, the first group to put down roots in Illinois was the French. The French settlers lived mostly in the southwest part of the state, particularly east and south of St. Louis. Some towns and buildings there still bear French names. The first Americans to build homes in Illinois were from the southern states, such as Kentucky and Tennessee. And through the state's early development, American colonists from the Southern states stuck to southern Illinois, and Yankees, people from the Northeast, focused on the Chicago region. Political and philosophical clashes between these two groups—the moderns (mostly Northerners) and traditionalists

(mostly Southerners)—occurred often, especially over the issue of slavery.

In the mid-1800s, as steamers and railroad travel became more available to the Midwest, immigrants came mainly from Germany, Ireland, England, and a few other European countries. They came here directly from their homelands and from other states, probably after reading promotional literature about the cheap, fertile land available here. In the 1830s German immigrants from St. Louis and Cincinnati settled in and near towns along the National Road, such as Effingham and Teutopolis. Chicago was also heavily German, although not as much so as Milwaukee to the north. Norwegians clustered in villages along the Fox River. The Swedes were mostly in the western part of the state, such as Bishop Hill.

Between 1890 and 1914, another wave of immigrants entered Illinois, this time from countries in eastern and southern Europe. This group included Poles, Italians, and Ukrainians. After World War II and into the second half of the 20th century, immigrants to Illinois originated from Central and South America, Asia (including Southeast Asia), eastern Europe, and some from Africa. While their point of arrival is almost always Chicago, some of the immigrants migrate to other towns in the state where the cost of living is lower and jobs are available. These cities and towns include Moline, Peoria, Carbondale, and Champaign-Urbana, which has a number of international undergraduate and graduate students studying and living in the area.

According to the 2000 Census, almost 90 percent of Illinoisans are native to the United States, with 20 percent claiming German ancestry, 12 percent Irish ancestry, 8 percent Polish, 7 percent English, 6 percent Italian, and 2.4 percent Scotch-Irish. English is spoken everywhere. But there are pockets on Devon Street in Chicago where you'll hear Indian and Pakistani. Along South Halsted Street you can pick up Greek phrases. In some of Springfield and Champaign's restaurants and ethnic stores you'll hear Korean, Mandarin, or Russian being spoken. In Amish country near Arcola and Arthur, you might catch the Amish farmers speaking German.

The state has a sizeable Jewish population estimated at 270,000, ranking the state seventh in terms of population of Jewish people. Most live in and around Chicago, particularly the north shore suburbs of Skokie and Highland Park. However, some Jewish communities can be found in central Illinois towns such as Bloomington and Champaign.

STATISTICS

Illinois had 12.4 million people according to the 2000 Census. In the state's very early days, most of the population centers were in the south, such as near Cairo and Shawneetown. That has changed drastically since the 1800s, and Chicago is now where most people live. Of the state's 12.4 million people, about 85 percent of them live in urban areas and more than 65 percent of the state's residents live in Chicago and its surrounding suburbs. Cook County itself has 5.4 million people. Chicagoland (Cook and the surrounding collar counties) is the only region in the state where visitors might feel crowded. Here you will often encounter long lines at tollbooth plazas, museums, and cafés.

Almost 75 percent of the state's residents are Caucasian, 15 percent are African American, and 7 percent are Asian. Of Chicago's nearly three million people, 66 percent of the city's residents are Caucasian, 19 percent are African American, and 5 percent are Asian. And about 26 percent of Chicagoans are Latino or Hispanic, compared with 12 percent across the state. In line with a national trend, it was the Hispanic category that saw the most population growth 1990–2000.

Chicago is a youthful town; college graduates and young professionals comprise a majority of the residents in neighborhoods such as Wicker Park and Wrigleyville. While Chicago and some large towns such as Champaign and

Urbana and Bloomington have a fair share of young adults, the average age of people in the rural counties keeps creeping higher, following another trend across the country. According to the Census about 70 percent of the residents are 21 years old or older. Illinois's population is fairly evenly distributed among men (49 percent) and women (51 percent).

Compared with national averages, Illinoisans are doing fairly well on a financial and educational level. About 10 percent of Illinoisans live below the poverty level. About 81 percent have a high school degree or higher and almost 27 percent have a bachelor's degree or higher, both a bit higher than the national average. The homeownership rate is at 67 percent, compared with the 66 percent national average.

ATTITUDES

At some point on your trip through the state you may hear a Chicagoan poke fun at downstate Illinois, calling people there naive or uneducated, out of touch with the latest trends (whether that trend is in real estate, fashion, or what have you). If you're in the south, chances are someone will refer to the know-it-all northerns and their obsessive consumerism. These jibes are nothing new. For almost 200 years, it's been the case of north versus south in Illinois. And that probably won't change any time soon. Just where is that dividing line between northern and southern Illinois? That varies depending on who you talk to. For some people, "downstate" is anything outside the Chicago region. For many people, though, it's anything south of I-80.

Northern Illinois residents tend to be more diverse politically as well as racially and ethnically. Chicago is without a doubt a global city. World travelers live and work there. But it still has a colloquial feel to it and people can't stop comparing it to New York and Los Angeles. It's the third-largest city in the country and yet residents and members of the media (including print, television, and radio) always seem to get overexcited when Chicago is mentioned in national media or when a celebrity visits and dines in a local restaurant.

IT'S "ILLINOY," NOT "ILLINOYS"

Illinois is squarely in the Midwest. But driving through the state, from Rockford in the north, Springfield in the center, and Carbondale to the south, you'll hear a range of accents. Essentially, northerner speech will sound more nasaly and staccato. Head south and you'll pick up more of a drawl, which becomes more pronounced the farther south you go.

The Chicago accent is perhaps the most mimicked accent of the state. Remember that *Saturday Night Live* sketch in which Mike Ditka–like actors cheer on "da Bulls an' da Bears?" The *a*'s were long, and the pace staccato. Some folks do talk that way. Born-and-bred Chicagoans will pronounce words such as Pulaski (as in the street named after the Polish general) with an accent on the *a*, i.e., Pulayski. Most Chicagoans will pronounce the city's name as Shicahhgo or Shicawgo. Mayor Richard Daley, by the way, whose family is from the south side, has a solid Chicago accent.

As you travel south, more and more people speak with a drawl and Southern accent. In the central region of the state, such as Springfield, Bloomington-Normal, and Champaign-Urbana, you'll notice that in-town residents have no sign of a drawl. But those who live just a few miles from the city outskirts have a slight Southern accent. In the southern part of the state, such as from Marion and southward, you'll notice that along with the Southern accent there often comes a friendly, casual Southern attitude. Don't be surprised when gas station attendants, wait staff, and others slip in a "sweetheart" and "honey" when they thank you for your business.

Some final words on pronunciations. Because the state was first settled by French, many town and place-names bear French names. Illinois is the French word for the Native American Indians who lived in the state when the French fur traders arrived here. But of course, Illinois is not pronounced as the French would pronounce it. Instead, it's Illinoy. (Ignore the *s* at the end.) Around the state there are a number of place-names that are pronounced nothing like the way you might think they would be said. Marseilles is Marsales. Okawville is pronounced Okaville. Vienna is Vayanna. And Cairo is Caro (like the syrup).

As you travel south, you'll notice people dress more casually and seem less hurried. They tend to be more conservative and religious. More folks (but not all) talk with a slight drawl, which intensifies the farther south you go. People are curious about visitors. If you walk into a local café, they'll all stop to look at you. But once you say hello and engage someone in conversation, you could while away the morning or afternoon chatting with him or her.

The phrase "Midwestern values" gets thrown around a lot, especially during election seasons. Just what this word implies probably varies per speaker. Generally you'll find Illinoisans are a welcoming, engaging, loyal, practical bunch. We donate to charities, try to recycle, and make sure the kids are getting a good educa-

tion. Illinois is predominantly Christian with a mix of Protestants, particularly Presbyterians, Methodists, Baptists, and Lutherans, and a good number of Catholics. Protestants and Catholics are the major religions, but in recent years a growing number of nondenominational churches have cropped up in the state. Mosques and synagogues are also found in most major towns. There's definitely a conservative religious contingent in the state (you'll notice several areas have quite a few Christian radio stations), but it probably does not have as many conservative or evangelical communities as the Bible Belt states.

Race relations have come a long way since the riots in the early 1900s and in the 1960s. Kids ride the buses together and attend schools together. Several nonprofit organizations around the state promote equality and diversity through school and workplace education. Most communities have human relations committees to iron out issues. Things aren't sparkling, though. In 1999 in Decatur, several black students were expelled for fighting at a football game. The action of the predominantly white school board was considered severe by many throughout the state, including Rev. Jesse Jackson of Chicago, who led a march in the city to protest the school board's decision. In addition, Chicago and many other cities such as Rockford and the Champaign-Urbana region remain fairly segregated. In Chicago blacks tend to live in black communities in the south and west sides. Latinos live with Latinos on the southwest and northwest sides. People of different races may work together, but they don't always live in the same neighborhoods.

Arts and Culture

MUSEUMS

From folksy Raggedy Ann and Andy Museum in Arcola to the Museum of Contemporary Art in Chicago, Illinois has a vast array of museums, large and small with collections that run the gamut. Museum Campus in Chicago is a trio of world-class museums: the Field Museum of Natural History, Adler Planetarium, and Shedd Aquarium. A few blocks away from those three museums is the Art Institute of Chicago with its famous French impressionist paintings and architecture collections. In Hyde Park to the south is the kid-friendly Museum of Science and Industry. And in Chicago's neighborhoods are a range of ethnic museums also worthy of a visit, such as the Mexican Fine Arts Center Museum and the Swedish American Museum Center.

The newest museum to open in Illinois is the long-awaited and much-anticipated **Abraham Lincoln Presidential Library and Museum** in Springfield. With a price tag of more than $100 million, this complex at more than 200,000 square feet has everything a Lincoln fan or historian could imagine, with exhibits that chronicle his life from his childhood to his time in the White House and assassination in Washington, D.C. Also in downstate Illinois, the University of Illinois at Urbana-Champaign has a few museums visitors might want to check out, including the Krannert Art Museum, which shows traditional and contemporary art, and the Spurlock Museum, which houses history exhibits from around the world.

Illinois has dozens of other lesser-known museums scattered throughout the state. These tend to be run by local residents or groups and highlight local history or a private collection of items someone or a group of people have amassed through several decades. One gem of a museum is the **Under the Prairie Frontier Archaeological Museum** in Elkhart, where owners have discovered and artfully arranged artifacts, such as a kettle, a tin cup, or part of an oxen shoe, that date from before the Civil War. In a small town surrounded by fields of corn and soybeans, the **National Museum of Ship Models and Sea History** in Sadorus is a find with a large collection of models in a renovated storefront. **Shea's Gas Station Museum** in Springfield takes a nostalgic look at Route 66 and two-lane highway travel. The travelers who collect vintage postcards will get a kick out of the impressive **Curt Teich Postcard Archives** in the Lake County Discovery Museum in Wauconda. The collection comprises about 10,000 postcards depicting rural and urban scenes in Illinois and the Midwest, but also from more than 80 countries.

HISTORIC TRAVEL

Illinois, the "Land of Lincoln," will not disappoint visitors who want to follow in the footsteps of the state's famous son, **Abraham Lincoln.** Lincoln spent some three decades here, from his early 20s to his early 50s. As a young man looking to find work and eventually as a lawyer on the circuit court and a politician, Lincoln traveled a lot throughout the state. And you can bet anything he touched, any building or room that he walked in, any town that he traveled through, if it's still around and someone knows about it, there's a plaque or sign marking the significance. There's no shortage of Lincoln sites in Illinois.

The must-see Lincoln sites are his home in Springfield and the surrounding historic district, the new Lincoln museum, his tomb in Springfield's **Oak Ridge Cemetery,** plus **Lincoln's New Salem,** a recreated village northwest of Springfield. This is where he worked as a postmaster and in a general store and taught himself law. In addition, you can visit the sites around the state where Lincoln debated with **Stephen A. Douglas** issues such as slavery. The **Lincoln Log Cabin State Historic Site** in Lerna, south of Charleston, is where Lincoln's father and stepmother lived. This sometimes-overlooked site is a living history farm and has informative exhibits on the Lincoln family and their backgrounds. In the former lead-mining town of Galena, you can visit the home of former president and Civil War general **Ulysses S. Grant** and stay or dine in the **DeSoto House Hotel,** where Abraham Lincoln and others have stayed.

For Native American history, one of the best sites in the state is **Cahokia,** a UNESCO World Heritage Site near East St. Louis. From about A.D. 900–1400, members of this thriving Indian village traded with other cities miles away, cultivated corn and squash, and built extensive earthen mounds, dozens of which still remain in the area. Northeast of Cahokia in the Illinois River Valley are remains of more mound cultures. The **Dickson Mounds Museum** near Havana highlights the histories and contributions of these people. The **Center for American Archeology** in Kampsville organizes archaeological digs of such sites for amateur historians.

Although many buildings associated with Illinois's French and British past are long gone,

you can visit the site of some of their forts, which have been rebuilt. Both countries built these forts to protect their Illinois territory, which in the 1700s and early 1800s was considered a remote and wild place. In the Mississippi River floodplain near Prairie du Rocher is **Fort de Chartres.** Several forts were actually built here, beginning in 1720. The massive stone fort you visit today was built to resemble the fort built by the French in the 1850s. Some archaeological remains of the original forts are on view there. Several forts also once stood in **Fort Massac State Park** overlooking the Ohio River near Metropolis. First the French built a fort there, followed by the British and finally the Americans. Virginian George Rogers Clark overtook the British fort during the Revolutionary War. During the Civil War the Illinois Calvary camped there. A replica of the American fort is on the site today and a reenactment of life in the 1700s is held in the park every fall.

Even if you're not Mormon, chances are you'll be fascinated with a tour of Nauvoo on the western edge of the state. Joseph Smith and his followers settled here in the 1840s and left behind a remarkably well-preserved village. The **Joseph Smith Historic Site** consists of several original settlement buildings, including Smith's former home, and shops such as the post office, blacksmith shop, gun shop, and more. Also included in the site is the Smith Family Cemetery. The Historic Nauvoo Visitors Center fills you in on the history of the village, temple, and the Mormons as does the recreated **Nauvoo Illinois Temple.** Steps from the temple, downtown Nauvoo has shops and restaurants for visitors. And a short drive eastward is the **Carthage Jail** where Joseph Smith was killed by a mob.

Two organizations you might want to become familiar with are the **Illinois State Historical Society** and the **Chicago Historical Society.** The state society (210 ½ S. 6th St., Springfield, 217/525-2781, www.historyillinois.org, 9 A.M.–5 P.M. Mon.–Fri.) publishes a number of books related to Illinois history and the glossy bimonthly magazine *Illinois*

Heritage, which you might want to look for in a local bookstore or order from the society before your trip through the state. The society also publishes the scholarly *Journal of the Illinois State Historical Society.* **The Chicago Historical Society** (Clark St. at North Ave., 312/642-4600, www.chicagohistory.org, 9:30 A.M.–4:30 P.M. Mon.–Sat.; noon–5 P.M. Sun., $5, free Mon.) has several rotating and permanent exhibits that focus on a person (such as Stephen Douglas or Lincoln) or an event in history related to the city or state. The store has vintage photographs and posters for sale a great selection of books for sale.

FESTIVALS

There's always something going on in Illinois, no matter what time of year. There are the traditional events, such as Fourth of July and Memorial Day parades held in most towns. And there are the untraditional ones, such as Morton's Punkin' Chuckin' contest, where participants shoot pumpkins out of cannons.

Whatever event it is, most likely it involves eating. We Illinoisans like to eat and drink. We like to listen to music. We like a parade. We like silly contests. Oh, and we like to eat. Here's a sampling of just a few food-focused festivals in Illinois: the Arthur cheese festival, the horseradish festival in Collinsville, the strawberry and chocolate festivals in the Historic Village of Long Grove, the crab festival in Alto Pass, and of course, the sweet-corn festival held in just about every rural town where someone grows corn. The mother of all food festivals is the enormously popular Taste of Chicago, where you can try hundreds of dishes from the city's restaurants.

Plenty of hot dogs and popcorn are on hand at the Illinois state fairs, held at permanent fairgrounds in Springfield and Du Quoin. These fairs bring in nationally known music acts, plus they feature 4H and other agriculturally focused exhibits. On a smaller scale, dozens of county fairs and farm shows are held all summer long throughout the state. They tend to include tractor pulls, demolition der-

bies, carnival rides, and plenty of food and beer tents. Stop by a county fair and you can learn how to raise a sow, goat, or other farm animal. The summer months are packed with music and art festivals from Chicago's world-famous Blues Fest to Peoria's riverfront blues festival, and Custer's Last Stand Art Fair in Evanston to Galena's Festival of the Performing Arts. Summer is also a time for many antique car shows, which pop up in many towns. One not-to-miss road party is the International Route 66 Mother Road Festival in Springfield.

Naturalists will enjoy solstice and equinox festivals at Cahokia Mounds near Collinsville, Decatur's Herb Fest, Lombard's lilac festival, and bird-watching events held in the cool months in towns along the Illinois and Mississippi rivers. In late November and early December tree-lighting ceremonies are common throughout the state. Several towns hold outdoor markets and ethnic festivals around the holidays. Chicago's Christkindlesmarkt always attracts large crowds for its German crafts, warm cider, and stollen. For that quiet, hometown feel, head to Bishop Hill's Lucia Nights, a Swedish festival of lights in mid-December.

SHOPPING

Variety, variety, variety. Whether you're hunting for a sleek outfit for a night on the town, a rare book from the late 19th century, or a ceramic dish circa 1950, you can satisfy your shopping impulses in Illinois. Chicago's got it all—expensive clothes and accessories, antiques, and kitschy collectibles. But don't forget to scour shops around the state. You might be surprised by the deals and oddities you could find in the barn turned antique store or tucked in the back of the storefront space on Main Street.

Chicago and Vicinity

State Street (otherwise known as "that great street") and **Michigan Avenue** in Chicago's downtown have long been the shopping hubs for the city. Department stores Marshall Field's and Carson Pirie Scott and ritzy boutiques such as Tiffany and Company line these shopping districts. Both are vibrant throughout the year, but effervesce during the holiday season with one elaborate window display and busking musician after the other. Upscale galleries are common in the **River North** neighborhood just north of the Chicago River and west of the Gold Coast. Funky boutiques are dotted throughout **Wicker Park, Bucktown,** and **Andersonville.** In-vogue fashions and home-decor shops are common in the gentrified neighborhoods of **Armitage** and **Southport.** Megamalls are mostly installed in the suburbs, such as the huge **Gurnee Mills** in Gurnee and **Woodfield Mall** in Schaumburg.

Antiques, Arts and Crafts, and Flea Markets

You won't have to hunt long for antiques or works by local artists. Several Illinois towns have charming main streets lined with storefront shops and galleries. Wilmington and Lincoln are well known for their bevy of antiques shops. The Fox River cities of St. Charles and Geneva have dozens of upscale art and antiques stores. You could spend hours in the mazelike **Illinois Antique Center,** in an old warehouse on Peoria's riverfront. For arts and crafts, the former Swedish colony of **Bishop Hill** has shops that sell handcrafted furniture, home-decor items, clothing, and jewelry. The streets of **Galena** are also lined with artisan shops run by friendly potters, weavers, and the like.

In addition, the **Illinois State Museum** highlights work of some of the state's best artisans at the Southern Illinois Artisan Shop near Benton and the Illinois Artisan Shop in the James R. Thompson Center in Chicago. At these shops you can learn about basket-weaving and quilt-making as well as buy some of these items. Other handmade items can be found in Illinois's **Amish country** near Arthur and Arcola, where downtown and homestead shops sell furniture, plants, produce, and everything you can imagine. Seeking bargains? The towns of **Sandwich** and **St. Charles** in the northern

part of the state both hold regular flea markets in the warm months.

FOOD

To be honest, it'll be tough to travel through Illinois if you're limiting calories and fat. As noted earlier, Illinoisans love to eat. We like doughnuts (Dixie Cream doughnuts in Tuscola are awesome, much better than Krispy Kreme), pizza, hot dogs, fish sandwiches, steaks, you name it. Here are a few common dishes in Illinois. First off is the **Chicago-style pizza.** Chicago-style pizza tends to be very cheesy and is usually a few inches thick. The crust, made of pressed dough, is topped with thick mozzarella slices followed by other toppings (popular choices are sausage or spinach), and then it's all topped with a layer of chunky tomato sauce. **Chicago-style hot dogs** are all-beef wieners loaded with green relish, chopped onions, sliced tomatoes, serrano peppers, yellow mustard, and a dash of celery salt. They're usually served in poppy-seed bun.

Outside of Chicago, the **horseshoe sandwich** is a common menu item, especially in Springfield, where it supposedly was invented. Every restaurant, bar, or drive-in has its own version of the horseshoe, but essentially it's an open-faced sandwich with 2–3 pieces of toast, layered with your choice of meat (hamburger, ham steak, turkey, corned beef, you name it), then topped with a pile of French fries, and on top of that melted cheese. What kind of cheese sauce it is varies per restaurant. And some places pour the cheese over the meat and then dump the fries over the sauce. Basically a horseshoe hits the spot after you've spent the day walking, hiking, biking, swimming, or engaged in some other type of activity for a long time, or after a night of partaking in more than a few drinks.

Food Markets and Farmers Markets

Illinois has about 200 regularly scheduled farmers markets throughout the state, held in places such as downtown parks and church or city hall parking lots. (Chicago alone has

© CHRISTINE DES GARENNES

Chicago pizza

more than a dozen markets.) Here you can find seasonal produce, from apricots to zucchinis, plus flowers, locally raised meats, and sometimes local artists play music or exhibit their creations. Check with the local visitors bureaus to find out about days and times the markets are held, typically on Saturdays May–October. In addition to the markets, several farms organize stands where you can buy a peck of apples or they allow you to pick your own strawberries or pumpkins, such as at Eckert's in Belleville or Curtis Orchard in Champaign. Farm stands are common in southern Illinois, where the sunny hills make prime spots for growing fruit trees. You can find dozens of apple and peach stands on the outskirts of towns such as Carbondale and Alto Pass in and near the Shawnee National Forest. Area visitors bureaus have orchard maps to help you navigate your way through the region.

Recreation

RESOURCES

Illinois has nearly 100 state parks in just about every region of the state, from the expansive Jim Edgar Panther Creek site in the center of the state to the small but scenic Apple River Canyon in the northwest. One of the best things about the state parks is that admission is free, no catch. Camping fees are nominal. **The Illinois Department of Natural Resources** (1 Natural Resources Way, Springfield, 217/782-6302, www.dnr.state.il.us) manages the sites, some of which feature historic lodges (such as Pere Marquette in Grafton) in addition to the standard hiking trails, lakes, rivers, and picnic and camping areas. The department partners with a custom publishing firm and prints a free guide to all these places. You can order it by calling the DNR or search all the sites online. In addition, the DNR publishes the glossy *Outdoor Illinois* magazine, which costs $15 a year. You can subscribe online or look for it in libraries and bookstores.

Another glossy magazine for naturalists is *Illinois Steward,* published quarterly by the University of Illinois. This one has more of a focus on environmental and natural-history issues important to the state. You can also find it at most libraries and bookstores or by calling 217/333-3650 or visiting http://ilsteward.nres.uiuc.edu. Cost is $16 for one year.

HIKING

Through river bottomland forests, restored prairies, or old-growth forests, Illinois has a network of trails throughout the state for hikers with varying degrees of ability. The southern and northern part of the state, where most of the hills are, have the most challenging trails. The central region has trails through restored prairies, offering opportunities for bird-watching and scouting for wildflowers. In the south, you can test your calf muscles by hiking along **Little Grand Canyon** by Carbondale. The

Mississsppi Palisades State Park has some challenging hiking trails.

© CHRISTINE DES GARENNES

steep, four-mile loop has several scenic overlooks of the Illinois version of the Grand Canyon. Nearby **Giant City State Park** has short nature trails, such as the Stone Fort Trail, which are less than a mile, or the 16-mile Red Cedar Hiking Trail winds around the exterior of this beautiful park. To the east of Giant City, hike past the remains of a Native American village and an ancient rock shelter at **Lusk Creek Canyon,** east of Eddyville. The **River-to-River Trail** is a vigorous 175-mile-long trail through Illinois that connects the Mississippi and Ohio rivers. Try a 12-mile section from Panthers' Den to Giant City State Park or a six- to eight-mile section from the Godwin Trail to the LaRue/Pine Hills State Recreation Area on the Mississippi River.

In the northwest part of the state, the Apple

River has carved 250-foot-high cliffs through limestone and bedrock. Admire the geology of the driftless region by hiking through the 300-acre **Apple River Canyon State Park,** which has short trails through bottomland and upland forests. Like Giant City State Park, **Starved Rock State Park** near Utica has a wide variety of trails for hikers of any level. There are 13 miles total at Starved Rock, from the .3-mile Starved Rock trail to the 4.7-mile Illinois Canyon Trail. You'll scale cliffs, maneuver along canyons, and view the Illinois River from on high.

Trails in the central part of the state are more level but no less scenic. One of the newest places to go walking is **Midewin National Tallgrass Prairie** near Wilmington. Once the site of an Army ammunition plant, Midewin offers miles of mowed-grass trails for hiking. The entire site is about 19,000 acres; however, only 6,300 are now open to the public. (More land is expected to open as the U.S. Department of Agriculture's Forest Service cleans and rehabilitates the land.) Moving southwest along the Illinois and Sangamon River valleys you'll find 24 miles of rough trails for hiking or mountain biking at **Jim Edgar Panther Creek State Fish and Wildlife Area** near Chandlerville. For more rustic trails (and by rustic I mean not paved or asphalt), head to **Sand Ridge State Forest** near Forest City. Situated along the Illinois River, the state forest has 44 miles of hiking trails, ranging from about 1.5 miles to 17 miles each. **Pyramid State Park** in south-central Perry County is another quiet park with about 20,000 acres to explore, with 17 miles of hiking and horseback-riding trails.

BICYCLING

Illinoisans love to bike. And why not? There are lots of trails to choose from and they're all accessible and fairly easy to navigate. Most of the state's bike trails are converted railroad beds with asphalt or crushed-limestone bases. And with the exception of the trails in southern Illinois, most trails wind through flat terrain with occasional sets of rolling hills, tunnels, or railroad trestles.

Although it's not yet complete, one day residents and visitors will be able to embark on the 475-mile-long Grand Illinois Trail, which will connect Chicago's lakefront with Rockford and Galena, the Quad Cities, and then back east to Chicago via the Hennepin Canal and Starved Rock area. For now, though, there are several other trails for biking. Here's a sampling. In the northeastern part of the state Chicago's **Lakefront Trail** runs along the lakeshore for about 18 miles, past landmarks such as the Shedd Aquarium and Museum of Science and Industry, sand volleyball courts, marinas, and sandy beaches. West of Chicago the 60-mile-long **Prairie Path** traverses a former railroad bed past Wheaton, Naperville, and many nature preserves. For a glimpse of the tony north shore suburbs, pedal along the **Green Bay Trail,** which follows the Metra line starting near Shorewood Park in Wilmette to Lake Bluff.

On the western edge of the state, the **Sam Vadalabene Bicycle Trail** connects the classic Mississippi River town of Alton with Pere Marquette State Park. It follows the Great River Road for about 20 miles. Another trail along the Mississippi River is the **Great River Trail** in the northwestern part of the state. It winds for almost 63 miles from the Quad Cities to Savanna to the north. You'll pass the Rock Island Arsenal and several lock and dams. One of the newest (and probably less crowded) bike trails in the state is the 96-mile **Hennepin Canal State Trail,** which carves a north-south path through the north-central part of the state through and near towns such as Bureau Junction, Princeton, Sheffield, Mineral, and Geneseo.

At the far southern end of the state, **Tunnel Hill State Trail** challenges riders for 45 miles from Harrisburg to Karnak. Pedal through tunnels, over trestles, and along the bottomlands of the Cache River basin. A short spur introduces visitors to the Cache River State Natural Area with its cypress and tupelo swamps. Also in the southern region is **Pyramid State Park** near

Pinckneyville. Fat-tire riders will never want to leave this 19,000-acre rustic park, which has a network of trails, including a 12-mile mountain-bike trail through woods, meadows, and past small lakes.

WATER ADVENTURES
Canoeing and Kayaking
Most visitors tend to think of Illinois as a water-deficient state. And compared to some of its neighbors to the north, such as Wisconsin and Minnesota, it is. But you might be surprised by the opportunities we have for paddling through quiet sloughs, along a national scenic river, and yes, even the **Chicago River.** Strolling through downtown Chicago early on a weekend morning, take a few minutes to peer over the Madison Street bridge or any other bridge in the Loop. You could stumble upon a curious sight: people kayaking along the Chicago River. Yup, those are actually kayakers. In recent years paddling the Chicago River has become a fairly popular way to see the city. Visitors can also have a go at sea kayaking on Lake Michigan, which, you might be surprised to learn, can become quite rough on windy days. Or, for a quieter, calmer canoe ride in the Chicago region, head to the **Skokie Lagoons** near Evanston. The Chicago area has quite a few clubs plus outfitters where you can rent and buy equipment, such as Chicago River Canoe and Kayak in Evanston.

If you're looking for a challenging paddle along churning rivers and rapids, two popular rivers downstate are the **Middle Fork National Scenic River** near Danville or the **Kankakee River** near Bourbonnais and Kankakee. The ultimate canoe tour in Illinois can be found in the extreme southern part of the state in the Cache River region. There you'll glide through cypress and tupelo swamps, past orchards while tree frogs sing. You can't beat it.

Before setting out on a canoe or kayak adventure, check out Illinois Paddling's website (www.illinoispaddling.org), which has links to several regional clubs and outfitters. Members

are working to develop and expand canoeing and kayaking opportunities in Illinois.

Boating
For more fast-paced boating action, you can find several public boat launches and piers along the shores of Illinois's many lakes. Because of the way the glaciers carved their way through the state, the naturally occurring lakes are in the northern part of Illinois (such as **Chain O' Lakes** at the town of Fox Lake), and the man-made lakes are in the central and south-central part of the state. The man-made lakes, such as **Carlyle Lake** (at the town of Carlyle), **Clinton Lake** (at Clinton), **Lake Shelbyville** (at Shelbyville), and **Rend Lake** (south of Mount Vernon) are huge and tend to attract people who are boating for sport or who are fishing. The largest man-made lake is Carlyle Lake at 26,000 acres.

Before launching into an Illinois lake or river, you need to register and have a title for your boat. (For more info, contact the Illinois Department of Natural Resources at 217/557-0180 or 800/382-1696). You'll also want to find out if there are any restrictions related to horsepower. Some lakes, for example, are restricted to boats with electric trolling motors. The DNR has a list of those lakes. If you aren't hauling your own boat around the state, you can rent anything from a paddleboat to a fishing boat with a 10-horsepower engine. **Eagle Creek Resort** on Lake Shelbyville, for example, rents personal watercraft. **Golconda Marina** in the southern part of the state rents pontoon boats. Check with the DNR for a complete list of boats available around the state.

FISHING
If you have a rod, bring it along on your trip through Illinois. The state has numerous accessible lakes, rivers, streams, and ponds for fishing. And fishing licenses are easy to get and cost just a few bucks. You can land a hefty chinook salmon while on a thrilling charter ride on Lake Michigan or a try for a channel catfish in the Illinois River valley. There are about 1.6

million acres of surface water and 26,000 miles of streams in the state, filled with trout (lake, rainbow, and brown trout), perch, muskies, walleyes, catfish, plus the usual crappies and sunfish. Salmon and trout are common in Lake Michigan, and muskies and bass are stocked in the big inland lakes such as Lake Shelbyville. Catfish and walleye make their homes in the streams and rivers.

Fishing licenses are available from the Illinois Department of Natural Resources Division of Fisheries (217/782-6424, www.dnr.state.il.us), bait shops, harbors, sporting goods stores, and some gas stations. You can buy a 24-hour license, 10-day license, or annual one. Daily licenses are about $6 for residents or nonresidents. Nonresidents can get a 10-day license for $13. An annual license for residents is $13 and $24.50 for nonresidents. You don't need one if you are under 16 years old or disabled. If you fish for salmon or trout in Lake Michigan you'll need a stamp.

The Illinois Department of Natural Resources publishes a fishing regulations handbook, available at most bait shops, harbors, and visitors bureaus. In addition to basic information on licenses and size limits, the handbook also includes the department of health's fish consumption guidelines, which might come in handy if you decide to fish in Chicago's harbors. In addition to the handbook, a great Internet resource is www.ifishillinois.org, which has a roundup of where to fish, lists of local tournaments, and weekly fish reports for lakes and rivers in regions around the state. For a list of places to fish call the DNR at 800/ASK-FISH (800/275-3474). The DNR's Division of Fisheries manages several hatcheries throughout the state, including the Little Grassy Fish Hatchery in Makanda and Jake Wolf Memorial Fish Hatchery in Topeka. These are open to the public.

If you have some time, take off on a half-day or daylong charter fishing trip on Lake Michigan to fish for salmon and trout. Dozens of charter boat companies offer trips launching from Chicago's harbors and the north shore marinas in Waukegan and Winthrop Harbor.

These trips can run several hours and cost several hundred dollars, but they're usually a quite an adventure. (From the shore, you might not realize Lake Michigan can kick up some tough waves pretty quickly. If you're prone to seasickness, don't forget the Dramamine.) For a list of charter boat companies, contact the Waukegan Charter Boat Association (103 E. Madison St., Waukegan Harbor, Waukegan, 847/244-3474, www.wcba.info); North Point Charter Boat Association (North Point Marina, 701 North Point Dr., Winthrop Harbor, 800/247-6727, www.salmonoid.com/npcba); or the Chicago Sportfishing Association (312/922-1100, www.greatlakes.org/il/fish-chicago/index.html), which represents tours that embark from several of Chicago's harbors.

HUNTING

Although primarily liberal and democratic Chicago tends to dominate the cultural and political landscape of Illinois, visitors and new residents are often surprised to discover that a devoted hunting (and progun) subculture exists in the state, particularly in the rural counties in central and southern Illinois. Perhaps not as ingrained into the way of life as in, say, Wisconsin or Michigan, hunting is something many residents do throughout the year. With the growing popularity of commercial game preserves and resorts, hunting as a pastime may continue to expand.

Essentially there are four hunting categories in Illinois: deer and turkey, migratory fowl (such as Canada geese and dove), upland game (such as quail and pheasants), plus trapping for fur animals such as fox, raccoons, and even squirrels. Hunting for wild turkeys is fairly popular and done in all regions, especially in the north in the spring. The deer season in Illinois runs from early October to early January, with separate weeks set aside for hunting with bows or shotguns. You can hunt deer in virtually all regions of the state.

Many state parks and wildlife areas are open for hunting, in addition to about 50 hunting

ILLINOIS WINE

In recent years the Illinois wine-making industry has really taken off. Ten years ago the state was home to a handful of vineyards and wineries. Now there are dozens. Some credit the state's wine and grape resources council (which had its budget slashed in recent years). Others credit the innovated and tireless entrepreneurs behind the operations. Illinois wineries are run by families who have been crafting wine for decades, retired teachers, former livestock farmers, you name it. Most wineries are open to the public according to set hours, and a few are open by appointment.

Illinois wines are primarily made from red and white French hybrid grapes such as chambourcin and traminette, grapes that are suited to the varied Illinois climate. Some vintners make wine from Illinois-grown fruit, such as peaches, apples, and berries. Bottles usually cost under $20.

The bulk of the state's wineries and vineyards are in the south. Grapes do well on the hillsides and in the mild climate there. While in southern Illinois, pick up a map of the Shawnee Hills Wine Trail, which directs visitors to five different wineries around the Pomona and Alto Pass region. Two good bets in southern Illinois are Von Jakob Vineyards near Pomona and Cameo Vineyards in Greenup. In addition to the Shawnee Hills wineries, you'll find wineries within an hour's drive from Chicago, such as Lynfred in Roselle and Glunz Family Winery and Cellars in Grayslake. To the far northwestern part of the state are the scenic Galena Cellars Winery in Galena and Massbach Ridge Winery in nearby Elizabeth. Both are set amid the rolling hills and near bustling small towns.

New wineries open annually. To get the latest scoop on where to go, check with the Illinois Grape Growers and Vintners Association's website, www.illinoiswine.com. Here's a sampling of Illinois wineries open to the public.

preserves (which are mainly for hunting upland game and fowl), which you'll find in just about every region except Chicagoland. Fees vary according to the preserve. Some have set fees based on the time you spend in the preserve (half-day versus full-day hunting trip) or based on the amount of birds the preserve releases for you to go after. A list of preserves is on the Illinois Department of Natural Resources website.

A seasonal hunting pass for residents is $7.50. For nonresidents, a five-day hunting is $28.50. Seasonal passes are also available. In addition to these fees, you'll have to buy permits specific to what animal you're after (deer, turkey, etc.), and permit fees can range from about $10–200 depending on the animal, whether you are an Illinois resident or not, and whether you choose to hunt with a shotgun or a bow and arrow. The Illinois Department of Natural Resources' *Digest of Hunting and Trapping Regulations* contains comprehensive information about

fees and rules of hunting in Illinois, plus maps of public hunting areas. You can download it from the website, www.dnr.state.il.us, pick up a free copy in most sporting goods shops, or call the DNR's regional offices: Sterling (northern), 815/625-2968; Bartlett (Chicagoland), 815/675-2385; Clinton (southern), 217/935-6860; Alton (southwest), 618/462-1181; Benton (southern), 618/435-8138; and Chicago, 312/814-2070. For special hunting permits call the DNR at 217/782-7305.

GOLF

If you're a newcomer to Illinois links, a good place to begin your search for a course is the **Chicago District Golf Association** (main office is at Midwest Golf House, 11855 Archer Ave., Lemont, 630/257-2005, www.cdga.org). This organization is not just about Chicago courses, but it's an association of golfers and 350 clubs in Illinois and parts of Wisconsin,

Collar Counties
Glunz Family Winery and Cellars,
Grayslake
Lynfred Winery, Roselle
Valentino Vineyard and Winery,
Long Grove

Grand Prairie
Hill Prairie Winery, Oakford
Furrow Vineyard and Winery, El Paso
Alto Vineyards, Champaign
Vahling Vineyards, Stewardson

Great River Valleys
August Hill Winery, Utica
Chateau Ra-Ha Winery, Grafton
Aerie's Riverview Winery, Grafton
Baxter's Vineyards, Nauvoo
Collver Family Winery, Barry
Waterloo Winery, Waterloo
Schorr Lake Vineyard and Winery,
Waterloo
Lau-Nae Winery, Red Bud

Northern Hill Country
Prairie State Winery, Genoa

Fox Valley Winery, Sandwich and
Oswego
Galena Cellars Winery, Galena
Massbach Ridge Winery, Elizabeth

Southern Illinois
Berryville Vineyards, Claremont
Fox Creek Winery, Olney
GenKota Winery, Mount Vernon
Pheasant Hollow Winery, Whittington
Spring Pond Vineyards and Winery,
Benton
White Owl Winery, Birds
Cameo Vineyards, Greenup
Von Jakob Vineyard, Pomona
Alto Vineyards, Alto Pass
Hedman Orchards and Vineyards,
Alto Pass
Owl Creek Vineyard and Winery,
Cobden Hills
Winghill Vineyard and Winery,
Cobden Hills
Cache River Basin Vineyard and
Winery, Belknap
Kite Hill Vineyards and Winery,
Carbondale

Michigan, and Indiana. It publishes course information (ratings, yardages, fees, etc.) online and in the bimonthly magazine, *Chicago District Golfer.*

As far as top courses in Illinois, here's a sampling: the Glen Club in Glenview (on the grounds of the former Glenview naval base), Cog Hill in Lemont, Lake of the Woods County Park golf course in Mahomet (a refreshingly hilly course in the middle of flatland), The Den at Fox Creek in Bloomington, and Eagle Ridge Resort in Galena.

BIRD-WATCHING

Whether you stroll through the prairie, river bottomlands, or atop sandstone cliffs, you will encounter and hear a variety of birds. Birding is a popular pastime in Illinois, and the

Illinois Audubon Society (425B N. Gilbert St., Danville, 217/446-5085, www.illinois-audubon.org), an organization that actually predates the founding of the national society, is active in protecting the state's flora and fauna, particularly birds. It maintains several wildlife sanctuaries in the state, mostly in the central and southern region. One is the Robert Ridgeway Grasslands adjacent to Prairie Ridge State Natural Area near Newton. Members also often organize bird-watching and counting trips to areas around Illinois.

Towns along the Mississippi and Illinois rivers, such as Havana and Alton, are often destinations for birders. Migratory birds, eagles, and other raptors congregate along those rivers in the winter and towns such as Havana hold bird-watching events. Some good spots include locks and dams along the rivers, trails within the Upper Mississippi River National Fish and Wildlife Refuge south of Savanna, Delbar State Park north of Oquawka, and the Chautauqua National Wildlife Refuge near Havana. If you like to look for birds with others, you can join organized tours held throughout the year at parks such as Starved Rock State Park near Ottawa or Midewin National Tallgrass Prairie by Wilmington. Take a short drive through the western town of Griggsville and you'll see why it is considered the purple martin capital of the nation. Houses for these mosquito-eating birds line the streets and front and backyards of the town's residents. Birders will want to check the Nature House Showroom, where you can buy houses for purple martins.

OTHER OUTDOOR RECREATION

Skiing

If you're itching to shush down some slopes, you won't have to drive out of state. Illinois is certainly not Colorado or New Hampshire, but there are a few hills where skiers get their kicks. Many offer great opportunities for beginners or intermediate skiers who want to brush up on their skills before heading elsewhere. One option (and perhaps the best one in the state for downhill skiing) is **Chestnut Mountain Resort** near Galena. Otherwise, novices and snowboarders can try **Villa Olivia** in Bartlett, **Four Lakes Villages** in Lisle, or **Ski Snowstar** in Taylor Ridge near the Quad Cities. If you want to slow things down, Illinois has plenty of spots for **cross-country skiing,** especially in

the state parks in the north. Stick to parks in the north, such as **Blackwell Forest Preserve** in Warrenville near Chicago and **Kankakee River State Park** in Bourbonnais. Snow often doesn't stick around long enough in the central and southern regions to make for a good cross-country skiing base.

Caves

Illinois has several hundred caves throughout the state, but the only one open to the public is **Illinois Caverns State Natural Area** in the southwestern part of the state near the tiny town of Redbud. Considered a wild cave (no electricity down here), Illinois Caverns has six miles of trails for visitors to explore. You'll trudge through mud and jostle around stalagmites and stalactites (those iciclelike formations common in caves). Visitors are required to explore in groups of four or more, wear boots, a hard hat, and carry three sources of light (i.e., a waterproof flashlight) per person.

Climbing

The outcropping and hills of southern Illinois make for some excellent rock climbing, especially for novices and climbers wanting to perfect their bouldering skills. You can climb at the following state parks: **Ferne Clyffe, Giant City** (both of which are in southern Illinois), and **Mississippi Palisades** in the northwest corner of the state. When you can't go outside, a few grain bins and silos have been converted into climbing gyms, such as **Upper Limits** in Bloomington and **The Silo** in Rochester.

Accommodations

HOTELS, MOTELS, AND BED-AND-BREAKFASTS

Rates for hotels vary widely throughout the state, the most expensive ones being in downtown Chicago, although there are some pricey resorts and inns in Galena and the Geneva area also. Midweek prices tend to be lower than weekend rates. Summer rates are almost always higher than those in February or March, when not many people, except business travelers, are visiting the state. If you reserve a hotel room with a credit card, you should be able to check in any time of night. But most hotels will give away your room if you don't show up by 6 P.M. and haven't given them a credit-card guarantee. Most bed-and-breakfasts require two-night stays on the weekends, and if you cancel, usually it needs to be done a week or so in advance, otherwise you may lose some money.

On the **Illinois Hotel and Lodging Association's** (877/4-LODGING or 877/456-3446, www.stayillinois.com) website, you can type in your destination, date of arrival and departure, and the server will check availability for all hotels, inns, and bed-and-breakfasts in the area. Or, call to make a reservation or order the free print version of the guide.

The **Illinois Bed and Breakfast Association** (6103 Old Hwy. 50, Aviston, 888/523-2406, www.go-illinois.com) publishes a helpful online guide and color booklet listing bed-and-breakfasts in the state. It includes lists of bed-and-breakfasts by region, plus info such as if the inn or bed-and-breakfast is pet-friendly, child-friendly, or wheelchair-accessible. The site also keeps a log of specials going on at bed-and-breakfasts around the state.

CAMPING AND CABINS

Do you want to walk a half mile through woods and then camp in a tent? Hook up your RV in a park alongside several other trucks? How about renting an air-conditioned cottage in the woods? In other words, how close to nature do you want to get? Illinois has plenty of camping options. This is a big RV state, and the **Illinois Campground Association** (866/895-2267, www.gocampingamerica.com/illinois) can help you choose where to park your truck. It lists campgrounds and RV parks online (through the National Association of RV Parks and Campgrounds website) and through a guide you can find at most travel information centers.

Otherwise, contact the **Illinois Department of Natural Resources** (1 Natural Resources Way, Springfield, 217/782-6302, www.dnr.state.il.us) to find out about its campgrounds, which vary from modern sites with electric hookups and shower buildings to remote hike-in sites where you haul in your tent and supplies by yourself. Camping fees at Illinois state parks range about $6–20 per night. Some state parks offer what's called "rent-a-tent," where for an extra fee you rent equipment such as the tent and flashlights for the night. Others have full-fledged cabins or cottages, complete with air-conditioning or heaters, such as Starved Rock State Park near Utica and Eldon Hazlet State Park on Carlyle Lake. Then there are the historic state park lodges, many of which were built more than 50 years ago by the Civilian Conservation Corps. Two personal favorites are the Pere Marquette State Park lodge overlooking the Mississippi River and the Giant City State Park lodge tucked in the Shawnee Hills.

Finally, there are 12 campgrounds in the **Shawnee National Forest.** Many are rustic (with pit toilets), but Oak Point Campground at Lake Glendale Recreation Area and Pounds Hollow have shower buildings. The forest is divided into two districts: Hidden Springs (Vienna and Elizabethtown area) to the east and Mississippi Bluffs (Jonesboro and Murphysboro) to the west. For more information on camping you can contact the headquarters in Harrisburg (50 Hwy. 145, Harrisburg, 618/253-7114, 800/MY-WOODS or 800/699-6637, www.fs.fed.us/r9/forests/shawnee).

Getting There and Around

BY CAR

Illinois is definitely a road trip–friendly state. Thanks to the Eisenhower freeway system, several interstates carve paths through the state, making it possible to zip through our state, stopping only at toll plazas or truck stops. Bring some quarters. A few tollways cross our state (I-80, I-90, and I-294). Fares vary, but tolls are generally $.75 a shot. (Although crossing the Skyway bridge, which links Chicago to Indiana) will cost a few bucks per car.) Residents and long-term, repeat visitors might want to invest in an I-PASS for about $40. Tolls for I-PASS holders are $.40 per toll booth.

If you're going long distances, say from Chicago to Carbondale, and have no plans to stop in between, the interstates are efficient. But if you have time, veer off them for some two-lane highway journeys through the main streets of small towns or the hilly roads through orchard country in the south. The mother of all two-lane highways, **Route 66** begins at Chicago's lakefront and winds southwest toward Chicago, mostly along I-55. Follow the **Great River Road** along the Mississippi River from East Dubuque all the way down to the southern tip of the state. The **Dixie Highway** (also known as Route 1) follows the eastern edge of the state through the Vermilion and Wabash River valleys. The **National Road** (or U.S. 40) cuts through the center of the state and takes you through many farming regions. The **Ohio River Scenic Byway** snakes along the great Ohio in the south and southeastern part of the state past quaint and historic river towns such as Elizabethtown and Golconda. All these historic highways are marked with signs that point you in the right direction.

The **Illinois Department of Transportation** releases road conditions on its website, www.illinoisroads.info, and records them on the hotline, 800/452-IDOT or 800/452-4368. For road conditions on the tollways, call 800/TOLLFYI or 800/865-5394.

BY BUS

Greyhound (800/454-2487, www.greyhound.com) services 38 cities in Illinois with several stops in Chicago (in addition to the main bus terminal building downtown on Harrison Street). Buses go to most of the other major towns and cities in Illinois, such as downstate cities such as Mattoon and Carbondale, and west to Galena and Moline. Not all cities have actual bus terminals, but buses will stop at places such as designated motels along highways. Hours at these terminals are always subject to change, so call ahead. Fares are usually under $30 for one-way trips, with discounts given to passengers booking a week in advance. Discounts are also available to seniors, students, and others. Greyhound also offers Internet-only and companion fare specials.

Other private bus companies operate in some central and southern towns, mostly to shuttle people back and forth to major airports in the region such as the Chicago airports and those in St. Louis and Indianapolis. Check with the regional sections for information on these companies.

BY TRAIN

Illinois is lucky. Several **Amtrak** (800/USA-RAIL or 800/872-7245, www.amtrak.com) lines crisscross the state, with Chicago's Union Station serving as a regional hub for many of these lines. Most of the trains run daily; however, sometimes they're subject to delays as they often yield to heavy freight traffic. You can hop on one of several "Superliner" trains. The **California Zephyr** train runs from Chicago west to Princeton and Galesburg before moving on through Iowa, Nebraska, Colorado, Nevada, and finally to Emeryville, California. The **Southwest Chief** links Chicago to Los Angeles, with stops in Illinois in Naperville, Mendota, and Princeton. The **Texas Eagle** connects Chicago with San Antonio via the Illinois towns of Joliet, Pontiac, Normal, Lincoln, Springfield, and Alton. The famous **City of New Orleans** train connects Chicago to New Orleans and stops in towns primarily along the eastern part of the state, such as the university towns of Champaign-Urbana and Carbondale.

For in-state and regional service, the **Ann Rutledge** goes between Chicago and Kansas City and the **Hiawatha** carries passengers between Chicago and Milwaukee. The **State House** train runs daily between Chicago and St. Louis, with stops in towns such as Dwight, Bloomington, Springfield, and Alton. The **Illinois Zephyr** train links Chicago and Quincy, with stops in towns such as Naperville, Princeton, Galesburg, and Macomb. **Illini Service** ties Chicago with Carbondale, with stops in towns such as Kankakee, Gilman, Rantoul, Mattoon, Effingham, and Du Quoin. Because Congress is always threatening to cut Amtrak's funding, check with Amtrak while planning your trip to make sure trains are running.

Before you take one of congestion-plagued interstate highways in the Chicago region, check to see if a Metra train line runs to or near your destination. **Metra** (312/836-7000, www.metrarail.com) has 12 train lines that cover all of Chicagoland and more. They stretch all the way north to Kenosha, Wisconsin, Fox Lake (by the Chain O' Lakes State Park), northwest to Harvard and Woodstock, and south to University Park. Metra train rides cost a few bucks each way, and Metra has special unlimited weekend fares that run about $5 per person. Plus, the trains are almost always on time.

BY AIR

Chicago's **O'Hare International Airport** on the northwest side is by far the busiest airport in the state (and in the world, as a matter of fact). It handled nearly a million flights in 2004. It's connected to the city via the Blue Line train, plus dozens of cabs and hotel shuttles are often lined up in the arrival and departure areas. On the southwest side of Chicago is **Midway International Airport,** a hub for economy carriers such as Southwest Airlines. It's linked to the city by the Orange Line train. In recent years politicians have been wrangling over the creation of a third airport in Peotone, south of Chicago. But that project, if it happens, won't start offering flights for many years.

Flying into Rockford is another option if you're visiting the Chicago region. About 80 miles from Chicago, the Rockford airport (officially called the **Northwest Chicagoland International Airport**) has flights to the Caribbean Islands, plus cities such as Orlando, Florida, Las Vegas, Nevada, Denver, Colorado, and Myrtle Beach, South Carolina. Parking there is free. Regional carriers such as American Connection and Delta fly into smaller airports such as the **Central Illinois Regional Airport** in Bloomington-Normal, which also offers free parking; Springfield's **Capital Airport;** the **Greater Peoria Regional Airport;** and the **University of Illinois's Willard Airport** in Savoy. Otherwise, if you plan to explore the southern and central regions, consider flying into St. Louis or even Indianapolis and then renting a car from the airports.

Tips for Travelers

HEALTH AND SAFETY

Plants, Bugs, Animals

There are no lions, tigers, or bears (wild ones, anyway) in Illinois, but there are a few critters you'll want to keep an eye out for. First, the mosquito. The **West Nile virus** was first detected in Illinois in 2001 after a laboratory confirmed two dead birds found in Chicago had the virus. Since then, the virus has been detected in all 102 counties (in birds, horses, and people). In 2002 the state registered more people sick and dead from the disease than any other state (that year 66 people died from the disease). The number of people infected who fall sick varies every year. Compared with 2002, in 2003 there were 853 cases of the disease in people and one death. Because people can get the virus by being bitten by an infected mosquito, the Illinois Department of Public Health recommends people apply an insect repellent with 25–35 percent DEET. Mild symptoms include fever and muscle aches; severe symptoms include a high-grade fever, dizziness, convulsions, and a whole slew of other unpleasant things. More information is available by calling the **West Nile Virus State Hotline** at 866/369-9710.

Critter No. 2: the tick. Although more of a risk in the northeastern United States than in Illinois, **Lyme disease** is something to think about when you're hiking through the woods or through areas with tall grasses. Illinois does have deer ticks, which can transmit the disease. Symptoms can include (but are not limited to) a ringlike rash around the bite (which gradually gets worse), fatigue, and dizziness. Check your hair and clothing for the insects after your outdoor adventure. You can use DEET to ward off ticks. As for other possible outdoor risks, if you develop a rash from **poison ivy** or **poison sumac,** pick up some cortisone cream from the nearest pharmacy. It should be available without a prescription. Illinois has a handful of poisonous **snakes,** including the northern/southern

copperhead, the cottonmouth water moccasin, timber rattlesnake, and Masasauga rattlesnake. Most live in specific areas of the state and don't really want to encounter humans. If you see a snake that could be poisonous, leave it alone. (For more information, see *Fauna.*)

Severe Weather

Anytime from spring through summer when it looks wicked outside (dark skies, shifting winds, hard rain), turn on a radio or television to listen for any weather alerts. Major towns have tornado sirens that will go off in case of a tornado warning. But if you're in a rural area, get out of your car and head to a low-lying area. If you're in a building without a basement, head to the interior of the building, away from windows. (For more on tornadoes, see *Climate.*) Also, use common sense when boating and golfing. Lightening does strike the ground, and it can kill people. If it looks as if it's going to storm, hop back onto the golf cart or turn the boat toward the marina. Don't go raising your irons or fishing rods to the sky.

GAY AND LESBIAN TRAVELERS

Not surprisingly, gay and lesbian visitors should feel quite comfortable traveling through the city of Chicago. Throughout the rest of the state, however, how the natives receive you can vary from warm to cool. Generally the slightly more progressive college towns and larger cities such as Springfield and Champaign-Urbana are more accepting of gay and lesbians.

In Chicago, the North Halsted and Broadway neighborhood is home to many gay-owned businesses, clothing and accessories stores, and bars. Andersonville, also on the far north side, is another gay-friendly neighborhood. As far as Chicago resources, there are several options. **Windy City Media** (1940 W. Irving Park Blvd., Chicago 60613, 773/871-7610, www.windycitymediagroup.com) publishes the weekly *Windy City Times* newspaper, *Night-*

spots, a weekly entertainment guide, plus other publications. You can pick these up at most convenient stores and book shops. Another resource is the **Chicago Area Gay and Lesbian Chamber of Commerce** (1210 W. Rosedale Ave., Chicago, 60660, 773/303-0167, 888/GL-CHAMBER or 888/452-4262, www.glchamber.org), which has a special section on its website for gay and lesbian visitors, highlighting galleries, theaters, events, and more.

Chicago's **International Gay and Lesbian Film Festival** sponsored by the Chicago Filmmakers is always a big hit. But the biggest gay and lesbian event in town, every year, is **PRIDEChicago,** held the last weekend in June. The parade and rally through the North Halsted neighborhood always attracts hundreds of thousands of people, gay and straight.

TRAVELERS WITH DISABILITIES

Visitors traveling in wheelchairs will find that most modern buildings (museums, restaurants, hotels) are accessible. The older, historic sites might be technically "accessible," but you'll have to enter through a rear entrance or other type of entrance and exit. Always check about wheelchair access with historic inns and bed-and-breakfasts.

If you're planning to travel to Chicago, there are several organizations that will help disabled visitors and residents navigate the city. Almost all of the **Chicago Transit Authority** buses are wheelchair-accessible, plus dozens of elevated train stations are wheelchair-accessible with elevators. Another option for getting around the city is the **CTA's Paratransit Service,** which offers door-to-door service for a fee. You'll need to apply and make reservations, but it's a handy service to have if you plan to stay in Chicago for a while. For information on any of CTA's programs, including the Chicago Taxi Access Program, which offers taxi rides to people with disabilities at reduced rates, contact the **Regional Transportation Authority** at 312/663-4357 or TTY 312/913-3122. Otherwise you can reach the CTA at 312/681-3098 or TTY 312/681-3099. A list of

accessible elevated train stations can be found on the CTA's website, www.yourcta.com. The site also has downloadable brochures for disabled people about getting around Chicago. Other sources for information include the **City of Chicago Mayor's Office for People with Disabilities** (312/744-6673 or TTY 312/744-7833, www.cityofchicago.org) or **Chicago's Open Door Organization** (773/388-8839), an accessibility advocacy organization.

For a national perspective on this topic, contact the **Society for Accessible Travel and Hospitality** (347 5th Ave., New York, NY, 10016, 212/447-7284, www.sath.org).

The **Illinois Department of Natural Resources,** through its Disabled Outdoor Opportunities Program (618/439-9111 or www.dnr.state.il.us), organizes special outdoor recreation events throughout the year for people with disabilities. The department also waives fees for hunting and fishing licenses for people with disabilities. Several state parks have wheelchair-accessible fishing piers and nature paths.

SENIOR TRAVELERS

Seniors can receive discounted admission at many of Illinois's museums, play performances, even restaurants, golf courses, and other places of business. Remember to ask for the discount, though. In addition, if you're a member of the **American Association for Retired People** (601 E St. NW, Washington, D.C. 20049, 888/OUR-AARP or 888/687-2277, www.aarp.org) don't forget to ask at the hotel or rental car company for a discount, usually around 10 percent. **Elderhostel** (11 Ave. de Lafayette, Boston, MA 02111-1746, 877/426-8056, www.elderhostel.org), a national nonprofit organization, holds daylong "day of discovery" events in cities around the country, including in Illinois.

TRAVELING WITH CHILDREN

If you are of the minivan set, Illinois has lots of stuff for you to do with your kids. First, there are more than a dozen children's museums in the state, from the multileveled Children's Museum of Illinois in Decatur to the small but growing Orpheum Children's Science Museum in Champaign. Check with the national **Association of Children's Museums** (1300 L St. NW, Ste. 975, Washington, D.C. 20005, 202/898-1080, www.childrensmuseums.org) for a list of museums in Illinois. There are also several water parks and theme parks to keep them entertained, from Six Flags Great America in Gurnee to Magic Waters near Rockford. For a list of water parks in the state, consult the **World Waterpark Association** (8826 Santa Fe Dr., Ste. 319, Overland Park, Kansas 66212, 913/599-0300, www.waterparks.com), which

not only contains information on the major sites, but also on some of the smaller, but just as refreshing, pools owned by park districts. While in the Chicago region, pick up a free copy of *Chicago Parent,* a monthly magazine that is a great resource for visiting and resident parents. There are several kid-focused travel guides to Chicago, such as *Frommer's Chicago with Kids, Fodor's Around Chicago with Kids,* and *The Lobster Kids' Guide to Exploring Chicago*

To keep the kids entertained in the car, buy a copy of *Illinois Jeopardy: Questions and Answers About Our State* by Carole Marsh and published by Gallopade International in 2000. It's a trivia book for kids in 4th–8th grade.

Information and Services

MONEY

Generally you should be able to find automated teller machines throughout the state in banks, gas stations, and grocery stores. Usage fees will vary; the average is $1.50, plus any charge you have to pay to your home bank. You can change money, cash checks and travelers checks at currency exchanges, which are in most major cities.

Sales taxes vary according to city and county, but it's generally around 6 percent, except in Cook County, where it's higher. Chicago sales tax is a whopping 9 percent. The state hotel tax is 6 percent, plus many counties and cities have additional hotel and motel taxes (taxes that usually fund convention and visitors bureaus). Expect gas prices around Chicago and the major interstates to be higher than in other areas.

Tipping

A standard tip at a restaurant is 15 percent. Giving 20 percent is not uncommon if you've had over-the-top service or are particularly generous. The tip amount is not included on the bill unless you are a large party of more than 8–10 people. Most restaurants automatically include tip for big tables. Shoe shiners at the

railroad station expect tips (10–15 percent is accepted), as do the folks who offer to carry your bags from your car to the ticket counter at airports (they're called skycaps). Tipping is optional for taxicab service. A tip of 10–15 percent is a nice gesture.

MAPS AND TOURIST INFORMATION

The Illinois Bureau of Tourism (800/2-CONNECT or 800/226-6632, www.enjoyillinois.com) stocks several rest stops across the state with tons of free maps, brochures, and coupons. Here's a list: I-24 (called Fort Massac, one mile north of the Kentucky state line); I-55 (called Homestead, eight miles north of the I-70 interchange); I-57 (called Trail of Tears, 32 miles north of the Missouri border); I-57 (at Rend Lake); I-57 (called Prairie View, 27 miles north of Kankakee); I-64 (called Gateway, 25 miles east of St. Louis); I-70 (called Silver Lake, 27 miles east of St. Louis); I-70 (called Cumberland Road, seven miles west of the Indiana state line); I-74 (called Salt Kettle, seven miles west of Danville); I-80 (called Mississippi Rapids, near the Iowa border); and I-90 (called Turtle Creek, two miles south of the Wisconsin border). There's also a tourist information center in the **Chicago Cultural Center** (78 E. Washington St., Chicago).

Instead of buying a map, order a free one (regular version or large print) from the Illinois Department of Transportation's website, www.dot.state.il.us, or by writing the department at IDOT, 2300 S. Dirksen Parkway, Springfield, IL 62764.

For more detailed information on back roads and topography, buy DeLorme's *Illinois Gazetteer,* available at most bookstores. Also, the **Illinois Geological Survey** publishes an array of topographic maps and geology field guides, some of which focus on a particular region or natural area in the state, such as Illinois Caverns State Natural Area. To review its guides and maps for sale, contact the survey's public information office (1816 S. Oak St., Champaign, 217/244-2414, www.isgs.uiuc.edu).

MEDIA
Newspapers
The two Chicago daily papers, the *Chicago Tribune* and *Chicago Sun-Times* are available in most towns around the state, in addition to in Chicago and the collar counties. Most visitors bureaus and chambers of commerce have links to the local papers. You can also check the **Illinois Press Association**'s website, www.il-press.com, which has links to regional and local newspapers.

Magazines
The Tribune-owned *Chicago* magazine (www.chicagomag.com) covers the Chicago social, political, dining, and cultural scene, plus some statewide issues. It's available in stores throughout Chicagoland, plus in bookstores downstate.

The University of Illinois at Springfield publishes the monthly magazine *Illinois Issues* (http://illinoisissues.uis.edu), which objectively explores a range of statewide issues, including political, economic, historical, and social issues. You can find it at bookstores and libraries around the state, particularly in the central region.

INTERNET ACCESS

Speedy and free wireless Internet access is cropping up at more and more places around the state, from coffee shops frequented by college students to truck stops along the interstate highways. If you have a WiFi-enabled laptop, all you have to do is have a seat at one of the tables to pick up the signal. Chains such as Panera Bread (in most Chicago suburbs and some downstate communities such as Champaign-Urbana) and Krispy Kreme doughnut shops offer WiFi, as do some public libraries. The website, www.wifi-freespot.com, lists such places.

Whether or not they have WiFi, DSL, or dial-up, just about every public library has Internet access. You'll have to sign in and might have to wait your turn (especially if you drop by after school or early in the evenings), but it's free. There are a handful of Internet cafés around the state. Most of them, such as Screenz, are in and around Chicago. Otherwise, you can always rent a computer workstation at Kinko's locations around the state. Finally, don't forget to ask about access at your hotel or bed-and-breakfast. More and more hotels and motels, whether they are national chains or locally owned, are offering Internet access free to their guests.

TIME ZONES

Illinois is in the central standard time zone, one hour behind New York (which is on eastern standard time), two hours ahead of Los Angeles, and six hours behind Greenwich mean time. The dividing line between central standard time and eastern standard time is along most of the Illinois-Indiana border. Illinois participates in daylight saving time by setting clocks one hour ahead at 2 A.M. on the first Sunday in April and one hour behind at 2 A.M. on the last Sunday in October.

BUSINESS HOURS

Typically your locally or independently owned boutiques and shops are open 9 or 10 A.M.–6 or 7 P.M. Monday–Saturday. Malls and shopping centers are open later, until 8 P.M. or 9 P.M. Monday–Saturday. Sunday shopping hours are typically 11 A.M.–5 or 6 P.M. Most of the shops in Chicago's Loop don't stay open past 5 P.M. on weekdays. Restaurant hours vary depending on the region and the season. Some close on Mondays or Tuesdays or reduce their hours on those days. Museum and historic site hours can run the gamut, especially November–March. Post office hours also vary according to the town. In big cities, you can bet the branches

there are open later than in rural towns. Most are open 8 A.M.–5 P.M. Monday–Friday and 8 A.M.–12:30 P.M. Saturday. The big holidays are New Year's Day, Easter, Thanksgiving, and Christmas. Just about everything is closed on these days. Tourist attractions tend to stay open on Memorial Day and Labor Day. Illinois celebrates a few obscure holidays, such as Casimir Pulaski Day, held on the first Monday of March. Chicago public schools shut down in honor of this Revolutionary War hero, but most businesses are still up and running.

Suggested Reading

LITERATURE

Algren, Nelson. *Chicago: City on the Make.* Chicago: University of Chicago Press, 2001. Or, *The Man with the Golden Arm.* New York: Seven Stories Press, 1999. Algren eloquently illustrates life in Chicago's Polish ghetto.

Masters, Edgar Lee. *Spoon River Anthology.* Urbana: University of Illinois Press, 1993. American poetry at its best. Masters, who was born in Kansas but grew up along the Spoon River in northwestern Illinois, chronicles life in small-town Illinois.

Sandburg, Carl. *Chicago Poems.* Mineola, N.Y.: Dover Publications, 1994. Or, *Cornhuskers.* Bridgewater, N.J.: Replica Books, 2003. These contain classic Sandburg poems. They're lyrical, poignant, beautiful, and accessible portrayals of everyday people and everyday things.

Sinclair, Upton. *The Jungle.* Tucson, AZ: See Sharp Press, 2003. This version is a reprint of the original, uncensored edition from 1905. If you didn't read it in high school (or haven't read it in a while), pick up this masterful portrayal of the Chicago stockyards, which also touches upon issues such as race, worker's rights, immigrants rights, and much more.

Wright, Richard A. *Native Son.* New York: Perennial Harper Collins, 1998. A page-turning, tragic story about Bigger Thomas and life as a black man in 1930s Chicago.

PEOPLE

Addams, Jane. *Twenty Years at Hull House.* Champaign: University of Illinois Press, 1990. Originally published in 1910, this book includes her thoughts on public and social policy, autobiographical notes, and stories about her experience at the complex to help poor and immigrant families in Chicago.

Higdon, Hal. *Leopold and Lobe: The Crime of the Century.* Champaign: University of Illinois Press, 1999. An account of the crime and the trial from the 1920s of two rich boys who killed a fellow boy and thought they could get away with it.

Royko, Mike. *Boss: Richard J. Daley of Chicago.* New York: Plume Books, 1998. Originally published in 1971, when Daley was still at the helm, this is a classic book about Chicago politics. Royko takes a hard look at the Democratic machine that dominated and still dominates Chicago politics and how Daley conducted business in city hall.

Royko, Mike. *One More Time: The Best of Mike Royko.* Chicago: University of Chicago Press, 2000. The best essays and columns about Chicago people and politics by Royko, a longtime *Chicago Tribune* columnist.

Russo, Gus. *The Outfit: The Role of Chicago's Underworld in the Shaping of Modern America.* New York: Bloomsbury, 2001. Not only do you learn about Al Capone here, but meet Frank "The Enforcer" Nitti and Mooney Giancana. The book spans about 60 years and includes stories about Chicago's beer wars during the Prohibition era to modern off-track betting and casino gambling ventures. With black and white photographs.

Sandburg, Carl. *Abraham Lincoln: The Prairie Years and the War Years.* Edison, N.J.: BBS Publishing Corp., 1993. This is the ultimate Lincoln book. The second part of this two-volume biography won Sandburg the Pulitzer Prize.

HISTORY, POLITICS, AND ECONOMY

Angle, Paul M. *Bloody Williamson: A Chapter in American Lawlessness.* Champaign: University of Illinois Press, 1952 and 1992. The late state historian Paul Angle dives into the history of what was once one of the most notoriously bloody counties in the state: Williamson County in southern Illinois. Now a quiet, rural county, Williamson once was the scene of several murders between rival gangs, violence between striking coal miners and the strikebreakers, and violence between the Klu Klux Klan and bootleggers.

Clark, George Rogers. *The Conquest of the Illinois.* Carbondale, IL: Southern Illinois University, 2001. Written 1789–1791, and reissued by SIU a few years ago, this book, in Rogers's words, describes what Illinois (and the Illinois Indians) were like before the state became a state. With plenty of footnotes with background information about historical events and people.

Hartley, Robert E. *Lewis and Clark in the Illinois Country: The Little-Told Story.* Westminster, CO: Xlibris and Sniktau Publishers, 2002. Before they set off on their westward expedition, Meriwether Lewis and William Clark spent six months in Illinois November 1803–May 1804. This book sets the stage for that endeavor, recounting how they recruited men and gathered supplies. It also provides a look into the makeup of the Illinois country, its early settlements of Cahokia and Kaskaskia, and touches upon its early history, such as the forays of George Rogers Clark (William's older brother) in the state.

Hill, Libby. *The Chicago River: A Natural and Unnatural History.* Chicago: Lake Claremont Press, 2000. A fascinating look at the history of the river, beginning with geologic prehistory from millions of years ago, through the creation of the Illinois and Michigan and Sanitary and Ship canals and modern efforts to keep the river clean.

Jensen, Richard J. *Illinois: A History.* Champaign: University of Illinois Press, 2001. In one of the few books about the prairie state's beginnings, Jensen writes in somewhat of an academic style about the state's early statehood years through modern times, particularly focusing on the clashes between traditionalists in the south and so-called modernists in the north during the Civil War era.

Klinenberg, Eric. *Heat Wave: A Social Autopsy of a Disaster in Chicago.* Chicago: University of Chicago Press, 2002. In 1995 a deadly heat wave struck Illinois, hitting Chicago hard. There were power outages and reduced water pressure because of opened hydrants, hospitals were overwhelmed with cases of heat-related illnesses, and an estimated 739 people died. Klinenberg examines what happened, the city's response, who died (mainly the poor, the elderly, and people who lived alone), and the societal implications of the event.

Terkel, Studs. *Working.* New York: New Press, 2004. The original Terkel, a Chicago institution, talks to people about what they do and what they think about their jobs.

Tilley Turner, Glenette. *The Underground Railroad in Illinois.* Glen Ellyn, IL: Newman Educational Publishing Company, 2001. Organized in question and answer format, with maps and historical and contemporary photographs.

Whiting, Biloine, and Melvin L. Fowler. *Cahokia: The Great Native American Metropolis.* Champaign: University of Illinois Press, 1999. This book not only discusses theories about the people who lived at this Native American village near the Mississippi River, but about all the modern development, archaeological research, and other activities that have occurred since the tribes disappeared hundreds of years ago.

GEOLOGY AND NATURAL HISTORY

De Vore, Sheryl. *Birding Illinois.* Guilford, CT: Falcon Publishing, 2000. This paperback guidebook, a little less than 300 pages, is divided by region and lists the top bird-watching sites in the state, nature preserves, rookeries, and more. It also includes plenty of maps and illustrations of birds, plus background information about the habitats of Illinois birds.

Jeffords, Michael R., Susan L. Post, and Kenneth R. Robertson. *Illinois Wilds.* Urbana, IL: Phoenix Publishing, 1995. A beautiful book with color photographs and essays about the state's geography and natural wonders. Divided into 15 regions, from the unglaciated woods in the north to the coastal plain forests of the south, the book explains how the state looks the way it does with its flat midsection, eastern forests, and bluff-filled northwest. With stunning photographs of green caterpillars, mushrooms, bluffs, and more.

Wiggers, Ray. *Geology Underfoot in Illinois.* Missoula, MT: Mountain Press Publishing, 1996. An engaging book that traces the state's history back to the Ice Age and millions of years before that. With illustrations and travel tips, this is a great resource for anyone interested in how the Illinois landscape came to be.

ART AND ARCHITECTURE

Clayton, Marie, ed. *Frank Lloyd Wright Field Guide.* Philadelphia: Running Press, 2002. About 100 Wright creations are highlighted here, with aerial, exterior, and interior photos. A great guide for folks who know about Wright's body of work; buildings are organized by his different periods, such as Prairie and Usonian. A thick book with a small trim size, it can fit into your purse or backpack.

Kanfer, Larry. *Prairiescapes.* Champaign: University of Illinois Press, 1987. Champaign resident and photographer Larry Kanfer captures the beauty of the prairie with 101 photographs of mostly rural scenes in east-central Illinois: corn and soybean harvests, abandoned farmsteads, foggy winter mornings on country roads. Kanfer has several other coffee-table books featuring Midwestern landscapes.

O'Gorman, Thomas. *Frank Lloyd Wright's Chicago.* San Diego: Thunder Bay Press, 2004. A slick coffee-table book, this book is arranged chronologically, from Wright's earliest designs to the late ones. Buildings are not limited to Chicago but also include estates in the suburbs as well as Michigan and Wisconsin.

Schulze, Franz, and Kevin Harrington. *Chicago's Famous Buildings.* Chicago: University of Chicago, 2003. A guide that you can slip into your backpack while touring the city. The guide, which has maps and black and white pictures, covers well-known and not-so-well-known buildings in downtown, plus some key historical buildings in the surrounding suburbs, such as Oak Park and those on the north shore.

TRAVEL AND FOOD

Avis, Ed. *The Lobster Kids' Guide to Exploring Chicago.* Montreal: Lobster Press, 2001. Small, convenient guide for parents.

Davenport, Don. *In Lincoln's Footsteps: A Historical Guide to the Lincoln Sites in Illinois, Indiana, and Kentucky.* Black Earth, WI: Trails Media Group, 2002. Another easy-to-follow guide from Trails, with maps and practical info and historical summaries of Lincoln's movement through the state.

Pohlen, Jerome. *Oddball Illinois: A Guide to Some Really Strange Places.* Chicago: Chicago Review Press, 2000. A lighthearted look at the state's kookiest attractions (people included).

Post, Susan L. *Hiking Illinois.* Champaign, IL: Human Kinetics, 1997. Easy to use with detailed maps and trail information, this book outlines 100 day hikes in regions throughout the state. Hike details include information about the region's topography, plant life, and nearby attractions. Pages are perforated so you can tear them out and carry the maps in your pocket or pack.

Shepard, Robin. *The Best Pints and Breweries in Illinois.* Madison: University of Wisconsin Press, 2003. The perfect book for those who enjoy a good brew. Shepard writes about 36 top-notch pubs and breweries in the state, with an explainer about how beers are made and a guide to rating beers.

Svob, Mike. *Paddling Illinois: 64 Great Trips by Canoe and Kayak.* Black Earth, WI.: Trails Media Group, 2000. A large, paperback book, this easy-to-use book is a must-have for paddlers. It comes with maps.

Know Illinois

Index

trips from 15–18; entertainment 47–51; festivals 48–49; food 58–65; history 30–32; itinerary 13–14; the Loop 33–38; maps 26–27; media 65–66; must-see sights 25; nicknames, city 55; North Shore 43–44; recreation 53–55; regional overview 7; River North 39–42; services 66–67; shopping 51–52; South and West sides 44–46; sports teams 54–55; tourist information 65; tours 66–67; transportation 67–69; trip planning 28–30

ment Center 120; Gurnee Mills 126–127; Kiddieland 84; Knight's Action Park 187; Ladd Arboretum and Nature Center 87; Lake County Fair 126; Lamb's Farm 127; Miller Park Zoo 141; Niabi Zoo 237; Orpheum 153; Perry Farm Park 136; Quincy Museum 270; Rainbow Ranch 383–384; Raven's Grin Inn 307; Rockome Gardens 200; Scovill Park 163–164; Six Flags Great America 126–127; Toy Station 94; water parks 103, 226

Farm Visits and Markets

Hiking

Parks and Protected Areas

Wineries

general discussion: 426–427
Aerie's Riverview Winery: 281
Alto Vineyards: 345
Baxter's Vineyards and Winery: 267
Cache River Basin Vineyard and Winery: 358
Cameo Vineyards: 391
Collver Family Winery: 274
Furrow Vineyard and Winery: 145
Galena Cellars and Winery and Vineyard: 296
GenKota Winery: 372
Glunz Family Winery: 125
Inheritance Valley Vineyards: 345
Kite Hill Winery: 339
Lau-Nae Winery: 286
Massbach Ridge Winery: 304
Owl Creek Winery: 345
Piasa Winery: 281
Pomona Winery: 344
Shawnee Hill Wine Trail: 345
Shawnee Winery: 358
Vahling Vineyards: 199
Von Jakob Vineyards: 344
Waterloo Winery: 287
Winghill Vineyard Winery: 345

Weldon Springs State Recreation Area: 162
Western Illinois University: 248

West Nile virus: 432
Wheaton: 107–110
Wheaton College: 109
whirlyball: 113
White Pines State Park: 310–311
White Sox, Chicago: 54
Wildcat Bluff: 356
Wilder Park: 111
wildlife: 402–403
Wildlife Prairie State Park: 252
wildlife refuges: *see* parks and protected areas
Williams Hill: 366
Williamsville: 174
Wilmington: 222–223
windmills: 116, 273, 307–308
Winter, Ben: 390
Wolf Creek State Park: 195
Wood, John: 271
Woodland Indians: 403
Woodlawn Cemetery: 332
Woodstock: 323
Wright, Frank Lloyd: 45, 76, 184
Wrigley Field: 44
Wyatt Earp Birthplace: 243
York Theatre: 111
Zion nuclear power plant: 126
zoos: Brookfield Zoo 82; Glen Oak Zoo 252; Lincoln Park Zoo 43; Miller Park Zoo 141; Niabi Zoo 237; petting 128, 136, 200, 383–384, 392; Scovill Park 163–164

ALSO AVAILABLE FROM

MOON HANDBOOKS®
The Cure for the Common Trip

USA

Acadia National Park
Alaska
Arizona
Big Island of Hawai'i
Boston
California
Cape Cod, Martha's
  Vineyard & Nantucket
Charleston & Savannah
Chesapeake Bay
Coastal California
Coastal Carolinas
Coastal Maine
Coastal Oregon
Colorado
Columbia River Gorge
Connecticut
Florida Gulf Coast
Four Corners
Georgia
Grand Canyon
Hawaii
Hudson River Valley
Idaho
Illinois
Kaua'i
Las Vegas
Maine
Maryland & Delaware
Massachusetts
Maui
Michigan
Minnesota
Montana
Monterey & Carmel
Nevada
New Hampshire
New Mexico
New Orleans
New York State

North Carolina
Northern California
Northern California Wine
  Country
O'ahu
Ohio
Oregon
Pennsylvania
Rhode Island
San Juan Islands
Santa Fe-Taos
Silicon Valley
Smoky Mountains
South Carolina
Southern California
Tahoe
Tennessee
Texas
Utah
Virginia
Washington
Wisconsin
Wyoming
Yellowstone & Grand
  Teton
Yosemite
Zion & Bryce

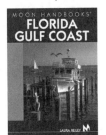

THE AMERICAS

Alberta
Atlantic Canada
British Columbia
Canadian Rockies
Vancouver & Victoria
Western Canada

Acapulco
Baja
Cabo
Cancún & Cozumel
Guadalajara
Mexico City
Oaxaca
Pacific Mexico
Puerto Vallarta
Yucatán Peninsula

Argentina
Belize
Brazil
Buenos Aires
Chile
Costa Rica
Cuba
Dominican Republic
Ecuador
Guatemala
Havana
Honduras
Nicaragua
Panama
Patagonia
Peru
Virgin Islands

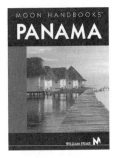

ASIA & THE PACIFIC

Australia
Fiji
Hong Kong
Micronesia
Nepal
New Zealand
South Korea
South Pacific
Tahiti
Thailand
Tonga-Samoa
Vietnam, Cambodia &
  Laos

www.moon.com

With expert authors, suggested routes and activities, and
intuitive organization, Moon Handbooks ensure an uncommon
experience—and a few new stories to tell.